VICTOR HUGO

BOOKS BY
MATTHEW JOSEPHSON

Galimathias (poems)
Zola and His Time
Portrait of the Artist as American
Jean-Jacques Rousseau
The Robber Barons
The Politicos
The President Makers
Victor Hugo

VICTOR HUGO

As a Young Man

Victor Hugo

A REALISTIC BIOGRAPHY OF THE GREAT ROMANTIC

BY

MATTHEW JOSEPHSON

DOUBLEDAY & COMPANY, INC.

GARDEN CITY 1946 NEW YORK

PRINTED AT THE *Country Life Press*, GARDEN CITY, N.Y., U. S. A.

CL

To My Wife

Foreword

THE LIFE OF A MAN like Victor Hugo offers the most tempting of subjects to the hand of the biographer. He was, in his colorful way, a pivotal figure among his people and in his century. He was, at one and the same time, a man of letters and a public man, that is to say, a political leader. Like nearly all literary men Hugo was a most articulate person. His writing is a long endeavor to know himself and explain himself—which, once more, offers great attractions to one who comes afterward to write his history. This articulateness in self-explanation is less often found in the cases of those who were purely men of action, soldiers, statesmen, or industrial captains. These, usually, for reasons of their own, have left large silences or blank spaces in their records.

For a long time I have been absorbed in the problem of the relation of the artist to society, the problem of his participation in public life. Several times, in other books, I have tried to explore this question from various sides. In Victor Hugo we have one of the greatest exemplars of the sedentary, meditative type of man turning from his study to service in public life.

To me it has always seemed that the artist, the creative man generally speaking, has two functions: one is to do his duty as a craftsman, unequivocally, disinterestedly, without regard to the demands of contemporary parties or regimes. The second function begins when the first has been obstructed, as often occurs in a time of social crisis. This touches the creative man's function as a citizen. To fulfill this he leaves his study and takes part in political campaigns, or fights in a war, or in a revolution, by the side of his fellow citizens, if only that he and his people may be able, later, to return to their civilized and creative tasks. These were not precisely Victor Hugo's own, calculated notions of his mission; yet he seems to exemplify them.

Victor Hugo lived in a time much like our own, and he lived through it courageously. His example is one of hope.

His century was "but two years old" when he was born and his lifespan reached almost to its final decade. The years of his childhood, under Napoleon I, were passed amid the scenes of something equivalent to world war; he saw revolutions, he saw republics give way to empires and Dark Ages succeeding eras of enlightenment. Yet he lived also to witness the collapse of tyranny—and from close by, as an active participant in the historic events of his age. He remembered that dictators do not usually enjoy long lives. For he was a poet and had a clairvoyance that went farther than the vision of men of affairs. He was a simple man, whose emotions and intuitions, however, were very strong and illuminating. In the presence of great human catastrophes he felt and expressed, now a mystic sense of "guilt," now a most expansive sense of pity always highly characteristic of him. He was a vital fellow: his passions and sentiments were never narrowly confined; he permitted himself to love family, women, children, and the common people toward whom he expressed a fraternally democratic emotion akin to that of the American poet Whitman. In the end he acquired something like a religious faith in common, ordinary humanity and its fruitful or constructive destiny upon earth. The transient victories of a despot never shook this faith for which he risked his wealth, his career, his life itself.

At the hour when a great dictator moved to seize supreme power over his country, Hugo's voice courageously warned his people and accurately prophesied the setting in of a "long Russian winter" for French civilization. "I do not know how long this eclipse will last," he said, yet he was as certain as he was alive that "daylight would return and the people and God triumph!"

Victor Hugo was often called "the most typical" of Frenchmen, typical of their courage and talent as of their human shortcomings. Over the span of the nineteenth century his poems and his books mirrored the character and the sentiments of his people with uncommon faithfulness. After a certain time his whole career became linked with the cause of democracy in France as firmly as was Lincoln's with a similar cause in America. Hugo could not abide life under a dictatorship and, as he went to his lonely exile, said: "For me, there is no fatherland where there is no liberty." He could wait and work patiently for the return of liberty, saying: "I like proscription, I like exile . . ." He suffered great trials, yet did not despair. France was in bondage, the people languished under a hateful dictator, under his police, his censors, his spies, his army—not for two years but for nearly twenty. Yet Hugo said repeatedly: "The people will awake one day. . . ." He who was called in his old age *Père la République* lived to see the triumph of a popular revolution.

Inevitably some large slices of European history and especially of French history in the nineteenth century enter into this biography. It seems timely to think of those other days. The French people (Hugo's hero) alternately knew fortune and disaster, yet could never be said to be wanting in courage. More than once they were completely betrayed, yet they understood this, understood the nature of the betrayal. The writer of these lines knew this brave and enlightened people well during long years of residence among them; he mourns for them in their present trials, yet refuses to despair for them. Victor Hugo knew them not only in the days of *la gloire* but in times of crushing military defeat, invasion, captivity, and famine that not only closely parallel the present but were in some ways more terrible. He said over and over again: "A great people cannot die."

MATTHEW JOSEPHSON

August 20, 1942

Contents

PART ONE
THE ARTIST

PART TWO
THE PUBLIC MAN

Illustrations

PART ONE

The Artist

CHAPTER I

Storm-tossed Childhood

He REMEMBERED VOYAGES. As far back as his memory could reach into childhood there had been hard, long journeys in pounding carriages over the highroads of Europe. His father, whom he knew but little, was then an officer in Napoleon's armies that moved in great sweeps over the Continent, halting but to advance again. Wherever the father took his stand at some new outpost of conquest, there the boy, together with his mother and his brothers, journeyed after him.

The first voyage of his far-wandering childhood, as he knew from hearsay, was made not long after he had come into the world. He was but six weeks old, just big enough to be carried in the arms of his mother or his nurse, when, by slow stages, he was taken from Besançon, on the northeastern border of France, to Marseilles, then overseas to Corsica, and finally to Elba. The return voyage through Italy, when his father was ordered to leave for duty elsewhere, he also remembered poorly because he was only two years old at the time.

But when he was almost six he set off again to rejoin his father on a trip of nearly a thousand miles from Paris to Naples. That was a long-enough ride in the opening years of the nineteenth century; but in those days of war, when there were long delays to make up convoys, it took three months or more. This journey he remembered vividly. For half a year he was a prisoner in the cab of a heavy diligence, bouncing and swaying along the roads over the mountains and down to the coast. But there was so much to see with his child's

3

eyes. He saw the vast barren Alpine passes and the snowy peaks, the incredibly blue Mediterranean, and Rome in a time of festival, when their carriage slowly followed a magnificent procession of pilgrims. Naples, gleaming in the sun and ringed with the azure of the sea, was fixed in his mind "as a white robe fringed with blue." To a strange, baroque, marble palace in Avellino they came to visit his father, governor of the province, who received them resplendent in the full uniform of a colonel of the Royal Corsicans. His father was not only very affectionate, but had many bonbons for him. Then mysteriously, disappointingly, the father was gone; after a few months' stay in Naples, whose dust and vermin and noise made his mother ill, they took the road back to Paris again.

Some two years later, the family again pulled up stakes and was off for a third great sweep to the south, this time to Madrid. They hurried, they packed everything they could get into a great *cabas,* as his mother called it, in her Breton style, a sort of huge basketlike vehicle led by six mules, so roomy that she packed a whole iron bed on top of it. At Bayonne, near the border of Spain, they joined a great military convoy and climbed the Pyrenees in a cloud of dust. At night the convoy halted and bivouacked. Ever present was the fear of attack or ambuscade by Spanish guerrillas along the winding mountain roads. Drums rolled, sentinels mounted guard, camp-fires blazed, horses were tethered, and the boy slept as in an armed camp. Sometimes guns went off at prowlers or merely shadows glimpsed. Then in the daytime they broke camp and rolled on through the dusty, sleeping towns of northern Spain. Some of these were simply made of a single long street in a gorge flanked by sheer mountain walls, with an ancient castle at one end and a church at the other. The peasants lined the street, sullen and proud, their eyes narrowed into slits beneath their sombreros, pretending not to be looking at the French train. Other towns they passed were simply smoldering ruins, the scenes of recent battles. The boy sensed the misery of the people and wondered at the hatred they felt for their conquerors. Spain was a fantastic and tragic land.

Yet there was not time to seek answers to all the questions that came to him. He was but a child, though one with a serious, almost wistful air. He thought of how beautiful were the hussars with their gold-glittering breastplates, the lancers with their snowy plumes, the dragoons, whose helmets flaunted "a mare's tail mingled with tiger's fur." When the convoy stopped one day at a ruined Spanish town, the scene of recent conflict, the boy jumped out with his brothers and other officers' children and played joyously at war among the heaps of rubble and stone, a bloodstained theater which the real actors had just relinquished to them.

His childhood was warlike. He grew up, he learned many things not commonly taught to children, in the intervals between voyages in the trail of his warrior father. Later, in poetic recollection, he fancied easily that his crib had been but a "drumhead" and the holy water for his baptism "drawn by a soldier in an iron helmet," while for his swaddling clothes the shreds of "battle-torn regimental flags" were wound about him; he reclined upon the "gun carriages of murderous cannon," while "a muse of the camps" sang him to sleep. Later he wrote with immense pride of his father as a hero of the Republican and Napoleonic armies.

Yet, at the time, his intensely stimulated child's imagination saw behind the lines a great deal more than the glory and parade uniform of warfare. It was curious how, since the time of his journeys across war-scarred Europe, certain cruel and dark scenes were fixed upon his mind and always returned, oppressing him, so that his heart secretly shrank at the thought of the pain and suffering associated with wartime.

Fifty years later he would draw from memories of childhood the picture of his ride down the Alpine passes into Italy. Entering a stretch of woods, he suddenly saw a row of human corpses hanging from the trees along the road. He had felt himself driven by curiosity and horror both to dismount from the carriage in order to make sure that these were really the bodies of human beings. Guerrillas or brigands, they had been left hanging there by the French authorities as a warning.

Or again, on the journey into Spain, several years after that, their convoy passed a regiment of invalided French soldiers going north. They were a ragged and crazy band, rigged up in all the uniforms and colors under the sun: some had monkeys or parrots with them as their pets; others, who had lost their arms, balanced themselves as well as they could on mules or asses, while guiding still others who were blind. The fresh troops of the southward-moving convoy saluted the war invalids with derisive laughter; the others, in turn, taunted them, saying: "This is how you will come back!" And they added, as a parting shot: "If you come back!"

Spain had snow-covered mountain ranges tinted with pink clouds, soaring cathedrals, and *alcázars,* or castles, carved by the Moors out of bright jasper and porphyry, as at Segovia. But, that

winter, how gloomy and damp had been the seminary at Madrid,
the Jesuit College of Nobles, where he had been sent to study with
Spanish boys. The priests who instructed him seemed "sinister," his
classmates were cruel to him in games. Each morning a little hunchback, dressed in yellow-and-blue breeches, deaf-mute and mon-
strously ugly, came to his chamber to wake him up. It was the first
face the child saw when he opened his eyes, and he remembered
forever how unutterably sad and deformed it was, though the poor
hunchback was kind to him. Did hunchbacks have souls like other
men?

But suddenly there would be news of some change in the battle
lines which he did not understand. His studies would halt while he
was taken off on another journey back to France.

Pulled to and fro by the changing tides of continental war, his
childhood was far-traveled, perilous, storm-tossed. There were, during long years, no fixed points, no safe harbors. The only anchorage
the little boy and his brothers knew was their mother, always near
them wherever they went.

Riding beside her, watching her, the boy marveled greatly at
his mother's courage and firmness of mind. She was of delicate appearance, with fine eyes, small hands, and tiny feet, yet she carried
herself calmly amid the confusion and danger of wartime travel.
He associated with her character always a "virile authority," which
came from her being frequently and for such long periods separated
from his father, and so forced to act as the real head of her family.
When he was small, his great fear was that their carriage might
go off a cliff in the mountains. One day at a sharp, narrow curve
of the road, a wheel actually slid over a ledge, and their vehicle
hung partly on the mountain, partly suspended in mid-air. Terrified, he and his brothers wanted to climb out at once. But their
mother sternly bade them to sit still. Though she admitted later
having been thoroughly frightened, she sat inside steadily enough,
giving directions to the grenadiers who came with oxen to haul
them back safely on the road.

"Learn never to show fear," she told her sons.

She had pride and carried herself well. In Spain, the officers
and ladies accompanying them always deferred to her, addressing
her as "Countess." But, though she could be stern with her children,
she could also fascinate and amuse them no end by her impetuous
and vivacious sallies; they knew that for them her store of affection
and understanding was bottomless. When she was away, her

youngest son felt that "all poetry and freedom" were gone. Wandering the world, suffering hardships together, they were brought to feel very close to each other, their ties growing always stronger, he knowing himself always surely protected by her, she pitying most of all her youngest-born and loveliest child.

Too often, however, he noticed the shadows at the corners of her thin, finely chiseled mouth as they rode on together. She would be silent for long hours, saying little, and that very deliberately, her eyes, usually so keen and steady in their gaze, avoiding his own, becoming veiled, furtive, a little melancholy. She smiled less and less as they approached the city where they were to rejoin his father.

Perhaps the boy's mind then intuitively called back terrible scenes between his parents in Naples three years before. He and his two brothers were bewildered and terrified by the voice of their father loud in anger at their mother. They could never forget it, much as they dreaded or hated to think of it.

So again in Madrid, upon their arrival, all joy in reunion was crushed by the bitter quarrel that was at once renewed between their parents. Even the youngest child, now nine, heard and saw everything and could not sleep. The anguish of his mother was a torment to him. But why? What did it mean? Why should his father, the general, be so cruel to his mother? Why did she weep at night? Then he suddenly knew what terror this discord could mean for him when an officer came and took him from her, as if by force, to shut him up in the somber Spanish seminary, where he saw her no more for long weeks.

The boy's early years had been made dramatically insecure by long voyaging between places that were no home to him; they were troubled by nightmare scenes witnessed in the wake of war. But worse, for many years his childhood and boyhood were oppressed by the dark shadow of parental strife. Of what caused it, he knew almost nothing until he was much older. Even then he was loath to think of it, and probably never knew the whole, tragic story.

2

The France, the Europe, into which Victor Hugo was born in 1802, "Year X" of the historic French Revolution, was a world much like our own, of world wars, upheavals, and revolutions. Only the modes were Roman; the Emperor Napoleon was budding already that very year in the person of the First Consul. The all-conquering tyrant of the age happened not to be Spanish or German, but French, or, more precisely, a Corsican, risen like some fabulous *condottiere* of feudal Italy to lead the fervent and "invincible" French armies. At all the frontiers of all the nations war ebbed and flowed. Up and down Europe, between victories and disasters, the military despot's battalions, officers, and agents went clattering about, "taking over" countries, cities, or provinces, plundering them, and yet also administering to them some of the blessings of the French Revolution's "new order." One of these plunderer-liberators was the father of Victor Hugo.

By many an allusion, in his memoirs and poems of personal reminiscence, the son tended to underline the profound differences between his father and his mother and the conflict they bred in himself. He would say: "My father was an old soldier of the Republic, my mother a Vendean . . ." His father was a native of Lorraine, the old, half Germanic border province of France; his mother a daughter of Celtic Brittany, whose pious folk, in the name of Church and King, waged such long and bloody combat within France against the French Revolution.

General Joseph Léopold-Sigisbert Hugo was indeed a true son of the great revolution. Born in Nancy, in 1774, he was a plebeian and not a descendant of the ennobled line of Chevalier Hugo of Spitzemberg, as was formerly thought. He was one of the nine children of the master carpenter Joseph Hugo and his wife, who had been a governess, both in turn the descendants of solid, industrious, ruddy-faced Lorraine peasants. His schooling at the Collège Royal of Nancy was interrupted by the arrival of the French Revolution, in 1792. With his father, one of the rising class of artisans, and his six brothers, he became a fervent partisan of the Republic, calling himself the Sans-Culotte "Brutus" Hugo. He volunteered as a mere boy for the army defending France against invading Allied troops and fought at Weissembourg and Valmy, where five of his brothers were killed beside him. At eighteen, "Brutus" Hugo was commissioned a lieutenant, and thereafter the army camps of the French Revolution were his home. "Hunger, thirst, sleeplessness, fatigue, and rags mean nothing to me any longer," he wrote home.

He was a short, broad-shouldered, high-colored youth, with brown hair and merry blue eyes and rather full lips. In battle he showed a reckless courage and was often wounded, once riding into action at the head of his men while still wearing crutches. By conviction he considered himself a disciple of the Friend of Man, Jean-Jacques Rousseau, whose writings he admired; hence a follower of Robespierre. Among his fellow officers he was known for his quick temper, love of fun, his quite florid way of speaking, writing, and even swearing, and his gallantry to the ladies. To amuse his friends he would compose light verses; he had pretensions as a student of mathematics and science; and in his leisure, professing to be an expert of military science, he busied himself writing certain technical monographs on the art of war, such as one "On the Escort and Defense of Convoys, with some Reflections on Pillage." These interests, however, did not prevent him—as he rode into Brittany in 1796 with the Republican columns sent to pacify the region—from entertaining as his traveling companion an agreeable young woman named Louise Bouin, clad in soldier's uniform, who became practically the toast of the regiment.

Captain Hugo, in the spring of 1796, was stationed at the town of Châteaubriant, near Nantes, with the battalion of his devoted friend Major Muscar. One afternoon, on reports of suspicious movements of disguised guerrillas outside the town, he was ordered to reconnoiter with a patrol as far as the farm property of La Renaudière, six miles from Châteaubriant. Near the farm, they met a young woman riding a bay horse, unaccompanied, toward the town. She was stopped and asked by the lieutenant to show her papers and prove her identity.

Her papers proved to be correct, recently drawn by the republican sub-prefect of Nantes who was her grandfather, and showed that she was Sophie Trébuchet, residing at Châteaubriant with her widowed aunt, who was one of the owners of the farm at La Renaudière. The young lady agreed willingly to go back to the farm with the "Blue" officer, identify herself further there, and also provide him with some refreshment for his men and horses.

She was then passably pretty, or *mignonne,* and rode well. Her hair was of a light chestnut color, her features were well-formed and delicate, though marked very slightly with the traces of the all-prevailing smallpox; her brown eyes were keen and proud. The young captain could not forbear to make himself as entertaining as possible on the way to the farm, and the young lady not only laughed merrily, almost nervously, at his sallies, but roundly complimented him, and urged him on. Arrived at the farm, they found wine as well as food. Captain Hugo and his men lingered until evening, and he did not fail to make an appointment to call on the young lady at her home in Châteaubriant the next day. While he lingered, his patrol naturally neglected to scour the neighborhood. From a house in the neighborhood, a dozen priests and a number of Vendean rebel leaders, who had been holding a secret meeting, had time to make good their escape into the dense furze. According to a long-established local legend, Sophie Trébuchet's ride along the road to Châteaubriant that day and her meeting with the "Blues" was no accident, but part of a preconceived plan to reconnoiter the road and send warning to them against danger. Certainly Sophie Trébuchet, on that day, in her whole manner of addressing the young officer, had shown a coquetry that departed widely from her customary reserve.

She was twenty-four, a native of Nantes, the daughter of a Breton sea captain who died young at sea. Her mother, too, had died when she was a child, and so she was brought up in a rather lonely, retired way by her aunt Robin, a widow of independent income, living in Nantes. On both sides of her family, however, she was a descendant of peasants, who had tilled the land near Nantes or Châteaubriant some sixty miles to the north, for two centuries, though some of them had risen to be intendants, or fiscal agents, for the land-holding nobles of upper Brittany. By tradition her people were, therefore, attached to the Bourbon and Catholic cause. But was Sophie Trébuchet a devout Royalist, like her fanatical compatriots who believed in all the saints, sorcerers, and werewolves? She was a Breton; she loved her people, as she loved her low, swampy, brier- and gorse-covered country, her gloomy Vendée. Sophie was given a good lay education; her aunt's favorite reading was Voltaire, the impious one, and he became Sophie's favorite too. Moreover, her relatives, after the Revolution arrived, showed themselves reasonable or opportunistic men, her grandfather even becoming a sub-prefect under the godless Convention.

But in 1794 the horrors of civil war overwhelmed Nantes. Sophie Trébuchet and her aged aunt witnessed and heard the mass executions of Loyalist Vendeans, men and women, priests and nuns, in the near-by central square of their city. Finally they fled northward to Châteaubriant, a smaller town, reported to be at peace, and lived there or at the family-owned farm, at La Renaudière, seven miles outside.

But here, too, guerrilla battles raged sporadically in the wild, thorny moors of upper Brittany. Repression was followed by acts of reprisal. The natives fought on from ambush, for their religion, their superstitions, their countryside, their local habits. Here, where her ancestors had always lived, Sophie Trébuchet knew all the neighboring partisans. Partly out of pity for them, partly because she was romantic, as Bretons—the Irish of France—so often are, she found discreet ways of giving them aid and comfort. She enjoyed the danger she ran in doing this, and such a precarious encounter as that with the young Republican captain.

He came once to call on the two ladies in Châteaubriant, and after that he came every day. A veteran of the Revolution's battlefields at twenty-three, he prided himself on knowing a thing or two about the world. He had a gentle smile, and presented himself as a young man of sensibility, having humane and liberal sentiments. Had he not saved the lives of twenty-two nuns, accused before him of being partisans of the old regime? The jovial young soldier set himself to conquer the Breton girl, but ended by conceiving a considerable respect for her intelligence, the intensity of her convictions, her firmness of character. Alas, in his turbulent youth he had known too few women of Sophie Trébuchet's type. When, after a few months, he was called back to Paris, to serve now in an administrative post at the Council of War, he remembered his evenings in her parlor with regret. On his part an effusive correspondence sprang up. Then one day, more than a year later— Louise Bouin, meanwhile, had left him for another paramour—he sent by letter his proposal of marriage.

She was twenty-five and had no dot, and Léopold Hugo, very young for a captain, was an ambitious fellow, a promising match. After some hesitation she accepted. Formal negotiations were completed by correspondence, and with a brother, Marie-Joseph Trébuchet, a government official at Nantes, she set off for Paris, where, on November 15, 1797, she was joined in civil marriage to Joseph Léopold-Sigisbert.

3

They lived simply at the old Place de Grève in the center of Paris, during the fantastic years of the Directoire, when the capital was filled with noise and fury and debauchery, when political conspiracy ran riot, when a leg of lamb sold for 1,248 francs. Sophie's early letters reported her husband as being an honest and generous man; he spoke of a rapturous contentment at the cleverness and goodness of his wife. A year after their marriage, in November, 1798, a son was born to them and named Abel. In the summer of 1800, after Napoleon's *coup d'état,* when renewed war was expected, they were in Nancy, where Captain Hugo had returned to combat service with the armies of General Moreau lying on the German border.

At Nancy, Sophie was often unhappy, mainly because she lived with her husband's mother and sisters, while he was off on campaigns. Besides, Léopold Hugo showed himself more and more a restless, wayward, unsteady fellow who often had trouble with his superior officers. Promotion now came slowly; he felt his ambitions thwarted and the posts of action he desired refused to him. When he introduced his wife into society—for Nancy hummed then with the social functions of the First Consul's newly-made officers and their ladies—Léopold noticed that she, at any rate, always made a fine impression, as though she were a lady of quality, and this helped him. It was thus that the extremely influential General La Horie, Moreau's chief of staff and a compatriot of Mme. Hugo's, met them, sought them out, and formed the habit of coming to dine with them often. Thanks to this officer's devoted friendship, Léopold Hugo was presented to General Moreau, received an active command in the Army of the Danube, and earned swift promotion to the rank of major and adjutant.

Victor Fanneau La Horie was the son of a rich merchant and landholder of upper Brittany, and had been given an extensive education in Paris; at the Lycée Louis le Grand he had been a classmate of Robespierre, whom he outshone in Latin. In the army he had been advanced rapidly. Like many high officers of the revolutionary government he was widely informed, given to furious labor at all hours, intensely ambitious, absorbed in elaborate political intrigues, thinking nothing of his personal comfort, or even the enjoyment of women—at a time that was notorious for its sexual license. But for Sophie Hugo, whose nature, reserved and yet ardent, was much like his own, he plainly conceived a strong attachment. They had much in common, sharing secretly their dislike for the "excesses" of the Republic and their hopes of an overturn. She reminded him of his own people. He, a slender man, clad always in elegant frock coat and fine boots, with brilliant dark eyes and a rather distant, aristocratic manner, reminded her of the great gentlemen of her own province. Then there was a great deal of high and secret politics going on with reference to La Horie's chief, General Moreau, the popular hero of Hohenlinden, and his chances of replacing the "Corsican upstart." This greatly involved La Horie, a busy negotiator between Moreau and Napoleon, and he found in Mme. Hugo an intelligent and sure confidante, who was always fascinated by the conspiratorial and to whom he could freely unburden himself.

In the late spring of 1800, La Horie, whom she saw almost every day, was gone from Nancy for months, busy with the details of the treaty of Pastdorf. She knew now what his friendship meant and how it filled her heart. He had made certain proposals to her, offering to be her protector, in a manner that was extremely earnest rather than gallant or frivolous. She had rejected them and the upheavals they threatened. There was nothing between them; yet she thought less tenderly nowadays of Léopold, her unsteady spouse, though he was also absent in the field. She was expecting a child again, and was nervous; living with the mother of her husband made her more so; she grew depressed, unable to sleep, "a prey to dark thoughts," as Léopold complained. Against his written wishes, she suddenly packed up and returned to her family at Nantes, with her infant son, leaving her husband a cold little note to the effect that she had gone to her native country to seek "tranquillity, and perhaps even happiness," and that he must come to find her there.

That spring there had been some stormy scenes between them before he departed for Germany. Léopold now wrote to protest his undying affection and entreated her to return. At the end of the summer she yielded to him and returned to Nancy. There she bore her second child, Eugène, in September, 1800.

In the autumn, the historic Peace of Lunéville was being prepared for defeated Austria. The First Consul's elder brother Joseph Bonaparte was to preside over the important proceedings at Lunéville, and there Léopold Hugo was transferred as commandant of the garrison, thus becoming attached to the "court" of Joseph Bonaparte. Here Sophie rejoined her husband in 1801. Consular France was now turning from republican simplicity to a tone and regime of imperial splendor. The diplomatic and social scene was animated and suited to Sophie's fairly patrician tastes. Her husband, moreover, owing to the recent death of his father, had come into an inheritance which he now proceeded to spend royally for her toilette or for his own uniforms. Their position seemed, by this new turn of the wheel, fairly brilliant. In the entourage of Joseph Bonaparte and Moreau she cut a figure and won friendships—even that of the future King Joseph himself—which would stand her in good stead. She was a somebody, a lady, as she had longed to be with all her secretive, romantic nature, and knew again moments of happiness.

It was the full springtime. They took a long carriage ride out into the country and halted to look at the surrounding mountains. The French have an expression, *revenez-y,* which may be translated as "a coming-back-to-it," a return, despite regrets or doubts, for a new trial. Reconciled, Sophie returned to her soldier-husband, even while her heart considered another.

Happy for the world that this last essay, this retracing of steps was attempted—else, what noble pages of prose, what thousands of resonant verses, what an abundance of golden rhymes might have been lost to the literature of France and all mankind!

"Thou wert conceived, among the eagles as it were, among the highest peaks of the Vosges," Léopold Hugo, in his babbling old age, used to remind his third son impressively. The place of his birth, however, was at a further remove, in the "old Spanish city" of Besançon, on the border of Switzerland, in the province of Franche-Comté, where, after the Treaty of Lunéville, Léopold Hugo was transferred to serve as commandant of a battalion.

Victor Hugo was born on February 26, 1802, very small and weak, "his neck bent like a reed," so that they almost despaired of his life. They had expected a girl, who would have been named Victorine. They baptized him instead Victor-Marie, after his godfather, General La Horie, their patron and friend. La Horie had said: "Hugo is a northern name. Let us soften it with Victor, which is of the south, and thus surmount the Germanic with the Roman."

The child was small and sickly. Only the unsleeping care of his mother saved him, so that, thanks to her, he would believe himself to have been "twice-born." Léopold Hugo's letters of the period testify proudly to his wife's fiercely possessive, maternal passion and unremitting devotion to her children, whom, in spite of the customs of the time, she insisted upon nursing at her own breast.

At this very moment, however, when the worn mother, but six weeks after her confinement, spent herself to keep her youngest-born alive, Léopold behaved with a light-minded disregard of their future which both exasperated and disheartened her. He squabbled with his colonel, whom he suspected of having committed irregularities with the regimental funds, and, irrepressible man that he was, denounced his superior by writing to Paris and fomented a perfect insurrection among the troops and lower officers at Besançon. An evidently painstaking investigation by the Inspector General of Napoleon followed, and Léopold Hugo was shown to have been extravagant and unjust in his charges, and to have injured the discipline of his whole regiment. Court-martial and dismissal were indicated; for Napoleon was now taking stern measures to discipline his armies and prepare for the change from Consular Republic to Empire. For the moment, while judgment of his case was pending, Hugo and his disaffected battalion were ordered to Marseilles, an inactive post, and a partial disgrace.

As they packed to move once more, under this new blow, Sophie felt as if a nemesis overhung them. She wondered if the tiny Victor would survive the hard journey to the south by carriage. Her husband, she was convinced, was a weak fool whose prospects were gone. Marseilles, once reached, was like a place of exile, farther than ever from the admired friend now stationed in Paris with whom she contrasted Leopold so unfavorably.

In the autumn of 1802, her husband, hearing that he was very likely to be cashiered, begged Sophie to go to Paris and appeal for the aid of the influential personages they had met at Lunéville, chiefly Joseph Bonaparte, General Henri Clarke (Minister of War), and General La Horie. He believed that she, by her cleverness, might succeed in winning pardon where he had thus far failed. She agreed, and departed late in November, 1802, though it cost her much to leave Abel and Eugène, and the tiny nine-months-old Victor, in the care of their father and a nurse. Yet their very future depended on her mission.

4

In Paris, Sophie Hugo succeeded by strenuous personal appeals in saving her husband from outright dismissal, but could not prevent his being indirectly degraded by an assignment to obscure garrison duty in Corsica; then after a few months, to still more insignificant garrison duty at Elba, in 1803. Meanwhile, she lingered on in Paris for an unconscionable time, while Léopold, usually the very soul of jollity, wrote her sad, reproachful little notes from Portoferraio, Elba, describing how faithfully he, the good nurse Claudine, and her husband (his manservant) attended to the three infants. There was no doubt that Léopold Hugo took joy in his sons, when he saw them and thought of them. To wring the withers of his absent Sophie he told also, in a letter of March 18, 1803, how the infant Victor, now just a year old and exceedingly pretty, was getting his first teeth; how he, together with Eugène, only three, cried often for his mama. He closed: "If the little one does not recognize you on your return, at least he will certainly make up for it quickly, for he looks all the time as if he has lost something." And again the officer wrote: "I could not help shedding a tear when Victor, carried in by Claudine, fixed his eyes on your chair, and directed all his regard with great anxiety to all the corners of the room. The dear child has not stopped looking for you everywhere and is not distracted from this search either by the mischief of his brothers, or by my caresses."

Léopold closed with protestations of his undying love for her, alluding to "burning fires which sear" and to "bonds which shall never be broken" holding him to his "adored Sophie." But by July, 1803, he was growing restive and wrote his wife: "Everybody here complains of the fact that I go out so seldom; everyone is surprised that you have not yet come back, and that I am in charge of the children. It causes some chatter which reaches me, but I say nothing . . ." Léopold-Sigisbert, however, had by now formed a tender and intimate connection with the daughter of an orderly in the Elba military hospital, Catherine Thomas. . . .

Why did Sophie tarry so late in Paris? Travel was long in those days; the trip from Marseilles to Paris and return to distant Elba, by way of Italy, might consume all of three months, but not eight. Her passion for her children was imperious. Yet this once she abandoned them entirely for a passion of another kind.

A week after her arrival in Paris in December, 1802, she had seen her friend General La Horie. The "Victor Hugo, Related by a Witness of his Life" (dictated by the poet himself in 1853), tells us piously that his mother visited with the Pierre Fouchers, Breton compatriots, who were old friends of the Hugo couple. We now know that she had gone to General La Horie's instead. She had surrendered herself to him, at last, with a firm resolution—despite her children and the danger she raised for their whole future.

There was, indeed, nothing light about their love. This meeting, this union, was the fruit of a long-weighed decision, a long-smoldering passion and faith in each other. No one saw them in public at the theaters and dancing places where lovers openly disported themselves. These two moody and impetuous Bretons moved together along solitary paths, finding happiness in each other, yet each suffering torment. Sophie was in an agony of suspense over her distant children as the days prolonged themselves. But La Horie was in very danger of his life, and it was characteristic of Sophie that she had resolved as at one throw to join him at this dark hour.

After the Peace of Amiens in March, 1802, Paris swarmed with returned priests of Mother Church, Royalists in disguise, disaffected soldiers in temporary retirement, and British agents. The breach between the mighty General Moreau (then forced into retirement) and the First Consul widened. Royalist and English plotters pushed into the breach, wooing the embittered republican general; and La Horie, long Moreau's most intimate counselor, also removed from active duty, worked day and night with the contrivers of the Pichegru-Cadoudal plot to eliminate Napoleon, in favor, possibly of Moreau, possibly of an ultimate Bourbon restoration. La Horie, though his career was interrupted at forty, had money and property worth some 100,000 francs, his prize at Hohenlinden. He had purchased a charming estate along the Seine, near Vernon, and, bringing Sophie there, in its garden unfolded his dream of a bucolic and scholarly future with Sophie and her children. But, first, he must help execute the great plan, which she cherished no less than he, of bringing about the *chute* of the dictator, for the sake of France, for the sake of liberty itself, as they conceived it. All the more she was drawn to him by his resolution, his daring aspirations—so lacking in her husband—which might, when the hour struck, carry him to Heaven knew what exalted place in the future regime.

She thought of her children. As the huge, growing conspiracy matured during 1803, she, probably aware of its timing, resolved to leave Paris, return to them and prepare to bring them back at the right moment, separating herself forever from Hugo. She had written him very rarely. But in July, 1803, after having further complaints from him, she set off for Italy, and reached Elba, via Leghorn, two months later.

Their meeting was stormy. Saying nothing for the moment of her connection with La Horie, or her ultimate plans, she proposed that she take the children back with her to live in Paris, for they could receive no education worth the name in barbarous Elba— and there wait for events more favorable to Léopold Hugo's career.

Because he could never refuse a woman anything, Léopold eventually agreed to Sophie's plan, and also promised to provide her, out of his appointments, with a meager 150 francs a month.

Later Sophie charged that he consented to this "in order to live at liberty with his mistress," Catherine Thomas. But it was true also that renewed war was expected at any moment, and Elba would be besieged by the British. It was better to evacuate the women and children then than see them made prisoners later. Afterward, Léopold Hugo (in his suit for a legal separation and control of the children) argued in different vein that his "inflexible spouse" had treated him with a great and cold indifference, "denying me all conjugal relations," as he said, and depriving him of his children.

Scrupulously she had kept her lips pure for La Horie, in a waiting that was half sensual, half mystical. Leaving Elba with her children in late November, 1803, she gained Livorno, after a rough sea passage—Léopold testified later that she had ignored the threatening weather in her haste to leave—then Marseilles and Paris again, on February 16, 1804. At once she hurried to La Horie's residence, in the rue des Petits-Champs. He was gone. But on his door was posted an official police bulletin, relating the recently attempted plot against the life of Napoleon, the arrest of Pichegru, Cadoudal, and Moreau, and the proscription of a long list of others who had escaped into hiding, for whose delivery large rewards were offered: first among them was the name of *Brigadier General Victor de La Horie!*

5

As soon as they had reached dry land and their carriage trundled northward, the three Hugo children were happy, first because they were with their mother, and then because they were in movement again and could look at the fleeing landscape through the carriage *portière* all day long. Victor, who, at the age of two, cried often, had huge blue eyes, golden hair, and a delicate, curving mouth. In fact all three of the children were golden-haired cherubs, and the passengers who rode with them could never praise them enough for their beauty and sweetness. Sophie Hugo had suffered immeasurably for being separated from them, and now clung to them all the harder for her sense of guilt in having abandoned them momentarily. Always self-possessed, undemonstrative, she knew proudly that her happiness was complete. She would never leave her sons again; she would fight for them like a lioness against those who might seek to take them from her. Her passion for them grew to be obsessive, almost morbid, and left marks, as of claws, upon their young unconscious minds.

In Paris, they lived for two years between 1804 and 1806 in a house at number 24 rue de Clichy, then at the outskirts of the town. All that Victor Hugo remembered of the place was the sheltered back-yard garden, with its horse trough, willow tree, and dry well, at whose edge he always played.

In May, 1804, Napoleon proclaimed the Empire, and Mme. Hugo, more mysterious than ever, rarely went out, and received few visitors. During these two secluded years Victor Hugo grew up to be a somewhat solemn little boy of four. His father, when he saw him in 1807, in Italy again, noted that he showed "an aptitude for learning. He is as deliberate as his elder brothers and very thoughtful. He speaks little and always to the point. His reflections have often struck me. He has a very sweet face."

During those two years in Paris, he did not know that his mother's friend lodged for a time directly across the street from them, at number 19 rue de Clichy. The police raided the place one night, but the man was not there, having gone to pass the night at number 24 rue de Clichy. La Horie lived as a hunted man in those days, moving from place to place, changing horses quickly, always, thanks to timely information, keeping a jump ahead of the Imperial secret police.

The presence in France of some of the surviving conspirators of 1804 was quietly tolerated. It was known that General Moreau, secretly released from jail on his promise to go to America, was given two years' time to liquidate his property. The same latitude was evidently allowed his aide, La Horie, by Fouché's police. But what they did not understand was his long delay in going abroad to safety; they did not know of the romantic, all-absorbing connection that detained him, and sometimes grew impatient and sent searching parties for him.

Meanwhile, Léopold Hugo felt himself rotting away at the army garrison in Elba. His pleas for more active service or advancement were refused because of his previous connections with Moreau and La Horie. Sometimes for months on end he cried his poverty and sent no money to Sophie for the support of his dependents, who would have starved if there had not been another devoted and generous protector. But in 1806 Sophie heard that Léopold was recalled to active service in northern Italy, with the army of the brilliant General Masséna; later, that he fought under Joseph Bonaparte, now King of Naples, who, finally overcoming his suspicions, rewarded Hugo for distinguished service by promoting him to a colonelship and naming him governor of Avellino, the city and province which Hugo helped to "pacify." It was this advancement—at a time when her lover had fled for his very life—that determined Sophie to make another long voyage, with her children, to Naples, in December, 1807. It was an attempt at a reasonable settlement between them, for the sake of their children.

Léopold had often reproached her for living far off in Paris, causing him added expense. But, now that she came to Naples, there were raging scenes between them, echoes of which certainly reached the children's ears.

They saw but little of their legendary father. He remained mostly at Avellino, living openly with his mistress, while they were lodged in Naples. The couple parted again, Mme. Hugo having his agreement that she should return to Paris with the children. He promised, now that his rank had improved, more generous sums for their support and education, some three hundred francs a month.

"Let time soften the memory of these unhappy circumstances," he said to his estranged wife. "Raise your children in the respect they owe us and with the education owing to them. . . . Let us live for them, and cling to them, since we have shown how impossible it was for us to be attached to each other."[1]

They arrived in Paris by the Lyons mailcoach, on February 7, 1809. At the terminal, a stranger soberly elegant in a long blue frock coat, and wearing a wig, was waiting for them.

"Don't you remember *M. de Courlandais?*" their mother asked the children. Vaguely they recalled having seen him, but they had never known him under this name.

In Paris, Sophie Hugo, after some hunting, found a charming old house with a large garden in a very rural quarter, at number 12 Impasse des Feuillantines, a small blind alley which intersected the old rue Saint-Jacques near the Renaissance dome of Val-de-Grâce. It had been an abandoned convent of the Feuillantines Sisters and was partly renovated, partly ruined. The house had high and spacious rooms, and the salon through tall, arched windows overlooked the greenery of a deep garden, like the great houses she had loved in Brittany. It was like a house set in a park, and she furnished it lavishly with chairs, rugs, tables, mahogany consoles, gilt vases, clocks, and curtains.

When the children saw the place they rushed about like savages.

[1] See Appendix, Note I.

The garden had been untended for years and was full of overgrown fruit trees, wild vines, flowers and weeds, not to speak of rabbits, insects and butterflies, and at the end of it stood a grove of shade trees. Mme. Hugo said to her boys: "Play, but you must not step on the flowers or climb on the ladders."

"May we climb the trees?" they cried.

"Yes, but you must not eat the fruit." They climbed the trees but ate only the grapes or fruit on the trees of the garden next door, with permission of a kindly old man, who was the astronomer Lalande. They played at war; they explored the attic rooms and on rainy days read all the musty books there, books full of old engravings, until night suddenly overtook them.

Here, in the old Feuillantines garden, from the age of seven, begin Victor Hugo's memories of happiness and of a first permanent dwelling place. He grew up at liberty, playing within these quiet walls with his brothers, who were nine and eleven, and with the two children of Pierre Foucher, friend of his family, who were named Victor and Adèle and were close to his own age. They had a swing in the tree, and Victor, who feared no heights, would swing himself almost over the tree tops. They would play blindman's buff, blindfolding little Adèle usually, wheeling her about in an old wheelbarrow and demanding of her, when they halted, where they were, tormenting her until she cried to be set free. The boy, in later years, wrote:

> The garden was large, deep, mysterious,
> Shut in by high walls from the eyes of the curious,
> Strewn with wild flowers and vermilion insects . . .

It was a poem that counted over in recollection the sum of unspoiled happiness, which had been not too abundant in his childhood.

But Mme. Hugo too was happy, or as nearly so as she could dare to be. One day she called the children into the salon and there was the man "M. de Courlandais," whom their mother also addressed as "General"—slightly pockmarked, with black hair, sideburns, and piercing eyes. That evening he joined them for dinner. He was there the next day, and the next. Soon they discovered that in the wooded depths of the garden a half dilapidated little building, formerly an old sacristy, had been cleaned up and he had been installed there as a permanent guest. The home in Les Feuillantines was now complete, as was Sophie Hugo's happiness.

The general was a little stooped, worn, with lined face, thanks to years of hunted life, though she would never believe him changed. For a period he had gained a secret reprieve from Fouché's police; his temporary hiding place in the sheltered corner of old Paris was known, as was his assumed name. He had promised to stay only until he had arranged his affairs and could go away to America. Meanwhile he lived with Sophie Hugo and her family, in the garden, much as Jean Valjean lived hidden in the convent garden of Picpus. The Hugo children who saw him every day were told to say nothing of his presence. He must lie low, never going out; occasionally a few sure friends called discreetly.

General La Horie loved the Hugo children; he knew how to tell stories, and also, as Victor Hugo recalled, he knew how to play games. On the broad stone steps leading from the house to the garden, in fine weather, he would cook campfire suppers for them and tell them of his campaigns. To his godson, whom he used to catch in his arms and throw up in the air, he was mentor, reading and translating Tacitus to him when he was but eight years old and inspiring him with his enthusiasms.

One day two friends of La Horie's came to visit him secretly, and the boy overheard them discussing certain repressive measures of the Emperor. To his surprise he heard them speak of the great ruler only as "Bonaparte." One of them exclaimed, as he recalled fifty years later: "Brumaire was the fall of the Republic. To efface Brumaire, I would make any sacrifice. I would give all my fortune." "I would give my life," said the other, adding, "France is not great, if she is not free." And then General La Horie, noticing that little Victor listened to them in his solemn way, turned to him suddenly and exclaimed: "My child, remember, liberty above all!"

During some eighteen months at Les Feuillantines, Victor saw more of General La Horie than he had seen of his own father during all his previous life. In some measure, the fervent, emphatic, and ill-starred man assumed the father relationship that was painfully absent in his boyhood. In a revealing passage of Les Misérables Victor Hugo himself has described the strange childhood of Marius, the young student who, much like himself, was brought up in alienation from his father—an episode based entirely, as he indicated elsewhere, on his own experience:

The child, who was known as Marius, knew that he had a father, but nothing more. No one ever let out a peep about all that. However, in the circles which his grandfather frequented, the whisperings, the half-words, the winks, had been going on about him so long that they had ended by reaching the mind of the small boy; and as he absorbed naturally, by a sort of infiltration and slow penetration, those ideas and opinions which were, so to speak, his respirable environment, so, little by little, did he come to think of his father only with shame and a stifling heart.

For his early education, Victor Hugo has said in one of his poems, he had only "a mother, a garden, a priest." Mme. Hugo had a power over her sons and seems to have held them in awe of her, yet she seems almost never to have punished them. Despite her stern airs, she believed in *l'éducation à la liberté*. She had read her *Emile,* and for years she simply permitted her sons to play out of doors, in the garden, to their hearts' desire. In addition Sophie Hugo had them read anything they liked. There was a lending library near by, in the rue Saint-Jacques, and the mother even had the two younger boys select and read books for her; that is, if they found them good, she read them afterward. Upstairs in the little shop was a mezzanine full of forbidden books, free in language and morals. The bookseller barred the way there, keeping these books under lock and key. But Sophie Hugo said, "Books never do any harm," and so he unlocked these bookcases and they read not only Voltaire but also Restif de la Brettonne.

In the autumn of 1810, however, she thought more must be done for them; Abel, who was twelve, was sent to a *collège,* while Eugène, ten, and Victor, eight, were sent to a small near-by pension as day pupils. The rather mildly ruled pension Victor attended was that of a former Oratorian priest, Father Larivière, who, in terror of the Convention, had long ago defrocked himself and taken his servant to wife. He was a kindly old man, as "naïve as a scholar, as malicious as a child," the boy remembered. Victor, whose precocity was always noticed by his elders, had already learned to read, at the age of four or five, simply by looking at letters. He was now, at about nine, taught Latin and a little Greek, as well as history and grammar—that is to say, when Father Larivière did not choose to take long naps and leave his wife and housekeeper to conduct classes. The other pupils were a half dozen boys from the neighborhood who were learning their three "R's." When school would be out, at an early hour, Victor and his brother, who were forbidden to play with the other school children in the street, would come running back to the garden and to "M. de Courlandais," who waited for them.

This tranquil, idyllic existence, in a sheltered garden and a house in a forgotten corner of Paris—chosen by Mme. Hugo for its seclusion—was rudely interrupted on one of the last days of December, 1810. Six years had passed since the Pichegru conspiracy had failed. La Horie hoped that leniency was now in order. He had even received word that Napoleon, hearing his name mentioned, had spoken of him on one occasion in friendly terms, saying: "La Horie? Why does he not show himself? Or address himself to me?" Openly, the fugitive now sent a petition to Savary, an old comrade in arms, who had succeeded Fouché as Minister of Police, asking for a chance to prove his innocence and the right to resume his duties in the armies, now greatly in need of officers. He had given his address and promised that he would appear openly at police headquarters on December 29, 1810, to make his appeal in person. When he put in his appearance on that day, he was told politely to return home and wait while the Emperor decided his case. "At last I am going to be a free man!" he told Sophie Hugo.

The following morning, while the family were gathered at the breakfast table, Mme. Hugo in her bonnet, the general in a dressing gown, the children ready to go to school, the maid announced two strangers who wished to see "M. de Courlandais." Cheerfully he went to the door. Then there was heard the sound of loud voices, a scuffle, the door slamming, a carriage rolling off. "Madame!" cried the maid, Claudine, *they are taking him away!*

6

The Feuillantines place was gloomy that winter of 1811 in Paris. Victor Hugo's mother was careful to keep her sorrow, her drama, locked up within the walls of the old convent park. "We must suffer and die in silence," he remembered her saying to him one day. Undeniably she was disposed to dramatize herself in her own proud way. But, in those times, who was not? Victor Hugo's mother was a daughter of the spectacular revolutionary era in France. She had seen, in her youth, all fixed points and institutions swept away in the storm, nobles, priests, kings, and brothers or friends in arms against each other.

Now, under the regime of Napoleon, there was law and order in France, yet many died horribly in battle; others, driven by their gambling ambition, were suddenly broken, or disappeared forever, at the whim of the tyrant, while still others piled up fortunes in plunder by his favor.

Napoleon, turning the revolutionary drives of anti-Royalist and anti-clerical impulses to his own ends, had become the Image of Authority. Victor Hugo, as a boy, saw him from close by one day of festival. It was at the plaza of the Panthéon, all illuminated and bedecked, where a great crowd waited and sang: *"Veillons sur l'Empire!"* ("Let us watch over the Empire!"). Then they fell silent as a procession of high military officials, with some princes and kings among them, all in uniforms of brilliant color, began to file out of the Panthéon and down its broad steps. To see the better, the boy slipped from his mother's hand and clambered between people's legs until he reached the edge of the cleared space. There he saw that small man "of solemn and illustrious face," but wearing an old cockade and a gray greatcoat that was shabby and worn, passing, "silent and grave, like a bronze god," through that multitude.

Victor Hugo was to be of several minds about this man. But to begin with he learned from his dramatic and "conspiratorial" mother to fear and hate him, Image of Authority that he was. She bred in him this hatred, not because she was a pious royalist, as he afterward tended to explain it. She had other and sufficient reasons. A portion of her heart was enclosed within Vincennes Prison by the orders of the dictator.

But while a La Horie, after years of hiding and waiting, lay in prison waiting for his trial as a traitor, which could have but one outcome, others enjoyed large, and sometimes, sudden, betterment of place and fortune. In the winter of 1811, Colonel Louis Hugo, Léopold's only surviving brother, arrived in Paris from Madrid with amazing tales of his brother's rapid advancement and glory. Serving now in Spain, under Joseph Bonaparte, the turbulent officer had shown his talent for dealing with guerrilla bands. The Bonapartist pretender had made him a general, marshal of the palace, first aide-de-camp to the King, governor of three provinces, and, finally, Count of Siguenza.

That this soldier of fortune gathered in plunder as well as honor was conveyed to Mme. Hugo by his Paris banker, who reported the receipt of some 51,000 francs, which she was instructed to invest in French land. Besides, word was brought to her that King Joseph, who remembered her favorably, desired that she and her husband should become reconciled and live together *en famille* at his court.

For the advantage of her children, to reunite them with their father, Mme. Hugo determined at once to take back her place beside her spouse. Drawing a very large sum on her husband's bank, over 12,000 francs, she set off with her three sons on March 15, 1811. That was the eventful voyage, in which they traveled in state, which Victor remembered most vividly of all, even down to the baron of beef, the slaughtered sheep, the keg of brandy, and the iron bed with which his mother burdened their large equipage.

Arriving in Madrid, they were installed in an apartment of the imposing Masserano Palace. Victor Hugo at nine had an eye which observed things in its own way, and a tenacious memory. Although his mother disliked antiquities or ruins as much as mountain scenery, he looked his fill at Burgos, Valladolid, and Segovia; at the tomb of the Cid, which French soldiers used as a target for musketry practice; and at the portraits in the gallery of the Masserano Palace where the grandees of other centuries looked down upon him as he played.

General Hugo had not known that they were coming. When, after several days, he arrived from Guadalajara, he was in a towering rage. On July 10, 1811, he brought with him a petition for divorce and papers authorizing the transfer of the children to his care. Abel Hugo, aged thirteen, was assigned to be a page of the King, while the two younger boys, Eugène and Victor, were placed in the College of Nobles, a large seminary that had only twenty-four pupils. Victor slept with his brother in a bare, monastic cell without a brazier to warm them in winter. His fellow pupils seemed to him vain and cruel, and there was often war to the knife between the Spanish and French boys. He feared the priests, his teachers, who concealed little of their hatred of France, and, since he could go out on only two days a week, the place seemed all the more a funereal prison to him.

Léopold Hugo had learned, by now, of his wife's transgressions with his old friend and superior officer, La Horie. Thunder and damnation! He would not forgive in her a frailty of which he himself, so often and easily, was guilty. King Joseph had been absent in July. When he returned, Sophie Hugo's entreaties were so moving that he imposed peace and restored the two younger children to her. But later, when General Hugo determined that the King should be informed of his wife's guilty connections with a conspirator against the Empire, he was of a different mind, and the children were sent back to the seminary. The indomitable Mme.

Hugo fought her case skillfully. Somehow, after long weeks, she succeeded in convincing the King of her "innocence" and of her husband's injustice to her. A settlement was made in her favor, with her children going back to her once more and a part of Léopold's large emoluments, 13,000 francs a year, assigned to her for their upkeep.

The repeated ordeal of forcible separation from his mother stamped in Victor Hugo's soul, as a boy, a fear of unbelievable, inexplicable cruelty, a fixation of hate and rebellion against the "tyrant father." (Upon his even more high-strung brother, Eugène, the effect was more morbid still.) Long years afterward, dictating his memoirs, he told of the strife between his parents by implication, or by vague allusions, rather than in detail. Even then, when the experience of life had reconciled him to a great many painful things, he wrote bitterly:

The children, by force of events, took the side of their mother; they never left her, she never troubled them in any way, she let them choose their future, she was for them *freedom and poetry;* whereas, their father was to them a sort of stranger who appeared before them in Madrid only to *imprison* them in the College of Nobles, and at Paris, only to *imprison* them in the Pension Cordier, and *to condemn them in perpetuity* to the study of mathematics.

But at last the two younger children were rescued again, reunited with their mother, and en route to France once more. Spain remained in Victor Hugo's memory as a reservoir of medievalism, chivalrous and cruel, mysterious and picturesque, inherently romantic. It was high time they left. Spain was rising again; Wellington with his mixed English-Iberian armies approached from the west and would soon fight his way into the valley of the Telavera, at Toledo, smashing the armies of Marshal Soult and sweeping all the Peninsula. As the horizon darkened for French Imperial power, the families of the officers and Empire nobles retreated to safety northward, back to France.

The Hugos fled northward with a great convoy of fearful compatriots. They were but three now, Abel having remained with his father. Mme. Hugo was more silent and preoccupied than ever. During her absence La Horie was to have been tried—only fragmentary, secret reports, passing through many hands, had reached her. Late in April, 1812, she was in Paris and, committing the children to the care of the servants, she rushed to Vincennes Prison.

She found him still there, waiting for her. He had not been ill-treated; as a political prisoner he enjoyed certain liberties, an apartment with a small parlor, books, and visitors. Napoleon had recently ordered extensive prison reforms—but under the dictator's secret police justice moved by mysterious ways. La Horie, though he had asked for judgment, had not even been tried after more than a year had passed.

Every few days Sophie Hugo saw her lover, in his parlor within the walls of Vincennes. Spring was poignant. Summer came and passed, and hope rose in the hearts of the two inveterate conspirators. La Horie, always in secret touch with his underground colleagues of various political shades, heard that the very throne of Caesar, departed to conquer Russia, was now shaking. With desperate humor a new plot was being cunningly woven. In fact, the highly theatrical adventures of La Horie and his associate, General Malet, not long after this time became a fruitful subject for the authors of popular melodrama.

At a given signal they were to leave their cells (then somewhat poorly guarded), open the political prisons, spread the news of Napoleon's "death," rally the host of oppositionists in Paris, and descend upon the government buildings in the center of the capital to complete their *coup de main*. Such things were not invented by Dumas, but were possibilities in those cape-and-sword days.

La Horie slept little. A passionate Latinist, he read Sallust and his bedside book was found afterward with the significant passage marked by his hand: *Audacio pro muro habetur. . . . Semper in praelio, his maximum est periculum, qui maxime timent.* In effect, "Boldness must be our rampart. The greatest danger is to those who have most fear!" It was as if the old Roman writer beckoned him to his mad enterprise.

At dawn, on October 23, 1812, General Malet was abroad, startling the police with his strange battalion; La Horie was set free and, at the head of a file of men, took over the Ministry of Police from his old friend and betrayer, Savary, the Duke of Rovigo. For four hours the conspirators "ruled" Paris; then they were swept from their comedians' seats by guards and police, rearrested, and quickly court-martialed.

Had Sophie received knowledge of all these desperate endeavors? She knew that something was to happen. Then from her friend Pierre Foucher, chief clerk to the War Department, she learned the details of the abortive uprising and the sentencing of her lover.

During the court-martial proceedings, so close were the Breton links, she was in the next apartment (the Fouchers'), waiting to hear the end. On October 29 the tumbrils rolled out, and La Horie and his friends faced the firing squad. The distracted woman walked the streets with her son Victor all that day. There were bulletins on the walls announcing the execution of the enemies of the regime. Among those heading the list, she pointed to the name Victor Fanneau de La Horie. "Look," she cried, "it is your god-father, 'M. de Courlandais.' They have killed him!"

They returned to the garden of the Feuillantines; she sat by the high windows overlooking the park, autumn brown, in shadow. It was the end of her love story. The passionate Sophie now more than ever lived only for her children. Most of all, the little godson, the *other* Victor.

CHAPTER II

The Restoration: Boyhood and Youth

At the end of the long journey from Spain in 1812 Victor Hugo found again his beloved garden of the Feuillantines in the old Saint-Jacques quarter of Paris, where he lived with his mother for three years in all. The swing was still in the tree, and the old wheelbarrow, the birds, the wild buttercups were still there.

He was now ten and had grown to be a sturdy boy. He had his father's big round head, and the same features which, though coarse and jovial in General Hugo, were in him exceedingly refined and delicate. His large, light brown eyes and his open and high forehead suggested something of his mother. The early portraits show him clinging to his mother with a solemn and somewhat wistful look at his full curving mouth, but having a face of great beauty and sweetness that often caused people to stare at him.

Both he and his elder brother Eugène had been made rather serious for their age, though they were very affectionate and devoted to each other. Returning to Father Larivière's, their instruction continued, incomplete, but in an individualistic manner that permitted them to go as far as they liked in their reading and in Latin. But at games Victor showed himself zestful, and even showed a touch of cruelty, usually toward the little Foucher girl, Adèle, whom he liked to slap. The games in those Napoleonic days were mainly war games; they were elaborate and violent, and Victor struggled to keep up with his brother Eugène and other older boys, one of whom always impersonated Napoleon. When it came to climbing, he was the most fearless one and had no sense of vertigo; the others would send him up into the highest branches of big trees to gather nuts or fruits. Victor showed ingenuity in carpentry, building most ambitious fortifications out of packing boxes he found in the coach house at Les Feuillantines. After he and his brothers had been taken to the theater, usually to see popular melodramas of the type of "The Ruins of Babylon," by Pixérécourt, they busied themselves producing plays of their own, together with the two Foucher children and the children of other military friends of their parents. Victor usually did most of the building of stage and dressing rooms out of old boxes, and also made most of the scenery, for he had a marked talent for drawing. His early lesson books were filled with skillful, careful pen drawings of human figures and animals in illustration of the Latin proverbs or fables of Aesop he had to memorize.

This phase of carefree play and undisciplined schooling did not last long. For the real Napoleon, playing at his real war games, disasters were accumulating in 1813. Taking a map, the Hugo boys traced the reported movement of the battle lines, which approached closer to France's borders. Not only was the Caesar of France defeated and driven back on Paris, but General Hugo, owing to French reverses in Spain, saw his fortunes sink swiftly. Soon the remittances from him dwindled to small monthly sums, or almost nothing. Early in 1814, Mme. Hugo removed to smaller quarters in what is now called the rue du Cherche-Midi, adjoining the residence of her friends the Fouchers in the Toulouse Mansion. At this same time, General Hugo returned to France and was assigned to the defense of the fortress of Thionville, on the northern frontier, and, with great gallantry, held this citadel until after Napoleon had capitulated and departed for Elba. The Imperial regime collapsed in a convulsive upheaval, whose spectacular epilogue was to be the Hundred Days and Waterloo in the following year. For the Hugo family, the repercussions of these swift historic events were a renewal of the bitter feud between Mme. Hugo and her husband, now living in the same country.

The general, as a Bonapartist officer, was confined, on parole, by the new Bourbon government, to residence in the town of Thionville, where he lived openly and in comfortable style with his mistress, Catherine Thomas, on the remains of his Spanish fortune. The legal force of agreements made under King Joseph was no longer valid now that that pretender had vanished; the general's mistress, moreover, urged him to reduce or even to eliminate the remittance he gave to his wife and children.

Whereupon the stout-hearted Sophie Hugo, in May, 1814, with her eldest son Abel as her defender, proceeded to Thionville and, in a military sense, invested her husband's home there. With her son she forcibly established herself in the house and required of the general that he provide for the support of herself and his children.

The Corsican consort swooned. The general, who now warmly hated his wife—he was a man of warm blood rather than of bad heart—flew into one of his famous fits of choler and threatened Sophie with his whip. But she held her ground, with composure, very much the "countess," and he was forced to retreat with his lady and take up residence at another villa outside the town.

Mme. Hugo now instituted, under French law, a lengthy process against her husband for legal separation and support—for which purpose she had established residence in his home—while the general prepared to give answer with a suit for full divorce, on the ground of her own infidelity. However, his own family and his old friend, Pierre Foucher, now appealed to him to avoid such an extreme measure as that of a public divorce on grounds that would stain his wife's character and darken the future of his own sons. Léopold Hugo relented—but court processes already initiated by him resulted in bailiffs' temporarily sealing all the rooms and furniture of Mme. Hugo's home in Paris, while her two younger sons, who had been cared for by the Fouchers, were placed in the custody of General Hugo's sister, Mme. Martin, whom they heartily disliked.

The feud of hate and vengeance vaguely felt, and yet raging around them, almost made Victor and his brother Eugène ill with grief. On May 30, 1814, Eugène Hugo, then fourteen, wrote to his mother that, during her absence, Victor and he were busy doing drawings, which they hoped to have all finished and ready to show her when she returned. On holidays they took walks with M. Foucher, in the Jardin des Plantes, the Paris zoo. He concluded: "Everything here is in perfect order, just as if you were at home." Eugène indicates, at this stage, the methodical and orderly way in which Mme. Hugo ran her home, and tries to assure her that he is keeping to her standards.

But from Victor, who is only twelve, there comes a poignant cry to the mother who has been his one rock of safety in a world of storm and danger:

A Madame la Comtesse Hugo, à Thionville
My dear Mamma:

Since you went away things are very dull here. We often go to see
M. Foucher as you told us to do. He suggested that we share his
son's lessons; we have declined with thanks. Every morning we work
at our Latin and mathematics. . . .

Come back soon! Without you we don't know what to do or what
to say; we are very confused. We never cease thinking of you.
Mamma! Mamma!—Your respectful son,

Victor

His mother returned eventually; but in September of that same
year, 1814 (the outcome of the case was undetermined for four
years), the general came to Paris and took charge of the education of his sons. He "imprisoned" them in a large pension, that of
Cordier and Decotte, where they were to live as boarding pupils
and receive an intermediate education to prepare them for the
Polytechnical School. It was his intention that they should be
trained to be artillery or engineering officers. He also gave strict
orders that they were to be kept out of the hands of their mother.
Abel, his eldest son, now almost seventeen, took a position as a
clerk with a business concern.

Victor Hugo's days of enchanted freedom were over. In effect
the pension where he lived was, if not a prison, next door to a
prison, the old *Abbaye,* on the grimy rue Margueritte, near the
Passage du Dragon; and he laid his own "imprisonment" to his
father's malevolence. Whatever might be said to him, on the few
occasions when he saw his father, he loyally protested and defended
his mother in his serious and measured way. One day in defiance
of orders, unable to bear his separation, Victor ran away from
school to see his mother and at last threw himself into her arms.
When he returned, he was slapped by his master and given deten-
tion, which he bore stoically.

The general, who was now in straits, living on a major's half
pay, made violent complaint of his sons' disaffection, saying: "It is
their cursed mother who is to blame for the conduct of those
children. Do they think they can destroy a whole new suit of
clothes every six months?" Mme. Hugo had never denied them
anything. He spoke of his wife as a "she-devil," or a "wretched
woman" who was "insatiable for money."

When Mme. Hugo one day showed her sons a furious letter from their father containing similar language, Eugène and Victor both sat down and, of their own accord, wrote their father a very brave and yet restrained and polite letter censuring his conduct:

We cannot hide from you the fact that it is extremely painful for us to see our mother treated as a *"wretched woman."* We have seen your correspondence with mamma. What would you have done, at the time when you knew her, when it pleased you to find happiness by her side, what would you have done to a person who dared use such language? She is always, she has always been the same, and we shall think always of her as you thought of her in other times.

Come what might, for all his wild temper, they knew and said where their hearts and their overwhelming sympathies lay. The general was wounded; for, at bottom, he wanted his sons for his own.

Later they were permitted to see their mother. Once a week she came into the dim parlor of the Pension Cordier and sat with them for an hour or two, scarcely able to say anything to them. She had come down a great deal in the world, and looked wan; her neat clothes were threadbare; she lived in two tiny rooms, alone, on an allowance of one hundred francs a month. Out of this terrible pittance she managed to save a few francs with which to bring them presents, bonbons, new shoes, and stockings that she knitted for them.

Now lodged in the "somber and confining" Pension Cordier, as he described it, Victor Hugo's education, which had been left so much to chance and liberty, began in earnest, assuming a far more rigid and conventional form. The pension was a long building of a single story reached through a court and giving on another interior court, which had little light and not a plant or flower in it, but had trees and foliage painted upon its surrounding walls, as if to lessen its gloom.

French lower schools in those days were in a state of confused transition from clerical to lay teaching. An air of dull routine still clung to them, however, emphasized by the black smocks the pupils almost universally wore. The Cordier pension was no better and no worse than others. Victor Hugo's headmaster was, once more, an unfrocked priest who suggested inevitably (as the pupil wrote in retrospect) "the old age of prejudice that takes dawn away from the child's soul and substitutes night." Maître Cordier was fond of rapping his pupils with a long metal snuffbox, though he professed to be a disciple of Jean-Jacques Rousseau, even adopting the great educator's Armenian costume. His associate, Decotte, who taught Latin and rhetoric, was pictured as irritable and even "brutal." The two Hugo boys, instead of sleeping in the large common dormitory, had a private bedchamber, together with a third boy. Because their learning had been so often interrupted, they were given advanced and more rapid instruction than their fellows.

In retrospect, Victor conceived a deep hatred of his schools and teachers and even his schoolbooks: *"Je maudissais Bezout,"* he wrote in a curious poem, published in 1856, alluding to a famous textbook of those days.

> *. . . I cursed Bezout . . .*
> *For I was then a prey to mathematics!*
> *Dark hangmen made me swallow algebra*
> *By force . . .*

On the other hand, offsetting the "hangmen" there was a poor young usher named Biscarrat, with a homely but kind face, who became devoted to Victor and his brother and stimulated their interest in Latin and literature, being himself a young poet of sorts. As a rule, most of the teachers Victor had at pension and Lycée were strongly attracted by him.

Many of Victor Hugo's first copybooks have been preserved. Their lessons are all written out in a firm, fine hand, with flourishes and arabesques at the ends of words, much like those in the models of penmanship that teachers frame and hang upon the walls. The copybooks, in which his mind's growth from boyhood to youth can be followed clearly, show that, after having been retarded a little, he rapidly became an advanced pupil with a special aptitude for mathematics (though he moaned over it) and Latin.

One of his prescribed tasks was to translate selected fables from French into Latin; his habit was first to make a quite literal version; then, although not required to do so, he would begin over again and rewrite the piece in more polished and natural Latin phrases, after which he would add some moral reflection of his own, or a suitable quotation. Thus, in translating the story of the clemency of Pyrrhus, it occurred to him to add the famous line of Virgil: *Parcere subjectis et debellare superbos.* This he followed up with a drawing representing two warriors, one extending his hand in mercy, the other, on his knees, disarmed.

One of Victor's greatest discoveries, at twelve or thirteen, was

Virgil, who became his most beloved teacher. He was reading the Eclogues of the stately Roman poet, and suddenly moved by their harmonious beauty and pastoral atmosphere, set himself to translating the First Eclogue into French hexameters:

> *Déjà les toits au loin fument dans les campagnes . . .*
> *Et l'ombre en s'allongeant descend de nos montagnes.*

The fashion had then set in for poetry at the beginning of the Restoration. Peace, a return to cultivated manners and civilized activities, called for a renewal of literary art, which Napoleon and his eternal warfare had tended to stifle or repress. Now, as in the days before the French Revolution, everyone wrote verse: Father Larivière did; Decotte, Biscarrat, Eugène Hugo and Victor Hugo likewise. Complimentary verses were often exchanged between pupils and teachers; they usually ran to chivalrous, eighteenth-century conceits, and were easily or artlessly made.

But with Victor the writing of poetry became almost a disease. From the very start, as we see in his copybooks, in his translations from Virgil, Horace, and Lucan, he groped his way toward the mastery of the caesura, or pause, that occurs in the middle of the French hexameter, and toward regularity in alternating masculine and feminine rhymes, in accordance with classical custom. By instinct and by ear he seemed to grasp the value of these traditional technical procedures in French versification, and his translations grew progressively more "regular." Then, as the fever gained him, he began to write poems of his own, at first fables in verse, acrostics, epigrams, and charades, for he was a little over thirteen. In short, poetry was a most dazzling discovery, offering a large outlet for his young mind.

One day, the "somber" Maître Decotte sneaked into his room and, opening the drawer of his night table, found copybooks filled with some three thousand lines of poetry. What vexed M. Decotte sorely was that he found a certain translation from Virgil among them. Only two weeks before he had read to the class his own translation of Virgil's First Eclogue, which the boy had evidently held to be so mediocre that he had set himself to improve upon it with a version of his own. The harsh teacher made a report of his pupil's bad habits, scolded him severely, and threatened to have him expelled, though nothing came of this.

Early in 1816, Victor suffered a painful injury to his knee during one of the pebble-throwing battles of his schoolmates, one boy having struck him down with a very sharp stone. He bled profusely, and the muscle bruise was so heavy that for several weeks he was confined to bed. Sitting up in bed alone all day, he read voraciously and was plunged into long reveries. Then, in a fever, he began to write poem after poem, poems in every form, odes, satires, elegies, imitations of Ossian or of Virgil's Georgics. They were no better verses than those the lyrical Shelley had written at the same age, about ten years before; but they were remarkable for their technical range, their effort to create vivid images, and their sense of design, or form.

From this year, when he was fourteen, dates a long poem of three hundred lines which he wrote in competition with his older brother Eugène, on the common theme of "The Deluge." Eugène, who was sixteen, and talented in his own right, wrote with considerable emotion and romantic power, but with a confused, ill-organized effect of nightmarish fantasy. Victor's poem, although uneven in quality, is composed of a series of definite scenes or pictures of the legendary Deluge, which are systematically built up to a climax. There were commonplace lines in it, echoes of other poets, but also signs of delightful boyish imagination expressed in vigorous lines; and there was an effect of control.

The disagreeable Decotte who spied on Victor, in jealousy of his poetic output, he imagined, would give him longer lessons to do, and would bustle into his room at night to snuff out his candle. Being persecuted, he would abandon himself rebelliously to his sin; to outwit the tyrant pedagogue he would lie awake in the dark, unable to sleep, inventing rhyme after rhyme, and completing in his mind whole poems which he learned to commit to memory and write down the next morning. Odes, elegies, even the lengthy dialogue of two long tragedies in classical style accumulated themselves, during 1816 and 1817. A very thick *cahier,* or notebook, dating from this artless period still exists, with the title boldly and gracefully written, with arabesques flowing about the letters:

POESIES DIVERSES, 1816–1817
VICTOR

It contained the exercises, the charming first flights of a mind that was immature, yet fresh and open-eyed. The events of the time were closely followed by the child poet, and one of his poems is entitled "Waterloo"; others treat of political issues of the period, usually in fervently Royalist vein.

On the opening page of this old copybook is a note, firmly written, dated September, 1816: *"I am fifteen, I have done poorly, I will learn how to do better."* Victor actually lacked six months of being fifteen, but his power of self-criticism was highly developed. After one of his poems, a long one of a hundred lines, he adds up at the bottom, "twenty poor lines, forty-two passable ones, ten excellent ones, two splendid ones, one terrible line, inadmissible." In another poem many lines and passages are crossed out, and a note gravely tells us: "The reader may honestly read the remaining lines."

Many of his early fragments show by many allusions the unusual affection ruling between himself and his brother, Eugène, with whom he often collaborates, and whose sensibilities, Victor, with delicate feeling, sometimes deliberately avoids wounding. Yet Eugène was undoubtedly distressed by the marked superiority of his younger brother, whose precocity everybody noticed. The eldest brother, Abel, no poet, but almost a grown man, earnestly encouraged him, and called the attention of his mother to Victor's striking talent. She found it hard to conceal, though she tried, her tremulous predilection for her youngest child. It was she he wished most to please. It was to her that he dedicated his longest and most ambitious creation, a first complete tragedy in fifteen hundred lines. At this period, when fourteen and a half years of age, he felt also the dawning influence of a famous contemporary writer, one who was to French youth, by his combined physical courage and eloquence, the literary-political hero of the Restoration—as Byron was the hero of the day to British youth. On July 10, 1816, the boy wrote in his copybook: *"I will be Chateaubriand or nothing."*

At fourteen, Victor was a long-headed boy who showed now and then qualities of force, of will. That he had imagination and talent of all sorts was evident to all who came close to him. These were stimulated remarkably during his much traveled, emotionally stressful childhood, which helped to make him "precocious." He had suffered and told little of that, though he had much to say. As Sainte-Beuve pointed out long before Freud, writing is a form of release for the secrets of the soul, even if they be divulged with indirection. Under the whip of Maître Decotte—perhaps a somewhat imaginary whip—the boy, during sleepless nights, was stimulated to ever greater mental efforts.

In the fall of 1816, while still boarding at the Pension Cordier he was entered in the historic Lycée Louis le Grand, one of France's great schools. In rhetoric he had no peer; but in physics, philosophy, and mathematics he also made his mark, as the record shows—he had an imaginative aptitude for geometry, and, to the delight of his professors, took high honors, an *accessit,* in the city-wide examinations in physics. He was, diligently enough, preparing himself for the Polytechnical School, as his father demanded; but in effect he was pursuing two careers at once, living a double life. His thickening manuscript books showed that he was determined to become a great poet, like Virgil, or a lord of letters like Chateaubriand, or something of both.

2

When, after an exile of twenty-two years, Louis XVIII, the stout, gouty, aging brother of Louis XVI, rode to the Tuileries Palace and all the people waved with banners and shouted *"Vive le roi!"* none among them was happier than Sophie Hugo. The return of the Bourbon monarch had the effect of a personal vindication for herself. To her, Waterloo had been a victory, avenging her dead Vendean compatriots and General La Horie. She could never speak ill enough of the Corsican ogre who, in the end, had wrought such large and bloody catastrophes for mankind. Apparently the Court had known something of her sentiments and former conspiratorial actions, for the Count of Artois, the King's fanatical younger brother (who was also to be King) sent her, soon after Waterloo, the emblems of the Royal Order of the Flower-de-Luce, with a diploma signed in his own hand; the lily was in silver and hung from a white moiré ribbon. Mme. Hugo wore this proudly, as well as a white dress, a white straw hat trimmed with tuberoses, and green shoes, according to the fashion of the hour—so as "to tread the Imperial colors underfoot." Thus costumed she went with her three sons to Notre-Dame Cathedral for the solemn ceremony of the royal *Te Deum.*

The Bourbons, for her, now had every grace and virtue in comparison with the Bonapartes, and were to restore the mythical monarchy, which seemed, after a whole generation, like a golden dream. It was inevitable that her son Victor should share her beliefs and remain apart from his father, who under the Restoration was a suspect character.

Gradually she repaired her situation, especially after 1818, when a favorable decision was handed down in her long suit for separation from General Hugo. Her sons, though still studying at the Lycée Louis le Grand, returned to live with her again, and she refurnished her home, now a modest apartment in the rue des Petits-Augustins, and its small salon, pleasantly enough, with the six mahogany chairs, the two *bergères* or armchairs, the Aubusson carpet, the tapestries, even the Lyons damask court gown, now used as a table drapery, that remained from her days as a countess of Spain. It was here that Sophie Hugo regularly received her Legitimist and pro-Bourbon friends, who were followers of the King's brother, the Comte d'Artois, the very soul of the Restoration and reaction.

A little circle of returned "Ultras" grew up around her, some of them men of distinction, such as the charming Comte de Volney, an erudite man of letters and a scientist, who repented having once been a liberal. Also the Marquis de Coriolis de l'Espinose, who wrote fervent poems and pamphlets to the glory of the Bourbons and took interest in Victor Hugo. These people had good manners, they were genteel; but they had long been exiled or suppressed or silent, and they had, some of them, seen their property confiscated and so were relatively poor. They were happy to find their place again even in the modest drawing room of Mme. Hugo. The boy Victor, who was bred by his mother "to speak only when spoken to," observed them gravely and marked them well in his memory. Almost a half century later (in a satirical passage of the Fourth Book of *Les Misérables,* describing the Royalist salon of "Mme. T.") he pictured these impoverished nobles and abbés of the old school vying with each other in recounting endlessly the horrors wrought by the Jacobins, their close escapes, and the sufferings of their kin and friends. Gravely they observed rank and precedence as in the days of Marie Antoinette. A worthy old marquise, who was reduced to one remaining servant, always spoke of her as "my people." They were conservative, they were "Ultras" —which was the term for extreme Legitimists—but they were very kind. As in the story of young Marius (in *Les Misérables*), sitting around the fireplace, taking their snuff, they made much of the handsome Victor. The old dowagers would say of him in tones of refined sympathy: "Such a pretty boy!" or "Poor child!" For was he not deserted by his father, who—Heaven preserve us!—was a "blood drinker," a Jacobin, one of Bonaparte's brigands, guilty of murdering so many of their devout brothers and sisters?

But these returned *émigrés* were no mere fossils to Mme. Hugo.

She hoped, always the ambitious woman, that her sons would play a signal part in the Legitimist regime for whose triumph she had labored. She hoped that men like Volney and Coriolis—who was close to Chateaubriand—would win favor for her talented sons, Victor and Eugène, who as adolescent men of letters promised to contribute richly to the peacetime literary revival that was now talked of as overdue.

The one great French writer who had appeared after the French Revolution was Vicomte François-René de Chateaubriand; his example, his glory, was also to have weight for the youthful Victor Hugo. Chateaubriand's career was a thing of romantic adventure: escaping the guillotine which claimed many of his aristocratic relatives, he had wandered to America and claimed to have hunted for the Northwest Passage (though no one was ever sure of that). Although, returning to France, he had won the favor of Napoleon by his lyrical prose, he chose to rebel against him and was exiled for a second time. Gradually he had become the leading voice of the Legitimist and Catholic cause, since he devoted the eloquence of a Rousseau to preaching a return to the ancient Christian faith. (Some held, however, that his *Le Génie du Christianisme,* was more aesthetic and pagan than Christian.) The new generation all took to their hearts his novel, *René,* with its tale of a melancholy youth who had fled from civilization, under the doom of some shadowy, sexual-religious tragedy, to the tepees of the unimaginable Natchez, "noble savages" of Louisiana. Everyone took it for granted that the returned author, soldier, explorer, orator, and Cabinet Minister under Louis XVII was "René" himself. Victor Hugo, who longed to emulate the strutting Breton noble, carried his books with him and read them in his classroom, behind a barricade of inkwells and papers, when the professor's lecture bored him. For this he was caught and punished one day, but he only read Chateaubriand the more fervently.

"The child but echoed the maternal faith," relates the Witness of Victor Hugo's Life (who wrote at his dictation). This is an extremely accurate statement in the psychological sense, far more so than those of Hugo's detractors, who held that he was given to exaggerating the influence of his mother and the Royalist milieu of his youth. His first ambitious writings, at the age of fourteen and fifteen, which were naturally cruel and bloody tragedies, *unconsciously* derive from the dilemma, the struggle between his father and mother, that tormented his whole childhood.

When he was about ten, Victor had shown great ingenuity in building theaters in the attic out of boxes. With no room for wings or dressing rooms, the Hugo children would wait for their lines and change costumes in a box under the table they used as a stage. But now they were bigger. At the Pension Cordier where they boarded until 1818, permission was granted them to give plays on holidays, with a whole classroom as their auditorium. Ambitious to become a dramatic author, Victor had set to work at once and written his first poetic tragedy, *Irtamène,* in five acts and fifteen hundred lines, with masculine and feminine rhymes alternating regularly, and with the caesura falling as steadily as in the coldly classical tragedies of Racine. The young playwright did not write a scenario; he made only a few notes dividing the drama into scenes, and then wrote it at one gallop, in ten days, usually during evening hours when he had finished his lessons in mathematics and physics. It was all done with great enthusiasm, the parts clearly conceived, the characters each holding to their parts without getting mixed up, or becoming the wife or child of another character.

One significant defect in his play, from a classical point of view, was his abandonment of the "unities" of time and place—though it had great unity of action. The subject (Victor never had any trouble thinking up a dramatic subject) was drawn from some mythical tale of ancient Egypt which had taken place at Memphis. It was a gory drama and full of surprises; whenever the hero found himself in a perfectly inextricable predicament, a concealed door or gate would open in the smooth wall enclosing him—like a theatrical afterthought. Yet apart from such bizarreries the piece had movement and suspense.

The writing of the play and its production were both secretly planned by the small playwright as a present for his mother on New Year's Day of 1817. In a long prologue he dedicates it to her, and expresses his gratitude for all she had done for him, as well as his eagerness, even his *impatience,* to have her approval. He warns her that she must expect delays, accidents, and even noise and whistling by "evil spirits," in the shape of his schoolmates, whom he begs her to ignore.

The very subject of *Irtamène* was calculated to please her, for it treats of the efforts of a heroic noble of Egypt, Irtamène, to restore to his throne an unfortunate king, Zobéir, whom conspirators and a tyrant usurper have flung into captivity. The hero knight, in his efforts to rescue the king, undergoes formidable trials of fire and torture in order to rescue his beloved monarch. At one point his position seems all but hopeless, and he faces his end:

> *Farewell, dear citizens, I now must die;*
> *Yet those unworthy tears I bid you dry,*
> *Since 'tis for the king's sake . . .*

But at this point the hero benefits by a thrilling rescue that comes not a moment too soon. The young playwright, too, seems beside himself with excitement—like a boy seeing a similar rescue in a "Western" cinema today—for he writes in the margin of his manuscript: *"Vive le roi!"*

Mme. Hugo was impressed. Although she was assured by her friends that the career of letters was a hazardous one, she encouraged her son to write all the poetry he wanted to, and it is to her credit. At this very time his father, who had retired to a small estate he owned at Blois, was writing letters to the headmaster of the Pension Cordier (where Victor now merely boarded), in which he noted, with pain, reports of the boy's addiction to verse, and ordered that he be kept firmly at his mathematical and scientific studies.

Victor Hugo's attachment in early youth to the Legitimist and Royalist cause is very plainly traceable to his emotional partisanship for his mother in her conflict with his father. A boy, and for that matter a grown man, writes of the experiences and emotions that have touched him most deeply. His mind, at this time, seems to be full of literary projects which symbolize his own subconscious conflict with his father. Thus his next play, a tragedy in mere prose, dashed off very easily, was called *Inez de Castro* and was the story of a prince of Portugal who defied his father, the king, by secretly marrying a daughter of the king's enemies. The king in a passage of fierce invective speaks in terms that might well be those of General Hugo in one of his famous fits of temper:

"Insolent son, rebellious subject! Do you not know that the laws of the realm punish with the supreme penalty him who defies his father and his king?" But the prince continues his resistance; and in the end it is arranged that not the rebellious son, but the father, is slain on the battlefield.

Victor Hugo, on the surface, appeared to be following his mother in her attachment to the extreme conservative party in France. But in his unconscious mind the real motive for taking such a position, the real driving force, is a kind of "rebellion" against the "tyrant father," which is one of the oldest themes of human legend. He was being conditioned inwardly to revolt against the Image of Authority. His royalism in youth is thus a paradox, born of his submission to his mother, inasmuch as he was learning to breathe the very spirit of revolution in embracing it.

In disobedience of his father, while he studied at the Lycée, he wrote constantly and with an ever increasing mastery of his medium. He taught himself the principles of French prosody. He changed, corrected, destroyed his pieces, and in the end images and rhymes came to him with abundance and seeming effortlessness. His translations of Virgil and Lucan done at fifteen—in contrast with his original poems, still boyish in tone—are examples of mature, finished poetic writing. Thus in his French imitation of Lucan, "The Cave of the Cyclops," he shows precocious qualities of craftsmanship quite like those of his own prime. He gives the very sound of the mighty hammerings of the Cyclops at their forges:

Sous leurs vastes efforts, l'antre tremblant résonne . . .
Ils frappent. . . . Soulevé par leur bras vigoureux,
Le marteau bondissant sur le métal sonore
Tombe à coups cadencés . . . remonte . . . et tombe encore.

He has the hammer "rebound from the ringing metal, fall in cadenced strokes, rise and fall again," in verses that are both powerful and harmonious.

Determined to strike a bold blow that would carry him toward his chosen career, Victor Hugo copied over his tragedy *Inez de Castro,* and submitted it to the director of a small theater known as "Le Panorama Dramatique." It was a melodrama and perhaps not much poorer in quality than those currently being played. For a time he had the impression that it would be accepted and that he had made a great stroke of fortune which would free him forever from algebra, physics, and the Polytechnical School that loomed as his unhappy future. But then it was returned to him as being unsuitable under the existing censorship rules. With its subject of parricide and poison plots it certainly, like many boys' writings, carried no useful moral lessons!

He was disconsolate at this first reverse. But then his eye fell suddenly upon the announcement by the French Academy of the subject chosen for the annual poetry contest to be held in 1817: "The Happiness Which Study Procures for Us at All Situations in Life." It was a subject that commended itself sufficiently to his then idealistic and virtuous temper. To be sure, established and skilled writers would compete for the prize in this nation-wide contest. But what did it matter? he thought; *Audaces fortuna juvat,* fortune favors the bold. In two weeks he had written over three hundred lines, while the usher, Biscarrat, and his mother beamed over his shoulder.

In his poem on this all too pedantic theme our young Victor assumed an elegiac and nobly Virgilian mood; he discoursed upon the beauties of quiet study in some rustic refuge, far from the vanity of the world, with a grave elegance, a grace and poise, which one still notes with astonishment—though he himself afterward detested this fairly artificial poem upon a prescribed subject. It ran:

> *Quand la fraîche rosée au retour de l'aurore*
> *Tremble encore sur le sein du lys qui vient d'éclore. . . .*
> *Mon Virgile à la main, bocages verts et sombres,*
> *Que j'aime à m'égarer sous vos paisibles ombres!*
> *Que j'aime, en parcourant vos aimables détours,*
> *A pleurer sur Didon, à plaindre ses amours!*

When the fresh dew, the poet tells us, at the coming of dawn, still upon the breast of the lily just opened, doth tremble, how he loves—O green and somber glades—with his adored Virgil in hand, to err among thy peaceful, bosky shades! how he loves to wander in those friendly groves, while weeping for Dido and mourning her loves. And thus he continues his sweet sustained harmonies, in this somewhat elegiac manner, like a youthful Milton, for hundreds of lines.

The poem was done, and only a few days remained before the closing date when it must be handed in. But how could the boy leave his class at the Lycée, or the pension where he still boarded in 1817, in time to deliver it? The masters would give him permission for no such purpose. Fortunately, the kindly Biscarrat, himself a poetaster, already living vicariously in the promise of his favorite pupil, conspired in his favor. He arranged to take a group of the boys at Cordier's for a walk along the Seine, during which they were to study certain architectural monuments. Pausing before the dome of the Institut, Biscarrat began a little discourse upon the historic building—when one of his charges detached himself suddenly from the rest of the group, dashed swiftly into the building, deposited a package at the door, and breathlessly returned. Like a bold soldier, Victor had outwitted the enemy.

Three months later, on August 28, 1817, the immortal judges of the Academy handed down their decisions.

To Victor Hugo they awarded an Honorable Mention, placing him among the first few, if not first, among the hundreds of poets who had competed. The poet had made an allusion, at one point, to having "barely attained five lustrums," and the judges in quoting his poem and reporting their award to him, noticed this and commended him warmly—"if *veritably* he was no older than that." This phrase gave rise to much polemical warfare over the significance of the word "veritably." Some cruel wits held that the Academicians wished to patronize so young a poet, or to encourage him with a Mention; others defending him, and Victor Hugo himself, hinted that the Academicians showed doubts about his extreme youth and, in fear of a hoax, avoided granting him a still higher prize.

Yet, whatever the intent of the Forty Immortals (few of whom are now remembered), there was no doubt that they contributed to the legend of the "infant prodigy," now for the first time mentioned in the Paris press. Because there had been some skepticism, as he felt, as to his age, he had written to the permanent secretary of the Academy, Raynouard, to say that he would be happy to submit a copy of a certificate of his birth. He was thereupon invited to visit the Institut and shown about its handsome conference rooms and library. He had then thanked his host by writing him a grave little epistle in verse, and M. Raynouard had responded with a few hexameters. All this was talked about in Paris, which was still a small city. His mother shone with pride. His professors at the Lycée complimented him warmly; at the Pension Cordier, the crusty masters who used to frown at him now assumed an air almost of fawning respect to the boy of fifteen who had brought Academy honors to their grimy little institution. But that year, 1817, was a year of miracles; he wrote one poem after another, and new honors were heaped upon his grave, round head that seemed almost too large for his body.

3

With the coming of the long-desired peace, a whole generation in France turned with relief to the pursuit of learning, letters, and the arts, whose development had been naturally retarded by twenty-five years of revolution and war. Louis XVIII was bookish and had decided literary preferences of his own. As a matter of policy he gave purses and pensions to writers favorable to the Bourbon Restoration. A severe censorship was practiced under the constitutional monarchy, but this only spurred the Opposition writers and journalists, the sons of the Jacobins, to effects of greater ingenuity.

Peace alone encouraged the contemporary "renaissance" and it was stimulated by the memories of the tremendously dramatic epoch recently experienced, which could only now be seen in some perspective. Thousands of persons wrote histories, memoirs (which are born of vanity, but are a great literary medium), and novels which, like Benjamin Constant's *Adolphe,* were but disguised memoirs. Almost as many wrote verse; indeed almost all educated Frenchmen were taught to write verse. French being an unaccented language, the writing of verse seems deceptively easy; true poetry, however, occurs more rarely than in England. Yet an increasing public showed an ear for poetry and read its exponents with enjoyment throughout the nineteenth century.

Officially, in poetry and drama, the influence of Voltaire, who had died forty years earlier, still prevailed, and many wrote in a pseudo-classical eighteenth-century style that wanted the wit of the old man of Ferney. The new giants of letters whom youth followed were Chateaubriand and Mme. de Staël, both formerly exiles and opponents of the Empire. Both were also exponents of the vital romantic movement that stemmed from Rousseau, advocating a literature of sentiment and passion, of "return to nature." Mme. de Staël, moreover, after her studies in Germany, had published in London, in 1810, her long-delayed book on the great German writers and romantic philosophers and their achievements in freeing literature of old bonds. This was not read in France until 1815. The posthumous publication of the lyrical poems of André Chénier, the pure singer who died on the guillotine in 1794, poems full of innovations and premonitions of romanticism, also had its weight. Soon, in the train of these writers, came the young poet Lamartine, with his first *Méditations* in 1820; in their obscurity Alfred de Vigny and Honoré de Balzac, only a few years older than Victor Hugo, were beginning to write in verse and prose; Stendhal, belatedly, almost in middle age, was turning from war to books; George Sand and Dumas, Sainte-Beuve and Alfred de Musset were to unfold their talent and play their part in the great cultural ferment of the early nineteenth century, a veritable "golden age" that was graced by great historians, political philosophers, and scientists.

Not only Victor Hugo but his brother Eugène, who also showed a marked literary talent, aspired to be a great poet or a writer. At this period, there was a younger and rival literary academy in France, that of Toulouse, which held annual contests and awarded prizes for poetry in honor of the *Jeux Floraux* (Floral Games) of Toulouse. Its spirit was considered less tradition-bound, more encouraging to young literary talent, and it permitted more freedom in subject matter. Eugène Hugo in 1817 had written a passionately Royalist poem on "The Death of the Duc d'Enghien," the last of the Condé princes, whom Napoleon had lured into France and had assassinated in 1804. While Victor had tried for the French Academy prize, Eugène had submitted his poem at Toulouse and won the second honors of the Academy there. Then, the following year, Victor sent the Academy of Toulouse an ode of suitably Royalist tone, on "The Virgins of Verdun," who had been executed in the time of the Terror.

At this time, the summer of 1818, he and his brothers to their great joy were reunited with their mother, whose long suit for separation had been won and yielded her a portion of the general's half pay. They had left the Pension Cordier behind them and also abandoned the detested preparation for engineering or artillery in spite of their father's wishes. Nominally they were enrolled in the Law School of the University of Paris, but actually they gave almost all their time to writing.

One day, in September, while taking a walk in the neighborhood of his home, at the square of the Pont Neuf, Victor saw a great crowd in a procession following a huge cart that bore a bronze statue. It was a large equestrian figure of Henry IV, which was being restored in place of the one destroyed under the Revolution. The boy at once joined the enthusiastic crowd and helped them, amid cheering and singing, to lift the heavy monument to its pedestal. When he came home he told his mother of the incident and she heartily agreed with him that it would provide a noble subject for an ode.

While Victor worked at his ode, his mother fell sick and lay in bed with fever. Victor insisted on attending her, and spent whole nights at her bedside. Then one evening she seemed better and said to him: "Have you written your ode? Have you sent it to the Academy?" The boy said that it was almost too late, as it must be mailed by the following morning. Recently, owing to his anxiety over her illness, he had been unable to write a line. At this, his mother seemed unhappy, but at length fell asleep again, while he gazed at her tenderly; then he went to the table near her, took his manuscript and set to work. He worked all that night. At dawn he had finished an ode of a hundred and twenty lines, and his mother, finding the manuscript beside her, gave him one of her rare smiles. He sent it off at once. The ode "On the Restoration of the Equestrian Statue of Henry IV" was an eloquent expression of patriotic sentiment, despite its rigorously classical style. As its climax the poem described vividly the poet's participation in the ceremonies at the Pont Neuf, with a directness of statement that rhyme and the complex demands of the ode in no way encumbered. For this poem, the Academy of Toulouse, on September 18,1818, awarded him its First Prize of the Golden Lily, and for the poem on "The Virgins of Verdun" (both are included in his first published volume) he was awarded the Second Prize of the Silver Amaranth. His brother Eugène, who received Honorable Mention for a poem he had submitted, was his closest rival.

Victor's prize-winning poems were printed by the Academy of Toulouse and reprinted in some of the Paris newspapers. A few months later, in May of the following year, Alexandre Soumet, secretary of the Academy of Toulouse, and an established literary figure, wrote him: "We have not prizes enough for the two brothers! Your seventeen years fill us with admiration, and, almost, with incredulity. You are an enigma to which the Muses alone know the answer."

With his fertile pen he worked busily at new odes, poetic tragedies, and even an *opéra comique,* though nothing came of this. Toward 1819 and 1820, with his two brothers—for Abel now aspired to be a writer of prose—his former teacher, Biscarrat, and some other young literary comrades, he held literary banquets at a friendly little *bistro,* called Edon's restaurant, on the outskirts of town. To his fellow diners, and anybody else who would listen, he would read his abundant new poems, which showed already an astonishing ease and virtuosity, although they still had a little of the air of rhetorical exercises. In December, 1819, he and his young friends decided to launch a literary periodical of their own. A year earlier, their great idol, Chateaubriand, had founded a weekly political journal, called *Le Conservateur.* In his honor, and to indicate their religious and political affiliations, they named their own journal *Le Conservateur Littéraire.* Poems, critical essays, and prose fiction were to be included in its pages. Because a novel was needed, and upon a wager, Victor Hugo offered to write one in two weeks. He returned with *Bug-Jargal* in its first brief version, the story of a slave revolt in Haiti, as narrated by a French soldier. When the numbers of the *Conservateur Littéraire* began to appear—during thirty months of existence it acquired only about two thousand readers—the official Royalist press commented upon it very kindly, calling attention to its loyal sentiments, and to the fact that the young "right-thinking" brothers who edited it gave their labor and inspiration in order to aid in the support of their "pious," staunchly Royalist mother. In her honor, Victor Hugo published in his paper a poem entitled *La Vendée,* and this was quoted in certain Royalist newspapers, one of which praised the precocious poet for singing the heroism of the Vendean counter-revolution "at the risk of being laughed at by the Opposition." The Conservative *Journal des Débats* spoke of Victor Hugo's group as "a holy alliance formed by several young people against that in-novating spirit which has invaded Montparnasse." On the other hand, writers in the much persecuted Liberal press, some of whom suffered imprisonment for their opinions, occasionally ridiculed the *Conservateur Littéraire* and its principal contributor.

On February 13, 1820, the Duc de Berry, as he issued from his carriage in a Paris street, was assassinated by a workingman named Louvel. With his death—he was the King's nephew, and Louis XVIII had no children—all hope of a direct heir seemed lost to the tragic Bourbon family. Stirred by this sensational crime and tragedy, as was all France, Victor Hugo within a few days completed an ode "On the Death of the Duc de Berry," which was published in the *Conservateur Littéraire* early in March, 1820. Once more, it was a most vigorous and eloquent poetic exercise, but it was timely; it spoke to a people whose emotions had been deeply aroused. For this reason and because of its pious sentiment, it was reprinted in the *Drapeau Blanc* (the powerful Bourbon daily of Paris) and very widely read.

The old King himself read the poem and was greatly affected by it, especially enjoying the ringing strophe which begins

> *Monarque aux cheveux blancs, hâte-toi, le temps presse,*
> *Un Bourbon va rentrer au sein de ses aïeux . . .*

and which he used to recite before the mournful circle of his in-timates at the Tuileries. He gave orders that a purse of five hundred francs should be awarded to the young author. A real public fame now came to the boy of eighteen that spread his glory far beyond the little Royalist literary coteries of the time and even beyond the narrow limits of the academies.

Chateaubriand himself had noticed the poem on the Duc de Berry and spoken well of it, and, when a colleague of his, a Royalist deputy who was an acquaintance of Mme. Hugo, offered to conduct the boy before Chateaubriand, the youthful poet was filled with mingled emotions of rapture and dread.

At a fine house in the rue Saint-Dominique, one morning, he and his companion passed through an antechamber and entered a large salon, where the writer and statesman received them seated at his fireplace, without moving. Chateaubriand, a small man, with a keen eye and a proud bearing, affected a military posture, all buttoned up in his frock coat, his head held stiffly in a high collar and thick, tight, black cravat. He said:

M. Hugo, I am delighted to see you. I have read your poems, those you have done on *la Vendée* and those you have just done on the death of the Duc de Berry. There are, especially in the last, things that no other poet of this time could have written. Unfortunately, my age and my experience give me the right to be frank, and I tell you candidly that there are parts of it I like less; but that which is fine in your odes is very fine.

Victor felt very small indeed, and was soon glad to be gone. Once outside, his companion asked him if he were now content.

"Yes, to be outside again," he breathed with relief. His companion, the Deputy Agier, assured him that M. de Chateaubriand had been very kind to him, for he had addressed him, he had actually spoken to him, while to others who came he sometimes gave only an icy stare and not a word.

Victor came again, however, some months later, and the great man, unbending a little further, encouraged him to continue with his poetry, which he called "the highest level of literature," adding: "You are on a loftier plane than I. However, I have done something myself in that way." He thereupon summoned his secretary and began reading huge sections of a poetic tragedy which Victor Hugo thought very dull, poor stuff, though he uttered only timid compliments. Chateaubriand then insisted upon his remaining while a valet brought him a tub for his bath. Affably, he undressed, sponged, rubbed himself, brushed his teeth, and continued an animated conversation with his young admirer. It was after this visit that the report that Chateaubriand had called young Hugo *"the sublime child"* spread all over Paris. This unique, legendary title clung to him for a long time, perhaps too long.

The painful struggles for self-mastery, as for public recognition, which most apprentice writers undergo, were never the lot of young Victor Hugo. From the time when he had scarcely outgrown childhood the applause of the world outside rang pleasantly in his ears: his precocious talents were freely announced, and laurels were placed upon his adolescent brows. He was the Sublime Child.

Yet in his chosen field he surpassed other young men who were older than he, because, in a sense, he had never been young. Thus he accumulated arrears that must be made up later at great cost. His temper and will were prematurely serious. Being young in experience, however, and human, the praise he heard affected him: from boyhood he carried himself as if he knew he was destined for some large success. When he was five years old his father, in a letter, had described him as "sedate and deliberate" and speaking always to the point. When he was seventeen he showed some affinity to those young *hidalgos* he had once known in Spain, who were austere and yet emphatic and magnificent, reserved but full of self-approval and self-esteem. In the *Conservateur Littéraire,* this almost absurdly grave young man wrote earnest polemical essays advocating a return to Christian piety, excoriating the "cynical" Voltaire, and calling for a fight to the finish with the Liberal or anti-Royalist faction in French literature and public life.

"Well, the boy follows his mother," his father, the former Republican volunteer, is said to have remarked at this period: "But time will change things, the man will think like his father."

Despite the honors and prizes that were beginning to come to him he did follow his "admirable" mother, as he called her, submissively, almost morbidly. Mme. Hugo's sway over her sons was maintained in full force even as they grew to young manhood, and they moved everywhere, steadfastly, by her side.

Between 1818 and 1820, almost every evening after dinner, Mme. Hugo would put on her bonnet and yellow cashmere shawl and, flanked usually by Victor and Eugène, set forth to visit her old friends, the Fouchers, in the rue du Cherche-Midi. Light and fuel were scarce and dear in those days. The Fouchers, living near by in an apartment of the War Ministry headquarters, the palatial (seventeenth-century) Toulouse Mansion, had these supplied for them by the state. Therefore these old friends, after six o'clock, spent almost every evening together. As Victor Hugo relates, Mme. Foucher would receive them in her boudoir, a large chamber with a deep alcove. At a corner of the fireplace Mme. Hugo had her chair always ready for her, sat down, took out her knitting from a bag with her, and began to work. M. Foucher, who was in poor health, always very tired after his day's work in the War Department, would sit at the other side of the fireplace in a deep armchair, with his book, a candle, and his snuffbox on a small table at his side. Between them, Mme. Foucher and her daughter Adèle sat around a little center table, also busy at needlework; while her young son, Victor Foucher, and Eugène and Victor, distributed on hard chairs, completed the family circle.

These soirées were extremely silent, and might serve as a tableau of the *ancien régime* in France. Nobody even asked the very reserved M. Foucher, a small dark man with an aquiline nose, for news, or how he felt. The Witness of Hugo's Life relates: "Eugène and Victor, thoroughly disciplined in their social life as they were free in their intellectual life, had been taught by their mother never to speak unless spoken to. Mme. Hugo from time to time would interrupt her knitting to look at the blazing fire or open her snuffbox, for like M. Foucher she took snuff. She would offer her snuffbox to her old friend, saying: 'M. Foucher, will you have a pinch?' M. Foucher replied yes or no as he felt, and that was usually, together with the good evening and good night, about all the conversation that was exchanged during the entire visit."

What was there so attractive about these long, monotonous evenings for Victor that made him hasten his mother on toward the Fouchers, or feel a pang of regret when by some chance, as rarely happened, they stayed at home or went elsewhere? Then suddenly it dawned on the Fouchers that Victor, for his part, had his reasons. All through the gloomy two-hour sessions the boy's eyes would steal over to rest on their daughter Adèle—eyes filled with ardor and flame—and her eyes would often turn boldly, as if with pride and pleasure, to meet his!

Adèle was barely sixteen in the spring of 1819, and Victor only seventeen. She had grown to be rather tall, and at that time was slender, with a round head, very dark hair, a beautiful moonlike forehead, and large, brilliant black eyes, set rather far apart under fine, long eyebrows. Her nose was aquiline and delicate; her lips red, fresh, warm; her complexion dark olive, almost like a Levantine's. Adèle, the awkward playmate of Les Feuillantines, whom he had known as his companion since the age of six or seven, had suddenly, at sixteen, become a wildly beautiful young woman.

All that winter, Victor silently gazed at Adèle with sultry eyes, and Adèle proudly returned his gaze. One day, by chance, they found each other alone for a moment in the parlor of the Toulouse Mansion. They felt constrained. Then the girl exclaimed: "Victor, tell me your greatest secret!"

"I love you," he said.

"And so do I love you," she replied as simply. He kissed her cheek quickly and that was all. It was in April, 1819, and they always remembered the date as that of their secret engagement, the twenty-sixth. From that day on they began to write each other, also secretly. Hitherto Victor had loved only his mother. It was his first treason to her.

CHAPTER III

Romantic Love: Model 1819

THERE ARE FASHIONS in love. At the romantic flood tide of the early nineteenth century the fashion in love was all for the solemn and tearful, as social historians later commented. Young lovers exchanged sentimental vows which embraced the most extravagant offers of self-sacrifice and the fiercest demands of jealous passion. In Victor Hugo the case was complicated further by a pose of magnificent "Spanish" pride that was derived partly from his boyhood visit to Spain, partly from his dramatic Breton mother.

He was seventeen. After his childhood, made sorrowful and shadowed by the conflict between his parents, he had grown calmer in recent years. His mind had opened and his will, stimulated rather than discouraged by insecurity, had hardened. At the same time he had tended to become reserved about his inward emotions. He had no real confidante save his mother. But desires were born in him which he sensed he must keep from her knowledge.

Now in the springtime of 1819, the remarkably elegant chestnut trees of Paris were blossoming and sending out their perfume. He loved, and knew that he was loved in return. He was so happy that he wanted to conceal his happiness from other eyes. Adèle, too, despite her sixteen years, had the wisdom of lovers and at first concealed her young emotions.

As it was difficult to judge when the precocious boy in Victor Hugo changed into young manhood, so it was not easy to recognize at what time in his life he had fallen in love. It was as if he had always known Adèle. Only yesterday they were children, playing in the garden at Les Feuillantines. He had grabbed an apple from her, slapped her when she cried, and rather enjoyed himself. Not long after that, as he related in personally reminiscent passages of an early novel, *Claude Gueux,* their mothers had said to them: "Go and play." They played tag in the garden, she running from him at top speed, her pelerine flying up behind her and showing her brown neck, until he caught her by the belt, made her sit down, and, while she laughed breathlessly, claimed a kiss "by right of conquest." Then she asked him to read something to her. He had a travel book in his pocket, and they sat reading it together all that summer afternoon, until the stars came out and surprised them.

"Oh, mamma! how fast we ran," she exclaimed to her mother when they got back to the house. His own mother looked at him with curiosity. But he said nothing, his heart was too full and even a little sad. He was twelve then, and, ever since that day when they had read the book together and kissed, his heart had been full of Adèle with "her large eyes, her mass of black hair, her golden brown skin, her red lips and rosy cheeks."

Now, they met for walks, or stole moments together when she came to pray at Saint-Sulpice. Their talk at first was innocent, artless, of a thousand things that could not possibly have interested any serious third person—quite as he described it all many years later in the idyl of Marius, the young student, and Cosette, in *Les Misérables.* At the same time it was "correct"; for Victor was "chivalrous," seldom daring to hold Adèle's hands; they almost never kissed each other.

"Both innocent beings, they unfolded themselves to each other; they told each other their dreams, their intoxications, their hopes, their illusions, their mistakes. . . . They confided in each other, with an ideal intimacy, that which each had kept hidden and mysterious. They related, with a candid faith in their illusions, all that love, youth, and the remains of childhood had left in their hearts."

Adèle was a naïve, unspoilt girl with the heart of an ingenuous and tender child, and it was as a child, with all the sense of surprise and fear of a child, that she yielded to love. Adèle's purity and innocence touched him. He placed her on a pedestal, himself at the feet of the pedestal, in the early-nineteenth-century fashion.

It was his duty, he would say, to cleave to her side, to surround her life with his own, to serve as her bulwark against danger, to place himself "between her and all suffering, without asking payment, without expecting anything in return." Must Adèle, therefore, feel constrained to love him in return? No, she could make sport of his devotion, reject, disdain him, and he would not complain. "And though all my days may be marked with sacrifice . . . on the day of my death I shall not have paid my infinite debt to you"—for having merely existed near him!

At another time (October 20, 1821) the young fiancé, in his voluminous love letters, expands upon his idea of real love. "When two souls who have sought each other in the crowd," he tells her, "over a long period of years find each other at last, when they see that they are suited to each other, know each other, in a word, resemble each other, then a pure and ardent union is established between them, a union that begins on this earth and continues beyond heaven. Such a union is *love*, true love, a love which, in truth, can be conceived by very few men. The world, Adèle, does not understand that type of affection, which is the lot of only a few beings, those destined for happiness like you, or for sorrow, like me. For the world, love is only a carnal appetite, or a vague impulse, which is overcome by gratification or by absence."

Here is defined the doctrine of love that is allotted to those Superior Souls who dwell apart from the common multitude, a doctrine which derives from Rousseau and the younger Goethe and is sung by Byron and Chateaubriand.

Some months later, during their extended courtship, to stress his "apartness," Victor confides to Adèle that he is a virgin and intends to remain so, come what may, to the very day of their wedding. He continues in slightly priggish vein:

I should consider a girl a very common sort, who married a man without being morally certain, through the known principles and character of that man, not only that he was *good*, but also, and I expressly use the word in its complete meaning, that he was a virgin, as virgin as she is. I am not unaware, in communicating these thoughts to you, that they are neither worldly nor do they belong to our century. But what of that! I have many other thoughts of this sort. . . . I also believe that the most severe modesty is no less an obligatory virtue for men than for women.

For that day, even romantic as it was becoming, Victor was advanced in his ideas of love. (Some of his friends also talked romantic love; but at night they prowled the streets, with coat collar upturned, seeking out street girls.) This confession had the effect almost of frightening Adèle.

Such was the extravagantly solemn and sentimental tone of the first letters he wrote her when he was less than eighteen.

Yet despite his desire to suffer and sacrifice himself, he had moods that were jealous and possessive too. One day, he flew into a wild rage because Adèle, crossing a puddle, lifted her skirt a trifle too high, and strangers in the street complacently stared at her ankles. Adèle would go to balls and receptions, which he shunned, since he never danced. He did not ask that she should refrain, but wrote her, on February 20, 1820: "Always keep me informed of what happens to you, of what you do, and even of what you are thinking. . . . I am, in truth, excessively jealous."

She wrote him in reply: "You have my entire faith. I have the pretension to regard you as my 'husband.' " Then very humbly, for she felt herself so greatly inferior to him in understanding, she gave him the report he asked for:

You ask me for an account of my actions. . . . What can I say? All the days of my life are so much alike that to describe one would be to describe a whole month of them. Every day I go you know where, and the rest of the time I work, or I take a walk with papa or mamma; then come the exercises for Carême, and there you are. . . . As to my thoughts, that is another matter, and I can assure you that I do not spend a moment without thinking of you. . . . I know that is very wicked of me, but I can do nothing else. Tell me a little, my dear Victor, when and how will all these torments end?

Adèle was so unfeigning and innocent that after a time she could not conceal her feelings toward him. On one occasion Victor seems to have asked her to "modify" her attitude, so as to keep their secret the better from parental eyes. Adèle, wounded by this, wrote him a sorrowful letter asking him if it was true that she had lost his "esteem."

Heatedly he assured her of his unfailing respect and single-minded devotion. He was her "slave." "I work for nothing else in the world but my wife," he avows. Then he tells her of some of the small "successes" he has gained. M. de Chateaubriand, named Ambassador to England, the other day invited him to go to London as his secretary. But Victor Hugo had politely declined, saying that he could not leave his mother. He told Adèle that it was also because of his wish never to be separated from her that he had declined—though his father, hearing of the rejected diplomatic post, had grown wrathful.

He pointed also to the prizes he had won already as a poet.

ADÈLE HUGO

After a Painting by Louis Boulanger

In certain salons he was spoken of as "an illustrious example." Alas, it seemed that she, and even her parents, had known nothing of all this. The lovely creature confessed that she had no ear for poetry. "I do not understand it. Are not *verses* poetry?" she asked.

And he replied: ". . . Your soul understands poetry"—for was she not both good and beautiful? As to his work, his ambitions, his successes—of which, he felt with a pang, she knew so little—he did it all for her. "I work for nothing else in the world, but my wife, dear Adèle." He adds: "You will consider me vain, just as you think me proud of what has been called my success, and yet, Adèle, God is my witness that I shall never be proud but of one thing alone, and that is to be loved by you." Romantic young man he might be but, unlike the Alfred de Vignys and Alfred de Mussets, his contemporaries in love and lyricism, he has hope instead of self-indulgent melancholy, will instead of sentimental despair.

She seemed to raise the question of how their "torments" would end, and what his "prospects" were. He assured her that he was ready to "stake his life" upon the chance of winning fortune by his pen, and thus extricating his mother from her difficulties and marrying his Adèle! Meanwhile, servants had seen them walking together, in secret.

Mme. Foucher spied upon her daughter, warned her and rebuked her, telling her that she had "tarnished" her character. She alone had been indiscreet and "at fault," and looked at Victor with bold eyes; he was a young man, hence blameless. Again Adèle was flung into despair: she believed herself "guilty" toward her mother, as she said, and "scorned" by her lover—which he denied most violently. Both suffered from the scrutinizing regard of the persons around them. It was at this stage, when they were extremely troubled in mind, that the elder Fouchers decided to go to the bottom of the whole business. For many months they had slyly observed everything that Victor, in his dread, had succeeded in hiding from his mother.

Pierre Foucher, head of a department in the Ministry of War, decorated, yet of modest means, with no dowry for his daughter, had been doing a heap of thinking out loud, together with Mme. Foucher. Then he had a talk with Victor and Adèle about their plans and proposed that he talk things over with Mme. Hugo. Victor showed fear of such a step, and tried to dissuade the Fouchers from approaching his mother, whom he loved but now also feared.

On April 26, 1820, a year to the day after the first avowals had been exchanged between the two young persons, the Fouchers called on Mme. Hugo, and asked her what should be done about their children. M. Foucher had a good opinion of Victor, but he was only eighteen and his prospects were uncertain. M. Foucher the modest bureaucrat, speaking tactfully, wondered if it were wise to permit an engagement at so early an age. Or whether it were safe to allow them to see each other often.

Mme. Hugo was completely taken by surprise; she had seen and suspected nothing. Then she was indignant. The two children together did not equal thirty-five years in age. Adèle was without fortune, and the "Countess" Hugo reared up in her pride. She had the most ambitious dreams for the career of her youngest and most gifted son.

"Such a marriage is preposterous," she declared flatly. "Never, never, never, while I am above ground shall it have my consent!"

The Fouchers retreated, angry and humiliated at learning how their friend Mme. la Comtesse rated *them,* coldly agreeing that their Adèle was to see her Victor no more. Their door was closed to Mme. Hugo as well as to her son.

Victor was called in during a part of this interview, acknowledged his passion, and heard the judgment against him without flinching. "Strangely enough," as Gustave Simon, editor of Hugo's *Lettres à la fiancée,* has remarked, "the young man felt no anger at his mother, but only at M. Foucher for having exposed his and Adèle's secret."

"Do you know, Adèle," he wrote that night in a farewell letter, "and it is an admission that I can make only to you, do you know that after it was decided that I was to see you no more, I wept! I really wept as I had not wept for ten years. When your parents had left, my mother saw that I was pale and silent, and became tenderer than ever as she tried to console me. But I fled and when I was alone I wept bitterly for a long time. . . ."

A year later, in one of those many letters to his young fiancée which were so carefully preserved by her in a beribboned package, Victor Hugo clearly hinted at the motives that led his mother to separate them. Money, security? She had shown that she cared nothing for them. "For a long time," he wrote, "she made me suffer because she carried too far her desire to see me happy. Her objections to our marriage were quite independent of you . . ." he added. His "authoritative" mother was *jealous,* simply because he loved another, a young girl. And he forgave her. He submitted to her. After Adèle, he said, "there is no other woman in the world for me except my mother." He saw Adèle no more.

2

In the small, confining quarters of his home in the rue des Petits-Augustins, an age-old drama of maternal-filial jealousy was being enacted. Victor Hugo lived under the domination of his high-willed mother, who, as he noticed, now lavished more tender affection upon him than ever before.

At eighteen, he faced most serious obstacles, struggled with himself, suffered sorely. The career of letters, for which he had, by now, wholly given up his university studies, was hazardous and brought as yet almost nothing with which to eat. His father, who was a stranger to him, opposed him. The very sight of the girl he loved was denied him by the will of his mother. He might well be melancholy, were he one of those romantic types then current in the literature of the day, given to sickly sighs and pallid despair.

But Victor Hugo was wholly unromantic in his robustness and energy. Healthy as he was in mind and body, a splendid youthful force rising in him urged him now to resist his mother, even by deception, while forgiving her. "I have learned from a strong mother that it is possible to control events," he wrote Adèle secretly after their separation began. Moreover he had a plan, which he was following with resolution. He said: "My family is as ambitious for me as I am for you. Some day, I hope, if I become my family's support, if I bring them peace and fortune, they will permit me to be happy, in other words, I shall have my heart's desire."

He now set himself hard at work, with a discipline astonishing for his years, and work helped him forget his pain. In the year that followed he had only a few glimpses of Adèle, sometimes in the street, once at an official ball, though their secret correspondence continued voluminously.

Over a span of two years he wrote most prolifically, publishing under various pseudonyms some 272 pieces of writing in the *Conservateur Littéraire* for 1820 and 1821, of which almost a hundred were new poems and the rest attempts at prose fiction, critical essays, and sketches.

Victor's new poems won him fresh laurels. His *Moïse sur le Nil* ("Moses on the Nile"), submitted to the Academy of Toulouse, was one of the best odes of his youthful, classical period, and brought him an "extraordinary prize" from the ever encouraging provincial academy in May, 1820, for he was now named *Maître ès Jeux Floraux de Toulouse*—in short a laureate and academician at eighteen. A little later in September of the same year appeared his fine ode in honor of Chateaubriand, entitled "The Genius," and this won several flattering notices, printed in the obscure corners of the Paris press reserved for literary comment. One of these, in referring to the indifference with which the public treated poets and their poetry, observed that "among those who have triumphed lately over this indifference we must count M. Victor Hugo, already renowned for numerous academic triumphs."

When, a little later in that year, a posthumous child was born to the widowed Duchesse de Berry, and became a future heir to the throne, all Royalist and Catholic France, with pious rapture, hailed the event as the birth of a "miracle child." On May 7, 1821, the important Paris *Quotidienne* saluted a new ode written by Victor Hugo, "On the Baptism of the Duc de Bordeaux," saying:

One finds at Lenormand's (in brochure form) an ode of M. Victor Hugo, young poet already known for a host of productions which indicate at once a fine talent and respectable doctrines.

Even in writing on subjects of a perfunctory character—there was no mistaking the fact—the young poet drew serious notice to himself because of his eloquence, his ease and directness of statement that seemed to overcome the rhymer's weakness of circumlocution, and his gift for vivid imagery which—though still cased in the rigid classical meters—made his work compare very favorably with the rather artificial stuff of his older contemporaries.

The Catholic Royalist faction in France seriously endeavored to encourage the revival of literature, as an ornament of the Restoration—in contrast with the war-making of Napoleon—and as a means of propaganda for spiritual and religious orthodoxy. For this purpose Bonald and De Maistre, the powerful literary advocates of Christian royalism, together with Chateaubriand, fathered the new *Société des Bonnes Lettres* (which was in reality an arm of the "Congregation," the supposedly Jesuit-dominated, semi-secret political organization of the extreme Right in France). It was before a meeting of the *Société des Bonnes Lettres* that the handsome young Victor Hugo arose, one day, in the spring of 1821, to read one of his odes. As the *Journal de Paris* related on May 14, 1821, an elegant and aristocratic audience "loudly applauded the young poet, full of vigor and energy . . . as notable for his youth as for his talent."

In the small literary magazine which he and his friends published, *Le Conservateur Littéraire* (which paid him nothing), he followed rigorously the Christian Royalist "line," quite like Alphonse de Lamartine, the young poet whose sentimental and religious *Méditations* in 1820 made him famous overnight. This meant that the Sublime Child repudiated the tradition of Voltaire, whom he set down as being a man without heart and truth; that he called for the stern repression of the "sons of Robespierre" and of the Liberals who fostered anew, secretly, the "Revolution of the Mobs." To one of his literary friends of this time, Victor Hugo applied a studied compliment in terms which he would undoubtedly have considered applicable to himself: "You are one of those young men of the Nineteenth Century who, by their gravity and their candor, astonish the false and frivolous old men of the Eighteenth Century." His vehement rejection of the great French Revolution —of which, by the way, his father had been a young partisan— contributed in large degree to the favor he won from the Court (where there was soon talk of a small pension to be awarded him), and to his winning the friendships of high personages in the Legitimist world. Little wonder that his conservative friends found in his boyish odes (as one commentator wrote in the *Moniteur Universelle* for October 29, 1822) not a pompous rhetoric, or artificial allusions to mythology, such as were fashionable then, but "an ode of pathos, the burning sighs of a young and pure heart, and the holy aspirations of a Christian soul." One day he met the young Duc de Rohan, who had pretensions as a man of culture; through him he met Lamartine, then about thirty and an officer of the Royal Guards, whose poetic style he tended, at first, to imitate.

"I still remember as I do yesterday the day," Lamartine recollects, "when the handsome Duc de Rohan, then a musketeer, since a cardinal, dropped in on me in my barracks on the Quai d'Orsay, and said: 'Come and see a phenomenon who promises to be one of the great men of France. You will be proud some day to have seen the oak in the sapling.'" Lamartine never forgot the thoughtful adolescent he met that day, "with a large, grave and beautiful head, who seemed a million miles away from the world around him."

Soon a whole circle of young Conservative intellectuals and writers gathered around him as his friends and literary comrades: among them Alexandre Soumet, the secretary of the Academy of Toulouse, who settled in Paris as a playwright, Emile Deschamps, Gaspard de Pons, Adolphe Saint-Valry—minor poets, some of whose work survives in comprehensive French anthologies—and finally the young Comte Alfred de Vigny, also, like Lamartine, an officer of the Royal Guards, and three years older than Victor Hugo.　•

With this slender, blond young aristocrat, whose manner toward most people was habitually sad and reserved, he formed a warm friendship. Vigny conceived of himself as a French counterpart of Lord Byron, and his first verses, with his early essay on Byron, were published in *Le Conservateur Littéraire*. They wrote each other warm letters, as Vigny moved with his regiment from one army station to another. When he was at Rouen, Victor Hugo wrote him bewailing the thirty leagues that separated them, declaring that he had read and reread a letter recently sent by his friend, "word by word, as a beggar counts piece by piece the gold he has found in a purse." To Vigny, Victor reports his small triumphs of the moment. M. de Chateaubriand, for instance, has said charming things about another of his odes; yet he adds humbly: "What is that beside your admirable elegy *Simoëtha!*" At this period, Hugo felt that his friend's "spontaneous" talent was superior to his own, "struggling in solitude with his Muse." The admiration was reciprocal. Vigny in one letter suggested that, since his own name was Alfred-Victor, his friend should call himself Victor-Alfred, in token of the lasting ties between them. When, in 1823, he departed to do battle in Spain, he committed the long poem, *Eloa,* unfinished then, to the care of his young friend, to be published faithfully, without corrections, "in the event that the bullets do not spare the poet." Fortunately his regiment never crossed the Pyrenees.

Hugo's physical beauty, his intense industry, his surprising command of the language, made his older as well as his young contemporaries grant him consideration, despite his extreme youth, as one who was marked among them, perhaps for *genius*—and in the time of Napoleon there was much thought of genius.

Alexandre Soumet, arriving from Toulouse, saw Victor Hugo at this time and spoke to him of his ambitions. The young man said: "I want to become a peer of France." Soumet added: "And he will!" He was now at about his full height, five feet seven inches, and of a graceful though solid figure. His long, straight hair was light brown, streaked with auburn, hanging down to his shoulders; and his "tiger-yellow" eyes were steady and keen. His mouth was full, yet delicate, and very expressive; his hands were small and fine. But what was always the most striking feature of him in youth as in age was his vast forehead, "like a tower," as Théophile Gautier would say.

At eighteen and nineteen, Victor Hugo learned much from the talk of young men who were a little older than he. From Vigny he received an influence that directed him toward the romantic, and made him read the "satanic" Byron (in translation). Then with passionate interest he began to read the novels of Walter Scott, who was at this moment, by the international success of his historical romances, virtually the dominant figure in world literature. In a time of disillusionment and unrest and change, Scott's romantic novels appeared with an effect that calmed the multitudes and distracted their minds. Seriously, Victor Hugo thought him worth emulating, pondered over his methods, and wrote a long study of his work in *Le Conservateur Littéraire,* giving an exposition of Scott's "minute exactitude" and the majestic grandeur of his historical tableaux. Scott's superb power of description undoubtedly stimulated the potentially greater one of the Sublime Child. Largely under the spell of Scott, he began to write his first real novel, "Hans of Iceland," upon which for more reasons than one he pinned great hopes.

He worked diligently at his craft; he prepared poems, novels, even plays which were to appear later. Yet despite his intense ambition, he could be remarkably self-possessed and planful for one of his youth. As a passage by him in *Le Conservateur Littéraire* shows, he believed in keeping his ambitions under control of the check-rein of his reason. Of others who in their haste to arrive showed too little wisdom of this sort he wrote:

One thing strikes us in the compositions of the youth who hurry to write for our theaters nowadays; they are so easily pleased with themselves; by gathering those wreaths they waste the time of their life which they should devote to courageous meditation. . . . Beware, beware young men, conserve your strength, you will need it for the day of battle: the weak birds fly straight off out of the nest, but eagles creep before taking flight on their wings.

In short, like Marius, in *Les Misérables:* "He was a youth who was ardent and cold, at once; noble, generous, proud, religious, exalted; honorable to the point of severity, pure to the point of savagery."

Sainte-Beuve was to write of him a little later:

The years 1819 and 1820 were undoubtedly the fullest, most ardent and decisive of his life. Love, politics, independence, chivalry and religion; poverty and fame, obstinate study, struggle against fate with an iron will—everything in him emerged and grew simultaneously to that degree of elevation which constitutes genius. Everything took fire, writhed and melted instantly in the volcanic flames of his . . . youth.

Although he worked constantly, he did not forget Adèle. His sleep was usually short. Every evening he would take a lonely walk, his steps usually leading him through the rue d'Assas, whence he would look up at a light in a certain room of the Toulouse Mansion, the room of Adèle. Then, wanting her, he would recall the time, so recent, when they were still free to walk arm in arm together, and her hand did not try to escape from his own, and their eyes met without constraint.

After meeting her at a ball, by chance, he wrote her: "You seemed displeased with me, and I had, all through the evening, the cruel pleasure of seeing you dance with other men." Early in 1821 he met her going to church, and learned that she took drawing lessons every day at a Mme. Duvidal's. He would watch for her, follow her and speak to her. Then she begged him not to do this, though agreeing that they might write to each other, in secret, at long intervals.

Thus restricted, he hit upon the idea of publishing poems to Adèle in his literary paper, whose purpose she alone would understand. One of these, the "Elegy on Raymond d'Ascoli," is the tale of a young man who died for love, taken from a medieval Italian legend.

Yesterday . . . dost thou recall, thou sweet and modest child,
   That yesterday by now so far from me? . . .

Tell me, O Petrarque, and thou, my love,
Is it not true that it were best to die?[1]

> [1]*Hier . . . te souviens-tu, fille aimable et modeste,*
>   *De cet hier déjà si loin de moi? . . .*
>
> *Dis, ô Pétrarque, et toi, ma bien-aimée,*
> *N'est-il pas vrai qu'il vaut bien mieux mourir?*

Then, in the spring of 1820, he had also begun his novel, "Hans of Iceland," an experiment in the manner of Walter Scott (and intended also for Adèle's eye). It was a series of romantic tableaux in which the love of a pure young couple, separated by political strife between their families, was to be the central theme.

Of "Hans of Iceland" he wrote candidly to Adèle that "the need to expand upon certain ideas weighed upon my soul and made me undertake a sort of romance in prose. My heart was full of love, and pain and youth; I had thee no longer; I dared not confide my secret to any living creature; I chose a silent confidant, of paper.

"I was trying to express, somehow, the turbulent impulses of my young and burning heart, the bitterness of my regrets, the uncertainty of my hopes. I wanted to picture a young girl, who would be the ideal of all fresh and poetic imaginations, a girl such as her I had dreamed of since childhood . . . pure, fresh, angelical. It was you, beloved Adèle . . . whom I had lost, and who seemed to belong only to the far-off future of my life. I wanted to put beside her, also, a young man, not such as I am, but such as I should like to be. . . ."

Here, as in the letter cited above, the young Hugo sings the love of Superior Souls. A characteristic passage that may have been written in 1820, at approximately the same time that he wrote to Adèle, runs:

Ordener, beside himself, had ravished from the lips of the girl, with her reply to his question, that first favor, that sacred kiss which suffices in the eyes of God to change lovers into husband and wife.

Both of them remained speechless, because it was one of those solemn moments, so rare and so brief on this earth, when the soul seems to experience something of the felicity of heaven. These are the indefinable moments when two souls thus address each other in a language which can only be understood by them; then all that is human is silent, and the two immaterial beings are united mysteriously for the life of this world and for the eternity of the other.

Ethel had slowly withdrawn herself from the arms of Ordener, and by the light of the moon they gazed at each other with rapture; only the flaming eye of the young man breathed forth a male pride and lion's courage, while the half-veiled regard of the young girl was marked with that shame, that angelic pudency, which in the heart of a virgin, is mingled with all the joys of love.

He wrote all this for her, when he was eighteen, often late at night, by a candle that guttered out. But did she still love him? He heard that there were now other suitors, and his tone with her grew harsh and violent. Hard pressed, as if in anguish, she answered: "If you but knew how many tears you have cost me, how much sorrow, how many sleepless nights, truly you would pity me. . . . You must think I have lost my head, and perhaps it is true. . . . I do not want to be reasonable any longer, I would rather faint and fall over a cliff. Little do you know, my Victor, how much a woman can love. . . ." This astonishing confession, and a lock of hair that went with it, made him happy again.

Then, suddenly, a first great blow, the first great sorrow of his life came to him. At the beginning of 1821, Mme. Hugo, who for some time had been ill with consumption, removed with her two sons to a small apartment on the ground floor of a house at number 10 rue de Mézières, which gave on a small garden. She felt that she needed the fresh air outdoors and the flowers. It was a small back-yard garden, yet she worked hard, directing Eugène and Victor at making alleys and garden beds, or wielding a hoe and spade herself, with a feverish activity. No one could keep her from working. In the early spring she took sick and went to bed with a recurrence of her chronic consumption. After several weeks she recovered, Eugène and Victor being her faithful nurses. But she was too active again, and at the end of May suffered a relapse. This time she lay abed for five weeks, while her fever scarcely declined. One night, while the two sons watched over her, she seemed to be sleeping easily. "It is her best night," said Eugène. "She has not stirred since midnight." Full noon had come. Victor went to touch her brow, and it was ice cold. She was dead.

Victor was distracted by his grief during the next two days. He had leaned so much upon her; now he felt a part of his life torn away. He felt truly alone, a veritable orphan. For his brother Eugène, the loss of the mother was an even more deadly blow. For some time during her final illness, Victor has related, Mme. Hugo was greatly concerned about Eugène's somber moods and odd ways. Now Eugène grew more "capricious and bizarre" than ever, keeping late hours, writing letters which he never showed anyone, borrowing money and disappearing.

On the night following the funeral, June 29, 1821, Victor wandered the streets of Paris. At last his steps led him to the rue du Cherche-Midi and the Council of War building from which he was barred. The home of the Fouchers was brightly lit, for it happened to be Mme. Foucher's birthday, and he could hear the sounds of

a large party. Victor made his way up the great stairs, looked
through the glass door and saw them dancing; Adèle "in a white
robe, with flowers in her hair, dancing and laughing." Adèle knew
nothing of his mother's death. Weeping, he crept away.

On the following morning, he turned his steps again toward the
Hôtel de Toulouse, toward the one person who might help him
and, in the garden adjacent to it, found Adèle. He was clad in
black and deathly pale. Adèle, who was alarmed at the sight of
him, burst into tears when she heard the news that had been up to
now concealed from her. "And to think that I was *dancing!*" she
wept. Their mingled tears were the sign of their reconciliation, and
the renewed plighting of their own secret troth.

M. Foucher, however, was less easily brought around. He had
come on the day of the funeral services to offer his condolences to
the sons of Mme. Hugo, but he had shown no desire to resume the
old footing with Victor. On the fifteenth of July he removed his
family to Dreux, sixty-three miles outside of Paris, almost in Normandy. It cost twenty-five francs to journey there by diligence, and
this alone, he must have reckoned, would hold his daughter's im-
pecunious suitor at a distance.

Victor was indeed poorer and lonelier than ever, owing to his
mother's death, for the annuities from her husband now ceased. A
cause of great bitterness to the late Mme. Hugo's sons was the failure of their father even to put in an appearance until some days
after their mother's burial in Montparnasse Cemetery. The distracted Eugène, in fact, had written his father a letter in the most
violent and threatening terms, for which Abel and Victor asked
his indulgence in a letter of formal regret. Not long afterward they
were to learn that the general, living at Blois, soon moved secretly
to legalize his relations with Catherine Thomas by a marriage ceremony which took place only a few weeks after his wife's death.
The general, living on half pay, had retained a small estate, a
fragment of the "million francs" he was said to have gained in the
Napoleonic wars, in the form of lands worth sixty thousand francs;
but it seemed now very doubtful that any of this would accrue
to his sons. Besides, when he did come to see them, he informed
Victor that he would continue to furnish him with a small income
only on condition that he "made up his mind to follow a steadier
career than that of letters." At the time of his mother's death the
young poet had a sum of eight hundred francs in his possession,
some of it saved from his own small winnings, and he estimated

that this might carry him for a year. He replied to his father's offer with a polite refusal, declaring that he would henceforth try to support himself. His chief concern, he said, was for his brother Eugène, who seemed not a little queer in the head; in a very manly way he asked his father only to aid his older brother, who needed help more than he did. Victor Hugo could be very gallant when he chose to be. He was deeply fond of Eugène, and thought simply that his brother was affected by his mother's death. He had no notion of the storm that was brewing in Eugène's darkening brain.

3

It was summer. The house in the rue de Mézières, which he was closing up and leaving for smaller quarters, seemed cruelly empty.

It was his habit even in youth to take long walks alone to clear his head. On the morning after the Fouchers had left Paris, July 16, 1821, he found himself on the road to Versailles, some twelve miles from Paris. Arriving there in the afternoon, he stopped with a friend of his, Gaspard de Pons, who had recently written an epistolary poem addressed to him as the Sublime Child. In the morning, instead of returning to Paris, he set forth in a westerly direction, toward Normandy, taking the road to the right which led north of Chartres. Mile after mile he walked in a burning sun, indifferent to the carriages that rushed past him covering him with their dust. Sometimes he sat down to rest, and wrote a few notes, which later took the form of his poem "On the Vale of Chérizy," published in his first volume. In this he pays his respects to a little hollow along his route where some sad cypresses lining the hills seemed to be attuned to his own mood.

The poem is a song of loneliness. The youth sits down wearily, thinking of his mother who is dead, his fiancée who is separated from him. As night comes on—he was on the road two days, and none knew where he slept—he feels himself truly a solitary voyager through life.

> Son sort est l'abandon; et sa vie isolée
> Ressemble au noir cyprès qui croît dans la vallée. . . .
>
> Déjà las de sa course, il est bien loin encore
> Du terme où ses maux vont finir; . . .
>
> Deux ombres désormais dominent sur sa vie;
> L'une est dans le passé, l'autre dans l'avenir!

He feels his "fate is to be abandoned," and his isolated life "is like that dark cypress growing in the valley." He is already weary of his journey, and yet "very far from the end, when his misfortunes are to cease." From now on "two shadows dominate his life"; the one (his mother) lies "in the past," the other "in the future"! It is the fear that he will lose his "lily," his "virgin with brow so pure, and smile so sweet," that makes him set his wide, round jaw and push on all the next day. For Victor Hugo, Adèle already replaces his mother.

As he walks on he thinks of his father, from whom he is alienated, only with anger and fear. Sometimes part of this hate is transferred to the person of Adèle's father, M. Foucher, the quiet, dark little man with the long nose, whom he also fears. He has already complained of him to Adèle, as having "behaved strangely toward me. . . . He is not frank and cordial and affectionate with me. I *want* to love him, as he is your father!" In other words he does not love him. Yet he walks on, with only the vaguest notion of what reception awaits him, resolved to demand a definite engagement with Adèle, and come to an understanding with her parents.

Weary and bedraggled, at the end of the third day out of Paris, July 19, 1821, the deep-chested young poet arrived at Dreux, the "town of the Druids." As he wandered about the town at dusk, M. Foucher, to his astonishment, saw him "prowling" around the cottage his family occupied. In Paris, M. Foucher had hinted to Victor that he would like him to favor Adèle with less frequent visits. Though he did not think ill of the youth, he feared having his daughter marry a man of letters, foreseeing, as he said, "little money and no end of trouble."

But, while Victor shadowed the Fouchers and wondered upon what pretext he should make a call, he was distracted from his purpose by a police officer who, unfavorably impressed by his growth of beard and his disheveled and dusty appearance, followed him in his comings and goings, and asked him suddenly for his passport. It was the time of plots and assassinations by the secret anti-Royalist society of the Carbonari. Victor, departing from Paris on the spur of the moment, had neglected to take any papers of identification with him. He protested with dignity that he was a law student and son of General Hugo, and was known to several persons in Dreux, though he forbore to mention the Fouchers. His assertion that he had walked to Dreux simply to see the country but hardened the policeman's suspicions, and he found

himself firmly led along to the local station. There he finally
thought of someone he knew, a Mme. Le Brun, mother of a young
playwright he had met in Paris. When the police proceeded to her
house with him, she kindly verified his identity and offered the
poor young man some supper.

The next morning, having washed, combed, and brushed himself, he walked out and promptly met Adèle and M. Foucher in
the main street of the little town. His first impulse was to approach
them, but then he recoiled. How would they consider his sudden
appearance? They would think he had followed them! He bowed
stiffly and retreated.

Returning to his cheap lodging place, bravely named the Paradise Inn, he wrote a letter which he brought to their house: "Sir: I
had the pleasure today of meeting you right here in Dreux and I
wondered if I were dreaming . . ." Thus ran his little deception.
"By the veriest chance" he happened to have been invited to visit
one of his friends residing outside of Dreux, and that friend also
by the "veriest chance" had left for Gap the day before Victor
Hugo arrived. He would have returned at once to Paris, had he not
had so many acquaintances in Dreux who pressed him to stay—
there was no mention of the obnoxious police official among them.
He continued:

Strangely enough, I left Paris much against my will. The desire you
indicated to have me stay away for some time made me feel that
way. . . .
I would not be frank, however, if I did not say to you that the
unexpected sight of mademoiselle, your daughter, gave me a deep
pleasure. I do not fear to say it openly, I love her with all the strength
of my soul, and in my complete abandonment, in my profound sorrow,
only the thought of her is left to give me happiness.

M. Foucher, who knew something of politics, saw through all
these subterfuges. But he was a kindly man at bottom, and a
reasonable one. Not for nothing had he held his seat, with equal
tact, under the tricolor of the Republic, under the Empire, and
under the white flag of the Bourbons. He found in the boy who
had walked sixty miles to see his lady a strength, a stubborn resolution "which opposed argument with argument," as he related
afterward. Victor came and made a speech in which he answered
for his career, boasting a little of the earnings he had been enjoying
as a writer, of the great persons interested in him, and the honors

he had already gained. He declared that he was writing a novel *à la* Walter Scott, and a play, in collaboration with another and experienced writer. He pointed out that a pension for him was under consideration at the Court. M. Foucher yielded. There was no mistaking the fact that Adèle was taken with him and wept often, and her father wanted peace. At last he agreed to an unofficial engagement between them, subject to the young man's finding a secure position for himself in the near future. "No one here expects you to abandon literature," he said, in effect; "that is and should be your principal vocation. But," he added sententiously and a little pompously, "above all, security, prudence. . . ." A further condition for the engagement required that he obtain the consent of his father to his marriage, for he was still very much a minor. But at last he was suffered to come and see his dark-eyed, languid Adèle, once a week, in the presence of her family. The clouds were lifting a little. He had gained a first victory by his audacity.

To Alfred de Vigny, stationed in Rouen with his regiment, he wrote, after his return to Paris, that he was "all broken up . . . but filled with glory at having done twenty leagues on foot." He felt scorn for people who rode in carriages. The journey, he added mysteriously, had "done him much good." But what good, he did not reveal—it was too important, and the battle was only partly won.

4

After his mother's death, he moved from the modest bourgeois home she had maintained, to bachelor quarters in an attic of a house in the grimy rue du Dragon, where for most of the next year he lived with young Adolphe Trébuchet, a cousin from Brittany who was a student. They had two small rooms in their unheated belvedere: in one were placed their two wooden cots; the other was their "salon." When young Trébuchet left Paris, Victor Hugo moved again to even smaller, cheaper quarters near by, in the old Latin Quarter.

His situation had certainly changed for the worse, with his mother gone, his allowance cut off. But with the small capital he had accumulated, 800 francs ($160), he resolved to carry on for a year or so, while he took measures to improve his own fortunes. It meant that he must live in the traditional style of the poor students and artists in the Latin Quarter. It meant eating on one franc a day or less, and paying rent of thirty francs a month. It meant that he cooked for himself: an omelette of two eggs and a glass of water was his lunch, a cutlet and a slice of cheese his dinner. He would sweep his own room in the morning, then go out and buy half a loaf of bread at three sous, and a chop from the butcher's at five sous.

And like Marius de Pontmercy, in *Les Misérables,* Victor Hugo would slip furtively into the corner butcher shop, among the chattering cooks and servants, his attitude seeming timid and angry at

Caricature of Hugo by Isabey

once. "He would come in, take off his hat, bow deeply to the butcher's wife, bow also to the butcher, ask for a mutton chop, pay the six or seven sous, wrap it up in paper, between the books he carried, and go out. . . . The chop which he cooked himself had to last for three days. On the first day he ate the lean, on the second the fat, and on the third day he chewed at the bone."

Victor Hugo had three linen shirts, one that he wore, one in reserve in his chest, and one at the laundress's for cleaning. He had two suits, one a new one for special occasions, the other, very shiny and threadbare, for everyday use. But at twenty he was a young man of note, who already knew great persons, and he could not appear in good society in shabby garments. Therefore he set aside the sum of 150 francs, a large part of his capital, on which he might have survived for six months, for the purchase of a blue-bottle coat with gold buttons, the kind of coat that elegant men of the age all wore. Thus, with his high-collared coat tightly buttoned over his poverty, Victor Hugo could go out to the theater when invited, or dine in town, and cut a certain figure.

Hungry as he was, he would call upon a Chateaubriand in his great house of the rue Saint-Dominique, bearing himself with that grave aplomb that he assumed from his earliest youth and seldom dropped. The third time he visited the author of *Le Génie du Christianisme* the great man conducted him into the salon, where Mme. de Chateaubriand greeted him with an effusiveness not common to her.

"Oh, M. Hugo, I was so anxious to see you," she exclaimed, "I am running a chocolate bazaar for the benefit of my indigent priests —can you buy some, at five francs a book?"

With a sweeping gesture, the son of "Countess" Hugo assured Madame that, upon his soul, he would be ravished to buy not one book of chocolates, but three, and forthwith gave her fifteen francs. Then, returning, he realized with a pang of regret that it was a sum upon which he might have eaten for two or three weeks.

There was always a Spartan, or Early Christian, side to Victor Hugo's nature. Living in solitude—after his cousin had left town— he enjoyed it. Not for a moment did he consider abandoning his chosen trade. In a sense, he enjoyed even contending with life on harsh terms, half fasting, and meditating alone, indifferent to everything around him, upon the poems and the books that he planned and wrote.

He would take long walks in the afternoon or in the evening— throughout his life he refreshed his body, and offset the terribly sedentary and mentally exhausting character of his vocation by walking. At night, he would sit by his candle, writing his abundant verses or his prose, or the endless and long *Lettres à la fiancée,* which are notable not so much for their wit, or persiflage, or purple patches, as for their very authentic and fresh revelation of his special character. They show him struggling with himself and the world, now downcast, now happy and boastful; they parade his vanity, but also show him, in extreme youth, taking charge of Adèle's unspoilt soul and possessively, masterfully, guarding her and instructing her to be what he desires her to be, in order that she might fill the form of his dream, his ideal.

Sometimes, as he cast about to earn a few francs, he saw no certain way out of his predicaments and his heart sank. Booksellers whom he approached refused the risk of printing the volume of his youthful poems, which already bulked large upon his table. He felt that the Republic of Letters, as he penetrated it, was a "morass," teeming with vile creatures who were already his "enemies," envying the favor he steadily won, determined to halt his progress and bring him down. Yet he persevered. *Perseverando!* was the motto he gave, many years later, to the hero of his symbolic novel, "Toilers of the Sea."

It was an industrious and silent life he led at nineteen, and so austere as to allow him few pleasures. An admiring friend, Alexandre Soumet, the middle-aged poet with the birdlike mouth and dreamy eyes, and also with a wig of long hair to cover his baldness, came one day and carried him off to dine with two actresses, who "knew his verses by heart" as he was assured. They were "décolleté almost to their waist," Victor Hugo remembered. He sat between them frigidly silent. His friend Soumet, a gay dog from the Midi, treated the ladies with an easy familiarity and called them by their second names: "Duchesnois" and "Levers," which shocked the younger man. Hugo's "grave and modest manner only stimulated them and they gave themselves to all sorts of mischievous annoyances that vexed him more than they flattered him," he has related. He felt that these actresses belonged to a world apart from that of mourning, courageous meditation, and ideal or chaste love to which he sternly committed himself. Returning home, Soumet remarked upon Hugo's success with the ladies and their evident eagerness to see him the next day, and asked him which one he would call upon first.

"Tomorrow I am going to see a priest, the Abbé de Lammenais," he replied severely.

French society at this time, at least on the surface, moved with the pace of a solemn reaction toward renewed faith in the Roman Church, and Victor Hugo, who was always a child of his century, mirroring his time, moved in step with it. Was it because of his mother's influence, as he later tended to explain it? Her influence here would seem to be superficial, as was her interest in the Church as such. Her own royalism was born of her *personal politics,* so to speak, rather than of the hope many Catholics shared, that the monarchy would be as a "rampart" for Mother Church. At Madrid, in 1811, Mme. Hugo had objected strongly to her sons serving as acolytes at the Mass, and, when told that this was the rule for all Catholic pupils, she had described herself and her sons, with something less than truth, as Protestants!

On the other hand, the contention made later by the anti-Hugolians that the poet was a mere time-server in his Catholic-Royalist phase as he was a time-server in the famous "conversion" of his later, Liberal republican years, is a judgment that is crude as well as false: crude, in the view of modern psychiatry, in its tracing of the complex development of his mind and character; false in building a thesis of "insincerity" from top to bottom; false in denying him the generous and courageous motives that ultimately predominated in his nature.

The truth is that Victor Hugo was always more disposed to religious worship than his Royalist, but Voltairean, mother. The gorgeous Chateaubriand, idol of Hugo's literary generation, had for a moment in his youth touched deep chords in Victor Hugo, with his *Génie du Christianisme,* and *Les Martyrs,* which stressed the artistic side of Christianity and mingled the marvelous architecture of Gothic cathedrals with the great images and symbols of the Scriptures. In time, Chateaubriand was exposed as being a "heretical Christian" rather than a rigidly loyal Catholic. But this was essentially the position that Hugo himself would take, that of a mystical and "heretical Christian" (as in writing the great *Légende des siècles*), when he systematically confronted the whole problem of faith, in his middle age.

But in the autumn of 1821 he was stricken by the loss of his mother, with whose memory he communed continually, as he said, and who followed him, amid storm or at dawn or in the night, "like an eye." He also felt himself frustrated in his love. Thus when he met, in Royalist circles, the pious young Duc de Rohan, who admired his poetry, he was at first greatly impressed with him, because the poor duke, too, had suffered a fearful loss recently. His young wife, immediately after their marriage, had perished in a fire, and, though an owner of great lands and châteaux, he had resolved to take orders, and lived in a bare cell of the seminary of Saint-Sulpice. Through Rohan, Victor Hugo obtained a confessor, the Abbé de Freyssinac, who was much in fashion at the time. But, when Victor Hugo confessed himself and spoke of his doubts in himself and his career, the priest assumed a very worldly line, arguing that he must develop his talents and attain success the better to spread faith by example and word. He must abandon his seclusion, and even prepare to pass from literature to public life, to politics, the field in which he could most aid Mother Church.

The young poet was repelled by all this "mundane" preaching, and asked Rohan to take him to the celebrated Abbé de Lammenais, the austere and learned Catholic Liberal philosopher. Lammenais turned out to be a small, shy, bilious-looking man, with fine expressive eyes and very nervous hands, clad in shabby clothing, wearing the coarse boots of a peasant. Victor Hugo had been introduced by the Duc de Rohan as a new "penitent," but the Abbé de Lammenais saw that he had no heavy sins to confess, and they passed on to a discussion of poetry and literature in general. Soon the author of the celebrated "Essay on Indifference" became a warm, steadfast older friend, giving his advice and moral support to the lonely youth. The Abbé de Lammenais also tended, in time, owing to his humanitarian and socialist tendencies, to become heretical, and was one day, in a mood of spiritual insurrection, destined to leave his Church. His influence upon Hugo can scarcely be considered an orthodox one.

I like your directness, your frankness and your elevated sentiments [he wrote to him, July 7, 1822], even more than your fine talent, which, nevertheless, I also admire. I do not doubt that the future will render justice to it, if the present refuse that. . . . But then, dear God, what are those vain noises that are considered glory or renown, and that are so soon extinguished in the silence of the tomb?

But, while Victor Hugo worked at his classical and generally Royalist odes, his mind opened. Just as his verses, at moments, already showed glimpses of the romantic in him, so his political opinions, at intervals, suggested shadings of heresy, and the critical non-conformist under his skin. When, in January, 1822, his idol, Chateaubriand, fell into disfavor, owing to clashes with the extreme reactionary group dominating Louis XVIII's government since the assassination of the Duc de Berry, Hugo defended him loyally before the Abbé de Freyssinac, who called Chateaubriand "no better than a Jacobin," and even before his prospective father-in-law, M. Foucher, who was always a conformist with whatever party was in power.

At this same time, a boyhood friend of his, named Delon, son of an officer who had been his father's comrade in arms, fell into trouble with the police, owing to alleged political conspiracy on his part, went into hiding, and was hunted all over Paris. Delon was a "hothead," Victor Hugo thought then, a violent republican who, after going into exile, some years later joined Lord Byron and died fighting for Greek independence. On hearing of Delon's danger,

Victor Hugo sat down and wrote a letter to his friend's mother offering her son asylum. He said: "I am so good a Royalist, Madame, that the police would never think of coming to look for him under my roof." The letter, sent directly to Mme. Delon's address, was of course opened by the secret police and even shown to the King, who loved to be kept informed of such little details. According to legends of the period, the King laughed over the incident and remarked that Hugo was a young fellow of worthy instincts.

But M. Foucher, when he heard of the affair, berated Victor for having "compromised" himself seriously. There was a heated discussion between them, and, to Victor's grief, Adèle took the side of her father. She had been brought up to be a good and pious daughter, and submitted easily to her father.

Her lover reproached her: "You seem always to range yourself with those who contradict me. I rarely have the pleasure of having you share my opinion. . . ." He adds: "Should one always ask if a step be useful or harmful, before doing what is just?"

Adèle was very good, very yielding, very feminine, and very innocent; her education was narrowly religious and she was taught a little drawing, for which she showed an aptitude. The environment of her family was essentially petty and commonplace, the home of a small government functionary, and there were times when Victor's grand airs and unbending, forthright opinions irritated them. "You should be more pliant," Adèle would plead, hinting at the vanity that the world found later written so large in him.

He answered her, in sorrow:

This observation wounded me. . . . If I am vain, I groan at finding among my faults the one I detest and despise most in the world. If you are wrong, if you mistake for self-love, a spirit, or if you will, a pride which I acknowledge and in which I rejoice, I am still more downcast at having been misjudged by the only person without whose esteem I cannot live.

He threatens to "keep his troubles to himself" hereafter, and reproaches her, saying: "You know me little, Adèle; you do not know my character."

Yet he continues in "bondage" to her, according her all virtue and all beauty. He declares that he is always ready to immolate all that he is and all that he has for her sake. "I am a thing that belongs to you!" he cries. Meanwhile the warmth, the tenderness, she offers him can never be abundant enough for him. He writes: "When I came and said 'Good-bye—until tomorrow at six,' nothing in your manner showed me that this period of separation seemed as long to you as it did to me. . . . A word, a gesture, a sign of regret, would have consoled me."

Sometimes, in a fit of jealousy, he tells her of his violent emotions, because of a word or a look somebody addressed to her, and of his desire to strike someone, to kill or be killed. She, the demure little bourgeoise, reproaches him: "For a mere word, perhaps meaningless . . . to risk throwing a whole family into mourning! One must be quite selfish to commit such a folly!" She is so right, and yet sounds so much like a passage out of a book on etiquette.

He is winning almost a national reputation, so far as literary circles are concerned, and she, his fiancée, she alone knows almost nothing about it, and finally asks him one day just what work he is doing.

He is made happy merely by her question. "I am delighted to see that you are not indifferent to what I am doing, as up to now I feared you were. . . . Should mere acquaintances know of my work and you . . . my inspiration, you, who are everything to me, not know?" He tells her of secretarial work he is doing for an Academician, of the novel he is writing, and of the play, to be based on Scott's "Kenilworth," which also engages him, adding that this last is "not a great literary undertaking, but a good financial speculation, which was all your father wanted . . ."

The late Louis Barthou, the French statesman and literary scholar who enjoyed collecting Victor Hugo's letters, remarks that the young poet was the "dupe of his heart, lost in his own lyricism," ignorant of the limitations of the young woman he loved and placed upon an impossible romantic pedestal.

But she was aware of her own limitations, and, fearing instinctively that the disparity between her own and her fiancé's talents and character would bring grief to them both, confessed her faults with a touching modesty. Obviously she struggles at times to rise to the "high tone" he sets for her, but feels unequal to it. She reads his poems, some of which, addressed to her, are already superb lyrics, and tells him sadly, "I am like a blind person trying to see colors." She fears that he will never forgive her ignorance. He replies: "Oh, Adèle, I implore you never to speak to me of your fear of my looking down upon you!"

But she, as if frightened by his very praises, tells him without vanity or coquetry: "Alas, you will have a wife who knows nothing, except to love you. Truly I regret that, but I am not to blame." How can she be his counselor and guide? And humbly she repeats later, as with a presentiment: "I am the most ordinary of women! I tell you honestly, and you will realize it some day and then you won't care for me so much, and I shall be wretched. I say to you that I am only a simple woman who loves you, and nothing more."

Meanwhile their engagement was prolonged for months, seemingly years. They had "misunderstandings," lovers' quarrels, and "forgave" each other. They saw each other only under the watchful eyes of the Foucher family; but, in the ripeness of youth, they grew desperately impatient. They began to write each other of their dreams. Victor, on August 27, 1822, told of how he attacked his pillow during sleepless nights: "Often . . . the most magical illusions transport you into the arms of your 'husband,' and he presses you to his heart with all his strength!"

He fasted and humiliated his flesh and yet slept not. "What solitude is worse than celibacy?" he wrote his fiancée, during one of those white nights. "You can scarcely believe what strange convulsions seize me, my dear; during the night when I cannot sleep, I embrace my pillow, like a lover, as I think of you; in my dreams I call you, I see you, I kiss you, I speak your name, I would grovel in the dust at your feet, be yours for once—and die. . . ."

Adèle answers in kind, saying innocently: "I too have had some sweet dreams, quite uncommon with me." There were moments finally when she assured him that, despite her family, she would fly to his arms at his command. But he, the pious young poet, proudly and fiercely guarded her virtue, even from himself.

5

In the summer of 1821 the good news came to Victor Hugo that the King had agreed to award him a pension. He was almost drunk with joy and, foreseeing an annual income of 1,500 or 2,000 francs in addition to his own earnings, looked forward to an early union with Adèle. Although, as he told her, various illustrious and brilliant careers were now forecast for him by persons he met, he was indifferent to all that. His own needs were simple. "I believe," he said, "I was made only for domestic happiness. . . . You, Adèle,

are my only goal, and all the paths that lead to it are good, provided I can go straight, without need of bending or crawling or
lowering my head."

But he had reckoned without the persistently bureaucratic spirit
of the French government. For many months, indeed for a whole
year, the question of his pension was postponed, or delayed by red
tape. Left in this uncertainty, he delayed, meanwhile asking his
father for legal consent to his proposed marriage. Although glory
and security, and the dark, exotic young beauty of Adèle, beckoned
him, all of it remained still tantalizingly out of reach, in the future
that was always just beyond the present. M. Foucher prodded him
with questions as to his prospects, and Adèle, too, grew restless.

"How can I believe," she wrote him, "that you really love me
and wish to marry me, when, in the eyes of other people, you appear to do nothing to forward our marriage?"

He answered her: *"I do nothing?* I am proud and shy, yet I
go to ask favors of the great. I wish to ennoble literature, yet
work for a wage. I love and respect the memory of my mother,
and I forget her, since I am about to write to my father."

He begs her to wait for him, or he will *"go to his mother,"* as
he hints in the moving love lyric, *A toi!* written in December, 1821.

He postponed writing to his father concerning his engagement.
In back of his mind was the unconscious fear of his father, since
childhood, as the one who would thwart his innermost desire if
he could. To write to his father meant to "betray his mother."
But, in the meantime, he saw to it that persons like the Abbé de
Lammenais and even the Duchesse de Berry petitioned for the
promised pension, and made repeated applications himself, pester-
ing the clerks at the Ministry of the Interior, who seemed to have
a good deal to say in such matters. But he was told to wait.

These were days of harrowing uncertainty. "All my future is
at the mercy of the waves," he wrote M. Foucher. "I would prefer
to be sure of something, even of misfortune; at least I could then
know where I stood. But now I must wait! My faculties for action,
for energy, are paralyzed, and what is required of me is patience,
a virtue which I lack. . . ."

Meanwhile he was no richer than before and had not quite
enough to eat every day. As he has described Marius in *Les
Misérables,* so it happened with him that, as time passed, he seemed
to "eat up" his watch and his clothing and other possessions. "But

more terrible were the days without bread, nights without sleep,
winter evenings without a fire or a candle; the weeks without work,
a future bereft of hope, a coat out-at-elbows and a hat so old that
the girls in the street laughed at it; the front door locked at night
because last month's rent was not paid, the porter insolent, the
neighbors mocking, and the waiter serving one with a sneer;
humiliations great and small, injured dignity, chores done for the
pennies they brought; bitterness, disgust and overwhelming misery.
Marius learned how a man may take all that—and indeed have
very little else to consume. At a time when his pride was most
sensitive, because he was in love, Marius felt himself a laughing-
stock, shabbily dressed, mocked because he was poor. More than
once he would lower his eyes to his worn boots, and know an unjust shame and misery. It is out of such dreadful and admirable
trials that the weak come forth infamous and the strong sublime. It
is the ditch into which Destiny flings a man who is to be made
either a knave or a demigod. . . ."

The spring of 1822 marked a low point in Victor Hugo's fortunes; the melancholy of a celibate youth, smoldering with the passions of an all too vigorous male, touched its depth. At about this
period he wrote to Adèle as if he feared that he would lose her:

I do not know what I am writing. I am assailed by somber thoughts
without even knowing their cause. Do not be surprised. In a certain
state of mind, there often come to us vague sorrows which the soul
cannot repel and can scarcely define. They are the memories of past
misfortunes and the presentiments of misfortunes to come . . . clouds
between us and our thoughts. All the smiling colors then turn gray,
all the sad ones grow obscure. But let some happy event come and, at
once, the clouds are broken, everything assumes its former shape and
color, and one is astonished at having been formerly so unhappy.

He had resumed his relations, lately, with his father, though on
somewhat formal terms. The general was engaged in writing his
military memoirs, and Victor gave him literary advice and aid,
while the general, in turn, relented somewhat on the question of
an allowance to his son. Then, finally in March, 1822, the son
ventured to disclose to his father, in a long letter, his protracted
courtship of Adèle Foucher, and asked for consent to their marriage. "I steeled myself against a terrible blow," he told Adèle
afterward. If the consent were refused, he would have to wait

five years until he would be twenty-five, and would probably then lose Adèle to another! On the ninth of March, 1822, he went to the great church of Saint-Sulpice for the service of Mass, and from afar spied his Adèle; he entered, knelt, and prayed with her. Then the reply came from Blois, on March 13, 1822, and he hastened to write to her: "Adèle, Adèle, I am drunk with joy. My first thought was for you. For a week I awaited misfortune, but it is happiness that has come instead."

Now he ran about all day to see the ministers and their clerks about his pension, so often promised, in return for his distinguished literary services to the monarchy, and as often postponed. At the same time, through a friendly printer, and with a little money supplied by his elder brother, Abel, he succeeded in having his first volume of poems, *Odes et Poésies diverses,* rather poorly printed on cheap grayish paper, and put on sale in several bookshops. Abel reported to him that, when he urged one bookseller to display his brother's work in the window, the man refused, saying that it would *"prevent people from seeing the real books he had on sale"!*

Victor Hugo's happiness was now ready to brim over. He was permitted to see Adèle every day instead of once a week. He was with the Fouchers, as their guest, at a summer cottage they rented in Gentilly, outside of Paris, on the day his first book appeared, June 15, 1822. It was reviewed in the Paris press at first, mainly by influential literary friends of his, such as Alexandre Soumet and the Abbé de Lammenais. But, soon after, other and more disinterested critics wrote of it in terms of unstinted praise such as only one other modern poet, Lamartine, had received, two years earlier. Hugo's friend Alfred de Vigny also, with good results, published his first volume this season, a few weeks after Hugo's appeared, and the two young poets were often likened or contrasted with each other. To the scanners of literary horizons the 1820's began to hold a golden poetic promise.

For Victor Hugo, the publication of *Odes et Poésies diverses* represented a first notable victory in the field of letters. The old King himself ordered several copies of the book, read and marked it, and announced his approval of it. Two months later, the promised annual pension, one thousand francs—somewhat below his expectations, and not more than was given to many literary mediocrities attached to the monarchy—was actually paid over to him.

The first edition of his poems, fifteen hundred copies, was soon sold out. Since his fortunes had taken a turn for the better (that is, after the day in March, 1822, when he received his father's consent to his marriage) Victor Hugo had written like an inspired man and turned out virtually a whole new volume of poems, much superior to his earlier work. Adding these to the first slender volume, he arranged for a second edition to be issued by the well-known bookseller, Persan, in December, 1822. His first work had earned roundly 750 francs, and the contract for its second edition, which won a surprising success, brought him an advance payment of seven hundred francs. This he devoted entirely to purchasing for Adèle a long cashmere shawl, without which no young lady of the period could properly go to the theater. The long-deferred wedding, after an engagement, secret or formal, extending over more than three years, was fixed for October 12, 1822. It was agreed that the young couple—Adèle had only a dot of two thousand francs in furniture and linen—were to live at the home of the Fouchers until they felt able to sustain an independent establishment of their own.

Victor Hugo sent paeans of joy to his father, to his friends, to the illustrious Abbé de Lammenais. The latter wished him joy, but virtuously urged him to remember his religion and prepare also to bear duties and sorrows. "The pleasure you show is legitimate, it is the order of God, and I am happy to find such a naïve and moving expression of it in your letter. But know also that it is a joy of the moment, and fugitive. There is another joy in eternity. . . . May Heaven, none the less, dear friend, spread over you and her, whom fate shall no more separate from you, the softest graces that it is pleased to accord young spouses. May He deign to remove from your path through this world all that may sadden your days and trouble your peace."

Then, and in later years, Victor Hugo tended to picture the drama of his youth and his first love, which was intense enough, as a struggle against mighty obstacles and deadly dangers. His first romantic novel, "Hans of Iceland," mostly written in 1821, but published two years later, is a slightly concealed allegory of the unconscious conflict he waged, now, as he imagined, with his father, now with his father-in-law, M. Foucher, or with others. He pictured himself as the young Danish knight, Ordener, and Adèle as Ethel—even the names were similar. The hero, setting himself against his own family, overcomes Gothic horrors and perils of all sorts to win the hand of his lady and be united with

her in a transcendent love. It was a theme that often returned to
him: youth at war with age and its authority.

In his disciplined youth something of "granite and iron" was
brought forth in him, as Sainte-Beuve observed, that few among
his contemporaries showed. He staked out his life and his work
much as a skillful, resolute general surveys his battlefield. Within
eighteen months of his mother's death, when he saw himself cast
off, alone, he had overcome poverty, won a rather brilliant place
for himself in the literary world, and had taken his Adèle to the
altar. Exultant, for he was often of a very sanguine temper, he
wrote her on the eve of their marriage: "Our story, dear love, will
have been proof of the truth that to will firmly is to win through."

General Hugo, in his letter to M. Foucher, according to custom,
had formally recommended his son's suit for Adèle Foucher's hand,
and called attention to his qualities of steadiness, his virtue. M.
Foucher, in reply, agreed with him, and commended the young
man for showing an unusual "gravity" which supplanted experience that was wanting. Everyone knew that Victor Hugo at
twenty was incredibly "grave" and resolute, moving forward always, with eyes fixed far ahead. Meanwhile, under his very nose,
stark drama burst forth.

After the solemn service at Saint-Sulpice, on October 12, 1822,
a wedding breakfast was served at the old Toulouse Mansion, attended by all of the immediate family of the couple, save General
Hugo and his new wife. The groomsmen included Alfred de Vigny,
Alexandre Soumet, Emile Deschamps, and Biscarrat. Everything
proceeded pleasantly, with the young husband, Victor, according to
an allusion once made by the poet, Lamartine, having the air of
"a vintner drunken with his wines . . ."

But suddenly Eugène Hugo began to act strangely, as was noticed
by Abel Hugo and Biscarrat, his old teacher, sitting beside him.
Six months before, when General Hugo, by letter, had sent his
consent for the marriage, he had also announced his own secret
marriage to Catherine Thomas, news which became the only
"cloud" upon Victor's happiness. But on hearing this, Eugène, who
had behaved queerly since his mother's death, suddenly disappeared, leaving behind him a strange note of farewell which made
his two brothers fear that he might attempt to kill his father. In
the papers of men who knew both brothers, such as the poet,
Gaspard de Pons, references have been found indicating that they
believed the neurotic Eugène was intensely jealous of his younger

brother Victor, and that, in a hopeless way, he too loved Adèle. In an *épître* to Eugène Hugo, Pons wrote:

Thou wouldst have done as Cain unto thy brother. . . .

Now in the midst of the wedding feast he was seen to give fierce looks and utter strange words. Quietly, Biscarrat and Abel Hugo induced Eugène to leave with them, and without disturbing the other diners. He was confined to a room, where Biscarrat stayed with him all night. When Biscarrat left for a short time he found, on his return, that Eugène had lit a score of candles and with saber in hand had proceeded to hack all the furniture in the room to pieces. Momently he is said to have cried out that he would kill his brother Victor. At dawn, Biscarrat and Abel Hugo called Victor from his marriage bed to help attend to the unhappy Eugène, who was stark mad. Victor had loved him well, without noticing too much what was going on within him. (He had thought sometimes that Eugène was mixed up with the Carbonari, the secret revolutionary plotters of the Restoration period.) Now, immediately after the wedding celebration, arrangements were made for the care of Eugène, who, with his disease progressing, was to end his days in the institution on the hill in Charenton. The tragic dementia of Eugène, bursting forth at the hour of the younger brother's nuptial joys, served as one of the first great antitheses in Victor Hugo's life of strong contrasts.

CHAPTER IV

"A Prince of Poets"

On summer evenings in the 1820's, residents along the southern outskirts of Paris, near the *barrières* (now called *boulevards*) of Vaugirard, Montparnasse, or Maine, would often see a band of from six to a dozen young men marching along, buzzing with talk, and yet with their eyes always fixed skyward, on the sunset or the distant hills and fields outside the city. At the head of the band there was always a very young man, of medium height but solid torso, having a very high forehead and long brown hair, and dressed in black frock coat and gray striped trousers. He was our poet, Victor Hugo, and was usually followed nowadays by a band, or, as one would say of some Scottish highland chieftain, by his "tail," composed of still younger or lesser men of letters and artists. These were his brother, Abel Hugo; Paul Foucher, his young brother-in-law; Adolphe de Saint-Valry, poet; Victor Pavie, poet and recent arrival from Angers; Charles-Augustin Sainte-Beuve, the small, long-nosed critic; Eugène Delacroix, the painter; David d'Angers, the sculptor; and Louis Boulanger and the two Deveria brothers, portrait painters. Sometimes Alfred de Musset, a handsome blond stripling of sixteen or seventeen, trotted along with them.

Usually, on fair days, Hugo and his band would proceed up the rue de Vaugirard, then like a broad highway, toward the open fields, making their way past the tempting little rustic taverns and garden cafés placed under grape arbors, whence came the sound of violins and dancing. Then the leader would order a halt, and they would stop and look toward "flowery Grenelle," toward the right of the Vaugirard highway, with its windmills and dairy farms and vineyards—then a verdant plateau, now a sooty, densely populated quarter of greater Paris. Sometimes they would sit there in a circle gazing at the sunset flaming over Grenelle and its thatched roofs and spires, at the bands of purple, pink, and blue— provided always there was a sunset—while their young leader would remain standing, his eyes fixed even farther away than theirs. Then, with mien exceedingly grave, his eyes almost closed, as in trance, he would begin to recite a poem of sunset in some exotic region of that unimaginable Orient which, in the 1820's, absorbed the young romantic mind. The cottages and cow barns of clay would become "crenelated castles," or towers, bridges, and soaring stairways leading to "immeasurable Babylons," or disappearing amid "archipelagoes of blood-tinted cloud." The circle of young admirers or disciples, literally sitting at his feet, would listen silently while he whom they called already "the prince of poets" recited, or even improvised with an eloquence so astonishing that those who heard him easily forgave him his vanity. When he was done, they would give cries of approval, each vying with the other to applaud him in those emphatic, affectionate, and sentimental terms which the literary 1820's and 1830's preferred.

Alfred de Musset, the gilded youth who turned up toward 1827, held that the leader of the band was a "monologist" who listened to no one else, which may have been more or less true. In satirical verses, he has reported that these excursions were not always blessed with good weather, and were held—

> In time of fog, precisely at the hour
> When the cat prowls and weeps; then M. Hugo
> Would issue forth to watch old Phoebus die.

But the Apollonian M. Hugo looked not only toward Phoebus in the heavens. Sometimes he would wind up with his disciples at some bistro, like Mother Saguet's, on the Vaugirard, and dine for one franc, with white wine "at discretion," to the sound of vague violins under the grape arbors. There he would grow happy, ruddy, full of programs and innovations, or even of paradoxes, his laughter ringing out above the other voices. Full of a sense of well-being, he would sometimes write a quatrain in the book of the inn, in a hand that was now very firm and large, leaving it there for the collectors and bibliophiles of posterity to discover.

At other times, instead of going to the country he would take his followers with him into the heart of ancient Paris, the *Ile de la Cité*. Then, at dusk, they would climb to the top of Notre-Dame Cathedral, and hang over its parapets, among the fantastic, tortured gargoyles and statuary of the Gothics, looking out over what was still a fifteenth-century town below them and toward the tossing ocean of old roofs and chimneys across the Seine. This too would provoke him to dream audibly and discourse with exuberance.

But he also *observed*. Sainte-Beuve, one of his younger disciples, related how one day from the spire of Notre-Dame they were looking at the old Arsenal building, hundreds of feet below and at the other side of the great square. On a balcony of the building, sat a lady knitting; she was Mme. Nodier, wife of Charles Nodier, their friend, who was the librarian of the Arsenal and resided there. Hugo's sight, according to Sainte-Beuve, was so keen that he could distinguish at that distance what Mme. Nodier was knitting. It was said in those days "Victor Hugo was an eye . . ."

Between 1823 and 1827, between the ages of twenty-one and twenty-five, the young poet, *pensionnaire* of the King, free to devote himself entirely to poetry, not only acquired a certain fame, but gathered a *cénacle,* a club or school of followers. He had come to be known not only as a poet of boundless promise, but as one who headed a whole movement—it was a position he enjoyed and insisted upon—that threatened to give a new turning to French literature.

To his friends there was already something of the hero about him, or the "archangel out of a stained-glass window," as one of them exclaimed. Freely they acknowledged his genius. To Théophile Gautier (who came to him some years later), he was a young Caesar, a demigod, with his confident pose, his pale, intense, smooth-shaven face, his finely chiseled, expressive mouth, his light brown eyes that looked straight at one, and his "monumental forehead like a white pediment," where, as it seemed to young Gautier, "the vastest thoughts could be written."

Moreover, he was in those days a happy and gracious hero to his friends. One, Saint-Valry, has related of that earlier time:

We were fascinated, seduced, by his gentle ascendancy—so much of purity, grace, and imagination united to so bold and vigorous a genius! All who came within his sphere of influence were touched by a feeling of friendship and enthusiasm as lively and as passionate, almost, as love itself. Genius was imprinted on his spacious brow, and something strong, puissant, inspired rang in his lightest accent.

2

To understand how swiftly Victor Hugo, by the age of twenty-five, gained a fairly complete ascendancy as the literary leader of "Young France," we must remember how great and persistent was the tendency to hero worship in the first half of the nineteenth century. With the termination of the great wars, men tended now to pay an homage similar to that offered the Napoleons and Wellingtons to the "geniuses" who led in the arts of peace—to the aged Goethe, to a Chateaubriand, even to a Byron.

Meanwhile literature in France was emerging from a long Silver Age. In England, Coleridge was saying that the French had "lost their poetic language." Few men understand nowadays how the pedestrian, pseudo-classical poetry of the Abbé Delilles or the forgotten Nepomucène Lemerciers won serious attention after the end of the brilliant eighteenth century. In the 1820's men of this stamp, interminably writing their old and abstract verses, still filled the seats of the French Academy but in no wise satisfied the thirst for genuine poetry. This appetite for poetry was a remarkable feature of the new literary audience not only in France, but even more in England, where Byron's "Childe Harold" was a best-seller, bringing him a veritable fortune.

From being merely à Sublime Child, a rhymer for a few literary coteries in Paris, Victor Hugo, who was, in his own way, and always, a painstaking craftsman, achieved a certain maturity as a lyrical poet by the age of twenty, and was fully recognized as the first in his field in France before he was twenty-five. Even earlier, in 1823, Stendhal, who disliked Hugo's poetry, writing his literary correspondence for the authoritative *Edinburgh Review*, reported that it was not Lamartine but "M. Hugo who is the real poet of the Ultra party."

If he had chanced to die young—as did André Chénier, under the guillotine—his place would have been firmly established in the history of French poetry with Chénier himself and with Lamartine, his own, slightly older contemporary. Although showing no marked originality of thought at this phase, Hugo's odes and ballads ceased to be merely skillful performances. They were executed with an increasing sonority and sweep of language, with a vividness and sensuousness of imagery, approaching that of the young Keats; toward 1827 novel effects of fire and color marked his work, which was already notable also for its great mastery of *mise-en-scène* or dramatic statement.

At the beginning of this fruitful period of lyrical writing, he declared in the first Preface to his *Odes,* published in 1822, that he saw no sense in the controversy which had lately arisen between the proponents of the "classical genre" and the "romantic" school. Declaring then that his intentions were political as well as literary, he implied that his position was that of a classicist who strove for the "elevation of *monarchical ideas and religious beliefs.*"

But soon the devil's hoof of the romanticist peeps out. His boyish novel, "Hans of Iceland," issued in 1823, had shown his disposition to follow in the trail of the "Gothic" or "Fantastic" school, exemplified in England then by the popular Mrs. Radcliffe and the much-translated "Monk" Lewis, and in France by Charles Nodier, successful author of several "horror novels." There were so many weird scenes in the caves of gravediggers or dungeons, there was so much of Hans, the monster, drinking blood and sea water out of human skulls, that Nodier, the established leader in this genre, was pleased and wrote in high praise of the young novelist. Hospitably he invited him into his romantic literary salon, which met regularly in a room of the old Arsenal Museum, filled with old armour. Other reviewers took young Hugo to task for piling up so much incredible horror in his romance and poked fun at him for holding too much intercourse with "the dead, with ghosts, vampires, fairies, goblins, and the secrets of the tomb."

Hugo was further reproached by critics of the classical bent, because in the third edition of his first poems, *Nouvelles Odes* (1824) which contained a group of his later odes, they already discovered metaphors and language usages of a "heretical" quality. In answer to one such criticism, in the conservative *Journal des Débats,* the poet cautiously denied these charges of literary "heresy," arguing that the same devices had been used by Horace and Virgil, as well as by earlier French writers. He still described himself as detached from the new "romantic school" and the quarrels it began to provoke.

But in his recent poems, such as *l'Antéchrist* and *la Bande noire* ("The Black Band"), dated 1823, all the germs of romantic tendencies may be discerned. The first was a fantastic, strongly colored word painting of the devastation befalling the world at the coming of the antichrist. The second is a rather wildly imaginary affair of "old ruins" and "rusty armour" and "shadowy corridors" and "funereal birds." A little later, in 1825, he wrote the technically brilliant, swiftly paced ballad, *Ronde du Sabbat* ("Sorcerer's Night"), a piece evoking an imaginary gathering of goblins and pixies in a haunted castle and their orgies and dancing. Here, full of a budding rhetorical violence, he showed already those romantic lapses from "good taste" which the academic authorities advocated in literature, and increasingly drew their censure upon himself. He showed also a strong disposition to use *antithesis:* calm before a storm, beauty beside ugliness. This, even while he still wrote stiffly classical odes ordered by the Court, which he served, in effect, as a young laureate.

One of his early poems of personal reminiscence, *Mon Enfance* ("My Childhood"), dating from 1823, recalls the years of perilous travel with thunderous military convoys through war-torn Europe. His recollections are woven around the names of far-off rivers, mountains, and cities: Rome, "queen of the world," and proud Madrid.

> *L'Espagne me montrait ses couvents, ses bastilles;*
> *Burgos, sa cathédrale aux gothiques aiguilles;*
> *Irun, ses toits de bois; Vittoria, ses tours;*
> *Et toi, Valladolid, tes palais de familles,*
> *Fiers de laisser rouiller des chaînes dans leurs cours.*

The strophe is made entirely of the names of cities, Burgos, Irun, Vittoria, closing with its very graphic brush stroke:

> *And thou Valladolid, with proud, ancestral mansions,*
> *Where rusting chains were hung across the courtyards. . . .*

This is a very characteristic example of the young Hugo's strongly visual feeling, which already differentiated his work from that of his contemporaries. He had remembered from his boyhood days in Spain how the conquered hidalgos had the custom of hanging chains across the courtyards of their great houses, as a mute sign of their enslavement by the invading French and of their undying protest. Thus, in the later editions of his first volume, poems of greater resonance, freedom, and even "feeling for truth and reality," as Hugo would say, jostled already beside primly classical odes written to order (which the poet later detested).

After the ode on the unfortunate Duc de Berry, whose assassination in 1820 brought a wave of reaction in France, he had written an ode on the birth of the duke's son, and another on the death of King Louis XVIII, late in 1824. Because of these literary services, his pension had been raised to two thousand francs a year. Then, in 1825, when Charles X, the former Comte d'Artois, fanatical Legitimist, prepared to hold pompous coronation rites at Rheims—as if to mark the deliberate turning of France from semi-constitutional monarchy to Bourbon absolutism—he indicated his desire that the two young laureates, Alphonse de Lamartine and Victor Hugo, should write odes in commemoration of the event.

It was a great distinction. Victor Hugo, at twenty-three, still partly under the enchantment of the Restoration, was unable to hide his enthusiasm and wrote to a young friend, Frédéric Soulié, on April 27, 1825:

. . . Royal graces rain upon me. . . . The King has named me a Chevalier of the Legion of Honor and done me the rare honor of inviting me to his coronation rites. You are going to rejoice, you who love me.

But his tendency to unclassical innovations in poetry were already being noticed and spoken of in literary circles in Paris. How would he now fit these with the new official honors given him? Would he not be obliged to change his style? However, he denies any such intention stoutly, writing to another young friend, Saint-Valry, on May 7, 1825:

I hear they are saying over there in Paris that I have abjured all my literary heresies. . . . Deny this for me as loudly as you can, and you will render me a great service.

His pious ode on "The Rites of Charles X" turned out to be a craftsmanlike exercise, and little more. There were too many such things included in his oft-reprinted first volume. But, at any rate, it was noticed that he did his task much more skillfully than Lamartine, the only other genuine poet discovered in France since the Revolution.

At heart, he had felt himself repelled by the elaborate and wearying ceremony, as he wrote to his wife, though all the notables of Europe and England seemed to have crowded into Rheims to witness it. It was an omen of renewed absolutism (which Louis XVIII had wished to avoid), and the French people understood it as such. Victor Hugo, who had been an ornament of the Royalist party, now for the first time began to wrestle with a growing disillusionment on their score and with vague doubt as to his real allegiance. In 1825 his royalism began to wane perceptibly. Meanwhile, under his pen the verses flowed, now in the quick, lilting, lyrical meters of the sixteenth-century song-writers, turning toward the grotesque or the romantic, or now in sweeping, resonant Alexandrines, or hexameters, which tended to shift the caesura at will —heresy indeed, in French versification!—or developed into runover lines, spontaneously breaking with classical laws of verse and unashamedly crying their lust for freedom, for untrammeled liberty.

At first, this feeling for liberty, this growing revolt against the old ways, was purely *artistic* in Victor Hugo.

In November, 1826, in a new preface for the augmented edition of *Odes et Ballades* (as his volume of poems was now called) Victor Hugo first openly "hoisted the flag" of literary romanticism. For four years previous to this the literary controversy between the romanticists and the classicists had been rising in heat—helped along by an attempt by a company of English actors to revive Shakespeare's plays in 1822, at the Porte Saint-Martin Theater. "Speak in French!" the unruly crowd had cried. "Shakespeare is an agent of Wellington!" The English actors were assailed with rotten eggs and apples. "In other words it was a great triumph for the national honor," Stendhal wrote sardonically. But the debate over the long-dead English dramatist, treated as the "savage" apostle of the romantic school, waxed hotter, aided by Stendhal's brilliant pamphlet, "Racine and Shakespeare," which was so caustic to French classical drama.

Victor Hugo, at last crossing his artistic Rubicon in his new Preface of 1826, also took up the cudgels for Shakespeare, and wrote his first manifesto for romanticism. His assertions, thus far, were moderate in tone. He contended, against those who held to Voltaire's notion that Shakespeare was barbaric and of a disorderly fancy, that the alleged barbarism of a Shakespeare was greatly preferable to the ineptitude of certain dull followers of classical style, now anointed members of the French Academy. Order must not be confused with dull regularity, he argued. A Gothic cathedral embodied a most admirable order in its irregularities. So with Homer and the Bible in literature. "The poet must take nature as his model and truth as his guide." Hugo, for his part, declared himself fed up with writing which was "orderly" in the manner of the formal gardens of the seventeenth century. "Regularity is the taste of mediocrity," he said. He preferred the primeval forests of the New World, with their giant trees and torrential rivers. The century thirsted for liberty, and he called for "liberty in art."

A new sequence of poems, romantic ballads based on old folk legends, written in 1825 and 1826 and added to his earlier series of poems, exemplified his new principles.

Over these, and over the challenging statements in his Preface, a controversy of unusual violence now began to rage, controversy such as he had previously avoided but which tended to cling to him and all his works from now on.

At this period the writers usually lumped together as romantics were most often Royalists in politics, like Chateaubriand. On the Liberal side, where a muffled agitation for political democracy was kept up, the writers tended to support the political tradition of Voltaire and seemed therefore aligned with the classical style. Liberal commentators, as in the small weekly, *La Pandore* (March 11, 1824), usually charged the romantics with being absurd and obscure, with some exception sometimes made for Victor Hugo, "despite his *hateful* [that is, Royalist] doctrines."

But now circumstances were altered. Political conservatives, as well as Academicians, were troubled at Hugo's cry for "liberty," and preached sermons against him, while in the brilliant and perceptibly anti-Royalist and anti-clerical semi-weekly, *Le Globe,* which Goethe called the most enlightened newspaper in Europe, a strong voice was raised in Hugo's defense. It was that of a young newcomer, Charles-Augustin Sainte-Beuve, then twenty-three, who on January 2 and 9, 1827, published an essay in two parts, which embraced a long and searching study of Hugo's poems. He spoke of the rise of this young poet as "one of those literary phenomena of which the muses alone know the secret." Possessed of a "fiery style, sparkling with images, abounding in harmonies," Hugo, by the high qualities of his soul, had risen to artistic achievements of a higher order than any of his contemporaries, and the young critic noticed with approval the growing richness of imagination and style in his newest work. He reproached those who, as if envious, treated this young writer with ridicule, noticing only the fantastic aspects of his writings and ignoring their noble parts. Sainte-Beuve made a few reservations on M. Hugo's conservative politics; then, in prophetic vein, closed by warning the poet against the abuse of his own splendid powers.

In poetry there is nothing more dangerous than power: if it is given free rein, it takes advantage of everything; and that which merely seeks to be original and new becomes only bizarre; a brilliant contrast degenerates into a precious antithesis; the author aims at grace and simplicity; he seeks only the heroic and renders the gigantic; and when he verges on the colossal he cannot avoid falling to the puerile.

Sainte-Beuve's first study of Hugo—he was the first man to devote a long and serious study to a writer barely twenty-five, whom he now ranked with the leading writers of France—by its boldness, made an initial reputation for the young critic himself. Victor Hugo, reading it, overflowed with gratitude, made efforts to learn the writer's address, and proceeded to his house, then almost next door to his own home in the rue de Vaugirard. He found him absent and left his card. On the following afternoon Sainte-Beuve returned the call.

The meeting with Sainte-Beuve at Victor Hugo's house that afternoon in January, 1827, was the beginning of a brief but dramatic friendship, and in the romantic manner, something like a love affair. But what was more, Hugo, who was attracting to himself a growing coterie of disciples and admirers, won for his ally a critical mind of rare power and sensitiveness, one with whom he could work out the ideas for many poetic experiments he was now undertaking. In talking with him Victor Hugo clarified his own thoughts. Sainte-Beuve was on one side a fledgling poet himself, and quickly grasped the value of the young master's innovations. On the other side, he was a young man of curious and extensive literary scholarship. He was, at this time, engaged in writing his "Historical and Critical Study of Sixteenth Century French Poetry," chiefly dealing with Ronsard and Du Bellay, the fresh and graceful contemporaries of England's Elizabethan song-writers. In them, he urged, was to be found a pure poetry superior to that of the men of the coldly classical age of Louis XIV, the seventeenth century's Racines and Boileaus, who were still used as models of literary perfection. Sainte-Beuve's researches brought an important fresh source to Hugo, who had known the older poets but slightly. His own groping innovations seemed but a harking back to the "naturalness" of a Ronsard. The freedom of the earlier French poets' metrical forms, their directness and fresh color, responded to his own disposition. Prompted by Sainte-Beuve, he would learn deeply from them. But in turn, Hugo, who was instinctively a great technician, would explain their secrets to the scholar and minor poet who was Sainte-Beuve.

"Up to then I had been antipathetic [to the Romantic School] because of their royalism and mysticism," Sainte-Beuve later recalled: "The conversation of Hugo opened my eyes and revealed to me the secrets of the poetic medium, the fingering, so to speak, of the new methods. Soon he won my utmost confidence. . . . Hugo showed me his ideas and his metrical processes, some of the secrets of rhythm and color."

Sainte-Beuve began to write verse, more freely, with a new verve. Their conversation centered endlessly upon poetry: "I soon seized the importance of these new ideas, which I then heard for the first time and which suddenly opened before my eyes new views on style and the technique of verse." While still writing his study of Ronsard and the "Pléiade" of the sixteenth century, Sainte-Beuve now recast his work, as he tells us, "in order to find examples and make applications illustrating Victor Hugo's theories." It is a commentary on the changeability of the critical mind. He adds: "From that day forward I was devoted to that branch of the Romantic School of which Hugo was the chief. . . . An enthusiastic period opened . . . the happiest years of my youth."

Now inspired by close study of the fresh songs of Ronsard and Bellay, the untamed poets of three centuries ago, whom Sainte-Beuve had presented to him in a new light, Hugo's poetic style became more decidedly romantic than before, and his subjects were drawn from medieval legends or the Bible—as if to draw the contrast more strongly with the Greek or Roman subjects favored by the classical writers. In 1827, he wrote some of the most colorful and pictorial of those ballads which made up the Third Book, the concluding section of the new edition of the *Odes et Ballades,* issued in 1828. Here in *Le Pas d'armes du Roi Jean* is the lyric of old Paris which has been likened to an old fifteenth-century woodcut:

> *Cette ville,*
> *Aux longs cris,*
> *Qui profile,*
> *Son front gris,*
> *Des toits frêles,*
> *Cent tourelles,*
> *Cloches grêles,*
> *C'est Paris!*

These lyrics were often made of short lines in three or four syllables, with rhymes or *rimes riches* occurring in glittering profusion, giving an effect of virtuosity that dazzled the literary public. But Victor Hugo had even more surprises up his sleeve.

At this period the eyes of all Europe were turned toward Greece, where the natives carried on their long rebellion against the Turkish tyrant. The martyrdom of Byron, Christian sympathy, and even obscure democratic impulses made the youth of France philhellenist in the 1820's; and Victor Hugo, always extremely sensitive to all the currents of opinion of his age, shared their sentiments and became a champion of the Greek rebels. He read various works on the folk songs and legends of modern Greece and the Near East. Through a friend, who was an adept orientalist, a government official named Ernest Fouinet, he also acquired translations of Arabian folk tales and songs. Then having absorbed the spirit of these things, he wrote his volume of *Orientales*, his oriental songs of Corinth and Sparta and Crete; of the Turks who massacred Greek prisoners by throwing them, at night, tied up in sacks, into the Bosporus; of Ali Pasha, who fought for Arabian freedom in Algiers; of the white reefs of the Greek Archipelago; of sultans and golden domes and seraglios and campfires in the desert and blazing sunsets. Soon he had a whole sequence of these poems which he prepared for a special volume, *Les Orientales*, to be issued later, but read to his friends from time to time on walks in the outskirts of Paris, in 1827, or at literary soirées in Charles Nodier's library in the old Arsenal.

The effect of these new poems upon his hearers was tremendous. Though artificial in their inspiration, they were like pieces of romantic and exotic program music in verse, aiming chiefly at effects of *color*. In this respect they certainly introduced an original, a "revolutionary," note into French versification—one of them, *les Djinns*, is now known to almost every French schoolboy, and the opening poem *Feu du ciel* ("Fire of Heaven") is equally read. In these highly colored exercises in verbal sonority a whole second generation of romanticists, that of Gautier and Baudelaire, was to find inspiration somewhat later for their cult of "art for art's sake." Orientalism was the literary fashion of the early nineteenth century in England as well as in France, where the painters, such as Eugène Delacroix, had already led the way.

Long before they were published, the *Orientales* excited something like superstition among the poet's friends, and passages were freely quoted from memory from his readings. "Hugo stands like a column among us," wrote one of them, Victor Pavie, in 1827, "throwing off an *Orientale* here and there. . . ." The young men with long hair who followed him about and imitated his style were convinced that he would go far. Two years later, in 1829, when *Les Orientales* appeared finally, "all Paris talked of nothing else for six months," according to Jules Janin, a literary historian of the time.

That he had a high and serious conception of his role as a poet everyone knew, for in some of his earlier verses he had aired himself on this subject: he visioned the poet surrounded by the listening people, "his word gleaming like fire," lightning playing about his head, and "his brow bearing the mark of God!"

With Victor Hugo the years of young manhood after his marriage were industrious, prolific, cheerful, and he moved from success to success, almost without appearing to undergo an apprenticeship, during the same ten years that his contemporary, Balzac, suffered in the obscurity of one garret after another. In his personal relations he "had much magnetism and a sort of imperious authority . . ." which tended to "subjugate" his friends, wrote one eyewitness, who was a friend of Sainte-Beuve. The poet's friends noted his ambition—to be the national poet of France, and its first man of letters. When he was twenty-five, he told the journalist Fontaney, who kept a diary: "I want the first place. . . . If I knew I was not to surpass and take rank over all the others, I would become a notary tomorrow." He recalled the example of the "regal Voltaire" who amassed great wealth so that later he might enjoy liberty of thought and action. Victor Hugo, too, intended to be passing rich. To this end he busied himself always with new and larger projects; he had plans for two novels; he read passages from a long play to Sainte-Beuve, after he met him early in 1827, and spoke of his dream of conquering even the theater. Sainte-Beuve, his daily companion and confidant and a youth of wavering character, was strongly impressed by his purposefulness. He was no less impressed by Hugo's virtue.

3

In the summer of 1823, on July 8, Hugo's friend Saint-Valry wrote in a letter: "My young friend, M. Victor Hugo, has just become a father; everything about him is precocious; genius and paternity. Nothing is more interesting to watch than this young couple; theirs is the love of angels."

Six months after their marriage, the two "angels," profiting from an increase in the royal pension on which they lived, flew from the parental roof at the Toulouse Mansion to quarters of their own at number 90 rue de Vaugirard. Here, in a small flat above a carpenter's shop they lived in security, though in very modest style. A young journalist who was invited to lunch with them remembered long afterward that he had been served only an *omelette au rhum,* but the rum was of so poor a quality that after repeated attempts they gave up efforts to ignite it.

Nevertheless, Victor Hugo in those early years knew a happiness he had scarcely dreamed of. After what he had seen of conflict between his father and mother he longed only for a pure and tranquil domestic life; he made this his ideal, holding to it long and stubbornly. He had been poor, hungry, and chaste. Now, in his days of uxorious contentment, he bloomed. Adèle also bloomed and grew more beautiful. Hers was "a strange beauty to which the eyes must grow accustomed," Sainte-Beuve wrote after he first met her. To Victor Hugo she was all goodness and tenderness. He could not bear to leave her even for a day, and in his poems to her he addressed her sometimes as his "virgin." She was tall; she had a native though languid dignity, and a gentle smile. The friends of the young couple sometimes spoke of her also as the "Madonna of the romantic *cénacle."* For years they saw her sitting by a window with a child in her arms.

Early in July, 1823, a son was born to them and named Léopold-Victor, after the poet's father. He was the first of five children Adèle bore in quite rapid order. Her husband was not only in the flower of his unspoilt youth, but on the Hugo side was a descendant of virile Lorraine peasants, his grandfather having had nine children, his robust father three, even in the brief, unhappy union with Sophie Trébuchet Hugo.

The naming of his first child after his father marked the dramatic reconciliation which had come shortly after his marriage. Besides, General Hugo had shown himself at last a generous father to the poor demented Eugène, whom he brought home and cared for himself.

It was the recurrent trouble over Eugène which had thrown the father and his younger son together. They discovered each other, fell into each other's arms, the one astonished and overjoyed at the strength, virtue, and beauty of his own long-lost son, the other recognizing the warmth and sweetness which, in ripe middle age, now predominated in the mixed and erratic nature of his father. At Blois, Eugène was gentle and quiet for a time, a "drowsy sheep," the general wrote to Victor. Then one day, at dinner, he seized a long knife and attempted—it is the key to his dementia—to stab his stepmother. Thereafter he was committed to an asylum under the care of the famous Dr. Royer-Collard; he remained there, a withered shell of himself, until his death in 1837. Up to the day of his death, he would ask affectionately after his famous brother, only the dim unconscious mind of him hating the other. His light had gone out—many had thought he would be an ornament of letters. Victor Hugo mourned him, and bade him a tender farewell in his ode "To Eugène."

It was as if, by his union with his beloved Adèle, some dark conflict within himself were at last resolved; fear of his father was gone. For the moment, the hypnotic power of his mother waned, and he could know his father again, forgetting at last the bitter struggles witnessed in his childhood. The general, now white-haired, had become a gentle soul, devoting himself to gardens and to books; like other Napoleonic soldiers he wrote memoirs and even verses, which his son applauded as "ingenious" or "pretty" but could not help him to publish. He was a warm man, and his warm instincts, his sympathetic tears, were as ready as his fierce temper had formerly been quick. More and more frequently he came to sit at his son's hearth in Paris, "like a knight of antiquity," and there to the spellbound young couple he told his stories of Italy and Spain, of desperate battles and near escapes, of Fra Diavolo whom he had captured in Italy, of Hohenlinden, of Napoleon seen in action, and Moreau, whom he had followed in battle. Little by little, Victor Hugo felt himself caught up by his soldier-father's fervor for the heroic days of the Empire. General Hugo was not always firm in his doctrine, yet something of the old Jacobin of '93 adhered to him. In his person, the poet came to feel himself consciously linked with the era he chose to regard as the greatest epoch of French or even of world history. Since the death of Napoleon, only two years before, in 1821, a new perspective upon the tumultuous past was being acquired by many thinking men. Reunion with his father contributed something, undoubtedly, to the beginning of a cult for Napoleon in Victor Hugo.

With the stepmother, too, Adèle had helped to effect a reconciliation—for Victor had never even acknowledged her existence. When the elder pair learned that the infant Léopold was sickly and weak, they offered to find a good wet nurse for him and keep child and nurse in the country with them, at Blois, until he had recovered. The younger pair agreed to this, and thereafter made frequent and lengthy visits to General Hugo's country place.

Victor Hugo thought of his father now as a brave soldier of France whose heroism had never been rightly rewarded or honored; he resolved to have the injustice repaired. Sentimentally he saw him nowadays only as wearing a "gentle smile":

Mon père, ce héros au sourire si doux . . .

In his waking hours he loved his father again; but in the night the memory of his mother still ruled him.

Adèle's first childbirth proved exhausting and, because she was so slow to recover, her mother, Mme. Foucher, nursed her. Then, when she was still too weak to go to him, the news was told her that the child had died, only three months after having been born. Her letter to her mother-in-law in Blois was a short, agonized outcry. But she strove to contain her bitter grief, because she knew that she was *enceinte* once more.

For years, hers was the simple, age-old drama of domestic love and childbearing, and it was drama enough for her young husband, who showed most powerful instincts of paternity. His poems, from now on, were full of the movement of children. After the first child's death, he promised Adèle that there would be a *"revenant,"* according to an old wives' tale of the Bretons that came down to him through his mother: the spirit of the dead child would return to them in another form. The second child was a girl, whom they named Léopoldine. She proved to be strong and beautiful and resembled her father.

According to a fragment of memoirs left by Adèle Hugo, the baby, whom she now nursed herself, slept in the same room as her parents, "and at daybreak she would climb from her cradle into their bed, and try with her tiny fingers to open the eyelids of her mother and father and make them understand that it was time to wake." They would wake, laughing drowsily, and "all morning there would be laughter for all three!"

A year and a half later, in November, 1826, Adèle bore another son who was named Charles-Victor; in 1827, there came another boy who was named François-Victor; and finally, in 1829, a daughter who was named Adèle. Five children in seven years, of whom four lived—it was a little wearying to the young mother, yet she bore it all bravely. At any rate, their home was filled with the sound of lively children, for whom the father proved to have stores of patience. They were free to climb into his study, draw houses and *bons hommes* on the margins of his manuscripts, and he cared little.

When Léopoldine was a baby (as Adèle Hugo relates) her parents took her with them on all their walks and outings: all swaddled up, carried by her nurse ahead of them, she would turn her face, beaming, to her parents and her young father could hardly refrain from rushing to seize her and kissing her repeatedly. When later, in 1827, they moved to larger quarters at number 11 rue Notre-Dame-des-Champs, with a walled-in garden of their own, the infants would play all day on the lawn below his study, and he would watch them as he worked. For them he wrote the sentimental lyric *Prière pour tous* ("Prayer for All of Us") and for their mother *A toi* ("To Thee!") with its impassioned vow of fidelity. In France, their fervently domestic tone was somewhat new and fresh.

In 1825, Pierre Dubois, editor of *Le Globe,* visited Victor Hugo at his home in the rue de Vaugirard to ask the poet to contribute to his Liberal newspaper. Nothing came of this first overture, though it is significant that Dubois hoped, at this time, that Hugo would one day join his republican band; that is, nothing came of it but the editor's memoir of the meeting:

I visited Hugo in his modest and charming sanctum in the rue de Vaugirard. There, in the *entresol* over a carpenter's shop, I saw, in a tiny drawing room, a young father and a young mother swinging to and fro a child a few months old, and stopping now and then to join its little hands in prayer before an engraving of some Madonna and Child after Raphael hanging on the wall. Although perhaps a trifle *arranged,* the little scene was none the less spontaneous and charming, for at every moment the impulse of the heart kept breaking through, especially in the case of the young mother, and I was touched and charmed.

Hugo's "prosperous hymen," his domestic felicity, was proverbial, a celebrated episode in the annals of the romanticists.

When, in 1825, three years after his marriage, he went on the journey to Rheims, he still addressed his wife in terms of the most lyrical endearment. Her absorption in the care of their two children and her housekeeping labors had not dimmed the aureole over her. He begged her to write him every day. Love in those times was not only tearful, it was freely epistolary. When her letters came, he assured her that they compensated fully for the pain and weariness of his journey. On the eve of his return, he declared: "The moment approaches when I shall see you. A moment in which one might well die of joy. Adieu, angel!" And she, in her unfeigned letters, brims over with the fullness of her happiness. Although his poetry is beyond her understanding, she encourages him, and takes joy in the reflection of his glory. "Write a beautiful ode, my Victor," she bids him as he goes forth to the king's coronation, "one worthy of you, and of your name; your glory is dear to me, and that will be my recompense for your absence." She was his Muse, his first Muse.

The home to which the Hugo pair removed in 1827, on the quiet rue Notre-Dame-des-Champs, was more spacious, in keeping with their improved circumstances. It was a square, old-fashioned house, with a garden of its own and trees, birds, even a little pond, reflecting the sky, and the open country of Montparnasse quite near. The Hugo apartment was on the first floor, reached by a little circular staircase starting from a small vestibule at the street level. It had a kitchen, dining room, two small bedrooms, a small study, and even a salon. The salon was called by Hugo's friends "the room of the golden lily" because his prize from the Toulouse Academy, the large golden lily, was placed upon a little table and formed the chief ornament in the center of the room. The room was decorated with pictures by his friends Boulanger and Deveria, inspired by his own poems. Here almost every night his friends came and heard him read his verses. Adjoining the salon was his study, which he called now his "cell," now his "beehive," where he often worked far into the night, sometimes to the injury of his eyes. In the neighborhood there was a legend that children would wake up at night, look toward the isolated little house among the trees, and ask: "What is that big star over there in the trees?" Often the big star did not go out until dawn.

Victor Hugo never smoked; he drank very little, usually only some table wine. A light sleeper all his life, he would rise early, not long after dawn, and set to work in his "cell." After his midday lunch, he would usually slip out through the back gate of the garden and cross over to the great park of the Luxembourg palace, a few steps from his door. There he would walk alone, watching the flowers, the birds, the old people, the students, the lovers, and soliloquizing to himself in rhyme.

Often he prowled about the old quarters of Paris, studying old ruins and ancient churches, which were then seriously neglected. He was something of a craftsman, with natural skill as a woodcarver, cabinetmaker, and amateur artist, and the Gothic or medieval monuments of old Paris, as well as those he studied during journeys to other cities in France, spoke to him a great deal. In love with the more romantic past, he became an antiquarian and collected old pieces of sculpture, medallions, vases, tapestry, with which he would fill up his home. From an early period of his life he began to agitate, by public letters to the newspapers, against the demolition of old monuments and against the redecoration of some of the Gothic churches then being restored in a false style—for he had learned to live among these things and to place his ballads, dramas, and romances in the vanished centuries they sprang from.

Ideas or inspirations came to him freely as he walked alone in the Luxembourg Gardens, in the street, or in the open country; he would retain them clearly in his memory, for he had great powers of concentration; returning to his desk later, he would fashion them into their final form. He wrote and produced regularly and voluminously during these early years of his marriage, a habit which would seem on the surface to be unromantic. But Byron, his great predecessor, was no less methodical; when he lived in Milan he would write a hundred lines of "Childe Harold" in a morning and rewrite them all in the evening.

4

Although he pretended, in his verses, to be a man of secluded ways, the circle of Victor Hugo's acquaintance widened steadily after his marriage. At least once a week, he and his wife would attend a soirée at the Charles Nodiers'. Nodier, gracious host and patron of the young romantic writers, was almost twice Hugo's age when they first met in 1823. A successful novelist, as well as an erudite bibliophile and a man of wit, he knew all literary Paris, and it was at the evening parties in the Arsenal library that Hugo met Lamartine (who, he felt, was his only peer among the younger poets). There, too, he met the rising young novelist and playwright, Prosper Mérimée (the future author of *Carmen*), and through Mérimée came to the salon of the Misses Clarke, where the reputedly sinister moralist, Henri Beyle, "Stendhal" by *nom de plume,* usually expounded his bitter paradoxes. Stendhal was a marginal figure among the young romanticists, and had already made mock of the Prince of Poets in occasional articles for the press. At first sight Hugo and Stendhal only "glared at each other like china dogs," then went their separate ways.

Through Nodier, in 1825, came a proposal for the writing of a travel book by Hugo, Lamartine, and himself in collaboration, which furnished a pretext and money for an exhilarating summer journey by carriage through Burgundy, to the countryseat of Alphonse de Lamartine, and then on across the mountains to Lausanne and Geneva and Chamonix. The book was never completed; but the vision of the Alps returning like a dream of boyhood inspired Victor Hugo both to lyrics and to a spirited narrative of the whole excursion, which was later dictated to his wife and set down in the *Victor Hugo Raconté*. Even more was he inspired by the ruined castles, the venerable churches, and other monuments seen on the way, so that Nodier was once driven to exclaim to him: "I declare you have Early Gothic on the brain."

Arriving at Lamartine's house at Saint-Point, Hugo had looked in vain for those "crenelated peaks," those "walls tinted by the years" and "ivy-covered" which the older poet had described for him in letters of invitation. Here was only a clean, whitewashed dwelling place.

"But where . . . is the château of your poetry?" he asked, wonderingly.

"This is it," replied Lamartine, "only I have rendered it habitable. The thick ivy made the walls damp and gave me rheumatism, so I had it taken away. The gray stones had a depressing effect, so I have modernized the place. Ruins are good to describe, but very inconvenient to live in."

Although the Lamartines offered the party lavish entertainment for two days, it was all a little formal, for Mme. de Lamartine was an aristocratic Englishwoman of fixed habits tedious to the French temperament. Hugo's relations with Lamartine, as with Alfred de Vigny, from now on—for he also had married an English girl, and a great heiress—were those of polite mutual esteem rather than of warm friendship and constant exchanges of visits.

A warm friend he gained at this period, in 1827, was Emile Bertin, a man of fifty, whose strong, grave figure still lives for us in a great portrait by Ingres. Bertin was the founder of the powerful independent daily, *Le Journal des Débats,* which had formerly, on occasions, defied Napoleon himself, and whose pages were soon hospitably opened to Hugo. Bertin, very rich, a patron of the arts, had a great rambling country house and park called *Les Roches,* near Brinvilliers, in the valley of the little Bièvre River outside of Paris. Here Victor Hugo and his family, together with numerous other artists and musicians, would be invited to stay for long week-end sojourns, sometimes for a whole summer. Here Hugo would ramble alone in the gardens and the deep woods and compose his poems in his mind, or upon scraps of paper he carried with him. In the evening he would read them to the Bertins and their guests. M. Bertin's daughter, Louise, who was very intelligent and learned, was also a gifted composer of music. Sometimes she would compose music to the songs of Hugo, and play them at the piano, in the salon, before a company that might include the Prime Minister Guizot, or Ingres, or Berlioz. Through the years a deep attachment grew up between Louise Bertin (who remained a spinster all her life) and the poet.

He drew closer to nature in the woods by the Bièvre; the more genuine and vivid pastoral poems that he wrote during the 1830's found their inspiration here.

But friendship among the young romantics was usually a passionate affair. "In those days, when one gave oneself to a friend," as a historian of the period, Léon Séché, has said, "it was body and soul without any restrictions, and with a sort of frenzy. Devotion had no limits, friendship resembled love."

Such a friendship Victor Hugo knew only for the young Sainte-Beuve at this stage. To others his affability had limits; with Sainte-Beuve he felt a deep affinity, and disburdened himself as to a brother. The first day they had met, Sainte-Beuve recalled, Hugo, after a time, "going like a torrent," had scarcely given him a chance to speak. They parted as if they had known each other all their lives. For years they saw each other usually twice a day, since Sainte-Beuve lived with his mother almost next door, on the rue de Vaugirard, and when the Hugos moved to the rue Notre-Dame-des-Champs, he too moved to a house in the same street, hard by.

When Sainte-Beuve timidly sent him his first poems, Hugo praised them warmly, saying: "I must declare that I divined, less from your so remarkable articles than from your talk and your attitude, that you were a poet. Permit me to be a little proud of my penetration and of having foreseen a talent of so high an order. Come soon again, please, as I have a thousand things to say to you."

From January, 1827, Sainte-Beuve enjoyed being the complete, trusted confidant of Victor Hugo, and soon the young master's literary protégé. Victor Hugo helped him to climb, introduced him to the salons. In turn he was to Hugo and his rising literary school a useful polemicist and advocate, pleading the cause of the new romantic movement vigorously before the press and public opinion. He lived almost in "servitude" to Victor Hugo, often writing and publishing critical pieces at his order.

Charles-Augustin Sainte-Beuve was the son of a lawyer, a native of Boulogne, born in 1803. Before he came into this world, his father died, and he was brought up by his mother under strongly clerical influences. These he threw off as his education proceeded —he was a most brilliant student—and he came to Paris to study medicine. Going about with the "sawbones" of the Ecole de Méde-cine, he lost his religious faith; growing melancholy, he had begun to write poetry; then essays, which were published by 1826, and this had encouraged him to abandon the career of medicine.

He was a small, thin fellow, with a pale face, a large round head, reddish hair, and a bad complexion. His nose was both long and bulbous. His eyes, often veiled and downcast, and his soft, moist handshake made him seem like a priest or at least a seminary student. But his smile could become very expressive or subtle. There was also something extremely sensitive about him; as Lamartine wrote at this period, "He was sensitive almost to the point of a disease, and a poet to the point of tears." After a time, his friends said, one found his ugliness interesting and almost pleasing. His shyness passing, his face would brighten, he would begin to talk, and his talk was delicate, seductive. At this period, in his early twenties, he bore himself with a certain air of mel-ancholy and frustrated stoicism—as his friend Dubois remarked, "an air of pretending to renounce everything, because one is on the eve of experiencing or enjoying everything."

He was a complex, tormented youth. He suffered over his own ugliness, as he wrote in certain introspective passages of his novel *Volupté*. He would peer into the mirror "as if fearing to see his ugliness increasing, disfiguring him still further . . . comparing himself anxiously to others, and learning to envy even the stupidest visages. . . ."

Meanwhile, with his awakening sensuality had come the bitter knowledge that he had neither physical charm nor the fortunate social connections of those heroes he admired in books. With the collar of his coat upturned to conceal his identity, he would range the streets of Paris late at night, driven by desire and curiosity to the *bordellos,* where, as he phrased it, "as an eternal dilettante, he tasted the sinister beauties of the flesh." Yet physical pleasure left him unhappy, and somewhat the worse for wear. Then he would analyze himself endlessly.

Beginning as a dissector of corpses, at the School of Medicine, he remained all his life an impassioned "anatomist" in literature, coldly probing with his scalpel not only the dead, but the quick, for that elusive motory mechanism which bound body and soul, mind and emotions, to physical circumstances.

This born dissector of souls, this biographer par excellence, was convinced that in Victor Hugo he had met a man of veritable genius, already steadfastly following his "star," though still in the years of youth. Fascinated, he studied him constantly, seeing him as akin to a military or political captain of the past fighting for power in the eternally agitated republic of letters.

Victor Hugo had a male and leonine beauty, a hearty and vigorous manner that often rang with authority; Sainte-Beuve's was an effeminate mind, with a disposition to hero worship. As Dubois, who employed him at *Le Globe,* said, "he needed always some master for the moment."

In the so patently autobiographical novel *Volupté,* which Sainte-Beuve wrote between 1832 and 1834, he used Victor Hugo as the original model for the character of the Marquis de Couaëns whom he disguises as a powerful political conspirator in the days of Napoleon. He disguises him further with "blue eyes . . . clear and hard . . . fixed yet never still," but with a manner proud and yet courteous, and "disposed to command"—in short, "a man of action." The disguised portrait of the "Baron" Hugo, under whose spell Sainte-Beuve came, continues with a representation of the man's supreme purposefulness, his overwhelming, single-minded determination to use all and everyone around him—wife, friend, ally—to the end in his view, yet concealed from others. Some of the opinions Sainte-Beuve credits to this character are quite literally those expressed by Victor Hugo years before in his love letters to Adèle, which Sainte-Beuve managed to read.

He had ambition, active talent for action, for audacity. . . . Like the majority of men of action, with a very keen grasp of material obstacles, he gave little heed to ordinary resistances . . . that might be encountered; he believed that *a given result could always be produced, if men who willed them strongly enough knew how to vanquish their chief adversaries.* . . . His most desired glory was to become one of those pre-eminent individuals who, at moments, dominate a large part of the world.

With a mind of great range, and which, at certain levels, easily handled any subjects, the Marquis was unevenly educated; in testing him, one was surprised to see both the extent of what he knew, in places, and what he was ignorant of.

In the romantic fashion, Sainte-Beuve "surrendered" himself to the fascination of his strong-willed friend, yet inwardly resented being "used."

He was tremendously happy, however, to be taken in as almost a member of the Hugo household. He had enjoyed few friends, and had known little of family life, often living apart from his mother. Adèle Hugo looked at him when he first came in—a timid, homely fellow—and returned to her knitting, saying nothing. So many literary people visited her husband, and she, deeply engaged with the children, often wore a somewhat distracted, dreamy expression, as if she understood little of all the talk that went on interminably about her. When at moments she entered the conversation and made some unguarded comment, Victor was equal to reprimanding her brusquely even before others.

To Sainte-Beuve, the home in the rue Notre-Dame-des-Champs was as a pure sanctuary. It made him want to be a good man and, almost, return to his religion. Leaving aside his mother, he had scarcely ever known a virtuous woman such as the adored wife and muse of his friend, with her dark and unfamiliar kind of beauty, seemed to his shifting glance. At first he had felt himself unable to look at her, and when she spoke to him he would avert his eyes.

5

Order, orthodoxy, and etiquette ruled French society, at least in its upper stratum, under Charles X. Parliamentary government became a dead letter, and a Court that was but a musty, priest-ridden, prejudiced coterie headed by the aristocratic Villèle, labored to suppress every trace of the Revolution and the limited political privileges that were its residue. The country prospered in peacetime, but the people were gloomy and restive. Even Chateau-briand and the French Academy itself protested at laws aimed at removal of the last vestige of freedom of the press, and in January, 1827, despite harsh repressive measures, a new election returned a Liberal majority of Deputies, creating a sort of deadlock in the process of government. Another sign of popular unrest was the spreading veneration for the memory of Napoleon among the masses; public controversy even over the question of the proper disposal of his remains now became the occasion for popular demonstrations of a renascent nationalism and even radicalism in France. With his death in far-off Saint Helena, the blood-drenched despot was forgotten, and the glorious conqueror who had spread a Revolutionary equality and the civilizing *Code Civil* to the ends of Europe was remembered with pride.

In a time of social tension, popular excitement—instead of moving logically against those who direct oppression—is apt to fix itself emotionally upon any accidental event that attracts its attention. This was what happened on February 7, 1827, when the newspapers reported how at an official ball of the Austrian Embassy a group of Napoleon's marshals, upon making their appearance, as invited, were deliberately insulted by order of the Austrian envoy. Legally these famous warriors, after 1814, were shorn of the title of nobility Napoleon had awarded them, usually to lands in Austria and Italy; but in the social usage of the day it was customary to call them by these titles.

However, upon entering the Austrian Embassy, they were simply announced as Marshal Oudinot, instead of the Duke of Reggio; Marshal Mortier, instead of the Duke of Treviso, Marshal Soult, instead of the Duke of Dalmatia. The very memory of Napoleon's glorious victories of yesterday was being rubbed out. Wrathful, they stalked out, and soon all Paris and patriotic France seethed with honest indignation over the snub, which became, unmistakably, an International Incident.

Victor Hugo, too, on reading of the incident in his gazette, felt as if outraged in his own person. Was not his father one of the Imperial generals? Did he himself not also possess an "upstart" or Bonapartist title—that of "Baron"? The Chamber of Deputies now rang with jingoist speeches against Austria. Yet the Bourbon government, installed by aid of the Austrians after Waterloo, could do nothing to avenge the insult.

Ostensibly Hugo was still a Royalist, but actually he had become by now completely alienated from that party. There were in him contradictory loyalties and sentiments. In poems he had written as early as 1819 there were seeds of a vague Liberalism jostling with his pious reflections. He himself, several years later, in 1834, looking back at his own record, could scarcely distinguish when he had definitely cast off the early Royalist influences. "There was, at any rate," as he surmised, "in the obscure, disordered flood of his youthful ideas and impulses one element at work, which would assimilate all the others—the spirit of liberty." There was also, as Sainte-Beuve would say later, a fairly shrewd instinct to "bow to the people" who on February 7, 1827, were so violently aroused by the Austrian insult to their war heroes.

Very quickly he dashed off an *Ode à la Colonne de la Place Vendôme,* an ode to the Napoleon Column, answering the national insult in stirring and martial words, singing in honor of the Emperor Napoleon—no longer the "Corsican monster"—a "colossus" whose hand moved the world, the Eagle whose "wing brushed Africa at Cadiz, Asia at Moscow." In verses full of a youthful ardor and bravura he paid his respects to the valiant men of the Imperial armies, to whose camps his own childhood belonged.

This timely and chauvinistic poem was published hastily on February 9, 1827, in the *Journal des Débats.* It addressed itself (though in a politic way, with eulogies for the Vendeans too!) mainly to all those who now embraced the whole myth of Napoleonism, if only out of hatred for the Bourbon regime in France and the Metternichean reaction elsewhere in Europe. The poem at once had an immense effect and was widely reprinted and sold as a small pamphlet. For the first time Victor Hugo, passing beyond his literary public, had spoken as with the voice of the whole nation, and his fame became nation-wide; all factions, even some of the Legitimists, joined in applauding him for his patriotic sentiments.

One of the Legitimists, however, an old friend of his mother, the Marquis de Coriolis de l'Espinose, noticed the *libertarian* accents he now sounded and wrote him reproachfully in later years: "In 1827, in your *Ode à la Colonne* you deserted the sane doctrines of the legitimate monarchy; the Liberal faction clapped and applauded; I groaned. . . ." Coriolis thus marked Hugo's change of heart as belonging to 1827. But his father wept with joy at reading this vindication of himself by the son who had once been lost to him.

Victor Hugo, as if with a foreknowledge of the terms of modern psychoanalysis, often alluded to the conflict "in his heart" between his "Royalist mother" and his father, "old soldier of the Revolution." With the writing of his *Ode à la Colonne* in February, 1827, it was as if he "pardoned" his father and sealed their final reconciliation. It is doubtful, however, that such profound conflicts, once lodged in the unconscious mind, are ever really resolved save in outward appearance. For Victor Hugo, this belated reconciliation became, at any rate, a favorite theme: the tragic tale of a son rediscovering his father too late was to cling to his mind even thirty-five years later and play a large part in the prose epic of *Les Misérables*.

During the last years of his father's life he saw him frequently at his own home in Paris, or in Blois. Once public honors and a little royal favor had come to him, the son exerted himself to improve his father's fortunes by having him recalled to active military service. He did not succeed, but with the aid of Chateaubriand won for General Hugo, who was still in his fifties, an honorary promotion to the rank of brevet Lieutenant General, in token of his brave action at Thionville in 1814 and 1815.

Victor Hugo spoke nowadays with an inordinate affection and pride of his father, whose earlier faults he evidently now forgave—having perhaps by now, quietly, learned something of the corresponding faults of his mother, or perhaps also repenting of his dark, rebellious thoughts in earlier years. He describes how he would make the journey in the diligence to Blois, and from the town climb the hill to his father's house in the outskirts, and at length, reaching its garden gate, he would find the veteran of France's heroic age, working peacefully with a hoe, a gentle, white-haired man, who came himself to open the gate for him. At sunset, father and son would climb the hill opposite the house, to look down at the view of the broad Loire, at the old town of Blois, and in the distance, barely visible on the horizon, the high turrets of the palace of Chambord.

To be near his son, General Hugo, in 1827, had taken an apartment in Paris in the rue Plumet. One evening—it was January 28, 1828—the younger Hugos dined at his house, ate and drank a good deal, and stayed until late. The general was in fine humor and full of reminiscent war stories. Victor and Adèle reached home after eleven, and they were undressing, when a strange man knocked at the door and demanded admittance.

"I come on behalf of the Countess Hugo to tell you that your father is dead," he exclaimed. Victor Hugo, who had just left his father in full force of life, thought it was some mistake, a horrible dream. Barely conscious of what he was doing, he dressed again and followed the messenger back to the rue Plumet, near by. He found his father stretched out, discolored, rigid, the collar of his shirt torn open, dead of a stroke of apoplexy. The doctor had been called too late. "The general died like a soldier; the heart stroke had caught him erect, struck him down with the swiftness of a bullet."

To a friend of his, Victor Pavie, he wrote:

I have lost the man who loved me more than anyone in the world. A good and noble being who looked on me with some pride and a great deal of love, a father whose eyes were never off me. And I am young to lose that support and comfort.

But this was not all of the truth.

6

On February 11, 1827, he wrote to his new confidant and brother in arms, Sainte-Beuve:

I communicated, the other morning, to M. Sainte-Beuve some lines of my "Cromwell." If he has the curiosity to hear more, he need but come Monday evening, before 8 o'clock, at my father's-in-law, rue du Cherche-Midi, mansion of the Council of War. All will be de-lighted to see him, and I especially. He is one of the auditors whom I would always prefer, because I like to hear them.

His very devoted,

R.S.V.P.   Victor Hugo

Cromwell was Victor Hugo's most serious effort thus far to win his way into the theater and address himself to its wider audiences. Many a writer and poet was drawn irresistibly to the candle-lit stage, but to Hugo's somewhat theatrical nature it had been beckoning ever since he was fifteen. At twenty he made another attempt in this direction, with *Amy Robsart,* an adaptation of Scott's "Kenilworth" in French verse; and, at twenty-five, he had completed *Cromwell,* in the very season of 1826–1827 when he had thrown himself, as the latest Preface to his *Odes et Ballades* revealed, into the struggle for "liberty" in literature and the arts.

He had spoken for Shakespeare, and the new play showed that

he had steeped himself in the work of the English poet. Indeed his strenuous efforts to approximate or imitate the qualities and even the license of Shakespeare—whom he could not read in English —make both for the originality of *Cromwell* and for its glaring weaknesses.

The idea of a drama based on the life of a great English dictator was probably suggested by the author's preoccupation with the figure of Napoleon and the reflection that Oliver Cromwell had been a forerunner. Nor was he the first to think of this subject: Abel Villemain, the literary critic, had written a biography of Cromwell in 1817, the still unknown Balzac had attempted to write a historical tragedy in 1819 (unpublished), and Prosper Mérimée another which was issued in 1823.

Victor Hugo, however, attempted a full-length, dramatic portrait of a heroic figure. The action of the drama is built upon a supposed plot against the Protector by the Royalist followers of the Stuarts, and among them Cromwell's own son is implicated, at least partially; a rebel against his tyrant father.

Scene follows scene in great variety and peopled with a host of somewhat outlandish English characters. They utter strong speeches against the dictator in exceedingly vigorous and picturesque hexameters, whose style breaks clearly with previous precedents of "good taste" and regularity. Besides, following Shakespeare's devices almost literally, Hugo endeavors to keep a minor love-comedy going within the major drama; that of the frivolous poet, the Duke of Rochester (himself one of the Stuart intriguers), appearing in disguise and suing for the hand of Cromwell's daughter. The introduction of clowns, humorous ditties, and love lyrics in such scenes is an added feature of the "comic relief" the young playwright attempted—after the Shakespeare pattern, and in violation of all existing canons of the French theater.

Surmounting the interest in the developing Royalist intrigue to assassinate Cromwell there is the further dramatic problem raised by the Pretender's being tempted to assume the royal crown. A high point in the play is the scene in which John Milton is presented as making a long set speech exhorting the dictator to refrain from such a fatal step and to preserve the democratic Commonwealth. Here, in one of the finest passages of his early writings, Victor Hugo shows a peculiar gift for a kind of poetic oratory, ample, eloquent, passionate, and suggesting, by the very sincerity of its accents, that the author himself is already no Royalist. Here incidentally, as also, in some degree, in the "Ode to the Napoleon Column," Victor Hugo has turned romanticism —originally belonging to the Christian Royalists—toward democracy; romantic literature becomes henceforth the medium of democratic movements in the nineteenth century, and that outcome is peculiarly Victor Hugo's contribution.

The play itself, however, is so long and diffuse, so poorly constructed, that by the time Cromwell defeats the conspiracy of his enemies one has grown fairly indifferent. An effort has been made to present the figure of Cromwell in realistic detail and not in "noble style" (as would have been usual in a conventional French play of this time); the effort is made to picture him as a plain bourgeois head of a family, yet he is not lifelike, and the other characters "come alive" even less. The play lacks local color and, as representation of history, is full of amusing inaccuracies for English readers.

Sainte-Beuve, after praising the play for its "revolutionary" poetic style and its strong opening acts, in a letter of honest and searching criticism, indicated its shortcomings, argued that the attempted scenes of comic relief—unlike those in Shakespeare— merely interrupted and overbalanced the drama, and advised extensive cuts, for the play as it stood would take six hours to produce. Victor Hugo thanked him, but, characteristically, made no revisions in his work.

Cromwell was one of those interesting "failures" achieved by an ambitious artist who reaches for the heavens. But, seen in the light of the time in which it was written, it is a landmark in French poetry and dramatic literature, because of its artistic innovations. First it was written in run-over verses, and with a varying caesura (or pause) which to the classicists appeared to be simply "free verse." It violated the classical "unities" of place and time, supposedly required by drama; it strove for an effect of crowded detail and reality and "naturalness," where the typical playwrights of the age, like Eugène Scribe, wrote thin stuff, utterly without feeling or true sentiment, and kept going merely by theatrical wirepulling. *Cromwell* was a long step in the campaign for the winning of that "romantic revolution" which others, long before Hugo, had been calling for.

The mind of the French artist always tends to reason, to theorize as it works—to a much greater degree than that of the English.

Victor Hugo introduced his play with a Preface which impressively announced a new dramaturgy and, at the same time, was an extensive and strongly argued manifesto in behalf of romanticism, in many ways more effective and significant than the play it introduced. The Preface to *Cromwell* was a charter for the romantic movement in France.

In the manner of Jean-Jacques Rousseau, Victor Hugo rested his case for the historic inevitability of romantic drama upon his somewhat arbitrary theories of the evolution of man from primitive to modern times. There had been three great ages in human thought, he believed: the primitive, "age of the ode" (or song); the pagan, age of the epic (Homer); and the Christian age, or the age of *drama* (that is, the romantic drama of "personal feeling," as differentiated from classical tragedy in the manner of a Corneille). He called for an end to artificial rules—"the three unities," time, place, and action—and to the absurd canons of taste, which required that certain words, such as "handkerchief," be avoided with pompous circumlocutions. Stendhal had urged even further that poetry be supplanted by prose in the French drama, holding that rhymed verses encouraged artificial locutions. But Hugo insisted upon retaining verse, verse that was set free. He also advocated the full use of *antithesis;* by representing the grotesque, effects of ugliness, intermingled with effects of the sublime and beautiful, and notes of comedy side by side with those of tragedy—as in life itself.

All these notions had long been "in the air," as long ago as the time of Rousseau, Diderot, and Samuel Johnson, and Lessing, Goethe, and Schiller in Germany. But the youthful Hugo expressed them anew with great vigor, and at a psychological moment, so that his sparks struck fire. Girding at the old conventions which still stifled drama and poetry in France, he contributed to a powerful, belated liberation and renewal of the romantic impulses that had already shown themselves in late eighteenth-century culture, but had been checked by the long years of revolution and war.

He preached liberty in art, urging that there were no conventions, no models or rules, that could not be changed in order to realize the fullest truth, the highest dramatic effects. Although there is much that seems arbitrary in Hugo's alignment of past literature and in his historical classification of literary epochs, the appeal of his manifesto was powerful, and its message of immense influence. He said in effect, "Know thyself, be thyself!" He said:

The poet of the modern world is not Racine (the classicist) but Shakespeare or Molière; for the object of modern art is not beauty but life; and that which gives us the keenest sense of life is not solely the beautiful, but the *characteristic,* even though that be ugly, odious or deformed. A multitude of figures, quantity of details, a sense of the scene, an impression of time and place startling in their exactitude, a realization of all that is individual, peculiar to a moment and a person; in fact an insistence on local color, on every exactest detail of Nature and truth, are not only permissible in drama, but necessary, though Tragedy, reserved for the Type and the Abstract, hold them beneath her notice. . . . The conventionalism of the eighteenth century may attempt to oppose the impulse of a young generation. It will be in vain! These severe young men who have seen Bonaparte refuse to be the train-bearers of an outworn superstition. . . .

Throughout the Preface there was an undertone of the revolutionary temper that nowadays seemed to smolder in Hugo and aroused such stormy controversy around him. In a warning passage he states: "There is today an 'old regime' in literature like the old regime in politics. The last century still weighs upon the new at almost every point. . . ."

Cromwell was too long for stage production. True, there was some talk of Talma, the Garrick of the Paris theater, being interested in it while it was being written, because of his desire to play a great character part, which few contemporary authors in France gratified. But Talma died without seeing the complete play.

It had its effect, however, in a more indirect way than that of stage production. Not long before this date, the influential *Globe* had been calling earnestly for a *coup d'état* in literature, saying: "The public waits, and minds are in movement. Literature is on the eve of an *18th Brumaire.* But Heaven knows where Bonaparte is!"

That evening, on February 12, 1827, as Victor Hugo read his new play and its Preface in a salon of the Toulouse Mansion before a brilliant gathering of about forty representatives of the theater, poetry, and art, including Lamartine, Vigny, Nodier, Soumet, Emile Deschamps, Prosper Mérimée, Sainte-Beuve and Baron Taylor (a theater director), they were all convinced that in this handsome young man of twenty-five the long-wanted leader of the hour, the literary Bonaparte, had been found. In peacetime France this was an auspicious hour for literature and the arts, concerning which interest and talk ran on feverishly and widely. The select gathering present at Hugo's reading were also still under the spell of his sensation-making ode to Napoleon, published only three days before. They were in a mood to be indifferent to the *longueurs* of his play and cheered its innovations, rose enthusiastically to its purple patches. They pressed about him to embrace him and flatter him, and, departing, talked of the new play in all the cafés and drawing rooms of Paris.

In October, 1827, *Cromwell* was published and sold very suc-cessfully. Over its challenging Preface a storm broke forth, the opening thunder of the battle for romanticism. Old Academicians were reported as "outraged" and "trembling with indignation." Eugène Scribe mocked at Hugo's words, whereas younger writers argued loudly that Hugo freed them from the uniform of servitude to rules; Théophile Gautier hailed the Preface to *Cromwell* as the "tablets of the law." According to Jules Janin, the charming his-torian of the French theater, a certain theater-going barber who had been highly excited by the whole controversy died suddenly, leaving as his last testament the slogan: "Down with the 'Sicilian Vespers'![1] Long live *Cromwell!*"

More than one theater manager now ran to Hugo (who was al-ready being freely compared with Byron and Goethe) and invited him to write a play that would be more than a mere success in the bookstalls. That same year, he had the frailty to take the old *Amy Robsart,* his adaptation of Scott, out of the drawer in which it had been gathering dust, and offer this for production. However, in secret fear of a humiliating public failure, and partly because his young brother-in-law Paul Foucher was burning to make a literary debut at any price—as he revealed much later—Hugo decided to pass off the play as the work of the other man, that is, of Paul Foucher.

It was a most curious trial flight. It was as if Hugo wooed Thespis clad in mask and domino. Yet a success was hoped for, and the magnificent Delacroix was engaged to paint the stage sets. In some inexplicable way the alert, but unromantic, Parisian audience learned that Hugo had a great deal to do with the queer new ro-mantic play. They felt it to be wild and poor stuff, and vigorously was the piece booed and hissed. The first night was one of turmoil, and the idea of a second night was abandoned. In the newspapers there was some tongue-wagging over the identity of the author, and

[1] A play by Hugo's opponent, Delavigne.

his tactical reasons for concealing it. Victor Hugo then came forward in chivalrous style and acknowledged by a public letter that he had "collaborated" to a great extent in writing the play, but that "the passages that were most hissed by the public" were written only by himself.

It was a first defeat in the theater, and it galled him. But Hugo was nothing if not determined.

CHAPTER V

The Battle of "Hernani"

STENDHAL, who had returned from a long stay in Italy where he saw something of Manzoni and the other Italian romanticists, noted in his diary how, after 1827, romanticism in France was becoming the cult of Liberal, and democratic, youth, who, inflamed with the desire for freedom, sought an outlet for their energies in literature and art. In short, romanticism was ceasing to be ultra-Royalist and mystical, a mere "German galimatias," as he had called it. And what was romanticism in the essence? It was a movement, he felt, which, while giving itself to certain excesses, sought expression for the secret aspirations of men in a new century, a new phase of social evolution. Very simply and brilliantly he defined it as "a manner of presenting to the people in literary works that which gives them the utmost immediate pleasure, in the light of the actual state of their habits and beliefs." In Stendhal's long view literature, like life itself, could never remain static, and the vigorous irruption of the new romantic movement in France proved this.

In this movement, Victor Hugo was freely acknowledged as the commanding figure or leader, and one of the nation's first writers, at so young an age, only twenty-five, that it was taken for granted his head had been turned. A contemporary work of literary history, published in 1829 by Toreinx, one of the opponents of romanticism, comments:

The author of *Cromwell,* after having been treated with unjust censure, saw himself suddenly placed upon a pedestal. He was praised and flattered as stupidly as he had been formerly calumniated, and now he was as if intoxicated by so much incense.

After the appearance of *Cromwell* late in 1827, a host of new playwrights studied its Preface and hurried to write bloody and extravagant historical plays in what they conceived to be the manner of Shakespeare. Alexandre Dumas appeared first among them with his romantic tragedy, *Henri III,* in 1829. Alfred de Vigny completed his faithful translation of "Othello" at the same time— others had greatly trimmed and "improved" the original. Hugo made haste more slowly with the new romantic dramas which he composed now with an eye to effective production on the stage.

The new edition of his *Odes et Ballades,* its closing section enriched with new ballads in his romantic style, had been published in 1828 with success. Few poets up to his time had ever had such a public. His *Orientales,* issued by the strong bookselling firm of Gosselin in 1829, sold 6,000 copies that season, which in those days of relatively high prices and printing costs for books made it a "best-seller." With Gosselin, that year, he signed a contract which assured him of a sum of 43,000 francs to be paid him over the next three years, against royalties for new editions of his earlier books and publication of several new works to be completed by him. His labors in the field of letters were enriching him. Yet the theater promised far ampler returns, and his family had grown sizably by 1829, when five souls depended upon him.

He desired a vaster audience, the "ocean" of the people, a figure he repeatedly applied to them in his poems. Even though he "opened the abyss of Revolution" he would "lead the people to their goal . . . the dawning century." More and more he turned to the people nowadays. "Genius has need of the people," ran one of his lines in 1827. His unkinder critics, on the classical sector or Right of the literary-political front, held that he bowed to the mob. But rather than continue with repetitions of the literary fireworks offered in the highly-colored *Orientales*—the Saint-Simonians, utopian Socialists of the period, already criticized such writings as being sterile and without heart—he moved, not directly at first, but by advances and retreats, toward an art of wider, more popular application. Nettled by the criticisms of the reformers, appealing for a "social art," he turned aside and wrote a short novel, *Le Dernier jour d'un condamné* ("The Last Day of a Condemned Man"), which was published in 1829. It was the simple story of a prisoner—whose crime is not revealed—waiting to be guillotined, and, in that early day, preached a powerful sermon against capital punishment. The abolition of capital punishment was to be, henceforth, one of Hugo's favorite causes. By strongly espousing it, as in accord with the Christian sentiments of mercy and pardon often expressed in his more pious phase, he was led by degrees to advocate broader social reforms.

Among the artists who were his friends was the sculptor David d'Angers, whose influence led almost directly to the writing of *Le Dernier jour*. The romantic painters in those days tried to "tell stories" on canvas, while the writers tried to "paint colors" with words, and they stuck closely to each other. David, who decorated the pediment of the Panthéon, was in politics a fervent radical and humanitarian. It was David who, one day, induced Hugo to go with him to the Bicêtre Prison to see the men who were condemned to the galleys and those who were waiting for the guillotine. These wretched humans stirred the poet's imagination, which was always intensely, almost sadistically, sensitive to pain and ugliness, as it was to beauty and pleasure. Crossing the square of the Hôtel de Ville, several times he had seen the tumbril carrying doomed men to their execution. Thus he had met Louvel, assassin of the Duc de Berry, at his last hour. Once he had seen preparations being made for the beheading of a criminal while a great crowd looked on as at a Roman festival, seats at near by windows or cafés being sold at high prices. A knot of people surrounded the slender red silhouette of the guillotine. It was only two o'clock in the afternoon; but the headsman was rehearsing his role, setting up his instrument, tightening a screw, oiling a joint or nut. The sliding knife seemed to give him some trouble; at last it worked properly. To see the man so prosaically busy with his tools, talking so calmly with the people around him, as he worked, filled the poet with a sense of horror, colder and more terrible than if he had been witnessing the act of execution itself. In a few days he had written his small novel, filled with an atmosphere of mounting terror, and having a very accurate or *realistic* scene of the execution as its climax. This slight novel of less than one hundred pages, which had but a modest sale, pleased Hugo's old friend the Abbé de Lammenais, who was growing to be a sort of Catholic Socialist, and also caused the republicans of *Le Globe* to entertain hopes that the poet would join with their faction.

He saw a grander stage for himself in the theater; he had large visions of a new national theater which would teach and lead the masses.

He saw (as he wrote somewhat later, in 1831, in the preface to

Marion de Lorme), that "the theater today can agitate whole multitudes of people, and shake them to their very depths." Art and literature, like politics, had been the enjoyment in earlier centuries of a few privileged people; but, with education spreading, this would no longer be true in the new century, of which he felt himself one of the predestined men. He told himself:

This would be the hour for him, to whom God would give the needed genius, to create a whole new theater, a theater vast and yet simple, unified and yet varied, national by its historical teaching, popular through its truth, human, natural, universal through its passion. Poets to work! Wonderful and great is the opportunity.

Had not the skeptical men of the eighteenth century told us that the great days were gone, that the time of conquerors and geniuses was past? Yet we had seen the French Revolution and the Empire. "Why, now," exclaims the intoxicated dramatic author, "should there not come a poet *who would be to Shakespeare as Napoleon. was to Charlemagne?"*

One of his fixed ideas, often expressed at this period, was that the great writer would, in the nineteenth century, play a part rivaling that of the great soldier in the preceding century.

The poet whom Victor Hugo then most admired among his contemporaries, Alfred de Vigny, was busily at work on his translation of "Othello," commissioned by Baron Taylor, the theatrical producer. The romanticists now pressed strongly upon the theater, and Vigny, who knew that Hugo also was occupied in preparing new plays, proposed in 1829 that they form a "syndicate" of romantic dramatists, who were to work together. Hugo replied that he would be glad to see Vigny at any time on this project, which was "alluring," yet also spoke of difficulties that occurred to him requiring that they "weigh, ponder, foresee everything possible in advance." He concluded, in this less than cordial response: "What a great good fortune it will be to be a member of this consulate of glory, of which certainly, I shall not be the Bonaparte."

Why did Victor Hugo *disavow* any intention of becoming a literary Bonaparte, when none suggested this?

Alfred de Vigny was troubled by this and other indications of overweening ambition in his friend. Sainte-Beuve saw design and cold determination in every action of the young author of *Cromwell,* whom he saluted in a poem: *"As an iron warrior, a valiant man of arms—yet noble and tender . . ."*

Hugo had appeared in the autumn of 1827 at the head of his band, to applaud the production of Shakespeare by an English company in which Kemble starred, making of this occasion a resounding demonstration for romantic drama. Then, as if directing a campaign, he showed himself at the head of the same swaggering clan of poets and artists, on the opening night of Alexandre Dumas's *Henri III* in February, 1829. This violent play, the first in the new romantic style, was both a popular success and an epoch-making event. At its final curtain, while the whole foyer cheered, the tall, exuberant young Creole, Dumas, rushed up to Hugo and embraced him as his friend and master. In his published version of the play, a few weeks later, Dumas wrote: "I do not say that I have founded a new genre, because in effect I have founded nothing. M. Victor Hugo and others . . . have pioneered before me."

A few days later, Hugo was present again, with his faithful lieutenant and propagandist, Sainte-Beuve, and the rest of his usual retinue or "bodyguard," at the opening of Alfred de Vigny's "Othello." His friendship was cooling for the count, whom he spoke of privately as "the gentleman," and Adèle Hugo was even more irritated at the countess, who frequented by preference the aristocratic Saint Germain quarter of Paris rather than the little literary salon of the rue Notre-Dame-des-Champs. There was also some competitive friction over Vigny's translation of Shakespeare being produced first at the Théâtre-Français, while a new play by Victor Hugo, which had been accepted for the same theater, was presented after it.

Yet Hugo, suppressing his vexation, felt it his bounden duty to support Vigny and Shakespeare (in undiluted form) at the historic opening night of October 24, 1829. "People are trying to disunite us, but I will prove to you," he had promised Alfred de Vigny, "that I am more than ever your good and devoted friend, Victor." The romantic "warfare" recorded a new victory, and Shakespeare was installed forever after in the French theater in his authentic style. Hugo and his friends "frantically applauded" all that night, as he reported, in order to subdue the bewigged, old-fashioned, doddering classicists in the audience.

Impatiently Hugo awaited his turn. Exactly four months before, in June, 1829, working from dawn to dawn in one round of twenty-four hours, he had completed the Fifth Act of *Marion de Lorme,* first called "A Duel under Richelieu," which he felt to be his most finished piece of work up to this date. The fate of this play, the circumstances causing the long delay in its production, had nothing to do with Alfred de Vigny, but rather with the dead hand of authority wielded by that *ancien régime* in France, against which an increasingly bitter resentment stored itself in Victor Hugo.

His chosen method was to use in his poetic dramas subjects drawn from past history, much as Scott had done in the novel. Thus he would gain the chiaroscuro, the deeper light-and-shade effects, and the atmosphere of emotional abandonment that romantic themes afforded. He would also circumvent the strict censorship of the Bourbon government, he hoped. After debating in his mind over the choice of a story of a young Spanish brigand chieftain of olden times suggested by his Spanish readings, and that of a famous seventeenth-century courtesan in Paris, he turned to the second idea and wrote *Marion de Lorme,* working over it most painstakingly for a period of many long months during 1828— only the last act being written in one mad gallop on a day in June, 1829.

Marion de Lorme, formerly as sinful as she was beautiful, falls in love with Didier, a virtuous young man of obscure birth. She has repented of her former frailties, and he pays court to her under the delusion that she is as pure and innocent as he aims to be. But a former favorite of hers reappears to create some uncertainty in Didier's mind, and feelings of fierce jealousy. There is a duel, and then, in accordance with recent decrees of Cardinal Richelieu banning all private dueling in France, the two young adversaries are apprehended by the Royal Guard and condemned to death. Thereafter the exertions of Marion de Lorme to save her young fiancé form the chief subject of the intrigue. A somber portrait of Richelieu is an incidental feature, and so is a rather satirical one of King Louis XIII (to whom Marion appeals in vain for mercy), pictured as but the weak, distracted tool of his all powerful minister. The action of the play is sustained with effects of suspense and pathos, up to the spectacular, foreordained execution scene of Act Five. Didier is the first of Victor Hugo's grave, dignified, humorless heroes; his emotional crisis, which appeared so original or authentically romantic in its day, comes as a consequence of learning the true character of the lady he courts. Then his mood turns to rage, to despair, to a refusal to escape and deliberate courting of death; most important, finally, to his "pardoning" Marion de Lorme and reconciliation with her, before his death.

In certain ways *Marion de Lorme* is Hugo's most effective romantic tragedy; its poetic dialogue, exceedingly sonorous, very free and full of verve, offers his authentic style and marks a very high point in French versification. Besides, it is written with no little wit, especially the first act, set in the apartment of Marion, in which there are amusing exits and entrances alternately of the rakish Saverny, a former lover, and the cloud-uplifted, pure-hearted swain, Didier. Introducing comic relief, like Shakespeare, Hugo sets an animated scene of gipsy players against the growing tragedy. Novel also, for the time, are the accents in which pure exalted love is celebrated in soaring passionate alexandrines. Some subversive passages are also to be found here, hinting at the waning Royalism of Victor Hugo: these include his irreverent portrait of the weak King Louis XIII and the scene in which the hero, Didier, when asked for his lineage—"*Didier de quoi?*"—replies with fierce pride: "*Didier de rien.*" Just Didier, Didier from nowhere!

On an evening of July, 1829, in the salon graced by the Golden Lily of the Academy of Toulouse, Hugo read *Marion de Lorme* to a crowded gathering not only of the romantic cenacle's original members, but also including Balzac, Armand and Edouard Bertin, the publishers of the *Journal des Débats,* Baron Taylor, Prosper Mérimée, Eugène Delacroix, Alexandre Dumas, and Alfred de Musset, who was soon, thanks to Hugo's inspiring example, to have a notable career of his own in the theater. Musset, then a blond dandy of eighteen, was said to have been dressed this evening, quite extravagantly, in a black frock coat with a velvet collar that came down to his waist; his trousers were sky-blue and very tight-fitting.

The host read his play for over two hours without sign of fatigue and with dramatic vigor, though, as one witness, Barbier, says, "in a range of voice that consisted of two extremely contrasting tones, one deep and the other shrill, and he went continually from one to the other." But the Parisian literary audience of that day was strong for poetry and sensitive to the original harmonies of Hugo's work. They rose to a pitch of enthusiasm that probably no other literary generation showed, interrupting the poet with volleys of applause and even cries of passion. They felt themselves called upon to express an unstinted adulation, and each outburst required new superlatives: "A cathedral! Monumental—an ogive! —a pyramid!"

One very young writer of the time, Edouard Turquety, who got himself admitted to one of these séances with some trouble, recalled afterward in his memoirs how in that rapturous springtime of romanticism he nearly fainted at the thought of finding himself in the salon of the "romantic Messiah." He felt he was hearing a new *Cid* being read, and was convinced that he stood in the presence of veritable genius. ". . . But in those times admiration was not enough. We had to become exalted, to leap, to shudder; we had to cry out with Philaminte:

One can bear it no more; one faints with pleasure! one dies!"

When the reading was over, Dumas, with Herculean strength, lifted the poet in his arms and carried him about, crying: "Hugo, we will carry you to glory! Hugo, you will make us all famous!" Everyone cheered and laughed—little Sainte-Beuve, in a corner under his ferrety nose, and with shifting eyes, rather feebly; Alfred de Vigny, applauding but lightly; Emile Deschamps looking over all the ladies while he clapped hands; and Prosper Mérimée joining in with the tips of his fingers. Then Adèle Hugo, tall and buxom, carrying herself proudly in silken evening dress, swept into the room with cakes and sherbets and ices. "I can still see the gigantic Dumas," wrote Henri de la Touche, another witness of this memorable literary banquet, "stuffing his mouth with cake, and shouting, with his mouth quite full: *'Admirable! Admirable! Admirable!'*" It was always thus with the romantics. The hero and the heroine died a hideous death in some Gothic dungeon, after drinking their love potion together and singing their tragic love in sonorous hexameters. Everybody in the audience wept, then turned to eat cakes and ices.

The next day, with all of literary Paris talking of Hugo's new play and its suitability for staging, a procession of theater managers came to the house in the rue Notre-Dame-des-Champs to negotiate with the author for its production. One of them, Harel of the Odéon, "a gentleman in black frock coat, white trousers, and enormous whiskers," tried to take the manuscript of *Marion de Lorme* by main force. When told that it was promised already to Baron Taylor of the Théâtre-Français, and was to be read before the committee of his theater, Harel exclaimed: "A reading? Why so? Here am I quite ready to accept it without looking at it." And he took a pen and wrote on the back of the manuscript the words: "Accepted for the Odéon Theater, July 14, 1829."

"There!" he exclaimed, "July 14—anniversary of the Bastille; well, I am taking my Bastille now." But Hugo, much flattered, extricated the manuscript from his grasp and sent it to the Français, where it was promptly accepted—subject to the will of "Mme. Anastasie," as the government censor was called.

At this point the whole project came to grief. The censor objected to the Fifth Act, the tragic Fifth Act written in a dawn-to-dawn intoxication, and the author would not conceive of changing it. He brought an appeal to the Minister of the Interior, M. de Martignac himself, the fiercely conservative and well-hated leader of the Cabinet, and Martignac sustained the censorship, holding that in the portrait of Louis XIII, who let his kingdom be ruled by Richelieu, the throne itself was turned to ridicule, and the world would see in it an allusion to the reigning King Charles X (who was quite as priest-ridden as his weak ancestor). To Victor Hugo's denials, the aristocratic Minister answered in his coldest and weariest tones that "the moment was serious" and that it was "not the time to expose the royal person to the insults and laughter of the public."

By now, over a month had been lost, and the young playwright was in despair over the disaster that threatened his cherished drama; he then appealed to the King himself and, the next day, August 7, 1829, was invited to an audience at Saint-Cloud. He stood before the once handsome, now "white-haired old man bent with the weight of years and of monarchy," as he described him in a poem he wrote years later. The former Comte d'Artois had been the idol of Hugo's Royalist mother, and had sent white lilies to Mme. Hugo for her sons at the time of Louis XVIII's coronation. He said: "I hear that you have somewhat maltreated my poor ancestor Louis XIII." Hugo urged his cause and begged for an early reply, which the King promised him earnestly. "I admire your fine talent," the King remarked, in dismissing him; "Victor Hugo and Désaugiers are my two favorite poets." Hugo was staggered at this observation, because the other man named was a writer of little music-hall ditties.

After a few days he was informed that the King regretted that he must sustain the censorship in this case. It was a hard blow to Hugo, impatient and ambitious as he was. It was driven home to him also how little room was left open for the careers of young men of talent who happened not to have been born into the old nobility. Nor did it appease him when a message was conveyed to him, a little later, through the Minister of the Interior, that the King desired, as if to compensate his loss, to grant him a pension of four thousand francs, in addition to the modest two thousand that he now enjoyed. This he refused—not with a haughty or angry gesture, as he later recollected it—but in a highly courteous letter to the Minister which was no less effective a refusal. While expressing gratitude for the favor he had previously received from the King, and alluding to the earlier pension, he hinted that he himself had done some little services to the King in return.

My Lord, that earlier allowance, modest as it is, will suffice me. . . . It is true that I have a wife and three children; it is true that I help to support widows and kinsmen who bear my name. But I have been fortunate enough to find in my pen the means of my independence. . . . Indeed it is chiefly precious to me as a token of His Majesty's good will. Living by my pen, I was obliged to count on the legitimate earnings of my drama *Marion de Lorme*. But since the production of this play, though written in all the probity of conscience, seems dangerous in the eyes of the King, I bow to his decision, while hoping that the royal will may change in this respect. All that I asked was that my play should be performed, and I asked for nothing else.

Will you therefore, my Lord, be good enough to say to the King that I beg him to permit me to remain in the position in which this latest expression of his good will finds me. . . . The King may expect from Victor Hugo nothing but the evidence of fidelity, loyalty and devotion.

It was a politic letter for a subject citizen to write to his King, but the phrase *"All that I asked was that my play should be performed, and I asked for nothing else"* had a note of pride hinting at the anguish caused by an incident which contributed largely to the writer's final alienation from the Bourbon monarchy.

Bitterly he turned to resume his assault upon the theater, setting himself now to carry out his alternate idea of a play based on the story of Hernani, a young Spanish brigand, named after a town he had passed through on his boyhood journey to Spain. He made haste; for his friends and rivals, following the new principles of dramaturgy he had presented in *Cromwell*, were busy producing romantic dramas in verse. With *Marion de Lorme* censored, Vigny's version of "Othello" had gone into production before his own work. He labored all night again, writing to Alfred de Vigny at this time: "I am one-eyed, and almost blind; I advise you never to work at night."

2

The drama, *Hernani,* opens in a castle of rugged Saragossa, in the early sixteenth century. In mood and atmosphere it suggests strongly Byron's dramatic poem "Manfred," written about ten years earlier, which had haunted the imagination of Young France. The opening scene of "Manfred," for example, is also situated in a remote castle, though in the Higher Alps instead of the mountains of Aragon, and the instructions run: "Scene One, Manfred alone —a Gothic gallery—time, midnight." Like Byron's ill-fated hero Manfred, Hernani, the hero of Hugo's tragedy, is a "soul that dwells apart," a rebel, alone against the world, an outlaw chief. There we have the opening chord that sets the minor key which the nineteenth-century romanticists preferred. Caught between the millstones of the Bourbon political reaction after 1815, and the oncoming business revolution that was already transforming European society, youth affected disillusionment, melancholy, and midnight moods. The young men of Europe were exhausted by the civil and national wars that had issued from the great French Revolution, and for the moment concealed their sympathy for the ideals of that revolution, seeking outlet for their emotions by adopting romantic poses and by turning to a past that was more shaded but lovelier than the harsh present. Later, in the 1850's, with a heightened pessimism they would cry—with Baudelaire—to be sent "anywhere, anywhere, out of this world!" But the romanticism of Victor Hugo, artistic parent of Baudelaire, was both more innocent and more robust, toward 1830.

The content of *Hernani* is fully in the key of the mental climate that nourished it. Hernani, who is really a young prince of Aragon, stripped of his lands and driven to brigandage by the enmity of King Charles for his family, falls in love with Doña Sol, the beautiful ward of the Duke Ruy Gomez, to whom she has been betrothed. Notice that Ruy Gomez, not only a "father," but one who stands as a living barrier to the marital desires of the young lovers, *is sixty years old*. Another rival is "Don Carlos," an elegant and noble young stranger who is also infatuated with Doña Sol, but has no honorable intentions whatsoever. He clashes in a duel with the wildly jealous Hernani, but they are interrupted by the arrival of the Duke Ruy Gomez who considers killing them both. "Don Carlos" then reveals himself as King Charles of Spain, and pretends to have come, in disguise, on a confidential visit to Ruy Gomez; Hernani, he claims, is one of his own men.

Later that same night, the King attempts to break into Doña Sol's chamber, but is caught by the watchful Hernani, who spares his life. However, the King soon returns with a company of guards to the scene of the duel, Ruy Gomez's castle, in order to seize his assailant. The old duke had, a little earlier, also returned, and, to his bitter grief, surprised Hernani and Doña Sol in each other's arms. His own reckoning with Hernani is only interrupted by the arrival of the King, at whose approach he places Hernani temporarily in hiding, in a secret passageway of the portrait gallery.

To the demand of his monarch for the surrender of the young bandit, the old duke simply discourses upon the portraits of his ancestors and the code of Spanish honor which forbids him to deliver a guest of his house. *Noblesse oblige.* The King is forced to retire, but takes Doña Sol as a hostage. Hernani then rushes forth crying: "But the King loves her!" The two men, the young lover and the aged guardian, then together swear a great Spanish oath to kill their King and rescue the young lady. On condition of furnishing his aid in this common enterprise, Hernani's life is spared by Ruy Gomez. In return for this kindness, Hernani pledges that upon the demand of Ruy Gomez he will yield up his life. He gives the aged fiancé a little silver horn, heirloom of his own noble father, with which he is wont to call together his fierce bandit followers. Whenever the old man desires to remind Hernani of his pledge and complete the bargain, he need only blow the horn.

For the Fourth Act we shift to Aix-la-Chapelle, where in the cathedral crypt, before the tomb of Charlemagne (a highly picturesque scene), King Charles meditates upon his approaching coronation that very day as Emperor of the Holy Roman Empire. Hard by, Ruy Gomez, with Hernani and his followers, skulking among the vaults, lies waiting to kill the King. The King undergoes a striking change of heart, promises himself to improve his character in keeping with his new role as ruler of the civilized world, pacifying his people, extending amnesty to rebels, and making reparation to those he had shorn of titles and properties. This solemn and eloquent monologue is a significant passage when seen in relation to events in France in 1829–1830, where the Bourbon King, Charles X, attempts one measure of repression after another. It is a piece of gratuitous advice offered by Victor Hugo to the King, who has just suppressed a play of his.

For Hernani, this change of heart also has import, for he is pardoned, restored to his estates, and united with the Doña Sol. In a final scene at Hernani's palace in Saragossa, the young lovers hold a dialogue which is an admirable operatic duet. Hitherto, Robin-Hood Hernani has shown himself, by self-confession, a combative and indomitable character, ready to brave a thousand dangers in order to fight his way into the castle walls and the heart of his Doña Sol. "I am a force who goes on! Whither do I go? I know not. Yet feel myself driven by an impetuous wind, an unseen destiny!" This and other passages have a striking resemblance to Victor Hugo's own letters to his fiancée, Adèle, in his early youth, and may easily be taken as a piece of self-portraiture by the poet, in mood of fierce ambition and reckless energy.

But now, in the final scene, life opens before them again, blissful and calm. The lovers issue from the dance floor, Doña Sol saying:

> Come see the lovely night! my lord, but for a moment ...
> All lights and music hushed—there's only night
> And you and I, while all around do sleep,
> And even nature seems but half awake.
> The sky is cloudless; everything reposes.
> Come breathe with me this air scented with roses ...

> (The distant sound of a horn is heard.)

It is, in the French, a memorable passage, an explosion of romantic and lyrical verse that translation cannot render. Then romantic fatality, always present in Hugo's dramas, breaks in: the old Ruy Gomez, in a black domino, appears and gives a blast of the little silver horn. Hernani starts from his dream; he recalls his pledge and his "Spanish honor," and takes poison. Doña Sol takes poison. Ruy Gomez stabs himself—all of this, naturally, with appropriate rhetorical flourishes—and the curtain falls.

The Fifth Act of Hernani, it was said in 1830, powerfully affected audiences and readers, though it was all a tale whose only moral lay, apparently, in the nemesis of "Spanish honor," and the story has since those days appeared so lacking in serious content as to seem absurd or infantile to later generations. English critics were given to saying in the 1830's that Hugo was but an

Hernani, Act II, Scene IV: Hernani and Doña Sol Alone

imitator of Sir Walter Scott, turning his predecessor's romances into plays, or that he was but an echo of Byron. There is a good deal of Scott here, but terser, more emphatic, more theatrical, and written not by an often careless Byron, but by a French lord of language and versification, with more natural grace than that of any poet since Ronsard three centuries before. Those who love French, or who are able to enter into a "sympathetic frame of mind," cannot even now read or hear the lines of *Hernani* without experiencing a very great sensuous pleasure. Actors of other days loved to render its sonorous verses. As in *Marion de Lorme,* so in *Hernani,* a certain enchantment was created, to which the generation of 1830 enjoyed surrendering itself. Moreover, the romantic drama, in its time, by its vigor, color, and movement, even by its heightened feeling for reality and for the free rendering of emotion, served to liberate both the French theater and French poetry from the bonds of an outworn and false "classicism." However, all this was achieved by Hugo, it has been pointed out by the older opponents of romanticism, without use of any serious ethical or intellectual content. His were but absurd and puerile romances for the stage, according to this view.

But is the content of the romantic plays of Hugo's youth so "puerile" as has been charged? The accusation holds only if we consider him as a "systematic" or purely rational thinker—which he himself sometimes pretended to be. But to modern critical analysis Hugo is essentially and remarkably rich in *symbolism* rather than in reason or logic. Seeking always to surrender himself to emotion, choosing subjects that command his "inspiration," writing as he does always in a state of extreme, trancelike concentration, he makes his literary productions to an extraordinary degree the outlet and the unspoilt representation of his subconscious mind. Thus he lends himself more perfectly than almost any writer of recent times to modern psychoanalysis, which seeks to learn its lessons from the symbols and the unconscious motives or reflexes of an artist rather than from his openly stated or expressed design.

Hernani, on the surface, is simply an affair of "Castilian Honor" (this is the actual subtitle of the play), and *Marion de Lorme* deals apparently with not much weightier stuff. But it is significant that the "mother complex" occurs very strongly in the *Marion de Lorme,* in a form very commonly occurring in dreams, with the mother seen as yielding to the father, therefore hateful (a "courtesan"), to the son's thwarted libido. The play with its shadowy drama of guilt and pardon therefore reflects clearly the "complexes" that haunted and shaped Victor Hugo in his unhappy boyhood. This, like the later play *Lucrezia Borgia,* suggests to us that he may have known ultimately much more about his mother than he revealed, and that he suffered deeply thereby and struggled for some solution.

Similarly, in *Hernani,* the young hero is a "rebel" dueling with the King (image of the "father," or of "authority"). Moreover, to Ruy Gomez, the aged guardian of Doña Sol, the father hatred, the "Oedipus complex," is also transferred, inasmuch as he enters into conflict with the young lover Hernani for the enjoyment of Doña Sol. It was a great deal like the story of Victor Hugo's relations with Adèle and her father, M. Foucher—when his own unconscious hatred shifted alternately from his own father to his future father-in-law as the being who seemed most likely to thwart his purpose. In *Hernani,* the hero who "kills himself" is represented as being (symbolically) slain by his own "father," for his dying words, in reference to the ancestral horn that shatters his dream, are: *"O father, thou vengest thyself upon thy son who forgot thee!"* In Victor Hugo's circle, and even in the Paris theater of that day, it was known that his tall, dark-eyed wife, Adèle, was the inspiration, the model of his Doña Sol in *Hernani.* Finally, as one follows the threads of suggestion in nearly all of Hugo's romantic plays, dealing with a far-off past, it is very significant that they are bound up consistently with a type of hero who is *in continual rebellion against authority* of one kind or another, as if typifying youth in conflict with age and paternal authority. Intuitively, the new generation of theatergoers, in 1830, responded to Hugo's plays, whose message became more and more explicit. Outwardly he was conservative, but within the dark, subconscious regions of his mind there was seething rebellion.

3

When Hugo announced to his friends that he would read his new play before a gathering at his house, the demand for invitations was so great that he and Mme. Hugo were compelled to limit the guests severely, since only sixty persons could be packed, standing, into their small salon. The séance of October 1, 1829, saw a repetition of the exuberant and flattering festival of June in honor of *Marion de Lorme.* This time the government censors passed upon the play, since it seemed to them both mad and innocent of political animadversions. Baron Taylor began rehearsals on October 31, 1829, at the Théâtre-Français.

Owing to the suppression of his preceding work, and the publication by the newspapers of parts of his letter to the King refusing an added pension, popular esteem for the poet had begun to rise strongly; both interest and controversy over *Hernani* were at fever pitch. Long before its opening, some passages of the play were smuggled from the acting cast and from censorship officials, as Hugo believed, and quoted or parodied in several music-hall skits and in newspaper comments by hostile critics who ridiculed its extravagant innovations.

As the hour of the *première* approached, which was for him as the hour of supreme battle, Victor Hugo felt that he had literally a world of enemies to contend with, and that many of them— former friends—were ready to ambush him at the first opportune moment. A writer named Henri de la Touche, whom he had aided and fed, published in the *Revue de Paris* for October, 1829, a vigorous satire entitled *La Camaraderie littéraire,* aimed at Victor Hugo and his "school." La Touche, having seen a presentation copy of a rare, richly bound volume of Ronsard's poems, embellished with many original verses by Sainte-Beuve, Lamartine, and others, in homage to "the genius"—from the "other geniuses"— conceived the opinion that the younger literary generation was fast falling a victim to "self-love," and that literary "comradeship" had become the curse of the age. He went on:

You may meet a small band of apostles, anywhere now, who calling themselves persecuted in the principles of their cult, have secluded themselves in order to lend each other encouragement; they are a congregation of strange rhymers who have entered into a conspiracy for mutual admiration. . . . If you are not endowed with the faculty for praising a man to his face, if you do not know how to reach the very heights of enthusiasm in an instant, we advise you never to approach this group that has boasted that "the century belonged to it" and calls itself a Cenacle, and offers its martyrs and its divinities.

Praise has become a slavery, an eternal bondage; in the little ultra-romantic church it is the morning and evening prayer; it is the tithe that every reading, every showing of a mere hemistich, in preparation, has the right to demand of the faithful taxpayers. And whenever one adept meets another they exchange meaningful glances as if to say: "Brother, we must praise each other."

These were hard blows that fell from unexpected, or sometimes hidden, quarters. Sainte-Beuve hinted that Alfred de Vigny was the "false brother" who had betrayed their confidences and prompted La Touche. La Touche's article had Paris laughing for many months and deeply embarrassed the romantic cenacle. To counteract its corroding effects, Victor Hugo commanded one of his young satellites, Gustave Planche, to fire an answering broadside in the *Revue des Deux Mondes*. It was entitled *La Haine littéraire,* and accused the opposition of working only to spread literary hate, but it had less wit and so was not believed.

On November 1, 1829, another blow fell upon Hugo, when Charles Nodier, one of his oldest friends and first patrons, suddenly published in the *Quotidienne* an article severely slating him for quitting pure poetry and running after the fleshpots of the theater. *"Et tu! Charles!"* Hugo wrote him in anguish, as Caesar to Brutus. "Little by little, from silence and indifference, I have seen you pass to eulogy, acclamation, enthusiasm for my enemies. . . . I had not perceived, in my perfect confidence, that this was a natural transition to warfare against me. . . . And what a moment you chose for that, when all my enemies gather around me, more numerous, fiercer than ever!" Their friendship of almost ten years was irreparably broken.

Many weeks in advance of *Hernani's première,* the new play seemed to spread storm in the world of polite letters. The fortnightly *Mercure de France,* in October, 1829, had announced that a whole young literary army, "fully armed, impatiently awaited the outcome of a major battle in which their leader wishes to be engaged alone. . . ." The *Journal des Débats* reported that the forthcoming production had aroused so much passion and hatred that it was being turned into a "field of battle," but this newspaper also tried to reassure the public, the government, and the police against rumored dangers of riot or bloodshed. Whatever might befall "the republic of letters," said the *Journal des Débats,* "the French monarchy need have no fear of the consequences."

Nodier, in a letter of January 11, 1830, to Lamartine, spoke of the danger of Hugo's precipitating "a small civil war," by his audacity; for "he sought now, in *Hernani,* to carry out his system, his theories, to their final expression." The effect of such strife, Nodier fears, would but embitter the young Hugo, over whom his "friendship" no longer holds empire, as it did ten years before. *"But when at the age of twenty-seven a man has formed a sect* (!) it is a rare thing for him to be able to listen to the cool appeals of reason. The enthusiasm of his young admirers must have the same effect on him as the song of the siren. . . . Would that the future would spare him the tribulations that go with glory!"

Well in advance, some of Hugo's older friends can be seen weeping crocodile tears for the poet's approaching decline and fall. Even Sainte-Beuve, practically a member of his own household, and not only his own constant companion but increasingly that of his wife—and most tenderly in the hours when Hugo is busy at rehearsals—even Sainte-Beuve retreats a little, warns him that he has decided not to write articles in behalf of *Hernani*, because he is convinced that his admired friend is now pursuing a mistaken course. Hugo wishes to bring a true poetic drama to the great public? Impossible! The public cares nothing for art, Sainte-Beuve insists. "Are you not, like Napoleon, trying to accomplish the impossible?" And then, "watching what has been happening for some time, your life forever at the disposal of others, your lost leisure, your paroxysms of hatred, the old and noble friendships broken, the idiots or fools who replace them . . . the lines and shadows on your forehead that come not from working over great thoughts, I can only grieve, regret the past, salute you from a distance, and hide myself somewhere." However, in this case, Victor Hugo imposed his stronger will upon the critic, and forced him back into line.

Hugo was accused of many sins and above all of a monumental vanity. Yet few have commented on the dubious character of those literary friendships upon which he was forced to count in his great hour of trial. On the eve of the "civil war" over *Hernani*, some of his best comrades seemed ready to desert, while warning him of disaster, vexing him with sermons, beseeching him to take care and mend his ways. How helpful they were! And what strange guises friendship assumed in the literary life!

But trouble flowed not only from close friends, but from the actors at the Théâtre-Français, where the playwright followed rehearsals daily in a most painstaking way. The cast assembled by Taylor was a strong one, led by Mlle. Mars, playing Doña Sol. She was fifty, she had been bred strictly in the classical tradition, and after thirty years of success had become an imperious queen of the French stage.

To an acquaintance who asked him if he were happy with the cast chosen for his play, he replied with some feeling: *"Mon dieu!*

I am in the position of a man who has put his wine in several bottles that have already been used and impregnated with the flavors of other vintages. I cannot always recognize the wine of my own barrel any longer."

"But at least," said the other, "you have in Mlle. Mars a decanter of gold and crystal."

"Yes," laughed Hugo, "but one in which a good deal of rose water has been poured."

Mlle. Mars protested bitterly to the author against certain of her lines which she considered in atrocious bad taste. Alexandre Dumas, in his memoirs, relates how she would try to make fun of these, reading them off wearily and derisively. *"You are my lion, superb and generous!"* How funny it was, she would remark, to address her leading man, M. Martin, a bald old fellow, as her "lion"! Did M. Hugo still hold to his lion?

M. Hugo did, he said, because he had thought it sounded right. Yet if Mlle. Mars would, perhaps, kindly suggest something better, he would be ravished to change it.

"But I am not the author," she exclaimed.

"Well, then, madame, let us simply follow the text."

During one spirited collision, Victor Hugo, in a temper, requested that the star relinquish her part. Feminine tears flowed and a reconciliation followed. The rehearsals went forward. It was a season of trouble and grief. One lost one's temper, and one lost friends. But Victor Hugo, always, instinctively courted, even enjoyed, opposition and difficulty and danger. To a friend of his, Adolphe de Saint-Valry, he opened his heart one night during this trying period, describing how he felt himself "crushed, overladen, choked." The Comédie-Française, the rehearsals, the gossip, the jealousies in the wings, those of actors and actresses, the maneuvers of the newspapers and the police, the troubles with his stepmother, who by legal processes had seized all his father's landed property— all this accumulated now and filled up his current life. "Well," he concludes ruefully, "I swim, I fight, I move upstream. . . . But you, Saint-Valry, take things easily. You are the wiser and happier one."

4

The opening night of *Hernani* was set for February 25, 1830. That winter was fearfully cold in France, and Victor Hugo went to the rehearsals clad in felt boots; braziers were lit in the cold, empty theater. Adèle Hugo, though approaching her fifth confinement in seven years, threw herself into the work of organizing their army of defense and attack. For, although her husband had announced, in revolutionary fashion, that he would have no paid, professional claque—no claque! an unheard of thing!—it was urgent that he and his friends prepare to fill a large part of the theater, on the opening nights, with the cohorts of romanticism ready to hurl back the expected onslaughts of the classicists. To such public battles over new departures in art and letters, Paris has always responded with all the Latin part of its collective soul, emphatic, enthusiastic, partisan, half in humor, half in transported passion or anger. There had been manifestations and "demonstrations" before, but that for the opening of *Hernani* by the "generation of 1830," which now came of age, was to serve as a historic model for a hundred years after.

Quietly and grimly, Victor Hugo, acting as his own chief of staff, with the aid of Sainte-Beuve marshaled all the phalanxes of the *Hernanistes*—or of Young France as he would soon call them—in order of battle. All day long, about eighty outlandish "volunteers" tramped in and out of the poet's home in the rue Notre-Dame-des-Champs, where orders were given them, and also some food, cake and wine, gratis. Arrangements were made for the allocation of the pit and the whole upper gallery to the regimented soldiers of romantic drama. Victor Hugo cut some red cards, and stamped upon them the Spanish word *HIERRO,* which means "iron." Any young artist who was *au courant* knew that this referred to the famous sixth poem in *Les Orientales*— which the advance-guard review, *Album National,* had called "the fairest literary monument of our epoch"—a poem they all knew by heart, which had as its epigraph the war cry of the ancient Spanish tribe of Almogavares, *Hierro, despiertale!* ("Iron, awake!"), and began:

To the war, oh warriors!

Armed with their red cards, the romantic clans of poets and novelists in bud, the embryonic journalists, the musicians and painters of the future moved into battle like the ironclad Almogavares of Gothic Spain. One band of them was led by a tall, blond volunteer, aged eighteen, named Théophile Gautier, whose hair came down to his shoulders, and who wore a scarlet satin vest and green silk trousers. He was a new recruit. As they left Hugo's house, his friend,

Gérard de Nerval, who led another battalion, cried to him: "Gautier, can you answer for your men?"

Young Gautier replied: "By the skull from which Lord Byron drank at the Abbey of Newstead, I'll answer for them!" And he waved to his young followers, bearded, long-haired, who at his signal, all shouted together: "*Hierro!* Death to the Wigs!" For the classicists, the men of the *ancien régime,* whom they planned to "scalp" with their "tomahawks," had no hair, alas. They were the Wigs.

The romantic brigade was manned with the scourings of the Latin Quarter and Montparnasse, mostly pupils of the painter Deveria. Also present among them were Hector Berlioz, the young composer, and Petrus Borel, the self-declared poet of vampirism, called horridly "The Lycanthrope"; another young lion of the Left Bank café terraces was Philadelphia O'Neddy, the vivacious half-Irish journalist, who headed a column of his own, his men dressed in red vests like Marat's and collars like Robespierre's. (Balzac and Stendhal came also, but stood apart and watched the proceedings with mixed feelings.)

Toward three o'clock, the day of the opening, between eighty and ninety of them were seen converging upon the Comédie-Française from all the neighboring streets, singing songs of the studios and uttering weird cries which brought people running to the scene. "You may well stare at us," cried O'Neddy, "we are the brigands of thought!" "We are the Wild Men of art!" yelled another. But as Gautier recollected:

They were not the wild, bristling, filthy Huns of Attila who besieged the theater long ahead of time, but the knights of the future, the champions of the ideal, the defenders of free art. What was more, they were handsome, young and free. Yes, they were hairy too—but you cannot be born with a wig, and many of them had hair that fell in curls . . . so becoming to their proud, dauntless, heads that the masters of the Renaissance might well have used them as their models.

Through a side door in the rue de Montpensier, which the manager, Baron Taylor, had opened for them, they entered the theater and camped in their assigned places, with three and a half hours to wait. They sang and they cheered; but the play was not to begin until seven o'clock, and so they grew hungry; opening parcels of food, they spread out ham, sausage, garlic, and cheese on the benches or on handkerchiefs they had brought, and opened bottles of wine, sharing each other's food, eating and drinking to their hearts' content. So much so, that soon a number of them began to search all about the House of Molière for a place where, as Rabelais phrased it, they might "expel the superfluity of that which they had drunk." In dark corners of the topmost gallery they quietly relieved themselves. At seven when the lords and ladies of Paris stepped out of their carriages into the theater—horrors upon horrors!—they smelled garlic, and even worse! The theater was in tumult; Baron Taylor in despair. The author, appearing in the room of the leading lady, Mlle. Mars, heard her reproach him through her tears: "It is your romantic young friends who have ruined us."

Then the footlights were lit, the theater grew dark. Victor Hugo stepped to the curtain, and looked out through a little peephole, as all authors have done throughout history. All of elegant Paris was there in the loges, from Delphine Gay, the young poetess, with her beautiful arms and golden hair, in a white robe and blue scarf, as in the portrait hanging in the Louvre, to the Duke of Saxe-Coburg, Chateaubriand, Mme. de Recamier, and Benjamin Constant. But up above, in the parterre, was "a band, wild and bizarre, bearded, hairy, dressed in all fashions save the current ones, Spanish, Italian, old French." They were still hurling insults and curses upon the classicists, with their shiny bald pates and high collars, in the balcony below them. "To the guillotine with the Wigs!" they cried menacingly. The theater gradually became nearly silent, and then the three fateful taps of the baton were heard. The author retreated to the wings. The curtain rose.

5

All reports agree that the spectators at the Comédie-Française, on that night of February 25, 1830, talked and acted as much as the actors, and no one remembered at what time the play came to an end. There were endless interruptions and apostrophes, and a continual cross fire between dignified old gentlemen and the young stalwarts upstairs, over the unorthodox usages and locutions of the new playwright. *"Hidden stairway!"* exclaimed one old gentleman at the opening line, according to Gautier's reminiscences. "You see the orgy begins in the first line, and it doesn't even scan." Hugo's foot soldiers berated the old gentleman warmly. There were cries of "Hush!" and "Throw them out!" Now the irreverent audience would interrupt, then listen, now incredulous at the extravagant and "antithetical" action, or now bemused in the spell of the Hugolian verse. But at the end of the Fifth Act, when the exquisite love dialogue of Doña Sol and Hernani was heard ("Come see the lovely night!" . . .), all were moved in spite of themselves, as if with a release of passion. After ecstasy, and fullness, and peace—the final dramatic antithesis arrives; suddenly, out of that silence, the horn sounds from a distance, then, louder and stronger, the music of fate. Hernani starts.

(*The horn sounds and dies, returns, prolongs itself.*)

The senile old man, in domino and grinning mask, appears, claiming his bond. Few persons present minded the thin story and character portraiture. No one wondered why a good, pious Spanish lady should love a bandit, or a generous, noble, virtuous old man of sixty should insist so annoyingly on demanding his senile pleasure at all costs. "The sound of the horn caused universal anguish," wrote Victor Pavie, one of Hugo's lieutenants, "in the four corners of the theater." In effect, like the Biblical horn of Joshua, it blew down the partly crumbled walls of French pseudo-classicism.

It was a sweeping popular success, a victory conquering the public of the theater for the new romantic genre, as even hostile newspapers admitted the next morning. The fairly official *Gazette de France* attributed "noble and deep thoughts, gleams of genius," to the new tragedy, and the critic of the *Globe* reported that long after he had left the theater the public still stood there, for an hour, applauding. The next morning the aging Chateaubriand gallantly wrote Hugo: "I am going, sir, and you are coming."

Victor Hugo had followed the progress of the battle from the wings, "preserving always his Olympian calm, despite the ill-humor of the actors, especially Mlle. Mars." With elaborate modesty he had quietly gone home before the final curtain. When the call for author was raised, he was not in the box with Adèle; but the first-night audience directed its applause to the stately, dark-haired lady, in a striking costume, with a white band under her chin, like a medieval headdress. With a gracious inclination of her head Adèle thanked the public. When she reached home, a crowd of Victor's friends were already there embracing him with all the effusiveness common to the literary warriors of 1830. He asked only if it were true that they had "enjoyed themselves."

However, for forty-five nights the hostilities continued. The friends of the classicists returned stubbornly to sneer and to whistle. Victor Hugo found it necessary to send his followers into battle each night. As he wrote on the second day of the engagement, to Paul Lacroix, publisher of his plays:

We must not fall asleep. The enemy holds vigil. The third representation must be handled so that it discourages them if possible. In the name of our cherished literary liberty, call together our host of strong and faithful friends . . . to help me wrench forth this last tooth of the old classical Pegasus. Forward march!

Sometimes the audience, entering into the fun, grew so unruly and profane that Adèle Hugo was forced to leave her box in protest. "We are worn out," Sainte-Beuve reported from the front, "because we have no fresh troops for every battle, and must give ground, as [Napoleon did] in 1814." But at the sixth performance a great coup was gained, when the Duchesse de Berry, brilliant representative of the court, made an appearance, her evident approval exerting a calming effect and serving to divide the opposition.

From a business point of view, the "battle of *Hernani*" was also significant, the receipts for the first two nights "breaking all previous records in the theater," as Hugo reported in an exultant letter to the publisher, Lacroix. His royalties for the run of about seven weeks, unusually long for the time, quickly brought him approximately twenty thousand francs; but performances in the provinces, revivals, and book publications soon added greatly to this sum. In a pecuniary sense he had made himself, at twenty-eight, one of the first, that is one of the richest, men of letters in France, and his tone and manner now reflected the consciousness of this with a quite bourgeois pride. Sometimes he even enjoyed referring to himself with the courtesy title of "Baron" he had inherited from his father.

Yet the principal effect of *Hernani* was to arouse *La Jeune France* which was prevailingly liberal and republican. "We must bring Victor Hugo over to fight for our cause," said one of these who watched the furor over *Hernani*. Had not the government suppressed his *Marion de Lorme* (though permitting it to be issued in book form)? Hugo in an ode had rebuked the Austrians and defended France's war heroes. Now in 1830 the hated Prince de

Polignac was Prime Minister, and prepared new *Ordonnances* of repression. Hugo was neutral today. "But tomorrow," one observer predicted, "he will be a revolutionist."

One day in March, 1830, Armand Carrel, the bold young leader of the republican opposition (a young politician of brilliant promise, who came to an untimely death in a duel), sought out Victor Hugo and invited him to join the republicans. Hugo demurred, but wrote him in self-defense:

I too have fought while M. Carrel fought; while he moved bravely against the political stream, I swam against the literary stream. In a sense we have both been proscribed men at the same time; although his has been the more serious and fairer destiny, I having only been outlawed by the Academy.

Yet here are already eight years that I have borne the heat and dust of the day, eight years in which I pursued my task without allowing myself to be turned aside by the need to defend myself against a thousand personal attacks. In an age when all was to be accomplished through the salons and the newspapers, I began and continued on my route without a salon and without a journal. Mine has been a life of solitude, conscience and art. . . .

I was destined to a large fortune under the Empire, but the Empire and my fortune went down in the same gale. I found myself at one and twenty a married man, a father with no income, save my daily earnings, living from hand to mouth, like a member of the working class, while Ferdinand VII enjoyed my revenues in Spain. . . . Obliged to live and keep my household together by the earnings of my pen, I have kept it free of all speculations or mercenary bargains. For good or evil I have written books, not engaged in bookmaking or bookselling. A poor man, I have cultivated Art as disinterestedly as if I had been rich, for Art's sake, with my eyes upon the future rather than the present. Compelled to make of my pursuit of letters both my business and my dream, I can say that I have never sacrificed the dream to the business.

Although there are, as usual, a few slight exaggerations in this piece of self-confession, there is a growing consciousness in Victor Hugo that he has triumphed by his own labor, rather than by inheritance and birth. But the bourgeois, the "self-made" men of France now fully shared with the working class a deep resentment at Charles X's government, which by July, 1830, had lost all hold upon the nation.

6

One unexpected effect of Victor Hugo's greatly increased celebrity, in 1830, was his expulsion from the apartment he rented in the rue Notre-Dame-des-Champs. Hundreds of young men had been tramping up and down the little stairway leading to his home; publishers, theatrical managers, and their agents besieged him; late parties and celebrations had been held there. Victor Hugo was now a public idol of Paris, his face well known, thanks to the portrait engraving by his friend Deveria, which was displayed and sold at almost every bookstall. Victor Pavie, an old-time friend, wrote to Sainte-Beuve of his regret at the passing of the smaller circle of other years and the old intimacy. "The hour of national renown, the popular hour had sounded for him; we were forced to share him; everyone and anybody crowded in, a host of new recruits. . . ." The landlord who lived below also regretted the change, and, saying that he was an old man in need of repose, gave the Hugos notice that they must find a home elsewhere.

They now removed to a much larger establishment in the rue Jean-Goujon, situated in the almost suburban but increasingly fashionable section of the Champs Elysées, on the right bank of the Seine.

Since 1829, Victor Hugo had been working intermittently upon a novel he had contracted to deliver, at a fixed date, to the bookseller, Gosselin, for which he had received very substantial advances. In the spring of 1830, Gosselin, furious at Hugo's sale of publishing rights in *Hernani* to another bookseller, threatened legal suit if the forthcoming novel were not produced. After a settlement of the quarrel, the author agreed to deliver his manuscript by December 1, 1830, failing which he must pay a penalty of one thousand francs for each week of delay. These were hard terms, but various booksellers who had at first besieged this author for his manuscripts already complained that he had a way—while protesting that he knew nothing of trade—of exacting extremely high prices for his services, in advances and royalties, sometimes leaving them little profit.

In the summer of 1830 the fear of penalties, at a thousand francs a week, spurred Hugo to a quite romantic fever of production. He had forgotten the glorious victory of *Hernani* and was fully concentrated upon his long-cherished project, a historical romance built around Notre-Dame Cathedral, when suddenly the

July Revolution burst forth. He dropped his pen. In fear and trembling he wandered the streets, watching the men who marched and fought, sometimes near his own house, during those three historic days, which ended with the flight of his old patron and censor, Charles X.

It was of King Charles X and his entourage of Royalist *émigrés* of the 1792 vintage that historians said in France, "they had learned nothing and forgotten nothing." Under his reign, the charter of 1814, which provided for limited suffrage and semi-parliamentary rule under a constitutional monarchy, suffered a steady decline in its force. Charles's principles held that, where the usually complaisant Parliament and the King did not agree, the will of the King must lead. After 1827, laws of Sacrilege had restored the Church almost to its old powers; laws on Indemnity had reimbursed the landed proprietors, in part, for expropriations. Then gag laws had been laid upon the press, in the Ordinances of June 26, 1830. The singular thing was that during this "black reaction," although society suggested gloom and decorum, France appeared more progressive, public opinion increasingly intelligent and resentful of the loss of popular rights. The more recent elections, in spite of every precaution to restrict their participants to a few hundred thousand citizens out of thirty millions, returned always more moderate or liberal representatives. The duel between the industrial and banking interests and the landed nobility, who had plainly overstayed their time, came to a climax with the proposals of the Polignac Ministry, which, as by a royal *coup d'état,* annulled the results of the latest election and restricted the vote still further. On July 27, 1830, the factories having been deliberately shut by their owners, the "uninvited guests," the people, the workingmen in their blue blouses, came into the streets. For three days they fought the Royal Guard and the Swiss mercenaries with the ingenuity and gay courage that the Parisian masses have always shown. Six thousand died before the King abdicated in favor of the infant Duc de Bordeaux. In reply the revolutionists uttered their byword, "Too late," and the old King departed for England, being succeeded—as a result of a new political compromise engineered mainly by Talleyrand, in which the people had been little consulted—by his wealthy cousin of the junior Bourbon branch, the Duc d'Orléans. The new King, Louis-Philippe, was the son of Citizen "Egalité" Orléans, who had embraced the cause of the French Revolution, and was supposedly a Liberal. But for two years the French masses continued to seethe with unrest, and the new government, only by hard fighting, put down the terrible workingmen's insurrections of Lyons, in 1831, and Paris, in 1832.

Victor Hugo, gradually alienated from the Bourbons, had felt lately that he must lead the romantic movement in literature into the camp of the movement of political progress. In some pages of diary notes, called "Journal of a Revolutionary of 1830," which, together with a similar piece, called "Journal of a young Royalist of 1819," published in a volume of essays, in 1834, he wrote:

My old convictions, my Royalist and Catholic ideas . . . have fallen to pieces, fragment after fragment, during the last ten years under the repeated shock of age and experience. Something of them still is left in my mind, like religious and poetic ruins. Sometimes I go out of my way to salute them with respect; but I no longer enter to say my prayers. . . .

I am no longer a Vendean at heart—though something of that still lingers in my soul.

He had felt the whole social and cultural edifice jarred as by an earthquake, he noted, and "the men of art, particularly stupefied, running in all directions after their scattered ideas." But, while he was confused or stunned for the moment, he felt always in his soul a need to be in step with the movements of his people and his century. He himself alluded to *"mon âme de cristal"* in a poem of this period: "my soul of crystal" responding sensitively to all the tides and changes of current of the time. He had a passion to know and experience them, even if his intellectual and rational powers were always relatively more limited than his intuitions, his senses, his emotions. In this connection, Professor Denis Saurat, in his searching study of Hugo's religious ideas, has called him essentially a "primitive," a man of intuitions. Yet he was eventually driven by his intuitions to attempt, courageously enough, to resolve for himself the great central questions of religion, morality, and society which possessed his century, an effort that brought him, in time, to suffer a profound spiritual crisis.

He made the gesture of saluting the heroic revolutionists of 1830, in a new ode: "To Young France." He sang of the men, women, and children who came running to the fight, of the whole turbulent city hurling itself upon well-drilled, heavily armed Guards, night and day, "while the panting tocsin, sounding from the belfries, constantly summoned the workers from their quarters, with its fearsome death rattle."

He had been brought up, during the Restoration, upon the "bogy-man" theory of the French Revolution as a thing of pillaging mobs. Such notions now left him forever.

But for the moment, in 1830, Victor Hugo remained "moderate" in his political sentiments, remembering with gratitude the patronage the Bourbons had formerly given him, and finally disavowing, with a certain regretful decorum, that which in his heart he had disavowed some years before. To his friend Lamartine, who was now embracing political action in earnest, he wrote on September 7, 1830:

On July 28, the cannonading caused my pen to drop from my hand as I was about to write you. . . . The atmosphere is full of contagion, which gains you in spite of yourself; no more art, or drama, or poetry in such a moment. . . . One literally breathes politics.

Nevertheless, this earthquake over, I have the conviction that we shall find our edifice of poetry standing more solidly than before the shocks that came. With us too it is a question of liberty; ours also is a revolution; it will march in solidarity with her sister the political one. Revolutions, like wolves, do not devour each other.

To another friend he wrote, during the "admirable revolution" of 1830, that he had feared to visit him in the provinces lest he compromise his friends by his present reputation as "a political and literary Liberal." The term Liberal in those days was a fighting word. Yet the Liberals of 1830, like Armand Carrel of the *National* group, envisaged little more than some form of "consular-progressive" government, which did not allow yet for too wide suffrage. Many, seeking a symbol of militant Liberalism, attached themselves to the cause of the House of Bonaparte, whose pretender, Napoleon's son, lived until 1832. If Hugo had Vendean ties through his mother, he felt also sentimental ties and hopes, through his "refound" father, which were lodged with the Bonapartes, as he wrote, in 1832, to the former King, Joseph Bonaparte, his father's friend. At this period he embraced no fixed party doctrines. He thought, practically speaking, that France needed "the *thing*, republic, the *word*, monarchy"—in other words a monarchy, like England's, under constitutional and popular limits. Nor did he consider participating directly in politics at this time, despite flattering invitations to do so.

He wrote, toward 1834, in his fragmentary "Journal of a Young Revolutionary," that what the people needed most of all was to be instructed. "To enlighten the people, to give them to read, is to civilize them . . . *humaniores litterae*. We must create, we must prepare the people for their humanities." This was mission enough for him, requiring the conquest of the theater and its crowds, the building of a great national drama.

On June 12, 1832, he wrote Sainte-Beuve:

Some day we shall have a republic, and when it comes it will be good. But let us not gather in May the fruit which will only be ripe in August. The republic to be proclaimed by France in Europe will be the crown of our white-headed age.

Hugo also expressed the hope that the government would not deal too harshly with the insurrectionists who were then, once more, setting up barricades in Paris. He felt that they were but "generous hotheads." He himself would join an uprising at once, he declared, if in that way he could help the rebels win relief. But at this time he joined no riots.

In these days, in the midst of life, plunged in a dozen different writing plans—for poems, dramas, novels—but prosecuting mainly his "war in the theater," his days were so filled that he sometimes scarcely knew what went on in his own household, or what his own wife was thinking.

Someone at this period asked Sainte-Beuve whether his famous friend believed in God or practiced religion, and Sainte-Beuve replied: "Victor Hugo does not concern himself with such things. He is a full man. He is happy." Jules Janin said at this time of his friend's fruitful and prosperous period: "I have known no one down here on this earth who laughs with such a hearty laugh."

He had been a mere youth, still in his twenties, when he became the laureate and first writer in France. His life had hitherto been carefully enclosed, an affair of long hours of work and habits of marital fidelity and paternal devotion formed by an early marriage. Evidently, as he approached thirty, he had arrears of life to make up.

Sometimes his friends, or even ladies seen in the salons he frequented, twitted him for being apparently ignorant, in the intimate sense, of passion, or of the interesting troubles and complexities it engendered. Oriental palaces and Castilian jealousy and courtesans of the time of Louis XIII, he had written of all these, and yet had known them only in books.

At times, Charles Nodier and, especially, Sainte-Beuve held up to him the example of Byron, who had experienced and suffered so greatly. They all but complained of Hugo's "innocence" and continence. One friend, Fontaney, called him "master" always to his face, but behind his back, writing in his diary, named him a bourgeois. But how needless or ill-advised such taunts can be! Life itself has a way of bringing to each man the full measure of passion and sorrow, of experience and knowledge.

CHAPTER VI

Sainte-Beuve: The Traitor Friend

For more than a decade, life, within the walls of Victor Hugo's home, flowed on calm and pure, no matter how rough or incidented his artistic career might be. With the unfortunate example of his own parents fixed in his mind, he had resolved long ago that his heart's desire was a tender and unclouded domesticity. That Adèle met these requirements in an ideal sense and made him his "soft retreat" he assured himself over and over again, as the years of their "prosperous hymen," fruitful in children, prolonged themselves. Perhaps more than any other French poet Hugo sang the joys of conjugal felicity. His third volume of poems, *Les Feuilles d'automne* ("Autumn Leaves"), issued in 1831, fully displayed the unchanging love the poet bore for his wife in many verses addressed to her, as:

O mes lettres d'amour, de vertu, de jeunesse. . . .

inspired by reading over the bundle of love letters of 1819–1822, letters "of love, of virtue, of youth." Then the long *Prière pour tous* ("Prayer for All of Us"), celebrated in five hundred lines not only devotion to spouse but to children, whom, in his tenderly sentimental canvas, he groups about his wife, all dressed in white. Without the sound and movement of children his home would be inconceivable, and so he prays for them.

But toward 1830 shadows touched this picture of a marriage idyl. The home was thronged with visitors of all sorts, and the scene of large dinner parties. Victor Hugo, who formerly could

153

not bear to be separated from Adèle, was gone much of the day, absorbed in theater rehearsals; or remained unseen for long hours in his study, talking with callers, or working late at night.

Adèle, the childhood companion, had become a tall, full-bosomed woman and, despite her languid disposition, busily absorbed in the care of her four children and the social duties which the position of her husband now involved. The people of the salons thought of her as a very simple woman, but also a very kind and loyal one.

After July, 1830, when her second daughter, Adèle, was born— it was her fifth confinement in seven years—she seemed for a long time very tired and *souffrante*. She went out with her husband less often. Pain, weakness, and an ailment of the kidneys clung to her for a long time, as the Hugo letters of this time reflect. Her own letters also show her a little weary and sad over her increasing burdens as a mother. A fear of new maternities showed itself in her, and these days she seemed to shrink from the arms of her virile young husband. To a certain extent she "refused herself to him," according to a tradition that was handed down by old friends of the Hugo family. At twenty-eight, still in young manhood, Victor Hugo had prospered enough to move to a big house near the Champs Elysées, with several servants and a porter; it also had separate bedchambers.

All this was noted and recorded by Sainte-Beuve, always present, watching everything through his half-veiled, watery blue eyes. Since early in 1827 the home of Victor Hugo was as a home to the young Sainte-Beuve, who for years had lived meanly and alone as a medical student. "I have always loved to live among others," this curious man said of himself later. *"I have always sought to make my nest in others' souls. . . .* I had a taste for intimate habits, private understandings."

He arrived usually twice a day, often for lunch and in the afternoon or evening. To Victor Hugo he was a brother writer, a comrade in arms, and a sympathetic critic, devoted, with seeming unselfishness, to advancing the poet's fame. The poems he himself wrote at twenty-five saluted in Hugo the "great genius," the "strong man" who had thrown himself into the field of literature "like a warrior," and before whom Sainte-Beuve "bent like a reed." It was in Hugo's circle, with his wife and children and friends gathered around, that Sainte-Beuve was induced, shy though he was, to read his early poems, and applauded and encouraged. Here the sun shone upon him and his young sensitive talent bloomed.

Then little by little he began to notice Adèle. He would steal a glance at her proud aquiline profile as she sat by the window, her feet usually raised on the bar of a second chair, a tambour in her lap, but her embroidery often forgotten while she gazed absently out of the window, only occasionally turning to him or to other visitors a gentle, almost maternal, glance. She was the muse, the "Madonna" of the romantic cenacle. He wrote in *Volupté* (of Mme. de Couaëns):

I found myself after six months of connection, entertaining only the vaguest impressions of her, as if in a suspension of sentiment, which far from resembling indifference, derived rather from a refinement of respect and my own extreme scruples about questioning myself on this. Coming in, I saluted her without speaking directly to her; yet I saw her without looking at her, just as one does with a young mother who suckles her child in your presence.

Then he began to look at her hungrily:

As I had avoided looking at her formerly, so now I became as avid to contemplate her: I haunted curiously with my eyes that noble and double visage; I penetrated that ingenuous expression, of a singular rarity, and which did not speak to me at the beginning; I spelled out, in some sort, every line of that great beauty, like a holy book, and a little difficult . . . which some friendly angel kindly held out open for me.

Gradually it all became a sweet habit. During the hours when the leonine spouse would be abroad, walking, or at the theater, or working alone, the long-nosed, shy young man, waiting for him, would sit talking with Adèle, forgetting the time.

Sainte-Beuve had just completed that sad and skeptical volume of minor poems, so much like that of Coventry Patmore, entitled *La Vie, poésies et pensées de Joseph Delorme*—even the name was taken from the title of the play which his friend Victor Hugo had read to him at this time. He had been long without religious faith; now he thought of returning to the consolations of Mother Church, and this, as he spoke with Adèle Hugo, touched her heart, for she had always been deeply pious. The poor, thin, round-shouldered, long-nosed young man! Yet so eager and bright in conversation; he told so many pointed little stories, even charming bits of gossip, drawn from people and books, which the readers of his twenty-eight sparkling volumes of *Causeries* would later relish. Sainte-Beuve's talk was enjoyable precisely because it was not always so tense or so elevating as Victor's. Accustomed as Adèle was to brothers and brothers-in-law, she came to enjoy being as a sister to him. For he filled a certain void—Victor, being so taken up these days, left her much more alone. At this time, Sainte-Beuve could not have told which of this "brilliant and happy couple" he loved the more.

Now he addresses certain poems to "Mme. la Baronne V—— H——" He opens his melancholy little heart to her, "his night, his void!" He sings of the "mother and chaste wife" who befriends him and comforts him, and compliments her as "one who, from the cradle, had been formed expressly for love by the secret designs of an amorous nature. . . ."

Their tête-à-têtes were long, "full of a thousand indefinable conjectures, recollections, bizarre experiences, situations, the changing human drama about us . . . never wearying of this mutual echo of our reflections, sometimes continuing thus late at night, before the dead embers in the hearth, and closing with a friendly and light good-night. . . . Our familiarity was all the more appealing because it was indefinite, and the relation left floating between us delicately, to be accepted or ignored as we pleased." These are the words Sainte-Beuve uses to describe the relationship between "Amaury" (himself) and "Mme. de Couaëns" (Adèle) in *Volupté*.

Then in a poem of his, dated July, 1829, inscribed to her, the line occurs:

A cloud passed over our pure friendship. . . .

The thought had arisen in her—she had confided it, as a presentiment!—that some day the deep friendship of the three of them might suffer a change, owing to some fault of his. Had he made some half revelation of his feelings? He answered in anger (as the poem describes it) with bitter denials, forgetting himself. Adèle seems to have thought once of dismissing him for good. But he begged her forgiveness. Then, "they shed tears together, seeing that they cared for each other, pardoned and forgot."

From those fragments—some of them privately published, or in manuscript, which Sainte-Beuve carefully preserved—we perceive that he is at this stage an imitator of the "sensitive" or sentimental lovers who were painted by Jean-Jacques Rousseau, Goethe, and Byron. In an anonymous article in the *Globe*, reviewing the new edition of his own book, *Joseph Delorme,* Sainte-Beuve, in December, 1830, admits that this "poor devil of a Joseph Delorme" is a product of the early romantic literature and the Restoration; "he feels his desires, dreams, passions rebuffed; he feels the need for some success, and his inability to attain it; he suffers in his pride, and grows bitterly discouraged"; sad, awkward and timid, he has "grown soft by weeping over himself." A born critic, Sainte-Beuve gives us here a very sharp and accurate estimate of himself in youth.

We see also that at some point he has concluded that he has fallen in love with Adèle. This makes for a remarkable situation. He loves his friend Victor, and he is *in love* with his friend's wife, the beautiful wife of a handsome man, a man of power, fame, wealth, genius, while he is obscure, and homely and poor to boot. Almost as soon as he has determined that he is in love and that the outcome can be only the most romantic sorrow for himself, he determines to write of it, at first in poems, then in a novel. It was thus that he came to write *Volupté.*

However, it is impossible to judge whether love inspired him first to write, or whether the very desire to write, to make literature, came first and prodded him to love. Toward 1830 the contagion of a furious literary production gained everybody. The eighteenth-century sentimentalists were complex enough; but the nineteenth-century romantics were sometimes *decadent* (as in the case of Sainte-Beuve) inasmuch as the composing of prose and verse, the self-conscious analysis of the self, went steadily hand in hand with courtship or love-making. Of this modern type of neurotic who holds a hand mirror to his face as he weeps or suffers love torments, Sainte-Beuve is one of the greatest models.

For example, he had a way of shocking and distressing the credulous Adèle Hugo by telling her that at moments his religious faith declined and he felt evil powers gaining over him. She, a pious Catholic, would respond with the pity he invited; she would become maternal and would preach to him. He would pretend to be consoled and uplifted. How cynically he managed all this he confessed many years later in his secret, posthumously printed journal, characteristically named by him "My Poisons":

I have done not a little Christian mythology in my time; it has all evaporated. For me it was like the swan of Leda, a means of getting at the fair lady and seizing a tenderer love. Youth has time on its hands, and uses all means to its ends.

Their friendship, Sainte-Beuve often assured Victor Hugo, was "a union of souls." But now it was fast becoming a union of three souls.

It continued in this manner with no overt tensions for more than three years. Sainte-Beuve devoted himself to a form of literary servitude for Hugo, writing articles expounding the meaning of his Preface to *Cromwell,* and in one case publishing such an article under his own name though it was actually written by Hugo. Hugo would go out and, coming back, find Sainte-Beuve in rapt conversation with Adèle. On more than one occasion they would own up that they had been talking of him. But he would join them, thinking nothing of it.

In the summer of 1829, Sainte-Beuve made a journey to England, hinting to one of his friends at the need to distract an unhappy heart by a voyage. In England he discovered the Lake Poets. They wrote of humble subjects; they loved nature and they loved God, as he reported in several absorbing letters to Hugo. He himself was *en route.* He wrote another little volume of poems, this time in the manner of Wordsworth, called *Les Consolations,* which was in effect a jargon of religiosity.

From England he writes to Adèle to tell her how he misses the happy domestic life that stems only from "my dear Victor and Mme. Victor." He continues mournfully, in the tone he ordinarily uses with her:

How mad it was of me to leave thus your hospitable hearth, the fecund and inspiring talk of Victor, and my two visits a day, of which one was for you. I am always troubled, because I am empty, I have no goal, no constancy, no work; my life is open to all the winds. . . . The only fixed points or solid frame for my mad *ennuis* and eternal divagations are you and Victor, your household, your home.

No, Madame, since leaving Paris, I have thought not once of Mlle. Cécile, nor of Mlle. Nini, nor anyone but my mother, and rather sadly (for certain reasons). I have thought of you as a consolation full of charm and good thoughts. . . .

His friends both reply to him kindly, as if he were the "sick brother." Victor Hugo assures him that since he has left there are no more good times at the rue Notre-Dame-des-Champs, no more *canapés,* no more *soirées* of conversation.

On his return, in the late autumn of 1829, the marriage of three souls was resumed on the old footing. Sainte-Beuve, who was sorely in need of steady literary work, was recommended by Hugo

to the *Revue de Paris,* where his first biographical and critical
studies, "Portraits of Women" and "Literary Portraits," now began
to appear regularly. In the summer of 1830, the Hugos' fifth child,
Adèle, was born, and Sainte-Beuve was invited to serve as her
godfather at her baptism.

A little later, Sainte-Beuve began to write his novel, *Volupté,*
and thenceforth the writing of the novel progressed more or less
in time with the drama of the three "friends."

In his foreword the author says:

Volupté is not precisely a novel: I have put all that I could of
observation and experience into it. I have painted true characters,
situations actually lived through: the souls described and exhibited
here in the nude were living souls. I knew them, I read them. Mme.
de Couaëns was no invention.

The hero, who writes in the first person, is Amaury, a spiritually
tormented young man who is bent upon becoming a religious
reformer. The friend at whose château he comes to stay is the
Marquis de Couaëns, a man of powerful attraction, energy, and
courage, who at the time is slowly preparing a great conspiracy to
overthrow Napoleon. Politics is his art. "Though our natures were
different, this energetic man was a large part of myself." But
Amaury, by stages, falls in love with Couaëns's wife, pictured as
dark-haired, dreamy, innocent, and mystical.

Amaury proceeds by little sighs and half hints to communicate
his feeling to Mme. de Couaëns. But she seems not to understand
his maneuvers; she is "naïve," almost without vanity, assumes
that he is simply using the exalted language of friendship, and
accepts his declarations as such. But one day, when her husband is
out, she ventures to show him a bundle of love letters exchanged
during her engagement with the marquis, though permitting him
to read only her husband's letters. He weeps over them; their
tears and emotions mingle, and, melting, they draw closer together than ever before.

The husband is much away, and Amaury on one occasion aids
Mme. de Couaëns when her child is sick. They practice their
devotions together, visiting churches and tombs and distributing
charity to the poor. Meanwhile he, by sly allusions, hazards some
bolder advances, which she rejects with a loyal simplicity or a
"calm wisdom." She does not conceal from herself that there is
a "portion of love" in this friendship, *"but her friendship has an*

air of purity and gravity from which she never departs." (Sainte-
Beuve is instinctively truthful here.) And then, *"tired of friendship without possession,"* as Sainte-Beuve phrases it in the novel,
and obeying "the imperious demands of the senses," the hero
returns to Paris, tries to forget the great lady he loves, and plunges
into a series of dissipations and vulgar affairs. Sainte-Beuve's own
procedure parallels this account closely, for in his leisure time, after
quitting the pure hearth of Mme. Hugo, he would leave off his
eternal sighing and pursue chambermaids and streetgirls relent-
lessly.

All would have gone smoothly as before, had it not been for
the tumult over *Hernani*. He who knew himself to be but a bookish
minor poet saw his friend, Victor Hugo, being exalted to the
heavens, escaping from his influence, and this pained him, for like
the parasite vine he longed to dominate the tree to which he clung.
He felt jealous of both of them. Even the dreamy Adèle now seemed
lost in the excitement of the battle, surrounded always by hosts of
strange, vulgar young men, who besieged her once quiet fireside.
He sat down and wrote off a bristling letter to Victor Hugo, on
February 20, 1830, a few days before the opening of *Hernani,*
conveying his urgent warnings that the poet ran dangers of com-
promising his "lyrical chastity" by immersing himself in all the
politics of the theater wings, busying himself with tactics rather
than art, and shaking hands with all sorts of low people. At the
same time, he acknowledges the fear that nothing he might say
to the poet would alter his view, "for minds like yours are unshakable, their vocation all marked out." But then in a postscript
feverishly written across the margin of the letter he ended with a
strange explosion:

And what of Madame? She whose name should not resound on your
lyre, except when men listen to your songs on their knees, she is now
exposed to profane eyes all day long, distributing tickets to over eighty
young men hardly known to her yesterday. That charming and chaste
familiarity, the true prize of friendship forever defiled by the mob;
the word devotion prostituted, the *useful* rated above everything;
ministerial combinations are carrying her away!

A most bizarre letter, full of an egoistic sentimentality that demands its rights and privileges in the "nest" and cries out its
jealousy.

Victor Hugo brushed aside his friend's warnings. Very firmly but kindly, as if dealing with a sick brother, he brought Sainte-Beuve around. At the *première* of *Hernani*, the young critic was obliged to sit up to a late hour, at Véfour's Café, near the Comédie-Française, expounding the beauties and hidden meanings of the play to a group of journalists, in short, helping them to write their review in time for the morning edition.

But the feverish accents of Sainte-Beuve's postscript may have served to open the husband's eyes a little, though he said nothing. In the spring of 1830, when the Hugos moved to the other side of Paris, to the house in the rue Jean-Goujon, near the Champs Elysées, they were situated a goodly carriage ride from the old quarters near the center of town, and Sainte-Beuve, this time, found himself unable to move after them. Nor was he encouraged to do so, for Victor Hugo felt that he needed a little more privacy. The younger friend's letters now became a prolonged lament at his loneliness. When he came to visit them one evening, he found the atmosphere chilly. Returning to his rooms, he sent to Victor the next morning, May 31, 1830, a letter full of reproaches, charging his friends with deserting him, comparing his own poor, unhappy lot to theirs, and calling upon everyone to pity him. But on the following day he sends a letter appealing for pardon and admitting that he had been tactless. He can no longer visit the Hugos so often, he says, but his heart's attachment to them will never change.

And yet how everything has changed! A few days later he makes the long trip by carriage across Paris, and the porter tells him that his friends are out, when, as he suspects, they are really at home! Victor Hugo, that very day, writes him: "And we were at home, dear friend—think of our disappointment!—we have stupid servants. Pay no attention to them and walk in the next time—next Sunday, then. You will dine with us, won't you?" Sainte-Beuve was wounded even by the terms of this note. They were making appointments with him now. He was no longer *chez lui*, no longer at home there, every day! His letters flowed with new tears, and to Adèle, quite openly, he remarks, while announcing plans to go abroad and take some university post in Belgium or Switzerland:

When I shall see you no longer, when I shall be lost somewhere hundreds of leagues distant from you without ever being able to write you, I shall none the less be the same in my heart, and the thought of you will be none the less my consolation, my good genius, my good deed.

2

So far the "friendship" of the author of "Literary Portraits" for Adèle Hugo had remained in that floating and undeclared condition which he analyzes so expertly in his novel. In effect he followed the tearful, romantic formula of love set forth in certain books he admired. So far there existed no sign or threat of one of the greatest mystery-scandals known to scholars of French literary history. What Sainte-Beuve's motives were in precipitating a crisis, he himself could scarcely explain afterward. In his old age he confessed to a young confidant, Emile Zola, that he had simply tried every possible kind of intellectual experiment or emotional stimulant. "To all these interior conflicts and contradictions," he said, "I defy anyone but myself to find the key."

Not a little of Sainte-Beuve's interest in Adèle Hugo, at least at the beginning, came from her proximity to a rising man and hence, to great events in the world of letters or perhaps public affairs.

Sainte-Beuve formed the habit of attaching himself particularly to women who could give him intimate news of the great men whose lives they shared. He paid court to Mme. Hortense Allart, the last muse of the aging Chateaubriand; ditto to the Marquise de Castries, because of her affair with Balzac; and to Louise Colet, because she knew so much about the mighty Victor Cousin. "Sainte-Beuve, in criticism, operates like the police in criminal investigation; he seeks the woman in the case. With delight he ferrets out the weaknesses of his contemporaries as if they served to excuse his own." Thus one of his most indulgent biographers, Léon Séché, explained him.

In the first volume of his *Causeries de Lundi,* Sainte-Beuve himself wrote later, apropos of the memoirs of Mme. d'Housset: "When the destiny of a nation lies in the bedroom of a mistress, the best place for the historian is in the closet."

We must always remember that, like many literary men, whose passions are compromised by their creative will, he was not only experiencing emotion, but was engaged, Narcissuslike, in watching the experience and "making literature" out of it. With this in mind, the behavior of Sainte-Beuve is more easily understood.

He had never yet, in his life, won the affection of a good woman. Ugly though he was, he felt himself made for love, made to enjoy all the *tremolo* of the human heart. Like his imagined Joseph Delorme he "longed for some success." And now that he had aroused a certain sympathy in Adèle, and believed that he could bring his assumed influence or ascendancy over her to a more decisive stage, Sainte-Beuve had suddenly felt a spasm of jealousy because she saw eighty young men who were strangers to her. The pangs of jealousy now convinced him that he must surely be in love, and his suffering increased.

To his friend, Victor Pavie, he wrote on September 17, 1830:

Well! pray for me and care for me, my friend: for I suffer terribly in my soul. All the poetry of me repelled, all my love without issue embitters itself and devours me. *I have become bad again.* Oh, when one is hated, how quickly one becomes wicked! But I am not hated, and at any rate worry little over those who hate me. But my evil and my crime is *not being loved* as I would like to be loved. There is the secret of my mad existence, without suite, without order, without work for the future. Since childhood, I dreamed only of one happiness, love; and I have not obtained it, nor even felt it fully. . . .

This letter, at this date, September, 1830, marks his disappointment, and gives no news of his having recently fallen upon some good fortune or having seized for himself the favors of some generous beauty.

Part of his suffering flows from the fact that he has resolved now to abstain from seeing the Hugos. In the summer of 1830, he goes to Rouen, to visit with his friend Pavie for a long time, and returning to Paris avoids Victor Hugo, who, he learns, is working steadfastly at his novel.

But suddenly, while keeping his distance, he struck two blows, one at Adèle, one at Victor. In the *Globe,* that summer, he published a brilliant biographical study of Diderot, with an account of his love affair with Mlle. Voland, later included in his series of *Causeries de Lundi.* To show the eloquence and skill Diderot devoted to the verbal expression of his passion, he cited one of his letters to Mlle. Voland:

In my heart, I raised a statue to you which I would never demolish. . . . With you, I feel, I listen, regard, caress, I lead the sort of existence that I prefer to all others. . . . It is four years since you appeared beautiful to me; today I find you more beautiful still, magic of constancy.

It was four years since Sainte-Beuve had first seen Adèle Hugo. (Because of this coincidence certain literary detectives in France have marked this essay as a secret message to Mme. Hugo.) Sainte-Beuve comments:

The love of Diderot for Mlle. Voland was one of those loves of the summer of life, profound, ripe, irremediable, which require only some obstacles in order to grow stormy. But the storms never burst forth, because the obstacles were almost nil.

From these remarks it has also been deduced that Mme. Hugo raised almost no obstacles to Sainte-Beuve's suit. But, whatever his intention, Adèle read little, and almost no literary criticism. Her husband read this piece, and if he had had any reason for suspicion, jealous man that he was, would have taken it as an open offense. But nothing came of it.

Then Sainte-Beuve, on the occasion of a new edition of his first poems, *Joseph Delorme,* in the autumn of 1830, wrote another piece in the *Globe,* an unsigned review of his own book. Here he airs a sudden disillusionment with the whole romantic movement, by pretending to disapprove of the book he himself had written only two years earlier, in 1828, under the influence of Hugo, and by recommending that it would be better for the poet nowadays to go over to the socialists, that is, to the Saint-Simonian or utopian socialists.

This Joseph, who consumed himself without faith, without beliefs, without action, this sick individual who followed his little path far from society and men . . . [found] the romantic association formulated under the Bourbon Restoration too restricted in itself, too far removed from the deeper movements of society. The Cenacle itself was nothing but a salon. . . .
Doubtless, at a certain stage of his career, he had come to cherish friendships and recognize God . . . but with him it was only domestic friendship and almost mystical religion. . . . He would have done better to proceed from that to the understanding and the love of progressive humanity and to a practical communion of the individual soul with God revealing Himself in humanity.

Thus the eternal dilettante seemed to signalize his desertion of the romantic camp—knowing that Victor Hugo would recognize the hand that wrote the anonymous piece, and feel the blow at himself. Adèle too would be shocked at his sudden turn from Catholicism to utopian socialism. But Hugo wrote him in terms that were magnanimous and affectionate, on November 4, 1830:

I have just read your article on yourself and wept over it. Pray, my friend, I beg you, do not abandon yourself so. Think of your friends, above all of him who writes to you these lines. . . . You know that your happiness poisoned poisons his own, because he feels the need of seeing you happy. Do not be discouraged. Do not spurn that which makes you great, your genius, your life, your virtue. Remember that you belong to us, that there are two hearts to whom you are the most constant and cherished concern.

Your best friend,

V.

Come and see us.

It was a warm letter, and thus far innocent of any knowledge of the cause of Sainte-Beuve's "despair." The critic later declared that Victor Hugo, whom he called a "crafty Frank," still needed to "use" him. Yet Sainte-Beuve had made a successful debut as the moon that followed Hugo in his bold orbit. The poet, who had enjoyed his qualities as a friend, continued to treat him with a patient forbearance, a serene and confident generosity, much longer than was warranted.

Sainte-Beuve continued to absent himself from the Hugo table. At length, one day in late November, or one of the first days of December, Victor Hugo, greatly concerned, came to look for him and pressed him for an explanation of his estrangement. Then Sainte-Beuve unburdened himself.

In a torrent of words, begging his friend's forgiveness, he confessed that it was Adèle, of whose beauty of soul and person he had been all too sensible; it was Adèle and his "guilty passion" for her that were the cause of his mysterious distress. Thus he could no longer come to see her "with impunity," and, for the time being, for the sake of their peace, he was determined to absent himself from their home. As to continuing his friendship for Victor, the "inconvenience" of his feeling for Adèle barred that. In all fairness, out of his very friendship for Victor Hugo, Charles-Augustin Sainte-Beuve must sacrifice himself, creep away to live alone in poverty with his sorrowing heart that was as a broken lute, with his memories and his despair. (Such were the terms in which an identical interview between Amaury and the Marquis de Couaëns is described in the novel *Volupté*.)

To Hugo this unexpected admission came as a hard blow. At this moment Sainte-Beuve was the only friend, of some time back, with whom he permitted himself, in his present position as a public figure, the relaxation of full confidence and intimacy. He saw the field of literature as a war, in which they fought together. Having climbed to a certain eminence, he was so made that he must press on for greater power and greater glory. He saw exhilarating campaigns before them, designed to burst in the doors of the Academy, to win over large newspapers, to dominate the theater, to place the whole republic of letters under the rule of romanticism, perhaps even the nation itself. And Sainte-Beuve, though unpromising as an imaginative writer, was rising to be a critic of mark, a strong ally. Identifying himself with a Cause, like all conquering men, Hugo felt that personal frailties must be held in balance.

It was not easy, for he felt that his friendship and his love for his wife—very jealous and possessive—was attainted.

Yet he recovered himself. He was the stronger one, generous and confident, determined to go forward on the path he had marked for himself, treating the evil or weakness that showed itself in others around him with indifference, ignoring even dangers that threatened. There need be no question of "choosing" between one and the other. He would manage; he would manage them both.

According to an account by Gustave Simon, who talked with him intimately in his old age, Hugo said to his friend: "It does not matter; it's all an illusion, impossible; do not change your habits; come to us as before." According to the account in *Volupté*, as reflected by Sainte-Beuve, Couaëns spoke to Amaury with a brusque good nature that removed all embarrassment:

"My dear Amaury," he said, at once, "I thank you for your cordial confidence. I had already thought of some such inconveniences as you indicate, but was not sure in my mind. You must consult yourself and not me. But do not begin to torment yourself, I beg you, over a situation that is fairly simple, that is guaranteed by the good and loyal sentiments of all parties concerned. Often men create troubles by dint of brooding upon them and fearing them, as one crushes a fine, full fruit, in the effort to learn what is inside. . . . I tell you that yesterday I counted on your early and constant appearance among us, and that today I count on it no less."

I was too ill at ease, too moved by the tenderness of the strong man, to say much in reply, I feared to raise my eyes and surprise a flush on his severe and chaste cheek. I shook his hand murmuring only that I placed myself under his orders, and we changed the subject.

In effect, the stronger man appealed to the younger and weaker to make a manly effort to master himself and keep everybody happy, and the other, like a sick child, promised to do all that was asked of him. A period of probation began. But unquestionably a certain reserve, a certain wariness, entered thereafter into Victor's manner.

3

In one sense Victor Hugo was the victim of his own literature. The new moral experiments and doctrines, the romantic philosophy implicit in his writings, held that passion was holy. Love had its mysterious and sacred laws to which all must bow. If a sinful courtesan, a Marion de Lorme, was equal to pure, self-sacrificing love, why not a poor young literary critic? How could Hugo condemn his poor friend?

Where the eighteenth century had regarded the sex impulse in a comic, sprightly, or candid spirit, the romantic nineteenth century held it as the passion divine, which neither worldly interests nor conventions must resist. There were many "trials" of love. Thus a George Sand alternated between the arms of an Alfred de Musset or a Chopin, as the lightning moved her. Prince Herzen, the romantic Russian revolutionist of the era, had his famous "family of three"; and the Hugos had their Sainte-Beuve.

They took him back on trial—it was tacitly understood—disturbed, yet not a little fascinated by his transports. Victor Hugo by his patient manner showed that he had no fear of losing that which he had possessed so fully. As for Adèle, there is reason to believe that, though she was vexed by him at times, she felt a genuine affection for the younger man. In her heart she could not hate him for his attentions, his raptures, his fits of spleen over her.

But the trial failed at once. A few days after the day when the two men reached their understanding, Sainte-Beuve came to dinner and stayed the evening. It was dreadful and glacial. Sainte-Beuve, the next morning, wrote Hugo one of his "wild" letters, declaring that the coldness and suspicion the other man was unable to hide had put him in a state to commit murder.

[December 7, 1830]

MY FRIEND:
I can bear it no longer; if you knew how my days and nights were passed and to what contradictory passions I am prey, you would pity me who have offended you. . . . There is despair in me, even, I dare say, rage; the longing to kill you, to assassinate you!—forgive these horrible impulses, but think of this, oh you who are given to so much

thought, think of the dreadful void which such friendship leaves—
What! lost forever?—I cannot come to see you sir? I shall not cross
your threshold? Impossible; yet it is so. And it is not because of my
indifference. Never, I beg you also to pray Mme. Hugo, never pro-
nounce the word *inconstancy* with regard to me.

He had sought in these two friends a friendship beyond earthly
love, and he felt in Victor now a veiled scorn and hate.

What then would I be doing at your home, *when I have merited
your mistrust, when suspicion steals in betwixt us, when your surveillance is persistent and when Madame Hugo cannot meet my regard
without consulting yours?* . . . You had the kindness to beg me to
come always as in the past; but on your part it was but compassion
and indulgence for a weakness that you thought to appease by this
mark of attention; I cannot go on with this; I should feel too much
torture, if you should feel even the slightest disquiet. That friendship
which was my cult is killed forever, and it remains for us only to
inter it with what piety we can muster.

Sainte-Beuve was tragic; Hugo's reply, on December 8, 1830,
was nearly so:

. . . Let us not inter our friendship; let us preserve it chaste and
whole, as it has always been. Let us be indulgent to one another, my
friend. I have my sore, you have yours; the painful upheaval will
pass. Time will heal all the scars; let us hope that some day we shall
find in all this only reasons the more to care for each other. My wife
has read your letter. Come and see me often. Write me always.
Remember that *after all* you have no better friend than I.

They did not see each other so often; they wrote at longer intervals. There is no doubt that Sainte-Beuve was tormented because
he willed to be so; he was determined to suffer for want of Adèle, to
whom he, like Diderot, "erected a statue he would not break."

Meanwhile Victor Hugo, who had no desire to be unhappy,
who moved forward so steadily, whose home had been so tranquil
and secure, suddenly felt the very foundations of his life shake
under him. His own emotions, once aroused, less febrile than a
Sainte-Beuve's, were fiercer and deeper. At this period the admission was torn from him: "I am no longer happy"—and it gave
Sainte-Beuve a deep, secret pleasure. Hugo faced a dilemma, he
was being forced to a choice that he had never asked for.

He had never doubted his wife; now the demon of suspicion
was roused in him, and the lion roared with pain. He suspected her

at least of some indiscretion in giving the other man room for encouragement—though she contended that she had done no wrong even in this regard. Nevertheless, the wounding thought would stay with him that she, at moments, could have entertained a weakness for the other man. At intervals Victor Hugo made honest efforts to conquer his own dark doubts, to hold both his wife and to hold his friend. He continued to play the calm, strong man in the situation. But heavily his gaze followed them about, puzzled, troubled; he "spied" upon them, as Sainte-Beuve wrote in his secret volume of poems, *Le Livre d'amour*. This, in turn, made Adèle unhappy. A poem addressed to her by Victor Hugo, dated as early as June, 1830, showed that he had noticed her moods:

> *Oh why do you hide? Why do you weep alone?*
> *Before your dreaming eyes what dark thoughts pass?*
> *What shadow floats within your soul?*

It happened that at this time also Adèle was weak and ill for many months after her last accouchement, and resisted his advances. In his distress, during the winter of 1831, he flung himself into his work, locked himself up day and night with his long historical romance, *Notre-Dame de Paris,* living with Quasimodo, the hunchback, and Esmeralda, the dancer, and Frollo, the alchemist.

4

He was late with the novel, and it became necessary to win from Gosselin, the publisher, a further reprieve for the execution of that dire clause that made Hugo liable to a penalty of 1,000 francs ($200) for each week's delay. Almost half of it had been written before July, 1830. Amid the wild street fighting of the July Revolution he had lost a whole section of the novel; then, to his delight, found it again and resumed his work. The private turmoil over Sainte-Beuve also did no good. Yet no matter how he felt, or what revolutions political or domestic engulfed him, he knew how to balance himself, concentrate anew upon his writing and carry on to the end.

The idea of *Notre-Dame de Paris* went back to his youth, his enthusiasm for Gothic art, and his association with Charles Nodier, who had charge of all the old armour in the ancient Arsenal. Climbing all over the ancient cathedral of Notre-Dame, investigating its structure, inspecting its stone carvings, and studying the ancient

books in the adjacent cloister library, he conceived the framework
of his rather satanic tale. Like Matthew Lewis, English author of
"The Monk," a "horror novel" much read in France, like Luther,
and like Dante, Victor Hugo became deeply absorbed in Lucifer
during his readings in medievalism. A long period of war, like that
of 1792–1815, has almost invariably been followed by one which
turns to contemplate not only God and His mysteries, but, by
antithesis, Satan, as well, and his dark works.

Hugo's accuracy and scholarship have been brought into question. Yet the old books he read on fifteenth-century Paris, by
Comynes, Jean de Troyes, and the later Sauval, with their exact
contemporary chronicles, were the best he might have chosen in
the 1820's. Ernest Feydau, the distinguished French archaeologist,
has declared that, compared with the work of the antiquarian
Sauval, which he borrowed from, or any other chronicler, Hugo's
romance pictured the life and atmosphere of the late fifteenth
century with remarkable clarity and fullness. From the old chronicles he drew French names of ancient flavor: Lewis's "monk"
must certainly have suggested the satanic alchemist, Archdeacon
Claude Frollo; the hunchback, Quasimodo, the cathedral bell
ringer, he drew from his own boyhood memories of Spain where
there was a deaf-mute hunchback porter in the seminary he attended; the gipsy girl, Esmeralda, her goat, and the cavalier,
Phébus de Chateaupers, were not difficult to invent. The character of the cathedral he absorbed, as he studied it stone by stone—
carvings, statuary, and gargoyles—sometimes in the company of
Deveria and the sculptor David d'Angers.

His larger purpose, aside from writing a diverting romance, was,
as he explained in the Preface to *Cromwell,* to picture—in contrast
with the seventeenth- or eighteenth-century classicists, who wrote
of pagan times—the little understood Christian eras, with their
saints and martyrs, their sorcerers and necromancers, their cathedrals and gargoyles, their heroism, their faith, their torture. In
effect, Victor Hugo clung to this plan for fifty years, for he returned to it in the epic *Légende des siècles,* written in the autumn
of his life.

Notre-Dame de Paris became the first great historical romance
in French literature. Before this, others had written garbled historical narrations: his friend Vigny had done one of Richelieu in
Cinq Mars (1826), and Prosper Mérimée had done something in
1829 on Charles IX. But no one reads these any more, whereas

Hugo's romance, despite its intellectual limitations, is so inherently dramatic—in this sense an advance technically over previous works in the field—it is so colorful and atmospheric in its descriptions, and even in its digressions, that it is still read in twenty languages, and, thanks to its crude representation some years ago in motion-picture form, has assumed almost a legendary character.

The story is, very simply, that of the infatuation of the alchemist, the amorous priest Frollo, for the gipsy singer Esmeralda, whom he attempts to kidnap through the agency of his devoted servant Quasimodo, the hunchback bell ringer of Notre-Dame. An officer of the Guards, Captain Phébus, rescues the girl from the hunchback and has him punished. Esmeralda falls in love with her savior, Phébus. But Frollo, spying upon their rendezvous, stabs Phébus and flees, so that she is accused of murder and sorcery, tried in splendid medieval style, and condemned to death. Before her ill-fated rendezvous with the officer, Esmeralda, in chancing to pass through the Place de Grêve had seen Quasimodo being lashed at the stake and pilloried, and in pity had given him water. Afterward, the poor monster, seeing her taken to be hung, with his supernatural strength seizes her from the hands of the guards and carries her to his towering belfry atop the great cathedral, where she finds asylum from arrest. There he faithfully guards her from all harm, including the attentions of Frollo.

The wild rabble of the Thieves' Quarter, in a sudden nocturnal uprising, tries to sack the cathedral and rescue Esmeralda, who had been identified with their band. Heroically Quasimodo, single-handed, defends the cathedral by hurling stones and weights from its roof upon them, until the Guards come and rout the rabble. In the confusion of this climactic scene, Archdeacon Frollo, however, makes off with the girl, and, failing to have his will of her, turns her over to the authorities. She goes to her death, in which she and Quasimodo are violently joined.

This fairly tall tale serves but as a frame within which Hugo hangs his immense, teeming, strongly-colored canvas of old Paris in the time of François Villon, with its thieves' dens, nobles, guilds, masques, holidays, and witch trials. Hugo is "an eye," and appears most effective in his large descriptions; the word painting of the city scene, viewed from the cathedral belfry in all its labyrinthine detail, makes up one of the book's many digressions—this, of nearly a hundred pages, like a smaller picture within a larger one—and is done with such intensity of feeling, such verve and abandon, that it seems today more interesting than his two-dimensional characters and their destinies. These are for the most part silhouettes rather than full portraits, save for the grotesque hunchback Quasimodo and the briefly-glimpsed, ill-favored King Louis XI. In his early period, Victor Hugo, like the other romantics, failed in the realization of character in detail. The characters in *Notre-Dame de Paris* he evidently regarded as symbols of Beauty or Evil; the cathedral was as a symbol of the age and its faith that broods over the whole drama.

The account of the nocturnal attack on the cathedral by the army of thieves, as a high point, has rightly been judged one of the great passages in the literature of the picturesque. He is eloquent also in achieving, by the use of technical detail (more or less accurate), effects of the grotesque and the satanic. His searching study of Quasimodo in all his ugliness and suffering and the coolness with which he dwells upon scenes of flagellation or torture also suggest a somewhat sadistic strain in him. Hugo's critics promptly remarked that his book was in no sense the work of a pious Christian writer. The social-minded Liberals as well as the literary Conservatives of the period reproached him for his apparent absorption in the merely picturesque and supernatural. Yet the book had a certain objective power, a sustained dramatic force, that created enchantment in its time and even today, by an overturn of taste, causes it to be greatly favored again, by the literary surrealistes.

The French novel had languished somewhat, in the late eighteenth and early nineteenth century—when mostly an ill-concealed and sentimental kind of autobiography was being produced. Not since Chateaubriand's rather vague romances, a quarter of a century before, had so much color and style been lavished upon a work of prose fiction—for Balzac's early work was in poor taste. The literary success of *Notre-Dame de Paris,* after it appeared in April, 1831, was so marked that a fashion was set which Alexandre Dumas soon began to exploit very profitably, and after him Gautier and even Flaubert likewise, though with more literary quality. The unity of action which Hugo achieved also gave new prestige to the novel form in France and stimulated his contemporaries, even a Balzac.

Owing to the revolutionary street fighting that flared up in 1831 and the depression of trade that year, Hugo's book did not sell widely at the start, but after a time its vogue spread until it was read all over Europe and America. When, many years later, Hugo journeyed to England, people who recognized him examined his back curiously to see if he had a hump!

5

On March 13, 1831, Victor Hugo wrote to Sainte-Beuve that his *Notre-Dame de Paris* was soon to be issued and told of how keenly he looked forward to his friend's criticism. They had often talked of the book, almost worked over it together. But Sainte-Beuve replied that, for various reasons, it would be impossible for him to do a review of the book in the *Globe*. It was strange that the young man who later became the most authoritative literary critic of his century in France refused to review *Notre-Dame de Paris*, was unjust to Balzac, attacked Alfred de Vigny (who was his friend), and ridiculed Stendhal.

He enjoyed playing the traitor to friends, as he did to ideas. According to Léon Séché, an amused and tolerant chronicler of his moral enormities, Sainte-Beuve constantly spread trouble between old friends like Hugo and Vigny; he spurned the romantic writers and joined the Saint-Simonian socialists, only to abandon these for the Catholics; but soon he managed to quarrel with the rather saintly old Abbé de Lammenais; finally, as an enthusiast of Pascal and the Jansenists, he wrote his *famous* tribute to them in *Port-Royal*, yet sincere Catholics held his faith to be spurious. A political radical in his youth, he wound up in middle age as a willing servant of the government of the Second Empire, against which the noblest characters of his own literary generation turned in revolt. But in 1831 he began his long series of betrayals by refusing support to his closest friend, the author of *Notre-Dame de Paris*, whose wife he was trying to seduce. In addition to throwing this pail of cold water at him, he deliberately precipitated a quarrel with Hugo, for he was weary of the game he had been playing, which had so little repaid his passion.

Hugo, he now said, had shown himself wanting in "confidence and frankness," while pretending to take a noble stand; he had, in fact, relegated him, Sainte-Beuve, to "an exterior place" in his life, yet selfishly sought his critical support.[1]

---

[1] In 1834, writing in his *Cahiers* (notebooks), published long afterward, Sainte-Beuve plainly refers to Hugo in describing a certain "gross man": ". . . He has absolutely no feeling for moral nuances. . . . If you praise him less, if you are silent, after having given him the greatest pledges, he says heavily: 'You are my

Hugo was so angered now that, as he says, he waited several days before daring to reply.

I could not believe, I must say to you, that that which passed between us, *that which is known to us two alone in the world,* could ever be forgotten, above all, by you, by the Sainte-Beuve I had known. . . . Truly you have changed much! You ought to recall, if your new friends have not effaced in you even the shadow of the image of the old one, you ought to recall to yourself *that which passed between us on the most painful occasion of my life, in a moment when I had to choose between her and you!* recall to yourself what you said, what I offered you, and what I proposed to you, you know, with the firm resolution of keeping my promise and doing as you wished; remember that and think of how you have just written me that I have been wanting in abandon, confidence, frankness! . . . For the present, I forgive you. A time will come perhaps when you will not pardon yourself.

Always, in spite of you, your friend,

V.

From this letter, some commentators have construed that a dramatic compact was drawn between the two men in their understanding of December 4, 1830, when Sainte-Beuve made his confession of "guilty passion." By this theory, Hugo would seem to have left it to Adèle to choose between the other man and himself. In the manuscript letter, which comes from the papers of Sainte-Beuve, the phrases, "that which is known to us two alone," and "to choose between her and you," are underlined by the hand of the critic, who adds in the margin: "False—he prevailed over her, while attributing to me things I had not said. . . . He lied to me at that very time and played me false—hence years of secret duel between us."

But, in truth, Victor Hugo never offered to give up his wife to the other man. It was hardly like him. One assumes rather that in the interview between them in December, 1830, Sainte-Beuve exclaimed in effect: "You will hate me, you will desert me, because I have told the truth about my feeling for her!" And Hugo had pledged that he would forgive, that he would preserve his attitude of friendship as before, in the hope of bringing his friend

enemy. . . .' If he wants to obtain a service of you which appeals to his *amour-propre,* the gross man is ready to introduce into the conversation even the name of his wife, knowing that you are a little amorous of her. . . . And when he unites a sort of genius to a vast pride, he becomes insatiable for praise. If you served him up a huge, thick slice every morning . . . he would soon have digested it, and by evening, half yawning, he would be asking you for more."

to himself. He had refused to make the choice between "her" and Sainte-Beuve. But was it possible to keep things as before? Therein lay Hugo's error.

Sainte-Beuve, after some delay, answered Hugo with a canting letter in which he ends once more with an abject plea for pardon. At heart he continues to believe, as his secret journals show, that Hugo is utterly insincere, refusing to credit him with any nobility of character, such as Hugo, as a high-minded romantic, really tried to show him.

The poet bore the rebuff to his beautiful novel, hastened to go and see the erring brother and pardon him.

They met more rarely, in the winter of 1831, at dinners in restaurants, in the company of other friends, though they continued to correspond with each other.

Two years later, at a moment when their relations had deteriorated even further, Victor Hugo himself tried to explain his long forbearance to Sainte-Beuve in accents that are simple and sincere. He wrote, on August 22, 1833:

You understand my nature very little, Sainte-Beuve. You have always believed that I live by my mind alone, and yet I live through the heart. I have need of love and friendship. . . . There, for better or worse, is the secret of my life, private and public. Hence more than one capital error of judgment, by you, of me.

Two days later, he added:

Do you not think that I too have suffered in the last two years? You have misunderstood in me a certain exterior calm. I need to love you and know that I am loved in return. *That has become a part of my life.*

Hugo was simply one who clung all his life long to his possessions, his wife, his children. He also clung to his friends and to the cult of romantic friendship.

In the spring of 1831, Sainte-Beuve worked at his brief biography of Hugo, the "great poet of twenty-nine," as he called him, completing the first version of the essay as it appears in his *Portraits contemporains*. In the summer of 1831, he visited friends in Belgium, was offered the chair of literature at the University of Liège, and reported to the Hugos that he had decided to accept it. This seemed like good news to them, for they were wearied of his exactions, and Hugo urged him on to Belgium. On July 1, 1831, Victor writes him from *Les Roches,* where the family is visiting with the Bertins, that they are enjoying themselves, that Adèle has recovered from a recent illness and is "gay, delighted, wonderful and well." He bids Sainte-Beuve not to forget to "write us from Liège."

At this message of too-evident satisfaction over his departure, Sainte-Beuve somersaults. Adèle's reported gaiety is too much for him. He decides not to go to Liège; he will not leave Paris. And he gives various lame reasons for his change of heart.

This was almost the last straw. Victor Hugo now answered him with a long and sorrowful letter. He expressed his disappointment at his friend's decision not to leave Paris, and declared roundly that he could not bear the thought of Sainte-Beuve living near him and prolonging an impossible situation. He concluded:

. . . This three months' trial of a half-intimacy, ill resumed and badly patched up, has not succeeded. . . . It is a torture. We are no longer free with one another, you see! We are no longer the two brothers we were. I do not hold you and you do not hold me, there is something between us. It is a terrible thing to feel when we are together in the same room. . . . Two hundred leagues apart, one would figure that it is the two hundred leagues that separate us. That is why I told you to leave.

Do you not understand all this, Sainte-Beuve? Where is our confidence, our mutual unfolding, our freedom to come and go, our endless causerie without afterthought? All is torture with me now. *The very obligation, which is imposed upon me by a person whom I must not name here, of being always present when you are there,* tells me incessantly and cruelly that we are not the friends of other times.

Let us then cease to see each other, believe me, for some time further, so that we may not cease to care for each other. Has your wound healed? . . . I know that mine has not. Each time I see you it bleeds. You must find at times that I am no longer the same. It is because I suffer with you now, which irritates me, against myself, and above all, against you, my poor and ever dear friend, and finally against another person, whose wish is probably the one I express in this letter. . . .

Let us cease then to see each other, in order to meet again, as soon as possible, and be reunited for life. . . . We will write, won't we? . . . Adieu,

Your friend, your brother,
VICTOR

I have shown this letter to the one person who ought to read it before you.

That was a dismissal, in very plain, but moving words, which no one could misconstrue. And Sainte-Beuve submitted to the order. The friendship between the first poet and the foremost critic of France had received its death blow.

6

Yet Sainte-Beuve would not have been himself if he had not tried to drag out the process of rupture with Victor Hugo by maintaining a continuous correspondence for some time after the death of their friendship. In this he reproaches Hugo for his unfounded jealousy, warns him of "chimeras," and denies having sought to return to his former intimacy "with a certain person," though she remains still the object of his "invincible affection." Meanwhile, he shows an unholy pleasure in provoking Victor into confessions of unhappiness, which no one had been able to wring from him hitherto. This even leads him to indulge in some hypocritically tender words of consolation. His letter is almost kind.

The new note of kindness touches Victor Hugo's heart, and without further reflection, on the same day that he receives the other's letter, July 7, 1831, he dashes off an impassioned communication:

. . . You are right in everything you say, your conduct has been honest, you have harmed no one. . . . It was all in my poor, unfortunate head, my friend! I love you more than ever at this moment, and hate myself, hate myself to the point of being sick or mad. The day when you need my life you may have it and it will be but a small sacrifice. For, you see, and I say this to you *alone,* I am no longer happy. I have acquired the certainty *that it was possible that that which had all my love ceased to love me* and that this could have meant very little to you! However, I try to tell myself all that you tell me—that this thought itself is madness—it is still the drop of poison that is enough to poison my whole life. Yes, pity me; I am truly unhappy. I no longer know where I stand with the two beings whom I love most in this world. You are one of them. Pity me, love me, write me.

Here are already three months that I suffer worse than ever. To see you in such a state would simply stir up all those fatal ideas. . . .

The usually serene Victor Hugo seems all at sea, while Sainte-Beuve seems all the more delighted. He begs his friend not to afflict that "dear and delicate person" with dark, unjust suspicions whose very violence may help to turn her heart against him. He hints that the leonine Victor is perhaps not always gentle enough with her. For this uninvited advice on domestic tactics, Victor Hugo thanks him politely, but, though they exchange letters, there is no thought of meeting again on an intimate footing.

Outwardly, so far as the world knew, they remained friends. Privately, Sainte-Beuve babbled everywhere of the wrongs done him and the madness of the poet. To Fontaney, who was filling up his "Romantic Diary: 1831–1837" with all sorts of tidbits, Sainte-Beuve described Hugo as a "wretch," saying, in effect: "He had made himself jealous, and through pride, and that is why his wife is sick!" There was nothing but granite and iron in the man's soul. As for the poor Sainte-Beuve, "he loved truly, and so was sequestered . . . recalled and banished again. Adèle was locked up, and Hugo and Sainte-Beuve see each other no more; if they did there would be bloodshed. . . ."

Sainte-Beuve was no ordinary knave. It was scarcely nice of him to try to take his friend's wife; but to speak to him about it continually was plainly a literary vice of his own invention.

He pretended to pray. The fragments of letters to Adèle, written by him (that is, copies) and found among his papers, reveal that he hopes to become purified by suffering and recommends the same to her. He addresses her in highly polished phrases:

. . . Love in me is . . . somber, mingling with the nuances of twilight in the churches we frequent. . . . My love has never known that robe of youth and grace and illusion. . . . As to a happiness crowned with pleasure, I have always believed little of that was intended for us poor mortals on earth.

But suddenly there would appear to be a change in his situation. To one of his new clerical friends, the Abbé Barbe, he wrote December 18, 1831:

. . . I have suffered much these last months. The passion which I had only half-glimpsed and desired, I have felt; it has endured; remained fixed. And that has filled my life with many necessities, hours of bitterness mingled with sweetness, and a duty of sacrifice, which has its good effect, but which costs one's nature dearly.[2]

[2]This note, found among Sainte-Beuve's papers, has led more than one prying scholar to deduce that in some manner Sainte-Beuve's long pursuit of Mme. Hugo was blessed with success. The late Louis Barthou, who held the largest collection of Hugo and Sainte-Beuve papers, assumed from this letter and some other signs that the critic's love earned certain "satisfactions."

At the same time he exchanges certain confidences, indeed he boasts of his conquest to certain of his friends. Ulric Guttinguer, one of the minor romantic writers of the Hugo circle, who was highly excited over an affair of his own, addresses Sainte-Beuve a brutally direct question, as early as February 18, 1832. Later, on August 11, 1832, he questions him again: "Tell me where you are at, please, and if nothing has changed in the great obsession of your life?" And on December 31, 1832, Guttinguer sends him good wishes and warnings: "May your happiness be preserved, my dear friend; but try not to jeopardize a future of genius, such as we await for you."

From such scraps of "evidence," and from the intendedly tell-tale volume of love poems by Sainte-Beuve addressed to Adèle Hugo, *Le Livre d'amour,* secretly printed in 1843, Barthou and other commentators have deduced and built up the thesis of Adèle's "complete fall" as occurring some time in 1831 or 1832. Most of this supposition is based on Sainte-Beuve's imaginative writings, and upon letters found among his private papers, all *copies* in his own hand of letters he may have written to her.[3]

For a long time the legend circulated about Paris that Sainte-Beuve used to visit Mme. Hugo in the absence of her husband, who was once more deeply engaged in the theater. According to this, he would come in, wearing a woman's clothing and a veil, and was once stopped and recognized by the concierge—a tale that might very well have been manufactured by Sainte-Beuve himself.

Sainte-Beuve in his later life did a good deal of boasting of his prowess in love intrigues, though Paris laughed at him and believed him unlucky in love. He invariably pursued blue-stockings and literary *grandes dames* and wrote them interminable letters. Most of these later friendships were with women of superior and virtuous character, like the widowed Mme. d'Arbouville and the brilliant Mme. Juste Olivier (who was happily married), and these usually, in a rather maternal way, tried to "improve" his character, while no gossip ever attached to them. Meanwhile his own home, presided over by a perpetually drunken housekeeper, was, according to eyewitness accounts, like a "disorderly house."

It is true that in 1831–1833, Sainte-Beuve by good behavior induced the Hugos to receive him again at their home. The system of "banishments and recalls" continued again. But, when

[3]See also Appendix Note II, for a further discussion of this episode.

he was in a phase of banishment, evidence shows that on two or three occasions Adèle Hugo went to see him secretly. This is admitted by Gustave Simon, friend of the Hugos in their late years, who wrote a very fair account of the whole case, arguing, however, that there was "but a partial fault" on Mme. Hugo's part— her only fault—in seeing Sainte-Beuve without her husband's knowledge on these two or three occasions.

Adèle was distinctly the maternal type of woman, to whom the brilliant rascal all his life appealed for sympathy, and who first tried to "improve" him. Very plainly it was her strong-willed husband and not she who usually decided upon the banishment of Sainte-Beuve. On occasion she thought Victor unjust. She was notoriously a charitable soul, and Sainte-Beuve held her if only through pity. For many years, even in her old age, as existing letters of hers show, she strove to bring about a reconciliation between the two men, though in vain.

But that she, with her very gentle, innocent, and somewhat indolent nature, should have betrayed her husband, who loved her still, jeopardized the future of her growing children, to whom she was most fervently devoted, and thrown herself at the head of the wretched little Sainte-Beuve seems far out of her character. A woman of towering passion might possibly have done this. But at this period, while Sainte-Beuve was winking his boasts to friends, she was ill, weak, and in pain.

In the autumn of 1831, confined to her bed, she is unable to accompany Victor on a visit to friends in the country and writes him news of her health, in very affectionate terms: "I was in great pain last night. The house is so sad when the master is not here, the very soul of the place seems missing." It was her very want of vitality—despite the dark, brunette cast of her beauty— that now brought a deep trouble to Victor Hugo, robust male, in the very prime of his young manhood.

Meanwhile, Sainte-Beuve in 1832 wrote a sequence of poems celebrating his love affair with Adèle. Its "secret history," as he hinted to more than one confidant, was to be revealed in the *Livre d'amour*, which alludes, by little suggestions, to a *satisfied* love and a mutual guilt. Some of these he published in various reviews, in 1832 and 1833, though without addressing them to anyone; most of them he kept in his closet. A passage in one of these, number XVI in the sequence, has even given rise to vague suspicions that the youngest child of the Hugos, Adèle, to whom Sainte-Beuve was godfather, may have been more than his goddaughter.

It is addressed *A la petite Ad——* ("To the Little Adèle," presumably) and draws a contrast between the youngest child and the elder daughter, Léopoldine, who completely resembles her father.

Adèle, or "Dédé," as she was called, also bore a striking resemblance to her father when she grew up.

> *Or toi, venue après, et quand pâlit la flamme,*
> *Quand ta mère à son tour, déployant sa belle âme,*
> *Tempérait dans son sein les fureurs du lion,*
> *Quand moi-même apparu sur un vague rayon,*
> *Comme un astre plus doux aux heures avancées,*
> *Je nageais chaque soir en ses tièdes pensées,*
> *Or toi, venue alors, Enfant—toi je te vois*
> *Pure et tenant pourtant quelque chose de moi!*

He pictures the mother now using all her soul to "temper in his breast the furors of the lion" (Victor), while he, the other poet, appears to her "as a softer star" and "swam each night in her tepid thoughts." Thus, according to his most secret revelations he *merely swims in her thoughts* while her "lion" takes her in his arms. And in this wise the other daughter came of their rites, *"nevertheless having something of me."* It is, of course, a metaphysical conceit; Sainte-Beuve was but present in Adèle's thoughts, he says. But other allusions are bolder still, as in XV:

> *Qui suis-je, et qu'ai-je fait pour être aimé de toi,*
> *Pour être tant aimé, pour avoir de ta foi*
> *Des gages si secrets, de si grands témoignages?*

Who was he, how did he deserve to be so loved by her, and to have such "secret pledges," such "great testimonials," of this love? In this poem also (dated August 12, 1832), he represents her further as pressing the brow of her friend "against her knees with her convulsive hands and her lips in his hair . . ." while murmuring the "tenderest avowals." This poem was published in 1832, though without dedication and with the concealment of "shadowed blue eyes" attributed to the lady. But in his manuscript, found among his private papers, Sainte-Beuve expressly indicates as instructions to his executors that the poem is to "A. H." And still other thinly-written verses describe secret trysts, carriage rides together around Paris at dusk, visits to churches where both lovers join in prayer, then hold sad colloquy in a churchyard. He thought it was all pretty strong stuff, and was determined to publish it one day, if not for its noble truths, then *because he had written it*.

In the early spring of 1833, he was absorbed in his series of little libels in verse when suddenly the tremendous news came to him that Victor—he, the chaste and virtuous one—was deep in the toils of a sinful Phryné of the theater. Victor abandoning his good "Madonna" and lost in a frenzied passion for another, a baser woman! It was one of the Great Events of 1833, and all Paris talked of it. Soon Sainte-Beuve, in a gloating mood, was spreading the news as fast and far as he could. Balzac, hearing of it, wrote to his Madame Hanska, so that it was known from Warsaw to London.

For Adèle Hugo, a life of unwonted loneliness, one in which she must share her rights, after so much wedded happiness and oneness, now began. She sat by her window brooding. But Sainte-Beuve, with indecent haste, renewed his suit, feeling that the road would now be conveniently clear.

According to a fragment among his papers, he wrote to her May 15, 1833:

I was saying to myself yesterday: how all that was beautiful, flourishing and blooming some years ago has fallen! . . . Hugo, the author of *Son Nom* and *A toi,* at the feet of a Juliette . . . all our poets sunken, our angels fallen! Oh, only we, my Adèle, have followed and accomplished our destiny strictly. Let us hold each other close, dear angel, and love each other unto death!—I love you!

But, not satisfied with trying to win the wife of his friend for himself, he began to attack his friend's books openly in the press, reversing his whole critical position as the exponent of the romantic school. In the *Revue de Deux Mondes,* of which he was a contributing editor, he reviewed a recently published essay by Victor Hugo on Mirabeau as a study in genius, damning it with faint praise while implying that in passing over or pardoning Mirabeau's moral frailties, because he "ended with greatness," Hugo himself now showed a certain lack of moral fiber and assumed wrongly that all things might be pardoned in a "predestined genius." These sermons coming from the perfidious critic were highly offensive and once more increased the strain between the two former friends.

Victor Hugo wrote a letter chiding him for failing to use a little "benevolence" or sympathy in this article, as he had formerly done even in his sharpest criticisms. Sainte-Beuve answered with an insolent allusion to the poet's domestic sins. They had once spoken of Hugo's home as a sanctuary or a *temple*. "I have no temple, and scorn nobody," Sainte-Beuve said now. "You have a temple; try to avoid scandal in it."

Victor Hugo was furious at these words. He was in no state to be tampered with at this time, since he was in the grip of a grand infatuation, felt himself assailed by scandal, and lived in a continual storm. Yet, perceiving that Sainte-Beuve besieged his wife again with renewed attentions during his absence, he remained as jealous of her as ever. He was resolved to hold his unhappy wife by his side as well as the beautiful young woman whom he now openly, according to common report, entertained as his mistress. He gave Adèle strict orders that she was to see Sainte-Beuve no more. Then he struck hard, in a curt, cold, briefly worded note, in which he broke with Sainte-Beuve forever.

Tuesday evening, April 1, 1834

There are so many hatreds and cowardly persecutions to be borne nowadays by me, that I can well understand how friendships, even the most extended, may be denounced and broken off. Farewell then, my friend. Let us each, for his part, bury in silence that which is already dead in you and which your letter kills in me. Adieu.

V.

But worse was to come. In September, 1834, a new collection of Victor Hugo's most recent poems was published, entitled *Les Chants du crépuscule* ("Songs of Twilight"). Sainte-Beuve, who had refused to speak of *Notre-Dame de Paris,* reviewed it at length and took occasion to point out to the public, as if with the knowledge of a favored friend, those poems which were addressed to Adèle, the virtuous spouse, and those poems of "adulterous love," which were addressed to the new mistress, declaring that the author showed a grievous want of taste in including these contrasting groups of lyrics in the same volume.

The twelve or thirteen elegiac poems of love which form the center of the collection in its truest, most sincere, part, are followed by two or three others, notably a last poem, entitled *Date Lilia,* intended, in some sort, to crown the volume and protect it. . . . This mythology of *angels* following after those of *nymphs* . . . seems to us to depart from a just sentiment of domestic poetry that good taste would have dictated. . . . The unity of the volume suffers from this [discrepancy]. It is as if the author sought to throw a handful of lilies in our eyes. He did not see that . . . a certain respected person would have been better honored and praised by an entire omission of her.

Possibly Hugo showed a want of taste or propriety in publishing poems to his mistress, followed with the *Date Lilia,* the elegy which celebrates his wife, though it is a strange and magnificent lyric. Moreover, it was sincere, for he was one of those men—they are not rare—who are equal to loving another woman and also a wife at the same time. But that Sainte-Beuve of all persons should reproach him was a piece of monstrous hypocrisy.

Even the tolerant Adèle was offended by certain indelicate allusions in the article, which were a betrayal of confidences and also advertised her domestic misfortune. But Victor Hugo—who heard that Sainte-Beuve was gossiping about his "shameful conduct" with the "other woman"—sent a second with his card to the critic.

Sainte-Beuve now showed considerable distress of soul. He came one morning to his bookseller, Renduel, still jesting feebly, but with an ashen face, and deposited for safekeeping a package of his manuscripts and his last testament and will to be opened in case Victor Hugo killed him. Renduel accepted the charge gravely, but remarked: "Is a duel possible between you, between *two poets?*" At this Sainte-Beuve cheered up a little and went off smiling.

Adèle, who was frantic with fear, moved heaven and earth to stop the duel, and other influential intermediaries aided her, so that no poets' blood was shed. The terror of those few days in the spring of 1834 was enough to keep Sainte-Beuve at a goodly distance from the unhappy woman thereafter. However, in his waspish soul, in secret, he devised and wrought a long-planned vengeance. He wrote the verses of *Le Livre d'amour,* set the book aside, whispered about it, but kept it always hanging over Hugo's head. Eventually he arranged (in 1843) to print it and circulate it privately at his own expense, knowing fondly that it would be the cause of a high scandal in the literary world, but unaware that scholars for a hundred years after would not only dispute its veracity, but would debate endlessly and pruriently over his dubious motives in publishing *Le Livre d'amour,* the so-called, badly written

"Book of Love."[4] Why, they would ask, if he had every reason, as he claimed here, to be grateful to a woman for the supreme favors she bestowed upon him, must he expose her to scandal? Why the need for vengeance? Exhibitionism? *Dementia litteraria?* The mad desire that none of his written words must perish? "To raise a monument to our great love . . ." he declared, in prefatory words, was his purpose. The boulevards, at the time the book was being passed about stealthily, were frankly skeptical. "Sainte-Beuve: why play the Don Juan, when nature destined you for literary glory, but not at all to be a Lovelace!" was an admonition uttered in 1843 by the witty journalist Arsène Houssaye. Others were repelled by his perfidy, but thought him his own worst enemy.

To defend his case before posterity, the artful scholar, inveterate searcher of historical and private papers of the dead, carefully sorted and classified all his papers and letters, and left instructions for their publication after his death. He had, in a spiritual sense, lived off Hugo; he had made his nest in his friend's home; he had tried to steal his wife. Now he was determined to libel them both. Hugo knew that the libel would be forthcoming, and left some strong lines among his own posthumous papers, describing Sainte-Beuve unmistakably, and the viperish look he wore when Hugo finally ejected him from his house.

Meanwhile the submissive Adèle obeyed her resolute Victor and, while pardoning all *his* transgressions, saw and even wrote to Sainte-Beuve no more. How little she seems here a woman of storm, ready to leap into the thin arms of little Sainte-Beuve! For this final sign of her surrender, her sacrifice, before the dominant strength and will of the other man—and at a time when he might be said to have forfeited her loyalty—Sainte-Beuve never forgave her. Across the top of the bundle of his old letters to her, many years afterward, he wrote the words: *"I hate her."*

[4]The scholars probed and pried like detectives, until it became one of the farce-comedies of scholarship. They uncovered his numerous lies—for instance, the time factor: Sainte-Beuve's absence on a voyage to England and Germany, in 1829, made his ambiguous hints about the parentage of "Dédé" Hugo utterly groundless—he had not thought of that!

CHAPTER VII

The "Firebird": Juliette Drouet

Love, love, nothing but love, still more!
For, oh love's bow
Shoots buck and doe. . . .
These lovers cry—Oh! oh! they die!
Yet that which seems the wound to kill,
Doth turn oh! oh! to ha! ha! he!
—Shakespeare: *Troilus and Cressida*

By the autumn of 1832 Victor Hugo's literary career appeared to have reached its zenith, though, in reality, it was but in its first phase. Within the past twelve months he had published three different works, each showing undeniable mastery in its separate field. In that of the novel, his *Notre-Dame de Paris* was acknowledged the most colorful historical romance known so far to French literature. In poetry, his third collection, *Les Feuilles d'automne* ("Autumn Leaves"), was read with deep enjoyment by his public; it showed a very marked advance over his earlier work and contained poems of intimate reflection, of domestic love, of the family and children, some of them dating from 1828, most of them written in 1830 and 1831. Finally his *Marion de Lorme,* the freshest and most lyrical of his early poetic dramas, was, thanks to the revolution, released from the censorship in November, 1831, and produced with great success at the Porte Saint-Martin Theater, with Mlle. Mars starring in the role of the historic courtesan. The very scene which had led to the play's suppression by Charles X—the one satirizing his "poor ancestor" Louis XIII—contributed to its appeal, after the overturn of 1830, for a popular audience in a very different frame of mind.

Taking him to its favor, the "July Monarchy" of the "Citizen" Louis-Philippe d'Orléans, through a new Minister of the Interior, invited Victor Hugo to write a hymn (to be set to music) to the men who had fought and died during the recent civil struggle. His "Hymn to the Dead of July" was given a musical score by Herold and sung before the new King, his retinue, and a vast throng of people at ceremonies held at the Panthéon on the anniversary of the revolution.

Thus, by the age of thirty, he had served as the official poet of two very different regimes. His most pejorative biographer, Edmond Biré, a younger contemporary of his, remarks that at this early period of his life no rival's glory compared with his. Byron and Scott were dead, Goethe was soon to follow them, Lamartine had quit the field to enter politics; "Hugo gathered the heritage of our great poets, becoming henceforth the first, not only in France, but in Europe."

From all these successes, fruit of so much tireless industry, wealth flowed to him—though chiefly from the plays—the wealth of a great bourgeois. Between 1830 and 1833, three of Victor Hugo's plays were reported to have paid taxes of over 47,000 francs; his annual earnings in the 1830's and 1840's averaged about 70,000 francs.

In October, 1832, the Hugos moved again, to still larger quarters at number 6 Place Royale (now called the Place des Vosges).

The Place Royale is a truly noble quarter of old Paris; it was even then, in 1832, engulfed in a busy commercial district, with the historic landmarks of the Temple, the Bastille, the Hôtel de Ville (then the original old edifice), and the Louvre all within easy reach. It is built entirely in late Renaissance style, being composed of an arcaded row of square, pink-colored brick houses, enclosing a small park or garden. Here, on the site of the Tournelles Castle, destroyed in 1563 at the will of Catherine de' Medici, King Henry of Navarre had caused a handsome residential quarter to be constructed in 1605 for his courtiers. Done by the best Paris workmen, ornate with wrought-iron grilles and heraldic signs (which disappeared in successive insurrections), the graceful little square with its statue of Louis XIII, its fountain, and its flowering lime trees still clung to its proud character. It was haunted by the ghosts of the Rohans who defied Richelieu and Louis XIV, of Corneille who dwelt here, and of the original Marion de Lorme, "the foolish virgin," who also held court here in her own fashion. Here too, finally, the nineteenth century's Prince of Poets made his residence for the next fifteen years. It was the home with which his life in Paris was longest and most intimately associated, and was eventually turned into the Victor Hugo Museum by the local government. The house had a great vestibule, and on the first floor a large salon and dining room. Upstairs were five chambers facing the garden, in which a rococo, terra-cotta fountain splashed musically. The farthest removed, in the attic, its windows overlooking the old pointed roofs and chimneys of the square, was Victor Hugo's study. From this room a secret passageway, such as he had always enjoyed, led down to a side door and out through the garden into an alley, so that he could escape unseen whenever he wished.

The Place Royale home was filled with ancient but sumptuous pieces of furniture, old tapestries, statuary, and huge vases in tremendous profusion. As soon as he acquired a goodly store of money Victor Hugo became one of the most passionate collectors of antiquities in an age when their cost was still reasonable. His dining room was filled with old armour, Spanish coffers, and Renaissance sideboards. His salon held Louis XIV chairs, Louis XV sofas, and was decorated with ornate old mirrors and gigantic gilt chandeliers. This vast, high room was dominated by two large marble fireplaces facing each other across the house, and to the left of one of them was placed a broad divan, surmounted by a splendid canopy which was said to have belonged to Mme. de Maintenon. Immense draperies of red damask overhung the tall windows of the salon—hence it was called the Red Salon—and the window recesses were so deep that at least two persons might easily pass into them, through the curtains, and hold a tête-à-tête. The Red Salon was also a veritable gallery of paintings—Delacroix, Boulanger, Deveria, and others, having contributed freely to the decoration of the "Master's" home.

Here the world beat a path to the poet's door. Here the Hugos received, night after night, in a long series of notable parties, Victor Hugo always standing in a corner beside one of the fireplaces, near the divan, his manner affable yet having a certain formal courtesy, recalling that *vieille école,* the old aristocracy of *émigrés* amongst whom his mother had reared him. The famous

writers and artists of the day, the older and also the very young
ones, like Gautier and Banville, came to him; also men of the press
and of politics, even prelates and princes, and strangers from distant lands. But not only were these receptions enjoyed by his
friends and social acquaintances, but on fine nights, in the square
outside, the ordinary working people of the neighborhood, with a
sprinkling of aspiring young writers, would gather below the windows or stand under the trees whenever there would be a brilliant
festival at number 6 Place Royale. They would wait and watch,
for hours, hoping to be rewarded by the sight of the Prince of
Poets, with his pale face, great gleaming forehead, and long hair
brushed straight back, stepping to the window with one or two of
his apostles, looking out at the street or the sky, talking for a moment, then returning gravely to the salon.

During the prolonged crisis over Sainte-Beuve, Victor Hugo
had never ceased working. Now at the very height of success and
fashion, though passing rich—only ten years before he had been
living on two francs a day—he labored unremittingly, as if it were
his one solace in life and as if with contempt for the idleness or
physical indulgence of others around him. In 1832, instead of
building upon his success as a novelist, he turned to the theater
again, perhaps because he was persuaded by Crosnier, backer of
the popular Porte Saint-Martin, that greater returns could be won
in this field. For ten years he bound himself by contract to deliver
at least one play each year. The theater became his religion. The
romantic drama was to be henceforth a medium for the dissemina-
tion of liberal ideas. To his friend in Angers, Victor Pavie, he
wrote at this period:

The theater is a sort of church, humanity is a sort of religion.
Think it over, Pavie. There is either a great deal of impiety or much
piety in that thought; but I believe I am accomplishing a sort of
mission. . . .

Although he considered himself a moderate in politics, disapproving of "hotheads" at this time, especially those who talked in cafés
of guillotines to be raised up and the Terror to come, he himself
was one of the crowd idols of the 1830's.

To the revolutionary crowd of 1831 and 1832 he threw his
popular dramas, in which, as in *Marion de Lorme,* the kings or
the nobles of the earth were pictured in all their human frailty,
so that the audiences roared their approval, sang *La Carmagnole*

and the *Marseillaise,* and cheered Hugo to the echo. Meanwhile the new constitutional monarch was proving himself none too liberal by the severity with which he suppressed popular agitation for free suffrage, at the beginning of his regime. Disappointment gripped France; and the government was forced to fight hard against attempted street risings and plots to assassinate the King, one of which missed fire on November 18, 1832, three days before the opening of Hugo's new play *Le Roi s'amuse,* at the Théâtre-Français. In this violently romantic drama (now chiefly remembered as the libretto of Verdi's opera "Rigoletto"), a famous King of France, Francis I, is represented, pre-eminently, as a frequenter of low taverns and debaucher of pure young girls, among them the daughter of his own court jester, Triboulet, who plots to murder his royal master.

After two performances, before turbulent crowds who repeated the scenes at the opening of *Hernani,* the government ordered the play suppressed. Victor Hugo perceived that an Orléans was much like a Bourbon king, so far as freedom of the theater was concerned. He determined to bring an action-at-law against the directors of the state-owned theater, as a means of rousing public opinion. The famous barrister and parliamentarian Odilon Barrot and Armand Carrel, the republican leader, were his counsel; but he himself used the court as a forum and in his personal testimony made a powerful oration in behalf of freedom of speech, for which he was much complimented. Montalembert, the Liberal Catholic deputy, exclaimed to him when he was done: "Well, if the theater is closed to you, you will always be able to fall back upon the tribune."

The case, heard before the Tribunal de Commerce on December 19, 1832, was of course dismissed. Victor Hugo was soon at work upon an alternate, non-political play, *Lucrezia Borgia.*

Clad from top to bottom in a rough gray woolen sleeping garment, like a monk, he would often work at night, by an open window even in winter; then he would rise at dawn and resume working; the afternoons he would spend busying himself with the details of rehearsals.

A relative of his, Paul Chenay, declared that at this time "no woman existed for him save Adèle." At the theater it was noticed that he treated the actresses "exclusively from a professional point of view—none of their provocations or allurements had any effect on him."

Yet he was far from happy. The portrait lithograph of 1829,

by Deveria, had shown him with his head alert, upward glancing eyes, and a rather proud smile curving at the corners of his full lips. But, in 1832, an oil painting by Léon Noël shows him unsmiling, with fixed, shadowed eyes, his whole attitude one of painful tension. His smooth-shaven complexion, also, is extremely pale, almost a dead white, save for the blue tint given by his heavy beard, which, it was said, dulled the razors of barbers.

Fragments of his poems and allusions of Sainte-Beuve suggest that his enforced continence troubled him sorely; he slept little and grew paler. Doubts and suspicions concerning Adèle assailed him— his pride had certainly been wounded by the complaisant interest she had shown in Sainte-Beuve. He had described himself, hitherto, to Mlle. Louise Bertin, as "a tranquil and serious man," of robust appetite. But this was no longer true.

Despite his exterior calm, as he had confessed to Sainte-Beuve, he lived by his emotions; the craving for love, or friendship, was the secret of his life. A passage in one of his recent poems (from *Les Feuilles d'automne*) betrays the torment of flesh he tries to hide:

> *Si jamais vous n'avez, à l'heure où tout sommeille,*
> *Tandis qu'elle dormait, oublieuse et vermeille,*
> *Pleuré comme un enfant à force de souffrir*
> *Crié cent fois son nom du soir jusqu'à l'aurore,*
> *Et cru qu'elle viendrait en l'appellant encore*
> *Et maudit votre mère, et desiré mourir?*

While everybody slumbered—while *she* slept, forgetful, flushed— "you wept like a child, crying out her name a hundred times from night to dawn, believing still she would come, and calling her again, and cursing your mother, and wishing yourself dead."

Sainte-Beuve too, in one of his secret poems, dated 1837, points to the same hidden conflict in his friend:

> *Adèle! tendre agneau! que de luttes dans l'ombre,*
> *Quand ton lion jaloux, hors de lui, la voix sombre,*
> *Revenait usurpant sa place à ton coté,*
> *Redemandant son droit, sa part dans ta beauté,*
> *Et qu'en ses bras de fer, brisée, évanouie,*
> *Tu retrouvais toujours quelque ruse inouie*
> *Pour te garder fidèle au timide vainqueur*
> *Qui ne veut et n'aura rien de toi que ton coeur!*

Adèle, as the rival boasts with great indelicacy, "like a tender lamb," would be struggling in the iron arms of the "jealous lion," returning to demand "his rights, his part in your beauty." And though "broken and fainting . . . you found always some unheard-of ruse" permitting escape from these importunities! And all this for Sainte-Beuve's sake, he assures us.

2

The play Hugo completed in the autumn of 1832 was essentially a melodrama based on supposed episodes in the life of Lucrezia Borgia, which, happily, was passed by the censor. Soon he was busily absorbed in the work of casting and staging the play (work which always interested him) together with the manager of the Porte Saint-Martin Theater, Felix Harel. Mlle. George, popular dramatic star, still a great beauty, though she was old enough to have been Napoleon's mistress, was engaged to play the role of Lucrezia Borgia. There was another, much smaller, female part in this play, that of the young and seductive Princess Negroni, who, though she speaks only a few lines for a minute, conducts the gay banquet and drinking orgy at which the enemies of Lucrezia are drawn together, entertained, fascinated, and poisoned. It was a pivotal scene. For the climactic appearance of the Princess Negroni, Harel had chosen a young member of his troupe, professionally known as Mlle. Juliette, who, the year before, had won some slight stage success, largely owing to her attractive face and figure, it was said. At first she had made some objections to such a small part, but in the end agreed to accept it with good grace.

When the dramatist came down on the morning of January 3, 1833, to oversee, with M. Harel, the manager, the final selection of the cast, he had an interview with Mlle. Juliette in the manager's office. Afterward he recalled that he had already met her once before at a recent theater ball. She had worn a magnificent white costume, and was quite surrounded by a little crowd of admirers when he was brought forward and introduced to her; he had bowed and retreated without even speaking to her. But, he recalled

> Her black hair shining as with a thousand gems,
> Her eyes startling against her white face
> And perfect shoulders, her movements full of grace,
> All of her laughing ardor, gleaming fire—
> And men crowding round her to admire. . . .

Now she was before him, seeming almost unable to stand still, balancing herself restlessly upon her small feet, telling him in a breathless rush of her decision to accept the part offered her. "There can really be no small role in a play by M. Victor Hugo," she concluded handsomely.

He had always been rather formal and prudently distant with actresses. He was still almost timidly formal as he thanked her; but now a bell rang in his head. He was suddenly, painfully aware of the advantages, the dangerous batteries, so to speak, that this young woman carried about her person. She smiled, her eyes playing almost impertinently with his. And he looked down at his shoes. He realized that he was probably very unfashionable: his black frock coat and sober vest were five years out of date and rumpled; his trousers were firmly braced above the waist, but were turned in and fastened under the instep of his boots by a steel chain; his long bushy hair hung rebelliously over his brow. He seemed almost like a provincial bourgeois. Then the rehearsals began; she was boldly coquettish. The actor before her recited his lines: "Friendship does not fill the whole heart! . . ." And she answered: "Ah, what is it that fills the whole heart?" but turned her large dark eyes to the author, in his box beside the stage, instead of addressing herself to the actor before her. During the rehearsals that followed the young actress openly, but with considerable *esprit,* paid court to the poet. But he, according to the others present, would simply bow respectfully, kiss her hand as well as that of Mlle. George, and leave directly after the performance.

Victor Hugo, by now, had mastered the difficulties and limitations of writing for the stage. His new play was written in prose, making its romantic scaffolding appear all the more deliberate and transparent. But on the night of February 2, 1833, when the play opened, his gaudy melodrama of Lucrezia Borgia regaled a Parisian audience which now had a marked taste for romantic violence. Never were more extreme contrasts used by Hugo in his plays. It was a spectacle indeed: these splendid Italian youths, banqueting in the hall of the Princess Negroni at Ferrara, were seen eating and reveling, when suddenly the chant of monks was heard, the Latin plain song, and the Brothers of the Misericordia, their faces shadowed in their black hoods, marched by bearing the coffins that are soon to receive the guests' bodies. And the damask, brocaded in cloth of silver, her superb neck and arms Princess Negroni, in her sixteenth-century robe of rose-colored wreathed in ropes of pearls, moving across the stage with her light effortless tread, was a veritable temptress, holding her victims to the banquet table by the enchantment she wrought. To the audience also she was an enchanting apparition for a brief scene, and one that contributed greatly to the success of the evening.

After the third act, the leading lady, Mlle. George, covered her with kisses. The author too paid her his warmest compliments. Despite her small part, the dramatic reviewers in the newspapers duly noted the "arrival" of the young actress and celebrated her beauty. Théophile Gautier wrote of her:

She created, with so little time and so few words, a ravishing figure of a true Italian princess, with a gracious and deadly smile, with eyes full of perfidious intoxication; a visage fresh and rosy . . . so charming that one forgot to pity the unfortunate guests and thought them fortunate to die after kissing her hand.

Victor Hugo, the next day, in his study at the Place Royale, wrote in the preface to the published edition of the play a special tribute to her:

In Lucrezia Borgia, certain minor figures are represented at the Porte Saint-Martin by actors of the first order, who perform their obscure parts . . . with perfect grace, taste and loyalty. The author is grateful to them. Among these, the public was particularly charmed by Mlle. Juliette. It can scarcely be said that the Princess Negroni is a role, rather a sort of apparition; young, beautiful, poised, Mlle. Juliette cast an extraordinary glow over this figure. . . . Here is an actress who, given the opportunity, will emphatically reveal to the public a talent full of soul, passion and truth.

Victor Hugo looked out at the Henry IV fountain below him in the Place Royale and dreamed of the "Princess Negroni." He continued writing the fragments of notes found later in his unpublished journals:

How beautiful she is! What a figure, what superb shoulders, what a charming profile! What a charming actress, what a reserved and yet distinguished bearing! Her interpretations are so true, her emotions so deep! . . . Her voice and manner are somewhat like Mme. Dorval but what a difference in simplicity and soul!

Mlle. Juliette had understood fully the meaningful spirit in which the author had uttered his compliments behind the scenes in terms which, to her joy, were reproduced very soon afterward in

JULIETTE DROUET

By Léon Noël

book form. Several times in the next fortnight they met in the
dressing room of Mlle. George, and the leading lady, who knew
the way of the world, would slip out discreetly and leave them for
a tête-à-tête.

In the dusk of a late afternoon, on Sunday, February 17, 1833—
it was carnival night and a masked crowd was celebrating in the
streets—Mlle. Juliette stood waiting by the window of her apartment in the rue Saint-Denis. She was to go to an artists' ball with
him that night. At last she saw, below, the solid figure in severely
cut black frock coat and silk hat turn slowly from the adjacent
Boulevard du Temple toward her door.

He hesitated for a moment, debating with himself over things
he had heard of the lady. With her dresses, her luxury, her admirers she was a figure in the more fashionable resorts of the demi-
monde of actors and artists. The lady seemed disposed to be sweet
to him, but was she not weakly fond of others as well? How he mistrusted actresses, and hated the gossip of the wings! There were
rumors of a sculptor and a journalist, even a certain Russian prince
who ordered her splendid wardrobe. The street was a fashionable
one, the house she lived in elegant. He looked at the revelers hurrying by, wondered if they recognized him, then averted his glance.
There were aspects of the case that troubled him. What should he,
Victor Hugo, conscious of his mission, of a determined and la-
borious life, what should he be doing in that galley? Then, in his
mind's eye, he saw her, in his memory he heard her as she turned
toward him exclaiming in a voice like Mme. Dorval's, *"Mon dieu,
what is it that fills the whole heart?"* Abruptly he turned and entered the house. A little black page boy in livery opened the door,
ushered him into the rose-colored, perfumed salon.

The gallant Théophile Gautier, in an enterprising study called
Les Belles Femmes de Paris, done at this period, described her as
follows:

Mlle. Juliette's head is of a regular and delicate beauty. Her nose
is pure, well cut, and well profiled. Her eyes are limpid and sparkling;
her mouth is lively, moist and red, and it remains small, however gay
and mad her laughter. All these charming features are enclosed in the
soft and harmoniously oval contour of her face. Her brow clear and
serene . . . provides a luminous crown for her delicate face, while
her abundant, gleaming black hair brings out marvelously the diapha-
nous glow of her face.

Her throat, shoulders and arms have the perfection of antiquity and are worthy of inspiring our sculptors. They would have been admitted into the trial of beauty in which the women of Athens let fall their veils before Praxiteles meditating his Venus. . . .

But, despite Gautier's classical allusions to the Grecian models of Praxiteles, there was absolutely nothing "marmoreal" about Juliette. How lightly she came to greet him, moving with that "aerial" bodily grace which the theater critics had remarked. She was full of quick sallies. Her large dark eyes were never still, and yet they could be very gentle. Her face (as the portrait by Noël showed) was intelligent and warm.

He was before her, reverent, awkward. But, after a few seconds, there was nothing awkward about his words. His compliments were so extravagantly earnest, given with such an old-world courtesy, that she thought how odd was her great man, who was yet so young and so remarkably handsome.

Victor Hugo may have seemed all too proud to the men who were his contemporaries and complained that they must either always listen to him or talk to him of himself. But instinctively, with a sweeping gallantry, he abased his pride before women, and they learned to love him for this way he had of casting his considerable laurels at their feet. His formally good manners and urbanity pleased them too. For them he was as a "god," but the "god" took on humanity. However, as Louis Guimbaud, the biographer of Juliette, keenly said, they always remembered his romantic cult and, with intuitive wisdom, were careful to pose also as "goddesses" before him.

He was saying to her, in effect, that he would simply adopt her, make her his own; that he was ready to share his own glory with the youthful renown of *la Negroni*. For her he would conceive and create the most marvelous roles. She felt that she was walking on air.

It was Carnival Night. (He was to have accompanied her to some ball, which was why he had called for her at her apartment.) But they did not go anywhere that night. The little apartment was warmly silent while, outside, Paris laughed and sang, "and the revelers passed by under the windows with loud cries." The great carnival passed them by. In the morning, when he left her, it was cold and raw; rain fell in torrents, while the maskers thronged past him wearily, just leaving their parties, their costumes frowsy, their masks torn. Many of them were drunk; he too, though he had drunk nothing.

3

For days and weeks that spring Victor Hugo lived as in a trance. He who was usually so methodical and punctilious would come home late for dinner; so attentive and courteous, normally, he was absent-minded to his guests; then in the evening, while his drawing room was crowded with men and women who had come to pay their respects to him, to see and hear him, his eye would be upon the clock. He could not wait to be off to the rendezvous at the rue Saint-Denis.

For Juliette gave herself to him unreservedly, with an abandon, a forgetfulness of self, he had seen too little of, for many years, in his Adèle. From the outset she said to him: "I am good for nothing but to love you."

Every day Victor Hugo wrote her messages, letters, and even lyrics. At his demand, and sensing at once his love of the word and its evidence, she too scribbled notes to him, from wherever she was, at all hours, on the backs of envelopes or scraps of newspaper, sometimes two dozen in a day. They were the naïve, authentic expressions of a devouring passion, direct, unashamed, fiercely jealous, insatiably hungry for him when he was gone.

Sunday, 8:30 P.M.

. . . I must write you one line of love, my dear little mad one. I love you—do you understand, I love you! This is a profession of faith which comprises all my duty and integrity. I love you, *ergo,* I am faithful to you, I see only you, think only of you, speak only to you, touch only you, breathe you, desire you, dream of you; in a word I love you. . . .

Do not therefore give way to melancholy; permit yourself to be loved and to be happy. Fear nothing from me, never doubt me, and we shall be blessed beyond words.

I wait for you, with warm and tender caresses which I hope will cheer you.

Your JuJu

And he wrote her years afterward:

Do you remember, my love, our first night? It was Carnival night in February, 1833. . . . Nothing, not even death, I am sure, will blot that memory out of my mind. All the hours of that night make their way again through my thoughts while I write, like stars going out before the eyes of the soul. . . .

In the midst of the popular carnival, we stood apart and hid our own sweet festival in the shadows. Poor angel, what beauty and love there are in you! . . .

Never forget, my angel, that mysterious hour which changed your life. That night was a symbol, a figuration of the great and solemn things that went on within you. . . .

Then, in his transports, the poet wrote for her some admirable lyrics, some of which were withheld for posthumous publication—such as the one beginning,

> *Oh! si vous existez, mon ange, mon génie . . .*

which was dated March 10, 1833. One of her early letters, in a group under the year 1833, appears to be in reply to this last poem in which she figures as both "angel" and "genius"; she writes:

It is not quite six o'clock in the evening, and I have just finished copying the poem you gave me yesterday; I am not very familiar with the kind of compliments used in fine society. All that I can say at this point is that I wept and admired the poem when I heard you read it; that I wept and admired it in reading it over; that I wept and admired it in remembering it. I thank you with all my heart for having thought of me in writing it. . . .

These words have the accent of sincerity, simplicity, and a natural dignity. So do other phrases that spring up spontaneously in Mlle. Juliette's letters: "When I hold your arm, I am as proud of you as if I had made you myself." Or: "I suffer a delirium of love, more than my poor heart can contain. Come then and take the overflow of my ecstasy."

In this strange young woman of twenty-five Victor Hugo recognized a grace that was unfeigned. And, without wishing to reproach the poor, and now lonely, Adèle more than she deserves, we must note that nothing in all her many letters responds to the many magnificent poems he wrote to her with equal warmth and earnestness. A trained actress, Mlle. Juliette loved to recite his poems by herself or before him.

He, for his part, made no effort to conceal the happiness that had come to him. Soon he plunged into writing a new play, "Mary Tudor," with the leading part of the queen for the imperious Mlle. George, and the second lady, Jane, for Mlle. Juliette. For he was convinced that a remarkable future as an artist was before her, and he had but to write her roles. Thus to the joy of collaboration in love was added that of planning and working together for the theater. With rehearsals as an excuse, he now, contrary to his former custom, formed the habit of lunching out, with Mlle. Juliette. Then they would set off walking about Paris, and even out into the country; for Paris in those days was not the crowded metropolis of seven-story houses it now is. At the foot of Montmartre, there were real windmills whirling their arms just overhead along the Butte aux Cailles; there was a little brook, flowing among the lilacs and syringas; and, on the summit, young couples, dandies and grisettes, picnicked and actually danced in the green grass to the sound of fiddles.

In her short, striped, pleated skirt, tight at the waist but flowing out wide at the bottom, wearing a little silken cape and a pink bonnet trimmed with black ribbons, Juliette would go forth proudly on the arm of her "friend," her eyes sparkling and her little feet dancing with happiness so great, as she used to say, that they scarcely touched the ground.

Victor Hugo, no longer pale, now "spruced" up his appearance. On his excursions with Juliette he would wear a quite elegant blue coat opening over a shot silk waistcoat and immaculate linen. To his delight he found that Juliette loved the country and was thoroughly at home in it, sharing his delight in flowers, beasts, and birds. They went to Montmartre and near-by Meudon, to Fontainebleau, Versailles, and the Saint Germain forest. Sometimes they walked silently, Juliette waiting reverently while he composed verses in his mind.

One evening when they were dining together under an arbor in the suburbs, Juliette cried out that there was something in Victor's napkin which he must open up and see. He unfolded a piece of paper, on which she had managed to scribble, in strictly legal form—for unfortunately she already knew a good deal about debts and promissory notes—the following document:

I acknowledge the receipt from M. Victor Hugo of a great deal of love, a great deal of happiness, and a great deal of devotion, which I hereby agree to repay on sight.
Signed:

JULIETTE

Victor Hugo, at once assuming an air of great haste, summoned the waiter and ordered him to finish serving their meal quickly, as he had important business to transact.

Everyone saw them together; all Paris talked of the "arch-angel" who had rushed into the arms of an actress, and smiled or frowned over the story. His friend David d'Angers, the sculptor, records in a letter:

It is very seldom that one can find Hugo at home now; he only goes there at mealtimes. Poor Mme. Hugo! . . . How fatally a liaison of this sort changes what was gold into lead! Not content with the struggle of romanticism, he has desired also the excitement of life, and he has become entangled like another Laocoön. . . . But I hope that some day his noble heart will realize its fall, and then we shall have some magnificent pages of self-reproach and bitterness at the weakness of man. . . .

Victor Hugo, for his part, felt no pangs of self-reproach. To Victor Pavie he wrote impenitently in July, 1833:

No one understands me. . . . I have never committed more faults than this year, and I have never been a better man—far better now than in my time of innocence which you regret. Yes, formerly I was innocent; now I am indulgent. That is a great advance, God knows. I have beside me a dear friend—an angel whom you also venerate as I do, who pardons me and loves me still. To love and to forgive—this is not of Man, it is of God or of Woman.

Nor did everyone find it in his heart to condemn Hugo, nor for that matter George Sand, the handsome feminist, at this very moment deeply engaged in her love experiments with Alfred de Musset. In popular interest the romantic flight of this couple to Italy rivaled the scandal of Victor and his Juliette, and made 1833 a year of romantic revolution in love. "You are not to be weighed in the same balance as the majority of common mortals," George Sand assured her young poet.

Alfred Asseline, a first cousin of Adèle Hugo, in his book of inti-mate recollections, reflected the attitude of Victor Hugo's family and circle when he remarked:

Conjugal fidelity, essentially a bourgeois virtue, has always been painfully difficult for poets to practice.

In the present state of our morals, it is admissible that superior men have the privilege of imposing upon what we call society . . . a friend —a female friend—the woman whom it has pleased them to choose as the veiled witness of their labors, who, legitimate or not, remains discreetly in the shadows beside the genius.

And Adèle?—Victor himself had brought her the news; she par-doned him, and they wept together.

She had resolved that it was owing to his genius that he should be free to "use other women," as Paul Chenay, a member of her family circle related. For there had been to some extent a "suppression of her husband's rights." And had he not been faithful eleven, nay, fifteen years, including their engagement? She said to Chenay, "Perhaps I had some reproaches to make to myself, or was wanting in submission?" Hitherto she had not always seemed a clever woman. But from now on, in her grief—for she was left alone a great deal of the time—she showed a true nobility of character.

She told her husband that most of all she wanted him to be happy. She wrote him, one day, in a letter that long remained unpublished: "I will never insist on the rights which marriage gives me over you. It is my idea that you should be as free as if you were a bachelor." She too was romantic; she submitted, she sacrificed herself. This submission was adjudged in later years by some literary detectives as the sign of a guilty conscience, rather than of her delicate health. Sainte-Beuve, however, by his statements after 1833 shows more than ever the bitterness of a disappointed suitor. He continues to make insinuations in public, but in private his reflections are full of anger at Adèle for her submission to her husband and her "credulity."

Adèle, with much dignity, continued as the *de jure* queen of Victor Hugo's household, remaining at the head of his table, living for her growing children, watching over his and their interests. Outwardly nothing was changed, which was what he most fervently wanted. Meanwhile he assured her that he "would always love her, though differently."

Besides, who knew if the affair would last? M. Foucher, her canny old father, became concerned at the rumors he heard. On June 27, 1833, he wrote to his sister, Mme. Asseline:

You know, about that woman, the lovely woman of the Porte Saint-Martin Theater . . . the "Princess Negroni." Is Adèle still worried about this? What is the state of the Princess's conversion? I should be glad to hear that the liaison that was going on when I left town had come to an end, and to my daughter's satisfaction. . . .

Then investigations were made, and the old man seemed pleased:

Many thanks for your information about the Princess Negroni. I am very relieved that Adèle is calm and that her conduct is still the same.

But the information received—unfavorable no doubt—was quite misleading.

4

Her real name was not Juliette Drouet, as she was now called, but Julienne-Josephine Gauvain. She was born on April 10, 1806, in the picturesque seacoast town of Fougères, in Brittany, the child of a poor tailor. When she was a few months old her mother died, and a year later her father. She was adopted by an uncle, Lieutenant René Drouet, a disabled veteran of the Grande Armée who had been given quiet employment as a coast guard.

She grew up, a pretty but badly spoiled little vixen, living with an indulgent old soldier and his companions, playing truant from the village school, swimming in the sea, dressed in rags and tatters.

When she was ten, Drouet, who had given her his name, decided that something must be done about her education and to relieve him of his responsibility. Through relations of his who were nuns, he succeeded in placing her in a school attached to a great convent in Paris, that of the Bernardine-Benedictine Sisters of Perpetual Adoration. It was the gloomy, padlocked institution of dark corridors and bare cells and fearful religious austerities later described in *Les Misérables*. Julienne received a strictly religious education and grew up under the sternest discipline. But she was also taught to write, to sing, and to paint in water colors. Certain *grandes dames* of pre-Revolution days, who had long ago retired from the great world, befriended her, and from them she acquired a certain distinction of manner and expression that was in curious contrast, at times, with the military vernacular and sailors' lingo she also used.

They had a saying at the convent, when a little girl was brought to them: "She is plain—she will be a nun." Julienne was as incorrigible as she was pretty. One day, as a grown girl, lying in penance on the pavement of a cloister, she wrote in chalk the confession: "Father, I accuse myself of being an adulteress. Father, I accuse myself of having stared at a man."

When she was sixteen, by an appeal to the Archbishop of Paris, she obtained consent to leave the convent. Thereafter all track of the girl was lost for three years. She disappeared as if into the depths of wild folly, or perhaps abandonment, hunger, and suffering, a period of which she would never speak. Then in 1825 she turned up again, at nineteen, as the model and the pupil of James Pradier, the fashionable sculptor who filled Paris and other

European cities with his imitation classical monuments, in many of which the fine head and firm figure of Julienne are still to be recognized. A pretentious *viveur,* he of course made her his mistress, though he was already endowed with a wife and children. In 1826, a child was born to her and named Claire. But soon Pradier, finding support of her burdensome, urged her to study acting, for which she had shown some talent, and sent her to friends connected with the Royal Theater at Brussels, while their child was boarded in Paris. Thereafter he would send her a little money, but more often sermons and homilies. By Felix Harel, the theatrical manager and political conspirator, then exiled in Belgium, she was given small parts to play, and he reported a successful debut. "Is this not a great pleasure?" Pradier wrote her. "How sweet is the bread one has earned *honorably!*"

After the July Revolution in 1830, she returned to Paris with Harel's troupe and appeared in several plays at the Porte Saint-Martin, under the name of Mlle. Juliette—"la belle Juliette," as she was called in theatrical papers, in 1831, though there was some division among the critics on the merits of her acting.

By 1832, her contract was fixed at only six thousand francs a year, but she lived in grand style—not with Pradier—but at first with Sechan, a poor, but talented scene designer, who showed himself a worthy fellow; then with Alphonse Karr, a young journalist who was destined for a considerable success as a light, cynical popular novelist and *raconteur.* In those early days, Karr had no scruples about calling Juliette Drouet his "dear wife," promising her marriage, and borrowing from her on the strength of this substantial sums of money which were never repaid. He continued to borrow from her after she had left him and passed under the protection of a Russian millionaire, Prince Demidoff, who established her in luxurious quarters in the rue Saint Denis. In Paris, the furnishers and the modistes credited her with specializing in distinguished foreigners; she became a popular figure, known for her free spending, but also for her generosity to her friends of the bohemian demi-monde. She was carefree, spirituelle, radiant, yet sometimes also nervous and sad. Save perhaps for young Sechan, the scene painter, she had never known the love of a good man. And now she had found her "king of poets"! There was something unspoilt, frank, and forthright in Juliette when she said, as she finished narrating her life to Victor: "Well, I am a daughter of the people!"

5

Her story moved him. Some of it he told later in those chapters of *Les Misérables* devoted to "Fantine" and "Cosette." His own life had been formerly a rather respectable and almost insulated affair, and much of what he had written was inspired by books he read or by historic events. But with Juliette he drew closer to life itself, to earthly beauty, and soon, as he realized, to a veritable grand passion. He was undergoing a sea change, whose effects were soon to be seen in a gradual alteration of his attitude toward many questions, a change of his interests, even his subjects.

Juliette had a genuine taste for literature, or for language—this was undoubtedly one of her attractions for the young lord of language beside her—and at an early date in their liaison she required of Victor that he write in a *livre de l'anniversaire,* a sort of daily journal she kept, poems especially addressed to her, on the occasion of the old and the new year, and regularly such thoughts, epigrams, or reflections as came to him after a night of love. Quite sincerely, he wrote her many a lavish tribute, some of them the most unaffected things he ever did. Juliette's *livre de l'anniversaire* became a faithful record of progress in love; it marked also the change in his attitude at this period. Among the first reflections are the following:

Your caresses make me love the earth; your glances make me understand the heavens.

The greatest happiness of life is love. That is why, when I look at you, my Juliette, I so often have at once a smile upon my lips and a tear in my eye.

When you look upon me, I would fill my soul with the sweet thoughts that I see in your eyes.

I prefer a smile of yours to all the canticles. I prefer love to religion. I prefer a kiss to a prayer. God only fills the soul, a woman fills the heart!

These reflections, a little godless at that, are vastly different from those of the author of *Odes et Ballades,* the "savagely pure" young man of 1820. Similarly with the poems that henceforth, so many of them, celebrate earthly love, of the type of *Tristesse d'Olympio,* written under the inspiration of the firebird of the Porte Saint-Martin Theater.

Also dating from this period were those impious reflections of Hugo's found in the posthumous "Post Scriptum to My Life":

How strange that after eighteen centuries of progress, the freedom of thought is proclaimed, the freedom of the heart is denied.

Yet to love is no less great a right of man than to think.

Adultery is nothing other than heresy. If freedom of conscience has the right to exist anywhere, it must be in matters of love.

Yet at the same time the poet wrote in his Juliette's book also in more transcendent terms:

At night, you are sleeping; I am awake; dream of me; I am thinking of you.

In this book are to be entered all the varying days of the season, by the month, the week, the day. But in my heart they are not different. What fills them is your name, your thought, your image, your presence, your absence. On this first day of the year, I shall write that I love you, on the last day of the year, that I adore you.

To be hated by base hearts, to be loved by a good heart, makes for a complete life. Do not fear hate if you have love.

If you could read in my mind, you would see that I love you; if you could read my soul you would see that I love you; if you could read in my heart, you would see that I love you. To my mind you are charming, to my soul you are heavenly, to my heart you are good. There is in you a woman whose feet I kiss, and an angel whose wings I kiss.

Beauty you have, intelligence too, and a good heart. If society had treated you as nature has, you would be highly placed indeed. Only do not mourn; society could not have made you more than a queen, but nature has made you a goddess.

In these long-hidden pages of Juliette's golden book (never divulged until the collector, Louis Barthou, opened them some eighty years later), there is shown a progression, a growth in Victor Hugo's passion. His attachment for Juliette Drouet becomes steadily sublimated.

It was not long before he realized that, in an undertaking begun light-mindedly with a young woman of easy morals, he had become all too heavily engaged. He was a prisoner. Even to Juliette it was a surprise. She had known pleasure; she had not been accustomed to such "Spanish" ways. He said to her: "If ever love was complete, profound, tender, burning, inexhaustible, infinite, it is mine."

From the *livre de l'anniversaire* one perceives at once that the course of their love did not run smooth. Juliette had certain habits; persons recognized her, smiled at her in a certain way. And all at once her king of poets, her King Toto as she called him, would go livid with jealousy.

Formerly he had tormented his fiancée, Adèle, because she permitted the wind to blow her dress above her ankles. But now, thinking of Juliette's past and of the gossip he still heard of Russian or Hungarian boyars who "kept" her, and full of dark suspicion, he would at first visit reproaches upon her. Then, doubting that she could be true to him—though she swore that she had severed all connections with her Russian prince—like some Othello, he would groan and rave and torment Juliette with a devouring, bitter jealousy the like of which she had never seen. She had longed for the love of some great, good man. It flattered her and it frightened her at the same time.

"You have been very cruel to me," she would reproach him stormily. "I swear I never saw those men. I am innocent of any crime. I can say no more."

But the picture of her past life rose before him; the prude in him suffered at association with a woman who had been perhaps no better than a soiled Magdalen, as he would have said. There were things she did not explain clearly—anxieties, "business affairs" that distracted her, which she concealed. Perhaps she was but devilishly cunning, like the others, he would reflect, and black anger would flow from his vehement nature.

There was trouble between them at the very beginning. The very difficulties into which Juliette was plunged at once derived from her resolve to be strictly faithful to him, cutting off all her former patrons and so losing their considerable financial support. Paris, alive with gossip about Juliette Drouet before 1833, never had any definite accusations against her after that date.

In June, 1833, she swore to him: "God is my witness, I have never once deceived you in these four months." It was four months since Mardi Gras. But he refused to believe her, or quarreled with her, and, as she wrote, "crushed" her by his references to her past life. She ran off to the country, leaving him a note: "I beg you not to attempt to see me again." But at his call she returned; they were happy, and they soon quarreled again.

In September, 1833, she wrote him: "I have been faithful to you for seven months." She inveighed against him for his "outrageous and unjust jealousy," which she said created "a wall a hundred feet high" between them.

They loved and they tormented each other. At two o'clock one morning she wrote him a tear-stained letter:

2 A.M.

I look up to you . . . as the noblest and most estimable of men.

It hurts me to feel that my past life must be an obstacle to your confidence. Before I cared for you, I felt no shame for it, I made no attempt to conceal or alter it; but since I have known you, this attitude of mine has changed in every respect. I blush for myself and fear lest my love have not the strength to erase the stains of the past. I fear it even more when you suspect me unjustly.

My Victor, it is for your love to sanctify me, for your esteem to renew in me all that was once good and pure. . . . I will become worthy of you if you will only help me. Farewell. You are my soul; my life, my religion.

Victor Hugo was her religion!

In the midst of this passionate experience, the Christian idea of redemption came to Victor Hugo. Like Marion de Lorme, the courtesan who had known only pleasure, Juliette would be redeemed by a great all-consuming love. "How true that play was!" Juliette exclaimed. For him she soon became a figure of repentance. She who was more Catholic than he, by training, abased herself before him—perhaps that is not always good for a man, but he seemed to demand it. She humiliated herself, and begged him to "purify" her.

Seriously, after the summer of 1833, she studied her role of Jane in "Mary Tudor," Hugo's new play. Miss Jane, it must be noted, is the young English girl who is betrothed to a workingman—but is treacherously seduced by one of Queen Mary's courtiers. Thereafter she goes about with "head lowered"; repentantly she begs her humble fiancé's pardon, promising him either to die for him or to live virtuously—as he wishes; and he pardons her. Such was the new part written by Victor Hugo for his Juliette Drouet (the "converted" Princess Negroni).

But she too was not without jealousy.

One day, at Juliette's wish, with his family away in the country, Victor Hugo brought her to his home in the Place Royale, only a few minutes' walk from her apartment in the rue Saint Denis. She studied the rooms, where he lived and worked. "It was so charming of you to allow me to come to your house," she said thoughtfully. She returned dejected, tearful, realizing "more than ever the depth of the chasm between your life and mine. It is no fault of yours, but so it is. . . . I am the most wretched of women. If you have any pity for me, my love, you will help me to rise above the lowly and humiliated position which torments body and soul in me."

6

Her troubles were great. For years she had been accustomed to live in a style far above anything indicated by her earnings as an actress. Thousands upon thousands of francs passed easily through her hands for robes, cashmere shawls, and jewelry, perfumes, and silks, and glorious hats—a great part of it, however, furnished on credit offered by tradesmen, who coldly estimated the time of her youth and the figure she cut. In her business affairs there had always been some disorder. But, once she had dismissed her Russian prince, she was confronted by pressing notes which she renewed now with increasing difficulty, at usurious rates of interest. Soon her creditors were hounding her as a woman who had left one man of large wealth for another who, though undeniably a great poet, suggested, as such, a less solid commercial risk.

The boarding and education of her daughter, Claire, whom she cared for and saw regularly, was also a cause of anxiety. When she appealed to James Pradier, the father, she received little more than advice, and would be forced to turn to new moneylenders to repay the old. Her recent trip to the country, to a friend in Brittany, was taken in the summer of 1833 partially in order to escape from pressing creditors. This sudden flight, as well as some of her maneuvers to raise money, appeals to her former lovers of which he heard gossip, but fanned Victor Hugo's suspicions, for she told him nothing definite about the seriousness of her predicament. She would run off and write him that she could not reveal her place of refuge "without exposing us both, but more particularly myself, to unnecessary annoyances . . ." meanwhile beseeching him to have faith in her.

He was a poet, and poets were supposed to know little about involved business debts and to live economically, certainly in comparison with a Russian landholder who owned a thousand serfs.

Hugo gave Juliette charming trinkets, usually antiques; he gave her manuscript poems, which were of immense value to her, and also gifts of money. But the scale of his private life was measured and prudent, for he had a sizable family, a large house, and numerous dependent relatives. Thus Juliette, at first, was left mostly to fend for herself. Her principal hope was pinned upon anticipations of the stage triumphs and larger earnings that would fall to her from her association with a great dramatic author.

However, the rehearsals for the prose melodrama of "Mary Tudor" were stormy. Mlle. George, playing Queen Mary, and other members of the cast keenly resented the new prominence given to one whom they had considered professionally a mere novice and their inferior. They retailed gossip and slander of Juliette Drouet; Mlle. George, the prima donna, is supposed to have told Hugo that Juliette was not only faithless, but dishonest, or at any rate irregular in money affairs. All these troubles, coming at a time when she faced the trial of her life, robbed the highly strung Mlle. Juliette of her professional confidence—and she was scarcely a practiced exponent of her art. In the small Paris theater world of that day, news of the "scandal" concerning the poet had set all the tongues wagging; half of the audience at the opening night, November 6, 1833, came to examine his new muse, and the other half to hiss her. The plot of "Mary Tudor" was one of the most preposterous Hugo had yet contrived; its deliberately arranged sensations and antitheses resembled the work of Dumas rather than of Shakespeare. From the start the play was not so well received as his others. But with the later scenes of the third act, where Miss Jane (Juliette) figures prominently, the hisses from all over the house—a whole claque was at work—drowned out the voice of the fair Juliette, and she soon lost her presence of mind.

In the authorized account of these proceedings, as dictated to the Witness of Victor Hugo's Life, it is piously stated that the actress playing the part of Jane, "owing to a grave indisposition," retired after the second night and was replaced by Mlle. Ida Ferrier. There is mention also that Victor Hugo believed the manager, Harel, had conspired to have a claque present to hiss the play and bring about its downfall. Some contemporary comment has held this to have been an absurd subterfuge on Hugo's part, as Harel would thus be cutting off his own nose, that is, causing loss to his own theater. But, we must remember that the star, Mlle. George (who was Harel's mistress), had shown herself as malicious as she was jealous of the younger and prettier rival. Harel might well have been driven to some intriguing by her demands. Besides, he had a wildly sensational play by Alexandre Dumas, with which he soon supplanted the "Mary Tudor" of Hugo. In this play a leading part was taken by Dumas's friend, Ida Ferrier, who had been Juliette's understudy and became later the wife of Alexandre Dumas. The whole tortuous theater intrigue was followed by a resounding public rupture between those two musketeers of the romantic drama, Hugo and Dumas. The failure of "Mary Tudor" meant some financial disappointment to the author, but in an immediate sense it spelled disaster for Juliette Drouet, who had conspicuously failed in the test.

7

It was all very well that Victor Hugo attributed her failure to intriguers and rivals, and strove to console her grief by promising to write new and greater roles especially for her, in which she would still win splendid triumphs. She was being hounded again by remorseless creditors who had noticed the downward fluctuation of the market. Victor had broken with Harel and transferred his services back to the Comédie-Française for his next play, also arranging that Juliette should be retained on their regular cast for occasional minor roles. Yet, with reduced earnings of but four thousand francs a year, her financial difficulties increased.

When finally he got from her a somewhat clearer picture of the nature of her troubles, of the heavy burden of debt overhanging her, he was shocked. She owed 12,000 francs to Janisset the jeweler, 1,000 to Poivin the glovemaker, 600 to her laundress, 620 to the dressmaker, 260 to the hairdresser, in all some 20,000 francs immediately due. She said nothing, at first, of further debts to moneylenders.

His scrupulous soul, very methodical in money matters, was offended at these evidences of sinful extravagance and indulgence. He and his family had been accustomed to live comfortably for several years upon such a sum as her jewelry bill represented. He wondered how far he dared go in attempting to aid her, and in his doubt and mental distress he began to give credence to some of the stories that circulated about her. As he began to raise such money as he could spare, and labored to bring some order into her affairs, even humiliating himself by addressing appeals for help to her former lovers, irritation and jealousy mounted in him, and his reproaches led to violent scenes. "You are tired of my love," she wrote. "You think of flying from me. My bad luck frightens you, you fear to share it any longer. . . . Oh, I could die," she wrote on December 20, 1833. And a little later: "You have crushed me by referring again to my past life, even while I assured you of my love and repentance and while I still hoped for a reconcilia- tion. . . ." She left to see her little girl then living in the country, bidding him farewell—"to protect us both from ourselves!"

This despairing letter he left unopened for two weeks. He was in a black mood. He told himself that he must leave this woman who brought disorder into his life. His need of her and his fear or mistrust of her destroyed his repose. In his notebook he wrote at this time: "January 13, 1834: eleven-thirty at night. Today still her lover, tomorrow * * * " The suspensive asterisks were his own question mark.

One evening, after avoiding her for many days, he came to her house and left a message:

If you are deceiving me, your duty as an honest woman is to leave me. I am going out and in that case, when I return in an hour, I expect to find you gone. If you are true to me, remain. Act as you would before God."

He found her there when he returned. She had resolved to re- fuse herself to his embraces, because he had once more outraged her with his reproaches and suspicions. Yet she yielded to him.

Forgive me [she writes] for having yielded myself to you after what had passed between us. I ought to have foreseen what would happen, and what did happen. God knows, I had resisted as long as I could and had given way only upon the solemn promise you made me never to refer to the stains of my former life as long as my conduct toward you should remain honest and pure. . . . Yet have you kept your word? . . . You are as ashamed of the insults you heap upon me as I am to receive them.

Spring came and there was peace again, though a peace that was constantly interrupted by the arrival of annoying creditors. From time to time Victor Hugo would leave her sums of money. On one day, finding a pressing bill presented during her absence, he left five hundred francs that he had just received for a news- paper article written on short notice. It was not enough, but, unlike Russian princes, he worked hard for the money he gained. He left a message:

This money is for you. I have just earned it for you. It is the rest of my night that I wanted to give you. . . . My pen almost fell from my hand twenty times, but I worked for you. . . . It is all fatality. Even in your downfall, I consider you the noblest and most generous of souls whom chance has injured. . . . No one should have the right to throw the first stone at you, but I. And if someone did, I should place myself between him and you.

He ordered her, despite her reluctance, to dispose of some of her finery in order to meet her debts, as one of her notes shows:

Today I had the notion of concealing from you the visit of one of my creditors, whom I found waiting for me at the concierge's. As you desired I found something among my possessions to sell in order to pay him.

In the summer of 1834 they went off together upon a happy vacation trip to the seacoast of Brittany. They took long walks by the sea and Victor Hugo wrote verses prolifically. But early in August, when Juliette returned to her home in Paris, she found bailiffs in possession of it, all her clothing and furniture seized, and sent him an urgent call for help.

Now he learned the full extent of her obligations to gamblers, loan sharks, and usurious tradesmen, some of whom had exacted as much as 100 per cent interest per annum. The total stood in the neighborhood of forty thousand francs. Forty thousand francs! In those days when workingmen earned two francs a day, when living costs were a fourth of their present scale, it was a fortune, a competence such as he had once hoped for, in order to have security for his family and independence for himself. His own life, all duty and labor, previously had been well ordered, his position in the world built up steadily, brick by brick. Now he must guarantee or underwrite the whole debt, or his Firebird would be rendered bankrupt, liable to imprisonment if she remained in Paris—because of "irregularities" laid to her—or hounded to some place of refuge in the country. But he could not conceive of providing such a large sum without endangering the position of his family, his own children—and all for his infatuation for a pretty actress. How could he defend his course to them, or to Adèle? He stopped at the brink of a grave danger. To her calls for help he now gave no answer. On August 3, 1834, she came to his house in the Place

Royale, as if for a last interview, entering his study by the secret passageway he had shown her. She informed him that she was resolved to leave him, to leave Paris and go with her daughter Claire to stay with a married sister living at Brest. It was very tragic. For a moment he broke down and begged her not to go. Then he grew wrathful and warned her of the terrible disasters that would follow if she left his protection. But, when she persisted, he finally gave her his hand very coldly, and she left his house.

As his friends well knew, he had always prided himself on his strength of will, looking far ahead, steering himself confidently. He had known intense suffering as a boy, and even hunger in his youth. He would bear this too; he would be free of the woman of storms, he told himself as he walked the floor of his study at the Place Royale. He would rid himself of this "shadow," this "night" as he was wont to say, which covered his life.

On her way to Brest, Juliette had sent him despairing little notes: "I was forced to fly from you. . . . It cost me a great deal to bear your supplications and then your angry looks. . . . I love and bless you. Be happy."

But then, in a second note, from Brest, she asked his pardon for the trouble she had caused him and reported that she was ill:

I shall die of this separation. I need you to be able to live. Since I told you everything, since the moment when my eyes could no longer rest upon yours, I have felt as if all my veins were being opened and my life's blood slowly drained away.

She was sick, and asked for pardon. Of all the teachings of Christ, that of mercy, of the principle of pardon, still moved him most. In the flood of emotion that swept over him he could no longer bear to refuse her his pardon, his help, his love. He rushed into the street, to go to the police office and obtain the passport then necessary for all travel even within France. Along a small dark street, the rue du Poirier, he passed two women and thought he heard one say to the other: "I spurned my own happiness. I went away." He thought it was the voice of Juliette—coincidences always moved him mysteriously. Through his mind there ran the memory of a letter she had written him some time ago, when they were happy—one of her pretty conceits, a document in legal form, like a deed transferring full title to her heart . . .

For the rest of my life, whenever presented, or whatever day or hour or minute presented, I am pledged to return the said heart in the same condition in which it is given today, that is to say, filled with a single love which is yours. . . . Executed at Paris, July 4th, at three o'clock in the afternoon.

Signed: JULIETTE, and witnessed by one thousand kisses with which this document is covered.

His mind was clear, and he knew what he wanted to do. He would go to her rescue, pay to the full; he would bond himself for her, and so he would have her back. As to his family and their needs, he would manage, he would work harder, he would hold and protect them too.

To Juliette he dispatched letters which were cries of burning devotion, and announced his early departure to join her at Brest. Before leaving Paris, he moved heaven and earth to meet the bills he knew were most pressing, disposing of a thousand francs he had on hand. He managed to stir the heart of James Pradier himself, who had been remiss in providing his share of the expenditures for the upkeep of his daughter Claire, and obtained some money from him.

Then at last, after days of carriage journey, he saw her. They stayed by the sea together. He wrote in her book: "After fog and storm, the weather has turned fine; the sea and the sky, grey during our separation, have made themselves blue and calm in order to smile at you as I do. Here our union is sealed in a solemn promise. Here our two lives are forever welded. Let us always remember what we owe each other. What you owe me, I do not know; but what I owe you, I know, is happiness."

Meanwhile the strange man, while en route to Brest, had also written to his wife on August 7, 1834: "I love you. You are the joy and the honor of my life." To his beautiful, vivacious 'Didine (Léopoldine), now eight years old, he now began to write letters that were tenderly sentimental, yet well suited to her age:

I have seen the sea; I have seen pretty churches, lovely fields. The sea is great, the churches are beautiful, the fields are green, the country is pretty. But the country is not as pretty as you are; the churches are not as beautiful as your mamma; the sea is not as big as my love for all of you . . .

As he sat in the sand beside his mistress, he wrote to his spouse also that he was very tired after his journey, "but that which is never too tired and always ready to think of you and to love you is the heart of your poor old husband who grew up with you as a child. . . ."

That season, those who, knowing of his marital infidelity read the tender elegy, *Date Lilia,* which he addressed to his wife, as if craving *her* pardon—it was even written at Brest, by the side of his Firebird—wondered at the complexity of the human heart. A Sainte-Beuve refused to believe him sincere, though the poem itself carried deep conviction.

But Adèle believed him, though he was absent again for long weeks, and she grew unhappier as the months of the other woman's ascendancy extended themselves into years. She answered one of his letters from Brittany: "I will say nothing that may make you sad when you are far away and I am not there to console you. Yet I believe that you love me in spite of all that, and that you must be enjoying yourself, since you delay your return. And in truth these two certainties make me happy."

CHAPTER VIII

The "Redemption" of Juliette Drouet

Fame, often enough, is made up of the evil, rather than the good, that is said of a man," wrote Balzac in one of his novels. Yet Balzac himself, hearing Paris laugh over the amorous trials of his colleague, Hugo, hastened to spread the current reports that the poet was insanely infatuated with an evil creature, that he was ruining himself for her, and that she was to bear him a child soon. To his own mistress, the Countess Hanska, the author of the *Comédie humaine* wrote:

I have already told you the story about H—— Well, then! He who married for love, having a wife and children, has taken up with an actress named J—— who, among other testimonials of her affection, has sent *him a bill of 7,000 francs owing to her laundress and H——* has been forced to pledge some of his property in order to pay this *love note!* Think of a great poet, for he is a poet, toiling in order to pay off the laundress of Mlle. J——!

The six hundred francs actually owing Juliette's laundress was bad enough, yet the wagging of the public tongues had multiplied it more than tenfold—which was a measure of the fame Hugo enjoyed now, in the sense of Balzac's own definition.

It was scarcely true that his character had disintegrated, as common report had it. On the contrary, he prepared with great energy of soul to meet strenuous trials ahead. He had become convinced that he could never part with Juliette, that a "fatality" bound his life to hers. Therefore, in the dramatic reunion at Brest, in August,

216

1834, he pledged that he "owed" her her happiness at all costs. Doing nothing by halves, he now proceeded to install Mlle. Drouet in a permanent and dominant place in his domestic life, making her his wife in all but name, his connection with her becoming as fixed as that with his wife had formerly been, her house conveniently near his own becoming his second home. To this new arrangement the somewhat ailing and resigned Adèle was brought to consent, though with the understanding that outwardly, for the sake of the children, a certain social discretion was to be observed and everything about their family life was to continue as before.

He had spoken often to Juliette of "redeeming" her past character. He was now faced, in all reality, with the quite tangible and untheological problem of redeeming her debts. This meant an additional financial burden which he faced determinedly. It meant that while he was still quite young and had only recently begun to enjoy large winnings from his playwriting—a source that was notoriously uncertain—he obligated himself to pay the large sum of more than forty thousand francs at some time in the future in full settlement of all claims against Juliette. At first, in 1834, he settled upon Juliette an income of 750 francs a month; but several years later, in 1838, as his circumstances improved, he increased this to 1,000 francs ($200) a month, and about half of these remittances, according to the understanding between them, was used regularly to retire the old debt during the eight years that elapsed by 1842.

All this meant also that he took charge of Juliette, body and soul (as he took charge of everyone—wife, children and friends—who came into his own life). She must do his bidding in all things, follow his program, learn to live under the severe economy he marked out for her, see him when he was free to come to her, see only those persons whom he permitted her to see—and submit her household accounts to his inspection each week. In short she must become his thing, his submissive slave, and learn to accept her allotted place in the discreetly sheltered corner of his life. Not only by a great love, but by suffering and repentance, by thrusting away silks and fineries, was Juliette, the once carefree demi-mondaine, to be "sanctified" under his guidance. Even in matters of love, Victor Hugo always had a great deal of the early Christian in him.

In her *livre d'anniversaire* there is an entry by Victor, at twelve-thirty one night, soon after the new regimen began:

"This is the last evening we shall pass in number 35½ rue de l'Echiquier. Let us keep an eternal recollection of this room in which we have been so happy and so unhappy, this room I love, after all, and whose ceiling has so often seemed like heaven to me. . . . Adieu to this place, but not to our love!"

The entry for the next night, promptly at 12:30 midnight, reads:

"This is the first night that we have passed together in your new house of the rue du Paradis. Oh! how well named is this street, my Juliette. Heaven exists for us, in this street, this house, this chamber, this bed. It is a new life that begins for us. Let us begin it with our old love. . . ."

Her Prince of Poets had transported his Juliette from the Street of the Exchequer and its spacious rooms to the Street of Paradise. But Paradise was much nicer for their exchequer—rent only four hundred francs a year, instead of fifteen hundred! It was a very plain and small home, too, consisting of only two tiny rooms and a kitchen. But would there not be always her manly "Toto" to make a heaven of it?

The wonder of it was how she was induced to accept the harsh new order. She who had lived for the moment was to own hereafter no real jewels and few dresses. Dress, he told her repeatedly, added nothing to the charms of a beautiful woman. But she was too much a woman not to suffer as she sold her fine robes and negligees, her ribbons and baubles, for loss of which her letters bear many laments:

My poverty, my clumsy shoes, my faded curtains, my cheap spoons, the absence of ornament and all pleasure apart from our love, testify at every hour and every minute that I love you with all my heart.

And then she must save money on fuel; her house was so cold that often she stayed in bed most of the day, reading and writing letters. She said to him: "If you seek warmth in this room you will have to seek it at the bottom of my heart!"

But to Victor Hugo's mind, there could be no true reformation or "redemption" without work. She must study her parts for new plays, sew and repair her clothes and even some of his, keep her house in order, and use such leisure as she had left to serve as his secretary—which she did very ably—copying many of his manuscripts, cutting out clippings from newspapers for him, classifying the notes he brought her. Finally she was required to write him at least once every day, recording each movement of her heart, each shade of thought that related to him—for he loved words, and sensed that she used them well.

Most remarkable and most exhausting of all, however, worse than everything else, was the form of claustration that her tyrant lover now imposed upon her. As Victor Hugo became completely bound to her, and she became an inextricable part of his life, his "Spanish" jealousy pursued her. He separated her from her former friends, female as well as male; he watched her, came in at unexpected moments; he demanded that she live alone, accounting to

A drawing by Victor Hugo

him for all her time. She was shut in, like the concubine of an oriental despot, receiving none but her lord and master.

But what he really preferred was to be alone with his chosen companion, either at her rooms or in the country. In July, 1835, when he and his family were invited to stay with the Bertins at their country house in the Bièvre Valley, outside of Paris, he arranged, with the permission both of Mlle. Bertin, his hostess, and of his wife, to have Juliette come quietly for a visit of a few days to a little inn about two miles away. Later they found a small white cottage with green shutters, in the near-by hamlet of Metz, in the same valley, where she remained for six weeks beginning in early September. It had formerly been a gamekeeper's lodge, attached to a neighboring château, and lay deep in the forest. From the Bertins' house at Les Roches Victor Hugo would walk by solitary woodpaths two miles across the valley to meet his mistress. She, dressed in a skirt of white jaconet, striped with pink, such as she usually liked to wear, and an Italian straw hat, would come running breathlessly to meet him at a fixed rendezvous, usually a gigantic hollow old chestnut tree. Walking in the woods, or sitting silently, or talking, or making love, half pagan and half mystic, they enacted what they called their "marriage of escaped birds." She would sit at his feet, playing the repentant Magdalen to his apostle or savior, while he devotedly "improved" her. Here, under the inspiration of Juliette and the wooded park, Victor Hugo wrote those sequences of lyrics which are the freest, the most genuine, and the most charming of his earlier poems. The love lyrics to Juliette, included in the new collections of Hugo's poems appearing successively as *Les Chants du crépuscule* (1835), *Les Voix intérieures* (1837), and *Les Rayons et les ombres* (1840), had a *natural* grace that was most rare in French poetry and the strongest contribution of romanticism, and Young France in the nineteenth century read them with the delight that English youth took in the lyrics of the ill-fated Shelley, or German youth in Heine. The fecundity of Hugo's genius continued to be astonishing and tended to throw some of his finest contemporaries (like Alfred de Vigny) into the shade. He was a conscious craftsman; he composed, he functioned steadily and often, but nearly always in a spirit that courted emotional intensity—though it is true that he seemed able to rise to intensity almost at will, with a theatrical flair. During the 1830's he wrote out of the fullness of emotional experience, under the sway of Juliette. His three small volumes appearing at intervals of two or three years, especially the last, *Les Rayons et les ombres,* showed him not merely sustaining his previous quality, but steadily surpassing it in effects of brilliance, variety, rhyme, and sonorous harmony. Inasmuch as he was destined in middle age to surpass again the best work of his younger years, under the whip of deepened experience, passion, suffering, and self-knowledge, his dominance over French poetry continued for an incredibly long period, indeed during most of his century. Yet to the English-speaking world the treasure store of his poetry is little known, save as a legend, owing to the difficulty of exporting or translating his skillful rhymes and his sonorous hexameters.

For Juliette he wrote, as he waited in the Bièvre woods, one of the most perfect love lyrics ever written in his language, numbered simply as XXIV in the volume issued in 1835:

> *Oh! pour remplir de moi ta rêveuse pensée,*
> *Tandis que tu m'attends, par la marche lassée. . . .*

Que ce réseau d'objets qui t'entoure et te presse,
Et dont l'arbre amoureux qui sur ton front se dresse
Est le premier chaînon;
Herbe et feuille, onde et terre, ombre, lumière et flamme,
Que tout prenne une voix, que tout devienne une âme
Et te dise mon nom!

His closing lines are memorable: "Oh leaves and grass, oh earth, wave, shadow, light and flame, let all take voice at once, let all become one soul, and tell her my name!"

The manuscript bears the date written in pencil: "September 19, 1834; 9:30 in the morning. Under the chestnut."

Another of the same vintage is that which begins:

Come, let me speak to you, O young enchantress,
Dante would have made you an angel, Virgil a goddess . . .
Come, the springtime laughs, the road is shaded,
The air is balmy, and yonder in the forest
The green thick moss beneath the oak invites us.[1]

Although one fears it may set no good example to say this, Hugo grew happier than ever before under the spell of his "Magdalen," and the tribute of youth and beauty she paid him.

In town the poet would come almost every night to the little rue du Paradis place. There were certain comforts and delicacies always ready for him which seemed to be lacking in his home—food he particularly liked, truffles or pie of meat or fowl. All his life he ate with a frightfully robust and heedless appetite.

Secluded with Juliette, he felt himself fortified against the world outside. He formed the habit of working in her apartment, where he could be established in complete privacy. There was a table in her boudoir, at a corner of the fireplace, a lamp, pens cleaned and cut. She would lie in bed pretending to sleep while he wrote, yet watching him curiously and adoringly. With her, after the storms of passion had blown by, he knew a deep peace, his life and heart, as he told her, were full—and here is the key to her thrall over him.

Gradually, as she understood his temperament more completely —mixture of enormous pride and secret doubt—she tended to

[1] *Venez que je vous parle, ô jeune enchanteresse,*
Dante vous eût faite ange et Virgile déesse . . .
Venez, le printemps rit, l'ombre est sur le chemin,
L'air est tiède, et là-bas, dans les forêts prochaines,
La mousse épaisse et verte abonde au pied des chênes.

address him in terms of the most extravagant and self-abasing adulation: he was her "god," her "adored tyrant" and her "great and sublime poet," and he was all this each day, unfailingly. Her praise of him, as she read and copied his writings, was each time more reverent and unstinted than the last. Some hidden fear or self-doubt in the poet needed this fairly maternal sustaining strength that she brought him.

In 1837, he wrote to his friend Pavie of the simple joy he took in escaping from the "tumult of [his] enemies in a sort of sanctuary with [his] wife and children. . . ." But this was a subterfuge. His sanctuary was with Juliette.

In his overflowing gratitude he told Juliette one day: "You are my beloved, my truly beloved before God and before men, ever tender, devoted, and beautiful to me. That which calms or agitates me, gleams in my nights, lighting the way before me, better than my study lamp, or in the daytime guides my solitary walks, my study, my dreams, even my labor, is the thought of you, the idea that you are there, that you love me, that you wait for me, that you think of me! If I have some genius, it comes from you. I have two wings in effect! They are yours, my angel!" The accent is gravely sincere, like those he once used for his mother. As from the earlier maternal embraces in childhood, the poet would rise from Juliette's arms, refreshed, his fears and passions calmed, his doubts at rest, his soul fortified.

Victor Hugo's dramatic mother, during his unhappy childhood, had left an indelible impression upon his unconscious mind. A child dominated by love of his mother often, when grown to manhood, seeks her likeness in woman. The high-spirited, passionate Juliette was now much closer to such a likeness than the fading and languid Adèle. One day, in 1835, when making a gift to his mistress of an old boyhood copybook in which he had written some early poems—dating from 1815—he inscribed it to her in these words:

It is twenty years since this was written by a boy who loved only his mother. Today, the boy is a man, he has no mother, but he has a friend, adorable and beloved; it is you. Heaven had given him a saint for his childhood, it has given him an angel for his years of ripeness.[2]

[2]Louis Barthou, who discovered and published this fragment, admits to being shocked at its terms. But today we find such expressions or comparisons illuminating, in the psychological sense, rather than merely impious. Long before the age of Freud, the romantics intuitively and unashamedly told what they felt,

2

Yet Juliette much of the time was deeply unhappy, despite the exclusive and jealous passion her lover showed for her and the literary immortality he promised. His poems to her and his written aphorisms in her book all reflect a continued unhappiness in her which he seeks to console, yet, like a sadist, manages to nourish at the same time. At times cries of grief, poignant calls for help, seem to escape from her in spite of herself:

. . . This sedentary life, this life of isolation, is really killing me. I wear out my soul waiting for you. I wear out my life pacing up and down in a chamber twelve foot by twelve. What I long for is not the world and its stupid pleasures—but *freedom,* freedom . . . to employ my time and strength in the useful business of my house and home; what I want is a respite from suffering, for I suffer a thousand deaths every minute. I ask for life—to live, *like you, like everybody else.* . . . Alas I hardly know what I am writing, my eyes are inflamed, my heart is heavy. I want air, I am suffocating. O Heaven, have pity on me. My Victor, I love you, I adore you, have pity on me. . . .

Many of Juliette's graphic letters, direct and genuine, show her prostrate for whole days with her grief and suffering. The "tyrant" would come then and would gently "raise Juliette from her knees." She would find him charming and noble again. Then, over and over again, she would flare up in momentary revolt at the isolation and boredom she suffered:

What am I but a dog in his yard? A plate of soup, a kennel and chain, such is my lot! But there are dogs whose masters come to take them out for a walk. How I envy them, the happy creatures. My chain is riveted on too firmly to be unloosened.

For some twelve years, between 1834 and 1846, Juliette lived, as if shackled by her lover, in this strange "claustration," the seclusion that his terrible sybaritic pride seemed to demand. Formerly she had been something less than virtuous, but had had her own life, free as a bird. Now she was virtuous, loyal, self-denying, and "redeemed" as her lover now assured her, but had no life of her own, was watched and confined. Only the powerful effect of her girlhood education at the convent could have led her to bear this life of real penitence. For long years she fought against

even likening an adored mistress to a mother, thus associating human sentiments which, as an elder statesman like Barthou held, should not approach each other.

it, but then resigned herself, became pious, and prayed a great deal. Eventually the bonds were relaxed, but by then she was much older, much changed, her thick black hair having prematurely turned white when she was about thirty-five—though her face, contrastingly, was as young as ever. By then too she had become accustomed to her lot and, as if to justify it, more than ever flattered and adulated her "tyrant," who was both the sole source of her happiness and the cause of her sorrow. In short, her obsession. The thousands of letters written to her lover by this latter-day votaress mirror these changes accurately; they form a unique modern document marred only by the constant note of extreme adulation of him which she maintained as if by some unwritten code. "I would not exchange the role you have given me for any riches in the world," she wrote him five years after they first met.

But there was a time when, for two or three years, Juliette still hoped, by Victor's aid, to return to the stage and win some success in her art which would permit her to escape. Victor Hugo like others was convinced that she had considerable histrionic talent. Her failure in "Mary Tudor" was laid to intrigue. Now, in the spring of 1835, Victor Hugo had completed another play, *Angelo, le tyran de Padoue,* and it was no accident that the piece departed widely from existing custom by having leading parts for two female principals.

Angelo, a prose melodrama, like "Mary Tudor" and the others before it, is placed in feudal times and leans much upon secret passages, staircases, labyrinthine intrigues, and some spectacular and funereal closing scenes—such as Dumas and Hugo consistently offered the theatergoers of the 1830's. Though it appears to have small merit now, the extravagant play, like most of the highly spontaneous writings of the romantics, reveals a great deal of Hugo's inward life at this period.

It is the story of a man who loved two women at the same time. The "Tyrant of Padua," Angelo, is married to Caterina, whom he keeps jealously locked up in a room of his castle, while he devotes himself to his mistress, the actress Tisbé. Caterina is pictured as being pure and innocent as a child and religious as a drop of holy water, a girl rather than a woman. Tisbé is a tigress of a woman, a spoiled child who had come up from the streets, and won her way through the world by her beauty and wit. Nor are these the only remarkable coincidences between the play and the life of the author. When the neglected Caterina is being punished by her strangely jealous husband with more stringent confinement because of the attentions of another man, Rodolfo, she declares that she had been true to both men, *without dishonor*. "I am not guilty, I am not *very* guilty. Perhaps I committed some imprudence . . ."

But Tisbé, a woman of the people, overflowing with life and talk, passionate, bold, slangy and gay (admirable portrait of Juliette) also loves the other man Rodolfo, and is torn between her conflicting desires, to ruin Caterina, or—seeing that Rodolfo loves the other woman after all—to sacrifice herself. Tisbé, comparing herself to the married rival, protests passionately at her own inferior social status, and denounces those hypocritical "women of virtue who pass veiled in the street, and pretend that they are better than we, courtesans. . . ." Meanwhile Caterina, the wife, also berates her tyrannical husband, saying: "You do not love me, and yet you are jealous. You have mistresses; that is permitted for you. Everything is permitted for men!"

The play is certainly full of the "counteraction of moral forces," as Hugo says in his preface, and much of it drawn freely from the emotional involvements of his own life. Eventually it is Tisbé, the courtesan, who is persuaded to sacrifice her life so that her rival, Caterina, may escape from her tyrant with Rodolfo. There, of course, is the message of the play, if it has any, the lesson of sacrifice which Hugo preaches to his own cherished concubine.

Juliette Drouet was greatly affected at reading this play, and memorized the part of the sacrificial courtesan, Tisbé, at once. She felt that she understood the role and looked forward to playing it at the Théâtre-Français as a means of escape from her deadly, dull isolation. Her lover, at first, did nothing to remove these fervent hopes. Then suddenly he brought the news to her that Mlle. Mars, the old queen of French actresses at the Français, and Mme. Dorval, the beautiful young star and mistress of Alfred de Vigny, had accepted the two leading parts in *Angelo*.

What were Victor Hugo's reasons for this change of heart? Fear of failure on Juliette's part? Hope of a certain success through use of the two famous stars, Mmes. Mars and Dorval, in one play? We must remember that in the spring of 1835, at this very time, Sainte-Beuve had called attention to the two contrasting groups of poems in Hugo's new volume, in short, to his two different muses. But to have the character of Tisbé (as we have sketched it briefly) played publicly by his mistress now would have been an indiscretion leading easily to more scandalmongering of the same sort.

To everyone's surprise, the play was a popular success from the day it opened, April 28, 1835, largely owing to the presence of two famous women in its cast. Juliette was heartbroken; yet she persevered and learned whole parts of other plays during her solitary hours in her apartment in the rue du Paradis or (after 1836) in the larger one at the rue Saint-Anastase. Then one day, in 1838, her great man laid before her a new play, *Ruy Blas,* this time in verse, and one of the best of all his plays. It was the lyrical counterpart of Beaumarchais's rebellious "Barber of Seville," for its hero, Ruy Blas, is a lackey who becomes prime minister and lover of a Queen of Spain.

The bold theme of this play is known to have been inspired by the admiration Victor Hugo conceived for the Duchess of Orléans, when he was presented to her in 1837, and by the friendship and favor which the Duchess of Orléans as well as the Duke of Orléans, heir apparent to the throne, showed him at this time. Owing to their patronage and that of the prime minister, Guizot, Hugo had at his disposal, early in 1838, the use of a state theater to be devoted principally to romantic drama, the Théâtre de la Renaissance, though he wisely decided to turn over its direction to his friend Antenor Joly. It was here that his *Ruy Blas* was produced before a brilliant audience in the autumn of 1838.

Victor Hugo's admiration for the young and cultivated Duchess of Orléans—she had grown up under the tutelage of another poet, the aged Goethe, at the court of her grandfather the Duke of Saxe-Weimar—was a source of anxiety to Juliette, who scolded him for spending so many hours at receptions in the Tuileries Palace. But none the less the tragic heroine of his new play, like the Duchess, was also a former German princess.

He wrote this play with greater pains and worked over it for a longer period of time than he had ever taken before. It was done at Juliette's apartment, where he had gone for refuge. She bathed his strained and swollen eyes, which from now on gave him trouble. She comforted him and spurred him on. When he was half done, she wrote him: "Oh, my two acts, my two acts! How I would love to hear them! I would give two years of my life to have them this evening." And soon afterward, she wrote: "You work, and I love you. We each do our separate task, you work for glory, and I work for happiness. But you will succeed more than I. . . ."

When she begged him to let her play the part of the Queen, he could not refuse her. Since the play was to be produced at the new theater under his own effective control, he instructed the manager, Joly, to sign an agreement with Juliette, which was done early in May, 1838.

She began to study her part. She was so happy that she was full of fear, fear that she was "unlucky."

Since you encouraged me to see a chance of my playing in your ravishing work, I am like a sleepwalker who has become drunk on champagne. I see everything double. I see double. I see glory and happiness, love and adoration, all in gigantic dimensions and impossible. I say impossible, because I know that you can never love me as much as I love you, and I can never, no matter what talent I may show, rise to the heights of your sublime poetry. It is not modesty on my part, because I think there is no one anywhere capable of playing these roles as you conceive them in your admirable head. . . .

Adèle Hugo, meanwhile, making head against the world as well as she could, maintained her position in charge of the Hugo family establishment with dignity. Normally, in the presence of others, her husband never failed to treat her with the most marked courtesy. He was always touched by her generosity to him. When he was gone for months upon a long vacation journey with his mistress, she wrote him, in July, 1835:

Do not deny yourself anything. I have no more need of pleasure, it is calm I need. I am quite old in my tastes. . . . What better is there left for me in this life? I have only one desire, and that is that those I love should be happy; happiness in life is gone for me. . . . Never shall I abuse my rights which marriage has given me over you . . . my poor friend, you who married at twenty, I do not wish to bind your life to the old woman I have become. Thus at least, whatever you give me you will give freely, and in all liberty. Do not trouble yourself about it. . . . I embrace you. Be happy, very happy!

But, though she seemed a fatigued and distracted woman as she grew older, what Adèle could never tolerate was the thought of the possible ascendancy of the other woman over her husband's mind and work. While having little taste for poetry, she had always been keenly interested in the theater and often occupied herself and helped her husband with some of the business and social details of this work. Upon learning that Juliette Drouet was to play the principal leading lady in *Ruy Blas,* she, usually so timid, was roused to action. It meant the official, public establishment of the other woman! For the first time in her life, Adèle intervened vigorously, against her husband's wishes.

To the director of the Renaissance, Joly, she wrote on August 19, 1838:

Doubtless you will be surprised to see me interfere in an affair which would seem to concern strictly only you and my husband. However, I think I have the right to act since I feel that the success of a play by Victor may be compromised and deliberately jeopardized. . . . For the role of the Queen has been given to a person who was one of the contributing causes of all the violent uproar made at the production of "Mary Tudor." I know that present conditions are now more favorable. . . . But sir, what you cannot do away with is public opinion, an opinion unfavorable to the talent of Mlle. Juliette, right or wrong. Granted that my husband takes an interest in this lady and that it is natural that he should wish to support her claims, I cannot admit that this interest should be carried to the point of imperiling the success of one of the most beautiful plays in the language.

Once more the fear of failure and the logical argument of Mme. Hugo carried the day against poor Juliette. It was the last time that she ever aspired to reach the stage again, a world from which the fierce jealousy and pride of her lover instinctively barred her. He strove to console her, but she wept endlessly and declared: "The thing I desire most shall never be realized. I have a presentiment that I shall die before succeeding in creating one of your roles on the stage. My heart is empty. . . ."

Thereafter she never emerged from the shadow in which Victor Hugo held her. Her happiness was to be, for a long time, only vicarious. When he won great honors, she enjoyed them by the dim reflection that reached her. When he went to give an address at some public reception, at the French Academy, or before the King's son, and on many other occasions, he would come to her, to have her pass upon his costume; he would read his prepared speech to her, and then go out warmed and heartened by her adulatory and ecstatic approval. He was always her "king" and her "Caesar." On the triumphant night when *Ruy Blas* opened at the new Théâtre de la Renaissance—with members of the royal family present—she sat in the rear of a box, clapping her hands in applause of the distinguished actress Mme. Dorval, who played the part of the Queen. She applauded, then wept, then laughed, and all at the same time.

CHAPTER IX

Olympio at the Place Royale

AFTER 1835 there appears in the poems of Victor Hugo an imaginary character named Olympio, to whom several elegiac poems are addressed, the finest of these being the long ode he wrote in 1837, *Tristesse d'Olympio* ("Sorrows of Olympio").

Who was Olympio? The voice of the poet, in a series of poetic dialogues, seems to address him now as a friend or now as some demigod, discussing and speculating with him upon his experiences and meditations. Olympio, it appears, has been subjected recently to much slander and denunciation; all sorts of enemies and the crowd of the envious pursue him, and the poet attempts to commiserate with him.

"Do not seek to console me and do not mourn for me," Olympio replies; "I am quite calm and at peace with myself. I am not concerned with the world that is too much with us but that which is invisible, yonder. . . ." Time, he declares, will justify his course, which men have attacked.

Why does Olympio always follow solitary paths? Why does he voyage alone to the depths of the forests, the mountains, and the sea? He declares that he has nothing in common with the herd of men, that "Genius must labor alone with the plough called Passion." Unswervingly he must continue upon his course. "Let us know how to be great," he says in effect, "while the vexations of the world vainly besiege us. Let us know how to bear our destiny under whatever name men call it. . . ."

Inevitably we receive the impression that Olympio is Victor

Hugo himself, or his double—to whom he speaks in the second person. He is or regards himself as a lonely and savage Titan, whose superhuman pride or self-esteem cannot be appeased unless he reaches those scarcely attainable mountain heights that recall to him his native Olympus. Olympio seems to emerge out of the woods of the Bièvre Valley, where he is accustomed to engage in secret rites, in spite of the censure of the world outside. From this time forward the luminous and mystic form of Olympio is super-imposed upon that of the poet himself.

To a friend who wrote Hugo of his suppositions upon the meaning of the poem on "The Sadness of Olympio," the poet answered, October 12, 1837:

You are right, Olympio is a symbol; every noble nature who is calumniated and misunderstood can find something of his own case there. You have well understood Olympio. . . .

Hugo was so pleased with this device that he thought of composing a whole collection of poems to be called "The Contemplations of Olympio," and wrote some notes for a preface to this work:

. . . There comes a time in a man's life when his horizon grows wider and he feels himself too small to continue to speak in his own name. He then creates, as poet, philosopher or thinker, a figure in which he personifies and incarnates himself; it is still the same man, but it is no longer his mere self. . . .

Although many knew him, Hugo was most of his life a lonely man. His house in the center of Paris and his table for many years were open to great numbers of visitors. In manner he was always polite to the point of affability, yet with a slightly formal old-time bearing recalling the tone of society in the days of the Restoration, after Waterloo. Sainte-Beuve had felt baffled by this reserve and composure of manner, and had reproached him for it. Victor Hugo had insisted that he lived through his emotions and his heart, but of course this was not true in the sense that Sainte-Beuve would have desired. At any rate, after the rupture with Sainte-Beuve, Hugo, made wary, allowed himself no more intimate friends, or any who were his peers. He had allies, disciples, pupils, acquaintances, but no friends. He was an Olympian! This was the valuation he set upon himself and demanded—arrogant though it might be—that the world accept. To this end his whole will strained.

Daguerreotypes of Victor Hugo done at this time show him sitting bolt upright, a hand thrust into his vest, his face impassive as a mask, yet tense and deeply lined, with eyes gazing far off beyond the photographer.

As he approached forty—indeed after the age of thirty-five—there seemed literally, at that period, no honors left for him to win in the republic of letters. (There was, of course, the traditional and rather hollow one of membership in the French Academy, which he had not gained.) For twenty years he had followed his mission as a poet and maintained himself on very high ground. The poet must be as a teacher and a leader of public opinion, "priest" and "seer" for the people, he said repeatedly. In *Fonction du poète,* written in 1840, he summed up his thought once more, as being opposed to an "egoistic art," that is, art for art's sake, which he had once temporarily espoused. The poet, writing of the past, was to expound the lessons of history, but was also to prepare mankind for its nobler future.

> *Le poète en des jours impies,*
> *Vient préparer des jours meilleurs;*
> *Il est l'homme des utopies,*
> *Les pieds ici, les yeux ailleurs.*

In these troubled days he was the "man of utopias, his feet upon earth, his eyes turned skyward," and, like a prophet, bearing a torch, heralding "better days."

In reality, Victor Hugo, as a national poet of France, in his first phase was more a sensitive reflector of his people and his times than a prophet. He himself had perceived this when earlier, in a self-revealing moment, he had spoken of his "crystal soul." His mind, predominantly lyrical in earlier years, was like a crystal that caught all the reflected light and color and movement of his age:

> *Tout souffle, tout rayon, ou propice ou fatal,*
> *Fait reluire et vibrer mon âme de cristal,*
> *Mon âme aux mille voix, que le Dieu que j'adore*
> *Mit au centre de tout comme un écho sonore.*

The shafts of light, the shifting winds of doctrine, good or evil, set to glittering or vibrating his "crystal soul," his soul of many voices, which God had evidently, with some profound design, "set in the very center of all things like a resounding echo."

Thus the succeeding volumes of poems, by 1840, reflected not only changes in style, but the successive changes of opinion and faith which had swayed France since Waterloo. The earliest poems were pious apologies for the Restoration of the legitimate monarchy, which had been overthrown by the French Revolution. But soon these were followed by invocations to the kings to give heed to the storms that gripped the masses of people—"Ah! the people! An ocean endlessly heaving. . . ." But, after the July Revolution of 1830, the tone of kindly advice ceases and though he refers but to the horrors witnessed at the time outside of France, in Poland, Greece, and Ireland, his new temper is wholly changed. He cries: "I hate oppression with a profound hatred. . . . I curse those kings who ride in blood up to the bridle!"

Under the slightly more constitutional monarchy of Louis-Philippe Hugo sings of the optimistic religion of material progress which now possessed his century, of the new age of "iron and burning steam," of "humanity that rises slowly, though tottering still." Meanwhile in matters of religion he turns more frankly skeptical; he reflects the century's increasing doubt of a personal God, and its moral agnosticism as well. If not exactly pagan, he voices already the sentiment of a pantheist who embraces unquestioningly the goodness and harmony of nature.

> *Aimer? haïr? qu'importe!*
> *Qu'on chante ou qu'on maudisse, et qu'on entre ou qu'on sorte,*
> *Le mal, le bien, la mort, les vices, les faux dieux,*
> *Qu'est-ce que tout cela fait au ciel radieux?*

Better to accept the radiance of sky and earth present before us, he implies, than to pray, hate, repent, or trouble oneself over questions of good and evil, death, and false gods.

Thus over the span of the years, his poems were a mirror reflecting the tendencies and sentiments of his time—rather than ideas in systematic form. When the French people, in disappointment over the shortcomings of two constitutional monarchies, began to think of Napoleon with regret, repining for the glory of the Empire, Victor Hugo also earnestly supported the renascent Bonapartism, a fact which contributed as much as anything else to his popularity as a poet. Indeed throughout his life, with few exceptions, Victor Hugo addressed himself very directly to his people, appealing to them, caressing or even flattering them, certain of his occasional poems being given the wide publication of the great newspapers' front pages. And France, in turn, accepted him as her favorite singer and maker of phrases.

But in the theater, during a decade of his ascendancy, since *Hernani* and the glorious Romantic Revolution of 1830, the relationship between the poet and the public was even closer. Year after year the spectacular romantic dramas whose genre and fashion he had created were played with bravura by actors who loved his sonorities, and were swallowed up, almost insatiably, by the delighted crowds. The timeliness and popular political direction of his plays, now little felt, were then very pointed. The crowds heartily enjoyed the lackey in *Ruy Blas,* who, by accident, became a prime minister and uttered tirades upon the corruption and backwardness of the court and the government of his country. Unmistakably, even in those early extravagant romances for the stage, he who was called the "French Shakespeare" consistently and truculently favored the "underdog": now it is a clown, or now a workingman, who has been terribly wronged by a king or a courtier and seeks vengeance; or now a gentleman of illegitimate birth, or a courtesan, who utters the noblest sentiments and appeals to the sympathy of the audience.

While the spell lasted, up to the moment when both the public and its chosen dramatic poet grew weary of the game, Hugo's power in the theater was immense and unchallenged, while even the old hands in the play-making business turned about and copied his methods. Of this power of his to sway multitudes by force of the word he was always keenly, almost jealously, aware. Again and again, while his plays held the boards, he himself would hasten to the theater. He came not merely to see them a hundred times over, but—as he confesses in verses written in 1837—to sit in the shadow of a box studying the faces of the crowd, watching "the response of the people in the theater to my thought."

Measuring himself proudly against other men, believing himself genius and Olympian being, he asked himself inevitably, insistently, how he might further extend this power of the word to wider zones. From his very first boyhood odes, as he himself has said, nearly all he wrote was "more or less involved in public questions." Now he conceived that only by entering public life, by becoming a political leader and orator in his own right, could he surpass and extend that which he had expressed by the written word.

As early as 1834, in a powerful essay on Mirabeau, he had betrayed his own ambition to emulate the immortal orator of the

French Revolution. He pictured Mirabeau as the Genius of Eloquence, riding the storms of revolution, loved and hated, yet imposing his will upon his epoch up to the hour of his premature
death.

. . . By the magic of words and by a sort of mysterious alchemy, he
converted into thoughts, into systems, into precise plans of improve-
ment and reform, the vague instincts of the multitudes; he nourished
the spirit of his time with all the ideas which his great intelligence absorbed and distributed among the crowd; with his arms he was always
pounding at the table of the tribune, at the men and things of his
century, as if to separate the chaff from the wheat which the republic
must consume in order to fecundate its revolution; he gave sleepless
nights to Louis XVI and to Robespierre, attacking Louis XVI's throne
as he attacked Robespierre's guillotine; he said to himself every morning when he awoke: *"What ruin shall I create today with my words?"*
He was pope, in that he led all spirits; he was God, in the sense that
he controlled events. . . .

But Mirabeau, Victor Hugo points out, was a leader of the
people:

. . . He held sway over the Assembly only through the people. What
Mirabeau said, the crowd repeated with applause; and under the
command of their applause, against its will, the Legislative Assembly
wrote as he, Mirabeau, dictated. Libels, pamphlets, calumnies, insults,
interruptions, menaces, whistling, laughter, all these were but pebbles
thrown against the torrent of his speech. . . . When the sovereign orator, seized by a sudden inspiration, mounted to the rostrum; when this
man found himself face to face with his people, when he confronted
the envious Assembly, like the man-God upon the waters; when his
gaze, sardonic and luminous, fixed from the height of that tribune
upon the men and the ideas of his time, as if measuring the pettiness of
men against the grandeur of ideas, then there was no calumny, no insult that could avail against him. . . . On the tribune, in his chosen
role, he became terrible and splendid and all opposition crumbled before
him. . . .

Victor Hugo, too, now desired that his words should assume
a direct political power, so that upon any given day he might
ask himself, like Mirabeau, what ruin or what miracle he should
create by his voice. "The slow and indirect action of literature,"
as the authorized account of his life (up to 1853) tells us, no
longer sufficed M. Victor Hugo, "and he wished to add to it the
immediate action of politics, augmenting the writer with the
orator." He felt himself free and independent, no longer attached

in any way to the fallen Bourbons who had patronized but also censored him. He was free to play a public part under the Orléans regime. However, he continues, "as a writer, he could not enter political life directly, owing to the electoral laws which then established strict property ownership as a requirement for a Deputy. There remained the Chamber of Peers. But to be named a Peer, one must fall within one of those categories which the King might choose from. The only one of these that was open to him was the Academy."

2

At various periods in recent times it has been said that France was "ruled" by a few salons in Paris. Victor Hugo's presence was courted by many salons and in demand at many public or literary functions. Yet he did not go out frequently, save to soirées at the Bertins' and the Girardins'. Bertin the Elder, as he was called, publisher of the *Journal des Débats,* was a man powerful enough to ask the Prime Minister, Guizot, to wait outside, one evening, when that great man arrived during the Bertin dinner hour at Les Roches. On another occasion King Louis-Philippe, who affected democratic manners, hinted that he would like to call at the famous country house outside of Paris. But Bertin said: "The King is quite well off at Versailles, and I am doing well enough at Les Roches." Bertin died in 1841, but Hugo's friendship was continued with his sons, who conducted his newspaper, and with his gifted daughter, Louise, who composed an opera, *Esmeralda,* based on Victor Hugo's *Notre-Dame de Paris.* The Bertins' extremely dignified and influential newspaper steadily furthered the poet's political ambitions.

Another powerful ally was Emile de Girardin, then in his early thirties, yet a rising figure in the newspaper world, who founded *La Presse* as a cheap popular organ, continually lowering its price and heightening its sensational and demagogic style of appeal until it had one of the largest popular circulations in France. Girardin was the natural son of Napoleon's well-known general, Comte Alexandre de Girardin. A dashing fellow, he had an adventurous youth, full of duels, love affairs, and daring speculations, which quickly brought him control of important newspapers and a large, and reputedly sinister, political power that was used in noisy support of Louis-Philippe. But much of Girardin's influence undoubtedly derived from his beautiful and brilliant wife, the former Delphine Gay. Her mother, Sophie Gay, was famous as a woman novelist; twenty years before she had known and encouraged Victor Hugo when he was but the Sublime Child. The blonde Delphine herself was an accomplished poetess who wrote witty *vers-de-société* and a successful writer of sketches for the newspapers and plays for the theater. Her friendship for Victor Hugo dated from her childhood, and—though Victor Hugo was known to disapprove sometimes of intellectual women—they remained on terms of pleasant friendship which, toward 1837, became like an alliance. Now Delphine de Girardin, with her riches and her wit, held enormous social power; she conducted one of the dominant salons of the Orléans period—which Hugo regularly visited—and made, if not kings, then Academicians, Peers, or even Ministers. Both in the Girardin salon and the popular newspaper, *La Presse,* which was an adjunct to it, Hugo's public ambitions were steadily fostered.

In 1839, when the death of the Archbishop of Paris, Monseigneur de Quélen, caused an unexpected vacancy in the French Academy, Girardin's *La Presse* reported: "It seems practically certain that Victor Hugo will succeed the Archbishop of Paris." Mlle. Dupont, an actress at the Comédie-Française, reading this while her hair was being done, took the words quite literally, and was heard to exclaim in amazement: "Just fancy! Here's some news for you! I don't deny Hugo's great talents. Assuredly he is a great man. But still I shouldn't have believed it possible. Why, here's Victor Hugo being appointed Archbishop of Paris!"

But the power he sought was temporal. Like most Frenchmen, Victor Hugo began by disliking King Louis-Philippe and ended by becoming resigned to him. At first Hugo had nursed special grievances against the July Monarchy for its suppression of his play *Le Roi s'amuse* in 1832. But later Guizot, as Minister of the Interior, who admired his writings, showed him much favor, and Thiers, the other political henchman of the King, he had been acquainted with since the days when the "midget Robespierre" was a student in Paris. Then, in 1834, he chanced to write to the young Duke of Orléans in behalf of some charity, directed by Mme. Hugo, for which royal sponsorship was wanted. The duke immediately made him a generous reply, offering his assistance, and also inviting Hugo to call upon him at his apartment in the Marsan Pavilion of the Tuileries Palace. In the early phase of the Orléans regime the family of the "usurper" anxiously sought friends abroad and at home. In their eyes M. Victor Hugo was an ornament of France and a power in the world of letters and the theater, and the young duke and heir to the throne, who passed for the liberal member of the royal family, showed a desire to draw Hugo, as well as other men who might sway public opinion, into his social circle. Victor Hugo found the duke a gracious young man who took a serious attitude toward the responsibilities he expected some day to assume.

The July Monarch in France had found European royalty conducting a form of lockout against the marital ambitions of his numerous children. But at length, in 1837, attempts at *rapprochement* with the King of Prussia were successful and the German ruler's consent was won to a marriage between his relative, the Princess Helen of Mecklin-Schwerinburg, and the Duke of Orléans, an event that was celebrated as a victory in foreign affairs. A few weeks after this, in the spring of 1837, Louis-Philippe announced that the huge, neglected, and largely uninhabitable Palace of Versailles, which he had been restoring for five years, would be presented to the people of France as a national monument and museum in which the relics and art treasures commemorating France's past glories were to be preserved. To celebrate the transfer of the great palace to the public possession, and to spread good will, the Fête of Versailles was held, in May, 1837. In accordance with his pretensions to being a citizen-king, Louis-Philippe invited a great number of commoners to the party, giving special attention to writers, journalists, artists, and scientists. Thus Victor Hugo, who had declared himself, in his poems and plays, a sort of Jacobin, found himself one day going to Versailles, dressed in the uniform of an officer of the National Guard—this was another of his recent honors. At the gate he met the paunchy Balzac, who was attired as a marquis of olden times—no one knew why—in clothes, as Hugo relates, "which were probably hired for the occasion and had certainly been made for someone else." The ceremony was ostentatiously democratic, but also confused and lacking in tone, Hugo thought. The King, a garrulous old man, showed marked attention to Hugo. But the poet enjoyed much more the compliments paid him by the handsome blonde Duchess of Orléans, who told him that the first thing she had gone to see in Paris was "M. Hugo's Notre-Dame Cathedral." She had capped this compliment by quoting some of his verses from memory.

Victor Hugo felt his Jacobin principles relaxing a little. Soon he was a familiar figure at almost all the receptions given at the Marsan Pavilion in the Tuileries, where there was to be found a coterie of literary men, very different from the crass financiers who frequented the aged King at the other end of the palace. The duke and duchess interested themselves in the charities that Mme. Hugo carried on; they lent their personal influence to Hugo's campaign (begun in 1836) for election to the French Academy; they sent him gifts, including a huge and rather bad painting in the romantic style, by St. Evre, which had won the first prize at the Salon d'Automne and which he gratefully hung in his house. At the soirées in the Marsan Pavilion, the duchess, as a devotee of good literature, held long conversations with her favorite French poet, and his Jacobinism of 1830 melted a little more.

The theme of Hugo's tragedy *Ruy Blas,* with its hero a lackey who sacrifices his life to protect the honor of the Queen he adores, clearly hinted that the poet dared to lift his eyes toward the princess. There would be a time in his life when he would pin great hopes upon the outcome of his friendship with one who was presumably destined to be Queen of France. Historians and memoirists paid tribute to her personal charm: "She was all the nobler in manner because of her genuine simplicity," related one eyewitness of the Orléans court. "One does not feel in her the cold nature of a princess," wrote another, the Duchesse de Broglie. "She was a woman who deserved happiness." Before her marriage, when she was warned of the fate that sometimes came to kings and queens of France, she was reported to have answered bravely: "I would rather be Duchess of Orléans in Paris for one year than sit here all my life looking out of the window of this castle." Yet she was to come upon evil days; and in later years Victor Hugo thought of her tenderly and mourned for her, as he wrote in memory of her some lines he left hidden among his posthumous papers:

> *Si le ciel m'eût donné, douce et charmante loi,*
> *Le grand devoir des fils qu'il te confie, à toi . . .*
> *Ah! comme elle eût dormie sous ma garde fidèle,*
> *Et lion pour autrui, j'eûsse été chien pour elle!*

Alas! how faithfully he would have guarded her, if the care of her royal children had been confided to him. A "lion" to others, he would have been "as a dog" for her! Assuredly there was a romantic quality in Hugo's new-found pro-Orléanism.

In 1840, even the popular press attached significance (sometimes humorous) to the prominence of Hugo in the counsels of the Orléans crown prince and princess. "The Marsan Pavilion nowadays recruits all the youthful hearts, the fair goatees and the floating manes that grace the lions of poetry," observed one Paris newspaper. Another commentator prophesied that when the duke mounted to the throne he would surely have a literary and romantic cabinet, with men like Victor Hugo as his Minister of Public Instruction and Théophile Gautier as Minister of Foreign Affairs.

Meanwhile the salon at number 6 Place Royale bowed to none for social brilliance of a certain kind. Sainte-Beuve was gone, and so were Alfred de Vigny, Nodier, and other old friends of the early days of literary-romantic "revolution." But Gautier, the exquisite poet and aesthete, still occupied a place at the right hand of the master, whom he treated always with an amusingly exaggerated yet good-humored deference, calling him his "Olympio" and his "sultan." Théodore de Banville was another poetic disciple, of the "second generation of romantics," who now held a prominent place at Hugo's court. Two younger writers, Auguste Vacquerie and Paul Meurice, both men of wealth, though of liberal ideas, also attached themselves after 1840 to Hugo and so fervently that they were said to form his bodyguard. The fat Balzac too came to the Hugo dinners, jovial, but observant and often a little sardonic at the master's expense. But more prominent than before among the guests were men of science, men of the press, and men of politics; while color and life was lent to these receptions by a host of beautiful and smartly gowned women. Outside, the poorer Paris neighbors stood under the windows watching people come and go or waiting for an occasional sight of the poet at the balcony.

How enchanting were those soirées of the Place Royale, as Théodore de Banville recalls them in his memoirs!

In the rear salon, around an enormous bank of flowers would be seated the young women, beautiful, magnificently dressed, happy to be at the great poet's, and Mme. Hugo doing the honors. . . .

In the large salon, a crowd of men and women moved about in a brilliant setting, and spilled . . . into the dining room decorated with old armour, coming and going, some of them young artists, sketching pictures in their open albums of the celebrities (of stage and press and public life) who were always present.

In the summertime it was more ravishing still; the huge door of the apartment would be left open; the perfume of flowers and foliage would come in through the windows, and the party would spread into the Place Royale outside as well as in the salons, for the young men would go out from time to time to smoke their cigars in the alleys, by the statue of Louis XIII; then they would come in again, drunk with the night, the stars, the glittering candles and the fair ladies who seemed like goddesses.

But one evening a crowd larger and more brilliantly dressed than had ever been seen before at the Hugo home arrived one after another in their landaus and barouches and climbed its iron-balustraded stone stairway. They dined and drank among the old armour of the dining room, then passed into the great red-damask-hung salon, where a still greater crowd foregathered after dinner. Then suddenly the hubbub of voices ceased. A tall, blond young man in the uniform of a major general, with a handsome and stately young woman of German type, entered. Isidore the butler announced in a tone bursting with pride: "Their royal highnesses, the Duke and Duchess of Orléans." The Hugos hurried forward to receive them. A chorus, directed by Mlle. Louise Bertin, now began to sing a passage from *Esmeralda*, the operetta composed from *Notre-Dame de Paris*; it was a song of welcome. In the chorus was a tall girl dressed in white, and of a strange, dark, and proud beauty. Who was she, the Duchess asked Victor Hugo? She had just come to Paris with her mother, the Countess of Montijo, and with Prosper Mérimée, who had been an embassy secretary at Madrid and made their acquaintance there. She was Eugénie de Montijo, then only sixteen. The crown princess, Helen of Orléans, for the first time looked at the young Spanish girl, who was to be the future Empress of France.

3

For Victor Hugo the road to political advancement pointed toward the dome of the Institut. In 1836 he announced his first candidacy for the French Academy, but was easily defeated. In 1839 he presented himself again. The Forty Immortals thought him too young. They were also predominantly Classical, and coyly resisted his efforts to woo them for four years. Although the customs of the Institut founded by Richelieu were extremely dignified, candidates were always required to go in person and pay their court to the members, while pleading for their vote.

Putting on silk hat, frock coat, and the cross of a Chevalier of the Legion of Honor, "Olympio" every winter season for four years regularly made the rounds of Paris in a cab and paid his formal calls.

By 1839, his campaigning grew more determined; numerous colleagues and high personages electioneered for him; the Paris newspapers followed the combat with mingled amusement and indignation. One young journalist wrote expressing his deep regret that a poet so unique as Hugo should *stoop* to become merely "one of forty." But the master replied to him serenely: "The academies, like everything else, will belong to the new generation. Meanwhile, I am the living breach by which the new ideas enter now and the new men will enter tomorrow."

When he came to see Chateaubriand, the arrogant old man said: "I knew you would come. The Academy is all a lot of nonsense. But you are quite right to stand for it. All the men of genius of the past have done it, like Corneille and Racine, you can't deny that. The title of Academician impresses the mob . . . otherwise it has no importance. . . ." Chateaubriand concluded his sermon by promising to deliver his vote.

But the obstinate Classical opposition was led in 1839 by Nepomucène Lemercier, a decrepit relic of the days of Louis XVI, who held Hugo's poetry in horror. Alexandre Dumas, with whom Hugo had graciously composed an old quarrel by kind services, went in his place to old M. Lemercier, heard his tirades, and replied, as he relates in his "Memoirs":

. . . You have refused Victor Hugo your vote, but there is one thing you will have to give him some day, and that is your place. Beware, lest in return for the evil you are now saying of him, he may be compelled to speak in praise of you before the Academy.

In truth, Lemercier died in 1840, and it was his chair that was finally awarded to Hugo, on January 7, 1841 (his fourth candidacy), by seventeen votes to fifteen. The leader of the Romantic school, as the popular journalist, Alphonse Karr, remarked, had entered the Academy by "bursting in the door."

"Thus he had a foot on the first step of the tribune," as his wife related, "and a new existence began for him." Very soberly he prepared his address to the Academy, to be delivered upon the occasion of his induction, June 3, 1841.

Perhaps never before in its two centuries had there been such a high day under the great dome of the Institut. For a week before the ceremony there had been a rush to obtain tickets, especially for the ladies who wanted to witness the historic induction of France's national poet, whom fame, and the breath of scandal as well, had made more romantic than ever. Mme. de Girardin (Delphine Gay), who had done her part to aid in Hugo's elevation, came wearing a scarf that was all trailing glory, as *La Mode* reported; the distinguished Mme. Thiers wore "Peruvian flowers." Shortly before two o'clock, amid a crescendo of whispering and rustling, arrived not only the Duke but the Duchess of Orléans (wearing a small white hat trimmed with roses), accompanied by her sister-in-law, the Duchess of Nemours, and the Princess Clémentine, daughter of the King. Not for many years had royalty so greatly honored a ceremony at the Academy.

The poet at this moment was described by one representative of the press as a man of "medium but solid build . . . his long smooth hair parted carefully off a forehead of pyramid shape. . . . His eyes gleamed with a restrained and dignified exultation. . . . His face, pale and grave, still seemed young." He wore his green, exquisitely cut and embroidered Academician's coat with effect. "M. Hugo carried his head high, and his manner was that of a conqueror entering a captured city. No wonder that his appearance excited intense enthusiasm among the ladies of the audience. His voice is strong and deep-toned, while his gesture and delivery —though a little pompous—cannot be fairly called affected."

If the poet fairly shone, and acquitted himself well in his speech, not a little of it was owing to the enormous efforts expended by a white-haired but still young and handsome woman who sat well back in the audience, out of sight of his wife, children, and friends. At the last moment she had worked with almost hysterical excitement to revise the fitting of his costume; she had made numerous copies and heard him deliver his vast discourse so many times that she knew it by heart. She had accompanied him, sitting and waiting in the back of his cabriolet, when he made his earlier rounds of courtesy calls upon the Academicians. Now nothing could have prevented her from witnessing the canonization of her idol.

To her he was neither grave, nor handsome, nor pompous—but simply a divinity. When he came to the pulpit, Juliette almost swooned in her seat. As she wrote him afterward: "From the moment of your entrance . . . there came to me a delicious astonishment, something between intoxication and ecstasy; it was like a vision of heaven in which I saw God in all His splendor. . . . My Victor, I could kiss your feet, carry you in my arms!"

Victor Hugo's address to the Academy ranged over broad subjects concerned with the future and past of literature and culture generally, of politics and governmental procedure as well, and embraced, in cursory review, a good deal of world history. It was, in short, a jumble of ideas and propositions, some of which strongly compromised each other, as the new Academician's more radical critics noted with disappointment.

He passed from the required eulogy of Lemercier, his predecessor (whom he had cordially detested), to some rather bold allusions to the "great and terrible" French Revolution which had, in some wise, "expressed the genius of the people." He paid an eloquent tribute to the genius of Napoleon, but also reckoned the cost of his long wars and his suppression of freedom of speech. In this connection he spoke strongly in behalf of the intellectual and political courage of Liberal writers like Benjamin Constant and Mme. de Staël, who had dared to defy Napoleon and whom he held up as models worthy of emulation. *The past century belonged to great soldiers; the new century, he prophesied, would belong to great writers!*

Yet, in turning to comment upon the present regime, he tended to discourage those who desired a republican system, perhaps fit only for "colonies" like America, while praising the "combined monarchical and popular" qualities of the Orléans dynasty. It was a regime that preserved the traditions of France while continuing some of the reforms of the Revolution. Nevertheless, the "expansion of liberalism" should not be halted, he urged. Hugo himself intended to labor, while remaining a non-partisan in politics, for the development of the social conscience among men, for the extension of human liberties, and for the introduction of humane laws designed to help "those generations who languished in darkness, wanting air and space," and who were sometimes driven, by suffering and passion, to "pound tumultuously upon the gates of the future." Then, in warning tones, he ended with an exordium to the noble eighteenth-century magistrate and philosopher, Malesherbes, who as Minister to Louis XVI, when there was still time, had pressed the King to conciliate the popular demand for reforms, though in vain. To Hugo, Malesherbes was the model of the intellectual turned into "a great citizen . . . who would have linked the tottering monarchy to the solid basis [of popular support] and thus saved state and King alike, if the cable had not broken. . . ."

The speech hinted at the role the poet conceived for himself, and reflected the curiously opportunistic course that "Olympio" pursued nowadays in his climb toward the political heights. It was the conciliatory expression of a moderate in politics, a man who accepted constitutional monarchy for the best. Yet, like everything Hugo did, it "engendered combat," as Sainte-Beuve remarked; for it sounded some unorthodox notes that jarred upon the ears of the King, as well as on those of the conservative Academicians who now received Hugo into their midst. It was significant also that this man of poetry spoke almost exclusively upon questions of politics, and finally of Malesherbes. Though he had died in 1793 upon the guillotine for serving as lawyer to Louis XVI, when the monarch was tried by the Convention, Malesherbes and his liberal ideas were never loved by Royalists even of the Orléans stripe.

The acting Director of the Academy designated to give a welcoming reply to Hugo was the Comte de Salvandy, former Minister of Education to Louis-Philippe. Where the man of letters had talked politics, the man of politics talked literature, making his speech a studied rebuke. He began by paying Victor Hugo an unprecedented compliment, expressing regrets that the Academy had not received him sooner. But then, point by point, he refuted the other man's political pronouncements. He closed with a pompous statement of his own views upon the proper literary ideals a Hugo should entertain. He should continue to cling to his lyrical heights and avoid mundane things. "Poet, this great star of Malesherbes should not be your polestar. The models that literature bids you accept, upon this solemn day of your coronation, are those of Corneille, Shakespeare, Dante, masters of eternal art regardless of the clime or regime under which they have lived."

Victor Hugo received this elaborate affront with his unvarying and "Olympian" aplomb—though his friends at the salon of the Girardins that night angrily protested at the "ambuscade" that had been prepared for him. Meanwhile his republican friends were disappointed; he came under vigorous attack, as men of all parties discussed his new political interests, his ambitions (as a writer in the *Revue de Paris* said) "to unite in his hands advantages of all kinds at the same time—fortune, power, and glory."

In the fortnightly *Revue des Deux Mondes,* on June 15, 1841, a noted literary critic, Charles Magnin, called attention to Hugo's remarkable change of interests and styled this "a solemn abdication of his past, a step toward the tribune, a candidacy for one of the Chambers." What did it all mean? The answer was: "peerage and ministry!"

A drawing by Victor Hugo

4

Ever since Waterloo the "legitimate" sovereigns of Europe had held France suspect, as the land of mob revolutions and *coups d'état.* But in 1841 this wariness was relaxed; more of Louis-Philippe's offspring married German royalty; an alliance between France and Prussia was much talked of, and England, ever watchful against the revival of French military dominance, grew agitated. It was at this stage that Victor Hugo, scanning the horizons, planned a book that would be no mere literary exercise, but would have the nature of an impressive political action, adding weight to his claims as a public leader. His plan was undoubtedly inspired by tête-à-têtes held with the German-born Duchess of Orléans.

In 1838 and 1839 Victor Hugo had spent his summer vacation touring with Juliette Drouet in Switzerland and Germany. In 1840 he visited the most romantic part of the Rhine Valley from Cologne to Bingen and on to Mainz and Heidelberg, spending two months in going over a distance of sixty miles, stopping at all the villages, exploring all the ruined castles and churches he could find. Victor Hugo now "discovered" Germany and the Rhine, just as Mme. de Staël had done thirty years before him. The medievalist in him, the lover of the "Gothic," was filled with delight. During the journey he devoted himself passionately to sketching and drawing the things he saw. He used pencil, charcoal, water color, or sometimes coffee grounds and tobacco drip from a pipe, with an untutored skill he had possessed ever since boyhood. His drawings suggested sometimes Rembrandt, sometimes Dürer; most often their subjects were ruined castles or ancient, crooked houses and towers perched on forbidding rocks. These drawings fully reveal the baroque side of Hugo, all the tangled, fantastic, nightmarish substance that appealed to his mind's eye.

From the Rhine he brought back what purported to be a travel book, entitled "The Rhine, Letters to a Friend," which was published in January, 1842. Its two rambling volumes were filled with spirited descriptions of journeys, scenery, and medieval ruins, interlarded with charming narrations of old German folk tales he had gathered along the way. But what was politically important was the concluding essay of more than one hundred pages appended to this work, in which he earnestly advocated an alliance between France and Prussia. It was an alliance, he argued, that would bring a long peace to Europe and end the uncertain equilibrium that had troubled the Continent for so many generations. France, he proposed, should aid Prussia by helping her complete her resources through the annexation of the territory of Hanover and the free city of Hamburg, in order to gain access to the sea and trade. In return, France must obtain the territory along the left bank of the Rhine. "The Rhine," he wrote, "is much more French than the Germans think." Whatever the Germans or the French thought, Hugo proposed a scheme for European policy, which, like many of his ideas, was already in the air and much discussed. For a few months it aroused international discussion. But soon the plan's doubtful feasibility became all too apparent, in the face of powerful British and Russian opposition. King Louis-Philippe turned to court England. Then occurred the sudden death of Victor Hugo's sponsor, the Duke of Orléans, on July 13, 1842, which completely changed the whole issue under discussion.

Leaving Neuilly, outside of Paris, in his carriage that day, the duke's horses were frightened and broke out of control. At some point in their flight he jumped from the vehicle and fell mortally wounded, dying several hours later. Louis-Philippe, the July Monarch, whose throne had never been too secure, was now an old man of nearly seventy. His eldest son's heir was only four years old and, if the King should die soon, his accession under a regency would legally follow, but would have doubtful effect in unifying the country. The prospects of the House of Orléans were darkened by this accident, which shook all Europe, as Lord Palmerston said. Among the so-called Intellectuals who were then attached to the July Monarchy, Odilon Barrot, Alphonse de Lamartine (a Deputy since 1834), and Victor Hugo all favored naming the Duchess of Orléans as Regent for her son. But the will of the dead prince, in agreement with his father's wishes, pointed to his brother, the Duke of Nemours, a dull and conservative fellow, as regent—for the fact that his wife, Helen, was a German and Protestant created delicate problems of internal and foreign policy.

Victor Hugo, who had written an official ode for the Coronation of Charles X in 1825, and another for the heroes of the Revolution of 1830, was now designated by the Academy to deliver an Address to the King, expressing the grief of the country, which he did, at a formal little court ceremony of July 21, 1842. He was now drawn closer than ever to the bereaved duchess. Many thought that, when her infant son would come into power, she as Queen Mother, and not the Duke of Nemours, would be the power behind the throne. Not only Victor Hugo, but other leaders such as the professional politician and "popular" orator, Odilon Barrot, based their calculations upon such an outcome.

The poet now also became one of the familiars of old Louis-Philippe. In terms of glory, which then still counted for much in France, the King seemed always disappointing: *la poire*—"the pear"—he was called, a term of ridicule in the French vernacular. Yet the old man merely laughed and gave pennies to the small boys whom he often found drawing caricatures of himself in chalk upon the pavement outside his palace. After having seen much of war and revolution, and having coolly escaped from assassins a dozen times, in his old age, he seemed interested in only one thing: money. He was said to be worth forty million dollars in his own right, yet always complained of poverty. Meanwhile, under this money-minded monarch, the industrial revolution surged forward, commerce flourished, railroad lines finally girdled France, and speculation in banks, factories, and mining enterprises absorbed the capitalists. Symbolic of the changing order were the new gaslights illuminating Paris after 1837, which, as Hugo's friend, Mme. de Girardin said, "made the night more visible than the day." And over all this rapid material progress, which was attended with much political and commercial corruption, the July King, as Hugo describes him in his diaries, presided cheerfully, a wily and patient man, plainly dressed, pretending to be democratic, yet determined always to curb and dominate rival political groups by intrigue, by methods of bribery, or even by pressure of the secret police.

Outwardly the Orléans regime appeared less authoritarian than the Bourbon regime, and managed to outflank its opponents for two decades; actually it was meaner and more corrupt. In the two Chambers political debate was stagnant, as compared with the days of the Restoration. But Victor Hugo now possessed the confidence of the King and enjoyed watching the game of politics from behind the scenes.

Louis-Philippe was loquacious and, putting on carpet-slippers, would sit talking with the poet by his fireside up to a late hour. He spoke of his early life, of his famous governess, Mme. de Genlis, who had followed the principles of her friend Jean-Jacques Rousseau in instructing him, and of his wartime experiences as a general in the republican army. Then, passing to the present scene, he spoke with bitterness of his Ministers, none of whom he really liked, though they might belong to Right, Center, or Left parties. Systematically he alternated Guizot and Thiers in power, the former a rigid Conservative, the latter a pretended Liberal, in accordance with their momentary usefulness as his instruments. The hour would grow late; all the servants and palace guards would be asleep, and old Louis-Philippe himself would go shuffling along with Hugo and usher him out by a side entrance of the Tuileries, bidding him a friendly good-night.

"I intend to be a Peer of France!" Victor Hugo had said in his youth. From time to time the question of his advancement was laid before the King. Finally, after determined pressure by the Duchess of Orléans and other friends, and in the face of considerable mistrust and resentment against the poet among professional politicians, Hugo, on April 13, 1845, was at last confirmed in the rank he desired, equivalent to membership in the British House of Lords. The royal proclamation read:

In consideration of services rendered to the State by Viscount Hugo, we have decreed and do decree as follows: that the said Viscount Hugo, Member of the Institut, be raised to the dignity of Peer of France.

Another long-premeditated step was completed, and Victor Hugo's self-satisfaction rose momentarily to its zenith. "Viscount" Hugo, indeed! Since the death of his brother Eugène in 1837 he had ceased to be "Baron," and had assumed the higher title, though it derived from the fleeting reign of King Joseph Bonaparte in Spain, and his late father's ennoblement, a dignity not only unrecognized by the legitimate monarch of that country, but never formally sanctioned by Napoleon I. At this time the poet also caused some genealogical searches to be made, which seemed to verify sufficiently the Hugo family pretensions to being descendants of ancient nobles of Lorraine, claims later proved to be completely unfounded yet passing current in biographical accounts of the new Peer. Juliette Drouet had once called his attention to the fact that the façade of Notre-Dame Cathedral, flanked by its two spires, had the shape of a gigantic "H." Drawing a large "H" in his bold hand, in the outline of a cathedral, the "Viscount" Hugo now adopted it as his shield. His motto was: *"Ego Hugo!"*

When his elevation to the peerage was announced, a hostile newspaper commented: "M. Victor Hugo has been made a Peer of France! *Le Roi s'amuse.*"[1] However, the stern republicans who wrote for *Le National,* many of them his former friends, greeted the affair with bitterly sardonic comment: "Victor Hugo is dead! Long live M. le Vicomte Hugo, lyric Peer of France!"

5

Was the poet in Victor Hugo "dead"? Olympio still stood in the midst of life, though he seemed vainglorious to his contemporaries, grew soft, indulged all his desires, and, while pursuing his worldly ambitions, seemed to lose his way. He was certainly very rich for those times. For the right to reprint ten of his books for ten years— he always limited the time covered by the contract and then renewed it at more favorable terms—he received from his booksellers upward of 30,000 francs a year, after 1838. But, in addition, the royalties of his plays, which were constantly revived, brought a far greater annual sum, one of the plays alone, the hugely popular *Ruy Blas,* averaging 40,000 francs in annual royalties over many years.

[1]The King was but "amusing himself," a pun on the title of the poet's famous play.

Nowadays there was sometimes open talk in French newspapers of Hugo's great wealth, and to the editor of one of these he wrote in self-defense, in 1845: "I have been working for twenty-eight years and have earned by my pen about 500,000 francs. I have brought up my four children . . . I support eleven people around me . . . do also a little alms-giving—so far as I am able. As to myself, I go about in a twenty-five-franc coat, and wear my hats until they are shabby. I work without a fire in winter, and go to the House of Peers on foot." Out of the 500,000 francs he had earned (a modest estimate), he had some 300,000 francs invested. In those booming Victorian days, investments in shares of railroads and banks were multiplied many times over. A large part of Victor Hugo's treasure, however, was cautiously placed outside of stormy France, or in the rising shares of the Belgian National Bank.

But in those days of moneyed ease and preoccupation with politics, he published new work less often than ever before. The volume of lyrical poems that appeared in 1840, *Les Rayons et les ombres,* was the last that came from his hand in the thirteen years that followed. His new play, *Les Burgraves,* followed the writing of the book on Germany by nearly two years and came four years after his last play, *Ruy Blas.* Then, after 1843, there was an extraordinarily long interval of silence, so far as new work was concerned.

In the later 1830's the fashion for romantic melodramas perceptibly entered its decline, hastened by Mlle. Rachel, who made her debut with brilliant revivals of Racine. Voices were heard now calling for an end to the gory extravagances that passed for romantic drama, and a return to more reasonable material. A new playwright, Ponsard, appeared late in 1842 and won a great success with his play *Lucrèce,* which seemed to embody the "romanticism of good sense."

Victor Hugo, feeling his dominant position in the French theater assailed, now returned to the wars with his *Les Burgraves,* a poetic drama of epic dimensions, intended to overawe adversaries and imitators alike. For his inspiration, this time, the poet went to the Rhine Valley and more particularly to those ruined castles in the crags above the river, now covered with ivy and wild vines but long ago the citadels of those hereditary Burgraves, or Robber Barons, who once preyed upon all that land and gathered in the loot of travelers and pilgrims passing their way.

The central figure of the drama is Job, the aged, retired Burgrave of Heppenheff, moldering away in his high citadel above the Rhine from which, for forty years, he has continued to wage combat with the Emperor Frederick Barbarossa. The old man lives with his remorse for an old crime, the memory of which haunts him, and for which his wild brood of sons and grandsons hate and curse him—though one devoted person, his great-niece Regina, and her fiancé, Captain Otbert, wait upon him kindly. Originally Job was a son of the German Emperor, we learn, and bore another name; his crime, which he waited to expiate, was that of killing his brother Donato, through lust for the brother's wife, then

THE RHINE
A drawing by Victor Hugo

selling the woman, who refused herself to him, into slavery. The setting of the play is thus a sort of gloomy family bedlam, and the presence of an old slave woman and sorceress, called Guanhumara, who constantly utters dark prophecies and eloquent curses, augments this turmoil. Then Regina falls seriously ill and lies at the verge of death, while her fiancé, Captain Otbert, is flung into despair. But the sorceress, Guanhumara, promises to administer a magic broth restoring Regina to health, if Otbert will slay the man she designates. He accepts, and learns to his revulsion that the man is Job. For Guanhumara is none other than the woman Job once sold into slavery. Thus she plots vengeance upon old Job, to be carried out by Captain Otbert, who—she had secret knowledge— is Job's natural grandson.

Here we have two significant underlying themes: that of the son driven to kill the father—the Oedipus theme (so recurrent in Hugo)—and that of "guilt," the Cain-Abel theme. (Did the poet's unconscious mind accuse him still of having contributed to the undoing of his own beloved brother Eugène in their old contest for the hand of Adèle?)

The drama develops to its climax in a grandiose poetry of horror and elemental passion—yet using one of the cheapest devices of melodrama: the continual revelation of "concealed identities." One of them is the Emperor Barbarossa, who introduces himself into the castle of Heppenheff in the guise of a beggar, but suddenly throws off his rags and asserts his authority over all the rebellious Burgraves, whom he imprisons, halting the plot against Job's life. Furthermore he shows himself to be the long-lost brother Donato, who had actually escaped from the raging torrent into which Job had thrown him long ago. Job is pardoned, and at the same time relieved of his terrible sense of guilt; he dies as one transfigured with joy. The witch, Guanhumara, also pardons him, and Regina and Otbert are married.

The fabulous drama of *Les Burgraves,* much assailed at the time of its appearance for its impenetrable thickets of fantasy and horror, has undergone an unexpected revival in recent times, many modern connoisseurs of Hugo's verse-drama preferring this work to all his others. But its deep and plangent poetry and its symbolic suggestions were ignored when it was performed at the Comédie-Française on March 7, 1843, for it took four hours to play. Mounting it had involved great trouble; the new star, Mlle. Rachel, had indignantly refused to have a part in it. Romantic youth, the long-haired rebels of 1830, failed to put in their appearance among the audience. When Hugo sent an emissary to the artist, Nanteuil, to ask for the aid of his pupils as a claque, the emissary was told: "Go and tell your master there are no more young men left." Even the loyal Gautier was forced to exclaim: "Our army is . . . decimated!" The *Hernanistes* of 1830 were mostly middle-aged, middle-class, married.

The play, received with the silence of boredom, closed after but a few nights, while at the same time, to Hugo's grief, Mlle. Rachel played to crowded audiences in *Lucrèce,* the rather restrained, almost unromantic, tragedy of his new rival, Ponsard. The heyday of Hugolian romanticism seemed over. One newspaper caricature that season showed the great Academician searching the sky with his lorgnon and asking himself why only the comet "had a queue, while *Les Burgraves* had none?"

In the authorized account of these episodes dictated by the

poet, it is related that he determined to retire from the theater after 1843. "M. Hugo no longer cared to expose his thoughts to easy gibes and anonymous hisses; moreover he had less need of the theater now, as he was soon to speak from the tribune."

6

Through the years, whatever his comings and goings, Victor Hugo treated Adèle Hugo, his wife, with much consideration, and maintained the warmest relations and ties with his family; for them he discarded the polite mask he donned before strangers, and no fonder paterfamilias ever doted upon his children than Hugo. Balzac, dining one night at the Place Royale, envied Hugo his handsome children, and thought them a credit to the parent. He was proud of his two promising sons, Charles and François-Victor, aged seventeen and fifteen, respectively, in 1843, and of his beautiful elder daughter Léopoldine, now over eighteen, and the pretty Adèle, now thirteen. He insisted upon holding them close to him. While traveling in distant countries with his mistress he would not forget to fire off numerous and urgent letters to his son Charles, when he thought the boy needed encouragement to face his examination at the Lycée, or to convey his exclamations of delight when Charles or the younger son, François-Victor, gained honors or "firsts." His letters to them were very simple and unaffected, but those to his eldest child, Léopoldine, whom he called 'Didine, were the tenderest of all, and she was something of a rival to Juliette Drouet.

Almost hungrily he loved her. Once when 'Didine was very sick he insisted upon sending everyone away and tending her himself day and night. Ever since she was a child he had been writing her gay foolish letters, full of charming fables. As a grown girl she would read to him when his eyes gave him trouble; she would answer letters for him when he was overwhelmed by his correspondence. She showed spirit and good sense, and seemed to understand her father very well. In appearance she resembled him strongly, with her chestnut hair, her longish oval face, and her firmly cut features. Both the existing portraits of her by Louis Boulanger show her, at ten and seventeen, not only as quite beautiful, but with eyes shining with the joy of life.

At eighteen she was engaged to Charles Vacquerie (the brother of Victor Hugo's earnest disciple, Auguste Vacquerie), a handsome and elegant young man and the scion of a rich provincial family living at Le Havre. After a very brief engagement, they were married on February 15, 1843, at the church of Saint-Paul, and a simple wedding dinner was held for them at the Place Royale with a small number of old friends as guests.

In the summer, the young couple went to stay at Villequier-on-the-Seine, at the country house of Vacquerie's mother. At the same time Victor Hugo, with his mistress and a party of friends, journeyed in Southern France, crossing into Spain, climbing the Pyrenees on September 2, 1843, and returning a week later. He had left no address and, in fact, traveled under an assumed name, a habit which he had found necessary since the early 1830's, to avoid being troubled by crowds and newspaper publicity. Just before leaving for the mountain climb he had written to Mme. Hugo describing his travels, and including a message for 'Didine, from whom, he said, he had just received a letter that was, "as always, full of gentleness and happiness."

Meanwhile, in Normandy, Léopoldine and her husband went boating every day on the Seine. On the morning of September 4, 1843, the young couple, together with Vacquerie's uncle and the latter's small son, went sailing in a small boat along the river's wide mouth. Out of the calm of that morning unexpectedly a violent gust of wind struck down from the hills along the Seine, swung the sail over, and capsized the craft. Only Charles Vacquerie, a strong swimmer, came to the surface. He called for help, then dived beneath the boat again and again, struggling to bring up Léopoldine. She remained submerged in the water, clutching the side of the boat in panic. Unable to save his wife, Charles Vacquerie perished with her—they were found clasping each other closely when their bodies were recovered, as were those of the other two dead. Mme. Hugo, staying near by at Le Havre, learned of the tragedy the next day and was brought to the scene, a completely stricken woman.

Down in the Pyrenees, carefree Victor Hugo walked back to the French side of the border on September 9. Because of his incognito no one had been able to reach him, and the Paris newspapers then took four days to reach the frontier. Tired and thirsty, he reached the village of Soubise, entered a café, and was brought a glass of beer and a newspaper, *Le Siècle*. He opened it and read. That was how he learned that she who was "the half of my life and my heart was dead."

Victor Hugo, as his poems reveal, was always afflicted by a mystic or symbolic "sense of guilt" for men, beasts, and things around him. It had deep bearing upon the sense of pity which grew strong in him in later life. But now, after 1843, he carried with him always a haunting sense of guilt and remorse for having passed so many days in "happy, thoughtless amusement and relaxation" while his favorite child, Léopoldine, lay dead.

The strange death of Victor Hugo's daughter and son-in-law moved all France; the press made much of the tragic circumstances under which the father remained ignorant of the affair for five days.

"Oh God! What have I done? What has thou done to me?" was his outcry. "She was too happy, she had everything, beauty, mind, youth, love. This complete happiness made me tremble for her a little. . . . God did not desire a paradise on earth." Thus he babbled out his despair to the friends who called or wrote him. No loss, one feels, had struck him so hard, since his mother's death twenty years before, and none would ever wound him so sorely again. Olympio, in his sorrow, shut himself up for a time in his great house in Paris. Stricken in the hour of his pleasure and triumph, he seems to lose faith in his God utterly, yet sits writing verses to Léopoldine that call back her soul. There is a shadow over him, and hereafter he moves more warily because of his wound, as if he fears always some evil stroke of that "fatality" or nemesis, which played usually so large a part in his romances.

"The house in the Place Royale is now all gloom and silence," one of his friends wrote, "broken only by the agonized sobs of the poor mother. . . . Hugo sits sadly with his two boys—while the little girl, Adèle, has not yet been told the truth. . . ."

Then he recovered, busying himself with the multitude of public and social activities that his ambitions required, and more than ever with those earthly pleasures that his nature nowadays demanded, more insistently, more grossly than before, partly in an access of cynicism, partly out of desire for forgetfulness.

CHAPTER X

The Strayings of Olympio

Hugo's achievements had been so varied and remarkable, his climb had been so swift, that it became somewhat fashionable to attack him, especially after his entrance into the French Academy. Désiré Nisard, one of the leading literary critics of the day, who had formerly come to praise him, now repented, and wrote of the lamentable spectacle offered by "the decline of a great talent." Nisard railed fiercely at his pretensions to play a large public role and dominate society.

But the hardest blow struck against him was delivered by his old friend Sainte-Beuve, and in the dark. In the early autumn of 1843, only a few weeks after the death of Léopoldine Hugo, the great critic prepared the proofs of the privately printed *Livre d'amour* with its so partisan account of the triangular drama of 1830–1832. The discreditable little volume was printed in an edition of 204 copies, and was duly registered, as of November, 1843, though at first only a dozen copies were circulated among carefully chosen friends of Sainte-Beuve, and especially certain ladies he desired to impress favorably.

It was a blow which, of course, bore most heavily upon Adèle Hugo, and this at an hour when she was a bereaved mother. Now was the time, one of his friends had counseled Sainte-Beuve, to become reconciled with the Hugos and "re-enter his [Victor's] heart by this wide wound." But he had flatly refused the advice, declaring that Hugo had "already given *him* trouble enough"(!). Nor did he think of sparing Adèle, the stricken mother. In his

diary, at this period, is written the cruel sentence: "One of the
truest satisfactions a man may have is to see the woman he has
passionately desired, and who has stubbornly refused herself to
him, cease to be beautiful."

In Paris the book was whispered about as a passing sensation
and even reviewed here and there in gossip sheets as an anonymous
work about anonymous but easily recognizable persons. It was
called by Alphonse Karr a "book of hate" and libel by a certain
"ugly poet" who dreamed that he was once the lover of a fair
woman, and set it all down in mediocre verses. Most people were
wholly incredulous of the book's claims and assumed with one
sprightly commentator that: "A man of honor never admits that
he has been the lover of a woman: but even less does he admit that
he has not been her lover."

Fortunately Adèle Hugo never saw *Le Livre d'amour,* though
Victor Hugo heard of it or saw it, and remained silent, as he nearly
always did when under attack.

When Olympio felt himself too greatly afflicted by adversity or
by the malice of his fellow men, he could always retreat to the
little nest of the rue Saint-Anastase, where the single-hearted
Juliette waited to give him comfort and adoration. Before her he
could discharge the secret bitterness or grief of the moment, as in
the poem dedicated to her, *Il Fait froid* ("It Is Cold . . .") published many years later:

> *Winter whitens the cold road. . . .*
> *Hate is the winter of the heart. . . .*

In her *livre de l'anniversaire* he wrote also at this time: "You
were telling me last night of all the words of hate that escaped
from those creatures in the theater wings. I walked home through
streets covered with frozen sleet, in a mist that stabbed my face.
Then I wrote these lines . . . *They hate us, we must love each
other.*"

He would bring her his burden of private sorrow or bitterness
and she would share it with him unstintedly—while his prosperity
and glory she enjoyed only in a faintly reflected or vicarious manner. For she lived always in retreat, in the background of his
magnificent and public life.

Juliette watched him anxiously, jealously. Her jealousy never
abated even when she was very old. She could not abide the thought

of his going to rehearsals and meeting actresses, or even to the Tuileries to see the Duchess of Orléans. On the other hand Olympio's jealousy subsided noticeably. The claustration of Juliette and all restriction upon her movements was finally relaxed by 1844.

Was it because he held the "redemption" of his Magdalen to be, as she told him now, a completed process? Or was it her white hair and fading lilies? Or was the cause of this moderation one such as Juliette, obsessed as she was, always desperately feared? At moments, she knew ecstatic happiness still at his side. At others, nowadays, she complained sadly of his indifference to her, of his treating her "as if she were a *sister*."

Moving in the great world as he did, confident, handsome, at the prime of his powers at forty, how could it be that women should not fling themselves at his head, as they had flung themselves at Byron's two decades before? His very poems which, as all France knew, recorded his intimate experiences and sang of a great and illicit love, were a provocation to the ladies of the romantic era.

Instinctively women stopped to pay him tribute. Meeting Théodore Pavie one day in the street, he took him by the arm and went into a shop, saying: "I must get a white tie for dinner tonight at the Tuileries. Come and help me choose one." The young lady behind the counter, according to Pavie, was extremely pretty. "As she tried on the silk tie around Victor Hugo's neck, her eyes lingered over him for a moment, examining him, evidently struck by the beauty of the poet's head and brow; and he did not fail to notice her admiration. . . ." But as with the midinettes in the shops, so with the ladies of salon and Court, who had come in crowds to witness his induction into the Academy.

That he was faithful to his "grand passion," Juliette Drouet, for something like a decade is a more or less historic fact. But as he approached middle age, moving in the fairly cynical milieux of Court, House of Peers, and great salons, his moral discipline relaxed, his ideas changed perceptibly toward the skeptical. Under the very influence of the purely worldly and public career that absorbed him so exclusively nowadays, he seemed to write, or at least to publish, no more for almost ten long years. Besides, under the immediate shock of Léopoldine's death—an experience that assumed a wholly different and deeper meaning in later recollection—his bitterness at the personal loss brought him to depths of unbelief. The hand of fate seemed meaningless and unjust, yet life went on, spring came again, and he donned his silk hat and frock coat to go to sessions at the Luxembourg Palace, or receptions at the Tuileries. Being essentially religious by nature, his thoughts soon again assumed a "religious" form, but were heretical, Olympian, and pantheistic. This mood, again, directly encouraged a certain liberty in private morals. Indeed Victor Hugo's moral progress moved in a distinct line, from the painful chastity and puritanism of his youth, to the incontinence and hedonism of his middle years and his incredibly virile old age.

2

Thus, one day in July, 1845, Parisian society was much diverted by a partly hushed-up scandal that was a nine-days wonder at all the café clubs and was spoken of in the gossip columns of the newspapers as "involving one of our most celebrated authors." Or, as the republican-minded *National* hinted: ". . . *An illustrious personage who combines the laurels of Parnassus with the ermine of the Peerage has been caught in criminal intercourse* with a certain well-known painter's wife, who has been arrested, while the (unnamed) statesman has been temporarily released."

Parisian legend, which eventually credited Victor Hugo with every conceivable variety of experience, credited him with the misadventure of 1845, alleged to have taken place in an apartment in the fashionable rue Saint-Roch. A certain *sofa*, according to legend, also played a notable part in the affair, for underneath it was posted a dull but patient *commissaire de police*, invited by an outraged husband to apprehend the statesman and the lady *flagrante delicto*. In fact the indignant husband, a successful portrait painter named Auguste Biard, had suspected his wife of entertaining adulterous relations with someone he described to the police as "an actor of the boulevards, with long hair." What was their astonishment when the man in the case turned out to be a Peer of France, who claimed parliamentary immunity from police examination. But M. Biard, desiring vengeance and having wealth and influence, pressed a suit for large damages, and prepared to carry the case to the Luxembourg Palace, that is, before the House of Peers, an unheard-of thing.

"Paris speaks of nothing but this affair," comments Sainte-Beuve in a letter of that season. "Think of my chagrin and my embarrassment over all this. . . ." For the lady in the case things went hard, according to another gossiping letter, by Lamartine, who says: "The amorous adventure of my poor friend Victor Hugo is desolating. They say that he has been forced to leave Paris in order to forestall a demand for prosecution of him in the Chamber of Peers; but what must be heart-rending to him, is to know that the poor woman has been flung into prison while he is free." In truth, the lady in question was committed to the Saint-Lazare prison for a night, but then sent away to a convent outside of Paris, for a confinement of six months—where she was later reported to have won the hearts of the nuns by reciting to them Victor Hugo's poems! Hugo, who was to have given his maiden speech in the House of Peers with a prepared address on industrial patents, delayed his debut, and was believed to have gone abroad.

Meanwhile, his wife, Adèle, turned heaven and earth to bring about a dismissal of the suit. With the aid of the Duchess of Orléans and King Louis-Philippe himself, the suit which "threatened to soil the ermine robe of the peerage," as the journalists said, was set aside. This was done by ordering a donation to the vengeful artist from the royal treasury, while a private sermon was administered to the poet by Pasquier, the president of the Chamber. All was hushed up, his debut in the upper chamber merely suffered a delay of six months. As Lamartine remarked: "France has an elastic spirit and a man can rise again *even from a sofa*." A whole police dossier covering this curious affair was prepared in 1845. But whether it described the piece of furniture implicated will probably never be known. For one day, during the revolution of February, 1848, Alfred Asseline, a young official of the Prefecture of Police who was engaged in removing secret documents to places of safety, came upon the Hugo dossier. He was a relative of Hugo and turned it over to him.

In May, 1844, about a year before the scandal burst forth, he had first met Léonie Biard at a salon gathering. She was young, only twenty-five, tall and blonde; according to the memoirs of Arsène Houssaye, she was not merely pretty but "mysterious" and "of an undulent and serpentine beauty." Her small, ugly, jealous husband—as Chopin once described him—was rich, but nearly twice her age, and she had determined to be separated from him. Born Léonie d'Aunet, the daughter of an army officer, she was well-bred and intelligent. She set literature, poetry, romance, love, above all things—then, finding all of this in the poet of the Place Royale, determined to conquer him and soon held him at her feet.

For years he was infatuated with her and wrote her burning letters and enchanting poems. This time the affair was conducted with a great deal of discretion and secrecy.

Mme. Biard was free to come and go in good society, or, even, when gatherings were held at the salon of the Place Royale, into the master's study, for she was known and indulgently treated by poor Mme. Hugo. She was known also to Victor Hugo's children, whose eyes missed nothing. After the scandal had blown over and Mme. Biard, separated from her husband, returned to Paris, they saw each other again—Victor Hugo being a determined man, and all the more so because of the discomfiture he had been subjected to. This went on for a long time.

The wonder of the whole story is that, while all Paris had laughed over the affair, Juliette of all people had heard nothing. Her friends out of pity for her kept the secret. Nowadays she saw him less often, because of state affairs, she thought. In 1845, there had been some malicious gossip about Juliette, and she had written Victor about it, and begged him to pay no heed to it. He had asked her to give no ear to malicious scandal about himself. If she heard anything, she gave it no attention, perhaps in very fear that it might be true.

For years, having acted as his literary secretary and copyist, she had the habit of going through the daily newspapers to cut clippings that referred to him, or might be of some interest to him. But on the morning when the story was printed in the two or three newspapers he could not reach with his influence—the *Débats* and *La Presse* were kept silent—Victor Hugo smilingly appeared at Juliette's door, and told her that he himself had already taken care of all the newspaper clippings.

Besides, he brought news that filled her with delight. He wanted to remain secluded with her for some days or weeks—for instead of flying abroad he had decided to hide at Juliette's apartment until the storm blew over. This alone, in ignorance of his real reasons, made Juliette very happy.

Thus he was punished again in consequence of his escapade with Léonie Biard, for, while infatuated with the other woman, he found himself locked up for many weeks in the charge of the assiduous Juliette.

When young Asseline later on brought the police dossier to Victor Hugo, he simply laughed and destroyed it. Perhaps it was at this time that he wrote the lines, included in his posthumous verses, *Toute la lyre,* upon the "unsolved problem of man and woman," lines that aspire for the time when

> . . . *The unhappy human race*
> *Would some day dare shake off the old dark yoke*
> *Of the heart, thenceforth free to love as the mind to believe.*

In 1847, when he was forty-five years old, Olympio was divided in his attachments between not two, but three households: that of his wife, that of Juliette Drouet, and that of Mme. Biard. But, as if this were not enough, like a middle-aged triton the Prince of Poets pursued his growing taste for women still farther afield. One day, in the company of his son Charles, now a high-spirited young man of twenty-two, Victor Hugo met the youthful actress Alice Ozy. An extraordinary beauty, she had already been celebrated by various poets, especially Théophile Gautier. The father, smitten at once, became a rival of his son for the favor of the charming young actress. She seemed flattered, and received the great poet with respect and sympathy, but, according to existing accounts, yielded the favors of her boudoir only to his determined young son. For various reasons the boudoir of Alice Ozy was famous in the demi-monde of Paris, partly because it had an immense antique bed as its *pièce de résistance,* one made of rosewood and incrusted with old Sèvres. One day, in response to his entreaties, Alice Ozy invited Victor Hugo to enter and see the bed "since the subject seemed to him worthy of his pen. . . ." He came, he saw, and wrote her a salty quatrain, which remained long hidden in the papers of the actress, to be discovered by latter-day bibliophiles:

> *Platon disait, à l'heure où le couchant pâlit:*
> *"Dieu du ciel, montrez-moi Venus sortant de l'onde!*
> *Moi je dis, le coeur plein d'une ardeur plus profonde:*
> *Madame, montrez-moi Venus entrant au lit."*

Mlle. Ozy, refusing to play Venus as invited, told Olympio that she found his verses "a little light," and tactfully refused his solicitations. Victor Hugo suffered a reverse, but evidently took it in good part; for he wrote her another quatrain beginning:

> *Un rêveur quelquefois blesse ce qu'il admire!*

Sometimes the dreamer wounds that which he most admires, he said apologetically, adding in his letter: "I certainly find you unjust, madame, but I am also compelled to declare that you are charming. I was wrong and you were right. I was wrong to think only of your beauty.

"Will you, then, with your gracious heart, excuse the license immemorial of poets accustomed to address themselves familiarly to kings as well as women, and permit me to lay before your feet, in prose, my humble respects."

For several months the poet seemed to enjoy calling on the young actress, in the guise of a paternal admirer. This did not prevent him, however, from writing the remarkable sketch in *Choses vues* ("Things Seen") entitled "After Nature" and describing an adventure credited to Alice Ozy. At a challenge from one of her lovers, the artist Chassériau, she engages in a trial of beauty, drops her robe, steps forth like one of the models of Praxiteles, and wins the day. When Mlle. Ozy, in dignified retirement of old age and wealth, forty years later, read all this, she cried out against Victor Hugo, then already in his grave, calling him not the King of Poets, but the "King of all the swine."

Romantic love as practiced in the 1840's by such famous devotees as a Victor Hugo or a George Sand and an Alfred de Musset, was part mystical, part hypocritical. The mystical aspect is suggested in the strange power the middle-aged poet was said to exercise over women who were both young and old. One report dating from the late 1840's refers to a mysterious viscountess, living in an aristocratic old quarter of Paris, who figured for a time in his rites; another to a young girl of seventeen, whose letters, found among his papers, were signed "Claire," and who even attempted one day to fly from her respectable family for the poet's sake.

One such letter, dated 1849, directed to Hugo at the Legislative Assembly, reads:

Sometimes, I am afraid I am doing wrong in seeing you like this without the knowledge of my family.

I come to you as to my beloved poet, in whom I have as much faith as in God, whatever people may say. If you love me ever so little, you will not take advantage of a girl of seventeen, whose only fault is to love you too well—that is, according to what people say. For you know that one can never love you too much, and that, in any case, it can never be wrong to do so.

Thus, in the full summer of his life, Olympio was as if intoxicated with liberties and magic powers akin to those exercised by the priests and kings of ancient pagan tribes. Out of this licentious season of his life flowed those many tales that long regaled France, of Hugo the Panlike peopling Paris with his natural offspring. In this period also his departure from Christian morality and his absorption in pantheistic and occult doctrine become marked.

These mystical qualities, in an earlier, weaker form, had been noticed years before, by one of the most curiously erudite of Hugo's many acquaintances, André Weill, the French-Jewish occult philosopher and exponent of the cabala. Hugo's poems had shown a tendency toward animism, or the belief in the spirituality of animals and matter; they reflected often a "sense of guilt" and on the other hand a sense of the poet's own "divinity," the belief that he was a soul apart in his function as a poet, one of the magi, one of the elect, with a mission to perform. These mystical tendencies—to anticipate events a little—grew ever stronger, and in time led Hugo, like Tolstoy, his younger Russian contemporary, to a profound and agonizing religious experience. But at the stage of his peerage, in the closing years of the Orléans regime, he was moved neither by remorse nor by the solemn aspects of his "mission" but lived rather like some prodigal satyr.[1]

Weill had greatly admired one of Hugo's poems, *A Mlle. Louise B——* (dated 1835), which, reviewing three possible ways of faith, Christianity, deism, or naturalistic pantheism, seemed to favor the last:

> *Good, evil, death, false gods or vice—*
> *What do they mean under this radiant heaven?*
> *No, Pan asks not that we pray . . .*

Weill called on Hugo, and soon they were friends. The poet enjoyed listening to Weill, as they rambled about the streets of Paris, expounding his versions of the cabala and other occult doctrines pleasing to his mind, which denied the Fall of man. Weill relates

[1] At this period, the Saint-Simonians (utopian socialists) whom Hugo had known through Sainte-Beuve at one time, not only preached economic equality but were mystics and occultists, sometimes solemnly preaching free love. Pierre Leroux, editor of *Le Globe*, one of the leading pre-Marxian socialists, was also known for his books on the philosophy of pantheism. Leroux was greatly attracted by Victor Hugo's writings, and often urged that he augment his pantheism with the true faith of socialism.

Regarding the influence of André Weill, the reader must note that this follower of Fourier and cabalistic philosopher was in no way connected with the orthodox religious thought of the Jewish communities, but was a heretic.

that Hugo conceived an affection for him and used him as a kind of "living reference book" on German history, literature, and occultism. He testifies:

Hugo knew woman very well, her charms and her dangers. After I had quoted for him several rather scatological (little known) poems of Goethe, current in the beer halls of German universities, he gave me some highly original advice about love, based on close observation, which I have never forgotten.

Weill also claims that he lent Hugo the occult books he was translating into French, "Zohar" and "The Mysteries of Creation," which supported the poet's own growing convictions concerning the "divine nature" of sensuality and the fecundity of "elect beings." Accompanying Hugo upon his rounds of Paris by night to certain salons, or even to the homes of lower-class women, Weill observed that the poet seemed truly to be playing Jupiter! In his *Mémoires* he comments:

Was this pride or poetic hallucination? It is a phenomenon of the will, such as one rarely meets in the history of letters. . . . Hugo, like Louis XIV, scattered his bastards everywhere. I know of . . . one son who is very proud of his origin (as a result of a certain brief liaison). I have known a very young girl who later became the wife of a journalist, who boasted everywhere, even in my drawing room, of being the daughter of the great poet, whose handsome profile she definitely had. . . . In a certain mansion of the rue des Capucines Hugo was adored like the god that he was, or thought he was, in good faith. Adultery seemed no more a crime to him than to Jupiter. And in fact, all the women of that period loved him, not exactly for his genius, but for his masculine beauty; for in the matter of love woman believes in the Holy Eucharist only under its real, or physical presence. Hugo was a veritable Olympian; his physique was convincing evidence of his metaphysics.

3

For several years Victor Hugo faithfully attended the séances of the French Academy, sat at its hallowed green table with the other Immortals, and gravely debated with them over the meaning, usages, and spelling of words being entered into the official French dictionary, a task carried on since the days of Cardinal Richelieu. The award of prizes, such as Hugo himself had once competed for, electioneering for new members, and ceremonial receptions of all sorts also occupied the Academicians. While serving for a time as "Director" of the Academy, it fell to Victor Hugo to make the address of reception, on February 27, 1845, to Sainte-Beuve (whose election he had opposed up to the last in favor of Alfred de Vigny). Even Sainte-Beuve admitted that on this occasion Hugo "behaved very well toward me—all the more because there were certain points in my speech which the day before . . . he had wished me to modify. Yet, in spite of my refusal to do so, he made no change in his complimentary remarks about me." Hugo's speech on Sainte-Beuve had an Olympian detachment from personal resentments and was a model of good taste. But when, a short time later, at an elaborate funeral ceremony for some Academician, the two former literary brothers found themselves riding together in the same cab, the poet's face was a graven mask and Sainte-Beuve's attempts at an exchange of amenities were coldly rebuffed.

Then, after 1848, Hugo suddenly wearied of the Academy and its tedious games, and came to its sessions no more, save on one occasion toward the end of his life—when the members almost failed to recognize him.

At the Luxembourg Palace, where sat the House of Peers, more ornamental than useful, Victor Hugo took the position of an independent. As long ago as 1833, in a letter to Thiers, then Minister of the Interior, he had declared that he preferred not to belong to any political party, but intended to judge or support each "in accordance with the degree in which it seemed to be working for the interests of the country, in my opinion." At that time he wrote also in his Preface to Les Voix intérieures: "One must be with all the parties on their generous side; and with none of them on their bad side."

It made for a most peculiar political position, which to the outside eye looked like political opportunism. Victor Hugo was considered generally an ornamental ally of the King and, with good reason, hoped for a Ministerial office. His diary notes show him in touch constantly with the highest political personages of the age:

June 12, 1846: Dined yesterday with the Duc Decazes; and met Lord Palmerston and Lord Lansdowne. Lady Palmerston is very beautiful.

January 14, 1847: At M. de Salvandy's I talked with the British Ambassador on the Irish question.

February 5, 1847: At the Tuileries, talked with people about Guizot's fine speech.

July 6, 1847: Attended the Duc de Montpensier's fête. . . . There were 4,000 guests. Dancing and splendid fireworks. All the princesses were there. . . . This display of luxury and magnificence makes the populace very discontented. They grumble. . . .

Among the men who surrounded Louis-Philippe, Hugo endeavored to distinguish himself by advocating what he called the "politics of ideas," that is, by assuming a more liberal or idealistic policy than the others. After his first prepared address on the prosaic subject of patents, which was coolly received, he made a speech (fully memorized in advance) upon the disturbances in Poland, now in the final throes of partition and extermination, urging that France give Poland the strongest possible moral support. Somewhat later, on January 13, 1848, he made a vigorous speech in eulogy of Pope Pius IX as one who "adopted the French Revolution and made of it the Christian revolution . . ." a speech which was disliked heartily by those Peers present who disapproved of Pius's temporary fervor for Italian democracy. The orator showed enthusiasm for charity and progress, but also did not fail to refer tactfully to King Louis-Philippe as "the most illustrious monarch of Europe."

One day, at the Luxembourg, Decazes, a former Minister, asked Hugo what his ideas of policy were. Hugo answered that he was for an alliance with Germany and the transfer of the Rhineland to France. Decazes went off shaking his head and exclaiming: "Poetry! Poetry!" The Peers neither took the poet seriously nor relished his enthusiasms. In truth, Victor Hugo, who had shown great integrity in his own field, had fallen into rather low company in the House of Peers: two of his colleagues, Teste and Cubières, were thieves, who were tried and sentenced for embezzlement from the government treasury; a third, the noble Duc de Praslin, turned out to be a murderer, killing his wife and committing suicide in 1847, this completing a series of current scandals that agitated all France and shook the government. Meanwhile hard times were putting in their appearance, the poor harvests of 1845 and 1846 combining with devastating floods to spread destitution.

There had been, in fact, no real revolution in 1830, as one French statesman observed; "only a simple change in the person of the head of the state . . . for a more acceptable member of the Bourbon family." Electoral liberty was harshly restricted, only about one per cent of the male population, that which owned property and paid 200 francs ($40) in annual taxes, having the right to vote for representatives. In other words, even small businessmen had no voice in the government. Wages were two francs a day for from twelve to eighteen hours, for unskilled laborers; labor unions were prohibited as being conspiracies against the state. In short it was an oppressively bourgeois government replacing with its own forms of repression those of its feudal predecessors. Now, after the swift industrial expansion of the 1840's, a crisis of "overproduction" appeared in 1847, and unemployment, beggary, larceny, and rioting were on the increase in the large cities. Meanwhile the government did nothing. But, for all its disappointments, 1830 had brought a revival of the fighting tradition of the common people in France. By a coincidence three great histories, giving a new and sympathetic interpretation of the French Revolution, by Michelet, Lamartine, and Louis Blanc, were published in 1847, and all had a wide popular hearing. Demonstrations by the republican opposition against Guizot, the Conservative Minister, grew bolder. The Liberals, in their press, loudly demanded a wider extension of the suffrage to all, or at least to much greater numbers of citizens than those paying 200 francs a year in taxes; parliamentary reform was also demanded, for by a system of job patronage many of the Deputies themselves were kept in the direct pay of the King. By rigid party votes all moves for reform were beaten in 1847.

Victor Hugo took no hand then in the rising republican opposition movement led principally by the groups directing the newspapers *Le National* and *La Réforme,* and including Ledru-Rollin, the popular orator, Louis Blanc, the defender of the unemployed workingmen, and Lamartine, now an accomplished orator but occupying a moderate position on the Left. The master of the Place Royale, though recognizing the evil omens of distress, collaborated with his friend Emile de Girardin, publisher of the erratic and sensational *Presse,* which still gave its support to Louis-Philippe.

On June 14, 1847, Victor Hugo spoke in favor of a motion to permit the return of members of the Bonaparte family, banished since 1815. Alluding to the popular unrest in France, he said warningly: "The people must not suffer! The people must not go hungry!" He continued:

As for me, when I see how consciences are debased nowadays, money reigning supreme, corruption spreading, the highest offices in the land invaded by men of the basest appetites, when I see the miseries of the present, I think of the great hours of the past, and I am tempted to say to the Chamber, to the press, and to all France: Let us speak a little of the Emperor, it will do us good! (Loud and prolonged applause.)

In this troubled hour, the orator called men's minds back to the patriotic and "heroic" age of Napoleon, "if only to occupy them with something else." His words "Let us speak a little of the Emperor . . ." were widely repeated, for the cult of Bonapartism always smoldered under the surface of French popular passion. The speech appears now like an all too clever maneuver, an attempt at political diversion, and one that ended, as usual, with a eulogy of the reigning King.

A student of Hugo's political career, Camille Pelletan, a younger friend and later an enlightened statesman himself, holds that the poet at this time was "a prisoner of the Tuileries." For Hugo it was a "sterile" period. He was obsessed by his fixed ambitions, his friendly alliance with the Duchess of Orléans, considered the future regent, and all these considerations made him try to cover the July Monarchy with some of the glory of Napoleon.

The motives of Victor Hugo were mixed; there were many strands of contradiction in the texture of his politics; his ambitions were as transparent as they were mundane. Certainly, he was then no ardent democrat who would give all power to the masses of people and their representatives, but a sort of Liberal constitutional monarchist. Moreover, he had been nearly all his life on poor terms with the coterie of intellectuals who (through the *National*) led the vigorous republican Left. These men, who considered themselves the spiritual heirs of Robespierre and Danton, worked feverishly to bring about *their* revolution—but also were prepared, as their private papers now show us, to use the most ruthless violence in putting down the "wild men" of the proletariat.

Curiously enough, Victor Hugo, while attached to the Court, always had many more points of contact with the extreme Left than with the middle-class republicans. Over the years he saw a good deal of the various utopian sects of socialists, followers of Saint-Simon, who advocated a scientific reorganization of society along co-operative lines, as a means of solving the problem of poverty. Now many of the early socialists (in those pre-Marxian days) preached indifference or neutrality in politics; many of them even believed that *a monarchy would be as favorable or more favorable to the realization of their dreams than a so-called democratic regime.*[2] Many of them, like Enfantin, the well-known successor of Saint-Simon, were preachers of a mystical religion of humanitarianism, now resembling a heretical Christianity, or now pantheism and occultism. Enfantin once addressed Victor Hugo in a letter as follows: "Poet and priest in one, it is through you that the male word of God will penetrate all men . . . bringing glory and love to all!"

Why did the utopian reformers (who lived in the slums of Paris by choice, or worked in Fourierist communities in the country) continue to look to Victor Hugo as a coming leader? Indeed, he was, with one or two exceptions, perhaps that of Eugène Sue, the favorite author of workingmen's reading circles that were formed at this period. For, from the very first, many passages in his volumes of poems expressed most powerfully the sense of pity for the poor and humble, an emotion which often appeared like some universal sense of guilt. One of his early poems, *Regard jeté dans une mansarde* ("Through a Mansard Window"), portrayed the life of a poor Parisian streetgirl in most charitable though sentimental terms. He had written two books advocating the abolition of capital punishment, a hobby with him: *Claude Gueux,* published in 1834, was a short novel upon the same theme as the earlier "Last Day of a Condemned Man," which it surpassed, with its powerful special pleading. All this had commended him warmly to the humanitarian-socialists. Finally, by his influence in high quarters he had several times interceded to aid political prisoners. On one occasion, in 1839, he was at a theater and received word that Armand Barbès, the fiery young revolutionist who had recently made an abortive attempt at an insurrection, was to die on the guillotine the following morning. At once, he wrote a brief message, in verse, to King Louis-Philippe, pleading for the pardon of Barbès. The King accorded a pardon at the last hour.

The idealistic reformers in the 1840's had the definite impression that Victor Hugo was "growing" in his views. André Weill, who was a Fourierist, reported in 1845 that the Academician and Peer was actually at work upon a long novel, which would soon

[2] See Appendix Note III.

justify all their hope in him. Hugo had shown some of it to Weill. It was entitled (then) *Les Misères* ("Misery"), and had an escaped convict for its hero, while another principal character was a fallen woman. Incidentally, Hugo's political theories of this period, 1845–1848, were clearly reflected in the career of his convict (then called Jean Tréjean, but later Jean Valjean), who becomes a rich but charitable capitalist and spreads prosperity among hundreds of poor people employed in his new industry.

"For the first time in fifteen years, I feel a certain fear for the future!" exclaimed Count Alexis de Tocqueville in the Chamber of Deputies, in 1847. In fragments of his notes, dated 1847, we see Victor Hugo also expressing the same concern:

Ministers—for seven years, nearly eight years, what have you done? Have you regulated finances? No, there are failures everywhere. . . . There are floods. Have you regulated the food problem? No, there is a famine. . . . Have you reformed the Chamber of Deputies, the election laws?

The July government suddenly becomes feeble—apologizing for doing nothing, without control over emotions and rumors in the public square, more fearsome of a riot than Napoleon of twenty battles.

Hugo felt that, for seventeen years, the government had left the masses without bread and given the country no glory. "We must turn ourselves to the people, the people, grave, calm, courageous and patient, who work and suffer and, gradually by a series of urgent reforms and improvements, create wealth out of their work and well-being, out of their suffering."

At the beginning of 1848, the movement for electoral reform was blocked in the Chamber of Deputies, then firmly tied to the King. Outside, the Liberals took to holding large "reform" banquets, since open political gatherings were prohibited, with speeches on the issues of the day and toasts to liberty and reform. The cries of *"Vive la réforme!"* grew louder, the speakers grew more caustic; some of them were even disaffected officers of the National Guard, the body of militia which had often defended the reigning government in street battles.

The King clung to Minister Guizot, who continued to bargain stubbornly with the reformers. Perhaps the voting restrictions might be compromised at 100 francs tax payment instead of 200?

On February 19, 1848, the government suddenly sent police to

stop an especially large banquet held at a gathering place on the
Champs Elysées. The Liberal deputy, Odilon Barrot, protested
against the police intrusion with an oration—but yielded peaceably
enough. However, when a still larger reform banquet was announced for two days later, with the guests invited to parade along
the boulevards to the meeting place, the government moved ener-
getically to suppress this demonstration, and announced that regular troops would be concentrated along a section of the Boulevard
de la Madeleine. At this order, in fear of a bloody clash, Barrot
and the other Liberals timidly agreed to call off the meeting of
February 21, and the government also agreed not to order in the
regular army. Both sides drew in their horns. But the public knew
nothing or would hear nothing of these delicate negotiations in
high quarters, and on the morning of February 22, 1848, the
streets of the capital resounded with running feet and loud cries.
Rioting spread widely. The people—the Uninvited Guest—had
arrived upon the scene.

Louis-Philippe had often shown steadiness in a crisis. But he
was seventy-five, and now grew weary and hesitant. He had thirty
thousand regular soldiers surrounding the city on February 22 and
23, but feared to send them in and shed blood. He was told also
that the National Guard would probably not obey orders if it
were called out. All day, on February 23, the King puzzled over
relinquishing Guizot and replacing him with the less hated Thiers,
another card from the same old deck—while the cries of the
menacing crowds outside the Tuileries thundered at his window.
But soon events took a much graver turn, rendering the King's
opinion or decision entirely superfluous.

At three o'clock on February 23, Victor Hugo, curious to learn
more of what was going on, walked over to the Chamber of
Deputies, passing a long column of men in shirt sleeves and caps,
who marched in close ranks toward the rue de Lille, near the
Chamber, which was guarded by battalions of infantry, with
rifles ready. "It is only a riot," some Deputies said to him, and
some of them seemed happy over it. He went out to look. At the
Place de la Concorde, mounted guards were protecting the bridge,
and other horse guards, wheeling about with sabers drawn, were
driving back a silent, passive crowd at the bridgehead. There was
no fighting; a flimsy little barricade was being knocked down by
soldiers, along the Champs Elysées. Everybody said there was
rioting in Paris, that people had been killed; but it was always

somewhere else and no one had seen it. Inside the Chamber, a bill regulating banking law was being debated dully.

Hugo walked the streets: he met an old literary friend, Antony Thouret, a Red republican, disheveled and weary after haranguing crowds all day, who assured him that the people were up in arms. That night, Paris celebrated wildly news of the removal of Minister Guizot. Victor Hugo, unable to sleep, walked about his quarter near the Place Royale. He passed a great procession heading toward the boulevards with torches and flags, gaily singing. His notes run:

Midnight is striking. The appearance of the streets is changed. The Marais quarter is lugubrious. I have just returned from a stroll there. The street lamps are broken and extinguished. . . . The Place Royale is guarded like a place of arms. Troops are in ambush under the arcades. In the rue Saint-Louis, a battalion is leaning silently against the walls in the shadow.

Just now, as the clock struck the hour, we went out on the balcony, listening and saying: "It is the tocsin!"

I could not have slept in bed. I passed the night in my drawing room, writing, thinking and listening. Now and then I went out on the balcony and strained my ears to listen, then I entered the room again and paced to and fro, or dropped into an armchair and dozed. But my slumber was agitated by feverish dreams. I dreamed that I could hear the murmur of angry crowds, and the report of distant firing; the tocsin was clanging from the church towers. I awoke. *It was the tocsin!*

The reality was more horrible than the dream.

For centuries the tocsin ringing called out the people of Paris in time of general danger. The crowd he had seen marching and singing had gone unmolested down the boulevards. But when it reached the Boulevard des Capucines a mass of regular troops, infantry and cavalry, stationed near the Ministry of Foreign Affairs, barred the way. The leaders of the procession were unable to turn the crowd about; the front ranks were pushed forward by the mass behind. Suddenly a shot was fired, "on which side is not known." A panic ensued, and a volley. Eighty persons fell dead or wounded. Then arose a general cry of horror and fury. The bodies of the victims were placed upon a great catafalque and paraded about the streets, by torchlight, accompanied by a grim, cursing crowd, ever swelling in numbers. At dawn Paris bristled everywhere with great barricades manned by thousands of armed workingmen.

PART TWO

The Public Man

CHAPTER XI

Revolution: 1848

P_ARIS WAS FESTIVE_ on the morning of the twenty-fourth of February. At daybreak, Victor Hugo, from his window at the Place Royale, saw and heard a band of the rebellious National Guards take over the adjoining Mayoralty building in his precinct, and force its occupants to deliver their arms. Restlessness gained him. He went out and walked the streets. Crossing the crowded Place de l'Hôtel de Ville with great difficulty, the poet felt himself in the midst of a "tumultuous human ocean." Here and there on his' route were barricades; he was recognized, and the insurgents good-humoredly let him climb over them and pass on. He sensed that the capital was firmly in the hands of the people of Paris. Once more they had risen with their old light-hearted courage—the students tumbling out of school to join the insurrection; workingmen in blue blouses; white-haired old men of distinguished countenance, who thought the days of 1792 had come again, and seemed radiant with joy; unemployed laborers in rags; gallant young hotheads, crying "Long Live the Republic!"; National Guards, in uniform, crying "Down with Guizot!"; and little street gamins, dragging arms or sabers they had stolen, singing songs, hundreds of Parisian foundlings, old beyond their years, romping about, spreading the news: "It is a revolution," in other words, a holiday.

Arriving at the Chamber of Deputies, Victor Hugo noted the confusion among the leading statesmen. The King, learning that the National Guard of Paris had rebelled and that the regular troops were permitting themselves to be disarmed, had removed

Guizot and named Thiers to head his cabinet, with Odilon Barrot included to represent "reform." But it was too late. Bullets whistled across the river at the Carrousel Bridge, opposite the Tuileries Palace. Inside the palace Emile de Girardin, the newspaper publisher, in a stormy harangue was urging Louis-Philippe to abdicate in favor of his grandson, the Count of Paris, naming the child's mother, the Duchess of Orléans as Queen Regent. (At the same hour, the Paris masses were invading the Chamber of Deputies, and Lamartine, the erstwhile romantic poet, standing on a chair, made a torrential speech that induced the people to leave in peace.) Weary, frightened, the King signed his abdication, though only in the name of his grandson, and took carriage for Saint-Cloud, the first stage of his stealthy flight into exile. Among the Deputies, Odilon Barrot, Emile de Girardin, and Lamartine had been committed previously to naming the Duchess of Orléans as Queen Regent, a task that remained undone. Hugo, eager to help execute this scheme, held a brief conference with his old lawyer, Barrot, leader of the Liberal opposition party under the Orléans regime, and acting in the last hour as Prime Minister— Thiers having been dropped. Then the poet, feeling as if he were acting in one of his own plays, rushed forth through the crowds to his own quarter to help lead the people in the desired direction, and proclaim the Regency.

But, hour by hour, direction of the uprising was passing to the radical leaders among the Paris crowd, who, according to an old tradition, gathered to set up a provisional government in the historic old Hôtel de Ville, seat of the Municipal Council of Paris. Barrot's speech to the Chamber of Deputies in favor of the Duchess of Orléans was a half-hearted effort. The duchess herself had been forced to escape from the Tuileries when a crowd broke into her apartment, and had taken refuge with military guards in the Invalides, where she awaited events. Hugo had sent word urging her to show herself before the masses at the Hôtel de Ville—"A mother and child—I will answer for the people." But it was thought by other counselors that the temper of the people was too menacing.

Hurrying back to the Place Royale, near the populous Saint-Antoine quarter, Hugo mounted the balcony of the *Mairie* and spoke to a large crowd, announcing the abdication of the King, the establishment of the new Liberal Ministry, and proclaiming the Duchess of Orléans as Queen Regent. He noticed that his

VICTOR HUGO

As a Deputy, toward 1849

words had an indifferent effect on his hearers. Then, although warned of the danger he ran, with a small retinue of political friends he hastened on to the Place de la Bastille, the very vortex of the insurrection, where about twenty thousand persons were gathered, many of them armed. Here he climbed the base of the July Column and struggled to make himself heard. The turbulent audience heckled him. "No! No regency," they cried. "Neither king nor queen! No masters!" Out of inexperience, Victor Hugo tried to answer those who interrupted him. For an orator this is fatal, for he must pretend that he stands above hostile interruptions, he must maintain his authority or give way. He swore that he himself would abide no personal rule, that the Queen Regent would guarantee liberty, unlike Louis-Philippe. "Look at Queen Victoria in England——" he argued.

"We are French. We want no queen!" the people shouted: "Long live the Republic!"

A man in a blouse shouted: " 'Let the peer of France be silent. Down with the peer of France!' And he leveled his rifle at me. I gazed at him steadily. . . ." But the attitude of most of the crowd was respectful and mild, and Victor Hugo, unable to make himself heard, was permitted to go his way. The whole February revolution against Louis-Philippe, the "revolution of contempt," as it was then called, was peaceful.

Victor Hugo, long immured in the conservative Orléans milieu, was utterly unaware of the forces of history already in motion; he was taken by surprise, as were other, far more experienced politicians. At this crowded hour, another romantic poet—for there was a great deal of romanticism in the revolution of February, 1848—Alphonse de Lamartine, his old acquaintance, used the power of the word to calm the crowd, but proclaimed the free republic they thirsted for, and for this was hailed as the hero of the day. When a little earlier the Duchess of Orléans, with her two children and the Duke of Nemours, had come to the Chamber, Lamartine had uttered the phrase that all powerful revolutions bring forth: "Too late!" He could no longer support her and must move with the tide. The duchess withdrew, and was soon on her way to England.

Before the great, insurrectionary crowd, by shouts of "yes" or "no" in a quickly improvised "election," a Provisional Government was named. It was headed by Lamartine (as Premier and Minister of Foreign Affairs) and included Ledru-Rollin, the Left republican orator; Arago, the distinguished scientist and Liberal leader; Louis Blanc, a moderate socialist (as *Commissaire* of Labor); and other less-known men, journalists and lawyers, who had been associated with the middle-class republican newspapers, *Le National* and *La Réforme*. A remarkable and motley-colored *de facto* Ministry, it was headed by a poet—though one with diplomatic and parliamentary experience—and included an astronomer, Arago. Yet it proclaimed the Republic in France, created order, functioned for three months until a regularly elected parliament replaced it, and issued a series of historic reform decrees: for the elimination of capital punishment, for the elimination of slavery in French territories, for the establishment of universal manhood suffrage, freedom of press and speech, and the "right to work," which involved government relief to the unemployed through National Workshops directed by Louis Blanc.

The "labor question" had raised its head in France, in 1848, and for about two months the Provisional Government appeared to be dominated by the working class of Paris, frequently petitioning, or demonstrating, or making noisy but peaceful incursions upon the Government officers to exert their pressure directly. The dark, crowded cities of Europe vibrated with an excitement that spread from the English Channel to the Vistula, and soon there were popular risings in many of the great capitals that made 1848 a memorable and "Red" year.

Under the industrial revolution, virtually no attention had been paid to labor as such. Official Government investigations made under the republic of 1848 showed that poverty among the workers took fantastic forms, that even women and children were driven to work fourteen hours a day, that in the industrial and mining sections of northern France laborers' families had only damp, squalid cellars to live in, that wages were barely at the level of animal existence, that only employers had legal bargaining rights. Under leaders chosen from their own class, the masses of Paris— who moved far beyond provincial France—wrested concessions from the new Government in the shape of work relief, much like that of the New Deal in the United States in 1933. The revolution had actually been engineered by the middle-class, who intended to exclude labor from any voice in government, but the proletarians had surprised them by their organized action and insistent demands for a "social" republic that faced the new industrial problems, for civil rights that gave the vote to nine million men, for the ten-hour day. Respectable France shuddered in fear of another 1793; business languished, and capitalists complained of the ruin being wrought by the "pampering" of unemployed workingmen. Recovering their composure, the conservative groups in society prepared to restore the balance at the approaching general elections of April, 1848. Meanwhile the Provisional Government, really a moderate affair, soon began to limit work relief.

To Victor Hugo the whole revolution seemed, at first, as incomprehensible as a nightmare. Before such sweeping changes, coming so much faster than the politicos themselves had foreseen, he, like many other moderate men, felt bewilderment, and some fear of a coming Reign of Terror.

He walked the streets studying the restlessness and tumult of his good people of Paris. On February 25, he dropped in to see Lamartine, whom he found resplendent in a tricolor sash. The Foreign Minister sounded him out on the proposition of joining the Government as Minister of Public Instruction. "It is impossible that Victor Hugo is not at heart a republican!" he exclaimed. But Hugo, up to yesterday a Liberal monarchist, and admirer of the Duchess of Orléans, would not yet be identified with the Provisional Government. To be sure, he was for the republic "in principle," but had its hour struck in France?

Nevertheless, like other former adherents of the Orléans monarchy, he pledged allegiance to the Republic; he accepted an honorary appointment as Mayor of his own *arrondissement*, to help keep order there; and early in March stood for election to the Legislative Assembly, as a Representative of the People—his old position and title of Peer having been abolished.

On March 2, a ceremony for planting a Tree of Liberty—one of many all over France—was held in the Place Royale, and Victor Hugo was called by the people of his quarter to speak. He responded in a little speech by saluting the Republic and ended: "Long live universal liberty! Long live the universal Republic!"

But the "platform" on which he took his stand in April showed that—though favoring universal suffrage, free education, even international peace—he was strong for private property as well, and feared the Left, feared the coming of a "Red" republic. To Hugo, even Lamartine seemed to have played the demagogue not a little. Yet when the mob of workers descended upon Lamartine again, pressing the red flag upon him, he had thrust it away. As Hugo wrote in a letter of May 24, 1848: "Lamartine . . .

spurned the red flag, he has abolished capital punishment, he has been for several weeks the bright star of a dark revolution. But today we pass perhaps from brilliant men to flaming men, from Lamartine to Ledru-Rollin, and may be expected to go from Ledru-Rollin to Blanqui. God help us!" He feared most of all Blanqui, the extremist leader of the Paris proletariat, who exerted pressure on the government through the new political clubs and workmen's associations of 1848.

2

Many writers felt the impulse to rush into the public arena—Balzac and Dumas, along with Hugo and Lamartine. But Hugo, as candidate in the national legislative elections of April 23, 1848, received 60,000 votes, not enough to elect him, but sufficient to encourage him to stand again in the complementary elections of June 4 for the Seine Département, which embraced Paris. Meanwhile new convulsions gripped France. The now class-conscious workers of Paris, who had helped to make the revolution of February, had tried to delay the establishment of early elections; they had feared that the preponderance of peasant, Catholic, and Conservative votes in the provinces might not only rob them of the social gains they hoped to win, but even of the democratic republic itself. Altogether 100,000 unemployed workmen had flocked to Paris to share in the meager benefits of the National Workshop. But the press denounced this new institution. Its benefits of only two francs a day were diminished; indeed, those who later directed it, by their own confessions tried to bring ridicule upon the whole project by holding the workingmen in relative idleness or at useless occupations. (Originally Louis Blanc had urged the establishment of genuine co-operatives provided with state capital, in those factories where private capital had ceased to work.)

Against the demands of working-class leaders, such as Blanqui, that the elections be delayed until the French people, subject to fifty years of misrule and tyranny, had had more time for reflection, Lamartine and his colleagues in the Provisional Government were obdurate. They insisted upon prompt recourse to democratic process and the voice of the whole nation. The result on April 23, 1848, was as foreseen; the Left republicans won less than 100 seats out of almost 900; the Conservative or bourgeois republicans had 500 seats, and some 300 went to the Catholic and Orléanist parties. The Provisional Government now dropped its two socialistic members, Blanc and Ledru-Rollin, and the movement to undo the reform laws of February and March got under way. This in turn led to increasing agitation among the Parisian populace, who, as Marx has written, hoped to eliminate the bourgeois parliament and carry on toward a socialist republic. A series of street demonstrations, beginning on May 15, 1848, was launched with the purpose of unseating the new Constituent Assembly. The expiring Provisional Government, headed by Lamartine, replied with orders for the arrest of Blanqui, Barbès, and other proletarian leaders, some of whom were imprisoned, while others were forced to flee abroad. The Revolution of 1848, which had begun with peaceful ceremonies in honor of fraternity and liberty, was settling down to a clear-cut class struggle. By June the mood of Paris was very ugly.

For the run-off elections of June 4, 1848, Victor Hugo campaigned as a middle-road independent, under a slogan of his own devising: "Vigorous hatred of anarchy, profound and tender love of the people." Actually, he was affiliated with the so-called Committee of the rue de Poitiers, a grouping of Conservatives who formed the Party of Order, headed by Thiers and the Comte de Falloux. Hugo scored a popular election success, being easily elected as one of the Representatives for the Seine Département, with 87,000 votes, which was 2,500 more than was given to the next successful candidate after him—Louis-Napoleon Bonaparte, nephew of the glorious Emperor, another new figure in the political lists who had just recently slipped back into France.

A few weeks earlier, in March, 1848, Victor Hugo had written down some private reflections on the current situation:

I do not understand why the people are feared. . . . The sovereign people are all of us. To fear them is to fear oneself.

As for me, for the past three weeks I have observed them every day from my balcony, in this old Place Royale . . . I see them calm, happy, jesting, when I mingle with groups of them, when they march in processions, rifle and pike at their shoulders, with drums and banners. . . . I swear that I do not fear them. . . .

In this moment of panic I fear only those who are afraid.

But the Party of Order acted out of fear. Early in June, the Comte de Falloux introduced before the new Assembly an innocent-seeming bill whose indirect purpose was to eliminate the "socialistic" National Workshops. On June 20, Victor Hugo, now an elected Representative or Deputy for the people, rose to make his maiden address in the Assembly and opened the debate on Falloux's bill, which he supported. He pronounced the Workshops a failure, and warned the socialists against precipitating "civil and servile war," which might undermine Order, Property, and Family, the triangular base upon which, he declared, our civilization rested. Yet, though the *Journal des Débats,* on the Right, called the speech "noble," and Louis Blanc's *La Réforme* called it "perfidious," its undertone was conciliatory. It ended with an appeal to all factions to show mutual good will in seeking solutions of difficult social questions—a spirit noticeably lacking in other spokesmen of law and order. Victor Hugo himself was ashamed of this speech, in after years, and emended it in issuing his public papers.[1]

The new labor associations had previously made unarmed demonstrations. Now, as they saw the doom of the National Workshops, they gave answer with the tremendous working-class insurrection of June 23–26, 1848. The Montmartre and the Latin Quarter, the Saint-Antoine and the Marais—which embraced Victor Hugo's residence—saw barricades set up in all their crooked, narrow streets, manned by a formidable urban army of workers, many of whom were members of the National Guard or former regular soldiers.

Rising in such determined mood, the Parisian masses had often had their way in the past. The problem of street fighting in those days, before the wide boulevards were opened up, was considered a thorny one. While feeling distaste for fighting fellow citizens, the regular soldiers and the bourgeois elements of the National Guard disliked those narrow streets, which became deadly ambuscades with enemies firing at them not only from barricades but from

[1]When, in 1875, Victor Hugo's public papers appeared under the title *Actes et Paroles* ("Words and Deeds") it was evident especially in the first volume, "Before Exile," as his persistent critic, E. Biré, has shown, that he had suppressed the most reactionary passages of his early speeches. This was done in the case of the speech on the *Ateliers Nationaux.* I do not know what vanity led him to try to eliminate evidences of doctrinary inconsistency. Nearly all public men have been inconsistent, from year to year, at one time favoring peace or high taxes, at another war or low duties. Hugo could well afford to stand on his final record, as we shall see, and needed no justification of his earlier errors. (The missing passages have been restored by his later editors.)

Moreover, in my view, the fact that Victor Hugo started with a series of prejudices typical of his own class at that time—that the proletariat was driven by envy, desire for loot, etc.—makes even stronger his later and so different convictions which, once arrived at, he never again altered.

cellars, doors, windows, and roofs in their rear. Then the Parisian proletariat traditionally fought with a desperate courage, indeed a fanaticism, which for long years their bourgeois brethren never understood.

Formerly the educated leaders of the middle class, that is, the capitalists, called out and led the workingmen in revolutions aimed at ousting the old dynastic factions and winning political privileges, which they usually appropriated for themselves. Now that this had happened again in February, 1848, the middle-class politicians were determined to stop at the political reforms they had won for themselves and pay no further attention to questions of hours and wages and unemployment. But that the "servile class," once peaceful expedients had failed, should show determination to improve its status by fighting seemed inconceivable. To the bourgeois it was but a "sinister" rising in quest of loot and plunder.

The Provisional Government had foreseen civil war; Lamartine had even discussed tactics with General Cavaignac, Algerian veteran, who was Minister of War. It is significant that General Cavaignac was not a disguised Royalist, but a bourgeois republican by conviction, his father having been a member of the Convention in '93. He made an elaborate disposition of his fifty thousand troops, regulars and National Guards, moving in two columns upon the enemy inside the city, and keeping a central base from which a mass of reserves was fed into battle. An evil tradition has persisted that Cavaignac deliberately took his time, permitting the insurrection to rise to its boiling point before moving decisively, in order to do his job with more sanguinary and lasting effect. We must note, however, that the Parisian workingmen in those days used very skillful street-fighting tactics, most exhausting to regular troops: they raised up barricades and vanished when artillery arrived, only to reappear elsewhere.

On June 23 terror engulfed Paris. In the mid-nineteenth century the rich still lived elbow to elbow with the poor in all the old quarters of the capital, the masters living on the main floors of the fine houses, and the laborers often occupying the basements or the unheated attics of the same or adjacent buildings. Victor Hugo found himself cut off by a line of barricades from his home, located in a bitterly contested battleground, and was forced to spend the night at the Assembly, unable to hear news or even to send a message through to his family. At 9:30 of the morning of the twenty-fifth of June, the third day, he attempted to reach his wife: "Situation grave. The fight will begin again, hotter than yesterday. The insurgents are growing in numbers." From one source he heard to his horror that his house had been burned with all his manuscripts and art "treasures." From another he learned that his wife and children had found refuge in a near-by quarter that was disarmed.

At the start of the insurrection a Committee of Representatives, with Victor Hugo as one of the members, was named to visit the barricades and attempt to treat with the rebels by peaceful means.

For three days and nights he stayed in the streets witnessing scenes of nightmare horror and massacre. He saw women, some of them prostitutes or workingwomen, "young, disheveled, terrible," or half nude, climb the barricades to defy the regular soldiers and urge on their men—by their example, as they fell dying—to fight without quarter. He saw laughing street urchins, manning the defenses with their elders, wielding muskets they could hardly carry. He saw in the Reds an inconceivable "heroism of despair." He would march up under fire, as at the barricade of the Boulevard du Temple, near his own home, with several companions, wearing the sash of a Representative of the People, and carrying a little white flag of truce. He summoned the rebels to yield and end the bloodshed. But some of them replied: "Ah, M. Hugo, you do not know what hunger means!"

A contemporary account (in *L'Emancipation* for July 2, 1848) reads:

Among the Representatives of the People who exposed themselves boldly during those bloody days we must cite M. Victor Hugo. . . . In his generous desire to spare the shedding of French blood he was not afraid to proceed all alone up to the barricade in the rue Vieille-du-Temple, in spite of those who tried to hold him back. When the insurgents took aim at him he advanced nevertheless, and told them that they were misled, but that they were all brave fellows, and not one among them would fire on an unarmed man walking toward them alone. . . . These unfortunate persons, moved for a moment by his speech, answered that they had sworn to die rather than give up, but that they thanked him none the less, and considered him a good citizen.

The (official) *Moniteur* for July 11, 1848, also spoke of Victor Hugo holding up an attack by troops, before another barricade, until all means of conciliation had been exhausted. Then the firing would, begin, and continue until all the insurgents were dead or wounded. On the site of one of these battles—there were many summary executions of those caught with gun in hand, or grimy with powder—he succeeded in spiriting away to the safety of Juliette Drouet's apartment in the rue Saint-Anastase four men whom he recognized. For at one barricade when the insurgents had asked for terms, offering to lay down their arms, they were told by General Cavaignac's officers that no terms would be given.

For three days the most widespread and deadly civil warfare ever seen in Paris streets raged on, exceeding in ferocity even the slaughter of French Revolution days. Once more it was said: "The Revolution devours its sons." Then it was suddenly over. The workingmen were crushed. The government's army lost over 3,000 in dead and wounded; some 10,000 insurgents were casualties, and 15,000 more were taken prisoner, sent to jails and concentration camps, and ultimately deported to tropical colonies in Africa and South America.

Victor Hugo felt his heart torn to its very depths by the scenes of somber horror he had witnessed day and night. In his letters of the moment, we find no cold hatred such as his colleagues felt for the revolutionists, but principally the spirit of pity and mercy. Late in the afternoon of June 25, when Cavaignac finally struck hard, he was able to write to his wife:

Today is expected to bring an end to it all. But what a sad end, with so many brave men killed on both sides! So many brave soldiers! . . . And oh! those poor misled workers!

The next day, he writes to Mme. Hugo: "Where are you? What is happening to you? For two days I have been roving about the quarter without being able to get home. My heart is torn with anxiety." He learned, however, that his family was safe, and his house left untouched by the rebels who had occupied it. Then to Juliette Drouet, he wrote on the twenty-sixth:

. . . I have used my authority to conciliate passions and stop bloodshed, and succeeded but to a slight degree. I am broken with fatigue. I have spent three days and three nights in the *mêlée*, without food, without a bed to sleep in, one moment almost falling asleep in the street. Some good person gave me a piece of bread and a glass of water; another gave me clean linen. At last this terrible fratricidal war is over. As for myself, I am safe and sound. But what a disaster! I shall never forget the terrible things I have seen in the last twenty-four hours.

The last hours were of course those devoted to taking prisoners or not taking them. Victor Hugo had shown courage in defending the Party of Order, more courage by far than many of its members who later attacked him; he had feared the coming of the Red republic; he had feared that France would sink into barbarism, that civilization itself might perish. But now that the nightmare was over, recovering himself, he was filled with a sense of pity, the emotion dominating his prose epic, *Les Misérables,* of which two volumes were to be devoted to the story of just such an insurrection as he witnessed in 1848. The days of 1848, even recollected in calmer moments, had the effect of changing the whole character of the work then in progress.

After the great insurrection was over, men asked what had caused it. "There is only one cause, poverty," said Louis Blanc. But few listened to him. The Catholic leader, Comte de Montalembert, declared that the insurgents were "less than human"; the Liberal deputy, Jean Marie, declared that "barbarism had raised its head," and must be put down mercilessly. Thus began the reprisals directed by General Cavaignac, who under the state of siege proclaimed on June 23, acted as military dictator of France. Victor Hugo was warned by a close friend, Baron Taylor, that he must refrain from urging clemency for the rebels, but in the name of family and country must do all possible to help destroy the men of "hellish doctrines." To this end, Napoleon had used force; but Hugo could accomplish the same mission by "the power of the word."

He, however, was of a different mind. On July 3, 1848, he issued a statement to a newspaper: ". . . It is true that my home was invaded by the insurgents; I owe it to them to say, and I say willingly, that they respected everything in my house, leaving it as they found it." The first two volumes of *Les Misérables,* in manuscript, he found undisturbed on the table of his study, where the rebels had camped.

His motives at this stage were mixed, his insight, as an amateur of politics, was as yet dim—though he was learning in a hard school—but there was no hatred in him toward the vanquished. His days were spent in answering and acting upon appeals from friends of the prisoners. In a fragment of diary he wrote some six months later, on January 11, 1849, he recapitulated: ". . . Before the barricades I defended Order. Before dictatorship I defended liberty. In the presence of *chimeras.* I have defended property, the family, inheritance, the eternal truth of the human heart. I asked for clemency toward those who had strayed and severity toward traitors; justice to all. I extended a fraternal hand toward the vanquished. . . ." This is an honest statement of his position following the bloody June Days of 1848.

Meanwhile he was outwardly still affiliated with the Party of Order and on at least one occasion attended its secret caucus in the rue de Poitiers. "I went only once to the committee of the rue de Poitiers," he wrote in his diary, later, on the back of an invitation from them dated August 21, 1848. "I never returned. To see it once was enough. . . ." Then in another note addressed, at this period, as if to the professional politicians of the Right, scheming for the restoration of a monarchy under the guise of Order, he wrote privately: "Gentlemen, I belong to your ranks, I have fought on your side. . . . Loyal and disinterested co-operation is not enough for you; you must have passive obedience. You will not get it from me. . . . I shall remain in the Party of Order, but you may as well know that I will never commit what my conscience calls crimes in order to avoid what your politics calls errors." In the fire of revolution Victor Hugo was changing slowly. In his conscience he questioned many things that he had formerly taken for granted, though he had scarcely begun to set his feet upon his road to Damascus.

3

Within a few history-making months, while the mills of revolution ground on, the national poet had risen to a certain eminence as a courageous public servant. He who had written so many glowing pages wrote no more save public speeches for the rostrum. Into this new life his whole mind was drawn ever more deeply.

On July 31, 1848, a new daily newspaper, called *L'Evènement,* was launched with much advertisement, and it was widely understood in France that Victor Hugo was its guiding spirit. Its financial backers were Moïse Millaud (associate of Emile de Girardin), who gave 50,000 francs, Fromentin-Meurice, brother of Hugo's young disciple, Paul Meurice, and, in a smaller way, Hugo himself, who contributed 17,000 francs. The editors were Auguste Vacquerie, Paul Meurice, and the two sons of the poet, Charles and François-Victor Hugo, aged twenty-two and twenty-one respectively. Hugo, in a public letter, stated that he was a friend of the newspaper but in no way were its opinions to be attributed to him. This was considered only a diplomatic gesture. The newspaper placed Hugo's slogan on its masthead: "Vigorous hatred of anarchy, tender and profound love of the people." Faithfully it reflected the shiftings of Victor Hugo's political thought; it rose and fell with his political fortunes.

He was no longer a mere man of letters, but a furiously absorbed man of politics, resolutely following his star, to serve the people? —or to feed his own ambitions, his lust for power? Many wondered then and later.

To a friend, who wrote expressing the hope that he would soon become a Cabinet Minister, he answered, December 10, 1848:

I beg of you, not to look on me as a possible Minister. I want to remain independent. . . . I want *influence,* not power, honest, upright, enlightened influence and nothing more, nothing for myself above all. And my whole ambition, when all of you shall have saved civilization and the country, will be to return to my plow, that is to my pen.

In truth it was a difficult time to remain cloistered, with the nation torn by class struggle, a new republic to be built, and a new constitution to be written. Hugo in his private diaries tells himself that he must avoid seeking office or power, that he must work with a pure public spirit and disinterestedness, remaining a "man of truth, obedient to my conscience." And though the statement sounds rhetorical, it describes accurately enough what he did, *what actually happened* to him. Many contemporaries, such as Edmond Biré (in his biased biography), scoffed at Hugo, attributing all his actions to selfish desire for power, and unconscionable scheming for it. Similarly, Pierre de Lacretelle, a later commentator, and one of very cynical spirit, goes so far as to accuse Hugo of conspiring against the Republic to win dominant power for himself. The scheme fell through according to Lacretelle chiefly because of Hugo's political "ineptitude," his "impractical" qualities, and his overweening vanity. For was he not a poet? How could he perform any services of value alongside of professionals like Thiers, Falloux, Barrot, and Montalembert? Yet history showed these veterans of the tribune to be monumental blunderers, and ultimately credited the "impractical" poet with vision and the courage to follow his vision.

Hugo did wish for power, in spite of his decorous statements to

the contrary. It was for this end that he and his associates had
founded a very enterprising and vigorous newspaper, acting in
support of him. But have not strong men in public life always
sought power? Have they not always said to themselves, with the
elder Pitt, that they alone and only they could save the state? In
Hugo's case it has been urged that he was utterly inconsistent; that
he began by following a narrowly conservative course, until his
hope of advancement through the Conservative groups proved
vain, and then turned selfishly and vengefully to the opposite
course. To prove this the record of his votes on specific bills is cited
by Biré and Lacretelle. But it happens that later search of the
record shows that these hostile commentators gave wrong reports
of Hugo's voting on certain measures, reports which for a long
time were widely accepted, to his discredit.

With the Conservative groups firmly in the saddle after the
June Days, the majority of the Second Republic's Constituent
Assembly proceeded to frame a Constitution and design an effective
executive power. The Constitution-making, which offers usually a
glorious opportunity for jurists and lawgivers, was in this case
meanly done. Its real intent was to nullify the reform laws enacted
in the first glow of popular revolution. For, once in power, the
men who had called the people to arms against King Louis-
Philippe formed themselves into a Party of Order, maintained
martial law for a long time, and with bayonets prodded the common people to quiescence.

The new Constitution created a President to be chosen by universal suffrage, but the right to vote was eventually restricted,
after 1850, by rules of residence, so that 3,000,000 out of 9,000,000
citizens, mostly laborers and farm hands, were disfranchised. The
President was to hold office for a single four-year term, but his
powers were left somewhat vague as compared with those of the
legislative branch. (Victor Hugo voted for the popular election
of the President rather than for his election by the legislature,
which a Conservative minority favored.) Civil rights were defined
and granted, but were left much more uncertain than under the
more precisely written American Constitution, and were restricted
by certain necessities of "public safety and order," also left vague.
A single chamber rather than a bicameral one was voted—though
Hugo favored the Anglo-Saxon system of upper and lower houses
of the legislature.

Meanwhile, as the country prepared for the election of a Presi-

dent, martial law was continued, and this drew from Victor Hugo
an earnest plea for restoration of full liberty of the press, which
the Conservative majority refused to heed. On September 15 he
also made a strong speech in favor of the complete abolition of
capital punishment, one of his favorite themes, and won the warm
applause of the Left. Somewhat earlier, the question of incorporat-
ing the "right to work" in the preamble of the new Constitution
was heatedly debated. The Conservatives regarded such a principle with horror as being tantamount to communism, though the
Provisional Government had already accepted it. Hugo has been
charged by his denigrators, Biré and Lacretelle, with voting
against the "right to work" clause. In reality he was recorded as
absent, but his newspaper, on September 12 and 15, 1848, published editorials vigorously urging its adoption—though in vain.

Hugo's independent or Liberal votes on bills providing poor relief, or extending free education and jury trials, also gave no assurance of his "narrow conservatism" to his friends of the rue de
Poitiers. Yet these first well-intentioned moves were ineffectual;
the lines of class and partisanship were being rigidly drawn. The
Second Republic was now governed by men who were profoundly
anti-republican and, above all, dreaded a recurrence of French
Revolution phenomena. At first moderate in their expressions, the
leaders of the Conservative majority later dropped their mask and
showed themselves to be nothing more than Royalists who waited
only for the restoration of an Orléans or a Bourbon. The Left, composed of extreme republicans and a few socialists, closed their
ranks and formed "the Mountain," in accordance with the 1793
tradition. But they were reduced to the position of impotent onlookers by the government's suppression of political clubs, censorship of the press, and imprisonment or exile of thousands of the
June, 1848, insurrectionists. Meanwhile the Catholic and aristocratic faction, led by the Comte de Falloux and the Comte de
Montalembert, fenced with the Orléanists—made up of financial
men and their followers, led by Thiers—to determine whether a
Bourbon or an Orléans prince would be recalled to power eventually. Then suddenly the adventurous Louis-Napoleon inserted
himself into the picture.

They had seen him elected to the Assembly by no great margin
and thanks only to his magical name. The son of Napoleon's
brother King Louis of Holland and of Queen Hortense seemed at
only forty a somewhat decayed gentleman with poor credit. He

had once tried to seize power in France by a small uprising at Strasbourg in 1836, and had been caught rather easily and let off without punishment, though sent into exile in England; he had then tried another uprising in 1840, landing from a small boat off Boulogne and nervously proclaiming himself Emperor—Napoleon's son the Duke of Reichstadt having died. But this attempt also proved abortive; he was taken prisoner by a sergeant, was locked up for a time, but managed to escape to America. Louis-Napoleon wore waxed mustaches and played the English dandy. But he seemed so timid that he could barely make himself heard when he rose to speak in the Chamber. Yet a motion was made to remove him from his seat.

Gallantly Louis-Napoleon resigned, and gained vindication in a new election. This improved his standing, but also definitely provoked debate over excluding from the presidency any family which had previously reigned in France. A vote on this question left the Bonapartes as well as the Bourbons free to pose as presidential timber, though no Bourbon, of course, would have taken to the hustings. As soon as it became clear that the President would be chosen by popular election, Prince Bonaparte borrowed some money—his English mistress's furniture was almost seized at this moment by a sheriff—and announced his candidacy for that office.

What was there in the name Napoleon? To the French a great deal. The Emperor Napoleon, after the First Republic had been sundered by internal divisions, unified the country and carried out the practical aims of the new business class that had made the French Revolution. When Napoleon, in time, became a Great Tradition, Victor Hugo by his Bonapartist poems had done much to keep the tradition alive. In 1831, the former King Joseph Bonaparte wrote a letter thanking Victor Hugo and speaking in warm terms of his deceased father. "I have not forgotten, Sire, that my father was your friend," Hugo replied. He declared that, if the heir of Napoleon (then still living) should give guarantees that he would support liberty and progress, Hugo would instantly rally to his cause, and with him "all that youth of France that venerates the name of the Emperor, and over whom, obscure though I am, I may have some little influence."

These words were written at the beginning of Louis-Philippe's reign, when the poet felt himself outraged by the restriction of his freedom as a playwright. But Hugo was not alone among Liberals in France who dreamed of an overturn favoring a Bonaparte.

Under two monarchical dynasties, the anti-Royalist opposition in France at first embraced the cult of Bonapartism before evolving gradually into republicanism—and Hugo's "crystal soul" clearly reflected this long evolution.

But in 1832 the young son of Napoleon suddenly died, then other heirs to the succession, leaving Louis Bonaparte as the sole hope of the family.

Victor Hugo had decided, after June, 1848, to remove his home to a more peaceful quarter of Paris than the old Place Royale. One day in October, 1848, he was engaged in unpacking crates of furniture at his spacious new home, in the rue de la Tour d'Auvergne, at the west end of Paris, when a short, dark man walked in, and announced himself as Prince Bonaparte. Hugo's first impression of him was "Distinguished, cold, intelligent, dignified—German in appearance—with dark mustaches—no resemblance to the Emperor." Later, Victor Hugo, like others, recalled how lack-luster was his glance, how his eyes avoided yours when he looked at you, how he tended to say nothing in reply to your questions.

There was only a wooden trunk in the room and the poet and the prince sat down on it together. Only a few days before, Louis Bonaparte had begged Thiers for his support in the coming presidential campaign; now he approached Hugo, who was becoming more than an ornamental figure in politics and controlled a growing newspaper.

"I have been calumniated," began the Prince. ". . . They claim that I want to be Napoleon over again." All that was mad, he asserted; he pretended to no genius, but to a desire to demonstrate his virtue. Instead of seeking to be a "guilty hero" like Napoleon, he desired to be a "good citizen" like Washington. In truth Louis Bonaparte had often declared himself a democrat, or even something of a socialist. In Italy he had fought beside the men of the *Risorgimento*. While in the French prison at Ham, he had written a book on "The Extinction of Pauperism." (Later it was learned that his favorite bedside reading at that period was Machiavelli's "The Prince.")

Victor Hugo was thinking of the power of his name, and felt pleased at the liberal professions of faith the prince made. There seemed nothing scheming and tenacious about him. Thiers, the great wire-puller of the Right, was convinced that Louis Bonaparte was a man who could be molded by his own hands and, in the Assembly, worked secretly to build him up as a possible counterpoise to other groups. Meanwhile, Victor Hugo was not yet a firm adherent of democracy; he was a humane man, who believed that the best results for France might be obtained by a statesman wielding large powers for the public welfare. The bloody dissension under the newly arisen bourgeois republic had tried his soul. The republican General Cavaignac, conqueror of the streets of Paris, now ruled temporarily under martial law but was spoken of as a "man on horseback." Louis Bonaparte was not hated, as was Cavaignac, by the common people of Paris. Might not this nephew of Napoleon the Great, as President of France, bring peace and conciliation? And might not Victor Hugo serve as counselor to the President, as he had hoped to serve under a Queen Regent? In return for his democratic pledges, Hugo promised Bonaparte his support; and soon Hugo's newspaper, now risen to a circulation of fifty thousand, aided in the election campaign of Napoleon's nephew.

"France needs a man to save her," declared *L'Evènement*. "We cannot help saluting a man named Napoleon. . . ." Louis Bonaparte's campaign statements were also praised as being "calm and Liberal, pregnant with a love of the people and devotion to order. . . ."

In November, 1848, Hugo voted to defeat a motion aiming to exclude any member of the Bonapartists from the presidency. On another occasion, before the elections, the proposal had been made that the President be required to "give his oath to the Constitution and to the Republic in presence of the Assembly"—this, also, Victor Hugo opposed, though it was adopted by the majority. Apparently Victor Hugo believed, in 1848, that the Republic might not long endure; but there is no evidence that he "conspired" at any time to set up Louis-Napoleon as a dictator, as has sometimes been charged against him.

That the mass of French citizens shared Hugo's sentiments at the moment was shown by the election of December 10, 1848. General Cavaignac was the choice of the Conservative republican politicians in the Assembly, Ledru-Rollin of the combined Left parties. Instead of Cavaignac, the man who carried the name of Napoleon received the overwhelming majority of the peasants' and townspeople's votes, or more than 5,434,000 to Cavaignac's 1,448,000 and Ledru-Rollin's 370,000.

The first impressions of the President were disappointing and in no way suggested the possible dictator of whom certain socialists had given warning. His ministry—after Thiers had refused the honor of joining it—was headed by Odilon Barrot, a former Orléanist, and included the Comte de Falloux, Catholic and Legitimist leader, as Minister of Instruction. Barrot, now a Conservative republican, had shown his feebleness in emergencies, and Falloux represented Bourbon reaction; the other appointees merely reflected the majority party of the Assembly, called the Party of Order, which in less than a year had made the bourgeois parliamentarians thoroughly disliked in France. Victor Hugo's newspaper commented on the noticeable lack of "eminent men" in this Cabinet and the spirit of compromise that seemed to underlie it. Yet, covering his disappointment, Representative Hugo continued to support the President. Accepting Louis-Napoleon's invitation with alacrity, the poet attended the first official dinner at the Elysée Palace, December 24, 1848. The dinner was attended mostly by Bonapartes and their open partisans. The food was mediocre, Hugo found. People addressed the President as "Monseigneur" or "Highness"; the servants wore Napoleonic livery; but the prince himself, after dinner was over, moved from group to group with the air of a timid stranger. It was all a "bourgeois-republican-imperial mixture," Hugo recalled, in his memoirs, but what did it mean?

The President appeared unable to impose a positive leadership upon the Assembly, as Hugo urged him to do. He moved at first against the restive masses in France, threatening to use a harsh hand in putting down disorders, and saying: "It is time that the good men come forth and the wicked tremble." The Assembly, which was dominated by Thiers, the little schoolmaster of French politics, pursued its own gait and repeatedly snubbed the President, or ignored his messages. The Legislative Assembly insisted upon its superior prerogatives under the Constitution. The effect of divided counsels within the government was just as pronounced after May 13, 1849, when new elections finally brought a new body of Deputies to replace the old Constituent Assembly. Both the Conservative majority and the extreme Left were more solidified by the election and remained bitterly hostile. Meanwhile the President seemed out of agreement with his own Cabinet Ministers, and played a curious game of stressing his differences with the leaders of the Parliamentary body. Soon he came to an open clash with them over the issue raised by the French expedition to Rome, in 1849, which had been voted by the Assembly just before his election as President.

Italy too had known a popular revolution in 1848, and Pope Pius IX, who had formerly been the friend of democracy and unification, found himself one day forced to flee from Rome, when the people rose against the Papal Authority that ruled it and declared for a republic, under Mazzini, in February, 1849. At this the Catholic world was in a furor: Austria, Italy's old oppressor, began to move its armies southward again, after defeating the Italian nationalists of Piedmont; France, too, not to be outdone, dispatched an expeditionary army to replace the Pope upon his throne in Rome, before the Austrians could get there. But republican France pretended that its soldiers were being sent to see that newly won Italian liberties were preserved—while Pius was being restored. However patriot Italian revolutionists under Garibaldi repulsed the French invaders before the walls of Rome, in May, 1849. Liberal or moderate men in France now realized that the expedition was a mistake, that it was begun in response to pressure by Catholic politicians in France and tended to impose by force an unwanted form of government upon the Romans—the undemocratic and repressive rule of the Papal Authority. Yet the French army before Rome, after receiving reinforcements, attacked again and seized the Eternal City from the republicans in a bloody battle.

On June 13, 1849, the ardent democrats of France in protest at the Roman expedition organized a large popular demonstration against the government in the streets of Paris. But though the marchers were unarmed, General Changarnier, military commander of Paris, cleared the streets with great violence, and the government used the occasion to eliminate the militant democrats and socialists. Ledru-Rollin, the foremost orator of the Left, was forced to flee the country; thirty other deputies were unseated and some of them condemned to imprisonment.

Reaction was swiftly overtaking the Second Republic, which had been inaugurated with so many fair promises of liberty. Victor Hugo watched the Conservative leadership that dominated the Assembly using unlimited force to suppress opposition at home and sending an army to crush liberty abroad. In June, 1849, his eyes began to open. A minor incident vexed him. On June 13, 1849, when government troops broke up the unarmed parade of the Left republicans and socialists they also burst into the offices of certain newspapers and smashed up their printing presses. Victor

Hugo, indignant at these excesses by the military, and fearing for the freedom of the press again, appeared at a large committee hearing in the Legislative Assembly, and vigorously interpellated the government officials and army officers responsible for these outrages. His charges against them were blandly denied, and he was now greatly blamed by his colleagues for raising such questions. "It was not the right moment to speak of such things," they protested angrily. But he persisted. For the first time he found himself in open, clear-cut opposition to the so-called Party of Order. It was a turning point.

It was in the summer of 1849, he recalled afterward, that he came to feel complete disillusionment with his Conservative colleagues. He had been in a waiting mood after 1848, he declares in the preface to his public papers (*Actes et Paroles*); "but after June, 1849, he waited no longer. The significance of events flashed upon his soul. . . . When he saw Rome trodden down in the name of France, when—after June 13—he saw the triumph of coalitions hostile to progress and marked their cynical joy, then indeed he was grieved—he sorrowed for France, he understood."

At this time a bill was pending before the Chamber providing for a commission of inquiry to study housing conditions among the poor and make plans for public relief. It was intended as a nonpartisan measure, and the Catholic philanthropist, Vicomte de Melun, who fathered the bill, was expected to head the commission—but there was also much talk that the whole affair was a sop thrown to the populace, and that nothing would come of it.

Hugo, always warmly interested in such measures, came to its support with more vigor than the sponsors of the bill cared for. On July 9, 1849, in the most aggressive speech from the tribune he had made so far, he called attention to the deep unrest in the country, and argued that the government must not merely attempt to suppress disturbances when they occurred but must eliminate the cause of the disturbances, must attack the problem of poverty. Then he uttered memorable words:

I am not one of those who believe that we can remove suffering in this world; suffering flows from a divine law; *but I am one of those who believe and declare that we can abolish poverty. Poverty is a disease attacking the body politic, like leprosy.* . . .

There were outcries and interruptions. "We are all agreed on that point," shouted a member on the Right. "You are refuting arguments which no one has advanced," yelled another. "The recommendations of the Committee have been unanimously supported. . . ."

Hugo continued, however, to urge that the work of the commission be prosecuted most earnestly and thoroughly, a suggestion which seemed to fill the Conservative majority with increasing anger at him. For the orator had touched a tender nerve. There had been a great deal of talk in the corridors of the Chamber, among the Conservative legislators, that an end must be made of all such efforts as the present one to "pamper" the lower classes, that what was needed was pitiless force instead of public relief. Prominent among the men who used such terms was the Comte de Montalembert, leader of the pro-Bourbon faction, in former times a Catholic Liberal who had worked together with Hugo's old friend the Abbé de Lammenais—in fact, an old acquaintance and admirer of Hugo himself. It was to such statements as Montalembert's that Hugo now openly alluded when he said that they held "there were no two ways of re-establishing order," that the sole remedy was "force," and that "all else was vain and sterile; and that the very proposal of the Honorable M. de Melun (on public relief) and all other kindred proposals must be thrust aside, *because they are nothing—I repeat the words they use—but socialism in disguise.*"

These words aroused the entire Conservative majority to fury, and brought a wave of applause from the Left. "Who said that? Give names!" many Representatives cried out, leaping to their feet and endeavoring to interrupt or distract the orator. Hugo, surprised at their violence, stood there proudly, saying: "I am happy that my words have caused such a unanimous protest." He had believed, he said, that it was better to bring these things out into the light of day.

But Montalembert, as if feeling himself singled out, rose to a heated interpellation and declared Hugo's assertions unfounded and irrelevant and a reflection upon the honor of the Chamber. The President of the Assembly, Dupin, a crooked old lawyer, in rather partisan manner called Hugo to order and indulged in some parliamentary jokes at his expense. Hugo then was permitted to close his speech on poverty; but from that day on he was a marked man.

He had like an amateur broken the polite rules of the game these professionals played; he had said blunt, unpleasant things right out, and this with a direct logic that went to the heart of the contradictions that tormented the politicians of the Second Republic. Yesterday these men had agitated violently against the King, his corrupt system, and his treasury deficits; they had protested in the name of liberty and justice and brought all the people to their aid. But, having ousted the old King, they needed the common people no more and wished only to temper their will for greater liberties and civil rights. In the dilemmas they themselves had brought on, the bourgeois politicians suffered, and Hugo's charges, which diagnosed their attitude correctly, gored them. Henceforth they were suspicious of Hugo, and attempted to interrupt, confuse, or ensnare this poet in their midst by parliamentary maneuvers. Meanwhile the clerical faction soon showed that it had only pretended to espouse social reform "in order to wrest the workers from socialism," as Lacretelle himself remarks. The *Commission d'Assistance Publique* got nothing done and fell apart, while Melun, author of the bill for public relief, was later repudiated by his own Conservative party—as Hugo, in his speech on poverty, had forecast.

In August, 1849, an International Congress of Peace was held in Paris, and Victor Hugo, elected as president, with the great English Liberal, Cobden, as vice-president, gave the opening address, before an audience of fifteen hundred delegates from many countries. It was a radiant vision of universal peace and fellowship between the nations that he unfolded in rolling periods. Delivered with powerful effect, it brought him a tremendous ovation. It was an early day to dream of world peace. Also, Victor Hugo was growing accustomed to sounding the idealistic notes; he began to associate with what his Conservative friends considered bad company.

President Louis Bonaparte, meanwhile, kept aloof from the class conflicts in the parliament, and if anything set himself at odds with the parliamentary machine (run chiefly by Thiers) that dominated France in the early period of his term. The President was mistrusted by Thiers and the financial interests; he was hated by the Legitimists and the Catholics. As a matter of policy he made systematic efforts to win the favor of the army, and on the other hand went to great pains to please the working class, whom he had the habit, at this period, of addressing in the streets of Paris or other large cities. Now playing the Liberal President, he suddenly raised the popular issue of the Roman expedition (which had been ordered before his election).

On August 18, 1849, he wrote a letter to his aide-de-camp, Colonel Ney, whom he had sent on a mission to Rome, arguing that the French Republic could not possibly send an army to Rome only to throttle Rome's liberties. "If France has intervened to restore the Pope, she has not done so with the intention of restoring the old absolutism." For the Pope, and the Council of Cardinals, on returning, had re-established the old system of ruling Rome and the Papal States by means of the clerical police and foreign guards, allowing for no civil rights or representative government. Bonaparte concluded bluntly: that he desired the Pope, as a matter of temporal policy, to grant general amnesty to political prisoners, secularize the governmental system in his territories, establish the Code Napoleon and a "Liberal government."

The President had sent off this letter without consulting his Cabinet. In mid-September it was made public, through the press, with the effect of a bombshell—though the Conservative leaders of the French parliament continued to ignore its statement of policy.

Pope Pius IX, in his reactionary mood, answered this move of Bonaparte's with his somewhat unsatisfying papal bull, the *Motu Proprio* declaration, offering amnesty only to certain categories of rebels but continuing the clerical form of government in Rome. But for the President this answer that was no answer mattered little. He used the incident to sharpen the conflict between himself, in the Elysée Palace, and the politicians in the parliament—for whom it raised the embarrassment of religious controversy. The President had taken the popular or Liberal side in the controversy.

For Hugo, this seemed a promising development; it represented an alluring opportunity to enter the fray on the side of Bonaparte, and against the Conservative majority with whom he was already on painful terms. His own hope, as editorials in *L'Evènement* indicated, now lay in building a "plain" between the Red *Sans-Culottes* (men without breeches) on the Left, or on the Mountain, as it was called, and the *Sans-Coeurs* (men without hearts) on the extreme Right. Into this middle ground he hoped to be able to carry along the President in the general direction of progress and liberty.

At a committee hearing on supplying further credits for the Roman expedition, Hugo heard the veteran Thiers complacently declaring his approval of the position taken by the Pope—it was another snub at Louis-Napoleon as a sort of "overzealous young man." Thiers also held that there was no difference between the President's demands and the Pope's reply. But Hugo vigorously opposed this view, saying that the government should take a strong stand, that there was a wide difference involved, that the President's letter recalled the Rome expedition to its objective of guaranteeing liberty, while restoring the Pope.

A week later, the sixteenth of October, Victor Hugo was invited to the Elysée for dinner, and on this occasion Louis-Bonaparte complimented him on his initiative and thanked him for the support he had given. By this Hugo was led to believe that the President, usually so taciturn and obscure in speech, but now angry at Thiers and company, meant to press vigorously for a liberal policy on the Italian question. However, the parliamentary regime, headed by the Ministers, Barrot, Falloux, and Toqueville, refused to follow the President's "personal politics" and continued to avoid the issue—while the Left, for the moment, enjoyed taking the side of the President.

Eager to follow the new path he had marked for himself, which the President's attitude seemed to encourage, Victor Hugo rose in the Chamber, on October 19, 1849, to make an important address on the Italian question. (We must remember that thousands of Italian patriot democrats languished in prison and all the world outside condemned the French army's occupation of Rome.)

Hugo pointed out that the original object of the expedition, as conceived under the Constituent Assembly in 1848, had been perverted from its "humane and liberal intention." Now a free republic was placed in the position of helping to impose by arms an absolutist-clerical regime upon an unwilling people!

. . . From the first the clerical authority (differentiated from the pontifical-spiritual authority), fiercely bent upon reaction, animated by the blindest, the most baneful and unforgiving spirit, wounded all generous hearts and wise men, alarmed all the thoughtful friends of the Pope and the papacy. Each of the acts of this authority was fanatical, violent, hostile to ourselves, irritated our army in Rome and our nation in France. We asked ourselves if it was for this we had gone to Rome, if France played a role worthy of her, and an aroused public opinion began to turn angry looks toward our own government. (Sensation.)

He referred to President Bonaparte's letter to Ney, admitting that it had created embarrassment, that it might have been "more ripe and premeditated in its terms," smacking less of the "personal rule" (which some said he aspired to secretly) yet insisting that it marked out for the Pope the serious program of a government of liberty. And what was the answer—the *Motu Proprio?* And its meager promises of amnesty? Hugo rose to an epopee, with a skillful rhetorical trick. He would speak always, he said, with a profound respect for the head of the Christian faith. But was the Pope now free? Or was he now a prisoner of the reactionary cardinals around him? Therefore Hugo took courage in his hands and was willing to say openly in plain words what his real thought was on the papal bull. (There was turbulence, then silence.)

The act of the Roman chancellery has two faces: a political side, which rules questions of liberty, and that I call the Christian, the charitable side, affecting the question of clemency (for the former rebels). In so far as political liberty is concerned, the Vatican grants nothing; as for clemency, it grants still less. (Applause from Left.) It accords only a mass proscription. (Quite right!) Only it has the kindness to call this proscription by the name of amnesty.

Hugo was being ironical, yet his simple, powerful phrases told what is known now to have been the plain truth. With indignation he described a Rome given over to mixed feudal and monkish rule, to a venal police, to secret trials at which no civil rights existed. And more—

They have just brought back the Inquisition! Oh—you are going to tell me that the Inquisition is only a name now; but it is a horrible name, and I fear it, for in the shadow of a dark name, there can be no good things!

The orator called upon the Assembly to choose between the directives given in the President's letter and the monstrous situation that had arisen in Rome with the aid of French arms.

This speech, more than anything Hugo had yet done, won the thunderous acclaim of the Mountain and the unforgiving hate of the Right. It had an embarrassing anti-clerical and libertarian tone that not only offended Hugo's former friends in the Party of Order, but also disturbed Louis Bonaparte.

The next day, the newspaper which officially supported the President, *Le Dix Décembre,* in honor of the date of his election, declared: "M. Victor Hugo has performed the duties of a Foreign Minister, since the government was abandoned or misunderstood by its own Ministry." The Royalist newspapers commented that the famous poet sought a portfolio as Minister in the Cabinet. The Right leaders now defended the Pope, and sought to curb the

President by attacking Hugo. Montalembert had repeatedly interrupted the orator with cries of "calumny." When Hugo left the Chamber—he usually did not wait for opponents' replies, as if not trusting his own impromptu reactions under provocation—Montalembert, one of the most skillful speakers in France, attempted to refute him point by point. Hugo, he charged, had shown "perfidy" to his former associates. "Gentlemen," he closed, referring to the applause given Hugo by the Mountain, "the speech you have just heard has already received the chastisement it deserved in the applause that has greeted it." There was tumult on both sides of the Chamber. He added: "If the word *chastisement* offends you, I will withdraw it and substitute the word *recompense*. . . . I say then that the speaker has received his recompense in the applause of the Extreme Left, but that the majority to which he has belonged until today, and the moderate electors of Paris who returned him to represent the Party of Order (loud interruptions) . . . that these electors, I repeat, will be entitled to ask whether it was to gain this sort of applause that they sent him to this House."

It was war. Montalembert was reading Hugo out of the Conservative party. The session ended in twenty minutes of uproar and then was adjourned. The next day Victor Hugo replied:

M. de Montalembert has declared that the applause of one portion of this Assembly was my chastisement. Well, I accept that chastisement and I am proud of it. There are other plaudits which I will leave to those who care to accept them—the plaudits which come from the hangmen of Hungary and the butchers of Italy! There was a time when the Honorable M. de Montalembert made better use of his fine talents. He has passed to the side of those who oppress, and I remain on the side of those who are oppressed.

Hugo was leaving the Party of Order, and the newspapers of the democratic opposition noted this with gratitude, saying that because he had never really been "one of us" he deserved all the greater honor and praise for speaking the truth.

Meanwhile for the scheming President in the Elysée Palace the situation was delicate. He was dissatisfied with his Ministers, who had rebuffed him, and he was displeased with Hugo, who had put the whole issue in such blunt terms that the clerical party in France seethed with anger. Hugo in helping him had gone too far! In "The Memoirs of the Second Empire," by Granier de Cassagnac, a young writer who, thanks to Hugo's favor, won high office under

Louis Bonaparte, it is recorded that Hugo, after his speech, went to see Bonaparte and received a severe dressing-down. Hugo left the palace unable to conceal his own anger at this treatment.

The President now tacked about. On October 20, 1849, he had taken a strong stand against the republican parliament on the Italian question. On October 21, 1849, he backed away, as if in fear of an open break with the majority party, and his official newspaper cravenly declared that the President now felt that Prime Minister Barrot had acted in "good faith." (In reality he never forgave Barrot, nor Thiers, who stood behind Barrot.) It was a ridiculous about-face, as the spokesmen of the Left all remarked, and Victor Hugo, who had boldly committed himself, was left where he stood. He was never a pliable man, and his rupture with the President dated from this day.

In the Elysée Palace, a raffish crew of personal partisans, soldiers, gamblers, and petty political adventurers formed the palace guard of Napoleon's nephew. There was a period of confusion. Louis Bonaparte needed money, and his 600,000 francs a year as President were not enough for his "political" expenses, for the army of street fighters in white shirts whom he gathered to fight the socialists, or for the newspapers he hired. But the legislature remained niggardly and obstructive. The strange little man had periods of hesitation; he held long conferences with his cronies. But then he returned to the tactic of bold action, for, though uncertain in knowledge and character, he could be extremely stubborn.

On the thirty-first of October, posing as the responsible head of the government, he suddenly sent a message to the Assembly demanding the resignation of the entire Cabinet. He expounded also his ideas of "personal rule," saying: "A whole system triumphed with my election, for the name of Napoleon in itself is a program, meaning: at home order, authority, religion and well-being for the people—abroad national dignity."

Secretly, without consulting the regular party leaders in the Assembly, he had prepared a new Council of Ministers, consisting of his own partisans and backers, men unknown or little known, whose appointment he soon announced. It was significant that he named no *Président du Conseil* (or Prime Minister) but appointed one of his retinue, General d'Hautpoul as vice-president or nominal head of the Ministerial Cabinet, thus indicating that he himself was to be its chief henceforth. There was, of course, no remote impolitic thought of naming Victor Hugo as Minister of Instruction.

These were far-reaching moves, yet the public seemed as if numbed by previous measures of oppression under the Republic, and made no demonstrations. In effect these steps undermined parliamentary rule in France—but the common people by now hated the Assembly, and took the change calmly. The rival factions of politicians who made up the Conservative majority remained passive, some of them, like Thiers, plotting in England with the Orléans family, and others conspiring with the Bourbon heirs. They waited, convinced of Louis Bonaparte's inability to wear his famous uncle's crown. Yet, out of the very uncertainty of the situation and the rivalry of factions, his opportunity was made for him, slow and timid though he was.

Bonaparte's military lieutenants quietly reinforced the regime of semi-martial law in Paris and other cities. In the salons they were saying: "The *coup d'état* is on the march!" This was repeated so wearyingly that few people believed it.

4

Thoughtfully, Victor Hugo watched these events, his eyes now wide open. In his diaries he wrote under date of November, 1849:

Last year I fought by your side, because you defended civilization, this year I fight against you because you attack liberty.

He had been accused of being a poor parliamentarian, of not being "practical," of saying blunt things at the wrong time. He soliloquized:

Because I have the stupidity to have a conscience, you tell me that I am no politician. . . . *Politician:* a queer fish, without a conscience. A rascal who puts up a systematic opposition or defense, and who says white when his leader says white, or black when his master says black.

He still thought of himself as belonging no more to the Left than to the Right. "I am not a politician. I am a free man still," he told himself. But as a free man he found himself as one against many, driven into an opposition that appeared more and more desperate. He knew now that his fight must be made for human liberty—how he knew, and why it had taken him so long to see this simple thing were other matters—but he knew. And with each passing day the prospect seemed more somber. In later years he recalled that at some point during this season of troubling conflict with others and with himself the light of truth seemed to burst upon him as with the effect of a mystic revelation. Then the bitter joy of combat itself possessed his soul. He thought: ". . . At the moment when the conquerors were extending their hands to entice me into their ranks, I felt in the depths of my heart that I was on the side of the conquered." For they, the coalition hostile to liberty, were destroying the Republic, which he saw already in imagination as a woman prostrate, bound, gagged, expiring, whom he approached tenderly, kneeling by her side.

Before him he saw downfall, defeat, ruin, insult, proscription—and he said, "It is well." From that day the Republic and Freedom were identified in his mind. . . . Every man, if he is sincere, may tread again for himself the road to Damascus—a journey which must vary for each individual soul.

A momentous law reorganizing the entire system of public education in France—then still half clerical, half temporal—was being prepared in 1849 by the pro-Bourbon Comte de Falloux and his associates. The Falloux Law, somewhat disingenuously called "A Law for the Freedom of Instruction," proposed to place the network of primary schools throughout the country under the direct supervision and control of local prefects—which many believed was but a devious scheme to have them run by the bishop of the region. In any case the law appeared to encourage indirectly both the revival of parochial schools and the more active participation of the priests in the free primary schools along with the local mayors and municipal councilors nominally in charge of them.

To Victor Hugo, who had aspired to be France's Minister of Education, this was an engrossing subject, and raised issues that might be decisive for generations to come. In truth, as historians have pointed out, France's education, her whole culture, since 1792, has been a battleground in which the men nurtured in her university and those who came from her great Jesuit schools have long dueled with each other. Today still, in the French village the schoolteacher and the curé usually stand as rivals wrestling for the souls of the pupils. To Hugo the lower-school teachers were as "an army of Progress." That this was no illusion on his part is shown by one of the outspoken statements of Montalembert, who had become a fairly fanatical leader of the clerical party and was one of the sponsors and contributors of the great Jesuit newspaper, *L'Univers*. Society, according to Montalembert, was threatened by vile conspirators and demagogues, and would perish unless "authority and respect" were re-established. He continued:

Who, then, defends order and property in our countryside? Is it the schoolteacher? No, it is the priest. I tell you that today it is the priests who represent order, even for unbelievers . . . represent moral order, political order and material order. . . . Today two armies confront each other in France, each having 30,000 to 40,000 troops; the army of the schoolteachers and the army of the curés. . . . *Against the demoralizing and anarchistic army of the schoolteachers we must fight with the army of the clergy!*

When Falloux's bill was introduced in the Assembly, early in January, Hugo noticed to his dismay that the new "Kitchen Cabinet" of President Bonaparte gave it their support. On the other hand, the minority parties making up the Mountain or the Left, militant democrats and socialists, rallied together to fight the bill, Victor Hugo resolutely joining with them on this occasion.

On the second day of the debate, January 15, 1850, he began a two-hour speech by declaring that compulsory education for all, free of cost, was the ideal of a republic of free men. Then he turned to the bill under consideration, to examine how much it met such an ideal, and soon was launched upon one of the most eloquent and passionate philippics in all the history of political oratory. Victor Hugo was a poet, but his broadening conception of his role, as we have seen, formerly required that he act as a "conductor" of the people, a priest and prophet to his age; now, however, he proposed to serve as a man of action and a soldier as well. Placing himself in the breach, as it were, convinced that the republic was in mortal danger, he delivered himself not of merely rhetorical phrases but of the most terrible general indictments of the clerical parties—accusations that gored and wounded the Conservative majority, while by their eloquent liberalism they sent a thrill to the hearts of all liberty-loving men. The scene in the Assembly as he proceeded was "indescribable" according to the parliamentary reporter—a mounting storm over which he soared triumphantly, as if intoxicated, amid applause and denunciation, finding the confirmation of his mission in the very hatred he evoked.

For his part he desired true religious education as much as anyone else, he declared, but insisted upon the separation of Church and state which the "fathers" had demanded. "The priest must not be mingled with the teacher" and religious instruction must be "within the Church and not without," that is, not partially introduced into free primary and secondary schools, as was proposed, by establishing a partly clerical surveillance over the school councils. He accused the clerical party of having written the main provisions of the new law, and burst forth fiercely:

I am resolved not to entrust to your keeping the instruction of our youth, the development of new minds opening to life, the spirit of the new generations, which is to say the future of France. I will not confide to you the future of France, because to entrust it to you would mean to surrender it to you. To me it is not enough that new generations should succeed us; I desire that they continue our work.

And that is why, men of the clerical party, I will have neither your hand nor your breath upon our younger generations; I will not have that which our fathers have done undone by you. I will not have this shame after their glory. (Strong agitation on both sides.)

The new law bore a mask, "liberty of instruction." That, he resumed, was the way of the clerical party. When they "forged a chain" they called it "liberty." Hugo drew a broad distinction here between the Church itself and the clerical party and the Jesuits, whom he dubbed "parasites of the Church." It was a distinction which, at this very period (when Hugo was under terrible attack by Louis Veuillot, in the Jesuit newspaper *L'Univers*), the bishop of Paris himself seemed to accept, since he came to Hugo's defense. Asserting his own faith in the Christian doctrine of mercy and its heroic apostles, denouncing those who fostered clerical obscurantism and tyranny, Hugo continued more wrathfully still:

Ah we know them well, the clerical party! An old party, guarding over the gates of orthodoxy for centuries, guarding indiscreetly, fatally, jealously, the gates of the Church. It is they who have discovered, in place of truth, those two Pandora boxes of ignorance and error; they who prohibit science and genius from going beyond the missal, and who would cloister all thought in dogma. (Renewed tumult.) Every step that knowledge has made in Europe, has been without them and in spite of them. Their history is written in the record of human progress, but in reverse. They have opposed everything. (Murmurs.)

. . . And you would be masters of education! And there is not a writer, not a poet, not a philosopher, not a thinker that you accept, and all that has been written, discovered, dreamed, deduced, imagined, illuminated, invented by genius in all times, the treasures of civilization, the secular heritage of generations, the collective patrimony of all minds, you reject! If the brain of humanity were placed before your eyes, opened to you like the page of a book, you would, I am sure, act to make emendations, corrections!

Wild laughter and howls of indignation or threats accompanied the speech, which closed with a striking epopee on intellectual liberty, and a prophetic warning to those who would halt and bind it:

Ah! you would stop it all! Alas, I say to you again, with deep regret, I who have no wish for upheavals and catastrophes, *if you reject progress, then you shall have revolutions! To those so mad as to say:* "*Humanity shall go no farther,*" *God answers with the trembling of the earth!*

The effect of the speech was so powerful that it seemed to the republican press as if Victor Hugo, single-handed, had "shamed and crushed reaction" by an immortal discourse. The *National*, though showing some reserve about the illustrious new recruit, reported on January 16, 1850, that, while Hugo, from the tribune, "sounded the anger of the masses of people, he sowed confusion and rage among the Right." Insults and impotent threats filled the air, but none was able to deny the truth of the orator's accusations. The printed pamphlet of the speech on freedom of education was sold all over France, but suppressed where martial law was enforced in large cities such as Lyons. Bonaparte's Minister of Instruction was forced to introduce certain amendments limiting the partial clerical supervision of schools, in order to quiet public fears of the Falloux Law. Thus, opposition led by Hugo forced some liberalization of the law, when it was finally passed, making it a compromise. In later years (amid fierce controversy) it was further liberalized, but it remained the basic law of education in France.

When Hugo had finished his oration on January 15, 1850, he stood silent for a moment upon the tribune while the storm of yelling and cheering, as in the days of the Terror-ridden Convention, continued for long minutes. Then at a signal, the nearly two hundred members of the Mountain, led by the democratic orator Michel de Bourges, and Félix Pyat, the socialist, marched down the steps of the Chamber and slowly, gravely, defiled past Hugo, saluting him warmly while he stood waiting quietly until they had all gone by. The Left, whose strongest leaders had been driven into exile the year before, had found a new leader.

CHAPTER XII

En Route

THE SECOND REPUBLIC, a year after its birth, fell completely under the control of the veteran Conservative politicians, such as Thiers, Molé, Berryer, Falloux, and Montalembert, who came to be called now the "Burgraves"—after the title of Hugo's play about the solemn old German nobles in the castles above the Rhine. They were men of different political color, Bourbon-Catholic or Orléanist capitalists and in some instances simply Conservative republicans like General Cavaignac. Their unity lasted so long as they felt themselves menaced by danger from the Left; once this was eliminated, the Burgraves found time and inclination to pursue their rival intrigues and, thanks to their own dissensions, became a fair prey for Bonaparte, the uneasy schemer in the Elysée Palace.

On March 10, 1850, special elections held for the seats of the thirty-one Representatives arrested or exiled the year before resulted in the return of twenty-one radical republicans or socialists. In the towns of France, despite all efforts to harass and discourage them, the democratic elements delivered a solid and disciplined vote, which filled the Burgraves with fear that their majority would not last. They were still more alarmed when another by-election, in Paris, on April 28, 1850, brought a sweeping victory to Eugène Sue, the romantic novelist, author of the "Mysteries of Paris," who, in politics, was a professed socialist. Panic even spread to the Bourse, where stocks and bonds fell heavily on a single day.

"The Barbarians are at the gate," the Burgraves said warningly, through their newspapers. The drive of reaction was pressed home.

Montalembert sounded a famous war cry: "We must make the expedition to Rome over again—at home. . . . As with the Roman republic, there can be no indifference and no complicity. . . . We ask for war!" The important thing, Thiers declared, was "to eliminate several millions of the most dangerous voters," by much narrower restrictions of the suffrage than was permitted as yet by the Republic's "absurd and impractical Constitution." To this end, the Burgraves who ran the parliamentary machine proposed an accord with the President and common action. With no little cunning, Louis Bonaparte pretended outwardly to be reluctant to follow such unpopular policies, and was reconciled finally to accepting them only under the pressure of the Assembly majority.

Against this strong tide of reaction (accompanied by many arrests and deportations, much vexing censorship and policing) Victor Hugo fought day after day, side by side with the leaders of the Mountain—though his real purpose was still, like that of Lamartine earlier, to rally the moderate republicans together as a coherent party. It was a task that became more and more hopeless as the lines of class hardened. (Lamartine, standing between Left and Right, mistrusted by both sides, had gone down like a rocket, and lived in retirement.)

Hugo by now had come to be a magnificent orator, with deep and strong voice, and simple but impassioned gestures. As Sainte-Beuve, who heartily disliked his course of action, admitted, Hugo and Lamartine both brought their lyrical and descriptive powers to their oratory; for this reason their legislative speeches are among the few that may still be read as literature now, Hugo's more than Lamartine's because of their extraordinary timeliness for us today. Hugo could use close-knit argument and a logic that was often very cutting; but he wrote also with a passion and eloquence and vividness recalling the orators of ancient Greece and Rome. He always read or recited from memory, never improvising his literary effects, as Jules Simon, his famous republican colleague, relates. Thus he was not adroit or easily useful as a fighting arm in an emergency, but could be brought out in carefully prepared assaults upon the Right, his words falling like mighty blows or stinging like whips, thrilling his sympathetic followers by effects of description that gave a foretaste of *Les Misérables*.

But, knowing his habits, the gentlemen of the Opposition constantly tried to disconcert him by insulting interruptions, until he would halt impatiently—

Hugo: Gentlemen, I know that you are indulging in deliberate and calculated interruptions—

A Voice on the Right: But we were just laughing.

Other Voices: It disturbed your speech which you have committed to memory!

Victor Hugo: These interruptions were intended only to disconcert or confuse the speaker.

Voices: You mean your memory! Your memory!

Victor Hugo: You are refusing freedom of thought and speech to me . . .

Voices: Your memory! Your memory!

Nevertheless certain of his speeches, such as one made on April 5, 1850, during debates over new Deportation Laws, had tremendous effect and were effectively used as campaign literature in elections. With the death sentence abolished, the Second Republic under the Burgraves sought to extend the system of exiling political prisoners to concentration camps in tropical colonies such as Guiana (Devil's Island). Hugo's speech on this subject was entitled by the socialist leader, Pierre Leroux, "The Dry Guillotine," and gave a picture of the sufferings of an exiled prisoner in some fever-ridden isle:

Criminal to some, hero to others, you seize him, in the midst of his renown, influence, popularity; you tear him away from his wife, his children, his family, his country; you uproot him violently from all his interests, from all that he loves . . . and you plunge him into the shadows, into silence, at an inconceivable distance from his native soil. And there you hold him, a prey to himself, to his regrets, if he had thought himself a useful man, to his remorse. . . .

You desire that slowly, day by day, this soul, this mind, this energy— even this ambition—should be buried alive, *alive,* I repeat, four thousand leagues from the fatherland, under a burning sun, under the horrible weight of this prison-sepulcher, twisted, tortured, devouring himself, despairing, begging for grace, calling to France, praying for air, life, liberty, agonizing, and miserably perishing! Ah, it is monstrous! I protest. . . . What you call expiation, I call martyrdom; your justice I call *assassination!*

Then, rising to his climax, the orator made a sensation when he recalled that "the sword of political punishment belongs not to justice but to chance, passing to the conqueror with fortune." He warned his colleagues that such a fate as they handed out now to their opponents might later be meted out to them by "that law of vengeance" which the winning party always called justice.

As for myself, in this troubled hour, I do not know what fate the future may hold in store for me. In my own heart I mourn fraternally all the victims of today, and those of tomorrow, in these revolutionary times. I hate and would break these arms of violence. . . . This law may have unknown consequences. Do you realize that I am defending you against yourselves! Do you know what may be done to you some day, under certain circumstances, thanks to your own law?

These warnings caused a tumult of protests and interruptions, even the chair calling Hugo to order and warning him that he slandered the Republic and used terms designed to spread terror. The old Burgraves, trembling with outrage, denounced the orator and drove through the new penal law—but Hugo's words on the "Dry Guillotine" were heard all over France.

At that time his entrances into the parliamentary debate were always greeted with roaring protests by the members of the Right, who never failed to call him "renegade" and "deserter." Camille Pelletan, a Cabinet Minister in later days, declared that the records of debate in the Chamber at this period show that no such disorders and partisan maneuvers by the chair as Hugo suffered had been known in France since the days of 1793, or even afterward at the time of the Dreyfus Case. But Hugo refused to be silenced.

In May, 1850, there were also widespread rumors of a coming *coup d'état*. When Victor Hugo rose to speak, May 21, on the question of universal suffrage, which the Burgraves moved to restrict, he was informed that his life was in danger.

Notes in his unpublished diary (*Moi*) under date of May, 1850, run:

Conditions are serious. I must base my conduct on circumstances. I desire no confidences from anybody. . . . Yesterday, May 14, a battery of artillery was brought to the Hôtel de Ville by night.

May 16.—Sinister rumors in the Assembly. Inevitable rioting instigated by the police. There is even talk of a few assassinations. The mistress of an aide-de-camp of General Changarnier said to Colonel Charras (a Liberal deputy) who told it to me: "Take care, in case of rioting . . . the parts are assigned." Colonel Charras will be killed by a pistol shot while crossing the Champs Elysées. Charras added: "You had better be careful, Hugo." . . . Yesterday I was advised in a *friendly* sort of way not to speak on the electoral question. I said: "That makes me all the more determined. I shall speak. Afterward, let God's will be done. . . ."

The Conservatives now moved, in May, 1850, to alter the law of universal suffrage by adding provisions for six months' residence, and other restrictions that eliminated almost a third of France's nine million voters. Jules Grévy, Jules Favre, and Victor Hugo spoke for the Mountain against the measure. Hugo's most impressive point was that, when the right of vote was denied to men, all peaceful means of expression were lacking, and they had no other recourse, eventually, but rebellion. To remove the vote of the poorest classes, as now proposed, would lead to an explosion that would wreck the Republic. The Burgraves indulged in much jeering at the poet-orator—though one wonders, now, what was so wrong in his prophecy and his diagnosis. Victor Hugo was a proud man, and at one especially insulting interruption, unable to win the aid of the president of the Chamber, the crooked old M. Dupin, he exclaimed:

I remark, and the *Moniteur* will remark tomorrow, that when I deplored the exclusion of a whole class of citizens from the suffrage, the men on that side *laughed* at me and said: "So much the better!"

But none cared for peace. It was during the debate on the restriction of the vote that Adolphe Thiers, the small, bespectacled leader of the Orléanist faction, assailed the Representatives on the Left for bowing to the common people, at whom he hurled the epithet—with the admitted purpose of exasperating his opponents —*vile multitude*. The tremendous explosion among the republicans that greeted these words, in Thiers's estimation, frightened some uncertain Representatives into supporting his measure and settling the issue at the expense of the same "vile multitude."

During the mêlée bitterly personal attacks, intended to discredit Hugo as a leader of the Left, were made by Conservative leaders like Montalembert. Speaking on May 22, 1850, in Hugo's absence, Montalembert declared:

If M. Victor Hugo were here I should recall to him the antecedents of his life—all the causes that he has sung, all the causes that he has flattered, all the causes that he has abandoned. (Cheers from the Right.) But he is not here. That is an old habit of his; just as he hides from the service of lost causes, so he runs away from the reprisals that one is entitled to inflict upon him. (Bravo! Bravo!)

Montalembert and others repeatedly taunted Hugo, alluding to the Royalist verses he had written twenty-five years ago. On the next day the poet was present and met his adversaries head on.

MONTALEMBERT: I say to M. Hugo: *Your France is not mine!* It is not ours! . . . I say he has sung in honor of the Restoration, of the birth and the baptism of the Duke of Bordeaux, of the coronation of Charles X, and that today he tries to forget and conceal all that. . . .

HUGO: I do not! Why—my monarchist verses? I wrote them in my youth, nay my childhood, some of them when I was fifteen!

MONTALEMBERT: After 1830, following the fall of King Charles X, he sang the obsequies of the "heroes" of the July Revolution, as if to atone for his faults. . . .

HUGO: I defy you to cite those verses of which you speak, M. de Montalembert.

MONTALEMBERT: But I pass over his poetry, I revert to his prose, and his prose delivered from this very tribune. Yes, I could not help my feelings of indignation when I recalled having heard him myself address King Louis-Philippe with the most adulatory phrases (laughter) and two years later, from the same rostrum, saw him come to felicitate the people of Paris for having burnt the throne of the old king he had once honored, and who gave him his peerage.

HUGO: It is untrue!

MONTALEMBERT: You will find him always using the same formulas. Here is what I predict: If ever there comes a time, as I fear, when this country upon the ruins of its liberties, lies dishonored and degraded by the party *to which M. Hugo has deserted,* if ever there arises a despotism of some kind, he will be the first man to flatter it, he will try to breathe upon this future despotism the incense which he offers today to the workingman and which he has already offered to two Dynasties. (Tumultuous applause.)

Hugo, taking the floor, pointed out that the complimentary words he had addressed to King Louis-Philippe had been on the occasion of the grant of a pardon to a condemned man. He ended by saying he had never deserted M. de Montalembert, since they had never been "in the same camp." (Montalembert had campaigned as a Catholic Liberal.)

MONTALEMBERT: You were elected in Paris by the Conservatives.

HUGO (quickly): And you were not, that was just what I meant. What! I am accused of being a renegade, an apostate! But gentlemen, *what a strange sort of renegade I would be, passing from the camp of the conquerors to the weaker side.* But no . . . I am only a man of order who sees reaction before him, that is, disorder, and who fights

it; I am a man of liberty who fights those who would spread servitude.
. . . The future will decide between M. de Montalembert and myself.

Victor Hugo pondered over his course in public life and the significance of the sharpening personal attacks upon him. In his
diary he wrote, as if addressing his adversaries:

. . . They tell me, *"You have changed!* In 1848 you were against
the 'Reds'; in 1850 you are for them." Let us be clear. . . .
. . . I was born into a class which made me a Royalist from childhood, before I knew what I was; then, as I grew older in experience,
and with the help of meditation, by degrees, like many of my contemporaries, I came to embrace the ideas of my age and my country. I,
in my obscure and limited person, am a living proof of the truth and
irresistible force of that movement toward democracy which you
oppose.

Here in Hugo's diary notes (only recently made available to
us) is the clearest and most searching explanation of his "inconsistency" in public life. He was, as always before, the "crystal
soul," echoing the changing times. He himself in his own person
was but "a living proof" of the force and truth of the whole movement toward democracy. He, wealthy, ennobled, famous, a favorite
of kings, having every reason to resist this movement, was convinced at last that he must embrace it, even to his own cost. His
"apostasy" was a conversion and a notable one for the democratic
cause; he passed from the ruling party to the side of the oppressed.
As to his being politically inconsistent in changing parties he was
no more so than an Abraham Lincoln passing over from the Whigs
to the anti-slavery Republicans, after 1852, and responding to the
same vibration-waves of democracy sweeping the world.

Was Hugo's change of heart but transitory, as Montalembert
insinuated? History would soon show the brilliant Montalembert
as a craven time-server, reversing himself, fawning upon the new
autocrat of tomorrow, and then broken and cast aside by that
shifty ruler, sinking into ignominious obscurity.

By contrast, the "impractical" poet in politics showed the far
broader vision and the courage to follow it unswervingly once it
had been fully revealed to him.

One evening, as he sat in his study—it was August 17, 1850—
a messenger brought news that Honoré de Balzac lay dying. At
once Hugo hastened to the great house which the novelist, thanks

to a wealthy marriage, had won for his middle age, hurried up a marble staircase, and entered the dying man's room. The author of *La Comédie humaine* at fifty had literally worked himself to death. He lay paralyzed by a sudden heart stroke, his huge round head almost purple in color. Hugo pressed his hand and left quickly, exclaiming: "Europe is about to lose one of her great minds."

Without being intimate friends, they had known each other well for over twenty years; their so different careers paralleled each other. Balzac, for all his pitiless hate of the *bourgeoisie,* turned into a mystical reactionary, while the aesthetic author of *Notre-Dame de Paris* became a leader of popular causes. Yet Balzac's novels were much admired by the working classes for their truthfulness. At Balzac's grave, Hugo delivered a funeral oration, very brief, moving, and simple, recognizing the genius of the man, now finally beginning to be accepted at its true worth. Balzac, he said, heralded for the nineteenth century "the domination of men of mind over men of the sword." He continued:

His life was short, but full; more filled with works than with days.
Alas! this powerful toiler who was never weary, this philosopher, this poet, this genius, lived among us through days of storm, struggle, quarrels, combats, common to our time for all great men.

But henceforth he would glitter among the stars over France. There would be no "night" for the man of genius.

Hugo enjoyed these ceremonial occasions at which he addressed a flock like a magus or a pastor in swelling yet vigorous periods, and opened his heart a little on questions of life and death. A great crowd had followed the Balzac procession on August 21, 1850. There was also present a contingent of workingmen who, according to *La Presse,* fervently saluted Hugo in his carriage, crying: "Long live the defender of the free press! Long live the defender of the people! All honor to Victor Hugo!" This was a new and heart-warming experience for the former laureate of kings.

Hugo's name was now mighty in the land, and in these unpredictable times—when the mere name of Bonaparte had brought one man almost accidental fortune—who knew what the future might not bring forth for a Victor Hugo as popular idol, or what role he might be called upon to play? Men were looking to 1852, since the Constitution forbade a second term to the President, and, with no famous leader now present among the Left republican factions, it was said that Hugo might well be their candidate, as

Lamartine had once been, though for a brief season, the inspiring leader of the moderate republicans.

Hugo was a mighty recruit, the newspapers on the Left observed. He had proved, as *La Démocratie Pacifique* commented on April 6, 1850, that the doubts he had felt concerning the Republic, and the illusions he had had about the so-called Party of Order, were gone, while his love of "liberty and progress" was sincere and grew stronger.

On the other hand the *Journal des Débats*, a long-time sponsor of Victor Hugo, on June 16, 1850, named him "the first demagogue in France, if not in Europe," and "always a socialist at heart."

Who knows what ambitions possessed him now, as they have possessed every strong man who enters public life? On August 8, 1850, his journalistic organ, *L'Evènement* (a highly successful newspaper) sent up a trial balloon in an editorial that said: "We must remark that for the last twenty years it has been shown that there can be no great opposition movement without a great poet. That of 1830 had Chateaubriand; that of 1848 had Lamartine; that of the great day in the future, we predict, will have Victor Hugo." For after having been the national poet he was becoming the people's orator.

But others, too, thought of the approaching elections in May, 1852. The Burgraves, with the country calmer now, and no longer fearing the Left, resumed their factious intriguing and their efforts to curb the President. Bonaparte, on the other hand, began to tour provincial France, making speeches that promised public works and other benefits to the masses, denied by the parliament. With elaborate modesty he now stated that, if special circumstances forced upon him, as head of the government, "new burdens," he would willingly assume them, heavy though they were. In this way the Republic would at least gain a more effective and energetic rule, he implied, than it had under the dominantly parliamentary regime. But President Bonaparte could not bring about the reforms the people desired unless he were given by the people "the power to accomplish them," a power of action that now, unfortunately, was unconstitutional. Therefore, he argued, the Constitution *might need revision*.

Soon the idea of changing the term of the reigning President from four to ten years was being broached by the Bonapartist daily, *Le Dix Décembre*. A new political organization, the Society of the

Tenth of December, was formed in Louis-Napoleon's honor by his Prefect of Police, Carlier; the members were drawn from the "slum proletariat" and, instead of paying dues, received five francs each day and a white shirt to wear as a uniform, distinguishing them from the socialists in ordinary workingmen's blue shirts, whom they systematically provoked and fought in the streets of French cities.

To Napoleon's nephew belongs the credit for evolving, from day to day, a general plan by which a man of ordinary mental powers but of persistence and cunning, could methodically use the machinery of the democratic state to overthrow it. As President, he wooed the army officers and promoted those who became his partisans. In June, 1849, General Changarnier, commandant of the Paris military forces, had cleared the streets and was called thereafter the "bulwark of society" in the Conservative press. He was reported to have some ambitions of his own and there was some doubt whether he would defend the Burgraves of the Assembly, in a pinch, or stand with Bonaparte. Then, with a sudden, gambling boldness that he showed intermittently, the President settled this problem by dismissing Changarnier on January 5, 1851, supplanting him with a tool of his own. The majority leaders in the Assembly felt a momentary panic, but were reassured by Thiers, who was certain that Louis Bonaparte was a blockhead and that the army would never move against the sacred tribunal. Bonaparte was uncertain and dull-witted on many sides; but even he could not fail to understand that the last military defenses of the Republic lay under his hand.

In the summer of 1850, Hugo's friends, the editors of *L'Evène-ment,* had been prosecuted by the government for publishing articles alleged to provide incitement to civil war, but by skillful defense won their acquittal. The next year, June 11, 1851, the government, still aiming to strike at Hugo, indicted his son Charles for a strong article attacking the government for the execution of a prisoner, and attacking the institution of capital punishment generally. After Léopoldine, Victor Hugo loved Charles best. Appearing in court, he obtained leave to speak in his son's defense. He asked that he himself be punished, since the son only adhered to the principles he had always taught him. "I . . . have fought this iniquity all my life and shall continue to fight it—I swear, in the presence of yonder great victim of the death penalty who is listening to us and watching over us all!" With these words he pointed to the picture of Christ hanging on the wall at the farther end of the court room. In spite of this dramatic appeal, Charles Hugo was found guilty and sentenced to a fine of five hundred francs and six months' imprisonment. Deeply moved, Victor Hugo exclaimed to Charles as he was being led away: "My son, you have been greatly honored today—you have been judged worthy of fighting and suffering for the sacred cause of truth! Be unshakable!" Soon afterward, the younger brother, François-Victor Hugo, was also tried and imprisoned for infringement of the new press rules. In this great emergency, the father found his sons, both devoted, courageous, and intelligent young men, removed from his side.

2

He lived in storm. The growing political crisis in France and the hazards of his own future absorbed him body and soul. Yet at the same time, in the midst of the tremendous social crisis, he was inwardly tormented by the increasing emotional strain of his divided private life. Two dark clouds hung over him, moved toward each other across the sky, and joined in one storm.

As Victor Hugo approached fifty his whole physical appearance was altered and already reflected the two-fold strain under which he labored. He was, of course, no longer the handsome youth of the *Hernani première* in 1830, but a man of very broad frame and proud carriage, still remarkably distinguished-looking, with his high, pale brow over which lank locks of iron-gray hair fell rebelliously, his dark eyes and jutting jaw, and, now, uncommonly deep lines about the eyes and mouth that told their interesting tale of hidden pain.

For seven years, up to the summer of 1851, the great man entertained (as many Parisians knew) two mistresses and supported, counting his own family, three households. By his new lights he seemed to have freed himself from the sense of personal sin, permitting himself the liberties of a Silenus. Yet, as in the case of Adèle in earlier years, he was not entirely freed from fear of the sorrow and pain that he might bring to others.

Juliette Drouet was now installed in a pleasantly furnished apartment of the Impasse Rodier, hard by his own mansion in the rue de la Tour d'Auvergne. Nowadays Paris called her "Mme. Drouet" almost formally—after these seventeen years—and recognized her as the "consort" of the poet. Leaving Juliette, whom he saw less often, owing to the pretended pressure of state affairs, he must run to Mme. Léonie Biard's home elsewhere in Paris. Léonie Biard was worldly and ambitious, and in the last years of the Orléans regime encouraged his public ambitions. But Juliette, a daughter of the people, was instinctively democratic and warned him against too close a pursuit of kings, princes, and duchesses, whom she considered disgusting. For his sake, she feared the tumult of politics and sought to defend him against it. She also regretted the new public life, which seemed to set distance between them. Sometimes she would come to the gallery of the Chamber, sit there with her knitting, listening to him. On April 6, 1850, she wrote:

When I think of the admirable speech, so religious, so noble . . . and conciliating, that you delivered yesterday, at the risk of your health, and then reflect upon the senseless uproar and idiotic and violent interruptions it provoked, I feel only hatred, contempt and disgust for political life. . . . Really, my treasure, the more I see of political life, the more I regret the time when you were simply the *poet* Victor Hugo, my sublime love, my radiant lover. I revere your courage and devotion, but I suffer in my tenderest feelings at seeing you delivered over to the beasts of an arena more brutal than that of Rome. I have conceived a loathing, not only for your antagonists but also for . . . this form of life. If I had the power to change it, I assure you I should not hesitate, even if I had to deprive you of your rights of citizenship. . . .

Was it not enough for him, she asked, to remain the "First Citizen of her own Republic" and Prime Minister of her heart?

So long as Juliette knew nothing, Victor Hugo was free to continue his divided affinities, receiving gifts he needed from her, but also from the other, more youthful woman. When the other woman, Léonie, pressed him to give up or send away the white-haired Juliette, the strange man refused; he could not bear the thought of it. But Léonie was made unhappy by her dubious situation, and was a determined woman. One day, June 27, 1851, Juliette opened a package sent her by mail. Enclosed in it was a bundle of letters dating since the year 1844, bound with a ribbon that bore Hugo's seal, her lover's proud device, EGO HUGO, and the mantle of peer added in 1845, *sur un champs d'azur, au chef d'or, aux merlettes de sable et aux casques de chevalier*, with which he augmented his glory so strangely. The letters were love letters extending over seven years to another woman, who now calmly invited Juliette to leave the field to her.

Juliette for two days wandered in the streets mad with grief and rage, yet "stopped now and then by a flood of tenderness that overwhelmed her, and causing tears from her heart to fall to the pavement . . ." as she wrote in a vivid letter. She sent for him, but two days passed before he came. He denied nothing. Was it a caprice of the senses? But it had all gone on for seven years, which excluded such a possibility. Juliette was resolved to go away, to live in Brest with her sister to whom she had fled seventeen years before. But Victor Hugo by his earnest supplications and signs of genuine grief prevailed upon her to stay. He pleaded for her pardon, which he had once given her. He insisted, and she believed him, that now he could not live without her. Yet he induced her to permit him to see Mme. Biard for an interval of time, three or four months, during which he would endeavor to break off their connection gradually, cost what it might. What he proposed for himself was a "period of trial," often resorted to by the romantics, during which he would determine which of the two women he must hold. Juliette consented and waited, filled with hope and pity. Victor Hugo also suffered. Sometimes he was wonderfully kind, sometimes cruel to his Juliette. Once, heavily veiled, she came suddenly to visit him at the Chamber. His attitude was cold; she wrote him:

I returned deeply troubled . . . at your haste to return to the hall, with the most confused and embarrassed air, like a man disagreeably surprised to be seen with me. How I suffered at that moment, and what I suffer now would be your condemnation before God if you were capable of a new betrayal . . . which would now indeed be a sacrilege. I refuse to believe this evidence, your pallor, your embarrassment, your flight! . . . My God, my God, what have I done to be so stricken. . . .

Léonie Biard too had had the habit of coming to the Chamber. Victor Hugo fought with himself, and Juliette too fought, in that foreboding summer of 1851 when Paris whispered again about an approaching *coup d'état*. Should he stake everything he had, burn his bridges and fight—whom? Bonaparte, Léonie, or Juliette? The two struggles, one public, the other domestic, merged into each other in his unconscious mind, and decision in the one plainly hung upon the outcome of the other.

Bonaparte, during the summer of 1851, moved to impose his

"personal rule" upon France, in the form of an "authoritarian" government, by forcing the revision of the Constitution so as to permit his election for a second term. The later Bonaparte revealed his consular character, attempted to assume in his own person and erect over France the Image of Authority. At this, a fierce atavistic impulse drove Victor Hugo to rebellion, though he knew he would be a marked man, and doomed if Bonaparte should triumph.

In a mood of weariness and apprehension he came one day to see Juliette, whom he had once likened to his mother, and she comforted him with her tenderness. Several years before, in 1846, her own daughter, Claire Pradier, a very beautiful young girl, had died of consumption. Victor Hugo had become quite fond of the pale Claire, who had such tragic eyes, and had contributed to her education and support more than her father. Juliette proposed now that they visit Claire's grave and pray for her immortal soul, and Victor Hugo accompanied her upon this melancholy mission, as he had before. He had once written a poem to Juliette in which he declared that the spirits of their two "angels," the dead Léopoldine and the dead Claire, always hung over them and united them forever. Once more he assured her, in 1851, as they prayed together before Claire's grave (for he always enjoyed prayer), that they were bound to each other eternally. In an access of generous passion (such as came to him also upon the tribune), he told Juliette that his mind was made up, and she threw herself into his arms, saying that she forgave him.

"I no longer see the wrong you have done; I see only my love," she said. "I do not know if my happiness will return, but I am sure that there will be for me no other lord but you." This was written on July 15, 1851, two days before Victor Hugo's speech on the revision of the Constitution.

In late October, 1851, he went with her for a visit of three days to the forest of Fontainebleau, now in its autumn colors. There he escaped from the passions and dangers of the parliament, and became again the poet. When they returned to Paris, he went to see Mme. Biard, then at midnight returned to Juliette, as he had promised. The "trial" was over. He told her that the other woman had agreed to a separation. He pledged himself to remain by her side. Juliette, driven by her single-minded devotion, had fought well. When he left Juliette, he was at peace with himself. He turned with renewed strength to the serious tasks that accumulated for him in the world of public affairs.

3

In June, 1851, Louis Bonaparte had given a speech at Dijon attacking "parliamentarianism," and had ridiculed the dissentious Assembly. Printed petitions appealing for the revision of the Constitution (to permit a second presidential term) had, thereafter, flooded Paris and other cities.

On Bastille Day, July 14, 1851, the great debate over the issue of revision—raised by Bonaparte's supporters—had opened in the Chamber, with Berryer and Falloux, the Royalists, favoring revision (for obscure reasons of their own), and Michel de Bourges and Hugo opposing it in behalf of the united Left. Victor Hugo's turn came on July 17, closing the formal debate, which had been temperate in tone thus far. But his speech was far from temperate. He had been brought out by the Left like a cavalry brigade in the final charge to destroy the enemy lines. His speech reviewed the evil deeds done under the Republic since 1849, girded against the Party of Order, against the Ministry, against Bonaparte himself. It was an immense four-hour-long diatribe, deliberately intended to insult and infuriate the adversary, and to warn the country of impending dangers—for it was plain to see that the political pot was boiling merrily. Recently, with the connivance of the President, a pamphlet entitled "The Red Specter," written by the journalist Romieu, a hanger-on of Bonaparte's, had been widely circulated in France, as if to announce a coming proletarian uprising. Hugo, referring to this propaganda, charged that men like Berryer and Falloux, leaders of the Right, had falsely raised this Red Specter, were attacking the Republic itself, and sought to destroy the very traditions of the great French Revolution. This he declared was a continuous movement, taking form in three successive revolutions down to 1848, and heralding not only the liberation of the people from the old monarchistic regimes all over Europe, but that "immense edifice of the future, which will be called some day the United States of Europe!" Thus, early in the day, he lifted his voice for world peace.

Montalembert (interrupting) cried: "Hugo is mad!"

M. de Molé, former premier, exclaimed: "What a thought; what extravagance! Oh, these poets!"

The orator accused his Legitimist adversaries of seeking by intrigues to restore one form of monarchy, while other (Orléanist) Conservatives plotted for another type of monarchy, none defending the Republic. He declared the idea of monarchy dead in France, for all time. He recalled the corruption and bankruptcy of Louis XV's reign and that of Charles X in 1830.

A VOICE FROM THE RIGHT (interrupting) : *And what about pensions for poets?*

HUGO (stops) : I would say to the gentleman who interrupted me that he refers evidently to a pension offered me by Charles X, which I refused.

M. DE FALLOUX: Pardon me, you received a pension from the funds of the King!

HUGO: Would you like to hear the real story?

M. DE FALLOUX: I rise to correct an error: M. Hugo said "I never received a pension under the monarchy. . . ."

HUGO: I did not say that (tumult—laughter—turning to the Right he continues). Listen well: You have laughed, I assure you that you will not laugh when I have finished. . . . I was nineteen years old; I published a volume of poetry; Louis XVIII, who was a king who loved books, you remember, read it and awarded me a pension of 2,000 francs. This act was spontaneous on his part, to his honor and mine . . . I had made no demand. The letter you have in your hand, M. de Falloux, proves that. Several years later, Charles X reigning, I presented a play, *Marion de Lorme;* it was suppressed; I petitioned the King, who received me, but refused to revoke the order. The next day I received from the King the advice that, to recompense me for my loss, I was to have my pension increased from 2,000 francs to 6,000 francs. *I refused this!* (Applause.) I wrote to the Minister that I desired only my liberty as a poet and my independence as a writer. (Applause on the Left.) There is the letter, M. de Falloux. . . . I see, gentlemen, you no longer laugh at me.

Thus, with uproarious interruptions the speech continued.

"You monarchists—you are all dead!" he cried, turning to the monarchists. "You do not belong in our century, in our world!" "No! No!" cried voices from the Right. The chairman pounded his gavel, exclaiming sarcastically: "Order. Silence. Do not resuscitate yourselves!"

Resuming his argument, Hugo warned the reactionaries in the Assembly against undertaking new intrigues for a Royalist restoration, declaring that the very stones and pavements of Paris were still red with the blood that had already flowed from such adventures, and that such a course could end only with new holocausts and new flights into exile for the "new royalty."

At this many Representatives of the Right crowded to the

rostrum, exclaiming that Hugo was "threatening them with the Terror." One man, an officer, drew his pistol and cocked it. The Representatives of the Left moved down to defend Hugo—some of them urging him to leave the platform in protest, because the chairman seemed to make no effort to preserve order now. But Hugo refused to yield to Montalembert, who tried to reach the platform, and yelled that he had revelations to make. The tumult subsided a little, and he continued to his climax in a passage that gripped the whole unruly Chamber.

This Government has throttled all our liberties, one by one—nay it is not a Government, it is one vast intrigue—history will call it one vast conspiracy. France lowers its head in dishonor, Napoleon trembles with shame in his tomb, while five thousand tramps cry "Long live the Emperor!" That is your glory. And now, my friends, let us talk a little of the "Empire"! They tell me no one is thinking of an empire; I have the habit of tearing off masks. What do these cries mean—Long live the Emperor!—who *pays* for them? What are these whispers we hear of a debauched pretorian guard preparing for attack on us?

Is it because ten centuries ago there was once a Charlemagne, who left to the world a sword and a scepter immeasurable; . . . and is it because another genius came, a thousand years later, who knew how to take up this sword and this scepter, and reared himself a throne over this continent, and made history, whose glory still endures, who spread the Revolution over Europe, who gave his name to those glittering syllables, Friedland, Rivoli, Jena? Was it because he, in turn, exhausted after ten years of fabulous glory, let fall the sword and scepter which had achieved these great things, that you come now, *you,* you dare to take it up after him, as he had taken it up after Charlemagne! (Rising tumult.) You would dare take in your puny hands the scepter of the Titans, the sword of the giants. After August—must we have Augustulus! *Because we have had a Napoleon the Great, must we have a Napoleon the Little!*

This unforgettable Hugolian antithesis—*Napoleon the Little!*— turned the Chamber into a frenzy of cheering or cursing men. They scarcely heard the orator's closing words on a coming "eclipse" for the Republic. How long it would last he did not know; but he was as certain as he was alive that "daylight would return and that the people and God would triumph!"

Napoleon the Little; Napoleon the Little. The words went ringing out over France and Europe and America. The amateur in politics had turned prophet and given his warning to men. From

England and Italy and many other lands, letters came to him applauding his forthright speech, and bringing him condolences for the imprisonment of his sons. Even the great Mazzini wrote him: "I have loved you since my days as a student; I admire you more than ever today for your burning words."

In the Assembly the commotion created by Hugo prevented passage of an act authorizing the revision of the Constitution, the measure failing to win a majority of three-fourths of the Representatives, as required.

Louis-Napoleon might be "little," but time grew short, and the defeat of revision barred all lawful approaches to renewed power after May, 1852. There was for him no other course, if he would survive, but the *coup d'état* of violence. At the Elysée Palace the band of conspirators and adventurers who surrounded him, headed by the Duc de Morny (his half-brother), Maupas, the new Prefect of Police, and General Saint-Arnaud, the Minister of War, grew desperate, as the summer of 1851 wore on, and made hurried preparations for action. Some of them favored carrying out the *coup d'état* in September, with the legislative branch in recess and the Representatives away on vacation. But General Saint-Arnaud argued that this would be unsafe since the politicians from their home districts might head uprisings which converged on Paris from the outside, as in the time of the Girondins, and more difficult to suppress. It was better to wait and take the Assembly later when it was in session, and when "the big fish could be caught in the net."

Louis Bonaparte waited. He scraped together some money from new loans, for the conspirators were out of cash again. "In this game we are risking all our hides on one big play," said Morny, always the cool, polite gambler. They passed out fifty thousand francs to be handed in ten-franc gold pieces to the regular soldiers of the Paris garrison on the appointed day. Quietly they emptied the great Mazas Prison of its criminals, who were sent elsewhere. Some news of this leaking out, certain police officials were dismissed and told to keep quiet.

In November, when the people's Representatives had returned to their sittings the President confronted them with a demand for the repeal of the unpopular Electoral Law of May 31, 1850 (which had disfranchised nearly three million voters). It was a bid for mass popularity. Puzzled, the Assembly majority hesitated and defeated a motion for repeal of the law by a narrow margin—it was supported by Hugo and the Left. The parliament thus nourished the hatred of the common people, who called its members the Twenty-Five Francs—after the daily salary they voted themselves. Cynically and stubbornly the Party of Order preserved its own acts of usurpation, which alienated the sympathy of the people and opened the way for another usurper.

Juliette Drouet had told her lover that she feared for the future but that she would guard him. She wrote to him one day: "I see that all your devotion, courage and genius will not suffice to prevent the coming catastrophe that will overturn the Republic." She strove to calm "her Robespierre" as she now called him in jest when he returned from forensic battle. One evening when he lay down to sleep, exhausted by an animated session, she bade him good night, saying: "Sleep well, my beloved Representative, there will be time later to listen to the thunder of the Mountain."

He slept uneasily these days, though it was not the thunder on the Left that made him wakeful. Once, on September 28, 1851, he rose late at night and wrote in his diary:

They strike at me. . . . Whatever may happen I see my purpose clearly, I do not turn my eyes from it, I shall march toward it. Every man has his *via crucis*. Calvary at the end of the road. . . .

As December approached, France seemed calmer, but the trap was ready. The Prince-President was a fearfully nervous man and slept poorly. Yet he had the brass to hold a large and splendid reception at the Elysée Palace on the night of December 1, 1851, showing himself very cheerful and friendly to all comers, up to a late hour. It was a reception that Victor Hugo, of course, was neither invited to nor cared to attend, for he was now one of the three or four chiefs of the republican Left.

The next morning, at eight, Hugo, who was at his own home, heard a pounding at the door, and two republican Representatives burst into his house crying: "The Republic has been *made prisoner!*" Soldiers, they said, had surrounded the Palais Bourbon, and Thiers, General Changarnier, and seventy leading citizens and officers had just been arrested while still in bed. Those of the republican Deputies who had escaped the net thus far were to meet and consult at a certain house in the rue Blanche. Would Hugo come out? He replied that of course he would come. But first he rushed into his wife's room to tell her of what was happening and placed on her bed a box containing nine hundred francs—

all that remained in the house after he had taken five hundred francs for himself.

"What are you going to do?" Mme. Hugo asked anxiously.

"I am going to do my duty."

"Do it," she said, and embraced him.

CHAPTER XIII

Coup d'Etat: Rise of a Dictator

AFTER HE HAD SALUTED his departing guests, smiling his vague smile at them through his waxed mustaches and imperial, on the evening of December 1, 1851, Louis Bonaparte proceeded to his study and opened a special dossier with the word "Rubicon" written over it. Here were the prepared orders for the next morning's operations. The Duc de Morny came hurrying back from the theater, where he had shown himself as usual that evening; General Saint-Arnaud, Minister of War, and Maupas, the new Prefect of Police, also arrived for the nocturnal conference. These were the principal directors of the coup.

Their plan aimed at taking over the capital, the Assembly, the Ministry of the Interior (or Home Office), the police and army command in the dead of night; second, arresting those prominent personages who might be active opponents, thus paralyzing France by the suddenness of the stroke. Even the smallest details had been attended to in advance: the bells of churches were muffled; the drums of the National Guard were removed; newspaper presses were stopped, save those assigned to print the new ruler's proclamations for the historic day of December 2; finally large bodies of troops (but no cavalry such as might wake the burghers) were marched all night into the main squares and stationed before the principal buildings and bridges.

At six in the morning, Parisians who went to work early first saw the white posters pasted on walls all over the capital during the night. There were three proclamations: the first presented Louis-Napoleon Bonaparte's "Appeal to the People" against a conspiring parliament, which he thereby dissolved. To end the "era of revolutions" and to satisfy popular demands for legitimate reform, the President asked for special authority; to obtain this, he announced in a second Proclamation, in the style of Napoleon the Great, a plebiscite to be held in the early future under universal suffrage, in order to sanction an "authoritarian" or consular form of government. A third Proclamation addressed itself to the soldiers of the army as the "elite of France," summoning them to obey orders unquestioningly, and promising them rewards. While taking the capital by surprise, the Prince-President posed as a sort of national Liberal, ready to save the people from a reactionary parliament.

Paris awoke to find its main streets lined with regular infantry. "It looked like Lisbon on one of its days of military overturn," the Austrian Ambassador, Huebner, reported. Seventy-four high politicos, including little Thiers (rather badly frightened) and General Cavaignac in his nightshirt, were caught in bed and placed under arrest—though Thiers and other extreme Conservatives were soon afterward released.

Toward eleven o'clock, when the Representatives arrived at the Palais Bourbon for their regular session, they found the streets and main approaches of the hall barred by soldiers with bayonets. A few managed to get inside by little-known side entrances. But the parliament of the Second Republic as a whole broke up into several blindly struggling segments. A group of about three hundred legislators, turned away at the door of the Assembly, arranged to meet at the mansion of the aged Count Daru, near by, but, being pursued and surrounded by soldiers, retreated through the garden and met in the *Mairie* building of the Tenth Arrondissement, at the square of the Croix-Rouge. There in solemn union they decreed that "Louis-Napoleon Bonaparte has forfeited the Presidency of the Republic." These were chiefly Conservatives, and they would go no farther for fear of creating a disturbance. However, a lieutenant of African chasseurs soon arrived and politely arrested them; though they assured him he was violating the law he said only: "We are soldiers, and must obey orders."

Inside the Palais Bourbon itself, some thirty Representatives who had managed to get past the guards, including Eugène Sue, called out the President of the Assembly, André Dupin (who resided in the building), and urged him to put on his sash, go into the Assembly Hall, and protest to the military officers who had taken charge. Dupin had to be thrust forward by his colleagues, and finally croaked out: "We have the law on our side, but those gentlemen have the power. Come, let us get out of here!"

While these painful, but somewhat comic scenes were going on, Victor Hugo, still at large, hurried to join a third meeting of parliamentarians, that of the Mountain, at a house in the rue Blanche. About half of the Left's Representatives, those who were men of military or organizing experience, had been arrested already, as Hugo noticed. Those remaining were principally the orators, theorists, and intellectuals, of whom sixty, headed by Michel de Bourges, Jules Favre, and Hugo, convened to plan resistance to Bonaparte's *coup d'état*. The Second Republic had been associated at the outset with a good deal of romanticism, in the shape of Lamartine; now in its hour of danger it depended principally upon men like Hugo, the poet, Edgar Quinet, the historian, and Favre, the philosophical jurist and scholar, to defend it against a powerful, secret conspiracy organized by the executive with the aid of all the military and police force of the state.

"Hugo, what would you have us do?" they asked.

"Everything," he replied bravely.

Asked to speak first, he called for active resistance, by making appeal to the soldiers in the street and to the people. If the troops yielded, march with them to the Elysée and seize Bonaparte; if the troops fired, scatter all over Paris and call the people to arms, in other words, to the barricades.

However, other leaders, such as Michel de Bourges, who possessed greater first-hand experience of such revolutionary situations, as Hugo modestly related, urged a policy of watchful waiting, to begin with. The people, they reported, seemed to be taken by surprise, but were not excited or angry. In the working-class districts of Paris there was no unrest similar to that of 1830 or 1848. For the workers were bitter at the majority party in parliament which had killed or deported their leaders in June, 1848, and disfranchised great numbers of them in 1850. They rather enjoyed the overturn of the Twenty-Five Francs (as they called the men of parliament) by Bonaparte, who had long been trying to woo and dupe the laboring class. It was important, therefore, to wait until the people began to open their eyes and grow warmly indignant, rather than hurry things and be quickly crushed by superior force. The program for the first day or two was to be devoted to agitation by cautious methods. The meeting chose a Committee of Insurrection which, on Hugo's motion, was named a Committee of Resistance, since he argued that it was really Bonaparte who practiced insurrection. Victor Hugo was named as one of the four members of this directing committee; the members, after agreeing to resume their meeting at night, scattered to communicate with their followers in Paris, to rally speakers and print pamphlets calling attention to Bonaparte's violation of the Constitution. By a majority vote the meeting refused a preliminary call to arms, and recommended spoken or printed appeals—but all printing presses had already been taken over by the army.

Victor Hugo and two other colleagues roamed about Paris all that afternoon, haranguing people from street corners and omnibuses, and watching cavalry and artillery riding past them into the center of the city.

What if he stirred up the people? How could he do it? Victor Hugo asked himself insistently.

Victor Hugo relates, in his own account:

As we reached the Porte Saint-Martin a long column of infantry debouched into the boulevard, which is here depressed well below the curb level, drums beating ahead . . . their undulating bayonets filling all of the Place Saint-Martin. An enormous, compact crowd lined the curbs on both sides, many workers in their blue shirts leaning over the iron railings to look down at the soldiers. As the troops marched by, a great cry arose from the throats of the people, as from one man: "Long live the Republic!" The soldiers marched on in silence, but it seemed to me that their pace slackened perceptibly and some of them looked at the crowd with an anxious air.

Victor Hugo was recognized and surrounded. People cried: "Long live Victor Hugo!" They asked: "What shall we do?" He cried: "Tear down the posters! Louis Bonaparte is a rebel. . . . We the Representatives of the people declare him an outlaw. . . . Citizens, you have hands; take the law and your guns and go for Bonaparte!" (Bravo!)

Hugo continues:

The enthusiasm, the indignation, the anger I felt in their eyes made me think then, and I think now (twenty-five years later) *that it was perhaps a supreme moment. I was tempted to capture this whole crowd and begin the battle.*

Charmaule, beside me, held me back, saying in a low voice: "You will cause useless bloodshed. These people are unarmed, and here is the artillery coming up."

To be sure, I saw several pieces of cannon, led by horses, coming up. . . . *I recoiled before the responsibility that I would have incurred.* To seize such a moment might bring victory; it might mean a massacre. Was I right? Was I wrong?

Victor Hugo's narration of these events, in "The Story of a Crime," written a few months afterward, but revised and published only in 1877, is admittedly a romantic history. He had resolved to set down as he saw with his own eyes the details of a world event, together with the testimony of others. His own part was not a little exaggerated, with his usual impulsive vanity and swagger. For there was, in truth, a good deal of "romance" in the whole innocent procedure of the improvised Committee of Resistance which attempted to thwart a vast military-police operation organized for a *total coup d'état*. (Technically, the *coup d'état* of Louis Bonaparte was a brilliant model for all later "inside" insurrections of the fascist type.) And yet, although Hugo may have been at the time excessively romantic and egoistic, as has been charged, we must remember that these traits in no way stopped him from showing fight. Unaware of or indifferent to the crushing force set against them, Hugo and his friends worked steadfastly to raise up a demonstration, which, to everyone's surprise, gradually assumed a most serious character.

At the start the efforts of the republicans seemed feeble and ill-directed. Unarmed, they were pursued in the streets whenever they tried to speak. The people seemed apathetic. Late in the afternoon of December 2, when Hugo returned to the rue Blanche meeting agreed upon earlier, he and the others grew downcast at the first reports of arrests and of strong measures being taken to shut off all means of communication.

But again Victor Hugo was in the van of those who urged more forceful action. A "romantic fool" who "dreamed of being President," his detractors called him. So be it! Sometimes there are not enough "romantic fools."

On behalf of his Committee Victor Hugo quickly dictated a manifesto appealing to the people to defend the Constitution (but not the hated National Assembly). It ran:

Louis-Napoleon is a traitor! He has placed himself beyond the law. . . . Let the people do their duty, the republican Representatives have taken the lead.

A man arrived with news that soldiers were pouring into the rue Blanche and surrounding the house. The republicans, making a rendezvous for midnight at another secret meeting place, a house in the rue Popincourt, fled by back doors and side alleys and scattered about Paris.

They harangued the populace. Once more Victor Hugo, riding with three other colleagues in an omnibus toward the center of the city, found his passage blocked among dense crowds and cavalry with naked sabers riding alongside of his omnibus and filling up the boulevard. He relates:

Suddenly the troops halted and the traffic came to a standstill. . . . The soldiers were close to us; from my place in the omnibus I could almost touch them. Unable to restrain myself any longer, I lowered the window and put my head out. Gazing steadily at that dense line of soldiers facing me, I cried: "Down with Louis Bonaparte! Those who serve traitors are traitors!"

The soldiers looked at him almost with a drunken stare but did not move. His companions also took up the cry: "Down with the traitors! Down with the dictator!" But the whole omnibus seemed seized with terror, and implored Hugo and his friends to desist "lest we be massacred."

I was in a whirl of excitement [Hugo continues]. An officer . . . turned to us in a threatening way and waved his sword; the crowd looked on, as if in a daze. . . . Vaguely I imagined that a collision must come, and that from the crowd, or from the troops, some spark would fly. I hoped for a saber stroke from one of the soldiers, or a cry of fury from the people. I had obeyed a sudden impulse. . . . But nothing came of it, no saber slashing nor shout of anger. The soldiers did not move, the people looked on in silence. *Was it too late? Was it too soon?*[1]

At night, after the wearying day of agitation, Hugo came to the secret rendezvous at the rue Popincourt and learned that the manifesto he had dictated had not yet been printed, for all presses were under military guard. Several members set off to find a secret press. The Left republicans were more hopeful and determined now to foment an uprising.

Were they too late? Too soon? Hugo and his friends asked themselves these questions continually, reflecting the uncertainty and

[1]A. F. Davidson's "comprehensive" biography of V. Hugo cites this passage, mistranslating in a manner to cast ridicule on the hero, and inserting boastful expressions not used by him. Davidson's work is a systematic English copy of the monumental work of prejudice written by Biré in four volumes.

inexperience of the Republic's defenders. A peaceful poet and several writers, editors, and lawyers were working night and day to rouse up a mass revolution against a dictator. So few seemed willing to listen and follow. He moved as in a trance, forgetting food and sleep. Where were his wife, his children? What would become of him? How would it all end? He dared not return to his house, certain that police waited for him there. Then he bethought himself of a brave young workingman whom he had saved from the soldiers in the bloody insurrection of June, 1848. He had hidden the man in the attic of Juliette Drouet's house. This man would surely be of help in calling out his working-class friends, and Hugo determined to find him. Thinking of his man, he remembered Juliette Drouet—recently nearly lost to him. He hurried through the dark streets longing to see her again, perhaps for a last time.

Juliette had rushed to his house, in wild fear, at nine o'clock in the morning, as soon as she had had news of the *coup d'état*. But he was already gone. Then, returning home, she had waited all that day outside her door, in fear and trembling. When he came, she was beside herself with joy. That day Victor Hugo had not eaten more than a bar of chocolate someone had given him. She fed him and urged him to hide there; he refused, saying that he would surely be hunted at the house of his mistress. He told her that he was obliged to go to the Bastille quarter to find the man they had once rescued, who was now a small wine merchant. She insisted upon accompanying him. In truth Juliette feared terribly going out on this night of terror, but she feared even more that she might lose sight of him.

A pall hung over the Paris night, they felt. On a zigzagging course they rode through streets lined with waiting soldiers and silent crowds. Yet Victor Hugo, sitting well back in the cab, was in carefree mood. Laughing, he pointed out to her the theater on the Boulevard des Italiens where Verdi's opera *Hernani*, based on his play, was being performed. But she was silent, fearful, thinking only of where she could hide him. At the wineshop, they saw Auguste . . . and other friends of his, and it was agreed that arms would be gathered and serious business undertaken. One of the men reported that a barricade was to be set up in the faubourg Saint-Marceau.

"In that case, I want to be with you," said Hugo. "Come and call me."

"Where?"

"Wherever I may be." How could he know or say where he would be tomorrow? But he meant apparently that his friends could find him at his post of duty, wherever it was.

Hugo, at midnight, put Juliette into a cab, and sent her on her way, while he returned to another secret meeting of his Committee at the rue Popincourt. During the meeting there, and at a café to which the members took flight on further news of police approaching, Juliette, who did not go to sleep, made careful arrangements to have Hugo sheltered at the home of a friend of hers in the rue Caumartin. She came back to bring him there in a carriage and saw him safely to bed before she left him.

On the morning of December 3 the streets of Paris were more animated. Barricades were going up; the small, hastily printed proclamation of the Committee of Resistance was being read here and there. Representatives like Jean Baudin, Victor Schoelcher, and Victor Hugo harangued the people in the streets and led them to barricades. In effect, the plans that were being shaped were not unskillful; they involved the gradual arousing of the people and the setting up of small barricades, whose defenders—when the troops descended in too heavy force—were to fly in all directions, but to return to them after the soldiers were gone. These were the street-fighting tactics used successfully in 1830 and 1848.

But suddenly things began to move faster. At nine-thirty in the morning of December 3, several of the republican Representatives were organizing a barricade in the crowded Saint-Antoine quarter. A column of soldiers arrived to clear the street. Schoelcher walked out toward them unarmed, calling on them to fall back. The soldiers motioned him aside with their bayonets and moved on toward the barricades whence scattered shots were aimed at them. They answered, killing the young Representative Jean Baudin.

Just before the engagement, Schoelcher related, Baudin had been sneered at by some workingmen near by who said: "Why should we kill ourselves for the Twenty-Five Francs!" And Baudin had replied proudly: "I will show you how a man can die for Twenty-Five Francs!" His words were repeated all over Paris and roused the city to a sullen anger.

2

The second day of the *coup d'état* was becoming interesting and bloody. M. Bonaparte, as the Parisians would say, had "drawn the wine." During the afternoon and evening of December 3, large barricades were rising in the dark, crowded Saint-Antoine quarter, the East End of Paris; workers in blue smocks were manning them grimly. The trade-unions were issuing proclamations. "Hugo's Committee," as it was called, was still at large and busily functioning. The *de facto* government authorities were showing a little confusion about what to do next, or whom to arrest.

Victor Hugo had not slept all night but, propped on cushions before a fireplace, sat listening to the sound of carriages, the tramp of soldiers marching by, the hour striking. Early in the morning, he had stolen away quietly, again accompanied by Mme. Drouet. He rode to a meeting fixed at a café near the Bastille. Passing troops, he could not restrain himself from haranguing them violently, for a third time—but Juliette tugged at his arm, saying fearfully: "You will get yourself shot." Arriving at the rendezvous by a roundabout course (where Juliette left him for the moment), he learned of the fate of Representative Baudin. He learned also of threats made by Morny, the new *de facto* Minister of the Interior, to have any deputies found behind barricades *shot out of hand*. A proclamation posted that morning by General Saint-Arnaud advised all persons to keep off the streets; those who were responsible for circulating or posting appeals to the population to take up arms in insurrection would be shot. Victor Hugo had already signed such appeals.

Friends of his now implored him to fly to safety. One said that Bonaparte hated him more than any other opponent because of the terrible epithet he had put into circulation: "Napoleon the Little." Proudhon (recently released from prison) and Pierre Leroux, both veteran agitators, warned him that his efforts would be vain, as the people were confused and would not fight for the hated parliamentary regime.

Victor Hugo did not know at the time that Prefect of Police Maupas, on December 3, had called the attention of the Duc de Morny to Hugo's leadership in the attempted rising, and asked what should be done about him. At first he was told to do nothing. Then, on repeated inquiries, Morny replied over the new telegraph set installed in the Ministry of the Interior: "You may use your own judgment with regard to Hugo."

Hugo continued working with his Committee, writing new appeals to the people, which were rushed off to secret presses. From the constantly changed secret meeting places he and his comrades would be forced to fly repeatedly—as sentinels warned of soldiers approaching—to new hiding places from which they directed their activities.

The evening of the second day seemed menacing: despite orders crowds appeared in the streets, loudly saluting the Republic and singing the "Marseillaise." Here and there big barricades were being built; during the night some twelve hundred armed working-men finally came out and took their posts, most of them at the old Saint-Martin's Gate on the boulevards. That night, Juliette Drouet ventured out, managed to find Victor Hugo again, and like a guardian angel led him to another safe hiding place, a house in the rue de Richelieu, where she left him in good hands. But early in the morning, when she hurried over, he was gone to a secret meeting place of which he had left no word with his hosts, and she realized with horror that she had lost track of him completely.

Because of his secret movements and his changed hiding places all about the great city, and also because of the fact that he was not killed at some barricade during the fighting of December 4, certain commentators have left accounts which disparage Hugo's courage. Maupas, one of the Bonapartist conspirators, in his memoirs, denies that he intended any harm to M. Victor Hugo. The police and government knew where Hugo was, and could have taken him easily, he asserts. In the next breath he reproaches Hugo for having remained in hiding and changing his address from day to day.

If Hugo were frightened, would not the most sensible thing have been to keep out of the whole business and, like Sainte-Beuve and many other luminaries, go to bed for the duration of the crisis? "Critics are seldom heroes," Sainte-Beuve remarks at his own expense. When the shooting was over Sainte-Beuve hastened to give his allegiance and lend his brains to the new regime. Montalembert, the retrograde Catholic Liberal, who had taunted Hugo as a time-server, was at this moment in the Elysée Palace, closeted with the new Caesar and his "Pretorians," framing the terms for a (somewhat temporary) entente between the Catholic party and the Bonapartists.

No, Victor Hugo and his colleagues were not the experienced organizers and fighting men of the Left—these were imprisoned at the beginning. Certainly they were visionary, and lost much precious time debating irrelevant questions. Hugo, in long arguments, even urged that the abolition of capital punishment be proclaimed and that the Central Committee pledge itself to spare Louis Bonaparte when he was taken! But to accuse Hugo of want of courage was an immense falsehood. It was chiefly circulated after the *coup d'état* by former friends of his (such as Granier de Cassagnac, whom he had once helped) who abandoned his cause and went over to Bonaparte, thus later coming under the fire of Hugo's terrible pen.

As a member of the Central Committee of four men upon whom it devolved to lead the uprising, as one of the generals of the popular movement, Victor Hugo, as far as possible, avoided direct exposure of himself in the front lines—though he carried away a bullet hole in his overcoat as a souvenir of the conflict. The tactical situation required that he and his associates avoid arrest, keep under cover, strike blows here and there, fatiguing and worrying the military power while waiting for the popular movement to assume massive force.

"The tide is rising," Edgar Quinet, the historian, told Hugo as he came in from the street during the afternoon of the second day, December 3. The common people, the workers of Paris, were coming out—they had always shown themselves the most courageous townspeople in the world. In the East End and the Latin Quarter students and republican-minded National Guards were reported in full control of the streets; at one point, a district *Mairie* building, filled with guns and ammunition, was captured.

In those days, as the regular soldiers debouched into silent, sullenly waiting streets, between tall, grimy buildings, they wished themselves in the open fields, rather than in the labyrinthine heart of a hostile metropolis of a million and a half enemies. Approaching a barricade before them, they watched uneasily for ambuscades, and were sometimes caught from the rear by murderous musket fire from rooftops or windows.

In his diary, Huebner, the Austrian Ambassador, noted: "The workers seem disposed to avoid battle, but try to wear down the soldiers. Also there is beginning to be some doubt as to the success of the *coup d'état*. This is scarcely concealed at the Ministry of Foreign Affairs." Indeed, Louis Bonaparte, at the Elysée Palace, had not slept a wink for two days. He feared the unexpected, the Unknown. His military henchmen had smilingly promised that there would be no bloodshed; now men were dying. Bonaparte was disappointed and also frightened. Soon he grew more frightened.

The police head, Maupas, now expected a general rising all over the city and sent frantic appeals to Morny during the afternoon of December 3, warning him that "socialist battalions armed with portable bombs" were converging upon police headquarters. The self-possessed Morny replied briefly: "Nothing can be done until tomorrow."

In the evening there were reports that the regular troops were being drawn back a little. In great alarm Maupas appealed again to Morny, saying: "The news is becoming extremely grave. . . . Insurgents are occupying *Mairie* buildings, acquiring arms. To allow the thing to spread itself from now on would be highly imprudent. . . . We need cannon and right away!"

Over the new telegraph set Morny replied, late at night, to the Prefect of Police: "Go to bed and be damned." (It was this badly frightened Prefect of Police, Maupas, who later accused Victor Hugo of lacking courage.)

The tactics had been carefully fixed, after the model of General Cavaignac's operation in June, 1848: to let the uprising come to full bloom before moving to crush it. General Magnan, commanding in the field, while drawing in his troops on December 3, 1851, remarked: "Tomorrow I will teach them a lesson they will remember."

The next morning, December 4, reports came to Morny of larger and more numerous barricades going up all about the center of the city. Now he sent word to Generals Saint-Arnaud and Magnan: *"Let my orders be executed. Strike hard along the boulevards."* Calling at the Elysée Palace, Morny reassured the pallid Louis Bonaparte, saying grimly: "I am going to close up the political clubs along the boulevards."

At one o'clock in the afternoon three strong columns of troops, numbering 30,000 out of the 80,000 actually held in readiness, marched toward the centers of disturbance, one along the left bank of the Seine, a second along the right bank, while the third and strongest column, including artillery, moved up the boulevards until it stopped before a small barricade erected at the old Saint-Denis Gate, on the Boulevard de Montmartre, which was manned by a few workingmen with guns.

A dense crowd now lined the avenue, singing and cheering for the Republic. The people in the streets were in holiday mood. Thrust back by bayonets, they crowded upon the curb and kept shouting insults at the soldiers, who began to pull down the barricade. Suddenly a shot was fired, perhaps from a window, as some eyewitnesses reported. In an instant the soldiers, who seemed tired and unnerved, began firing volleys on all sides of them into the unarmed, dense crowd of people on both sides of the avenue; they reloaded and discharged their muskets into cafés, shop-windows, houses, and hotels. One officer of artillery sighted his cannon at a building down the avenue, with a café at the street level, and soon demolished its whole façade. Women, children, old men, shopkeepers at their trade, idly curious passers-by fell wounded or dying in heaps. Before Jouvin's glove shop there was a pile of corpses—an old gentleman with his umbrella, a studious-looking young man with eyeglasses, among the heaped-up workingmen's bodies. The popular Café Anglais, the Café de Paris, Tortoni's all ran with blood, targets for the troops. A little boy of thirteen, flee-ing into a toyshop for shelter, fell dead over a heap of toys; Dr. Piquet, the scientist, seventy years of age, died as he sat reading in his study; an artist fell before his easel with a ball through his skull; a chemist in his shop was riddled by the lancers who rushed in. Before the Théâtre des Variétés there were fifty-two corpses, eleven of them female. It was a massacre.

The soldiers advanced steadily along the Boulevard de Mont-martre, their musketry fire increasing in fury. All who could move in time fled in a horrible stampede. An English correspondent of the London *Times,* looking on from a hotel window, declared in his remarkable eyewitness account—no French paper published any news of the affair—that the firing was wholly indiscriminate and could be attributed only to sudden panic or drunkenness among the soldiers. It continued for at least a quarter of an hour—though some reports said for half an hour or longer. The toll of this modern Saint-Bartholomew's Day was officially counted at 380 dead (in the back files of the *Moniteur*) though some historians have placed it at 900, without counting the wounded.

Victor Hugo, who had been attending a meeting near by at the house of Jules Grévy, one of his republican colleagues (and later President under the Third Republic), heard the shooting and can-nonading and hurried toward the boulevards to see for himself what was happening. Near the Saint-Denis Gate he was in time to see the corpses piled up, the people running in all directions, blood flowing in the gutter, the wounded calling for help. In a moment the Boulevard de Montmartre, alive with merry-making people, had been transformed into a deserted shambles.

"It was indescribable," he wrote later. "I saw this crime, this slaughter, this tragedy. I saw death raining blindly down upon the people; I saw the massacred crowd fall all around me. That is why I sign this book ["Story of a Crime"] as written by a Witness. . . . Destiny watches mysteriously over the future historian. She allows him to be present, involved in a scene of carnage, yet spares him death, desiring that he should live to write of what he has seen."

The deliberate, cold-blooded slaughter of December 4, 1851, Victor Hugo wrote afterward, opened his eyes and that of the world to the true character of Louis Bonaparte. In the crisis he showed himself a "Jean Mandrin," a bandit chieftain, underneath his intellectual guise. Hugo was horrified at the recollection that he had once known the man, received him in his own house, and sat at his table. He had thought of him as a calculating gambler, but now he had thrown off the mask. Louis Bonaparte was a criminal, a murderer.

Truly, as Hugo said, "It was this carnage that made Louis-Napoleon emperor." He became master of France, historians would say, *by and with the army,* on December 4, 1851. Orders had been given to take no prisoners, and the few workers who rose again in 1851, after their sufferings in 1848, were pitilessly crushed. All militant republican leaders were arrested, unless they fled into exile. The democracy established by the common people in 1848 was ended on December 4, 1851, and the people would always remember that day. They would always remember Louis-Napoleon for "the day of the massacre of the boulevards."

3

Early that morning, Victor Hugo had gone to his home in the rue de la Tour d'Auvergne, got a change of clothing and some personal effects, and fled like a hunted man. The police had come to arrest him the day before. Spies had hovered about the house; his daughter Adèle, in a letter of December 19, 1851, spoke of these visitations as a "nightmare" from which she longed to awake. Mme. Hugo, rendered ill with anxiety, had taken to her bed. Fortunately his two sons, still in prison, had been prevented from sharing the dangers of civil war with him.

At the Boulevard de Montmartre, he stood swayed by emotions of horror and despair which would never leave his memory. At this rate—when even bystanders were slaughtered without warning—he saw, as everyone else saw, that resistance by the people's Representatives was useless. Exhausted, dazed, sick at heart, he turned to take a few steps, when one of his associates in the Assembly, Xavier Durrieux, came up and seized him by the hand, exclaiming: "Ah, there you are. I have just seen Mme. Drouet. She is looking for you."

Juliette, at the sound of firing, had turned faint with fear, yet managed to dress and set off toward the boulevards, hoping against hope that she would not find him killed or mutilated. At one street corner she came upon a heap of corpses and uttered a cry of horror and indignation. A cavalryman menaced her with his pistol, and she fled through an open doorway. Yet she continued her search through the death-ridden streets until, by chance, she met Durrieux, whom she knew as one of Victor Hugo's associates, and who remembered where he had gone. She found Victor Hugo standing dazed, not knowing where he was, flung herself into his arms and begged him to hurry away to a place of safety. He obeyed her. And she led him to a new hiding place.

That night scattered barricades continued their resistance, but on the following day fighting ceased. Hugo remained in hiding at 19 rue de Richelieu, with the Montferriers, friends of Juliette. He slept badly. In the morning he would hear her key, awake in terror; then she would come in, bringing cold food from her house. Moreover she guarded the door outside. One morning, after he had been hidden in the rue de Richelieu for three days, she stood downstairs at the door waiting for him, or walked up and down the street outside. Then she suddenly felt herself being followed by two policemen, and she set off walking in a blind direction; she shook the police off, and then doubled back to watch them and make sure they were not now covering the house in the rue de Richelieu. She went in again, ran upstairs to warn Victor Hugo, and found that he had not come in the night before, doubtless out of fear of being followed. All that morning and afternoon she waited downstairs in the cold hallway until he came in. Then she sprang at him, saying: "Do not come in here."

"Am I discovered?"

"Yes."

"Are there police outside?"

"No," she said, and led him away. They walked casually to the Place Royale, near by, and hired a carriage.

"Where do you wish to go, Monsieur?" asked the coachman.

"I don't know," replied Hugo.

"But I know," said Juliette, laughing, and an hour later they were in a new place of refuge. Victor Hugo hid in a room that was divided from the salon of the apartment by a thin partition. Through the wall he could hear his friends talking about the news of the day, saying that a price had been placed on his head, even discussing rumors that he was dead.

France was calm again, and mournful. The Conservative politicians were being released from jail now, and the republicans were being imprisoned.

On the evening of December 11, 1851, clad in a blue shirt, a workingman's cap pulled over his face, and carrying a tin food basket, Victor Hugo entered the Gare du Nord and took the night train to Brussels. He carried with him a false passport authorizing a man named Lanvin to cross the frontier. Four days earlier, Juliette Drouet had gone to Brussels to prepare for his arrival and await him there.

As the iron monster of a locomotive puffed away northward, Victor Hugo's heart, filled with emotion, vibrated with every revolution of the wheels. Napoleon the Little, Mandrin, was driving him from France, from those he loved, from the city that was his native land, where his whole adult life had been passed. And tomorrow the wealth he had earned by such terrible labor of mind and heart might be taken from him, his books suppressed, his plays condemned. What would become of his sons, still in the Conciergerie? And his wife and daughter? How would they live? Ruin faced him; hard days were beginning, leading he knew not where.

Yet moments of elation and self-righteousness also gripped him. He had spoken out, exhorted and called men to arms, he had fought hard. Now he rode to join the illustrious company of exiles —Dante, the noble son of Florence; Voltaire, the defender of Calas against murderous bigots; Rousseau, the father of the French Revolution; Chateaubriand, the rebel against Napoleon the Great. From moods of anger he veered to a mood of peace and serenity; he would know how to bear everything. He said to himself (as he wrote in letters at this time): "I am going to continue with my pen the war I have waged by my speech." It would be a new life: "The writer must replace the orator. . . . We must lay our hands on Bonaparte." A new life of struggle and privation; but he was ready.

As he neared the border he thought of Juliette Drouet, and his heart filled with gratitude. For all the rest of his life he could never forget her unfailing devotion to him. He recalled to her in later years: "When in my hiding place, after a night of suspense, I heard the key tremble in your hand, danger and darkness ceased to beset me: light came in through that door. Oh, let us never forget those hours so terrible and yet sweet when you joined me during pauses in the struggle. . . ."

Even eight years later, in 1860, writing fragments of his diary on proofs of the *Légende des siècles,* found among his posthumous papers, he rendered justice to Juliette:

The order to shoot me if I were taken had been given in the first days of December, 1851. I had been warned of it in the course of a meeting which took place at Landrin's on the third of December. . . . The fact that I was not captured and shot, and that I am alive at this hour, I owe to Mme. Juliette Drouet who, at great peril to herself, saved me from every trap, watched over me unceasingly, found me shelter and rescued me; with what remarkable intelligence, zeal and courage, God alone knows and remembers. She was awake day and night, wandering alone through the murky streets of Paris, avoiding guards, throwing off spies, boldly crossing the boulevards under gunfire, sensing always where I was and when my life was in danger, always finding me. . . .

In the morning the train slowed up at Charleroi, and customs guards came on. "M. Lanvin" huddled in the corner of his third-class compartment. Would his false passport hold good? His own brother-in-law, and his old playmate, Victor Foucher, a high Bonapartist official, had conveyed the document to him. Very possibly the police in Paris knew who this workingman with white hands was and were relieved to have him cross the borders. The customs guards examined him briefly and passed on. The train rode into the safety of Belgium, and at last he descended at the station in Brussels. There at the platform was a familiar, tall, womanly figure, Juliette Drouet waiting for him.

CHAPTER XIV

The Road of Exile: Brussels

On the morning of December 12 he reached Brussels and his first feelings were of immeasurable relief, as if a terrible weight of dread were lifted from him. For days he had felt like a hunted animal, for he was convinced that a price had been put on his head —though none knew then or later if reports to this effect were authentic. After December 4, 1851, a wave of repression swept over France: in preparation for the "free plebiscite" of December 14–21, Bonaparte had more than twenty-five thousand citizens arrested. The "eagle" in Victor Hugo could not have borne the prison atmosphere that hung over France henceforth. His instinct to fly had been sound.

To his wife, who now lay ill in Paris, he hurried off a letter, addressed to "Mme. Rivière" and signed "Albert Durand," informing her of his safe arrival. He sent her instructions as to what to do with his papers, his securities, his effects. The plan was for her and her daughter Adèle to remain in Paris and protect his considerable possessions as well as they might. In a returning wave of tenderness for his wife, he closed: "Have courage, I beg you. I know that you have a great and strong soul. Tell my children that my heart is with them. Tell my little Adèle that I don't want her to turn pale and thin. She must be calm. The future will belong to those who are good!"

He tended to see the future darkly, penetrated by the thought that he had probably ruined himself and his family; certainly he had jeopardized his whole fortune by leading in the resistance to

Louis-Napoleon. His revenues from the theater would be cut off, his books which sold so widely would be condemned, his stipends as a Representative and doubtless also as a member of the Academy eliminated. It meant the loss, he estimated roughly, of 60,000 francs a year. Happily he had about 7,500 francs of *rentes* based on Belgian and English securities, or little more than a tenth of his previous income. At fifty, after living somewhat in the style of a millionaire author for nearly twenty years, he was stripped of his wealth and driven into exile. He would go to work again, he would write, he would rescue them all by his labor.

His first lodgings were in a small hotel; then after several days he established himself in a furnished room of an ancient building at number 27 of La Grande Place de l'Hôtel de Ville, the central square facing the ancient town hall. His room, which was above a tobacconist's shop, was very long and high, "like a hall," he related, and cost only one franc a day. It had a low bed, two rush-bottom chairs, and a chest. He ate dinner with beer at one franc at the Grand-Café; living costs were very cheap in Belgium in those days, and he reported in his next letter to Mme. Hugo, which he sent by an intermediary, that he planned to live in Spartan fashion on three francs a day, or 100 francs a month. (Mme. Drouet was established as frugally at a small hotel near by.) He listed his expenses as follows:

Lodging	1 fr.00
Breakfast (cocoa)	0 fr.50
Dinner	1 fr.25
Fire wood	0 fr.25
Total	3 fr.

From his window he looked out at the old quarter of the Belgian capital, notable for its medieval guild halls and its beautiful Gothic Town Hall with the lacy spire, one of the finest examples of its kind in Europe.

Very discreetly, the Burgomaster of Brussels, who had met the distinguished exile at some dinner in Paris, dropped in to pay his respects and offer what friendly assistance and advice he could.

In spite of the great troubles now afflicting him, Hugo at once led his visitor to the window and called his attention to the Town Hall, where some workmen on scaffoldings were repairing and painting the old spire white. He implored the Burgomaster not to have the building whitewashed but to leave it black. The Burgomaster promised to follow his wishes.

Victor Hugo was not alone in exile. About ten thousand French citizens had crossed the border into Belgium after the *coup d'état,* some of them Royalists as well as republicans and socialists. But Hugo was considered the soul of the opposition to Louis-Napoleon.

In the streets little crowds sometimes followed Hugo or watched him eat at his café. A young Belgian accosted him one day in the street and exclaimed: "M. Hugo, you and Louis Kossuth [the Hungarian revolutionist of 1848] are the two greatest fighters for human liberty!" At a dinner of Belgian printers a toast was offered to Victor Hugo, Mazzini, and Kossuth, as "the three men who personified resistance to despotism." Hugo reported to his wife that he found himself more popular than he had believed.

One day Victor Schoelcher, the social-democrat, one of the bravest of the republican leaders, turned up in Brussels wearing the long black cassock of a priest, at which everyone laughed because he was known to be a confirmed atheist. He came to pay his respects to Hugo and said: "Citizen Hugo, I always regarded you previously with some suspicion. . . . I doubted that you had become a sincere republican. This doubt lasted three years. It was ended in three days, the second, third, and fourth of December. I am Victor Schoelcher. Here is my hand."

Other exiled political leaders, besides Schoelcher, were Louis Blanc, Pierre Leroux, Félix Pyat, Colonel Charras, and General de Flotte, and these at once surrounded Hugo and held conferences with him all day long upon plans for continuing their fight. Other friends of his, such as Jules Janin, the distinguished dramatic critic, made special trips from Paris to see him and offer their help in the form of money or confidential services. Thus, in his straits, he found himself treated as a hero, with the acclamations of freedom-loving men coming to him from all sides. In spite of the secret police, many tributes came to him from France, one of the most moving of these from his own younger son.

The elder son, Charles, was soon to be released from prison, for his term expired on January 15, 1852. François-Victor still had seven months of incarceration to face. He had not always been perfectly happy in his father's hands, but now he was inspired by his father's actions and reflected the sentiment of many persons in France when he wrote: "My poor dear father, I see you as strong and great. That is what gives me strength, that is what gives me courage too. Prison—as long as you are not discouraged what does it matter? Your existence will have been one of struggle and combat. That has been the fate of all geniuses. We are torn apart now, yet never have we been more truly united. I feel that I have never loved and admired you as much as I do now."

Nor was the sojourn in Brussels all feverish and gloomy political activity. Alexandre Dumas, the tall, swarthy, exuberant romancer, Hugo's old-time friend, was also there, not as a political exile, but as a financial exile, in flight from his many creditors. Though he filled the newspapers of the world with his swiftly manufactured newspaper fictions and earned millions of francs, he consumed and squandered everything and was forced now to make Brussels his temporary headquarters. At once, on news of Hugo's arrival, Dumas rushed to him and covered him with kisses. Thereafter he tried to cheer up the exiles by giving large banquets to them as well as to crowds of hangers-on and actresses from the Vaudeville of Brussels—to whom he gave away cashmere shawls and other regal gifts. Dumas astounded the Brussels public by his extravagance, while Victor Hugo, also reckoned as a millionaire writer, astounded them no less by his frugality. Dumas, going back and forth to Paris in connection with his own affairs, carried many letters and documents for Hugo, in secret.

"I have become as a center of activity," Victor Hugo wrote his wife. "My hall—for my chamber is like a hall—is never empty, sometimes holding thirty persons, and I have only two chairs! I must make some effort to close my door, for all my time is being taken up and I need it more than ever."

Soon he found that there were disadvantages as well as gratifications in a glorious exile. He was forced to give up eating in public restaurants because of the crowds. Also, the Belgian government, in some fear of its powerful neighbor, began to exert pressure upon Hugo in order to learn what his intentions were and to induce him to behave quietly or leave the country.

What was he now to do? His first letters, as soon as he had taken rest, breathed a courageous resolution. He wrote to his wife, on December 14, 1851:

During twelve days I felt myself between life and death, but I was untroubled. For I was at peace with myself. I knew that I was doing my duty and my whole duty. That brings one contentment.

A few days later he wrote with much feeling to Adèle, his daughter of twenty-one, who, he learned, had been prostrate with fear for him:

MY BELOVED LITTLE ADELE:

. . . Thanks for the flower, which still smelled sweet. It was as if, dear child, you had sent me your soul. . . . I am living alone, banished in the north, the fog, working without letup. I gather strength thinking of you.

The *bad times have come at last that you sometimes heard me predict.* . . . Let us be strong, let us stand together. That is the only real happiness that merely material disasters cannot take away from true hearts. Courage, dear child, something tells me that we shall soon see each other.

On January 9, 1852, news came that Victor Hugo was formally banished from France, together with a large number of other opponents of Napoleon the Little. When the long roll of the proscribed was definitely published, even the bravest of the refugees felt himself poorer and sadder. Frenchmen, and especially Parisians, never prefer foreign strands to their own. By chance, one of the leaders of the Committee of Resistance, Michel de Bourges, who had participated in the street fighting, found that he was not included in the list of exiles. He wept with joy and returned quietly to France. Hugo wrote to his wife on January 10, 1852: "Our two sons in prison, and I in exile. It is hard, but it is good also; a light frost often improves the harvest."

To an old friend of his youth, Victor Pavie, he wrote also in a mood of calm resignation to the will of God:

Dear friend, dear poet, many thanks for your letter which moved my heart. I am banished, proscribed, exiled, chased out, what not? It is all for the best, since I feel the joy of a clear conscience before my country which sees and judges. . . . You know I have a deep faith. I suffer at being far from my noble and good wife, from my daughter and my son Victor—far from my home, my city, my fatherland. But I feel myself nearer to the true and the just.

I bless Heaven; all that God does is good.

Victor Hugo, like one of the Early Christians, felt himself strong in his righteousness and welcomed the test of adversity. But again, like an Early Christian, he was filled with the wrath of the Lord against the tyrant; he thirsted for a just vengeance, and often cried out to Heaven to aid him. He felt in himself a will, exceeding in force that of any of his comrades in exile, to continue the fight by all means possible. On the day that his formal banishment was proclaimed, he wrote to Mme. Hugo: "I feel myself invulnerable in the fullness of right and the serenity of my conscience. *The people will awake one day;* and then each will find his proper place again: I, in my home, and Monsieur Louis Bonaparte, in the pillory!" He added: "I like proscription, I like exile. . . . I love all those who suffer for liberty, for their country, for justice. . . ." Decidedly he was undergoing a large emotional experience, and, as if in revulsion at his own too comfortable and too worldly existence of recent years, he seemed to exult in his present ordeal and fall. Indignation, pity for France, horror gripped him; he flung himself into his task with all the ardor of his nature.

2

At first he had no precise plans. "In a few months, more or less," he wrote hopefully to Auguste Vacquerie, "we shall be reunited either in Paris or elsewhere." All that the men in exile heard from France induced them to believe that the days of Louis Bonaparte would not be long. The newspaper publisher, Girardin, turning up in Brussels, assured Hugo that it would be a matter of three months. Others thought a year or two at most, following a war that was expected momently.

The present picture of France, as Hugo phrased it, was that of a land under a "long Russian winter." Authoritarian government, as it was then called, headed by a single man and supported by a single party, was promptly instituted by the Prince-President. To put himself in funds quickly he "legally" confiscated the vast estate of the Orléans family, his predecessors and rivals, which appeared like a gigantic theft committed in broad daylight. Censorship and police law fastened themselves again upon France in most drastic form; clubs and political meetings were prohibited. Denunciations by neighbors of persons opposed to the regime were encouraged and rewarded; all men known for their independent opinions were shadowed and hounded, sometimes arrested and deported, though no evidence could be brought against them. When local uprisings by the poorer peasants took place in the southern provinces, in 1852, they were put down with a heavy hand, and many thousands were sent to the galleys, or to Africa and Cayenne.

Bonaparte, soon to turn Emperor, ruled by decree. Soon a fictitious Constitution prohibited all but the single party in power from electoral campaigning, and a fictitious Senate merely "advised" the dictator, its members being given appointments of thirty thousand francs a year, an outright bribe. When Montalembert told Bonaparte that he thought prominent men would be ashamed to serve in such a body, the dictator said lightly: "Just wait and see."

After six years of the authoritarian regime had held France *in terrorem* the spirits of the people sank so deeply that many wondered if anything could ever raise them again. One day a former Representative murmured at a private dinner in Paris: "How six years of servitude have laid us low. Stories of the kind we have been hearing—if they were told about Russia, in former times—would have made us feel like setting off on a crusade. Today we hear of such things going on right in our midst, and we listen almost with indifference."

To those who watched from beyond the border it seemed that the French people, who had acted with heroism in 1830 and 1848, would not long abide the "bandit" who had suddenly stolen into power over them. And yet the world of letters, the theater, the arts, even the sciences lay under a pall of gloom. The great historian Michelet retired, unwilling to give his oath of allegiance to Bonaparte; year by year others quit the universities and the schools, many like Edgar Quinet taking the road of exile. A few writers had gone over to the new regime, notably Sainte-Beuve, Hugo's old friend; but most others wrote with a guarded irony. Yet one or two sometimes spoke out boldly. In March, 1852, Jules Janin, in an essay on recent French drama, generously praised Victor Hugo, whose name was seldom mentioned, nowadays, in the press. Hugo then wrote Janin thanking him and remarking that his words were "as a ray of light in Siberia." He closed: "I see that you still care for me a little over there. . . ."

Jules Janin had not always given approval to Hugo's writings, but now he answered in a letter of twenty pages, which gives a graphic picture of the state of culture in France:

Surely you could not for a moment doubt the strong sympathy and deep respect that have surrounded your exile. You are our chief, and you are our god! Now you march before us, and we dwell in your kingdom, absent though you are. . . . Was it not you who, with a valiant hand, first cleared the soil we are all now cultivating after you. . . . You gave the first call; you were the Resurrection and the Life! It needed only a little distance and great misfortune that you should be

seen in all your greatness. Today you are complete, nothing is lacking
for you, neither hatred of the victors of a day, nor the persecutions of
the parricides, nor the insults of venal pens, nor the hideous spectacle
of France shorn of all her liberties. Ah, if you but knew how wretched
we all are, and how on waking, each of us finds it shameful to see himself one of the blind, oppressed millions! . . .

We are gagged, we are silent, we are lost, we are the butt of ridicule
and the sport of the whole world. A yoke weighs upon our humiliated
heads, a scepter of iron rules the art of speech and thought. . . . The
most honest men have continued honorably to protest as long as possible, and show their resistance and their scorn. Others have become
silent and reserved. . . . Ah if you but knew how many brave fellows
(journalists) would rather die of hunger than beg a little work of the
present régime, surely you would be pleased.

Janin assured Hugo that during this dark night in France men
looked with hope only abroad, to their illustrious exile, who was
now likened to Dante and Themistocles. Thus, at mention of his
name in a class of the University of Paris the students spontaneously
burst into cheers and the class was suspended. The gang in the
Elysée Palace thought they were rid of Hugo, but, Janin reported,
great numbers of people were waiting to see what he would write
and what vengeance he would take with his pen.

It was no secret! All Paris (even the Prefecture of Police) knew
that Victor Hugo was furiously at work writing his account of the
coup d'état. But two days after his arrival, he had begun writing
full tilt, from the dossier of notes and testimony gathered during
his last days in Paris and fortunately carried in his workman's kit
to Belgium. He worked rapidly at his "Story of a Crime," by
which he intended to bring Bonaparte to book and lay bare the
complete record of the conspiracy of bloody violence which had
throttled democracy and liberty in France.

In writing this book, he said, "There is something sacerdotal
in my function: I replace the magistracy and the clergy. I judge,
which the judges failed to do; I excommunicate, which is what
the priests have failed to do." To his disciple Paul Meurice, who
was still in prison, he sent word: "I am going to grab Louis Bonaparte by the ear and lead him around before all posterity."

For one thing, he was in temporary straits, not knowing whether
he could draw upon income from his investments in France. He
begged his wife, who wrote tactfully of her need of money, to be
patient, to economize severely, and promised that he would soon

have a book done which would repair their fortunes a little, and then they could live more comfortably again. Hetzel, of the large publishing firm of Hetzel & Lacroix, assured him that his historical narration of the Bonapartist *coup d'état,* if done quickly, would sell 200,000 copies even with France excluded as a market.

On the other hand, the launching of this work of chastisement was part of a major plan for conducting an unwearying propaganda fire from outside France's borders. "The Republic is not dead," Hugo would say to his comrades. *"The Republic is our religion."* There were plans on foot to launch a newspaper-in-exile, backed by Louis Blanc, Hugo, Mazzini, and Kossuth, the banished heroes of liberty. They hoped to publish the paper in Belgium, or England, and have copies of it smuggled into France. In addition to running this newspaper Victor Hugo thought that he would be able, with the aid of his friends and his sons—Charles arrived in February, and François-Victor joined him in July, 1852—to launch a free publishing company and sell books written by Blanc, Edgar Quinet, and other exiles, in Belgium, Switzerland, and England, and, secretly, in France. The plan, he informed his wife, was "to build a citadel of writing and publishing from which we would bombard the Bonaparte." The practical details of these plans seemed less difficult at the start than later.

Victor Hugo, who had grown fairly stout during ten years of public life, now ate little and wrote furiously. At times he paused and read passages from his book to his comrades in exile, noted their comments, and took down evidence from them of things they had seen. He worked at all hours. Once, the concierge came up to tell him that his son Charles, now lodging with him, had not yet returned, though it was midnight and she must now lock the doors and retire. Victor Hugo told her that he would go down to her post in the tobacconist's shop, and would work there at his writing while waiting for his son. He then stood at the counter—he preferred nowadays to write standing up—and worked until three in the morning, when his son came in and was taken aback at being admitted by his father instead of the concierge. The father said nothing; but thereafter Charles Hugo came back at a more respectable hour.

At moments, Hugo would pause in his furious prose writing and turn to verse, also on the subject of recent events in France and the Bonapartist gang. In these, after a long rest from verse-making, he found a new style, satirical, edged with anger, and yet sonorous and eloquent still. He put these aside, thinking they might some day make a sequence and that there was much that could be said in verse better than in prose.

Meanwhile spring came to Paris, where Mme. Hugo, in the big, lonely house at number 37 rue de la Tour d'Auvergne, was sorrowfully winding up their affairs, arranging to sell the Hugo *lares et penates* and join her husband permanently in exile—she had already made two or three brief visits to Brussels. At her husband's orders, all the treasures of twenty years' collecting were placed under the auctioneer's hammer on June 8 and 9, 1852. It was like a decline and fall, the end of everything. Hugo's friends, Théophile Gautier and Jules Janin, tried to organize a club to purchase the Hugo *bibelots* and return them to him or hold them and present them to the state some day. Janin wrote Mme. Hugo that the auction was an event that "shamed all France." Nevertheless the bourgeois, beside themselves with curiosity and bargain-hunting passion, came in a great crowd and haggled for the chairs and tables of carved oak, the Boule clocks, the marble busts, the vases, the tapestries, armor, books, pictures, and bric-a-brac of every kind, and bought them up cheaply. In the attendant confusion there was a certain amount of quiet pilfering too; so that Hugo's son could report that what the grimy, half-naked working-class insurrectionists had spared when they broke into the house in June, 1848, the *bourgeoisie* had defiled in the June, 1852, invasion. A mere 12,500 francs ($2,500) was realized from the sale; when it was over and everything carted away, Mme. Hugo and her daughter Adèle remained sitting forlorn and alone in the empty house, by the window, looking out for a last time at the pretty garden below.

At this moment, Jules Janin was completing the fourth and last volume of his rambling and delightfully anecdotal history of the French theater (*Histoire de la littérature dramatique en France*), a work that has remained of great value to this day. The concluding volume treated of the Romantic Revolution in France, a part of Janin's own carefree youth, when, over twenty years before, he himself had witnessed the meteoric rise of young Hugo. In retrospect, it was now easy to judge what a great impetus, what breath of renewed life and poetry, the author of *Hernani* and *Marion de Lorme,* despite his faults, had given to the formerly moribund theater, and what a host of imitators and improvers he had engendered. In his book (which was published with great success at the outset of the new Empire), Janin devoted some of his best chapters to Hugo and his school, placing him definitely among the immortals of France's drama and poetry, paying him a public tribute that was not only generous but courageous as well.

While he was working on this, the auction took place, and Janin set off from his quarters on the Right Bank of the Seine (as he wrote in a letter to Hugo) and paid a last visit to his friend's dismantled home.

Alas I wished to see for one last time that poetic refuge, and Saturday, in the moonlight, I passed its wall. Everything was ended. A great silence hung over your house. A star cast its beam over the little garden where you used to walk in the evening. Of the two windows that gave on the garden, one was closed, the other open. At the open window, a white shadow, a quiet, attentive figure contemplated in silence the city she must leave tomorrow. I believe it was your daughter who sat there in revery. At the other window there were your wife and son talking in low tones, their words calm and sad. . . . They were saying farewell to the charming nest where the paternal glory was once sheltered. . . .

As the gentle Janin, playing Boswell to Hugo, watched the two women who sat there, in imagination he saw something apprehensive and yet patient and stoical in their attitude, as if like the Trojan women of old they waited courageously for the next blow to fall upon them. A Golden Age of literature had just gone under the hammer, he felt, and the pages Janin wrote (he too was growing old) flowed with genuine tears:

Of all that luxurious interior, that heap of fine things, those draperies made for queens, those rugs, those gilded vaults above, there remained only . . . two straw-bottomed chairs borrowed from the house porter.

And I spying upon them tenderly . . . thought back upon the enchantments that once filled those desolate salons with the endlessly charming conversations, parties, and obeisances for the man of yesterday. I called to mind again the poets, the musicians, the renowned painters, the fair women, the great names of all Europe; I heard the happy murmur of bright wits, young and old, gathering to pay homage to the glory of our age. Ah, misery! . . . From the depths of my heart I sent my adieux toward those two women and the great poet, and all the memories of the springtime of our youth that is gone.

When Victor Hugo in his bare furnished room in Brussels read this he wept the bitter tears of an exile, thinking of how low was the estate to which he had fallen. He wrote Janin a brief note of acknowledgment that was almost inarticulate with emotion. Yet soon he was master of himself again. Janin, in his book, also records a special visit he paid Hugo at the time of his stay in Brussels, his last sight of the poet for long years. He arrived by the night train at five in the morning, he relates:

. . . The sun had just begun to climb the heavens, dissipating the mists of night. At the great square, where Egmont and the Count van Horn were executed to satisfy the vengeance of the Inquisition, there opened, in a somber shop, a narrow door; one mounted by a ladder in back to the refuge where dwelt this Peer of France, this knight of the Golden Fleece.

The door was open. One entered the proscribed man's home freely, as before. He was stretched out on a carpet on the floor, asleep. He slept so deeply that he did not hear me come in, and so, I could admire, at my leisure, those solid limbs, that deep chest where life and breath took so much space, that well uncovered brow, those delicate hands. . . . One would have said it was the sleep of a child, so even and calm was his breathing.

At last he awoke . . . he smiled at me coming out of his sleep, and as I threw myself into his arms, holding back my tears, he embraced me so hard I choked for air.

3

Victor Hugo slept with a sound conscience. He worked so busily that he minded little how or where he dropped off to sleep. Once, in a note to his faithful Mme. Drouet, he alluded, by means of a metaphor, to the determined, dedicated mood he felt in himself these days. "As I write you," he says, "I see a man who is laboriously raising a great stone at the end of a rope to the top of the belfry on the Town Hall, where a sculptor is perched, waiting to carve it. There is the very image of one's life: by the sweat of our brow we raise our name to the summit of some mysterious edifice, where posterity, the unknown sculptor, will take it and give it its final form; we lift up this stone which is the memory of us; the future carves it. Well, it is a rude labor, harder perhaps for me than for many others."

The "Story of a Crime" ran to two volumes and was finished in May, 1852. Victor Hugo had been forced to change it numerous times as new evidence and altered reports came to him. It was a "personal history" of the *coup d'état,* describing the plotting of the Bonaparte crowd, their sudden surprise attack on the sleeping city, the invasion of the parliament and humiliation and arrest of its members, the rallying of the republican and socialist group to opposition—he called it *defense,* of the existing government— the calling of the people to arms, the street fighting, the massacre of December 4, and the defeat of the popular party. Throughout the historical narrative, written with all the warmth of indignation he felt at the moment, there were many personal reflections and narrations of incidents he himself had participated in.

However, as soon as he was done, many difficulties arose that made the printing and sale of such a long work impractical. The Belgian government, in a friendly way, for it was under a strongly Liberal regime arisen from the barricades of 1848, put pressure upon him to learn what he was doing, and to urge him to remain passive, which he refused. In the end a tacit agreement was reached by which Hugo promised that so long as he remained in Belgium he would not publish anything that might disturb the relations be- tween Belgium and the new French government.

Indeed, the Belgian legislature was preparing a law, the Faider Law, prohibiting the publication of works criticizing the head of a foreign power—which took effect only at the end of 1852, and eliminated, in the future, such embarrassments as Hugo provided. Meanwhile, he learned that an alternate plan to publish the "Story of a Crime" in London might be long delayed, despite the sup- posed liberty of the press reigning there. It is also possible that he was dissatisfied with the material available to him then, and doubted that he had made an accurate history of events that had taken place so suddenly and with such speed.

Regretfully he decided to put the whole work aside, and kept it unpublished, among his private papers, for some twenty-five years, up to 1877, when under special and timely circumstances, he issued it as a memoir, with strong effect. But in 1852 he felt, discouragingly enough, as if his labor of five months—at a period when he needed money—was all misspent. Therefore he turned at once (in June, 1852) to an alternate plan, of writing a short, simple, fiery, satirical pamphlet or portrait of Louis Bonaparte, a direct personal attack upon him under the challenging title of "Napoleon the Little." He had noticed that the more independent Belgian newspapers currently used this term to refer to the new despot of France, that the epithet had entered into common speech. He now worked in desperate haste and in about three weeks completed a short book of two hundred pages, which was simply a diatribe or philippic against the dictator.

He was driven on by his indignation, his hate, and the fear that time was short.

I take Bonaparte to task [he told himself in his diary notes] and raise myself before him like remorse, while waiting for all the others to rise and chastise him. . . . Will he fall?—Yes—When? I do not know— But surely? Surely. A man cannot be embroiled in all these colossal contradictions without being lost. . . .

Bonaparte *must* fall. Victor Hugo would see to that.

"Napoleon the Little" takes on the semblance of a personal duel. Hugo catalogues Bonaparte's hypocrisies and lies; he names him "Mandrin" or "Cartouche" or "Schinderhannes," the names of old French and German murderers and bandits. In part, the book is a mordant pen portrait of the man, Louis Bonaparte, as a mediocrity elevated to supreme power by a military conspiracy; in part, it is devoted to the men of his entourage, his band, whose shady past is raked up and whose debauchery and corruption is outlined in detail. But here and there the anger of the author abates, and he tends to laugh or mock at his adversaries with effects of Rabelaisian wit and burlesque such as he had used only rarely before. Then, in turn, he grows wrathful and passionately eloquent, for he feels, he suffers, in every fiber of his being the tragedy of France, and when Hugo feels deeply his pages take fire. In his century perhaps only Zola was to rival him in achieving such effects of power with language.

The essence of his argument is that Louis Bonaparte, who had given oath to uphold the Constitution of the Republic, has very simply taken over power by turning liar and crook, by using cheap ruses to appeal to the basest appetites of soldiers and peasants— and all this for the sake of "law and order"! But what future, what stability, what order could there be in a regime founded on violence and dishonor? A shadow had fallen over the whole social system. "Public morality has gone into eclipse," he exclaims. "All guarantees are lost, all points of support have vanished." What, then, would the common thief, haled before a judge, say when he was accused? He could argue that the head of the state had stolen 25,000,000 francs, violated his oath of office, snatched for himself a throne. The common murderer would say also:

"The head of the state has shot, sabered, and strangled innocent passers-by in the street"—and all the crooks, counterfeiters, bandits, thieves, assassins, false witnesses, and pickpockets would retort: "You judges, you bow before that man, you praise him for being a perjuror, compliment him for having falsified, glorify him for having cheated, congratulate him for having stolen, and thank him for having assassinated—and now *what would you have us do?*"

There had been a "plebiscite"—after thousands had been killed, other thousands seized and imprisoned, millions intimidated—and so the *coup d'état* and the new "Constitution" were as if legally "sanctified." Hugo likens this ruse to that of a highway brigand who holds up a diligence and has his confederates go through the pockets of the passengers, while he addresses them as follows:

"In order to put myself straight with the law, I have written a statement here on this paper that you freely recognize that all I have taken from you belongs to me and you surrender it in full agreement and of your own free will. . . . Extend your right hand and sign. If anyone moves or talks, there is the muzzle of my pistol. Otherwise you may go free." They sign; *they vote*.

Thus they voted "yes" for the dictator, in 1852, and thus they have voted ever since when invited to do so by new dictator-brigands. Hugo with his poetic insight made the whole scheme of the popular plebiscite terribly transparent to us long ago.

But now men lived in France only "under rules, discipline, passive obedience, with eyes lowered, silence in the ranks, and all marching in military step. . . . We are in Russia! The long Russian night has fallen over France . . ." and in the midst of it goes that "sinister sleepwalker" Bonaparte, haunted by his crimes, yet driven to plot new ones.

Victor Hugo, as pamphleteer, is a conscience in eruption. France sleeps, and that to him is the gravest evil. Evil and scandalous also is the indifference with which the civilized world has received these events. *"This monstrous sleep of the conscience must end!"* he cries.

But Hugo not only flays the nineteenth-century French forerunner of all the later models of the leader principle with an apocalyptic fury, but like one of the prophets of old he has the courage to forecast his end. Those who are prone to despair he reminds that the days of tyrants are always numbered; the Dark Age must pass:

Do you not see that it is all a chimera! Do you not see that December Second is but an immense illusion, a pause, an *entr'acte,* a sort of painted curtain-drop behind which God, the miraculous Stage Manager, rearranges and sets up the scenery for the last act, the supreme and triumphant act of the French Revolution! Mistakenly you gaze at the curtain, you look at the figures painted upon the thick canvas, noticing the nose of one, the epaulettes of another, the big saber of a third . . . the whole group of caricatures and specters, and you take this to be the reality! But do you not hear the muffled sound of One who comes and goes, do you not see the curtain already trembling with the breath of Him who stands already behind it!

"Napoleon the Little" was quickly printed and published in London, at the expense of Hugo and his publisher, Hetzel, and put on sale in England and on the Continent on July 29, 1852. In England two different translations were issued at a low price, in editions numbering tens of thousands, making the new French ruler a much hated man among the English.

In France the work was of course banned and was never openly mentioned (even in Belgium, though it was permitted to be sold, it was not reviewed). But many hundreds of copies were smuggled into France in fishbaskets, or wrapped up as packages of sardines in tin cans, and circulated from hand to hand. An organized smuggling service steadily forwarded copies of the book across the Swiss and Italian as well as the Belgian and German border. In one French town two hundred persons read a single copy of the book. In at least one case, a workingman of Saint Malo who was caught reading it was given a prison sentence of three years. Therefore many read the book all the more avidly, and as a work of combat it had an immense effect.

A mediocrity who assumes power over a great nation inevitably takes on, in the popular mind, a certain wrapping of augustness and vague, fearful authority, no matter what his past character. But Hugo by holding up the man to universal scorn, by insistently harping upon his crimes and reminding men of the brutal coup, injured the growth of the imperial myth. That the tactics of the pamphlet were right is shown by a statement of the Empress Eugénie many years afterward, to the effect that the Second

Empire dragged with it the cruel memory of the massacre on the boulevards, "like a ball and chain on its foot." Victor Hugo's purpose had been to make this ball and chain as heavy as possible.

Some held at the time that Hugo conducted a sort of "personal squabble" with the dictator, because he had once aspired to be President in his place. (This was often said in the Tory press of England, after Palmerston's Ministry about-faced and moved toward *rapprochement* with the French despot.) Certain hostile French commentators spoke of the monumental vanity that distracted the poet's mind. To them it appeared that Hugo, a single man, a mere writer, was insane with pride to set himself against "the mighty Emperor having 10,000 cannon and 500,000 soldiers," as Edmond Biré put it. Well, madness or pride, it was a heartening sight. It needed a strong sense of one's worth and one's right as a free man to challenge the absolute military despot before whom half of Europe's thrones already trembled. Undoubtedly the bitterness of personal disillusionment gave edge to Hugo's hatred; but his passion, his unfailing desire for vengeance, was also influenced now by his growing sense of having a "mission" to perform. In France, his friends, in secret correspondence, cheered him on and lamented his exile. He answered them proudly, saying that, under present conditions, he did not suffer at absence from his native France. "For me there is no fatherland where there is no liberty. You are right not to mourn for me, dear friend . . . I was chosen from among better men to stand on the side of intelligence and civilization; chosen not by Bonaparte, who knows nothing of what he does, but by Providence to whom I am grateful. What an honor to represent you thus!"

It was because he felt that he had a mission to perform here that he attained such accents of righteousness and pride and wrath. But, whatever fault men might find with Hugo's attitudinizing, he seemed heroic and gigantic, compared to the indifferent, the writers who stayed in bed, the sheep who quietly did as they were told. By his exaltation he kept a flame burning, which he fed steadily and fervently with his boundless indignation, a flame that glowed beyond the border of France, whose lights had gone out. For twenty years, long after other men had cravenly made their peace, accepting the best terms they could, and had crawled back to their places of submission, that flame burned on brightly.

4

It was not long before he began to feel highly uncomfortable in Brussels. How could he fail to suffer anguish for want of those luxuries, advantages, and powers he had yesterday enjoyed? How could he forget the dreariness of banishment among strangers— none knew how long—and far from the places and things that were home, family, and native land to his memory? He was far from home, and yet a little too close for comfort. Sometimes he heard rumors that the new Napoleon plotted to send secret agents across the near-by border to kidnap him and bring him back to France. He slept fitfully, until he received assurance from his friend the Minister of the Interior that, at his call, the Belgians would come running to his aid from the great Town Hall across the square.

Other rumors, no less curious, told of how Bonaparte regretted the "fatality" that threw Hugo and himself into opposite camps, and hesitated for several days before adding Victor Hugo's name to the rolls of the banished. Reports appeared one day in the Belgian newspapers saying that Victor Hugo was unofficially "authorized" to return to France. When journalists came to make inquiries of him, he answered that he had once, in 1847, in the House of Peers, helped to win authorization for the Bonapartes to return to France, "but now—M. Hugo has nothing to ask of M. Bonaparte." On the other hand there were many rumors that, owing to Conservative and clerical protest at his presence, he was soon to be banished from Belgium as a troublemaker. He knew that the publication of "Napoleon the Little" would create an international episode if he remained.

He found himself in the center of a large band of unhappy refugees, men of ability and rank in their own country but now come down in the world, hungry, and embittered. There was little agreement among them and much factious spirit. Some were rigid socialists, like Félix Pyat; others utopian and peaceable theorists like Louis Blanc; others still simply bourgeois who disliked *"les Partageux,"* the "sharers," the Reds.

When Louis Blanc and Mazzini planned to launch an international newspaper, Victor Hugo, after some deliberation and with the advice of his family, decided to have no part in it. "I fear," he explained to Mme. Hugo, "that connection with it would lead to my losing the independence of my position up to now, attaching me to the past record of other men, and, as a result, linking my future with factors unknown to me. That would strongly affect the disinterestedness that I now typify, since I have not been mixed up in any parties, nor held power, nor hazarded any theories, but have only upheld the flag and risked my life for it."

But such a stand caused some of his fellow refugees to show disappointment in him. He was a difficult man to use for party organization purposes. Certain refugees vexed him by spreading gossip in the local press about his closefistedness. Many were starving, and begged him for money. The truth is that although he supported nine persons, Mme. Drouet along with his personal family and several aged Hugo relations, and now felt himself in straitened circumstances, he gave a little money regularly to many refugees, though not with the careless grace of the oft bankrupt Dumas *père*. He helped raise funds for the refugees by speaking at public banquets; he donated five hundred francs of the proceeds of his first book published in exile. He paid for the lunches or dinners of those hungry ones who followed him about. But what he gave was never enough. Some of them maliciously accused him of being a stingy man who invited them to one-franc dinners, then went off and ate sumptuous repasts in private. It was true that Victor Hugo ate with a voracious appetite, but usually very simple food, and barely noticing what he ate. He cared nothing for fine clothes after he went into exile. However, he was always a careful man with money and had a very strong sense of its importance in a pecuniary society, which was sometimes a cause of vexation to his wife and sons.

Meanwhile the Brussels authorities, some of whom were very friendly to Hugo, quietly informed him that they were under pressure from France, and hinted that if he departed for England of his own free will—before the publication of "Napoleon the Little"—it would spare them the embarrassment of expelling him somewhat later. He fixed his mind upon going to England, settling in the country, rather than in London, and staying preferably on the island of Jersey, where the natives still spoke an old Norman French. When the exiles in Brussels heard of his plans, in mid-July, 1852, they came to him in a body and petitioned that he remain in Brussels until the government was forced to expel him.

"But if we make trouble over the affair," he argued, "it may lead to all of you being expelled." They answered touchingly that they would follow him to England. Here they said, he was the "center" of a movement, a force; in Jersey he would be alone.

What irked him now was precisely the business of being the "center" of a political organization, even a loose and incoherent one. The events of recent months had stirred him deeply; he had a longing to be at work, after ten years of semi-retirement from writing; he had many ideas and plans, for at least four new books, but too little privacy. Besides, his own idea of how he could be of maximum effectiveness in warring against the despot of France—he had not the slightest intention of relaxing his grip on his familiar devil, Louis Bonaparte—was by working with words rather than by organizing men. His combat must be a lonely one carried on, henceforth, by the power of the written word, already demonstrated in "Napoleon the Little." Meanwhile, to keep his word with the Belgian authorities he must leave the country before his book came out.

Sadly he prepared to depart again (a day before the publication of his book) for a strange land, yet hoping that he could find some permanent dwelling place, unite there the scattered members of his family and a few close friends, and carry on. For "the bandit" in Paris looked as if he would reign yet another year or two—M. de Girardin's prediction of three months had been overoptimistic.

On July 31, he made his farewells and proceeded to Antwerp to take the Channel boat for England. A small band of his fellow exiles, headed by Alexandre Dumas, Arago, Noël, Parfait, and Colonel Charras, insisted on following him in a pilgrimage to Antwerp. There a luncheon banquet was given to him by a democratic society of Antwerp; they toasted the great exile, crying: "Long live Victor Hugo!" and "Long live the Republic!"—for they were almost synonymous terms—until the great man and his son Charles wept openly.

Hugo's farewell speech, "On Leaving Belgium," was a challenging statement to the world. He said:

In replying to so many cordial expressions addressed to me permit me to speak but little of myself and my own plans. . . . What difference does it make what happens to me? I was exiled from France for having fought the ambuscade of December, and I am exiled from Belgium for having written "Napoleon the Little." Well, then! I am twice banished, that is all. Bonaparte hunted me in Paris, he hunts me down in Brussels; the criminal defends his crime. I have done my duty, hence I am punished. Very simple. I shall continue to do my duty, and I shall continue to be punished. Still very simple. Naturally I suffer at leaving you, but were we not born to suffer?

One of the preceding speakers had alluded to the danger of an invasion of Belgium by the armies of the French autocrat, and of the readiness of democratic Belgians to lay down their lives for their country. Hugo, now a citizen of the world, added his own exhortations in terms considered treasonable in official Paris, and so violent that the audience was almost petrified.

Yes, if M. Bonaparte comes, if he invades your country, if he comes some night—for that is his favorite time—to cross your frontiers, dragging in his train, or better, pushing before him—for it is not his way to march at the head of his troops—pushing before him what he calls the French Army, an army now denationalized, those regiments which he has turned into hordes, those pretorians who have violated the National Assembly, those janissaries who have sabered the Constitution, those *soldiers of the Boulevard Montmartre!* who might have been heroes, and whom he has turned into brigands—if he comes to your frontiers, bringing you shame, where you have had honor, bringing you slavery, where you have had freedom, bringing you crime, where you have had probity, oh, then, arise Belgians! arise! Receive him as your ancestors the Nervii received Caligula! Run to get pitchforks, stones, scythes, ploughshares; take your knives, take your guns, take your carbines. . . . Call everyone to arms! . . . It is not Hannibal at the gate, it is *Schinderhannes!* Ring the tocsin; beat the drums; make war in the fields, in the towns, in the forests; defend yourselves step by step. Remember your fathers who bequeathed you glory! Remember your children to whom you would bequeath freedom! Take up the funereal battlecry of Waterloo: Belgium dies but never surrenders!

But accompanying the electrifying battle words were reflections that breathed also a religious spirit, the spirit of the Early Christians. The soldiers of liberty, the exiles, he said, were born to suffer.

There are some who say: The Republic is dead. . . .
Fellow-exiles, if the Republic is dead, let us watch over her corpse; let us illuminate our souls and let them be consumed like candles around her bier; let us kneel before the Idea that has died, and after having been soldiers who defended it, become priests to give it decent burial.
But no! I say the Republic is not dead!
Citizens, I say that she has never been more alive. She has been driven into the catacombs, which is good. Those believe her dead who take the catacombs for a tomb. My friends, the catacombs are a sepulcher, the catacombs are a cradle. Christianity emerged from them bear-

ing a diadem, the Republic will emerge with an aureole on her brow. . . .

As priest or prophet of his own lay faith Hugo always closed nowadays with appeals to his listeners to contemplate the fate that overhung the despots, and the bright tomorrow which beckoned free men. He prophesied the coming of "the United States of Europe." He concluded his speech with the salute of the socialists of 1848: "Long live the Universal Republic!" Victor Hugo was in fine voice that day and spoke with great effect. He had become a force to be reckoned with, heading the revolutionary opposition that stubbornly fought the thrones of Europe at all the borders during those benighted years after 1848. His hearers cheered him jubilantly and followed him to the dock, where the good ship *Ravensbourne* got up steam.

A goodly crowd filled the pier, though a heavy rain was falling, everyone refusing to leave until the ship was out of sight. The effusive, romantic old rascal Dumas insisted upon being the last one to embrace Victor Hugo. From far out in the harbor, Hugo could still distinguish the tall Creole by his white vest, waving a handkerchief.

He walked the deck, wrapped in his cloak. The boat pitched and rolled as it entered the Channel waters; the drenching rain beat in his face as he stared toward the unknown country behind the veil of fog.

CHAPTER XV

Jersey: Duel between a Writer and an Emperor

Since noble arts in Rome have no support,
And ragged virtue not a friend in court . . .
'Tis time to give my just disdain a vent,
And cursing, leave so base a government.
Where Daedalus his borrowed wings laid by,
To that obscure retreat I choose to fly . . .
—Juvenal, *The Third Satire (Translation by Dryden)*

H E STAYED in London, with his son Charles, but three days. During this time, as an emissary of the refugees in Belgium, he was supposed to hold conferences with Ledru-Rollin and Mazzini on the question of co-ordinating the work of the various groups among the exiles. Nothing came of the conferences. For all his determination to continue revolutionary pressure from abroad against Bonaparte and his government, Victor Hugo grew warier, convinced that he must hold himself at a certain distance from the immediate strife of political factions, bitterest of all among men of theory and statesmen without power, who rule uncertainly *in absentia*. Besides, he detested the gray vastness of London. He said to his son, as soon as they arrived: "How do we get out of here?" On August 4, 1852, he took ship for Jersey, arriving at Saint Helier port the next day. Discreetly, Mme. Drouet and her servant Suzanne followed him on the packetboat the next day.

Jersey, largest and most fertile of the Channel Islands, lies about one hundred miles south of the coast of England, in sight of France, sheltered within the balmy Gulf Stream, all verdant, rampant with flowers and orange and lemon trees, almost a subtropical isle, a jewel set in the western ocean, which is here so incredibly blue. The zestful animal and poet in Victor Hugo now supplanted the man of political revolution, and gave thanks fervently as he set foot on this Norman island long ruled by free England. "Sonorous island!" Victor Hugo named Jersey; for the waves raged eternally against its shore, its rocks and cliffs, and the old granite bulwarks of its port, as if echoing musically the storms of the world he had left outside, and the storm in his heart. But in this beautiful refuge, to which so many famous French exiles had turned before him (Chateaubriand too), he wanted, above all, repose, repose in which to complete the work he had set for himself, the poems and books that now clamored to be written. "It was a ravishing country," he wrote, on his arrival, to a friend in Belgium. "One passes in a moment, from woods to piles of rocks, from a flower garden to a reef, from a green field to the sea. . . . From the shore one can see France. . . ."

But how could he win the repose he craved? Before him, as he landed at the dock in Saint Helier, he saw the "lugubrious little army of the sacrificed" already waiting for him, about seventy French refugees, together with a crowd of Jersey natives who had gathered to give him a fraternal welcome. They were headed by his old acquaintance, the loquacious philosopher and utopian, Pierre Leroux. In response to a welcoming address by Leroux, he made a brief speech in which he laid special stress upon the good will and harmony reigning between all the different groups of republican exiles in Belgium. They had shown themselves able to bear their trials, to love each other and sustain their faith in their common ideals, he said.

That is what I saw in Belgium, *and that is what I know I am going to find here*—this fair picture of fraternity, this great example of accord among the banished which France has need of. Oh! let us seal and cement this union, abjuring all dissension and discord. Since we have but one color for our flag, the purple, let us have only one sentiment in our souls, fraternity!

After stopping for a few days at a hotel, the Sign of the Golden Apple, he found a furnished house which he rented for a year. It was in a somewhat isolated corner of the island, near the beach and near the hamlet of Georgetown, outside of bustling Saint Helier, and was called Marine Terrace. It was a square cube of a stucco house, painted white, with large square windows and a flat roof. It was glacially English to Hugo, after the bright peasant houses of France—"Methodism in brick and stone" he called it. On the ground floor was the kitchen and a small drawing room and study, overlooking the road; on the upper floors were the coldly painted sleeping chambers, sparsely furnished, with white shrouds for window hangings. The north facade gave on the road, the south side gave on a spacious garden terraced into the rugged shore, planted with tamarisks and roses, and having a splendid, undisturbed view of the sea. The garden was protected by a granite wall bordering the beach, and from the house Victor Hugo could hear the waves lapping or, in hurricane weather, crashing against it day and night.

He had come first to spy out the land with his son Charles. Mme. Hugo, Adèle, François-Victor Hugo, and Auguste Vacquerie (a part of the family since the death of Charles and Léopoldine Vacquerie) joined him in mid-August and together the reunited family set up house and cultivated the weedy garden.

As they installed themselves, Hugo wrote to a friend in Paris: "We aim to spend a year here, then we shall perhaps go for a visit to Madeira. After which Sire Bonaparte may fall, and we may all return to France to chant the final chorus. Don't forget to tell him our plans."

With the proceeds of the Paris auction Victor Hugo busied himself buying pieces of antique furniture, with which Jersey abounded, and decorating the drawing room and study in his favored baroque style. November came, the rain fell continually, the wind blew, even in the house one was deafened by the roar outside, and Victor Hugo sat one morning with his younger son, looking out of the drawing room windows at the storm, like brooding castaways.

"What do you think of this exile?" François-Victor asked suddenly.

"That it will be long."

"How do you intend to employ it?"

The father answered, "I shall gaze at the ocean." There was a silence. "And you?" he resumed.

"I shall translate Shakespeare," said the son.

A few minutes' walk from Marine Terrace, in an apartment adjacent to Nelson Hall, a small hotel overlooking the sea, he had established Mme. Drouet, as she was respectfully called nowadays, faithful companion of his fortunes, guardian angel, and now more or less officially recognized as such by all his friends, and even his sons, though cautiously snubbed by the anglicized natives who were subjects of Queen Victoria.

Taking up the thread of Juliette's story, so firmly interwoven with the poet's life, we find her now an extremely distinguished-looking lady in her middle forties. Her young face against the suddenly altered color of her hair led Victor Hugo to refer to her in poems of this period as *"ma beauté blanche,"* his white beauty. In Brussels for six months, the misery of exile had turned for her into a season of poignant fulfillment. She had been forced to live with extreme discretion and self-effacement at a little hotel, near Hugo's residence, her allowance a meager 150 francs a month, less than a fourth of the sum she had been permitted in Paris just previously.

What made her happy was that Mme. Hugo was absent in Paris, save for a few brief visits, and she, although forced to see her "god" only at stated times of the day for walks, had him entirely under her own sway. She watched over his health, repaired his worn clothing. Out of her small means she prepared one good meal a day, his lunch, which she sent to him: usually a broiled cutlet. When his son Charles came to Brussels, she sent two cutlets, and the son did not refuse his portion. That was the thin opening wedge.

Soon Charles Hugo, a tolerant young man of advanced political ideas, like François-Victor as well, was compelled to acknowledge the "other woman's" rare qualities of devotion and self-denial. Their father told them plainly that he owed his life to her. Often the two sons would be present at lunches or meetings between their father and Mme. Drouet, and came to accept the situation with good grace. In addition, during these emergencies she entered more or less directly into the family counsels, advising them with firm common sense and tact. All this made Juliette wonderfully happy; her life, formerly a mere shadowed corner of the poet's life, was now filled to the brim, with all her mental resourcefulness in full demand. When there was need of her, when there was trouble, Juliette, the former actress, the "lost" girl of yesterday, always rose to the occasion.

One incident during the Brussels sojourn showed Victor Hugo how generous his mistress could be, and how much she deserved the respect of all men. Mme. Hugo had been staying in Paris, working to protect her husband's publishing rights and interests, with which she was quite familiar, she too rising to this cruel emergency and demonstrating unexpected reserves of courage and dignity. Late in December, 1851, a few weeks after the *coup d'état,* Mme. Hugo made a quick trip to Brussels to consult her husband on their problems. Juliette, before her arrival, tidied up his bare quarters—always besieged by the exiled politicians and filled with the ashes of their pipes—and provided everything needed to make the stay of Mme. Hugo more comfortable: food, linen, even silver. On another occasion, Mme. Hugo announced her early arrival for a second visit, and Juliette, effacing herself, wrote to Victor Hugo:

Do not concern yourself with me, my poor beloved. . . . Devote yourself entirely to your courageous and noble wife during all the time of her stay here. Do not deny her any of the pleasures which may atone for the cruel experiences she has been facing. Make of my resignation and my courage a sort of litter for her with which to soften the shock of stones along her road, while she is here. Give her all the consolation you can and all the respect and affection she merits, and do not fear that you will exhaust my confidence and patience thereby.

Mme. Hugo, as well as her daughter, did not "recognize" Juliette. But she learned to respect her.

In Jersey she saw that Mme. Hugo had trouble in finding efficient servants, that the Marine Terrace house was poorly managed, and from a distance tried to help solve its problems. Above all, she wanted to take care of Victor Hugo and to give all her time to doing this!

"It needs all my stubborn watchfulness to deal with those inept and indolent creatures, the servants," she wrote him early in 1853, as they were settling into their home. Hardest of all for her was to wait and look on with folded arms, she said, while her poor poet contended with men and fate. "How I regret all the prejudice which prevents me from consecrating myself entirely to your service. It would be so sweet to me, who am afflicted by the futility, the uselessness of my life. . . . Oh how I would wait upon you day and night! rendering you all the little cares that you always seem to lack." And, again, she complained that though she exerted all her love and tenderness to help her endure her situation, "in the hope of attaining to the right to devote myself to you, I have not yet reached that point." However, in the days of exile, she was far happier than before; she approached her ideal more closely.

Not that life and love with Victor Hugo ran ever smooth! There were still moments when the straying glance of her Silenus's eye gave her reasons for jealousy. She suffered at these moments, and fought him. We must remember that unlike his wife, Adèle, Juliette could be not only "mother" to him, but also his "tigress," as he once remarked. At Brussels, in late January, 1852, provoked by some negligence on his part, she suddenly wrote him a stormy note offering him his liberty: "If you told me to go away, I would leave without turning to look back!" Once more he begged her to stay. Days of exile, wandering in a foreign land were to be his lot. He begged her to share it, to follow him abroad. Almost superstitiously he told her that they were fatally bound to each other and he was sworn to die in her arms: ". . . Are you not my breath, my life? Oh, my beloved, it seems that you have become a part of myself, and when I speak to you, I speak to my own soul."

In Jersey, Mme. Drouet's little apartment at Nelson Hall, consisting of chamber, salon, small dining room, and kitchen, was cheerful and well run, while the house at Marine Terrace was a little gloomy in winter, its table dull. Almost every day, the poet came to Nelson Hall and walked with her. Then he grew accustomed to taking supper with her on frequent occasions; thus she was able to "find the road to his heart by way of his stomach."

At Marine Terrace, too, Victor Hugo was besieged by visitors and occupied with political work on behalf of the proscribed. There were not a few controversies and dissensions among them. Pierre Leroux, the utopian socialist headed one camp, Hugo the other. By temperament the old pioneer of socialism was incompatible with the poet. Leroux was gravely dignified in manner, rigid in his socialist and pantheistic principles. He would call frequently and address Victor Hugo always as "my neighbor," for Leroux operated a farm near by on some co-operative plan. As Hugo's financial circumstances grew easier, his earlier books being permitted to sell in France, his income from investments flowing to him again, Leroux, in conversation, would call attention to the difference between the poet's status and that of his fellow exiles, who had lost all. This was most vexing. Hugo disliked being contradicted, and, besides, had no intention of sharing the wealth that remained to him. Even Juliette bridled with indignation at the "egalitarians" who sometimes offended her great man.

From the importunities of the exiles and the problems of a confined family life—with sons, daughter, and wife often showing themselves bored, unhappy, and vexed with each other—he would

take refuge at Mme. Drouet's house each day. At first he had
pretended to meet her by chance and take random walks with her,
or carriage rides along the sea or into the interior of the island,
which "nature had made a garden . . . where all seemed perfume, sunlight, laughter." But noticing that the prudes of Jersey
showed discretion in pretending to ignore Mme. Drouet and her
situation—the whole island knew about "that woman," and looked
the other way—he formed the habit of escaping from his house,
after lunch, and going directly and openly to her apartment.

Once more, as in Paris, at the rue Saint-Anastase, a writing
table, with paper, and a few books were set out in the parlor by the
fire, and he would work there in peace. He would have supper
with Juliette and stay on. Then the fellow exiles, learning of his
habits, would come there to look for him. Certain of these, such as
Hennet de Kessler, a young scholar, now in greatly reduced circumstances, he grew very fond of. They would partake of
Juliette's food, and liked it. Soon there were large suppers for
exiles held regularly at the Nelson Hall place rather than at Marine
Terrace, and Charles and François-Victor joined them, while
Juliette Drouet, a very gracious and competent hostess, presided
happily. Assuredly her life was fuller than ever before. Charles
Baudelaire, who met her in Brussels, had called her the "servant
of the great heart."

Life in Jersey had its good points. The people spoke an old
Norman-French dialect; they were a picturesque, seagoing folk,
and hospitable or respectful to the distinguished exile—for they
were accustomed to receiving exiles from France. Victor Hugo
studied them at work and at play, found their speech, their simple,
unspoilt manners and their curious old customs of absorbing interest, and determined to write about them some day. The governor
of the island extended certain courtesies to the Hugos and they
were welcome to official balls, which, however, only the sons attended.

Mme. Hugo wrote with astonished delight of the freedom from
police surveillance they enjoyed under British rule. "No passports,
no identity papers," she reported in letters to France. It seemed
incredible. But life in Jersey was provincial too. The people were
puritanical, and, for the escaped Parisians, Sundays were a mournful ordeal. In the basement of Marine Terrace, the Hugos would
shut all the doors and windows so that neighbors might not hear
the click of billiard balls.

Mme. Hugo felt much older these days; while Juliette bloomed, she repined and grew lonely. A letter of hers to Janin in 1854 runs:

Our life is always the same. Exile is base, it is monotonous. My husband rises with the dawn, and works all morning; we do not meet until noon for lunch, then we greet each other and converse. . . . My son Charles has turned into a lively talker, and his father and I listen to him with pleasure. After lunch, each goes his own way, my husband for a walk in the countryside, my second son into town—he is the fashionable one—and Charles stretches himself out on a hard horsehair sofa and dreams, smoking his pipe. . . . The piano music that floats down from above is that of my daughter, Adèle. . . .

2

Autumn came to Jersey Island, and winter. The winter was wild. "The heavens pour, the wind howls like a beast, the trees twist themselves on the hills, nature rages furiously all about me," Hugo wrote in a letter to friends in France. "I have wedded the sea, the hurricane, an immense beach of sand and all the stars of the night." The sea became his companion. He was a prodigious walker, and now, very sensuous and very visual, he roved the beach of Jersey daily, scanning the sky and the waves, noting every change of humor, each turn of the wind, alteration of light and sound, the endlessly varying colors and moods, the sobbing and chanting of the sea. The ocean suited his leaping imagination—a companion he loved, and yet also feared and hated.

Spring came—here April came through the window early in March—and he wrote to the former Representative Alphonse Esquiros, a brave comrade of the Paris street fighting, now living in Belgium:

I have spent the winter writing somber poems. The book I am doing will be called: "Castigations." You can guess what it is about. . . . "Napoleon the Little" was written in prose and so was but half of my appointed task. The wretch was only roasted on one side—I am turning him over on the grill.

Alone with the sea and sand, like Saint John at Patmos in flight from a hateful Emperor of Rome, Victor Hugo's mind turned constantly, obsessively, toward the new Emperor who had risen over France, and at thought of him was seized with apocalyptic fury.

While in Brussels, as if speaking to himself, he had written some notes found long afterward among his papers, which fully reveal his state of mind. A mystic conviction gripped him that he could, by the power of the word, bring down, or help to bring down, the House of Bonaparte.

Well, then! I shall kick in the door of that palace and enter with you, history! I shall seize the guilty by the neck. . . . I shall light up with a blazing, noonday illumination their dark night lair. I shall show him for what he is . . . and his court, his gang, opulent, triumphant, degraded, horrible . . . filibusterers and buccaneers, false priests, spies, crooks, butchers, hangmen, from the henchmen of the condottiere who sells his sword, to the Jesuit who bargains with the Lord. . . .

And at Jersey, he wrote other fragments, bitter, self-questioning, as if with accents of persecution mania that echoed in his continual soliloquy by the sea:

And so I am proscribed, exiled, banished, hunted . . . one whom wisdom, prudence and success no long favor. I live alone by the sand of the sea, having nothing but my dog; from time to time the English reproach me for using what they call their hospitality. . . . I go, I come, I walk at random, by the sea, in the woods or the fields, a republican, a demagogue, a "communist," a kind of blood drinker, pariah or wolf. Peasants see my French face and insult me; I thank God they do not throw stones at me. . . .

Some time later, the lovely Mme. Delphine de Girardin, poetess, playwright, and *grande dame,* arrived in Jersey to visit with her old friends the Hugos. It was a happy reunion. She brought a new invention and cult just then spreading over Europe: spiritism, table turning, the communication with the souls of the absent or the dead. Victor Hugo and his sons became absorbed in this new game. He, with vibrant hands, became especially adept; night after night they would extinguish the lights in the salon at Marine Terrace, and the table they gripped so feverishly together would begin to knock and speak to them! To Hugo it was far from being a game; it was a new and profound religious experience that changed his whole way of life.

One of the spirits he calls forth and converses with is Louis Bonaparte, whom he accuses and judges:

What feeling do you have toward me?—Hate and respect? . . . Tell me the name of the man you think most of?—Olympio?—I am bound to you by chains—I am afraid. . . . How much longer will your reign last?—Two years?

Victor Hugo was bound to the man Bonaparte. The duel must go on between the writer exiled in his distant island and the Emperor. Many contemporaries thought Hugo mad with pride, like the fallen Lucifer. There was no mistaking the pride which drove him on and the suffering he felt. Portrait photographs made of him in Jersey, between 1852 and 1855, show him with ravaged, deeply-lined face, mouth drawn down at the corners, and eyes sunken, fiercely glaring, their fixed regard bespeaking the flaming will behind them.

In Belgium, while writing the "Story of a Crime" and "Napoleon the Little," he had from time to time thrown off verses, doggerels, and puns aimed at his personal devil. One named *Toulon,* written a few days after the *coup d'état* of December, 1851, was a vigorous piece and ended with a keen turn of wit:

> *Ville que l'infamie et la gloire ensemencent,*
>   *Où du forçat pensif le fer tond les cheveux,*
>   *O Toulon! c'est par toi que les oncles commencent,*
>   *Et que finissent les neveux!*

Toulon was famous both for its convicts, perpetually working on the hulks, and as the naval fortress where the "bandit's" famous uncle, Napoleon the Great, had begun his career of glory by giving battle to the invading English. Thus Hugo spiritedly apostrophizes Toulon as "the city of infamy and glory, where uncles begin and nephews must end up."

Assuredly, there was much to be said in the form of poetry that could be better said than in the form of prose. Why could he not sing of the Inferno of December 4, or send forth a great chant of hatred and indignation against the criminals who had assaulted free France and debauched her in the night? He thought of Juvenal's bitter diatribes at the Rome of Domitian and Nero, and of the laments of Dante, driven from Florence. He cried: *"O Muse Indignation,* come to me! thou whom Juvenal loved and whose light shone in the fixed eye of Dante, come let us raise over this content and glittering empire of knaves, and that stolen victory, enough pillories to make an epic!" This was the thought of the last strophe of *Nox,* the first poem in the new series of *Les Châtiments* (Castigations) written at Jersey. His guiding conception was to paint, in the form of a series of satires (like those of Juvenal), but in more passionate and Dantesque style, a poetic tableau of the Bonapartist conspiracy and insurrection. The true hideousness and wickedness of the conspiracy could best be rendered by metaphor, invective, grotesquerie, and poetic intuition. He desired to infuse his work also with the portent of a doom, thus giving to his satire an Old Testament or apocalyptic character. Possessed with this plan, Victor Hugo worked through the winter of 1853 in a perfect frenzy.

It was nearly ten years since he had last completed a large literary production, *Les Burgraves*. He had at first grown somewhat soft with prosperity, but then many things had happened to him and he had suffered greatly. Now he had much to say and on his walks, or in his study, or while he tried to sleep, words and images came to him, formed themselves, and swiftly were written down. By the side of his bed, he kept papers ready and, waking at night, would scrawl hastily, feverishly, the phrases and ideas and rhymes that came to him in the darkness.

Living constantly by the sea, the broad view of its shaken waves, its onrushing and fleeing storms always in his eye, its wild strong music in his ear, he was possessed for a long time by the oceanic violence. Besides, in his exile, in his relative poverty and isolation, the iron will he had shown in his youth, the almost primitive ferocity in combat with himself and his adversaries—qualities little called upon in recent fat years—now returned to him. Steadily he built up again the pieces of his life, ruled sternly over the members of his family (whom he set to work at one literary task or another), meanwhile feeding the flame of his anger and, by grace of the Muse of Indignation, writing *Les Châtiments,* an epic of "six thousand lines of hate" as Lamartine termed it.

One must not assume, as Lamartine tries to suggest, that this new book of poems was monotonous in effect. On the contrary, it is the most original piece of work by Hugo thus far; it is conceived with the skill of a great artist, given variety of style and mood, verging from effects of wild fantasy and ribald wit, to those of repose, of pity, of philosophic reflection. In all French literature no such work of poetry had yet appeared. Voltaire's satire corresponded properly with that of the cool, neat Pope. One must go for comparison in recent times to English literature, and to Dryden's "Absalom and Achitophel" if one could conceive that cruel portrait of Shaftesbury done upon a huge canvas, peopled with all the lesser figures around him. Something of Milton's vigorous line is here, and Swift's derision, and Byron's comic rhyme (as in "English Bards and Scotch Reviewers"). Then, on the visual side, by effects of caricature, the qualities of a Hogarth and of Hugo's own younger contemporary, Daumier, are rivaled.

He was satisfied that the scoundrels who lived in his own age were equals of the most monumental knaves of all other epochs painted by the older poets. The theme of bandit-into-emperor was simple enough; he resolved to fill in the picture with all the minor characters of the Bonapartist gang. Maupas, the Prefect of Police, the illegitimate half-brother, Morny, the financial intriguers, the military adventurers, the generals, Magnan and Saint-Arnaud (who had personally known and hated Victor Hugo), the crooked Bonapartist Ministers, Baroche and Rouher, all the literary turncoats who had gone over to the new regime, and the Catholic or Jesuit leaders, such as Montalembert ("the viper Judas"), Falloux, who had ridiculed him, and Louis Veuillot ("Iago"), who had malignantly lampooned him for ten years. Lately Veuillot, in France, had been calling Hugo "Jocrisse in Patmos"—Jocrisse was a well-known clown—thus, the "clown Saint John." All these men who were his adversaries, Hugo branded and put in their allotted place of eternal torment in his Second Empire Inferno. It is the plenitude of particular names, of historical personages now forgotten or obscure, that has made *Les Châtiments* a little neglected by readers outside of France. A large glossary of names would be needed nowadays. Moreover, translation of this bold poetry has presented obstacles that, in English, would tax the skill of some modern John Dryden.

On the whole, he tried to avoid vulgarity and give his "Castigations" a certain dignity; some scabrous lines referring to alleged diseases of Louis Bonaparte were emended by him at the beginning. A good example is *Nox*, the long opening poem. It begins with a narration, in hexameters, of the secretly prepared assault upon the sleeping capital of the Republic, led by the "Emperor Soufflard" (the name of Eugène Sue's fictive criminal who prowled in the sewers of Paris); the conspirators win their treacherous victory, carry off their loot. Then, as France falls under a kind of "night," the mood changes, and in quicker-moving strophes (tetrameter) the poet pictures the chief conspirator, "furtive, pale, dull-eyed," discussing his real plans, counting the gold he will seize, contrasting his own destiny with that of his uncle, who had "the fanfares of glory," while he would have the "bags of money." A following section shows the bandit-emperor being coronated at Notre-Dame, acclaimed by his dupes as the "savior of order, defender of religion and the family!" Then the poet, in a long and very lyrical digression, turns and contemplates himself and his own lot. He is seated upon a great rock by the abyss of the sea, dreaming and sorrowing; the sky is pure, the sea now murmurs and sings to him enchantingly, calling upon him to look at the birds, the waves that come like white flocks, the blue water of the distance, the fishing vessels:

> *Tu me montres ta grâce immense*
> *Mêlée à ton immense horreur.*

Give me your soul! the sea demands. Exile, extinguish your flame in me! But no, he replies, rallying himself. O somber sea, I hate you. Is it not you, who, dragging upon your moving waters toward Cayenne those black hulks, like great coffins, bear away forever our martyrs to their last agonies, covering their desperate, suppliant cries with your beautiful, yet guilty music! The closing section of *Nox* evokes memories of the titanic revolution of 1793, calls upon the half-naked workers, who once saved French liberties and conquered Europe, to remain strong, to prepare to hasten the promised day of deliverance.

Similar in form is the poem called *Floreal,* in which the exiled poet rests in a forest clearing, vibrating to all the odors and bird sounds of early April in Jersey; but then he notices a newspaper from France in his pocket—and suddenly the sky grows dark, all the joy of springtime vanishes, while he stands up to hurl imprecations at Napoleon the Little and his gang. Other poems deal with various aspects of the conspiracy, the "inside story" of its preparation, the secret executions by night, the tale of an innocent child killed by soldiers and its sorrowing mother, the humiliation of the parliament, the incidents of heroism or cowardice among the individual legislators with the craven ones held up to universal derision. One of the more violently satiric poems, *On Loge à la nuit* ("Lodgings for the Night"), is done in the manner of the feast of Gamache in "Don Quixote," showing Bonaparte as a modern "Tom-Thumb Attila," reveling with his fellow Huns in the Tuileries Palace, which they have just captured. From the great fireplace a sinister light is reflected on their livid faces and bloody hands. A whole ox is being roasted on the fire:

And yelping in his corner, Baroche the dog doth sit,
Crawling to lick your feet, while turning o'er the spit.[1]

But, while the wicked revel within the castle, their noise conceals the ringing hooves of a black horse approaching by "unknown roads" through the dark night, bearing the avenging "gendarme of God"!

Les Châtiments, as a book, is organized into separate sections, entitled: "Society is Saved; Order is Re-Established; the Family is Defended; Religion is Glorified." The climactic poem, *Expiation,* which has become best known of all this collection, is a genre painting of the martial career of Napoleon I, closing with the retreat from Russia, and prophesying the same dark end for his nephew. Meanwhile the obscure heroes and martyrs who fought on the people's side in the *coup d'état* of 1851 are commemorated. The book ends (like Beethoven's Ninth Symphony) upon a grand *finale* of hope, with *Lux,* a song to hearten the weary exiles, rejecting despair, reaffirming the poet's undiminished faith in the idea of progress and in the ultimate triumph of humanity and right, through the irresistible advance of science and rational knowledge—after each ebbing movement—a faith which he shares with the other nineteenth-century seers of France, Comte, Quinet, and Michelet. It is a triumphant chant in honor of the coming of peace and fraternity. As he wrote his closing lines, he had reason to hope, for a new war, the Crimean War, threatened France with disaster again. In a poetic postscript, Hugo noticed this event and forecast the renewed operation of that "law of revolutions" that would, in war's bloody aftermath, bring the doom of the tyrant and the liberation of the people.[2]

Throughout his life Hugo had been a natural master of the craft of poetry. *Les Châtiments,* by its virtuosity, fully equaled his last and quite brilliant volume of 1840, *Les Rayons et les ombres,* but greatly surpassed the earlier work by its sustained tone of towering passion, which seemed to carry the poet to new heights of linguistic eloquence. For the first time in the literature of France, satire became both lyrical and dramatic. Hugo no longer declaims: he suffers, struggles, laments, curses. A Prosper Mérimée,

[1] *Et jappant dans sa niche au coin du feu, Baroche*
Vient te lècher les pieds, tout en tournant la broche.

[2] In the case of the Crimean War, to Hugo's chagrin, the expected retribution suffered a serious postponement. But fifteen years later he saw himself vindicated and called attention to this fact in the 1870 edition of *Les Châtiments.*

who had gone over to the service of Bonaparte, exclaimed, on reading the book, "Hugo is mad; he grows drunk on his own words!" But Francisque Sarcey, a noted critic, commented: "Hugo wrings the neck of his adversaries with strong Alexandrines, until they fall off. . . . Never have such resounding epithets and maledictions been heard before save in the Old Testament."

Les Châtiments was printed in Jersey, in October, 1853, at the author's expense, and then shipped to the Continent for smuggling. Many persons in France had heard advance rumors of the new "Eumenides" awaited from Jersey. In bales of wool, in crates of sardines, and literally in every traveler's trunk thousands of copies entered France, some of them even by mail, cut up unrecognizably into seven or eight parts, and sent to different addresses to be assembled later. Pirated editions were also printed, many being run off in fine print on onion paper or cigarette paper. France read *Les Châtiments* with delight and memorized its songs and purple patches. The very abundance of particular names of personages then in the public eye made it relished all the more, especially by the young generation which grew up under the "authoritarian" regime of the Second Empire. France knew *Les Châtiments* much better than *Napoléon le Petit*.

When the new Emperor was shown a copy of "Napoleon the Little," he had said mockingly: "Well there! Here is 'Napoleon the Little' by Victor Hugo the Great!" Victor Hugo flew into a rage at hearing report of this pleasantry and included a short poem in reply, "The Man Laughed," which said: "He mocks at me, the knave, but I hold Bonaparte by the neck, I *brand* him!" It was true. Bonaparte, who is said by some to have had his own good intentions, was ill-starred not only in peace and war, but also in literature, for he went down in history as a butt of ridicule. He held, in a militarized France, an absolute power precisely comparable to that of Mr. Hitler today in Germany. But Louis-Napoleon Bonaparte has remained somehow *branded* as a fool and a rascal; and when one searches for the source of this legend, the powerful, unremitting pamphleteering of M. Hugo from his island appears to be the largest part of it.

For nearly twenty years the flame of his anger continued to glow, and mistrust, skepticism, even hate of the French dictator was nourished among the youth of France. Young writers like Emile Zola read these verses, as if thereby committing an act of secret revolt against the regime of shame that made life seem vile and sad and seemed at times to banish laughter itself from the land of bordeaux and champagne.

Victor Hugo became a legendary figure. They saw him as he pictured himself in this book (in *Ecrit le 17 Juillet, 1851*) standing alone upon the tribune and assaulted by the majority of the Assembly:

> . . . *My soul calm and inviolate,*
> *Scorning your esteem, esteeming all your hate.*

What pride the man had! But he, at any rate, was *a man*. In the legend (as in many engravings of the period) he was also pictured as standing on his Rock of Exile—a picturesque eminence on the Jersey shore, actually frequented by the refugees—whence he could see the coast of France; a man of broad frame, with vast brow, flowing hair, and burning, deep-set eyes, standing against the wind and the tide spray and sending forth apocalyptic maledictions, like lightning bolts, over the sea. The legend of Victor Hugo on this island grew to the proportions that the legend of the Man of Saint Helena had assumed for a preceding generation. His very departure had left a terrible void in the republic of letters, which was only beginning to be fully estimated, as Jules Janin wrote him:

> You are as a distant orb hovering over a world which feels your absence and likens you to Brutus. . . . What an arch of triumph will greet you and what acclamation up to heaven, at the return simultaneously of our Liberty and our Poet. Courage and patience! *Homo fortiter miser.* The greatest spectacle that a mortal can give is that of supporting misfortune with dignity.

3

"Oh, my dear comrade in arms and thought," Victor Hugo wrote to Alphonse Esquiros, in 1853, "let us not be discouraged. Let us persist, fight, redouble our efforts, persevere in the war against that which to us is evil, hate, and *night*." Esquiros was one of the socialist members of the Assembly who had fought in the barricades of December, 1851. Later he had come to stay for a time in Jersey. A few notable men such as Quinet, Leroux, Etienne Arago (nephew of the great scientist), and certain persecuted Polish, Hungarian, Italian, and Russian revolutionists were numbered at times—not all at the same time—in the little colony of some three hundred refugees, mainly French, who continued the struggle from Jersey. They were not happy, nor were they all uniformly brave. "Some yield out of hunger. We aid them as much as we can. Some weaken," Hugo wrote to Gustave Flaubert's friend, Louise Colet, in December, 1852, "and then they accept the infamous permission to return that the Criminal calls amnesty. They leave after having signed a statement that they had been 'led astray by evil counsels.' I forgive them and mourn them."

The exiles were a mixed community, including people from every walk of life, peasants, vintners, scholars, doctors, teachers, writers, even one (Legitimist) nobleman, the Comte de Valleareau, who, like Pierre Leroux, the utopian, worked a small farm and sold greens in the market of Saint Helier. Several gave lessons in French; others did domestic labor; one ran a small inn; others simply idled, or lay on the *Rocher des Proscrits* (the Rock of Exile) and gazed toward France. Among the French, there was agreement on the need for overthrowing the dictator Bonaparte, but very little agreement on the method of doing this. They plotted insurrections every night, and abandoned them the next morning.

In their wretchedness, they fell to quarreling. There were two groups or societies among the exiles, one called *La Fraternité* and the other called *La Fraternelle;* it was almost the same thing—but, as Victor Hugo wrote afterward in reminiscence, "they did not live together fraternally."

Once a year, on November 29, there would be a Polish festival in honor of the Polish revolution, and Victor Hugo would speak as the principal toastmaster. On such occasions, Tsar Nicholas would supplant Louis Napoleon as Hugo's target. Or when a refugee would die—often they were not church members, or were nonbelievers—Victor Hugo would be asked to give a funeral oration. Then, over the plain grave, he would stand, not merely a tribune, but something of an oracle, something of a priest, and would give what was in effect a sermon and a prayer in accordance with his own present deistic and social-democratic faith. Sometimes there were imprecations in these little speeches against those who had driven a poor, hungry exile to his lonely death in a strange land, but often they were very grave, calm, very beautifully conceived and spoken; some of the simplest and finest things the poet ever wrote were these little funeral orations for his deceased comrades, recited before the remaining exiles. Such was the funeral oration for Louise Julien, a sort of socialist sister of charity, who had helped the republican fighters in 1851, was imprisoned, lay sick in jail, and came to Jersey to die in 1854.

This woman, by her patriotic songs, by her kind and sympathetic words [said Hugo], by her good actions, made the name of Louise Julien famous in the working-class districts of Paris. Daughter of a working woman, she had supported her sick mother ever since childhood. In the time of the civil war, she made bandages, and went in an ambulance to tend the wounded of both sides. This woman of the people was a poet, and she was a mind; she sang of the Republic, loved liberty, appealed to the fraternity of all nations and men, believed in God. . . . This is what the woman did. And M. Bonaparte killed her.

Ah, such a tomb is not mute; it is filled with sobs and moans and clamors to Heaven!

Citizens, the tyrant, for his part, deceives himself. God does not wish this silence, this darkness, to continue; God does not wish that liberty, which is His word, should die. Citizens! at the moment when despots appear to have triumphed, God . . . rebuilds slowly, in solitude, that which has been destroyed. He rebuilds with the grass of the cemetery, with the shadow of the cypress, with the deathly mound that is made by coffins buried in earth; and out of this solitude, this grass, this cypress, these vanished coffins, do you know what comes forth, citizens? There comes the rending cry of humanity, the denunciation, the inexorable accusation that causes the despot to turn pale, the mighty protest of all the dead! . . .

O dead ones who surround and listen to me, malediction upon Louis Bonaparte! O great dead, let this man be execrated! . . . Malediction everywhere in every clime, in France, in Austria, in Lombardy, in Sicily, in Rome, in Poland, in Hungary, upon all those who violate human and divine law! Malediction upon those who fill the hulks with prisoners, those who raise up gibbets, who destroy families, who torture the people! Malediction upon those who proscribe fathers, mothers and children, those who whip women. O exiles, be implacable in your solemn demands for justice and humanity. . . .

One cause of trouble was the occasional intrusion of certain of Bonaparte's police spies in their midst, disguised as poor, starving exiles, stationed to overhear and watch. "Exile is not glory," Hugo said later, "but it resembles glory in this sense, that both are infested with vermin." He relates, in the foreword to his published speeches, with a touch of persecution complex that seems pardonable under the circumstances:

A foreign prince, who murders the language, comes to pay his respects. . . . Is he a real prince? Yes, he is of the blood royal, and also straight from the police. A pedantic professor is introduced; you come upon him reading your private papers. . . . Your exile is haunted by that specter the spy. A stranger, with a very mysterious air, comes to whisper something in your ear; he tells you that if you wish it he will undertake to assassinate the Emperor; he is Bonaparte offering to kill Bonaparte. At your fraternal banquet someone in a corner will shout: "Hurrah for Marat! Up with the guillotine!" If you listen carefully you will recognize the voice of Carlier. Sometimes the spy begs for alms; it is the Emperor who is begging through his *agent provocateur!* You pay the tavern bills of a certain exile; he turns out to be a policeman. . . . As you walk in the street you hear someone say: "There goes the real tyrant!" It is of you he speaks. You turn around and ask: "Who is that man?" And the reply is: he is a refugee. Not at all. He is paid to do his business. He is one of Maupas's republicans.

All this diatribe referred to men who were far from imaginary, for the Imperial Police in Louis-Napoleon's time were as patient and persistent and ubiquitous as were the "vermin" they were named after. They kept themselves well informed in Brussels, London, Jersey, and elsewhere. One of these human vermin named Hubert, living in Jersey, was always noticeably noisy in his denunciation of Bonaparte; after a time he excited some suspicion and was suddenly given away by the jealousy of a woman friend, who turned up with papers of his, proving him a spy.

The exiles were worked up into a fury, and some were for killing him outright. In the cellar of a tavern at Saint Helier port, Hugo participated in a grim trial of the man and, according to his professed doctrines, preached pardon, or at least some mild punishment. The man was momentarily in debt to his landlord, and the latter, a democratic French native of Jersey, was persuaded to use his privilege of having the spy imprisoned for debt, according to an old local law. Hubert was put in the jug, and the cost of his upkeep—again according to an old law—was defrayed by his accusers, which meant mainly Hugo, the only one able to pay about 1 shilling 3 pence a day to the jailor.

But the business of paying regularly for the imprisonment of the enemy became a wearisome and unnatural expense, incurred in enforcing a debtors' law a law of medieval origin. Hugo felt that he must dispose of the case honorably. "What if I do not pay?" he said one day to the official who called for the weekly subscription. "In that case the prisoner will be set at liberty." Hugo replied: "Very well, then I decline to pay." The man got off the island as fast as he could. Victor Hugo had the dual pleasure of pardoning an enemy and economizing at the same time.

The terrible thing about exile, Victor Hugo said long afterward, was the sense of being stripped of all legal rights. The poor man in his native town or village had friends and rights. The substantial man, walking the streets of his city, not only had rights but enjoyed privileges. In a foreign land, all these intangible but fundamental advantages are suddenly lost.

At first the English-ruled island of Frenchmen seemed to offer refugees from continental Europe a delicious and novel sense of liberty. They were no longer shadowed or disturbed by government or police officials. Mme. Hugo wrote:

This country is freedom itself. No controls are exercised. The gendarme, the police sergeant, is nowhere in sight. . . . Each man may come or go at his own free will.

Such privileges in Anglo-Saxon lands were ever surprising even to former citizens of the erstwhile French Republic. But soon, underneath the appearance of full civil liberty, friction with the authorities arose and gradually increased.

Britain, following the lead given by Queen Victoria, had at first shown herself shocked at the brutal *coup d'état* of Bonaparte and the menace of a new military captain rising over France. But the "Russian peril" now hung over the Balkans; Turkey had become England's "Sick Man of Europe." Under the provocations of the Russian government war suddenly flamed up in the Near East, and Constantinople and the Dardanelles became the declared objective of the Tsar. Protestant England soon prepared for foreign war to aid the Moslem empire, and Bonaparte in France appeared as a useful ally, offering the contribution of a big land army in a "brilliant" war adventure designed to rescue the Turk and preserve the balance of power. The Emperor Napoleon III, as his title now read, had definitely failed to win true popularity in France, and looked abroad for martial glory. In April, 1854, in pursuance of the policies favored by Lord Palmerston, the British government signed a treaty of alliance with France, and several weeks later the Crimean War was on.

In September, 1854, Victor Hugo in his Jersey retreat denounced the Anglo-French pact as boding no good for either nation. It was in his opinion a bargain made by the English commonwealth with one who was no better than a swindler, and so imbued with the spirit of treachery. This speech was noticed with displeasure in the London press, though it was given at one of those little funeral services for a deceased exile in obscure Jersey.

On November 29, 1854, Hugo spoke at a festival for Polish refugees in Jersey. By now some news from Russia had been arriving, thanks to the reporting enterprise of the modern press (especially the London *Times*). Not only were the initial, sanguinary reverses of the Allies at Sevastopol known and discussed, but reports of the enormous casualty rate, owing to disease and inadequate medical care, sickened all men of humane feeling and stimulated Florence Nightingale and her trained nurses to a magnificent pioneering effort. Victor Hugo was merely one among many humanitarian speakers who denounced the agents of a great military catastrophe and made complaint against the horrors of modern siege warfare, the rivers of blood flowing on Crimean soil. For this he was naturally excoriated as "unpatriotic" in Paris, but was also strongly censured in the British press, which now began to find his presence in English territory an embarrassment.

Some months earlier, pursuing his fixed principles on the question of capital punishment, he had also intervened publicly in a celebrated criminal trial, held in the neighboring Channel island of Guernsey. A man named Tapner had committed murder under gruesome circumstances and was sentenced to be hanged; but Hugo, as if feeling himself guilty for the unfortunate criminal, addressed public letters to the people of Guernsey and to the Prime Minister, Palmerston, demanding a pardon. Now one passage in the letter to Palmerston was more vivacious than tactful, for he addressed the famous dandy as follows: "I once met you at a dinner. . . . What impressed me was the expert way in which you knotted your tie. I had been told that you were celebrated for the expertness with which you did that. I see now that you know how to tie a knot around another man's neck too!" This was the sort of barbed wit that ruffled the feelings of British statesmen. It led eventually to an interpellation in the House of Parliament, during which Sir Robert Peel summoned the English government to put an end to the "sort of personal quarrel between Mr. Victor Hugo and the distinguished man whom the French people have chosen as their leader."

The exile at once replied with a belligerent statement, published December 22, 1854, in the British press, declaring that come what might, he would continue to assault Bonaparte from the ends of the earth. He concluded:

Yes, the gentleman who speaks of a *personal* quarrel is right. My quarrel with M. Bonaparte is a personal quarrel—the old personal quarrel that goes on between the judge on his bench and the accused in the dock.

M. Bonaparte was, in his gloomy way, a tenacious man. He sent reinforcements to the Crimea in 1855 which brought improved results in his military business, and also in the spring of the same year undertook a formal visit to Queen Victoria, as a means of cementing the new alliance. Diplomatic and social circles in London prepared for a grand welcoming festival, but Victor Hugo on his distant island, learning of the approach of the dictator, flew into a terrible fit of wrath, and wrote a short pamphlet, "Letter to Louis Bonaparte," which was circulated on April 9, 1855, a few days before the Emperor's arrival. It was "Napoleon the Little" over again, but in six pages, and therefore devastating:

What are you doing here? Whom are you after? Whom do you come to insult? England, through her people, or France through her exiles? . . . I say to you, leave the exiled in peace; hands off liberty.
. . . Are you going to put your hand on your heart and swear allegiance to the pact with England as you did to the Constitution of the Republic . . . with touching accents and moist eye? What oath are you going to swear now, what affirmation of eternal fidelity, what inviolable pledge . . . what coin stamped with your effigy are you going to put into circulation now, counterfeiter that you are?
What do you bring to this land? The land of Thomas More, of Hampden, of Shakespeare, of Milton, of Newton, of Byron? They do not ask for samples of the bloody slime of the Boulevard Montmartre. Have you come in quest of a *garter*? Well, you are covered with blood right up to your garters.

Thus the castigation continued lustily, overhauling the man's crimes, including the more recent ones in conjunction with the government of Her Majesty, the Queen. It ended on a strange note, one not usual with Victor Hugo formerly. From his observation of the dictator in former years he had guessed that he was a man who slept uneasily. Hugo cared nothing if he added to Bonaparte's sleeplessness. He now announced that he had lately been consulting the oracles (the turning tables), and that their auguries for the future were not good. Like a prophet of doom he exclaims:

Ah, miserable one! What is your tomorrow? What does the future hold for you upon this earth? Sometimes in the night, being sleepless—

for the slumber of the fatherland makes for the insomnia of the exile
—I gaze toward the horizon where lies the darkened coast of France,
and regard the eternal firmament, visage of eternal justice, and I put
questions to the Ghost concerning you, I ask the Shadows of God what
they think of your future—and I must say, sir, I mourn for you. Only
a terrible silence comes as the reply of the Infinite.

A brief version of Hugo's "Letter," done into English, was
posted on the walls of buildings in London on the morning of the
Emperor's arrival, but was torn down by the police.

4

In 1855, Victor Hugo still hoped fervently for the fall of the
dictator. Had not Napoleon the Great come to grief in the desolate steppes of Russia? "There can be only one issue to 1855," he
wrote to Mme. Delphine de Girardin, "and that is 1812!" He
added that the "turning tables" told him some remarkable things,
and that everyone, his son Charles reported after a trip to the
Continent, was awaiting an early deliverance for France.

But in the Crimea, by dint of terrible exertions, French and
British arms wrested a face-saving stalemate out of disaster. A peace
which placed limits upon the westward advance of Russia was
imposed, and the Emperor "Boustrapa" held triumphal celebrations in Paris, where, in August, 1855, Queen Victoria went for
a return visit.

The little colony in Jersey was plunged into gloom by these
developments and especially at news of the royal visit, which promised to postpone indefinitely the day of their vindication and return. At Saint Helier, the refugees published a little newspaper of
their own, *L'Homme,* edited by Ribeyrolles and some others who
had been on the staff of *La Réforme* in Paris. On October 10,
1855, they reprinted a "Letter to Queen Victoria," by Félix Pyat,
already published in London. In this Her Majesty was rudely
twitted upon the advantages and pleasures she had gained during
her visit with the ruffian in Paris. It closed with the parting shot:
"You have sacrificed everything—your dignity as a Queen, your
womanly scruples, your aristocratic pride, your English sentiment,
your rank, your sex, even your modesty—for the sake of your new
ally!" The piece was considered libelous by some of the citizens
of Jersey, and a public indignation meeting was held in the Assembly Rooms of Saint Helier, which only the police prevented

from turning into an immediate raid upon the office of the exiles'
newspaper. On the following day, notice was sent by the Lieutenant-Governor to Ribeyrolles and two others held chiefly responsible for the journal *L'Homme* that they must leave the island
in six days.

Victor Hugo was highly indignant at the expulsion of his colleagues. He had been growing more and more restive lately among
the Jerseymen. He despised their society—and the provincial big-
wigs who ruled over it—and he resented their prudery. He came
and went as he pleased, dressed nowadays with a studied negligence, and, as if in defiance of the puritans, had "the air of a
genial brigand," as Juliette put it. In fragments intended for his
diary, under the heading, "Ocean," he wrote at this time:

To the English, I am *"shocking," "eccentric," "improper!"* I wear
my necktie incorrectly. I have myself shaved by the barber at the
corner . . . like a *workman*. I run up against *cant;* I attack the death
penalty, which is not respectable; I say *monsieur* to a lord, which is
impious; . . . I am French, which is odious, republican, which is
abominable, and an exile, which is disgusting, defeated, which is shameful. . . . I may say the English have received Hugo in the same way
in which they chased out Byron. . . .

One thing, alas, for which he cherished his "Lemnos," Jersey:
that it was within sight of his native land. An Italian Liberal nobleman offered him a refuge near the beautiful Lago Maggiore; a
Spaniard, at a time when Spain seemed moving toward a Liberal
government, offered him a castle. They tempted him with sunlight
and blue sky, as he wrote to Louis Colet, in June, 1854. "But alas,
to go farther away, again! From here I can see France. . . . The
sea, France at the edge of it, how sad it would be to lose this
horizon."

But at news of the banishment of his already banished friends,
he was ready to risk his security—though he had had nothing to do
with the letter of Pyat to the Queen, and in private said it was
tactless and ungallant. How could Victor Hugo have remained
silent and forsaken his comrades? He rushed off a tremendous
manifesto of his own, called "A Declaration," in which he charged
that Bonaparte and his French police had pressed the hand of the
British government to move against the refugees in Jersey. England,
he implied, and English liberties were falling under a shadow.
"Another step in this direction and England would be but an annex

of the French Empire." He closed with the challenging words: "And now, let them expel us."

That the "crime Emperor's" consuls watched over the exiles in Jersey and elsewhere was true enough; his diplomats also exerted some pressure on England to curb anti-Bonapartist agitators—yet the English, reading of Hugo's manifesto, which was posted up in Saint Helier, thought he suffered from delusions. Ten days after the manifesto was issued, on October 27, 1855, at ten in the morning, the constable of Saint Clement Parish in Jersey, together with two other officers, presented himself at Marine Terrace and asked to see M. Hugo and his two sons.

"To whom have I the honor of speaking?" asked Hugo, coming to the door himself. The constable introduced himself and informed the master, with expressions of polite regret, that, in consequence of the recent publishing and posting of the said "Declaration," and under instructions received from the London government, His Excellency, the Lieutenant-Governor of Jersey, ordered M. Hugo and his two sons to leave the island within a week, that is, by November 2, 1855.

Hugo answered gravely: "Very well, sir." Having given the same notice to the two sons, the constable and his attendants sat down, while the Hugos remained standing.

Then began one of those extraordinary scenes, romantic or quixotic and yet very moving, which occurred so often in Hugo's stormy life. One was not a poet for nothing. He remained standing, and began to harangue the officers, while his son Charles noted down the subject of the conversation.

HUGO: Gentlemen, do you understand the large import of the action which you have just now taken?—with so much decorum, I grant. . . . I do not hold you responsible for this act: I do not ask for your opinion; I am sure that in your own consciences you are indignant and unhappy at what the military authority has made you do today.

THE THREE OFFICERS (silent, bow their heads).

HUGO: Your silence tells me enough. Between the consciences of honest men there is an invisible bridge through which thoughts are communicated without having to come through their lips. Nevertheless, I repeat, you must be made to realize to the full the enormity of the action to which you have been obliged to lend yourselves. Mr. Constable of Saint Clement, you are a member of the Council of this island, you were elected by the free suffrage of your fellow citizens a representative of the people of Jersey. What would you say if the

Exterior of Hauteville House, Guernsey

The Lookout at Hauteville House

military governor sent his soldiers to arrest you in your bed one night, if he threw you into prison, if he tore up your mandate, and treated you, a representative of the people, as the lowest malefactor. . . . If the Governor of Jersey were to do all that, what would you say? (Silence.) Answer me!

The Constable: I would say that the Governor was *wrong*.

Hugo: Would you limit yourself to saying he was wrong? No, you would say he was a criminal. Is not the man who kills liberty and butchers the people a parricide, a criminal? Answer me.

The Constable: Yes, monsieur, he commits a crime.

Hugo (after explaining that he had but performed his duty by taking a stand with his comrades in exile): We are writing a page of history, monsieur. We are three historians here, my sons and I, and one day this will all be recorded. Answer me, then: In protesting against crime, would you not be using your right, would you not be doing your duty?

The Constable: Yes, monsieur.

Hugo (reads off his "Declaration" of October 10, protesting the banishment of his comrades, and at each clause asks): Had we not the right to say this?

The Constable: Yes. Yes. But you disapproved of the expulsion of your friends.

Hugo: I disapprove of it entirely and I am proud to do so. But . . . does not your liberty of the press permit the criticism of an arbitrary act by the authorities?

The Constable (confused, miserable): Certainly, certainly.

Hugo: And it is for this that you have come to announce the order of my expulsion—for this "Declaration" which you admit does not exceed the bounds of established liberties, and which you would have written if you were in my place?

The Constable (lamely): When do you intend to leave, monsieur?

It is all both comic and sublime, and also so futile; all this triumphant reasoning, and the officer merely repeats the lesson he has learnt, the orders he brings. Hugo starts with anger, but calms down, when the constable hastens to explain that he desires to know in order that he may come and pay his respects before the great man's departure. Victor Hugo then proceeds:

I do not know yet what day I shall leave, monsieur, but you may rest assured, I shall not wait until the expiration of the time set. I am in haste to leave Jersey. A land where honor no longer exists burns my feet.

And now, M. Constable, *you may go.* You will return to give an account of the execution of your order to your superior, the Lieutenant-

Governor, who will give an account to his superior, the Government at London, who will render an account to *their superior, M. Bonaparte.*

The account of the dialogue between Hugo and the Jersey police officers was recorded by Charles Hugo in his *Les Hommes de l'exil* ("Exiled Men"), and some of it, as published in Belgian newspapers, was subsequently denied by M. Lenepveu, the constable. English commentators found the whole scene worthy of the extreme vanity of the French poet and ridiculed him for his pompous behavior. Yet Hugo was being true to himself. With his French temperament, he was disposed always to endeavor to face life's great emergencies with suitable words—he believed in the power of the Word! The more commonplace type of mind assumed, because he spoke with such gravamen and gestured with such éclat, that he must be a fool and a poltroon who would do nothing. But Victor Hugo both uttered his magnificent phrases and then took action, with fine courage. "Words and Deeds," was the fitting title he gave to this period of his life as a public figure, and to the three volumes of his speeches and manifestos. He was penetrated with the sense of the drama of his life; out of this sense, and out of his suffering, great words came to him often. Having said his piece, with a heavy heart he prepared to leave the Jersey isle and undergo a third exile.

He would go on, he would continue the fight, he would raise up his voice, he would protest—though many smug persons told him that he was a fool, and that he could easily have reconciled himself or made his peace with circumstances beyond his power to alter.

At moments, as he recalled in a reminiscent passage of *Actes et Paroles,* he hears voices debating within himself:

Be reasonable. You are in the wrong. Who forced you to find the *coup d'état* wicked? What an idea, to fight for the right? What caprice entered your head? . . . To defend the right and the law, when nobody is for them! Mere demagogy, absurd, stubborn. A man takes a dagger and kills justice. Probably he has his reasons. Be with that man. Success makes him right. . . . All the world will sing your praises. Instead of being proscribed, you will become a Senator and you will no longer go about like a fool.

Do you not see that the priests, the soldiers, the bishops, the generals are with him! . . . All the respectable people are against you. . . . Come, think, repent, come to your senses. . . .

He continued upon his course. He lifted up his great voice and protested again and again. Then, his anger abating, there would be a *détente,* a fall of tension. He felt a great pity for those who wronged him and for those who were deceived and misled. He grew tender and even calm. He meditated.

That the episode of Victor Hugo's banishment from Jersey was considered far from ridiculous was shown by the fact that large indignation meetings were held outside of Jersey—in London, Glasgow, Newcastle, and elsewhere—by democratic and workingmen's associations, which were addressed by popular leaders like Joseph Cowen, and passed resolutions condemning the action of the Palmerston Ministry. Hugo packed up his trunks, and answered these many friendly messages with heartfelt thanks, saying that they sustained his hope in "great and generous England." From all parts of the world, famous men and women wrote him their condolences. The account of his statement to the constable, the story of his new trial and banishment, aroused sorrow and admiration for this great latter-day martyr among the friends of democracy everywhere, from the English Channel to the Vistula. "You are the real emperor of the French," one of these wrote to him.

He had learned to enjoy the climate and the beauty of the Channel Islands. Although he had a passing thought of seeking refuge in America, he had really fixed upon the near-by island of Guernsey, forty miles to the north of Jersey, smaller still, more rugged, more isolated, and more completely Norman-French in population.

On October 31, 1855, accompanied by his younger son, François-Victor, he embarked on the packetboat *Dispatch,* arranging that the rest of his family should follow him after he had found a home. With him he took the large chest in which he carried all his manuscripts. "The sea was heavy, the wind rough, the rain cold, the fog dark," he wrote to Mme. Hugo. "Jersey can no longer be seen, not even as a distant cloud."

In disembarking at Saint Peter's Port, Guernsey, a few hours later, it was necessary, owing to the smallness of the harbor in those days, to go ashore in a tiny lighter, which danced perilously beside the steamer. The father and son jumped into the small boat. Then the sailors unceremoniously, "as if it were a basket of fish," flung down the chest, which landed at the edge of the bow and teetered there uneasily for a second—a large part of *Les Misérables* was already stored in the chest—then, fortunately, fell back inside the boat, and was carried with them to the landing dock.

He had been told that if he caused no disturbances the local authorities at Guernsey would let him be. At the dock a picturesque little crowd of fishermen, sailors, and burghers waited for him. They were silent, but looked on sympathetically. As Victor Hugo stepped upon the land with his ever youthful stride, they all uncovered their heads.

CHAPTER XVI

Religious Experience

"W HY WAS I NOT exiled before!" Victor Hugo wrote in 1854 to his publisher, Hetzel. For him persecution and misfortune had no such disheartening effect as one would normally have expected. In Brussels, in his cheap furnished room, he had shown himself busy and carefree. In the Channel Islands, as Michelet saw him during a visit, he seemed to have the strength of a "driven man, who walks without halt and takes two sea baths a day." Driven from one island to the other, he took the change of habitat more calmly than his family and his adherents. He was at last wholly preoccupied with his writing: "I am lost in poetry," he wrote to a friend, "among rocks and fields, flowers and sea and clouds."

Exile from France and the fall from his high position in her public life had brought some powerful release, so that, ever since the beginning of 1852, he who had been silent for a decade had begun to write volume after volume. In 1853, at Jersey, *Les Châtiments* had followed hard upon *Napoléon le Petit* done in 1852. Some of his most memorable poems were written in two or three days and nights. After the long pause he returned to poetry with a riper, surer mastery of the craft. Problems of style no longer restrained him; ideas, memories, experiences thronged to his mind. In the year and a half that followed the summer of 1853 he wrote most of a new sequence of poems, forming the two large volumes called *Les Contemplations,* a work of apologia and, indirectly, of poetic autobiography. He put this aside, then he gave it its finishing touches in 1855. In this same period, 1853–1856, were largely completed the long prophetic poems, *Dieu* ("God"), and *La Fin de Satan* ("The End of Satan"), which he withheld for posthumous publication. The next two or three years that sped by for Hugo in the island of Guernsey saw the completion of *La Légende des siècles* ("The Legend of the Centuries") a sort of "story of mankind" in epic and narrative poetry and, in many ways, a summation of nineteenth-century thought. This historic volume (to which another part was added many years afterward) was published in 1859. The two years after that were given over to finishing the huge novel, *Les Misérables,* which he had been dragging about with him since the late 1840's; most of its ten volumes (as issued in the French edition) were written by the end of 1861. Thus the ten years since the beginning of his exile in December, 1851, most of them spent in the lonely, rugged island of Guernsey, were years of incessant literary production—in contrast with the preceding decade of public life. These were the years of a Cyclops toiling alone—miraculously inspired years during which books that were far stronger than everything that had gone before, the books of the greater Victor Hugo who now made himself known to the far corners of the earth, came from his hand. At the age of fifty he became twice the size of the man he had been before. Little wonder that he fervently wished he could have been exiled sooner.

Jersey was half English, half French; but Guernsey, the island of the prehistoric Druids, was predominantly Norman and Celtic. The tiny old port of Saint Peter was picturesque enough, with its Gothic church and its small houses jostling together on crooked streets that were terraced into the bluff overhanging the small inlet that was its harbor. Down below, the harbor was so filled with fishing vessels of all sorts that their spars almost pierced the windows of the houses standing on the quays. And from the top of the bluff, at Hauteville Street, where the Hugos came to live, one held the whole blue sea in the hollow of one's hand. Once again there was the scudding sea, the craggy shore, the queer form of Sark in the distance, and now farther off than in Jersey, but still within view, the coast of France, "the shores that call to us," as Hugo said.

He resumed his long walks, often with younger friends visiting the Hugos, such as Alfred Asseline and Paul Chenay, his wife's relatives. He would go with his sons to wild and isolated promontories, and he loved to bathe in the sea. At the beach, Chenay re-

THE KING OF POETS
Caricature by André Gill

calls, his voice would ring out clear and young, his laughter as frank and joyous as a boy's. His body remained surprisingly young and graceful; the natives knew him by his springy pointed step. He preferred to go out without a vest under his coat, indifferent to cold. If there was a threat of rain, he usually threw a light overcoat casually over one shoulder as he set out.

Guernsey had a somewhat smaller population than Jersey, and also very few French refugees. Here he was able to withdraw into himself, and avoid that day-to-day agitation against the Imperial regime that had left him no time almost for private thought since 1851. To be sure, he continued his political action, his battle for democracy, but at a certain remove, which permitted him the leisure and calm requisite for writing and for exploring certain deeper questions or mental speculations that wholly absorbed him nowadays.

Victor Hugo was not a systematic thinker, and his learning, as Sainte-Beuve said, was uneven. But the violent upheaval of his whole life in recent years, the private and public tragedies in which he had participated, led him now intermittently to re-examine all his past beliefs and his own course of conduct; he began to probe the meaning of the extraordinary adventures that had befallen him; also, growing older, he thought of the future. He meditated more and more intensely, and gradually found himself in the grip of a psychological crisis, a form of religious experience, that brought him alternately to states of exaltation and agony. For several years this crisis of his whole inward life endured (between 1852 and 1855), and with the phases of suffering, of resolution and immense relief from terrible tension, that finally came to him are bound up the inspiration and the completion of his greatest writings.

What did it matter what emperors or constables might do to him? He struggled tragically amid shadows day and night; he wrestled with himself. Then at last he was freed, and went forward again without stopping to look back.

This trancelike and mystical phase of Hugo's life dates from the beginning of his exile and the time of his stay in Jersey, in 1852–1855, to which we must revert for a little. At this period it was his habit to sink into long spells of revery. Alternately he called himself the Dreamer and the Meditator. On the naked sands alone, facing old age and an unknown future, he found himself besieged by pressing memories and by endless reflections upon "man, nature, and God."

His friend Jules Janin, publishing an intimate account of Hugo's life in 1853 (in the fourth volume of *L'Histoire de la littérature dramatique*), pointed to the tragedy of his daughter Léopoldine as marking a turning point in Hugo's life. It was a just view. The sudden loss of the beautiful elder daughter who had first taught him the joys of paternity, and his favorite among the children, had struck him as with the force of an avenging blow at a moment of careless prosperity and self-complacency. He bore with him a sense of "guilt," but became embittered and skeptical. He had given himself to a round of pleasures; he had entered public life, at first as a friend of the reigning monarch, hence out of vanity— only later had he turned to the people's side, fought for them, and "fallen" in their behalf. Was there some meaning in it all? he asked himself. Would his banishment ever end? Was he right? Wrong? And what lay before him?

Years had passed, and, despite his fierce polemical onslaughts, darkness hung over France. The common people, he noted with deep disappointment in his diary notes of 1855, were fooled by the momentary victories of Bonaparte, by "the bustle of public works, bright lights, *Te Deums*, parades, a whole glittering imperial spectacle." Business was good, and none cared how the national debt grew, nor thought of the iron collar at his neck!

Would liberty return? Were men moving in the direction of progress, or were they retrograding? Were his own efforts of any avail? Would his voice be heard; would he win vindication? Was there a just God? (once more). Would he ever see and speak again to Léopoldine? The poems written at this period when doubt heavily assailed him, those included in the new sequence, *Les Contemplations*, have titles such as "Insomnia" and "Melancholia." In one of these, *Paroles sur la dune* ("Words Spoken on the Dunes") he interrogates the sea and the wind, inconsolably asking if "all life, love, joy and hope are empty?" In another of the same genre, *Horror*, he walks as in the dark night of the soul, asking whence we come, where we go. Black is the gulf upon which the exiled wanderer floats like a ship submerged. Man, from the depths of his woe, "watches, continually turning in a tragic sky, the zodiac of the tyrants." In the companion piece *Dolor*, on the other hand, he speaks as if he has reached a state of resignation.[1]

> *O Pain, thou key of Heaven!*
> *Atonement key that opens a closed door!*
>
> *Ascent is sacrifice; the summits are austere.*
> *Olympus changes, fades, till Calvary is here,*
>   *Sun-scorched or winter-iced.*
> *The Cross immensely spreads, like a long shade unfurled.*
> *Look! At the four wide corners of the world*
>   *Bleed the Four Nails of Christ!*

[1]His manuscripts show that *Horror*, pitched in the mood of stark despair, was written *on the day following the writing of Dolor*, with its message of peace and resignation. Hope and desperation alternated swiftly within Hugo. The verses quoted here are from the translations of Mrs. Mary Robinson Duclaux.

He recalls his lost daughter also in the great elegy entitled, *A Villequier,* the name of the village on the Seine River where she had died in 1843. In the tones of a Job he chants a mighty protest against Heaven, then slowly forces himself to a state of resignation, which has underlying it more irony than faith, the gentle resignation of a Dante.

> *O God, Thy world is dark! the music of the spheres*
>   *Is made of sighs and sobs no less than songs, I think.*
> *Man is an atom lost in an endless vale of tears,*
>   *A night wherein the Good rise and the Wicked sink.*
>
> *I know Thou hast no time, Creator that Thou art,*
>   *To hear us when we cry;*
> *And that a child who dies, wringing a mother's heart,*
>   *Is nought to the Most High.*
>
> *When the wind shakes the bough, I know the fruit must fall,*
>   *I know the bird must lose the feather from its wing;*
> *Creation is a wheel that rounding on us all,*
>   *Grinds into dust at every turn some precious thing.*
>
> *Our months, our days, our tides, our tears are things that pass,*
>   *Like clouds 'twixt sky and sod;*
> *The grass grows; children die; I know it well alas,*
>   *I know it! O my God!*
>
> *Perchance createst Thou unknown immortal things*
>   *Wherein the grief of man is a chief element?*
>
> *Perhaps the vast designs of Thine unnumbered plans*
>   *Need that our children die,*
> *Drowned in the eddying dark—the black wide swirl that spans*
>   *The whole space of the sky?*

There was no mistaking the evidence of a tremendous inward crisis, mounting in intensity in nearly all the elegies in the sequence of *Les Contemplations.* Victor Hugo's was not a logical spirit. But among the superior qualities he had was the will to carry his meditation—passing, as in a trance, and by long vigils, from that which he saw and knew—to the "edge of the Infinite," to the unknowable and immeasurable. Thus in a psychic state, with his mind "dilated," revelations and emanations from the unknown seemed to reach him, an experience far from uncommon, and perfectly acceptable in the light of modern psychology.

He had been in youth, as Renouvier, the French philosopher, points out, a Christian out of habit and custom; then, after 1830, merely his language habits had remained Christian, while his tendency was pantheistic; but in 1853–1855 he became spontaneously and unconsciously a real Christian—though a heretical one, suggesting the gnostics or Manicheans of olden times. He saw always, in his mind's eye, tormented and suffering souls in the form of dwarfs, monsters, or hideous animals who seemed to bear the "guilt" of man imprinted upon them. He saw symbols everywhere, embracing as he did the Pythagorean doctrine of metempsychosis—the transference of souls of men after death into animals, or plants, or even mineral matter, in accordance with the degrees of virtue or vice those souls had attained.

In ancient, more credulous times, a man with such visions (as those expressed in the concluding or religious book of *Les Contemplations,* and in *Dieu* and *La Fin de Satan*) would have been hailed or stoned by the people as prophet, saint, or deranged heretic, in accordance with varying circumstances. In recent times many lay figures, having no less powerful religious experiences than those of the canonized Christian saints, a Rousseau or a William Blake or even Hugo's contemporary, Tolstoy, strove to win others to accept their visions, and to launch their own religious systems or sects, outside the Church. In this course Victor Hugo also persisted for long years, under the illusion that he was constructing a system of his own.[2] In Hugo's new "system" there was a familiar pattern of doctrines often used before and again reaffirmed by various mystical groups, such as the Saint-Simonians in France, especially Leroux and Reynaud, who tried to reconcile socialism and Christianity. But within Hugo's "system" there were also variants that appeared in some measure to be original with him. Since his early youth he had conceived of the function of the poet as that of Seer. Now, in his poetic discourses written in Jersey such as *Les Mages,* he went on to affirm that it was the poets who were the predestined Magi; the supreme geniuses of mankind were the "solar men," touched with rays from Heaven, who transmitted

[2] It was a time when the "materialistic" nineteenth century everywhere, in Europe and in America, appeared to be shaken by a profound soul-searching. The books of various latter-day mystics were in Hugo's library, his favorite reading at this time.

light from age to age. Why have priests, he asks, when there were conductors of souls in the poets, such as Virgil and Dante, much like the earlier Isaiahs and Ezekiels, in whose spiritual company he now ranged himself. In one quite remarkable poetic discourse, *Ibo*, he endeavors to discover the mysteries of the Unknown, which, as Seer, he hopes to reveal to the peoples, "ever plunged in ignorance . . . dwelling in the night."

> *Les lois de nos destins sur terre,*
> *Dieu les écrit;*
> *Et si ces lois sont le mystère,*
> *Je suis l'esprit. . . .*

> *Donc, les lois de nôtre problème,*
> *Je les aurai.*
> *J'irai vers elles, penseur blême,*
> *Mage effaré.*

The laws of our destiny, God had written; but he, "the spirit, pale meditator, affrighted Magus," he would dare to approach them, would win to understanding of them.

2

Victor Hugo always had much of the "primitive" in his nature; like men of the so-called primitive races he tended, when events surprised or mystified him, to pass over obvious or immediate "causes" and imagine mysterious or occult causes. He had been drawn to cabalism; an animist, he saw symbols, if not spirits, in birds and beasts, even in certain "horribly frowning" rocks or crags along the Jersey shore. In a poem done at this period he wrote:

The flower suffers and closes its eyes under the scissors. . . .

This was written generations before scientific experiments recorded actual evidence of sensation in plants. During these days of "struggle and revery," as he described them, he knew these things because voices told him of them.

Then in September, 1853, his old friend, Mme. Delphine de Girardin had suddenly arrived at Jersey, as already noted, and brought with her the new spiritist cult of table-turning that swept from America to England and Europe at that very moment. Now a whole chorus of voices out of all ages and all climes spoke to Hugo, who showed himself a remarkable adept as a "medium," with his son Charles and Mme. Hugo scarcely less so—for it was a highly neurotic family.

What was the vibrant turning table, once the lights were extinguished, but the Pythian tripod of old? Soon Hugo was communicating voluminously with those other "solar beings," with the spirits of Luther, Socrates, Moses, Shakespeare, Molière, Galileo, Jesus, Aeschylus, Isaiah, Charlotte Corday, and even the "Lion of Androcles" (at whose explicit order, he declares, he wrote a poem having that title, for the "Legend of the Centuries"). He talked with the spirits of Tragedy, Drama, and Criticism, with the Shadow of the Sepulcher and Death—although uncertain whether they were ideas or beings. He communicated with a Frog, with the Blade of the Guillotine, the Ocean, and the Angel of Light!

He became exalted. His frequent acts of enormous pride are more understandable in this light; for he had the exaltation of his mission as surely as Saint Theresa had hers. Occultation, the process of throwing off hindersome earthly bonds and obstacles (kin to "inhibitions") in order to pass to a state of unrestrained and semiconscious trance, permitting communication with the spirits of the dead, all this is an experience nowadays considered valid enough so far as it reflects the reality of the state of transport in the individual subject, or "medium," himself. There was no doubt of the reality of Hugo's religious experience: the visions that he found *within himself*—as we now tend to say—the records of his communications and conversations with spirits were all set down at length and preserved.[3]

Wonder of wonders, the Hugos were able to communicate with the spirit of Léopoldine Hugo at once. "They wept and they believed . . ." relates Auguste Vacquerie, a member of the family circle who did not join in their rites. They experimented with an engineer's plane-table having attached pencils, alphabets provided with an indicator needle, or simply knocks, the method they mostly used. Charles Hugo also proved to be an adept "medium"; generally he "transmitted," while his father provided the points of departure, the questions.

At this period Charles Hugo suffered from hallucinations. Re-

[3] They were published, however, only after a very long delay of nearly seventy years, in 1923, by Gustave Simon, as *Les Tables tournantes de Jersey*. The poet and his heirs had feared the laughter of the incredulous.

turning home late one night, in Jersey, he saw lights and heard voices in the salon upstairs. Hurrying in, he found the candelabra all lit and nobody there, as he related. In terror he threw himself into bed and pulled the covers over him. His father, also, after communicating with a certain White Lady, unknown to him, heard her make an appointment to meet him at three o'clock of the following morning. In the early morning darkness Hugo awoke and distinctly heard three knocks at his bedroom window. "How punctual the spirits are!" he exclaimed, but wretchedly buried his head under the pillow and refused to stir.

Soon, they were all prey to hallucinations—there had been insanity in the case of Victor Hugo's brother Eugène, and one of his own children, alas, was now *en route*. In the darkness, with taut nerves, the spiritists invoked their unconscious thoughts (which answered always with echoes of what lay in their own subconciousness, spoke in their own language, and in conformity, as Hugo noted, with his own doctrines). It never troubled him that Aeschylus, Dante, and Shakespeare *spoke to him always in French* and even used his own literary style and meter.[4] He was convinced that he was an instrument of God, and that the spirits had chosen the table at Jersey to reveal themselves to him, in the shape of the Frog (of whom he wrote in the *Légende des siècles*) and the Angel of Light (whose pantheistic system he outlined in the posthumously published prophetic poem, "God").

He wrote to Mme. de Girardin, on January 4, 1855:

The tables tell us the most surprising things. I wish I could tell you about them and kiss your hands—or wings! . . . A whole system of cosmogony that I have been brooding over—and partly written out— during the last twenty years, has been confirmed by the tables, and with magnificent elaborations. We live nowadays in sight of a mysterious horizon which changes all the perspectives of our exile; and we think of you to whom we owe the opening of this window.

The tables recommend silence and secrecy—except for two details, important ones it is true—you will find nothing concerning them in my book *Les Contemplations*.

---

[4]Once he invoked the spirit of André Chénier, the poet guillotined in 1794, and asked why one of his poems, entitled "XIX," had been left unfinished. The spirit answered by promptly dictating the missing passage. However these lines, included in the "spiritist" works of Hugo by Gustave Simon, are plainly written in Hugo's style, and not Chénier's. What is most remarkable is that the poem by Chénier was not at all unfinished, but appeared in fragmentary form only in the old first edition of his works that Hugo had with him at Guernsey.

It was at this period, we learn, that Victor Hugo had himself photographed by Auguste Vacquerie, sitting in an ecstatic pose, with his eyes closed. Upon the only proof remaining of this photograph he wrote in his thick, bold hand: *Victor Hugo listening to God*.

In spite of his fear of the spirits, Victor Hugo included several poems written "under the dictation" of the turning tables, in the final section of his new volume, *Les Contemplations*. The first two-thirds of this volume are devoted to fairly material and worldly themes; the immense prophetic poem at the end of it, *Bouche d'ombre* ("Shadow-Mouth") frightened many of his most devoted readers a good deal, for it discoursed openly upon the "revelations" that now came to him. In this poem (which he justly considered one of his profoundest and most beautiful pieces), as in the posthumous *Dieu* and *La Fin de Satan*, the cabalistic and Pythagorean mysteries he had been brooding over for many years were unfolded in the form of philosophic or discursive verse. The central theme of all these longer prophetic poems is the triumph of divine virtue over the forces of evil and darkness.

His "system" as here exposed (also partly revealed in passages of *Les Misérables*) held numerous contradictions, but ignored them, much like the religions of primitive peoples, or the ancient Magi. With Walt Whitman, he seems to say: "Do I contradict myself?—Very well then, I contradict myself!" Hugo believed in transubstantiation: all matter lived, felt, thought (Pythagoreanism) and mounted by stages toward God. Everything, even inert matter was part of God (pantheism). Everything was metamorphosed and progressed toward a higher state (utopianism, or optimism)— first by way of suffering, which is reparation, and explains all evil in the world; then by knowledge, which liberates us from evil; finally by love, which emanates from God. Thus there was for Hugo no "absolute" evil; the Fall, central idea of Christian theology, was not recognized by him as such. Why did God create evil and shadow? Because He needed that there be "lesser" creatures, instead of having all uniformly of His own stature; and in the second place evil was "necessary" so that man himself *might have the power to create*. For if man had lived always in perfect felicity, what great things, what masterpieces would he have made? It was only through suffering and disaster that man discovered the divine force in himself. (For example, through being betrayed and banished by some Louis Bonaparte to the Channel Islands.) Here

Hugo, of course, departs from established Catholic tenet, and evidently condones a certain element of evil in himself—a convenient doctrine, for, like Martin Luther, our magus was disposed both to the sins of the flesh and to religious meditation.

The guilty, according to Hugo's occult revelations, were punished by transference into the forms of certain animals, plants, and even stones. By communicating constantly with their spirits the poet introduced powerful effects of animism and symbolism into his writing from now on. A certain cavernous rock formation on the shore at Guernsey, by its ravaged and threatening expression, always filled him with a wild dread, and he would discourse upon the condemned soul locked within it. One night, a companion witnessed how he walked the beach of Guernsey in the moonlight, at the point where the ruins of great Druid stone monuments lay sprawled about, addressing himself to them in passionate and amazingly eloquent invocations. And on another day, walking in a field with some friends, reading them one of his prophetic poems, he noticed that a Guernsey cow steadily followed them along the fence in the next field, pausing when they halted, as if listening to him. "Do you not see," Hugo exclaimed, "that the cow understands poetry, the cow has a soul!"

But though the guilty were punished by transference of their beings into baser form, his religion conceived of pardon as one of its principal doctrines. It was a religion, as he said, "that loved the hated, and saved the lost." Thus hate, which had ruled Hugo's heart for years, after the *coup d'état* of 1851, gradually dissolved and vanished during the period of his religious experience, leaving him a man of far greater serenity of temper than ever before.

Although God had suffered evil to exist, He had arranged to have His "solar beings" (as Hugo wrote in his mystical study "William Shakespeare") in whom the force of divinity was concentrated, to "bring the central fire to the planet." Hugo was convinced that mankind would be redeemed by the Magi, his chosen Great Men (Shakespeare, Socrates, Galileo, Dante, and others) whose powers would ultimately overcome those of the Caesar Borgias or Louis Bonapartes. That he himself was one of the company of the Elect (as his cabalist-spiritist revelations told him) he never doubted. The tables confirmed this on many occasions, when he appealed to them.

In February, 1855, he asked the tables: "Who will lie in my tomb, a poet or a prophet?" The reply was a trifle obscure and reserved, as the spirits' replies often are; but after many renewed trials it was apparent that their answer was favorable, for their instruction became more and more explicit.

One of his communications, as recorded by his sons, reads:

The beings who inhabit the unknown and who see into our thoughts know what I have been writing. On more than one occasion the table has spoken to me of this work: the Shadow of the Sepulcher has ordered me to finish it. . . . These mysterious and great beings gaze at will into my thought, as one looks into a cave with a torch. . . . So much is this true that I have been all but wounded in my poor human vanity by the precise revelations coming to me, which cast, far beyond my little miner's lamp, an illumination as of lightning and meteor. . . . The being called Shadow of the Sepulcher *ordered* me to write poems calling forth pity for those captive and punished beings who compose, in the opinion of men without vision, only dead matter. It said: "There is no longer any Hell. . . . O men, O plants, O beasts—all is love. O firmament, O living beings, all is a supreme pardon. And now you may die." In this state of mind I wrote the verses which the Idea asked for.

In pursuance of his "mission," regarding the lesson of pardon, Victor Hugo wrote the extraordinary poem (in *La Légende des siècles*) describing a horse, flogged to death by its master, turning up its eyes pitiably to Heaven and praying as it expires. It is a poem expressive of a sense of expansive pity that he has never before attained, the sense of pity which is later to be incorporated in the martyred figure of Jean Valjean. For as prophet, or magus, he saw himself charged with the mission of preaching universal pardon and fraternity, in short, with "abolishing hell" and "completing the work of the French Revolution." To him the French Revolution is a decisive stage in the march toward human redemption, obstructed from age to age only by the negative forces of evil. His long, posthumous, and unfinished prophetic poem "The End of Satan" (written in 1854) consists of a series of allegories beginning with the Calvary of Christ, and reaching (as projected) a final stage of liberation of man—"Satan pardoned"—following the resumption of the French Revolution in future times. This is also the underlying theme of "The Legend of the Centuries," three volumes of "small epics" tracing the story of mankind, in its march toward liberty, which Hugo wrote mostly in Guernsey.

For many months, Victor Hugo slept little and wrote furiously, as if under a hypnotic compulsion. His "communications" show that he still suffers alternating moods of hope and tormenting doubt up to 1855; for the tables, the oracles, have a way of being less than clear in their replies, as he learns at repeated séances. Indeed they sometimes seemed to resent his too great importunities, as he pressed them for definite instructions. He wrote on February 10, 1854:

> *Return again to silence, snuff your candles,*
> *Return to that Night whence once you issued,*
> *The human eye must not read eternal truths*
> *Over the shoulder of the dead. . . .*

A residue of doubt also clung to him, and he learned to accept its presence with resignation, as "necessary." In the end, after a long, agonizing effort of meditation and occultation, he says, in accents of the deepest and most philosophic humility:

I shall no longer insist; it grows plain to me that the sublime world, though consenting to communicate with our shadowy world, is reluctant to be forced, even when one's curiosity is motivated only by adoration of God and respect for the infinite. The sublime world desires to remain sublime . . . but not exact; it desires our vision, but not our science. Not even to render its intentions more humanly understandable will it accept the aid of scientific evidence and the effort of our reason to penetrate and observe. In a word it prefers that men should continue to doubt. That is noticeably the law, and I resign myself to it.[5]

[5]The same concept of the approach and recoil of thinking man from the mysteries of the metaphysical infinite is very beautifully expressed in Hugo's "William Shakespeare" (1864), which is not a critical study, and touches only in small part on the English poet, but is actually a discourse upon those poet-prophets of all the ages who lead mankind in its "collective voyage" toward some "splendid Canaan beyond the horizon." This much misunderstood book, sometimes poor in detail and, like Hugo's other prose writings, given to much overemphasis, nevertheless rises to superb philosophic statements. Edouard Renouvier and Denis Saurat, the philosophical scholars who have given much study to Hugo's "religion"—his mystical side, which literary historians for a long time tended to ignore or belittle—hold that both in the prophetic poems and in "William Shakespeare" he expressed in poetic formulae certain metaphysical conceptions that have nowhere been more vividly stated. Thus in "William Shakespeare," Book I, Part V:

"Each man is free to go out or not to go out on that fearful promontory of thought whence one perceives the shadows. If he does not venture there, he lives during all his ordinary life, with a normal consciousness and a normal faith, a normal doubt, a normal virtue. For his own inward repose, this is the better course. But once he dares to go out upon that extremity he is caught. The profound waves of the prodigious have appeared before him. No one may gaze into that oceanic abyss with impunity. Henceforth he will be the *dilated*

The Orphic tables warned him to show restraint and humility before the Unknown.

One day, he had put insistent questions to the Shadow of the Sepulcher.

Hugo: Do you know the poems I wrote eighteen months ago, which are identical with the things you have just said to me?
Shadow: No.

Thus he learned that his work was incomplete and must be continued. Then he asked the Shadow if the being who was to bring about the New Revelation was to be a man "like Moses and Jesus."

Shadow: No.
Hugo: Is he living among our generation?
Shadow: No.
Hugo: Will we see him in our lifetime?
Shadow: No.
Hugo: Is it I who am to be the prophet, or is it not I?
Shadow: Every great soul does two works in his life span: his work as a living being and his work as a ghost.

Victor Hugo was now able to judge that the revelation of the new religious system that he had been "ordered" to transmit *was destined to come only from his tomb.*

At repeated séances, he was instructed by the Shadow that he must not frighten his contemporaries by too brusque or bold revelations for which they were not prepared, but must initiate them gradually:

Beware, O mortal man, O proscribed one, O man of a century . . .
Better to do a positive work for the Twentieth Century than a doubt-

thinker, aggrandized, yet floating; that is to say, the meditator. At one point he is the poet, at the other the prophet. A certain portion of him henceforth is touched with shadows. The immeasurable has entered his life, his consciousness, his virtue, his philosophy. . . . He sees in diffused prayers, clinging, so strange a thing, to an indetermined certainty, that which he called God. He distinguishes in this twilight enough of his anterior life and his ulterior life to seize the two ends and revive his soul. . . . Stubbornly he clings to the edge of this haunting abyss, continues his probing of the unexplored . . . this effort to sound the impalpable, this searching of the invisible. He is drawn by it all and repelled; he goes back and forth . . . He goes toward it again, takes a step or two, and thus plunges into the impenetrable. . . .

"But however greatly one struggles for free will, one does not resolve these problems. One puts pressing questions to the abyss. Nothing more. As to the replies, they are there, but mingled with the shadow. The enormous lineaments of the eternal truths seem to rise before us for an instant, then fall back again into the abyss. . . ."

ful one for the Nineteenth. Jesus was resuscitated only once; thou
canst fill thy tomb with many resurrections . . . and the generations
will view with wonder this prodigious tomb marching on during a
century of human life.

HUGO: Thou hast given me a sublime counsel, and if thou but
leavest me time, I shall follow it.

By 1856, at Guernsey, he had fairly completed his prophetic
books ("God" and "The End of Satan"), then put them away to
be published after his death. He feared that his irreligious republican and socialist friends would mock at his belief in metempsychosis, in the transference of souls. One of his posthumous fragments runs:

> *Thou wilt return like old Voltaire himself,*
> *Laden with years, to thy beloved Paris. . . .*
> *Thou'lt think like him with the same honest joy:*
> *I am so good they hold me for a fool,*
> *I am so foolish that they think me good.*

He kept his new religious certainties somewhat hidden from prying eyes, and that which he permitted to be seen he did not defend
or explain. Thus many "exalted" personalities face the world with
a spirit of reserve about their deepest convictions.

It is no coincidence that the poet in communicating with the
spirit world absorbed religious doctrines that answered his own
deep-felt needs and longing. His sense of fulfilling a sacred mission and the utility of it was reinforced. The presence of evil and
suffering, and even of guilt within himself was explained and
pardoned. Even his own earthly frailties seemed to be in accord
with that "universal prostitution" which, according to certain
types of occultism, was directly connected with the force of crea-
tiveness. (Thus he was permitted to continue his apparently "sinful" relations with Mme. Drouet and also to deceive her in turn,
which he continued to do up to a very advanced age, with various
laundresses and servant maids. And when betimes his conscience
was pricked by his own sensual philanderings, the Shadow assured
him that this was all a mystery that he must respect and question
no more.) Nor did these apparent contradictions prevent him
from believing in God in his own way, while becoming henceforth a fierce and scornful antagonist of the established Church.
The orthodox Church, in his conviction, no longer observed the
spirit of mercy with any sincerity, whereas Hugo preached "uni-

versal pardon," human fraternity, and the perpetual revolution
of progress, which he held was the will of God, although it had
been propounded earlier by the brilliant unbelievers who spread
the eighteenth-century Enlightenment.

However at Guernsey, after 1855, his religious transports tended
to subside. He ceased to importune the turning tables; he retreated from the abyss of infinity, returning to regular hours of
work and exercise and sleep. His new books of poetry and prose
now gushed forth in a perfect torrent, but nearly all of them had
a deeper breath than his earlier writings, they were in some
measure "touched" by the tremendous religious exaltation he had
experienced at Jersey, his own "isle of Patmos."

Hugo in Guernsey, by André Gill

CHAPTER XVII

The Voice of Guernsey

When liberty returns, I shall return!

—Hugo

Eᴀʀʟʏ ɪɴ ᴀᴘʀɪʟ, 1856, *Les Contemplations* was published in France, in two volumes, the grudging permission of the Imperial censorship having been won by the publishers because it was a non-political work. To a certain extent this book is an autobiography in poetic form, since it documents much of his life; though mainly written in days of exile, it also includes certain poems done over the twenty years since 1836—which he had felt to be of too intimate a nature to publish while he was a member of parliament. Many of the poems, moreover, are works of reminiscence, recalling his childhood, his mother, his father, his youth, his early struggles, his militant campaigns or controversies on behalf of new artistic doctrines, his amorous and social adventures, the tragedies that he experienced (Léopoldine's death) and, by somewhat veiled reference, his exile, and discovery of new faith and hope. To augment the effect of a spiritual and sentimental autobiography (or pilgrimage) the book is organized in two parts, one retrospective, entitled "Yesterday," the other entitled "Today." The large mystical poem, *Bouche d'ombre,* which may be likened to some of Blake's or Ralph Waldo Emerson's mystic discourses in verse, is placed in the concluding section.

This large collection of Hugo's poetry, the first new one published in sixteen years (aside from the satires of *Les Châtiments*) used a great variety of different forms—the lilting song, the epistolary poem, the ode, the elegy—and many different manners of

approach, now descriptive and "realistic," now lyrical, now philosophical. But it had consistency, and was mainly cast in Hugo's
later or "grand style" (some of the earlier poems, in manuscript,
indicate the most painstaking revision). In the heart of the work
were the series of elegies to his dead daughter, among the greatest
things of their kind ever written, and contributing a predominantly
tragic tone to the book.

Out of this seminal book, many schools have sprung. The lyric,
La Fête chez Thérèse, dedicated to the poet's second mistress, the
blonde Léonie Biard, is a festive pageant in a garden, with amorous
maskers and entertainers and music—which inspired Verlaine and
a whole school of "symbolists" to writing *Fêtes galantes.* Another
poem, *Réponse à un acte d'accusation,* is a tour de force proudly
asserting the poet's innovating or "revolutionary" role in the
republic of letters, and may be likened to Rimbaud's later tour de
force about "the alchemy of the Word." Hugo wrote:

> *I blew up a wind, blustering and revolutionary,*
> *I placed a red bonnet on the old dictionary . . .*
> *Set the naked muses dancing the Carmagnole . . .*
> *Crying: To arms! prose and verse! Form your battalions!*
> *I besieged and took the Bastille of Rhyme,*
> *And said to words: Be now republican!*

On the other hand, the concluding prophetic poems caused baffle-
ment among Hugo's readers, and were misunderstood or derided
much as William Blake's prophetic poems were abused—though
modern poetic taste now greatly favors the mystical writing of
both these poets. But this formed only a small part of the work,
which possessed a great many points of appeal to Hugo's public.
There were a few who abused Victor Hugo for turning both
"democratic and Pythagorean" at the same time, though generally
the press in France gave him only small and cautious reviews. But
nearly everyone acknowledged that his poetic power had increased,
rather than diminished, and wondered where Hugo had found his
fountain of youth. The enthusiastic poetry-reading public of those
days rushed forward and in the first season alone bought almost
ten thousand copies of *Les Contemplations,* though it was issued
at the relatively high price of twelve francs. For Hugo in exile
was the glamorous Dante of his day. Today, still, we find much of
the best and most representative work of Hugo as a poet in *Les*

Contemplations—he is, at any rate, France's long-lived Shelley, and France had never had a Shelley. In the middle of the nineteenth century, a "silver age" both in England and Germany, Victor Hugo was easily the first poet of Europe.

One of the results of this success was Hugo's purchase of a house in Guernsey for the sum of a thousand pounds sterling—in Jersey no aliens were permitted to buy property. Thus he became a permanent resident of Her Majesty's realm and somewhat less exposed to persecution. Patiently, persistently, he built his home in exile. He wrote to Janin:

Imagine, I am practically building a house. Having no fatherland, I seek to have a roof over my head. England has been no gentler to my hearth than France. . . . Now with the patience of an ant I am rebuilding it here. This time, if I am chased out again, I want prudish Albion to be forced to do a violent deed: to destroy an *at home* . . . *Les Contemplations* will pay for it all. That book has given me a roof, and you who liked the book must come to share the shelter it provides.

He had become tired of living in furnished houses. Actually, he did not build, but purchased and altered a sizable old mansion standing in Hauteville Street, on the bluff overlooking the sea, and said to have been constructed in the eighteenth century by a retired corsair. Guernsey always was a haven of smugglers. Also of legends; for this house was said to be "haunted." Victor Hugo thought of naming it "Liberty Hall," but then compromised on "Hauteville House."

The Hugos moved into Hauteville House in the late fall of 1856, after laborers had completed six months of alteration work according to the poet's ideas. But, in truth, he spent the next three years, up to 1859, altering and decorating his Guernsey mansion, until the house itself might well be called one of Victor Hugo's principal "works," as astonishing and as full of antithesis as any of his writings.

The house had a sober, gray façade, with fourteen narrow English windows, and was fronted by a garden and a grilled gate. Once inside the paneled vestibule and corridor, the visitor passed out of modern England and into a shadowed, romantic baroque interior of heavy carved oak walls, pictorial tapestries, brilliant damask hangings, great carved oak fireplaces, and massive sixteenth- or seventeenth-century furniture. In addition to all this there was a forest of pictures (many by Victor Hugo), statuary, bas-reliefs, inscriptions, Gothic candelabra, curios, death's-heads.

Hauteville House (now a museum owned by the City of Paris) bears the full imprint of Victor Hugo's late romantic and theosophic spirit. The ground floor, for example, was decorated with a series of drawings by Hugo, very elaborately framed by himself, of birds and insects, each of which had its legend and meaning. Passing through the billiard room, one entered the "little salon" which gave on a rear garden overlooking the sea. Its central feature was a fireplace reaching to the ceiling, ornamented with woodcarvings of Saint Paul holding "The Book" and of a monk bearing the inscription: "The Heavens." Upstairs the large dining room, which also looked out on the sea, was a fantasy of colored statuettes, grotesques, porcelain animals, Sèvres and Dresden vases, Delft tiles, and old choir stalls remodeled into pieces of furniture or paneling by Hugo, who was himself a gifted wood turner and cabinet-maker. Its great hearth of faïence tiles was built in the shape of a gigantic "H." Everywhere the woodwork was carved with legends such as: "Life is an exile"; "Eat, walk, pray"; "To wake at six and retire at ten, makes a man live ten times ten." There was even an old painting here of a Madonna and Child, under which Hugo had inscribed the legend: *"Liberty Carrying the Infant People Who Will Grow Up."* Thus he *laicized* the Virgin Mary and made her the Mother Image of democracy! At the head of the dining table was placed a huge Gothic armchair, with a chain across its arms to prevent its being used, and a brass plate that read: "The absent are here!" It was "the armchair of the ancestors," Hugo said; it remained always unoccupied while the family ate.

The grand salon on the second floor was in late Venetian style and decorated in red, as at the Place Royale, in Paris, with ornate mirrors, gold-embroidered screens, and oriental draperies. Its *pièce de résistance* was a huge Venetian baldaquin (said to be the work of one of Veronese's pupils) supported by six sculptured African slaves, in lifelike color and almost lifesize, each holding a tall candelabrum. On the third floor, reached by an enclosed stairway of oak paneling, was the Oak Gallery, entirely carved and paneled by Victor Hugo, with the aid of an old Guernsey wood-worker, out of Flemish chests which they dismantled and reworked. On this floor were various bedchambers, the master bedroom having a monumental Gothic bed of dark carved oak and being called the Garibaldi Room. Victor Hugo, who greatly admired the Italian soldier of democracy, had once, after arranging for a visit, prepared a royal reception for him—but Garibaldi never came, and neither he nor Victor Hugo ever slept in the vast bed-chamber.

Indeed the master lived and worked almost exclusively on the topmost floor of the strange house, in a small glass-enclosed belvedere or "lookout" perched on the roof, an apartment austerely furnished and overlooking the port of Saint Peter, the whole archipelago of the Channel Islands, and a limitless expanse of sea and sky. It was the brightest, cleanest, least encumbered room in the house that the poet himself chose to work in, its light almost blinding after the theatrical gloom below. Facing to the East, toward France, was a tall pulpit, before which he always stood and wrote. This high room, where the poet wrote *Les Contemplations, La Légende des siècles, Les Misérables,* and also "Toilers of the Sea" and "The Man Who Laughs," has become a shrine. Here he also slept, upon a low hard bed that was recessed into the floor, had paper beside it for writing at all moments, and near it a heavy Spanish trunk of iron, in which his manuscripts were kept. It was a cold room, but he preferred it so. At daybreak a servant would bring him a basin of cold water; he would bathe quickly and spring to his work, seldom leaving off until the lunch hour. Victor Hugo awoke at dawn and wrote for four or five hours every day for over sixty years.

One more detail concerning the living arrangements at Guernsey: a few minutes' walk from the Hugo mansion, higher up on Hauteville Street, Mme. Drouet was established in a pleasant little cottage. Gradually the interior was furnished with pieces of furniture and objects of art brought from the last Paris home of Mme. Drouet, until it fully resembled that romantic and private bower. Hauteville Féerie, as Victor Hugo called it, had a terrace that overlooked not only the sea, but even his own high lookout. From her terrace, the white-haired Juliette, now somewhat stout, gout-ridden, and slow-moving, could spy the white figure of the poet undergoing his daily hydrotherapy in the morning. She could watch over his comings and goings, even knowing when he slept well, or when he worked late at night; and she could signal messages to him, or he to her.

But their love life was calmer, perhaps ended and now transformed into a deep, unchanging friendship, as one of the poet's posthumous fragments inscribed to Juliette (in *Toute la lyre*) hints:

> *When two hearts in love have grown old together. . . .*
> *Love purified, all passion spent, still keeps*
> *Its afterglow . . . and knows the peace of evening,*
> *Yet still remembering noon, still being love.*[1]

Victor Hugo now celebrated their growing old together in verses that had a classical harmony. He took pride, nowadays, chiefly in the "moral beauty" of Juliette Drouet.

2

France lived in an intellectual darkness—Louis Bonaparte showed no sign as the 1850's passed of flying before the verbal thunderbolts of Victor Hugo. The poet, therefore, reconstructed his life in Guernsey, his lonely island of exile, in more permanent fashion. He filled his house with a plethora of books, pictures, and art objects that peopled its solitude and spoke to his eye and his imagination. He surrounded himself with the members of his united family, and often with relatives, or friends and younger pupils, such as Auguste Vacquerie and Paul Meurice, who visited with him for long intervals and worked at Hauteville House. At least one of the small number of French refugees who lived in Guernsey, Hennet de Kessler, an aristocrat who had become a militant republican and exile in 1851, became a cherished companion and when he became ill and could earn nothing was invited bv Hugo to live at Hauteville House.

"A little work is dull—much work is exciting," Hugo would say. Driven by the unflagging will of the master, everybody around him worked. Mme. Hugo wrote an "official" biography of her hus-

---

[1] The poem entitled *L'Amour*, XLVII in *Toute la lyre*:

> *Quand deux coeurs, en s'aimant, ont doucement vieilli,*
> *O quel bonheur profond, intime, recueilli!*
> *Amour, hymen d'en haut, ô pur lien des âmes!*
> *Il garde ses rayons, même en perdant ses flammes.*
> *Ces deux coeurs qu'il a pris jadis n'en font plus qu'un,*
> *Il fait des souvenirs de leur passé commun*
> *L'impossibilité de vivre l'un sans l'autre;*
> *(Juliette, n'est-ce pas? cette vie est la nôtre!)*
> *Il a la paix du soir avec l'éclat du jour,*
> *Et devient l'amitié, tout en restant l'amour.*

band's life, though only up to the year 1841, partly from letters, partly from his dictation at mealtimes. It was published anonymously, in 1863, as "Victor Hugo Related by a Witness of his Life," an interesting document despite its errors and deliberate, prudent omissions. Charles Hugo wrote light novels and, with the aid of his sister Adèle, gathered the materials for a "Journal of the Days of Exile," including their conversations with the spirits. Auguste Vacquerie wrote plays and travel sketches of the Channel Islands. Adèle Hugo, a nervous, sad young woman, with large dark eyes, played the piano and composed music. François-Victor Hugo, the more scholarly and intellectual son, was launched, at his father's urging, upon a vast project of translating the plays of Shakespeare, a labor of ten years, completed by 1864, the year of Shakespeare's Tercentenary. In the winter, storms would go raging with unbelievable force through the Channel, between Guernsey and the Norman coast, while floods of rain beat against the windows—yet all Hauteville House throbbed with labor. His son François-Victor wrote to a friend: "If all our books are completed they will have to add a new wing to the National Library in Paris."

There were few distractions here; letters from friends, the daily newspapers from London and Paris, arriving a day or two late by packetboat, were big events. But in work one forgot, one buried oneself. And there was so much to be done, and so little time!

His working plans, his opinions and principles were fixed, scarcely ever altered in the thirty years that followed his "religious experience" of 1852–1855.

"Did he still *hate* the tyrant?" he asked himself. "No. He fought him, that was all. . . . The exile did not complain. He worked. He reconstructed his life and that of his family. And all was well. . . ."

Visitors from France and elsewhere, such as Alexandre Dumas and Jules Janin, came to Guernsey, attracted by the legends which grew up about the island asylum and the poet's fantastic mansion there. Dumas, during his visit, had insisted on seeing *Hauteville Féerie* also and paying homage to the aging muse who resided there. All these visitors testified to Hugo's extraordinary self-discipline and to his remarkably youthful vitality and energy, which almost exhausted his companions in exile and wore down his family. While they often suffered from ennui, he worked like a tireless and happy giant.

After his cold tub at dawn, he would eat four or five oranges including the skins, and, pacing up and down, begin to work. By eleven or twelve o'clock he would have written a hundred lines of poetry or twenty pages (two or three thousand words) of prose; for, on occasion, after 1856, he would turn from poetry to carry on with the immense prose novel that had long occupied him.

At this period, he was unmistakably driven along by a sustained exaltation. He had an imperious desire to fulfill his "mission," to impose his thought, his message, upon his century. All his work at Guernsey and Jersey had the quality of "inspiration," though he said always that this came to him (not infallibly) or was courted in regular hours of labor. The new poems he wrote between 1856 and 1859 were now all connected parts of a tremendous poetic project which he conceived as "legends" or "small epics" picturing the march of mankind through history—thus the primarily lyrical poet now strove to master the epic style. He worked incessantly at his "Legend of the Centuries," though there were times when the weakness of his eyes frightened him and he was forced to make long trips to see a specialist in London. At one time while working over this book he was afflicted with anthrax, suffering a malignant infection of his legs and such pain that he could not sleep. All night long his gentle friend, Hennet de Kessler, stayed by his bedside to minister to him. But soon he was up—in all his long life he experienced only one or two minor illnesses—and hard at work again.

His noon *déjeuner* was a long meal which he ate with a ravenous appetite, chopping and mixing all his food in a peculiar *mélange* that he liked, eating anything and everything, cracking nuts with his teeth or consuming crabs and lobsters in their shells. Then he would be off on his daily walks along the beach or in the interior country with his daughter Adèle, or Juliette, or other companions, with whom his conversation sometimes appeared a perpetual monologue as if he talked his poems and prose to himself.

Those who met him along the beach remembered always the vigor of his movement. His hair was iron gray and its lank, rebellious locks always fell down about his face. Usually he dressed in a black coat or vest, with gray trousers, a shirt with a low and comfortable collar, and a black, loosely knotted cravat that floated freely in the wind.

His manner seemed affected to the English—Robert Browning, his great Victorian contemporary, and Elizabeth Browning found him "too affable." But French acquaintances were aware of the formal quality of his manner, and thought him reserved. Those who gained his intimacy, like the young Paul Stapfer, a French instructor at a Guernsey school, found nothing commonplace in his conversation when they walked or held tête-à-têtes with him. He showed, then, much affectionate and personal warmth. He was full of his work and his ideas and his settled opinions. His memory astonished people up to the very end. It was only when there was company, an audience before him, that he was inclined to perorate and grow "theatrical."

"My husband loves this island," wrote Mme. Hugo, who did not love Guernsey, to Paul Meurice, in 1856. "His sea bathing is very good for him; he seems younger than ever, and in superb health, and produces beautiful works. . . . He has not forgotten France, but feels himself detached from the present generation. . . . Ah, you see, one may not live far away from one's country for five years with impunity." Mme. Hugo added that the grandeur of the "aureole" her husband now wore atoned, in the eyes of her daughter and herself, for the pain of exile. But both Hugo ladies pined for France, and Paris. Often Mme. Hugo sat alone in Hauteville House, for in the evening Victor Hugo always dined with Mme. Drouet, very often in the company of his two sons and his friends.

Mme. Hugo felt even older than she was, and in her later years always had a distracted air. Sometimes she even committed the unpardonable fault—which Juliette never did—of not listening to what her husband said. One night, at Guernsey, he was speaking in her presence to a group of friends of his theories and doctrines, and was launched upon a great flight of words. Suddenly he turned about, interrupting himself, glaring at the rocking chair where Mme. Hugo sat nodding and drowsing over her sewing, and cried in a high voice: "Adèle, are you asleep?" She awoke with a start, exclaiming: "How could it be possible for me to sleep, my great and good friend, when you speak?"

One autumn day, she told her cousin, Alfred Asseline, then a guest at Hauteville House, that he was not to dine with her that evening, because the other gentlemen of the house had arranged a little party at Mme. Drouet's. He insisted upon remaining. She said: "You will displease me. I insist on your going to Mme. Drouet's house. There are few distractions here. . . . They are counting on you. There you will have a good time, you will laugh."

Asseline drew up his chair and took the hand of his cousin; she was pale as marble, her eyes as if glazed. They plunged into long and tender reminiscences. At last she exclaimed: "Ah well, go now. You will make me weep."

3

Charles Hugo wrote in a letter of 1859:

My father has just read us an admirable "legend" called *Ratbert,* in the vein of *Les Burgraves,* but magnified and idealized. And this splendid piece is only one small portion of his work! Anyone who did that alone would be assured of immortality. . . . Unfortunately we must wait; my father has two or three large poems to finish, before he can give "The Little Epics" to the printer. However, the great man works without pause, even at night. And, as a sign of his present absorption and seriousness, he no longer reads the newspapers.

"The Legend of the Centuries" was to have been originally a series of simple narratives of myths and legends drawn from various periods of history which appealed to Hugo's imagination. But when he wrote these poems Hugo was under the "command" of the spirits. He was determined to make his series of "small epics" the vehicle for that optimistic faith he held in the triumph of humanity over the forces of evil, the triumph of the idea of progress, which the turning tables had recently confirmed for him. His legends were to be selected as illustrating certain moral traits at various periods in man's history and to be arranged according to a chronological order. As he said in the preface to the book, he proposed to treat "the human species as a great collective individual accomplishing from epoch to epoch a series of actions, regarded from two aspects: the historical and the legendary, the second no less true than the first." The poems, he said, would picture the changing human profile *"from the time of Eve, mother of men, to the Revolution, mother of peoples. . . ."* At the time he completed the work, he also wrote in his diary: "History, tradition, legend, fable is my inspiration; religion, philosophy, nature from man to the ass, the people, humanity seen in its epic sense, in its heroic aspects . . . man become his own spectator in an enlarging mirror—such would be this book if it were ever complete or completed."

In truth, the opening legend or poem drew its inspiration from Genesis; the concluding poem, in the later, much augmented edition, pictured a mighty ship of the air (a dirigible balloon) as the vessel of the future by which man navigated and conquered unknown space.[2]

Hugo's socialist neighbor in Jersey, Pierre Leroux, had often urged him to confine himself no longer to "mere art." "Be an artist *with a purpose!*" Leroux implored. The two men often quarreled. Hugo, referring to this conversation, wrote resentfully in his journal: "Those who say that I have written art for art's sake have been inept; none has done more than I for an art of society and humanity: I have always tended in that direction. . . ."

In the "Legend of the Centuries" he came to write what was primarily the epic of the nineteenth century's humanitarian and evolutionary faith. (French literature had known no epic poetry since the "Song of Roland.") His legendary tales not only were moral fables, but symbolized the successive stages in the ascending movement of humanity: man discovering himself, as it were, by love and pity, by suffering and knowledge. He intended this work to be as a large literary "cathedral," in process of building, which he was to complete and ornament later on with additional "small epics,"—as he did in the 1870's—until it reached its present dimensions of three volumes. Together with his posthumous prophetic poems ("God" and "The End of Satan") it was also intended to represent the whole of his mystical philosophy.

But taken at a simpler level, disregarding their occult and animistic symbols, the poems of the "Legend of the Centuries" held an exceptional interest for the general public. They were mainly dramatic narratives of Biblical, ancient, medieval, and even modern episodes, down to the battle of Waterloo; they were dramatically told, and written in the grand style achieved in the "lookout" at

[2] Like Leonardo da Vinci, Victor Hugo was fascinated by the prospect of future aerial navigation. Toward 1860 he was in close touch with the famous photographer and inventor, Nadar, even subscribing for funds to help build a balloon.

One day, walking with Emmanuel Arago, near the Observatory in Paris, he saw a balloon, gilded by the afternoon sun, slowly rising above the city. He exclaimed: "There is the egg that floats, while waiting for the bird to come; but the bird is within and will come forth." Arago cried out: "And on that day *Geo* will be called *Demos!*" Hugo and the scientist's son both associated the airship, as symbol, with the future liberation of mankind. Today, in the midst of the much hoped-for twentieth century, other and darker views are often entertained upon the same subject. But may not the difference be derived simply from an alteration in the "will to believe"? Both these great citizens of the nineteenth century had suffered long years of exile at the hands of a military dictator; and both saw the same vision of hope in the heavens at what was one of the most tragic hours in French history, for it was the time of the siege of Paris in 1870!

Guernsey. In the range of French literature this book holds today a position corresponding to that of Milton's "Paradise Lost," if we may imagine an unpuritanical Milton bringing the subject of his epic almost down to the present day.

To give readers who know no French even a fragmentary notion of its richness and variety of color and verbal sonority is well-nigh impossible. Hugo's vocabulary alone was the richest of any French writer's. The very opening poem, "Eve," reveals the artistic boldness and power of this work. Hugo begins with a vast word painting of the dawn of creation, the springtime of the world. Everything —birds, beasts, trees, mountains, and stones—stirs, speaks, or sings. The mood is reverent. Then, the first man and the first woman are described standing in the midst of this primordial world, the man thoughtful, the woman eager, proud. Soon all nature, heaven, and earth, indicated by precise images, begins to chant in celebration of these two beautiful creatures, a song of joy that rises and fills the universe. Why? What miracle is taking place? The last line tells us briefly, dramatically: "Eve felt her womb trembling." Human love and conception are presented as no original sin, no Fall from grace, but an event upon which all Nature smiles.

Other Biblical subjects are treated with no less freedom, and sometimes with a richness of symbolic and allegorical suggestion that is most intriguing, in the modern, Freudian sense. Thus, in "Boaz Asleep," the old man is shown sleeping in his tent. Boaz dreams suddenly that an oak tree has begun to grow out of his stomach and grown so high that it touches the heavens; a whole race of people stem from it; on high a god died. Boaz wondered much at this dream. He had not known that during the night, in her despair, the starving Ruth had crept into his tent and lay sleeping at his feet.

Then, from Biblical times, the poet passes quickly through Rome and Greece, and dwells at length upon the Middle Ages, with its ample Carlovingian folklore, which is treated far more saltily than Tennyson's "Idylls," and makes up the most memorable part of the work for Hugo's French readers; finally he comes to the legends of the Renaissance in Italy and Spain, and to the French Revolution and the Napoleonic era.

The work is a mixture of queer erudition, fantasies, memories, and visions, and contains not a few glaring historical errors. When the proofs of the "Legend" were being sent off to France, Paul Meurice, who often acted as Hugo's literary secretary, timidly asked him why he did not look up some of his facts in the Encyclopedia Larousse. The master simply shrugged his shoulders with impatience, looked scornful, and walked out of the room. As in Shakespeare's plays, there were many factual errors in the "Legend of the Centuries"; these have been indicated by Paul Berret, the contemporary French scholar who spent long years preparing a commentary upon the work. Yet Berret, who traced all the poet's borrowings and sources, ended by conceiving a deep respect for Hugo's knowledge and insight into history and mythology, though it was based often on the most casual reading. Lanson, on the other hand, who considered the work incomplete and contradictory, even as an allegory of the ascent of man to civilization, confesses that its sensuous beauty and sonority, as in the case of works of music, is stimulating even to readers of philosophic temper. No systematic thinker, Hugo nevertheless, by metaphor, imagery, and emotional power conveys "sentiments and tendencies," an awareness of evil and suffering, an attunement to Nature and the unknown, a passion for humanity and progress. This vast synthesis of ancient, medieval, and modern legend also contained many poems that held personal and timely allusions in allegorical form. One powerful "Legend," for example, was a portrait of a medieval tyrant of Norway, whose conscience harrowed him, who heard always the tocsin sounding from an invisible belfry calling his people to rebellion and vengeance. The symbolism here unmistakably suggested Louis Bonaparte, as did another poem in which that dictator was quite recognizably metamorphosed into the shape of a poor frog.

In its concluding passages, "The Legend of the Centuries" reaffirms Hugo's messianic faith in the coming of the Revolution, heir to Christianity, and a rule of "universal love," bringing man a step forward in his ascent toward realization of his divine nature. Here, like so many other nineteenth-century thinkers, Hugo sought to reconcile the Gospel of Christ with the utopian-socialist ideals he had embraced in his later years.

The new work was permitted publication in France, in September, 1859, and benefited from a quite elaborate campaign by its publishers. For a work of poetry its popular sale was unprecedented in France—so many, to be sure, purchased the book out of reverence for the martyrized national hero, that one hostile journalist observed that Victor Hugo used his exile as a "speculation." Conservative and Catholic comment showed irritation at the poet's growing impiousness. But the foremost literary figures of the time, from George Sand and Gautier to the young Gustave Flaubert, all recognized that the old poet's art had only grown mellower with time. Even Sainte-Beuve conceded of this book that "the art of Hugo was magnificent," while Flaubert exclaimed at a literary dinner in Paris, "Hugo is not a thinker, he is a pantheist, and has the sap of trees in his veins."

"Salad in one man's head," a contemporary caricature

The period in France was tinged with pessimism: some writers lived in a sort of "intellectual half servitude," it was said then, while others, like Baudelaire, ignored political reaction, and followed the cult of art for art's sake. Victor Hugo, on his far-off isle, was isolated from all these transient mental fashions. He seemed, as the Goncourts wrote in their journal (after noting the reception of his new book), both remote from his contemporaries, as if living in another age, and at the same time "far above them" in stature.

On settling in Guernsey, Victor Hugo had given the government authorities there his word that he would take no part in political demonstrations such as Jersey had witnessed in 1855. He kept his word and there were no unpleasant incidents. At first the good society of the smaller island, consisting of the legendary "sixty families" who had long ruled it, treated the poet with cold disapproval, as a violent democrat who maintained open relations with an aged mistress and who had been known to insult the Queen. This referred to an occasion at a concert when he had conspicuously remained seated while the orchestra played "God Save the Queen."

However, the average citizens of Guernsey showed him a great deal of consideration and even held him in some awe. They believed that he had been a candidate for the throne of France and might become one again. Toward 1860, the relations of England and France became strained, owing to Napoleon III's floundering intrusions in Italy and elsewhere. In the event of war, an attack was expected upon Guernsey. "They will want to carry off Mister Hugo," one of the lesser Guernsey officials was heard to say. And he added determinedly: "But it will not be easy!" To Blick, his barber, Victor Hugo (partly because of his amazingly tough beard) was always a hero.

"When Monsieur will be on the throne of France, will he not have himself shaved twice a day?" Blick asked him.

"Blick, I shall never be on the throne of France, and I will not be shaved twice a day," Victor Hugo answered firmly.

Soon the local notables, especially the bailiff of the island, Sir Stafford Carey (whose daughter greatly admired the poet's work), showed him many courtesies and even persuaded him to appear with his family at the Carey residence on state occasions. He was able to report to friends in France that he had the status of a resident and Peer, and, according to an ancient law, was obliged to send two hens each year to the Queen of England.

His attitude growing more detached, Victor Hugo now preferred to devote himself more exclusively to his writing as his principal *modus agendi,* and to participate in public political agitation against the dictatorship while standing at a farther remove, and solely through the power of the word. For was this not, after all, his special power, his supreme talent, which no other man of eloquence in his time rivaled? Far from slackening his political activities, he extended them now, in a rhetorical form, over a much wider field, intervening by means of open letters, pamphlets, or speeches, contests for civil liberties or in democratic uprisings, not only in France, but in many far-off parts of the world. And, far from being forgotten in his island retreat, his fame and influence over public opinion extended itself most remarkably.

He was now a citizen of the world, in constant communication with that great company of Europe's exiled democratic or revolutionary leaders who, from various foreign countries where it was discreetly permitted—such as England or Switzerland—toiled secretly and unremittingly to launch uprisings and unhorse the reigning despots of their respective fatherlands. Mazzini and Garibaldi for Italy, Kossuth for Hungary, Herzen for Russia, and various Polish, Irish, Greek, Swiss, Spanish, Portuguese, and even Mexican and Haitian leaders wrote to Hugo for a public statement, here a pamphlet, there an inscription, or even for contributions of money. Hugo's principal contribution was in the form of words, and often the most powerful and eloquent words.

Mazzini appealed to him in April, 1856, saying, "It is a long time since we have heard your voice. . . . A word for Italy! She leans, at this moment, on the side of the kings. Warn her, rally her!" Hugo replied, June 1, 1856, with an open letter that was published in English and Belgian newspapers, warning the Italians against being gulled by small concessions that were just now being offered them in place of the liberty and national unity they thirsted for. "No sleep, no truce!" he cried. "Agitate, agitate, agitate! Agitation today . . . insurrection tomorrow. Your work is at once destructive and civilizing. It cannot fail."

The Greek insurrectionists of Crete appealed to him, and he wrote a plea for their brave men who fought the Turks. In Ireland, the Fenians rose in rebellion, and were crushed, their leaders sentenced to be hung. Irish wives and mothers wrote to Victor Hugo, begging him to lift his voice before the Queen in a plea for pardon. He penned an earnest appeal, which he believed helped to bring the commutation of their sentence in certain cases. He sent an appeal to the Russians pleading with their soldiers not to shoot their Polish brothers. To the Mexicans he wrote eloquently in 1863 encouraging them to fight to the death under Juarez, against the invading army sent by Bonaparte to establish a foreign monarch over them. Later, when the Emperor Maximilian was captured, he wrote again to the Mexicans begging that they show mercy, now that they had conquered, and spare the life of the royal prisoner— but this was in vain. In short, Victor Hugo, as the most famous victim of injustice, made himself an advocate-general of oppressed humanity everywhere in the world.

It was because he felt that he must fight ceaselessly on behalf of a world-wide fraternity, excluding no race, color, or creed, that Victor Hugo, on December 2, 1859, from his island refuge, attempted to save the life of John Brown by sending forth a thrilling call, "To the United States of America," demanding that the leader of the slave uprising in Virginia be spared. *"None of us can be neutral,"* he said. He was impressed by the coincidence that John Brown was sentenced to be hanged on December 2, anniversary of Bonaparte's *coup d'état.* He was also filled with the thought of the Christ legend, and saw John Brown as a latter-day saint, whose martyrdom would breed disaster for the American union. He wrote:

At this very moment, in Washington's fatherland, in the Southern States—and this monstrous contradiction arouses the indignation of the pure and logical conscience of the North—a white man, a free man, John Brown, has tried to liberate these Negroes, these slaves. . . . This austere Puritan, filled with the spirit of the Gospels, sent forth a cry of freedom to these men, his brothers. The slaves, weakened by servitude, failed to respond, for slavery numbs the soul. Deserted, John Brown fought alone with a handful of men. . . . They were captured. This is what is known as the affair at Harper's Ferry. John Brown and four of his men . . . have been tried. What sort of trial were they given?

John Brown lay on a pallet with six unhealed wounds. . . . "Justice" was done in haste. . . . Forty minutes of deliberation and three death sentences pronounced. And this happened not in Turkey, but in America.

Such things cannot be done with impunity in the face of the civilized world. The universal conscience is an unblinking eye. . . . Europe is looking at America at this moment. . . .

Before such a catastrophe, the more one loves this republic, the more one venerates it, the more one admires it—the more one's heart falls. . . . However great the indignation of the generous Northern States, they are associated with the Southern States in this murder. All of us, whoever we may be, all of us whose common country is the symbol of democracy, feel ourselves injured and shamed by this sentence. . . .

And when we reflect that this nation is one of the glories of mankind . . . one of the organs of civilization, in certain respects having surpassed all Europe, that there shines on its brow the immense light of liberty, we affirm that John Brown will not die, for we recoil in horror at the thought that so great a crime may be committed by so great a people.

Politically the murder of John Brown would be a fatal error. It would introduce into the Union a latent fissure which would end by breaking it open. Brown's martyrdom may perhaps reinforce slavery in Virginia, but it is certain that it will shake the whole structure of American democracy. . . .

As for me, a mere atom, yet feeling in myself the conscience of humanity, I kneel, weeping before the great starry banner of the new world, and in deep, filial respect, supplicate the illustrious American republic to give heed to the universal moral law, save John Brown and pull down the menacing scaffold. . . .

Hauteville House, December 2, 1859

John Brown was granted a reprieve, to December 16. There were some reports that he would be spared. Then suddenly the news came that he had been hanged. Victor Hugo, on his island, on a day of gray winter storm, mourned. Then he took his brush and pen and painted a powerful sketch, of a hanged man against a ghastly sky, every line of whose body droops in the last agony of death. *Ecce,* he entitled it. The drawing was engraved by his wife's cousin, the young lithographer, Paul Chenay, and thousands of copies of it were sold, the proceeds of the sale being sent by Hugo to various charitable funds, including those to provide medical supplies for soldiers in the American Civil War.

After 1861, he followed closely the course of the great Civil War whose coming he had predicted, and on two or three occasions wrote to President Lincoln, expressing his fraternal feelings. The Great Emancipator, in 1865, sent the man of Guernsey a photograph of himself, inscribed: "To Victor Hugo, Abraham Lincoln."

Recovering from the gloom and disillusionment into which Europe's democrats were flung after the year 1848, men took heart from the resolute example of their paladins of liberty, many of whom lived as wretched exiles. Beyond all the borders, Poles and Russians, Italians and Hungarians organized, agitated, and conspired tirelessly. Mazzini wrote to Hugo: "In the epoch of degradation and corruption through which we are passing—there is only one thing that can save us, and that is action, action!" Garibaldi with his brigade of one thousand "Red Shirts" suddenly descended upon the shore of Sicily, and defeated a mercenary army twenty times greater than his own, arousing the entire world to frenzied admiration for the romantic courage of Italian democrats. Later the much idolized soldier-democrat showed himself politically feeble, but in 1860 the friends of liberty everywhere cheered him on, and raised funds for his movement. Even the

British government, for its own reasons, helped him discreetly.

At Jersey, whence Hugo had been expelled in 1855, a large meeting to raise funds for the Garibaldi movement was scheduled for June 18, 1860. Several leading citizens of Saint Helier, who had vainly opposed the expulsion of Hugo, now begged him to address the meeting on behalf of the Garibaldi fund, assuring him of the approval of the government. Victor Hugo came; he was welcomed at the dock by a large and enthusiastic crowd and a banquet was held in his honor, which was both a tribute and a triumphant vindication.

His speech that day, for a free Italy, was one of his best efforts. The way of democratic revolution, he asserted, was the way of God; truth and right were divine and could not long be suppressed. In a very powerful climax he laid stress upon the oneness, the fraternity, of suffering and oppression everywhere in the world, called forth by the sinister partnership in crime of all despots. Against this unity of the despots Hugo invoked a universal and concerted resistance by the common people of all lands.

Oh! let those who suffer be consoled, let the prisoners take hope again. . . .

Yes, hope drawn from the four winds of heaven! Let the mujiks, the fellahs, the proletarians, the pariahs, the Negro slaves, the white victims, let them all hope; their bonds are a single chain; these hold together; but *once one link is broken the whole system falls apart. Hence the solidarity of despotisms.* . . . But that is all doomed, I repeat. How beautiful is the force of events! superhuman deliverance! Liberty is a divine gulf which draws on the enemy; the irresistible is at the bottom of revolutions. Progress is only one of the phenomena of gravitation—who can arrest it? . . . Oh dictators, I defy you! I dare you to stop the falling stone, stop the torrent, the avalanche, stop Italy (if you can), stop the march of '89, stop the whole world propelled by God toward the light!

More than a hundred thousand copies of this speech for Garibaldi's movement were printed and circulated; translated into Italian it was recited everywhere by the patriots. Victor Hugo was thus becoming a world leader. "I do not miss Paris any longer," the Goncourt brothers heard him say, when they saw him during a brief visit to Brussels. "What is Paris?—the Rue de Rivoli, and I have seen enough of that." For now his voice resounded in many lands at once. A poem that he wrote during the 1860's is entitled suggestively: "The Voice of Guernsey."

JOHN BROWN

Wash Drawing by Victor Hugo

From France, where minds now suffocated in emptiness and silence, young men, such as the poet Gustave Rivet, addressed poems to him:

Here where men's heads are sadly bowed to earth . . .
Gladly we hearken to your ringing voice,
Admiring the sacred fury that exalts you,
Silently blessing the sword you take in hand,
To inflict chastisement! . . .

Exile for him came to be an apotheosis. One day a letter reached him addressed simply to "Victor Hugo, the Ocean." From many lands came written tributes, such as one from Arrigo Boito, an Italian follower, who vividly described the singular role Hugo now played:

Warsaw cries: "Help save us!" A voice comes from an island and replies to her.

Rome calls: "Deliverance!" A voice issues from an island in response.

Crete cries: "To arms!" The voice speaks from the island to hearten her.

This voice, terrible and grand and sweet, is the conscience of our century. No crime can be committed, but this voice condemns it. No great and noble action is taken somewhere, but this voice blesses it.

Fraud, cowardice and tyranny hold Germany, France and Russia in thrall; but the right has a stronger power on its side: *The Voice of Guernsey*. . . .

That voice is yours, Victor Hugo!

They have done much to silence it. . . . Yet it thunders on. The storm which might drown it but augments its breath, the sea but increases its force. . . .

4

On August 18, 1859, following celebrations of French military victories at Magenta and Solferino, the Emperor Napoleon III issued a declaration of amnesty for all political exiles who had been banished in consequence of their defense of the Republic in 1851. Victor Hugo, after more than seven years of wandering in foreign lands, was now free to return to France—a prospect which delighted his family. But, after a conference with a group of his fellow exiles at Guernsey, he issued a statement to the press of England and Belgium:

No one will suppose that I personally would take any notice of the thing called "amnesty." In view of present conditions in France, protest—absolute, inflexible, eternal protest—is my one duty. True to the engagement I have made with my own conscience, I shall share to the end the exile of Liberty. *When Liberty returns, I shall return!*

He was henceforth a self-willed exile. "The real greatness of exile begins now," he wrote to his son François-Victor. To George Sand he wrote also that he considered the amnesty decree of 1859 as "the crowning insolence of that wretched *arriviste.*" That the guilty one should pardon the innocent was inconceivable! Hugo had vowed in *Les Châtiments,* many years ago:

Et s'il ne reste qu'un, je serai celui-la!

If but one remained, it would be Hugo. For it was a war to the bitter end—either the fall of the dictatorship or the death of the exile, as he told himself in his diary. "I intend to remain free," he said. Whether because of the immense pride or the shining constancy of it, his action caught the eye of the world. But how could Victor Hugo have lived at the mercy of a dictator; in the stifling air of France he would have suffocated. He remained wedded to his exile.

But his wife, his daughter, his sons languished in Guernsey. There were no diversions but Victor Hugo, no conversations but with Victor Hugo. For the sons there were no girls in this provincial little community. For the daughter, who was now nearly thirty, there was no marriageable choice. Adèle Hugo sighed after a young English officer she had met in Guernsey, but, forbidden to see him by her father, she grew listless and moody, and sat upstairs in the salon playing the same piece of music over and over again all day, until her mother thought she would go mad.

Mme. Hugo mourned for Paris. She said:

"Our exile is a fact. We must endure it. This house is bought and furnished at great expense—too great. Well, we must live in it, or at any rate make it our principal home. But it is undeniable that we have acted as though Adèle did not exist!"

"I am doing my duty to God and to France!" her husband would reply. She answered: "It is true, this remote island is a perfect frame for your glory—but are we doing our duty by Adèle?" But the father would not hear of their returning.

At this period, the younger son, François-Victor, translator of Shakespeare, had as his mistress a young Polish actress whom he had met in Paris and saw only on occasional trips to the Continent nowadays. At moments he thought of marrying her. His father, who had his own ideas on such questions, counseled him to bring the girl to their island, live with her in austere poverty, educate, "purify" her, and if she endured all this, then marry her. The girl came—but after a few days fled, never stopping until she reached Warsaw, and François-Victor was left desolate. His brother Charles was even more restless, made frequent journeys to Belgium and, after 1859, to France, but, though he longed to live a life of his own, usually came back at the command of his father.

Behind the walls of fantastic Hauteville House a good deal of unhappiness accumulated. They quarreled, wept, and were reconciled. Victor Hugo insisted upon holding them all close to him, yet he himself was far away, absorbed in his mission, in the writings the spirits had "ordered." In winter it was worst of all. The rain fell in sheets, and at Hauteville Féerie even Juliette wept and prayed. Victor Hugo wrote to Janin:

A storm has been raging here for a month. My house night and day resounds like a reef at sea; in this uproar I sleep poorly; the howling of the abyss outside makes my dogs bark—I have dogs now. Do you know what I do when I cannot sleep? I work, I dream, I think of France . . . I write for my country and for myself.

For many long months—amid his many other activities—his main thought and labor, in the morning and at night, had gone to the vast novel he now resumed writing, which pictured the passage of a convict, Jean Valjean, who was yet a man of God, through the "Inferno" that was modern society. Hugo's diary reads:

Today, December 30, 1860, I returned to work on *Les Misérables*. From April 26 to May 12, I read the MS. over; from the 12 May to December 30 I spent seven months in meditation and penetrating the entire work with the light present within me, in order that there should be absolute unity between that which I wrote twelve years ago and that which I am going to write today.

All through 1861 he stood before his pulpit in the lookout and wrote. Almost two thirds of the book was written in that year.

Only when his eyes became inflamed, and he feared he might go blind, did he consent to leave Guernsey for a visit to doctors in London and a brief change of air, which they ordered. Then he returned to his task. "I beg of God," he wrote to Paul Meurice in February, 1861, feeling himself again worn and ill, "that He permit me to finish what I have begun."

CHAPTER XVIII

Les Misérables

French of the French, and lord of human tears!
—Tennyson

At the end of march, 1861, Victor Hugo arrived in Brussels, accompanied by Mme. Drouet and his two sons—Mme. Hugo was gone on a long visit to Paris. Now real crowds followed him about, and reporters for Belgian, English, and even French newspapers tried to interview him, though he secluded himself a great deal. In some way the world knew that the illustrious exile had completed or almost completed an immense novel, the work of long years of his life, and knew even its title: *Les Misérables*. Harassed by questions as to the nature of the novel, Hugo, who was not averse to publicity, said to one of the journalists: "Dante once made a Hell out of poetry, I shall write of the Hell that is the real life of our age." Then having spoken these words, which were widely reported, he quit Brussels for a country retreat, unknown to the public, near by.

He stayed mainly at a small inn in the little hamlet of Mont Saint-Jean, which was on the site of the Battle of Waterloo. He had completed the writing of his novel, save for the section that described the Battle of Waterloo, which by a somewhat arbitrary literary device he introduced almost in the center of his work. He regarded Waterloo, and rightly, as the turning point in recent world history, and was resolved to have a huge word painting of this battle as one of the prominent—though digressive—features of his "universal" novel.

For several months he brooded over Waterloo, and wrote his

description on the scene or during quiet visits to the Royal Library of Belgium at Brussels, where he completed his research. Then in September he slipped out of Brussels and returned to Guernsey, where for eight months more he worked at the revision of the entire novel. Numerous publishers bid against each other for the right to issue the long-awaited book. Rumors of the fantastic price paid for it, reports that it would be suppressed in France, and denials of these reports aroused international curiosity. At last, on April 3, 1862, the first two books of *Les Misérables* were put on sale by Lacroix of Brussels and Paris (aided by a supporting syndicate of publishers) in nine different European capitals. The advance payment to the author had been fixed at the unheard-of sum of 300,000 francs ($60,000). But the profits realized by the publishers far exceeded this sum; in Paris the bookstores were besieged by crowds who in a week or so carried off all available copies of the first installment of four small French volumes. Then six weeks later came the second installment of three volumes, and on June 30, 1862, the final group of three volumes were bought up thirstily by those who had begun the novel in April. Much the same scenes were witnessed in London, Leipzig, Amsterdam, and other centers. Ultimately *Les Misérables* (mainly in popular editions) sold approximately 7,000,000 copies by the end of the nineteenth century, and became the book by which Victor Hugo, the poet, has been known in the four corners of the earth, as a novelist. From generation to generation, since 1862, it has never ceased to be read widely and included in all lists of the ten, twenty, or one hundred "world's greatest books."

The word *misérable* may mean both "wretch" and "wretched" in the sense of the poor. "The Wretchedly Poor" might be a literal translation, though the easily understandable French title has always been retained in English. The title truly conveys the intention of the book, which was that of a *social* novel—characteristic or dominant feature of nineteenth-century prose literature.

In this novel Victor Hugo's guiding interest, like that of his contemporary, Dickens, was social and humanitarian. In 1828, when Charles Dickens was a boy of sixteen, Hugo had already visited Paris prisons and written pityingly of the "Last Day of a Condemned Man." Six years later, he repeated this theme with variations in *Claude Gueux,* which some thought, perhaps wrongly, Dickens imitated in "Oliver Twist." But, though he did not read his contemporaries widely, Hugo undoubtedly learned something from the brilliant successes of Charles Dickens in the 1840's, a translation of at least one of whose novels he read appreciatively. In 1848, when Dickens came to call on Victor Hugo at the Place Royale in Paris, the poet received him with great marks of sympathy, and the young English novelist reported that he had greatly enjoyed his visit and admired the French master. They had certain points of resemblance, even in their domestic lives. The greatest study of a child waif, outside of Dickens's novels, was that of Gavroche, in *Les Misérables*.

Like Dickens, Hugo had known a brief but impressive taste of poverty in his youth, and never forgot it. In France, the greatest popular successes in the novel during the 1840's were not Balzac's but the unsocial, purely entertaining romances of Dumas, especially "The Count of Monte-Cristo" (1841–1845) in twelve volumes. The current taste then, as now, favored long novels; but, aside from this, Dumas's novels were plainly inspired by Hugo's success in the historical romance, *Notre-Dame de Paris*. It was not unlike Hugo that he should resolve—after having been checked in the theater—to exceed Dumas, or Eugène Sue, or for that matter Balzac, in his own field. But he desired that his own novel should be, in great degree, a social tract. About a year after abandoning the theater, in 1845, he began to work on the novel he first called *Les Misères*—he had signed a contract as long ago as 1832 to produce a novel in two volumes on this theme.

Though he was a rich Peer and a royal favorite, he made studies of penology, upon which subject he gave one speech in the Luxembourg; he persisted in his interest in the victims of poverty and society's injustice. In the august Chamber of Peers he rose one day in 1845 and remarked that he desired to represent no political party, but "the camp of the convicts." No one understood him then, because none knew that he was absorbed in the case of the convict Jean Valjean, whose story was based upon that of a real man. For two years he worked regularly upon the novel, completing all of its first two parts, most of the third, and outlining the fourth —when the revolution of February, 1848, interrupted him.

Looking backward, we perceive that Hugo had some cause to resent those who misunderstood his motives in the 1840's, who thought he pursued but vain ambition and self-indulgence or was insincere in his professions of humanitarianism—when at that period, for two years, he gave his mornings and nights to the tragic case of the released convict, Jean Valjean, to the story of the fall of the poor working woman Fantine and her foundling-child, Cosette, and to the study of an armed, popular insurrection in Paris, which was to form the dramatic core of *Les Misérables*.

The years of strife under the Second Republic caused him to halt halfway through his novel and try to help the popular cause by his active leadership, by his voice, rather than by his pen. But finally, in the days of exile, twelve years later, he returned to the novel. The air of permanence that Louis Bonaparte's regime assumed in 1860—after the decree of amnesty to the exiles—had something to do with this decision. Now, by dint of so much experience and suffering, Victor Hugo was a man of much finer stamp than in 1848. He reworked the first half of his novel, introducing everywhere a much deeper sense of compassion. He had had his religious ecstasy, and in 1860 inserted a whole new section, that of the interview between the saintly Bishop Myriel and the dying Jacobin in the first part: here the old revolutionist makes his profession of faith in an impersonal God, in the French Revolution, in the utility of its Terror, and in a predestined human progress, while refusing the last rites offered him by the bishop. But the bishop, the same one who was to succeed in "winning over" the soul of Jean Valjean from evil, ends by kneeling before the dying Jacobin and asking for *his* "benediction."[1]

Much of the substance of the book is based upon documentation. Hugo, as long ago as 1829, through a friend of his, came upon the story of the saintly bishop in Provence who, by the earnestness of his Christianity, succeeded in winning over the dangerous ex-convict sheltered in his house. Valjean's subsequent good fortune in business bears, of course, a superficial resemblance to the career of Monte-Cristo. For the description of the great convent in Paris, Hugo drew upon the memories of Juliette Drouet; on the Paris street fighting in 1832, and even the death of a little street gamin, like Gavroche, at one barricade, he had exact information. Other materials he drew from his own memory, especially the portrait of Marius, the student, who represents the author himself, as a young Royalist converted to democracy, and joining the popular revolution.

At Guernsey, Victor Hugo extended the scope of his novel twice

---

[1] This section, Volume I, Book I, Chapter X, has often been omitted in the most common, abridged English translations. It incorporates Hugo's religious ideas, as of his later years.

over, to the present 2,800 pages, working in a sustained transport over the second and more mystical half of the book. Very often he wrote up to twenty manuscript pages each day, or some 3,000 words. He worked in a very high state of tension which he was able to produce almost by self-hypnosis, and actually rewrote only to a moderate extent. There were numerous and long digressions—one commentator counts almost a third, 900 pages—but the quantity of concentrated writing giving effects of titanic power, or of sustained pathos, or of horror and terror, or prolonged suspense, or of large-scale description and crowd movements, is almost incredible in its extent, and explains the close grip *Les Misérables* has always had upon its readers.

2

The action of the book is set in the quarter century between 1807 and 1833. Its main thread, pulling all others together, is the life story of the released convict, Jean Valjean, and the successive steps of his passage through a modern purgatory. Within his varied experiences is exemplified what Hugo asserted in his preface to be the "threefold problem of the century": the degradation of man into proletarian, the decline-and-fall of woman through hunger, the destruction of children in a social Outer Darkness. In short his story and that of the characters grouped about him illustrate the misery created by man himself, by wrong penal laws, and by other evil laws and customs that make for social damnation.

Jean Valjean's adventures, which are very exciting in themselves, being often directed by the author's decided taste for melodrama, show his struggle against the ostracism of his fellow men, and his long flight from police persecution at various times and in various forms. His struggle with his own conscience (after a brief relapse into crime) is, however, a very searching and original piece of analysis, for its time. It is truly a "tempest within a skull," as Hugo says. Then, having found his soul, Jean Valjean's life becomes mainly one of penance and good works. He becomes (under an assumed name) a successful manufacturer, a work-giver, a mayor who befriends the poor of a whole large community. Then (in the second book) Fantine, the Paris workingwoman, comes to work for him and enters his life; but she is at her last extremities.

The downfall of Fantine, deserted by her lover and left with an illegitimate child, occupies most of the second book, and is done with sustained effects of extreme *realism* which even now require a fairly strong stomach in the reader. (Realism and romanticism were but two sides of the same medal; the "naturalistic" school of Zola certainly stemmed from Hugo and was also inherently romantic.) Indeed the description of Fantine's strayings and sufferings are well-nigh "sadistic." When Fantine dies, Valjean, realizing that she has been the victim of her fellows, determines to care for her child, Cosette, whom he tries to rescue from a baby farm. But he is obstructed by the exposure of his identity, thanks to Javert, one of the early police detectives of nineteenth-century fiction. The devoted Javert is but a cruel symbol of social oppression itself. Although the millionaire ex-convict might have escaped, he chooses to offer himself up to sentence—on learning that another man bearing a physical resemblance to him has been wrongly apprehended.

Committed to the galleys again, he escapes once more, thanks to his Herculean strength; for he is convinced that he has a mission to perform as a free man. He regains the money he has hidden away, seeks out the little Cosette, daughter of Fantine, and, after paying for her release from her cruel guardian, retires to live with her in Paris, under another pseudonym. He is now much altered in appearance, his hair all white. For an interval he is happy, engaged in charitable activities and in bringing up his ward, thanks to whom he discovers a long-denied paternal passion in himself, very beautifully portrayed here. But Javert discovers him again— the whole book is inherently a long "chase." This time Jean Valjean, only by the most miraculous exertions and melodramatic coincidences, escapes from his nemesis by dropping into the great tranquil convent of Picpus, and into a new disguise as a gardener, his adopted daughter being educated by the nuns. At this point occurs a digression of 116 pages, long even for Hugo, a remarkable essay in itself on the convent as an institution, upon the Christian church as a whole, and on the persistence of the medieval in modern times.

The third book is once more a vast digression, the Battle of Waterloo. (It has provided a classic work of description for French textbooks ever since.) After the battle is over, a wounded officer, who greatly resembles General Léopold Hugo, is rescued. He, as a former Revolutionist and Bonapartist, is forced into retirement during the Restoration. But the story concerns his son thereafter, Marius de Pontmercy, who is reared by Royalist relatives to hate his father and everything pertaining to the Republic and Napoleon.

Marius is a law student whose young friends in Paris are busy plotting an insurrection to overthrow the monarchy, but Marius ignores them, is indifferent to their doctrines, until he falls in love. He falls in love with the former foundling Cosette whom he sees, by chance, in the Luxembourg Gardens with her guardian, the disguised Jean Valjean. By falling in love he comes into conflict with his terribly strong-willed old grandfather, who both adores him and oppresses him (like Hugo's own mother). Marius now learns that his own father is dying; he reaches his home too late, but discovers at last the true nobility of his father, and thereafter, as if with a sense of guilt, sets up a shrine to him in his heart. At this period he rebels, runs away from his home, lives with fellow students, through whom he is drawn into the revolutionary movement of 1832, showing himself now an ardent republican and a hero.[2]

The long and sentimental idyl of Marius and Cosette is rudely interrupted by the explosion of a street insurrection. The people are discontented at the turn of affairs which has brought Louis-Philippe to the throne; they also suffer from hard times. In their uprising, they are led by heroic and idealistic young intellectuals of middle-class origin, including Marius. This provides occasion for the large epopee of the Rue Saint-Denis, the story of two days' insurrection, in which the Christian pacifist Jean Valjean, with the unremitting bloodhound Javert still on his trail, is involved. Hugo also introduces here the subsidiary story of little Gavroche, the Paris street urchin, who serves as a very colorful soldier and martyr of the insurrection. Gavroche, with his slang, his street songs, and his precocious Parisian wit, is Hugo's happiest character invention in this book. Here also, the crowd scenes of Paris and its common people in action make up a magnificent canvas; this, and the poet's lyric passages of prose in honor of Paris, which he named *La Ville Lumière* (the City of Light), did much to make him, in his time, the idol of the masses.

In the "Epopee of the Rue Saint-Denis," Hugo also writes his profession of faith in popular revolution. He "glorifies" the continued revolution that carries on the work of 1793 at recurring cycles. The revolution, he says in effect, is the law of God; it is "resurrection"; it incorporates violence and evils within itself, yet only in this way can man march toward his distant Canaan.

[2] In his notes for *Les Misérables*, the author remarks: "I must have Marius's joining in the revolution coincide with the time when he falls in love."

The later Hugo thus becomes, like the historian, Michelet, an apologist for Robespierre, and Marat, and the Great Tradition of 1793.

At the final hour of the "Epopee of the Rue Saint-Denis," he shows the young leader of the insurgents, Enjolras ("ideal revolutionary"), addressing his grimy, powder-stained band of rebels, and exhorting them to stand fast unto death. The human species, he declares, is but seeking to accomplish the laws of its being, to establish harmony between the soul of man and nature. "My friends, the hour we have reached, in which I speak to you, is somber; but that is the terrible price we must pay for the future. A revolution is a toll. Oh, I say the human species will be saved, uplifted, and consoled! We affirm it upon this barricade! Whence comes this cry of love if not out of the heart of sacrifice? O my brothers, this is the great meeting place of those who think and those who suffer . . . this barricade is a mound of ideas and sorrows. Misery meets the ideal; the day embraces the night and declares: I shall die with thee and thou wilt be reborn with me."

But the uprising is put down with great loss of life. Marius, badly wounded, is saved by Jean Valjean (who out of paternal jealousy had formerly tried to prevent his marriage with Cosette), and is carried by the gigantic ex-convict through the dark, slimy, labyrinthine sewers of Paris to final safety. Here is not only a most dramatic narrative of "escape," but a remarkable piece of allegory or symbolism strongly suggesting Grecian mythology and other types of "race-memories."[3]

[3]Despite the enormous length of *Les Misérables* it carries from beginning to end the excitement of a "serial-novel." Hugo's style has a deep, sustained breath, yet is also vigorous and nervous and not without a continual play of wit and poetic fancy (at some times a little labored, but at others most brilliant).

Hugo can be extravagantly sentimental, but sentiment with him is often enough quite genuine. He can write a hundred pages upon the *paternal* love affair between Jean Valjean and the little foundling child, Cosette—a subject that modern fashion would prohibit and that certainly never occurs in the terse novels of a Hemingway or an Aldous Huxley. But has prose fiction gained in stature by abandoning the simple human themes that a Hugo or a Tolstoy favored?

In representing emotion and in his intellectual approach Hugo is simple and direct, compared with modern talents, and ignores the moral "complexities" now much favored. Here, as in other examples of his art, the sin of disproportionateness is heavy.

But on the other hand one is strongly impressed by the richness of his intuitive or symbolic qualities. As a romantic, following his passions and obsessions, and striving always for effects of spontaneity, he touches everywhere upon the themes that concern our *subconscious* thinking; all his work, poetry and prose,

In the end Jean Valjean wins a final release from the Nemesis who has been pursuing him across two thousand pages; his Cosette marries Marius, but the old man dies. Because Hugo himself wrote as a changed man when he resumed work on the last two books of *Les Misérables,* Jean Valjean appears much more a mystic or a magus than at the beginning—his death scene is pictured with a veritably religious terror.

No summary or critical *aperçu* can convey the wealth of incident, or the cumulative power, the panoramic and encyclopedic picture of an age and a nation that this long work holds. Hugo wrote at a time when it was still permissible to idealize one's subjects. As the English novelist George Meredith said when the book appeared, it was "conceived in pure black or white"; yet in the same breath Meredith acknowledged that it had the "blood and bones" of great drama, and was "the masterwork of fiction in this century." It was certainly a seminal book. Despite its romantic method of organization and its simplified and weak character-portraiture—only the minor characters, like Gavroche, are profoundly drawn—it had the effect of advancing the tendency toward social realism in the novel. Later followers, like Zola, avoided leaning upon the device of coincidence; they made their work terser, and learned also to avoid Hugo's lengthy digressions. But none exceeded him in effects of sustained emotional power through the written word; none suffused his work with so much passion and so much pity. "Lord of human tears," Tennyson called Hugo in the sonnet he addressed to him.

"Through this book alone, you have advanced the revolution by ten years," one reader wrote Hugo from benighted France. Dealing as it did with events of thirty years before, the book was tolerated by the Imperial censorship. But some have held that the wide circulation of *Les Misérables* helped to pierce the political gloom in France. In 1863 local elections in Paris showed that the whole city was still anti-Bonaparte. In the *Corps Législatif* a courageous

is exceedingly rich in suggestions for the modern psychoanalyst. One suspects that part of his great appeal to the readers of his time was because he always stirred deeply the chords of their subconscious thought relating to conflicts between father and son, or between brothers, or love between father and daughter, or the impulse to rebellion against the Image of Authority—the themes which constantly recur in what are called his most "excessively romantic" writings, but now, to modern psychiatry, appear far from extravagant.

The later portions of *Les Misérables,* written after an interruption of twelve years, are predominantly allegorical. In his next novels, "Toilers of the Sea" and "The Man Who Laughs," Hugo becomes almost exclusively a symbolist.

but very limited and merely vocal opposition now showed itself, led by Ollivier, Jules Favre, and Jules Simon. Meanwhile the new generation of writers, such as Zola, and the younger men of politics, such as Gambetta, nourished themselves upon Hugo's books. It became fashionable to make fun of the Empire, direct criticism being still prohibited. Some of the democratic leaders who worked quietly again in France wrote to Hugo urging him to return and take advantage of his immense popularity to aid the gathering struggle to overthrow the dictatorship. Hugo refused to terminate his self-imposed exile, but maintained closer touch with advanced elements in France, and met a few of them at a large public banquet tendered him in Brussels on September 16, 1862, by his publisher.[4]

The "banquet for *Les Misérables*" was attended by a distinguished international gathering of writers, scientists, and statesmen from England, Germany, Italy, and Spain, though with only three or four well-known French figures among them. One of these, Eugène Pelletan, an opposition member of the existing "parliament," commented bitterly on the fear that most Frenchmen still showed to be seen or associated with Victor Hugo. Many persons in Paris had spoken of attending the Brussels dinner, but at the last moment had become suddenly "indisposed." Nevertheless, when one speaker after another had offered a toast or speech in honor of

[4] Following the banquet at Brussels in honor of *Les Misérables,* Sainte-Beuve, the old friend and traitor, now a devotee of the Bonaparte family circle, wrote to the Princess Matilde on November 12, 1862, sending her a full report of this gathering, and likening it to the conclaves of the exiled Bourbons at Coblentz in the days of Napoleon I.

"Well," he warned her, "our youth reads these things . . . and grows enflamed, believing all those big words implicitly . . . Are these men not our invaders, our returning *émigrés* of tomorrow? That which seems ridiculous today is quite otherwise tomorrow." The agitation of a Hugo he termed "menacing." A little later, in 1863, Sainte-Beuve told the Goncourt brothers that Hugo "had snatched the greatest popularity of our time under the nose of the very government that exiled him. His books go everywhere: the women, the common people, all read him. Editions go out of print between eight in the morning and noon . . ."

It was true that a furious literary and theological controversy raged in France over *Les Misérables.* Orthodox Catholics assailed the book because of its portrait of the saintly bishop as a kind of heretic within the Church. But many persons of deeply religious temper, including also many devout Catholics, strongly admired the novel.

At the same time many political conservatives attacked Hugo bitterly for laying all human evil to "society" and so working to undermine its very foundations, as they held. Their argument was that a great writer should never have permitted himself to say such things!

the poet, all the thousand diners rose in a prolonged ovation. Victor Hugo tried to speak, but the ovation continued for long minutes. Hugo stood waiting. Usually rigid or impassive in public, he at last bowed his head and, unashamed, let the tears stream down his cheeks.

His speech that evening was on behalf of freedom of the press. But soon he turned to discuss recent events in Italy, where a short time before events had taken a dark turn for the cause of national unity and democracy. Napoleon III, after intervening on the side of the patriots and engaging the Austrian armies in battle, suddenly decamped. The King of Sardinia went down to defeat, Garibaldi was made prisoner, and the Pope was still lef. temporal ruler of the Papal States in central Italy. Hugo believed that the shameful about-face of the French government and the subsequent disaster were to be attributed not only to the dishonest character of M. Bonaparte, which he had so often and pitilessly exposed, but to the pressure of the Catholic party in France, behind which stood the Papacy. To his mind recent Catholic intervention in politics was answerable for Italy's being plunged again into disorder and civil war. He now gave vent to an explosion of anger at the Church of Rome. He recalled that the late Gregory XVI had strongly opposed granting freedom to the press, which he characterized as the Beast of the Apocalypse in a famous encyclical that ran: *Gula ignea, caligo, impetus, imanis, cum strepitu horrendo.* This Hugo translated as meaning, "Mouth of fire, smoke, fearful speed, tremendous noise. . . . Yes! It is a locomotive rushing by—the press, immense and holy locomotive of progress!" And where was it going? It was passing through a *tunnel,* and he continued:

The tunnel is long, obscure and terrible. For we may well say that humanity is still underground, so much does matter envelop and crush, so much do superstitions, prejudices and tyrannies weigh upon it like a thick vault, so much darkness surrounds us! Alas, ever since man's beginnings history has always been subterranean. . . . But in the nineteenth century, since the French Revolution, there has been hope and certainty. Before us, a point of light appears. It grows, it grows from moment to moment, the future, fulfillment, the end of our miseries, the dawn of joy! . . . Courage to the holy locomotive! courage to thought, knowledge, to the press, to you, o minds! The hour approaches when humanity, delivered from the dark tunnel of six thousand years, suddenly brought face to face with the sunlight of the ideal, will make its sublime escape into the dazzling sunlight! . . .

At this rhetorical climax the audience rose again in long and violent applause. They cheered wildly for old *Père* Hugo because he showed himself unvanquished, steadfast as ever in his faith, but also because, now in 1862, they had more reason for hope. The despots of Europe were growing weaker; Bonaparte had no allies and was now at odds with powerful Britain; his treachery in Italy had shamed all decent men.

When the applause died down, Victor Hugo, in conclusion, turned to address the little contingent of French writers who had dared to show themselves at his side. "My friends from France, and my other friends," he said, "eleven years ago you saw what was practically a young man leave France, and now you see him again—an old man." He pointed to his head. In truth he had changed greatly in appearance. By the time he finished *Les Misérables* his hair had turned entirely white. Moreover, for the first time, he wore a beard, well trimmed, but also pure white. His appearance, with the deep lines of his face concealed, was now much gentler than before. He was a white-haired old man with a mild, faraway look.

"My hair has changed, but not my heart," he continued. "I feel that among you I breathe my native air. You bring back something of France, recalling the light and the smile of the fatherland. . . ."

3

"*Les Misérables* has helped me to restore my fortunes a little," Victor Hugo wrote to his publisher, Lacroix. This was a pleasant understatement, for, reckoning in French gold francs, he was easily a millionaire. Among his many talents, Victor Hugo had a *flair* for business. His letters of instruction to his new publishers, Lacroix & Cie., are extremely shrewd. He had literally cudgeled them into paying him the largest advance payment in the history of French letters against all royalties accruing over a contract period of twelve years. Within a few months Lacroix covered all his huge expenses, and thereafter, through lower-priced editions, gathered millions of francs in profits, none of which Hugo shared for eleven more years; thus it appeared as if Lacroix had overreached Hugo. But Lacroix threw himself into a frenzy of speculation and was soon utterly ruined. Hugo recovered the rights to his book in 1874 and by issuing cheap editions earned ultimately more than he had received in 1862.

Returning to Guernsey, after the fall of 1862, he now felt free to indulge himself more extensively in charitable activities. He himself nowadays felt most comfortable in an old coat and a worn felt hat; but as the author of a famous social study of human poverty and misery he received letters from all parts of the world, in a profusion that would have embarrassed a Rothschild, letters appealing for pecuniary aid, and felt obliged to gratify some of their writers, at least in a small degree. When a sergeant in a regiment quartered in Besançon (Hugo's birthplace) wrote him that he had lost two hundred francs belonging to the regimental treasury and would be cashiered unless he could replace it quickly, the poet, after a prudent investigation, sent him the money. At Guernsey, Hugo gave careful instructions to the cook, "Marie-Sixty,"—so-called in honor of her previous service with some of the Sixty Families of Guernsey—to give alms to all beggars who came to his door:

Bread is to be given to all who ask for it, but not money—without first consulting me. (Money is easily turned into gin.) All requests for work are to be referred to me at once, and employment is to be given, by preference, to old people, wherever possible: no distinctions to be made between Catholics and Protestants. . . . Soup and meat every week to the old rascal who describes himself as a Catholic, when he calls on Abbé Lemenant, and as a socialist, when he comes here. He is eighty years of age. . . .

With similar punctiliousness he instructed Paul Meurice, who often acted as his business agent in Paris, to pay fifteen francs a month to an old woman who, as a dresser at one of the theaters, had befriended Juliette Drouet.

He also supported numerous Hugo and Foucher relatives; he aided some of the French exiles, and supported at least one of them, Hennet de Kessler, entirely, when he fell ill. This Kessler was a devoted confidant who knew his Hugo well. Once in the excitement of an argument with the master concerning the value of a certain passage in *Les Misérables* he burst out: "But my dear master, you simply *do not understand* that book!" Yet Hugo loved him none the less.

On occasions, however, he gave alms for his own amusement. One day some years later, an old soldier he met in the street saluted him and said: "Great Citizen, Father of Democracy, I am a socialist and a faithful reader of all your books. . . . If you

VICTOR HUGO IN 1879
After a Painting by J. L. Bonnat

don't give me fifteen francs I shall be put in irons!" Hugo liked the cut of the man's jib, gave him the money, and told a companion of his of the incident. The friend said at once that he had been accosted by the same soldier, who had called him "honorable citizen," declared that he was a person of *conservative* principles, and accepted five francs from him. Hugo laughed: "You only gave him five francs. . . . But if he had called you 'Great Citizen' and 'Father of Democracy' as he did me—surely you would have parted with fifteen!"

A more serious venture in 1862 was the launching of the Poor Children's Dinners, held in the billiard room at Hauteville House every other Sunday evening. These probably developed out of Mme. Hugo's charity bazaars; soon between forty and fifty children came regularly, and, according to the ritual established, Victor Hugo, Mme. Hugo, and their sons waited on them. The Poor Children's Dinners (by a coincidence, beginning in March, 1862, at the time *Les Misérables* was about to be published) were talked of in the press as far away as London, and aroused much sympathy for the exiled poet. Some sermons were preached, and a movement among English philanthropists in London was begun in emulation of Victor Hugo's charities.

But his son Charles, a strong radical, vigorously disapproved of such individual distributions as being not in accord with true socialist doctrine. Charles had once had a dispute with his father because only beer was served with meals at Hauteville House instead of the French table wine he longed for. His father had berated him. In a fit of anger, Charles Hugo had rushed from the dining room into the garden outside, while the raging father rushed after him. After a time the other guests saw the father and son walking back and forth, arm in arm, or embracing each other warmly. But from that day on wine was served.

Now, again, Charles Hugo risked his father's wrath by arguing that the Poor Children's Dinners were ostentatious and ill-directed efforts, and that the ritual that always accompanied them, a form of grace Victor Hugo required, written by himself according to his own theosophical cult, was highly unnecessary. The father answered: "The true socialist must combine practice and theory. . . . While we wait here on earth let us share a little of our bread with the ragged children. I do not mind if it be said that Victor Hugo's door is open twice as wide to the poor as to the rich. . . ,

And I believe in God, and try to persuade others, large and small, to believe in Him as I do."

But, following sharp differences, Charles Hugo left Guernsey in 1863 for Brussels, and remained there permanently.

Victor Hugo fascinated his children, strove to hold them close to him, to possess them body and soul, and ended by exhausting them. But, as one visitor remarked, the members of his family were all persons of inferior will to his own. "They were amiable, devoted satellites, who found their source of life in him, while he, independent of them, obeyed a 'higher law.' " On one day, when Charles Hugo arrived late for an appointment, his father scolded him violently before a company of guests, and Charles stood the punishment silently. They seemed to bear his control willingly, even *proudly*. François-Victor, in a letter written to a friend, in 1859, discussing his father's recent work, apologized several times for his "excessive eulogies," adding: "You will smile at my enthusiasm, undoubtedly. . . . But it is not my fault if I am the son of Victor Hugo! . . ."

But now Charles was gone for good, and was keenly missed. His father wrote him in 1864: "Come back! We miss you here, I most of all, as you well know. Come back, come back. Come back, not only by train and in the flesh; but in heart and mind; end the material separation which . . . has kept us so long apart. . . . Come back! I can think and speak of nothing but your return!" Charles came back, but only for a short visit. In 1865, he was married to Mlle. Alice La Haene, the ward of the distinguished French parliamentarian, Jules Simon, and made his residence in Brussels. Thereafter, Mme. Hugo divided her time between Brussels, Paris, and Guernsey, where she stayed least of all. For three years, between 1864 and 1867, she was almost continually absent from Hauteville House.

The poor lady, now in her sixties, had become much effaced, so far as Victor Hugo's life was actually concerned. When she was away for long periods, or stayed with her son, Juliette Drouet would preside over Hauteville House, which she managed much more effectively than her rival. When visitors came, however, Mme. Drouet would hold herself discreetly apart, closeted in her room.

Very gentle and indulgent by nature, Mme. Hugo gradually became fully reconciled to her husband's unofficial but permanent consort. Some related that she was broken-hearted at the other woman's ascendancy, but in later years her ideas on such questions had become greatly broadened with experience. Once, after a visit in Paris with a worthy old couple who had long lived in irregular union, she wrote: "I can conceive that there may be a barrier between irregular and regular households, because in general un-married women come of a class that is unrestrained. . . . But, in appearance, Mme. A—— is as legitimate as possible. Her devotion and her love of her household legitimize her. . . . The poor woman suffers under an absurd law and is necessarily a concubine. Her virtues beat against the impossible. My ethics are not those of society. . . ."

These were brave sentiments for the time. But Mme. Drouet by her dignified reserve and her retired life had ended even by soften-ing the hearts of Guernsey respectables. As Chateaubriand once said of another famous *liaison:* "By dint of holding on for a long time, illegitimacies become legitimized."

At Christmas, in 1864, before leaving for the Continent, Mme. Hugo wrote Juliette a very gracious note inviting her to attend the family ceremony at Hauteville House. But Juliette replied that this kind thought was happiness enough for her. They became, after their fashion, good friends. One day, at an intimate dinner to Hugo in Brussels, they even appeared together, Mme. Hugo sitting on one side of the old poet, and Mme. Drouet on the other. The guests saw Mme. Hugo, with a sad smile, lift her wine glass to Mme. Drouet, saying: "I drink to you, madame!" In 1868, when she was very ill, Mme. Hugo gave Juliette a beautiful old cameo brooch which her Victor had given her fifty years ago, during their engagement.

Her increasing separation from her husband was not caused by the ascendancy of Juliette, but by another and far more tragic development.

Her daughter, the pensive Adèle, toward 1863, showed notice-able signs of melancholia. There she would be again, upstairs in the vast drawing room, alone, playing the same melody over and over, all day long!

That year Mme. Hugo completed as much as she wished to write of the anonymous biography of her husband's "great and sorely tried life," as written by a Witness. Before the book appeared, she wrote to Emile de Girardin, the old family friend, asking him, without the knowledge of her husband, for a loan of five hundred francs upon the security of the new book. Her purpose, she said, was to obtain funds permitting her to give her daughter a change of scene by going with her to England, which her husband firmly opposed.

Since 1862, the dark-eyed, glossy-haired Adèle had been wildly in love with a young English officer named Pinson—as her mother knew. She had met him during a journey to Brighton. Returning, she said to her father: "I am thirty, I want to be married." He answered in anger: "Since you have referred to your majority, and think of disposing of your person without consulting me, you are a bad daughter, and there is nothing for me to do but retire and reflect on what I should do." He left the house, and set off walking at a terrific pace along the beach.

With the help of an English governess who accompanied her on trips to Brighton when her father was absent she met her lover secretly. In the summer of 1863, learning that he was about to leave for service in Canada, she determined to fly with him. Suddenly she disappeared. From London word came from her, after a time, that she was married and had sailed with her husband for Nova Scotia. Her father, in unforgiving mood, sat at Hauteville House, raging at her. Mme. Hugo, who had been away in France at the time, on learning of her daughter's elopement, came back to Guernsey early in July, 1863, and strove to soften his wrath. "Has not her young life been sacrificed to political needs?" she said to him in one of the notes she would often write him from her room nowadays. "Was not Adèle made unhappy because of our chosen place of exile? Had she no right to a life of her own? You are generous, indulgent, and *will understand* what I mean. These dear children have their irresistible impulses. . . . We have not long to live; while we live, let us show them kindness and sympathy."

Victor Hugo, who had so often followed his own irresistible impulse, the "higher law of his genius," after a time understood his wife's point about Adèle's right to live her own life. He agreed to give his approval to the marriage. An announcement of the wedding was therefore placed in the local newspapers and stated that the young couple had left in October for Nova Scotia. But the announcement by the Hugos provoked an immediate denial by the family of the young English officer that any marriage, or even any engagement, had taken place. Victor Hugo and his wife and sons, who also heard further news from Adèle, were flung into the depths of despair. At last, after many anxious months, a letter came to them from Adèle, saying that Pinson had deserted her,

that she was ill and needed money. Late in 1864, her brother
François-Victor set off for Nova Scotia and brought her back. She
was terribly changed, and sadder than ever. She insisted, upon
being questioned, that she had been properly married and ever
afterward insisted upon that. But, when they pressed her, her
mind wandered, she assumed a fixed stare, and soon they perceived
with silent horror that she had become demented. After a time
she was quietly sent to an asylum in France, where she lingered
in an obscurity of life and reason for more than fifty years, until
her death in 1915. (For a long time nothing was known of her
story, until a vengeful and somewhat libelous book, by Paul
Chenay, a nephew of Mme. Hugo, was published in 1890.)

After 1865 Victor Hugo had no more daughters.

Only one son, François-Victor, remained with him. He was a
sensitive and gentle young man, of delicate features, decorated
by the thin side-whiskers then in fashion. His translations of all
of Shakespeare's thirty-seven plays, which his father had inspired
him to undertake, was completed and issued in 1864, in time for
the great Shakespeare tercentenary festival in England and France.
In honor of the festival for the English poet, and also to stimulate
interest in his son's translation, Victor Hugo now issued his study,
"William Shakespeare," but its occult tone greatly mystified the
public and it had no popular success.

During part of his long labor over the translations, the son
had been aided by a charming young girl, Miss Emily de Putron,
descendant of an old island family, who was a literary scholar and
Shakespeare enthusiast. They became engaged in 1864. But at the
beginning of January, 1865, a few days before their marriage was
to take place, Miss de Putron, who had always been of very
delicate health, having sick lungs, suffered a severe attack of
phthisis, and swiftly sank to her death.

Tragedy followed tragedy in the vast, high, thickly draped
rooms of Hauteville House. Once more the poet, still very erect,
assumed his role as pastor and magus to his own little tribe, and
before a new grave in a churchyard of Saint-Peter's, delivered one
of those funeral sermons that he wrote so feelingly and in which
he embodied his cherished doctrine of the transubstantiation of
human souls.

Where was the beautiful young girl gone, he asked? To the
shadows? No. It was those who remained who lived in shadows.

She remained in the light, hovering above and very near them, "a tender spectator." He addressed his stricken son:

You who have seen a beloved being vanish into the tomb, do not believe that she has left you. She is always there, closer to you than ever. . . . She, whom you mourn, has disappeared, but she is not gone. We no longer see her sweet face; we feel her wings. The dead are invisible; but they are not absent from us.

The magus then declared gravely that his own life had been most persecuted, and tragic, as if he labored under a curse. In his exile—as in the desert one meets with an oasis—he had encountered this fresh and innocent being who had consoled him by her mere existence.

. . . I bless her in the name of all whom she loved, I bless her for her beauty, her youth, her gentleness, in life and death. I bless thee, young girl in thy white robe of the sepulcher, in thy bier which has been covered with flowers and which God will fill with stars.

But François-Victor was inconsolable and left for Paris. Mme. Hugo, prostrated by the two tragedies, and now almost blind, accompanied him, saying as she left her husband: "My life is over. There is nothing left for me to live for any longer."

Her widowed sister-in-law, Mme. Chenay, came to Guernsey to act as housekeeper, while Juliette Drouet actually directed the management of the establishment. Victor Hugo stayed on in tragic Hauteville House, now almost empty. As before, he went on working, writing, meditating.

4

In the wake of *Les Misérables* and the world-wide audience it had won—American soldiers read it in the bivouacs of the Civil War, Protestant pastors in Holland read parts of it into their Sunday sermons—Victor Hugo resolved to devote himself to the novel, and between 1865 and 1868 completed two sizable ones, *Les Travailleurs de la mer* ("The Toilers of the Sea") and *L'Homme qui rit* ("The Man Who Laughs").

Like his obscure American contemporary, Herman Melville, Hugo was fascinated by the life of seafaring men which he saw all around him at Guernsey. In 1865, in preparation for "The Toilers of the Sea," he took copious notes on the construction of ships and navigation, and on the folklore and oceanography of the Channel Islands region. To his poet's ear the mariner's technical vocabulary seemed entrancing, and he filled his novel with a wealth of nautical lingo.

The narrative content here is extremely simple, even slight, compared with that of *Les Misérables:* the central theme is the story of Gilliat, the young fisherman, who makes a heroic, single-handed effort to salvage a small steamboat, wrecked by conspirators upon a wild reef on the coast of Guernsey and abandoned there high and dry. By salvaging the heavy engine of the ship Gilliat will save a beloved neighbor, its owner, from ruin, and in reward hopes to marry his handsome daughter. *Les Misérables,* originally intended as a social tract on the lives of the poor and downtrodden, had wound up as a work of dramatized symbolism. So in "Toilers of the Sea" Hugo's method becomes predominantly that of symbolism rather than of realistic narration. The digressions (*hors d'oeuvres* they were called then by critics) overbalance the narrative in length, and include the most powerful and significant passages of the book. As in a work of music or painting, one may interpret such a mysterious episode as the struggle of Gilliat with the devilfish as one pleases. To read it is like having a supernatural experience. The ship itself, which the determined workingman salvages intact, after a titanic struggle, is one of the first modern steamboats to be used in the Channel Islands—the superstitious natives had hated it—and all the power of the sea, in a long-sustained paroxysm of rage, seems bent upon destroying it. The steamboat is plainly a symbol. Yet when the storm, which is presented in one of Hugo's epic descriptions, is finally over, Gilliat is still there holding his steamboat safe, and Nature herself finally smiles upon this obscure hero, who in his struggle has demonstrated a superhuman will. "In every great heart is written the word: *Perseverando!*" Hugo comments. (Much the same moral, he implies thus, might be read in a great thinker's or writer's lonely struggle with himself and with the elements.) The engine of the steamboat *Durande* is finally brought back to port amid the applause of the people assembled there. The ship sails proudly again upon its errands. But Gilliat is not fated to win the shipowner's daughter, for she prefers another to him, and the humble giant dies in the sea.

In this book, which encompasses only two volumes in French, there is even more digression, proportionately, than in *Les Misérables,* yet also much of Hugo's most eloquent and lyrical prose in honor of man's courage and labor. Although he was bent upon delivering social messages, the late romantic in Hugo turned toward symbolism as a method, the method later used by Maurice Maeterlinck in the drama. Today, once more, modern novelists, surfeited with a rigorous realism, are disposed, like Hugo, to experiment with the symbolist method.

"The Toilers of the Sea" was published with considerable success in 1866—though arousing no such excited controversy as followed *Les Misérables*. Literary taste by now favored realism in the novel, which was exemplified already by Flaubert's *Madame Bovary,* and the early work of the Goncourt brothers, Daudet, and Zola. Yet Hugo's next novel, "The Man Who Laughs," was a historical romance, set in early eighteenth-century England, its characters picturesque gipsies, castaways of the sea, and members of the British aristocracy. This novel too had pronounced symbolic and even occult qualities.

Gwyneplaine, kidnapped English boy of noble blood, reared by the gipsies, is a noble being who bears engraved upon his face the hideous, frozen grin the gipsy surgeons gave him in early childhood, so that he might be of value to them as a clown juggler. Is it a symbol of the terrible and secret deformity that goes side by side with man's courage and virtue? And Dea, also, the beautiful waif found by the gipsies after a shipwreck, is, significantly, blind. She grows up to love Gwyneplaine, the juggler, with a pure and self-denying passion, in blessed ignorance of his deformity. (At the time when Hugo wrote this, Mme. Hugo, the muse of his happy youth, was going blind.) There is elaborate intrigue and startling adventure in this romance; but it is often interrupted by some remarkable digressions upon English life and customs and social evils in Queen Anne's time. These are usually pronounced by Ursus, a philosophical old gipsy, who carries a lamp with him day and night, and is accompanied always by a kindly wolf whom he has named Homo. But one of these eighteenth-century discourses—a socialist speech!—is pronounced in the House of Lords, and by Gwyneplaine, as his maiden speech, for the deformed juggler has finally turned out to be the long-lost descendant of a great Peer. Gwyneplaine, giving an oration on behalf of the wretched proletarians of England, evokes only a storm of mocking laughter (much like Hugo, in the Paris Assembly). Gwyneplaine also suffers great distress of soul owing to a torrid liaison with a dissolute young countess who pursues him because of his very deformity. At last he escapes from her and from the laughter of his enemies, to return to Dea, the blind girl, whom he finds dying. In his despair he kills himself.

Once more, there is an alternation of extravagant incident, picaresque adventure, symbolism, lyrical descriptions, declamation, social pamphleteering. Because the time of Queen Anne was not too far off, Hugo was accused of grave errors in recording English life and history, not only by the English critics, but by the French, when his book appeared, in 1869. English commentators ridiculed Hugo's documentation and declared that the romance cried out "its impossible absurdities." The names of the characters themselves were un-English, aside from their general unreality. The poet, Swinburne, on the other hand, praised the book, as he praised everything Hugo wrote; and Mrs. Duclaux, herself an English poetess of talent, has pointed out that Hugo, with his foreign eye, had a very significant vision of English life and customs: he had perceived "the medley of the medieval with the modern that characterizes England." "The Man Who Laughs" was intended as a study of the aristocratic bias present in English life and the failure of an elite, ruling in disregard of the wretched lower class, to make a nation. However, the virtues and purple patches of this romance, to a public that now strongly favored realism, did not offset its defects of disproportion, its overemphatic horrors and fantasies, and "The Man Who Laughs" became one of the least successful of Hugo's novels. For a good many years thereafter he ceased to write novels, his attention shifting to other things. Besides, the caldron of European politics had begun to boil furiously again.

In 1867, Mme. Hugo was in Paris again. At almost sixty-five she was but the ruined shell of the "Muse of the romantic *cénacle.*" By a coincidence, during the Paris Exposition that year, the Imperial government relaxed its prohibition of Hugo's plays, and *Hernani* was revived with great fanfares. Although it was thought that the invalid condition of Mme. Hugo would not permit her to attend the play's reopening, she insisted upon going, saying: "I would go, even if it caused me to lose my eyes!" No demonstrations occurred this time; the play was received with a solemn enthusiasm. Proudly she wrote her husband how young men had come to her and declared: "Victor Hugo is our religion!"

More and more her thoughts turned to the past. She sent for Sainte-Beuve, and with some reluctance he came. He too was but a desiccated relic of his old self, and another year or so was to bring him to his grave. Recently, when he had come to lecture at the Sorbonne, the students insulted him and broke up the session, owing to his professed attachment to the much hated Imperial regime.

But Mme. Hugo's business now was to bring about a reconciliation, such as she had long prayed for, between him and her husband. But they had moved in opposite ways for too many years and nothing came of her efforts. "You would have been touched at the warmth with which he spoke of you," Mme. Hugo wrote to her husband. It was true that the attitude of the twisted little man toward his old friend and master was ambivalent, compounded of unstinted admiration and lingering hatred.

In the summer of 1868, Mme. Hugo was in Brussels again, staying with her son Charles and his wife. Lately Victor Hugo, under doctors' orders, had formed the habit of making summer vacation trips from his island to the Continent, together with Mme. Drouet. In late August he arrived in Brussels and there was a family reunion. Mme. Hugo had been feeling stronger again, and on August 24, 1868, she went for a carriage ride with her husband and her son, full of laughter and chatter as they rode about the city. The next day she was down with a heart attack, and on the following day grew weaker still. Husband and son watched over her constantly, doctors were called from Paris, but she lapsed into a coma for two days, and died early in the morning of August 27, in Victor Hugo's arms.

There had been so many tragedies lately for Victor Hugo; the words of grief he uttered now were very simple and reverent as he mourned for the sweetheart of half a century ago.

Mme. Hugo had expressed the wish that she be buried beside her daughter Léopoldine, at Villequier, scene of the boating tragedy of 1843. The coffin was placed on the Paris night train, and was accompanied by Charles Hugo, Auguste Vacquerie, Paul Meurice, and other family friends—for the poet by his own iron-bound pledge could not enter France. Slowly the train puffed off into the darkness, while Victor Hugo, who descended at the border village of Quiévran, on the Belgian side, stood on the platform, alone, with bowed head, watching the remains of his Adèle being carried back to France.

5

When would he see the fatherland again?

"Before long, I think," he wrote to a friend in 1867, "the barriers of honor that I imposed upon myself . . . will fall."

The very revival of Hugo's old plays, after 1867—even the popular *Ruy Blas* with all its democratic allegory was soon put on the boards again—was a symptom of deep change. With unexpected generosity, the dictator now announced a new phase: the "Liberal Empire." By 1868, surveillance of elections was largely removed, the press laws were greatly relaxed, France breathed more freely and with more animation. But all this liberalism arose from sheer, desperate need.

There comes a time in the tide of each dictator's fortunes—and no despotic regime seemed more overbearing, more *total* than that of M. Bonaparte—when everything goes steadily downward, when wrongs and errors accumulate, and the directing hands that were once so firm tremble uncertainly for familiar points of support, yet find them no more. Hitherto, the strong dike had been the tacit will of the people to bear, to submit to the existing rule, and reject other alternatives. But slowly and unseen, the mounting tide eats into the bulwarks. There is an interval when the piling is corroded, and yet few know or guess its weakness, for outwardly the defenses seem as massive as ever before—a moment that is like a vacuum in history, an ominous pause before the inundation.

The indecent maneuvers of Bonaparte in Italy, between 1859 and 1862, had been followed by his tragic blunders in Mexico, after 1863. Not only was Britain alienated, but the highly armed United States, by direct threat, helped to frustrate his New World excursion in 1867. Meanwhile the quick victory of Prussia (led by Prince Bismarck) over Austria, at Sadowa, revealed France's isolation and danger in Europe. At home, the Emperor saw the very combinations that had once strengthened his hands, the Catholics and the peasants and the middle classes, fall into discord. Even the Catholic party joined with the republican minority in attacks upon the Imperial Government; sweeping election reverses followed the slightest lifting of police controls; and Louis Bonaparte was an ill and tired man. The Liberal republican group grew bolder, led by eloquent orators such as Gambetta, who inflamed the crowds and challenged a weakening regime to persecute them. When the press gag was removed, new opposition newspapers sprang into being. Victor Hugo's sons Charles and François-Victor returned to Paris in 1867, and with Vacquerie and Meurice, and the brilliant young journalists, Henri Rochefort and Edouard Lockroy, revived the old "Hugo newspaper," now called *Le Rappel* (the "Recall" or "Call to Arms"). Its main weapon now was humor and satire, chiefly provided by the fiery Rochefort, and soon its circulation mounted to 100,000 copies a day. Emile Ollivier, the Liberal leader, in 1868 was called to head the Ministry, as a concession to popular pressure—though this proved to be but a maneuver (too cunning by far) to create at first a Liberal façade, behind which renewed repression was to be devised, and new appeals for a popular plebiscite arranged in preparation for the great war that all men now expected. Early in 1870, Ollivier was summarily dismissed, and replaced by Bonaparte's old palace servant, Rouher (one of the "scoundrels" commemorated in Hugo's *Les Châtiments*). Soon his heavy hand struck at the opposition newspapers; including *Le Rappel,* which, on various pretexts, was barred from the streets, or stopped for days at a time, while Charles Hugo sat in prison again consoling himself with his father's heartening letters.

As the exiled leaders outside the border, especially Victor Hugo, divined the growing weakness of the Imperial regime, their agitation also was redoubled. Late in 1867, the ardent Garibaldi erupted again, landing with a raiding party at Mentana, on the soil of the Papal States, but he was defeated and taken prisoner by superior forces, partly consisting of French regular soldiers. On November 19, 1867, Victor Hugo wrote *Mentana,* a powerful polemic in verse, in the vein of his *Les Châtiments,* which called on everyone to oppose the Pope's temporal government and the French dictator who still aided it. Published as a small pamphlet, *Mentana* was widely read and extensively smuggled into France, where its circulation had been suppressed. To punish Hugo the current revival of *Ruy Blas* was halted, which the poet declared deprived him of fifty thousand francs in theater revenues—a blow that he expected but was ready to bear cheerfully if he could hasten by a little the departure of the detestable usurper.

In 1870, Victor Hugo wrote many "open letters" and manifestoes. He had seen something of history, and now heard voices and began to hope. On July 14, 1870, the French national holiday in honor of the taking of the Bastille, Victor Hugo presided over a curious little festival in the garden of Hauteville House, planting an oak tree which he dedicated to "the coming United States of Europe." To the assembled citizens he recited gravely a poem which prophesied the early deliverance of the French and other oppressed peoples. The reply came two days later, from the East, in the roar of Prussian and French cannon. "War is declared," his diary entry for July 16, 1870, reads. "It begins with France and Prussia." At first he busied himself only with humane efforts to help in the preparation of medicines and bandages for the wounded of *both* armies. He waited.

The attitude of the "Hugo group" so-called, as shown by editorial statements in *Le Rappel* a few weeks earlier (in July, 1870), was that the expected war with Prussia (in which France was placed by Bismarck in the position of the aggressor) was a tragic blunder. "May it be short, may it be the last," was the newspaper's wish. "We pray that it may be crowned not by the triumph of a Caesar, but by the apotheosis of humanity . . . a disappointment for despotism, vengeance for the Revolution!" These words, signed by François-Victor Hugo, resembled what his father was saying: that the war was not one "of liberty, or justice, but of *caprice*." In other words, France was divided, its democratic elements bitterly mistrustful, as the great war opened.

On August 7 and 8, the diary of Victor Hugo, waiting in Guernsey, shows his excitement at the "stunning news" of great disasters to the French armies at Wissembourg, and of preparations in Paris for a siege!

Under August 9, 1870, his diary reads: "Charles (visiting him then) and all my guests are leaving for Jersey where there is a telegraph. . . . I am going to pack up all my manuscripts in trunks, and put myself in readiness for all emergencies and for my duty." Very calmly the old poet wrote out instructions to literary executors, for the future publication of his remaining work—"in case I and my two sons are killed."

On August 13, 1870, he received a letter from Paul Meurice in Paris, advising that his presence would soon be needed in the capital. Two days later Victor Hugo left for Brussels, and waited there for further word, expected by a code telegram. "I want to return to Paris, openly, but simply, as a National Guard, with my two sons by my side. . . . I desire no share in power, but wish to share the dangers." Thus he wrote Meurice at the moment.

The reappearance of Victor Hugo in his "good town" of Paris could well have an electrifying effect, if it were timed with a revolutionary change in the country. A supreme battle loomed. He longed for "victory for France . . . overthrow for the Empire." What would it be, Jena, or Rossbach? August dragged to its gloomy end, and on September 1, 1870, he sent word to his faithful lieutenant, Meurice, "I am ready, but I do not want to go to Paris except in one case . . . *Paris calling the Revolution to its aid;* then I will come." The day after he wrote these lines, September 3, the Battle of Sedan began; the sickly Emperor yielded his sword, and on September 4—for events moved with terrible speed—the people of Paris rose, called a provisional government into being, and proclaimed the Republic.

On September 4, 1870, Hugo received a telegram from Meurice saying: *"Bring children with you at once."* It was the signal he awaited. At the consulate in Brussels he applied for a passport and, though declaring that he gave no allegiance to the Empire, was treated with courtesy. Mme. Drouet, Charles Hugo, and the young writer, Jules Claretie, accompanied him. Claretie later described the deep emotion with which the old poet ordered and paid for "a ticket to Paris!" At Tergnier, on the French side of the frontier, he descended and ate a hurried meal at the station restaurant, putting an unfinished crust of bread into his pocket, which he always preserved, "to commemorate the first breaking of bread in his native France," after nearly nineteen years of exile. For a few minutes also he stood, there, at the French side of the line, silent, with head bowed, his face covered with his hands.

CHAPTER XIX

Return of the Exile: "L'Année Terrible"

Victor Hugo returned to his own city of Paris at one of the darkest hours of its history. There had been a succession of military catastrophes. In the name of the provisional government a Committee of National Defense, headed by Léon Gambetta, Jules Favre, and Thiers, two Liberals and one Conservative, attempted to rule France and continue the war, though save for the young firebrand Gambetta the leaders seemed lukewarm about further resistance. France's second regular field army, under Marshal Bazaine, was bottled up in Metz; her remaining military forces were untrained and unready; the Prussians, virtually unopposed, methodically converged upon Paris.

But as Hugo stepped off the train at the Gare du Nord, on the morning of September 5, 1870, neither he nor those who came to welcome him thought of the future with fear. After nearly twenty years the moment he had awaited and prayed for had come. He was *vindicated;* he had triumphed. He thought only that France was at last free. The common people in whom he had placed his faith and whom he had unwearyingly summoned to action had once more shown themselves ready to "scale the walls of heaven." They had risen en masse and cast out their Caesar, Hugo's "personal devil." And now "their poet" *Père* Hugo, the bearded old man with shining face, was miraculously restored to them from his island of exile. It seemed that his very presence in this threatening hour lent a strength that could help them win through.

Before the station and in the adjacent streets thousands of peo-

ple joined spontaneously in a great democratic and fraternal celebration in his honor, one such as kings or dictators have seldom
known or cared to experience. The people unharnessed the horses
of his carriage and led him down avenues lined with a cheering,
singing multitude. *"Vive la République!"* and *"Vive Victor
Hugo!"* they shouted, for Hugo and Republic were identical.
Women threw flowers in his path. Workingmen rushed up to him
and said: "We only want to touch your hand." He thought afterward that he must have shaken hands with six thousand persons
that morning. Repeatedly he was forced to make speeches from
his carriage, or from café terraces at public squares. He said: "You
repay me in one hour for twenty years of exile." But only after
two hours, by pleading fatigue—for he was now in his sixty-ninth
year—did he win release and reach the safety of his friend
Meurice's home.

Long ago, as a young man, Hugo had ventured to define the
"function" of the poet as prophet and tribune for the people. But
even he had scarcely dreamed how fully this mission would be
realized in his own case. His long-prohibited pamphlets against
Bonaparte could now be read, and *Les Châtiments,* his "Castigations," were quickly given their first French edition, on October
20, 1870, and sold in unheard-of quantities, great bundles of them
being laid out in the open markets where (during the siege) people
traded or bartered for goods of all sorts. The aptness of Hugo's
warnings against the dictator in these challenging poems of 1852,
their prophecies of a debacle of blood and shame resembling the retreat from Moscow, this all seemed uncanny to French readers
after the Battle of Sedan in 1870. No less prophetic and timely
were the ringing verses that promised the resumption of the great
tradition of the French Revolution.

Les Châtiments, to the many who had only heard of the book,
seemed veritably a work of magic. While Victor Hugo became the
"moral leader" of the war of defense, his volume of satirical and
prophetic poetry became the "book of the siege." Patriotic con-
certs were held at large theaters, with famous actresses such as
Sarah Bernhardt reading its most dramatic passages, and the proceeds were devoted to the benefit of the soldiers. Victor Hugo
gave several readings himself to large theater crowds, and some
fourteen thousand francs he gathered in were used to order and
forge new cannons. The troops named one cannon *"Châtiment,"*
another "The Victor Hugo." Thus he could say that after having

bombarded Louis-Napoleon *Les Châtiments* were now bombarding the German invaders.

In those days of bright efflorescence Victor Hugo could have had any gift within the power of his people—they named a street of Paris and also one of the new balloons after him. It must be remembered that he was peculiarly the idol of the Paris population, for he had sung of their courage, dedicated magnificent pages to the humblest and poorest among them, and promised even these liberation. In wartime elections held in the Seine Department (the Paris district) for members of a new Assembly of Deputies, he received the second highest vote—Louis Blanc, the old friend of the unemployed and his old companion in arms, being first. Would he enter the Government? The returned leaders of the Left invited him to do so, but he refused, saying: "It is almost impossible to amalgamate me."

The Left statesmen, who knew Hugo's failings as well as his talents, refrained from urging him, and so he served mainly and very effectively as an unofficial head of a department of propaganda and morale, which, in those days, was usually an impromptu activity.

Four days after his return he rushed forth with a pamphlet entitled "A Letter to the Germans." It was a most curious document. Hugo's own associates on the Left, such as Henri Rochefort, felt that he treated the whole desperate war situation from a merely "poetic point of view." The times required that the defenders be imbued with hate, and Hugo's attitude toward the Germans was, in part, paternally affectionate. He argued that it was the Empire of Bonaparte that had declared war upon Prussia, while the Republic that now ruled France was innocent. He therefore invited the enemy to be reasonable and depart so that a fraternal peace might be established that would lead to the creation of a United States of Europe. Bismarck, Von Moltke, and company paid no heed to the old poet's elevating exhortations.

But if he was visionary—and some of his notions had proved more accurate than those of prosaic men—he had the virtues of his defects. He closed his pamphlet with some quite remarkable forecasts (which were one day fully borne out). The German people, he said, had "rendered a service to France" by helping to remove her despot, her Emperor. But let not the Germans take the same course as the French Empire, let them not become infatuated Imperialists, or they too would suffer from military despotism, making it necessary for the French people, in turn, to come and inflict upon them a great military defeat in order to destroy their Caesar. But, peaceful appeals failing, Hugo promised that the City of Light would know how to defend itself; it would turn itself into a volcano. "I, an old man, will be there to the end, unarmed." In this last remark, some acerb commentators have seen the suggestion of an appeal for mercy to himself. But Hugo had recently given a clue to his own fervently pacific principles, by his portrait of Jean Valjean, in *Les Misérables,* as a model of heroic nonviolence. Undoubtedly in his pamphlet he meant to call to mind the impassive courage and dignity of those ancient Roman magistrates who sat calmly in their curule chairs, awaiting the arrival of the barbaric Gauls outside the gates of Rome.

On September 17, 1870, the German armies were outside the gates of Paris, and Hugo issued a second pamphlet, "To the French People," calling for a mass rising, for a guerrilla struggle, for women and children to join the fight. This violent message was evidently justified, in the mind of the poet, by the German army's rejection of his first pacific appeals.

Many faint-hearted persons had been leaving Paris day by day, but two weeks after Hugo arrived, on September 19, the city was completely invested and all travel stopped. Victor Hugo, who had ample time to leave and might easily have been excused for doing so, in view of his advanced age, stayed for the duration with most of his two million fellow citizens.

Fortified Paris itself, and, within the walls, a sizable army that had escaped from Sedan, held the main German force at bay. The National Guard was also called up, and every able-bodied man between thirty and sixty was given arms. Victor Hugo's sons, both over forty, went into active service, while Charles Hugo's wife and two children were left in the care of the grandfather. Donning a kepi and a National Guard uniform, Victor Hugo paraded about Paris with the troops, or showed himself among them at the outer fortifications.

The French leaders hoped to hold on at Paris until large levies of new troops could be prepared south of the Loire River and, joining with regular forces, might come to the rescue. But the surrender of Bazaine's large army at Metz, on October 28, 1870, made the relief of Paris almost hopeless. Heavy siege artillery was dragged up by the Germans, and from three sides flaming shells crashed into the armed metropolis constantly. Two million men, women, and children grew hungry and cold as autumn came.

Hugo's journal of the siege is written with detachment:

October 8.—Feverish unrest in Paris. . . . The deep-toned Prussian cannon thunder continuously. They recommend unity to us. There has been no sugar in Paris for six days. The rationing of meat began today.

October 16.—There is no more butter. There is no more cheese. Very little milk is left, and eggs are nearly all gone.

Père Hugo was much occupied with the search for nourishing food because of his concern for his two grandchildren, Georges and Jeanne, who brought him great joy, and with whom he played happily every day. In his journal he relates tersely:

October 21.—We are eating horsemeat in every style. I saw the following in the window of a cookshop: *Saucisson chevaleresque* [equine sausage].

December 1.—We ate bear's-meat for· dinner. . . . It is freezing. The cannonade recommenced at daybreak.

December 3.—I told Schoelcher that I want to go out with my sons if the battery to which they belong is sent out for a sortie.

The sufferings of the Parisians increased day by day as winter approached. There was a moment when it occurred to Victor Hugo that simply by sacrificing his life he might gain world-wide sympathy for the cause of his tormented people. He broached this to his friends. But soldiers of the National Guard came to him with petitions urging him to "refrain from getting himself killed," since his life was necessary to the cause.

But, aside from this one fleeting whim for patriotic suicide, Hugo showed himself amazingly and consistently cheerful throughout the siege, more so than almost any other resident of the beleaguered city. He had already won a kind of deliverance; neither hunger, nor the chance of defeat, nor death could be worse than the long wait in the outer darkness, the protracted moral agony he had previously borne. In his old age, Paris saw a Hugo who was not only generally cheerful, but almost debonair.

Though living with the Meurices, he had one of the beautiful apartments of the Pavillon Rohan in the Tuileries Palace (which was thrown open for public use) placed at his disposal. Here he came every day and held court. All sorts of persons, from Ministers like Gambetta and Favre, to mere office-seekers, came to call on him. Foreign diplomats, such as Elihu Washburne, the American

Minister, consulted him upon plans for an armistice. The military leaders also came. "The generals are asking me for commands," he related; ". . . I reply that I am nobody."

Long-interrupted friendships were also renewed. A whole young literary generation, many members of which, like François Coppée and Catulle Mendès, were his professed disciples—for Hugo, as a craftsman, had always held the esteem of the most fastidious younger *littérateurs*—now came to pay him homage. Long secluded from men and cities, he tasted the pleasures of an intensely convivial social life in time of war. As a point of pride, and for morale's sake, intellectual and literary activities, parties, plays, went on as in peacetime among the Parisians of 1870–1871. The Goncourt brothers, calling with Gautier at the Pavillon Rohan, found the great man in his salon besieged by a host of visitors of all degrees, but prominent among them lovely ladies and actresses who quite "covered" him—this was a form of homage he could never refuse—while his stout, snowy-haired *inamorata,* Mme. Drouet, did the honors. The Goncourts' memoirs show him full of gaiety and verve, discoursing freely and uttering the most positive dicta upon everything from balloon navigation and the topography of the moon to the chances of the siege.

As a memento of the siege of Paris he wrote puns and comically rhymed couplets with which he often entertained his visitors, for it was fashionable to laugh at the suffering they all endured. Many of these light verses referred to the exotic animals from the zoo or strange fowl now sent to him as gifts for his table.

> *Mon dîner me tracasse, et même me harcèle,*
> *J'ai mangé du cheval! et je songe à la selle!*

His dinner had bothered him. For, having eaten of horseflesh, he dreamed of the "saddle" (and/or W. C.). Other verses are devoted to the joys of eating rat pie or elephant steak. Inviting his friend Théophile Gautier's lovely and gifted daughter Judith to dinner, he promised her "one of Pegasus's wings." To another lady the aged poet sang tenderly, bequeathing to her not his ashes, but out of his own rump

> *A beefsteak, luscious morsel fit for kings!*
> *Then will you know how tender I can be!*

During his "audiences" he would often jest even with sober official delegations. One day a committee for the relief of refugees from the province of Franche-Comté called on him for a contribution of money.

"Oh!" cried he, "I am not a native of Franche-Comté, I am a Lorrainer!"

A member of the committee quoted from his own poem referring to the place of his birth: "One day in Besançon. . . ." Besançon was the capital of Franche-Comté.

"Oh yes, perfectly true, I remember now. I was born in Besançon —but that was by chance, a mere accident!"

However, on a second visit to Hugo, Edmond de Goncourt found him in soberer vein. He stood erect before a small group of friends, very noble and benign, "like one of Michelangelo's prophets, with his thick white locks of hair falling, rebellious, about his face." In these dark hours he spoke always with a steadfast courage.

One chill dark evening in November, Mme. Edgar Quinet, walking with her husband on the Boulevard Montparnasse, as she recalls, almost collided with a passer-by, and by his voice recognized him as their old friend and fellow exile Victor Hugo.

"Who would have believed, a year ago, when we attended the International Peace Congress at Lausanne," she exclaimed, "that we would all be reunited in a beleaguered Paris?"

"Yes," replied Hugo, "but I should have been inconsolable if I had not been present during these great days." He then reminded the Quinets of one of his former predictions of a war to come, one that was to be greater and more horrible than anything yet seen. "But no, France is not lost," he declared. He continued to hope, even after the fall of Metz, that a breach might be made through the wall of 800,000 German troops now surrounding the capital. He hoped for France, even though secret treason and reaction showed itself among the ruling councils of the provisional government. "Europe will perhaps experience an epoch of Pan-Germanism," he said, "as we experienced twenty years of Empire—but a nation like France cannot go under!"

Mme. Quinet related that in taking leave of the "wise, brave, gentle old man" who was now Victor Hugo, she felt as if new strength had been given her to bear the trials of the terrible siege.

In these days the people of Paris showed their traditional high courage. Often their hopes hung upon some expected miracle. Hugo cheered them on, while Gambetta strove to inspire them with his torrential improvised orations and by his own physical daring, for he was a young spark of little more than thirty. Hugo relates:

October 7, 1870. This morning, while strolling up the Boulevard Clichy, I perceived a balloon at the end of a street leading to Montmartre. A small crowd surrounded it. . . . In the crowd it was whispered that Gambetta was going aloft. Sure enough I saw him in a group near the yellow balloon wearing a heavy overcoat and a sealskin cap. . . . It was half past ten. The weather was fine. . . . All at once the yellow balloon rose, with three men in it, one of whom was Gambetta. Beneath his balloon hung a long tricolor streamer. "Long live the Republic!" shouted the crowd.

Those were almost the first days of aerial navigation. The fiery Gambetta, to the astonishment of the world, landed successfully in Tours, and attempted to rally provincial armies for the relief of Paris. Hope would rise, and minor victories would be reported from the Loire front as "great news." But some persistently urged capitulation. Because of the uneasy fear of betrayal from within that spread among the militant workingmen of Paris, on October 31, 1870, a small uprising, led by the revolutionists Blanqui, Flourens, and Delescluze gripped the city for a day, but was put down on the next by regular soldiers, while Blanqui was arrested. Hugo had been invited by the would-be insurrectionists to participate in a proposed socialist government, but refused, and indeed now showed a marked desire to avoid public office.

At last, on January 29, 1871, when all the horses, dogs, and sparrows were eaten, after four months of heroic resistance, of bloody sorties and trench warfare, starved, disease-ridden Paris surrendered. Victor Hugo and his grandchildren could eat again, but he was most bitterly disappointed, for, with Gambetta, he had preached resistance to the bitter end, and pinned his hope on continuing the war from the provinces of France. The septuagenarian wirepuller Thiers, who had principally labored outside of Paris to rally support of foreign allies, had ended by exerting pressure for an early armistice with the Germans. Once more the wily, business-minded politico catapulted himself into the post of leadership. On February 8, 1871, elections were held for a National Assembly that was to negotiate terms of peace with the conquerors, and Victor Hugo was elected a Deputy by a tremendous popular vote. Together with other members of the Left republican and socialist bloc, and accompanied by his son Charles, he set off for Bordeaux, seat of the new Assembly, where he arrived on February 15, 1871. The men from Paris, "democratic head" of France's body politic, had sternly opposed surrender, and differed sharply with the majority of deputies from the provinces who had favored peace at any price. From the very start of the new Assembly sessions this division led to conflict with the Paris republicans, who formed a minority in opposition to the disguised monarchists and Conservatives from the country districts.

As Hugo and his colleagues left Paris, *Le Rappel* hinted, in an editorial, that under certain circumstances, rather than accept dishonorable terms of peace, the Paris delegates might come to an open break with the pro-Royalist majority and quit the Assembly at Bordeaux. Hugo's first impression, as he wrote to Meurice, was of a dark outlook for the Republic. "We are in the proportion of fifty against seven hundred; it is 1815 combined with 1851." Those were the years of extreme reaction in France.

Yet the common people in the great southern seaport, at the close of the first day's session, gave Hugo a tremendous ovation, fifty thousand persons filling the streets outside the Assembly hall and shouting, *"Vive la République! Vive Victor Hugo!"* During this scene, he relates, "the Conservative members of the Assembly filed out past me with furious looks, keeping their hats on, while all the other people around them waved their caps at me."

The irrepressible conflict between the two party groups over the Draconian peace terms offered by Prussia came swiftly to a head. The Left was for rejecting these terms; the Right was for submission—even though Alsace-Lorraine were lost. In this struggle, Hugo played a prominent but also a very singular part—for which he was afterward most bitterly assailed as being "unreasonable" or "fantastic" and "unpatriotic." But Hugo's peculiar contribution to public life was not destined to be that of the professional and practical politician. Of this sort, alas, and in the narrowest and meanest sense, the Third Republic was to have all too many! The *Père* Hugo was too old to change. He had been a splendid amateur in politics, and he remained in character, following his own inward lights until he could do no more, then passing from the stage. Yet in the perspective of time Hugo's "absurd" utterances appear like far-sighted and humane wisdom in comparison with those of the collaborationists of 1871. Of these men the leader was, of course, Thiers, that middle-class Machiavellian, who had survived so many regimes, and now, in the interests of property, was resolved both to end the war and to impose firmly conservative controls upon the newborn Republic. Behind the struggle over the treaty terms and all other issues there was always present nowadays a clear-cut class conflict—and in the distance, from turbulent Paris, the rumblings of social revolution could already be heard.

The Right moved roughshod over the minority, determined to sanction the so-called "Thiers-Bismarck Treaty." The leaders on the Left fought for delay, or threatened a mass resignation that would arouse the country. On March 1, 1871, Hugo took his turn among the notable statesmen of the Left, from Gambetta to Félix Pyat, in speaking against the peace terms:

If the deed of violence, which they call here a treaty, is really perpetrated, if this Carthaginian peace is concluded, then the repose of Europe will be lost forever! There will be henceforth in Europe two redoubtable nations; one because she is victorious, the other because she is vanquished.

As has been said by Professor Elliott Grant, an able American scholar, in his recent study of Hugo's political career: "No more judicious analysis of Europe from 1871 to 1914 could have been made. Even Thiers recognized its validity and interjected: 'It is true!'"

But the treaty terms were quickly ratified by the war-weary majority. Hugo, who had been serving as chairman of the Left bloc caucus, resigned that post to permit his party a free hand, and also expressed a wish to resign at once from the Assembly. Several leading men, Ledru-Rollin, Henri Rochefort, and the socialist, Félix Pyat, did resign in disgust. Hugo believed that an Assembly that had agreed to the mutilation of France should give way to a new body, rather than have the Republic born in their disgrace. However, he was persuaded to remain a little longer in the Assembly in order to help safeguard the Republic itself, for the majority appeared more and more violently anti-democratic. Hugo, once more, was one of those who tried to bring about conciliation between the more moderate factions in the Center and Left groups.

The final rupture soon came, however, when the Assembly turned to problems of internal government, and discussed the question of returning to Paris or continuing its sessions in Bordeaux, or some other city outside of Paris. Thiers moved for Versailles as seat of the Assembly, which was adopted. He mistrusted Paris, now seething with indignation at the peace treaty, which seemed like a gross betrayal. The transfer of the seat of government to Versailles came as an added insult to the people of the historic French capital, who had yesterday won the admiration of the world by their tenacious courage in the long siege. What would come next? The desperate masses of Paris feared that the Republic itself would be strangled by men like Thiers. How many times before, as in 1830 and 1848, they had been called out to fight for the overthrow of the old regime by the capitalist politicians—then seen the fruits of their sacrifices and victories stolen from them! To be sure, the working classes of Paris were in a minority in France; but now, largely converted to the "scientific, German socialism" of Karl Marx, they demanded a voice in the government, a measure of home rule, and a series of systematic social reforms.

Meanwhile, at Bordeaux, Victor Hugo burst into revolt over what appeared to be but a minor incident, yet one that was in reality symptomatic of the deep-rooted division within the Assembly. General Garibaldi, the soldier of democracy, in his latest military enterprise, had volunteered to come to the defense of France in the guerrilla phase of the late war, and at the head of a small army had fought nobly. In reward, he was elected a Deputy to the National Assembly, but, since he chose to keep his Italian citizenship and indicated that he would resign, the election was annulled by the Assembly's Credentials Committee. He was also needlessly insulted by being refused the honor of speaking before the Assembly. Then admirers in another district, this time in Algeria, elected him once more, and the majority party quickly voided this election too. For Victor Hugo this was the last straw.

On March 8, 1871, he took the floor, and in brief but passionate words defended his favorite hero. "None of the powers of Europe came to our aid, and this man intervened, a power in himself. . . . His sword had already rescued a whole people [Italy] and it might have saved another. . . . I do not wish to wound any member of this Assembly, but I would say that he is *the only one of the generals fighting for France who was not beaten.*"

They were not tactful words at the moment, and they aroused an indescribable tumult in the Assembly, with the majority members all on their feet howling imprecations at him, or denouncing him as "Liar!" and "Traitor!" For a few minutes he stood there receiving the full impact of their hatred, choked with rage himself. The President of the Assembly demanded that he explain his words.

Hugo answered impulsively: "Gentlemen, I will satisfy you, and

I shall go even further. Three weeks ago you refused to hear Garibaldi. Today you refuse to hear me. That is enough for me. I hereby tender my resignation." Seizing a pen from a stenographer, as he descended from the tribune, he wrote out his resignation in exactly the same words, and left the place while the hall mocked and howled at him.

The Conservative press reported the affair as a childish outburst on the part of a great poet who really had no place in politics. But quite a number of the popular leaders from Paris, such as Georges Clemenceau and Rochefort, had already resigned from the Assembly in protest at the railroading of the peace treaty and other measures. In sharp contrast with the Republic of 1848, the Third Republic was overwhelmingly reactionary from the start. Hugo had simply and impulsively seized upon the first pretext to dissociate himself from it.

2

Full of forebodings for France, which were shared then by many moderate democrats like Gambetta and Clemenceau, Victor Hugo prepared to return to Paris. The evening before his departure, March 13, he invited several friends and associates to dine with him at Lanta's restaurant. Charles Hugo, who had accompanied his father to Bordeaux, was also expected for dinner, his wife being present when the company met at six-thirty in a private room. But seven o'clock came while they waited, and no Charles. They ordered food.

While they were eating, the proprietor came in and asked to have a word with M. Hugo alone. They went downstairs, and the man gravely imparted the news that Charles Hugo, while driving home in a cab an hour before, had suddenly died of a stroke of apoplexy. The cabman had found him on the floor of the vehicle all covered with blood from a ruptured artery. Charles Hugo had been in weak health ever since the siege.

Victor Hugo had enough strength left to go upstairs again to his friends and inform them that he must be excused at once because of bad news which suddenly called him home. Pale and impassive, he begged them to finish their dinner without him. Later they wondered at his self-possession. Mme. Alice Hugo, Charles's wife, who thought the news might concern her children, followed him quickly. Together they returned to their quarters, and found the dead Charles. The old man bent over his son and kissed his brow, while Alice Hugo swooned away.

Victor Hugo felt himself growing very old. All of his family had been taken from him, save his son François-Victor, and he too, after the starvation diet of the siege, had been left ruined in health. Writing to Meurice on March 14, Hugo said: "I cannot see any more. I write through my tears and the sobs of Alice. My heart is broken. Charles is dead."

On the seventeenth, the bereaved father and his daughter-in-law took the train to Paris, which also carried the son in his coffin. It was decided to bury him in the Père Lachaise Cemetery. At ten-thirty in the morning of the following day they arrived in Paris, Victor Hugo having been without sleep for several days and feeling very worn.

On that day the atmosphere of the great city was strangely quiet. From the Orléans station the funeral hearse departed at noon for Père Lachaise. "Here and there," as *Le Rappel* relates, "barricades had been set up. And those who guarded them came forward to present arms respectfully. A way was opened for the procession through the barricades. The people of Paris, though possessed by their own tragedy, bowed to the great poet's grief."

At the Place de la Bastille also a spontaneous guard of honor was formed by National Guards, and all along the route their battalions were drawn up, presenting arms, with drums rolling and bugles sounding. The funeral of Hugo's son, instead of being celebrated with religious rites, became the occasion for a solemn tribute to the father and the cause he represented. "Long live the Republic!" the people shouted as Victor Hugo marched by behind the hearse.

Edmond de Goncourt, the indefatigable memoirist and reporter, fell into the procession and noted how many men wearing soft caps—the mark of the proletariat—had joined the march to Père Lachaise. Not all of them, however, were proletarian "looters" as Goncourt called them. At the grave, Hugo saw a big hand outstretched toward him, and a deep voice exclaimed: "I am Courbet!" "I saw an energetic and cordial face smiling at me with tear-dimmed eyes," wrote Hugo later. "It was the first time I had ever seen Courbet." He was one of the greatest painters of his era, and at the same time a revolutionist.

Did Hugo know what was going on elsewhere in Paris? He was a weary man, in need of repose. Two days later, on March 20, he left for Brussels to dispose of the affairs of his son, long a resident and property owner there.

"How the people love me," Hugo writes in his diary of this period. On March 18, 1870, he wrote the poem included in *L'Année terrible* ("The Terrible Year") which sings the praises of the Paris populace for their gentleness and sympathy:

> *O peuple! O majesté de l'immense douceur!*
> *Paris cité soleil, vous que l'envahisseur*
> *N'a pu vaincre. . . . .*

But the temper of the great city was far from gentle. Thiers, who was also a historian after his fashion, has written that at the beginning of 1871 "the business world felt a great anxiety at the thought of so many workers in Paris having arms." Quietly he had talked over plans for subduing the Paris population with one of his generals named Thomas.

On the very day of Charles Hugo's funeral, Thiers, as Premier, had ordered Generals Thomas and Lecomte to enter the city at the head of regular troops and remove the cannons that the local National Guards had used during the siege and then gathered together, in defiance of the Germans, on the heights of Montmartre. However, upon demand being made, the National Guards in Paris —who had been keeping order fairly well in the city—refused to give up their arms. In the streets approaching the Montmartre bluff great crowds of unarmed people gathered and barred the way to the regular troops. General Lecomte ordered the regulars to fire at them; but instead the soldiers disobeyed him, began to fraternize with the people, and shot and killed their somewhat ruthless general. A little later that same day, General Thomas was also seized and shot.

3

Feeling had been running high in Paris, bitterness at the peace treaty augmenting the effects of the sufferings borne during the siege, with the removal of the Government to Versailles fanning suspicion that the Republic was soon to be overthrown. Meanwhile, feeling their political separation from the rest of France, the people of Paris demanded a greater measure of municipal self-government than had formerly been allowed by law. As the crisis mounted, many moderate leaders, such as Clemenceau, then a young Deputy and Mayor of the populous 18th Arrondissement, pleaded for conciliatory measures by the Thiers Government, in order to avoid violence. They were rebuffed.

The "Hugo group," through *Le Rappel,* declared that the Assembly majority sought to "overthrow the Republic and . . . decapitate France," while the "irregular" movement originating in Paris struggled to maintain the unity of France and made just demands for a degree of self-government equal to that of other cities. *Le Rappel* was then the leading organ of the educated and Liberal middle class. Ignoring such appeals, Thiers, by arrangement with the German armies of occupation outside of Paris, ordered regular French troops to attack the city on April 2, 1871, and civil war began.

In Brussels, Victor Hugo, mourning his son, was engaged in writing a series of elegiac poems dedicated to his memory, when the news from Paris robbed him of all peace. Thiers had "thrown a spark into the powder barrel," he commented. "Wishing to extinguish political strife he has ignited the class war. . . . What a poignant thing, Frenchmen fighting each other!" While Hugo at this period condemned the excesses of the communards who seized control of Paris, he, like many other observers, placed responsibility for the civil war upon the statesmen of the Right.

Once the popular movement in Paris came under fire it passed into the hands of the revolutionary socialists, or communards, led by Flourens, Delescluze, Blanqui, and others unknown before. The communards favored establishing units of local self-government, called communes (or common councils), all over France, with the national government made up of a federal body of representatives of these communes. The communards thus tried to formulate their own new political institutions, which were to be copied about fifty years later by the Russian republic of *soviets* (councils).

Paris presented a picture of tremendous contrasts: at its ramparts the armed population defended it; within, an emergency government enacted sweeping reform laws including measures to help small businessmen, which there was of course no time to carry out. Actually few business properties were disturbed during the seventy-three days of the Commune. The American consul in Paris, staying at his post, reported no disorders or pillaging and less crime than before, up to the week of defeat. Many Parisian bourgeois joined in the active fighting against the regular troops of Versailles. They said: "We are simply defending Paris."

Early in April, Hugo, in Brussels, received first-hand reports of the situation from an editor of *Le Rappel* who had managed to escape from Paris. He judged that the Commune had inevitably reached its stage of violence, its rulers holding council every day with revolvers in hand. He said: "The Commune is as foolish as the Assembly is cruel. Madness on both sides." The Commune, in short, was "a good thing badly done." To *Le Rappel* he sent two poems, published on April 18 and 21, 1871, which embodied appeals to the people of Paris to refrain from bloody reprisals. The collection of poems inspired by the whole "terrible year," written during and after the siege, reflect a Hugo whose sympathies are divided, and who condemns violence whatever the end in sight. For this reason his heart was all the more torn because he recognized the "patriotic, republican, and proletarian character" of the Paris movement.

But, in this season of raging civil war—France's double tragedy —more terrible by far than foreign war, Victor Hugo was to be furiously reviled and persecuted for having distinguished even the faintest human features in the Red communards, bogymen of the nineteenth century.

In the week of May 22 to May 28, the troops from Versailles finally broke into Paris and the civil carnage proceeded from house to house, while the German soldiers from the hills looked with stupefaction at the great metropolis which seemed to be consuming itself in flames. The young unknown socialist leaders died at the head of their men, in the streets. Those who were captured fared no better. The Thiers Government's troops proceeded to terrible reprisals, estimates of the executed ranging between twenty and thirty thousand and including women and children. The aged statesman who, by his own admission, represented primarily "the world of business," showed that his Government could be more ruthless than any Royalist dynasty France had formerly known.

Those who succeeded in escaping from Paris now streamed toward the northern frontier; but the Belgian government moved to close the border to the hunted men. In Brussels, Victor Hugo was roused to anger at this harsh decree.

On May 27, 1871, he published in *L'Indépendance Belge* a letter offering asylum to the fugitives.

I protest against the declaration of the Belgian government relative to the *defeated men of Paris*.

Whatever may be said of them, they are political fugitives. . . .

Their violence has revolted me as the violences of the opposing party have also filled me with indignation. . . . But let us not turn our indignation only upon one side. The crime is as much owing to the Assembly. . . .

As for myself, I offer the asylum which the Belgian government refuses to these vanquished men.

This open letter caused a fearful storm in Conservative circles in Belgium and elsewhere in Europe. On the night following its publication, May 27, at 11:30, a band of young men of aristocratic sympathies surrounded Hugo's house, one of them ringing the bell and answering in response to a question by the master that his name was "Dombrowski." Victor Hugo knew that Dombrowski, a communard leader, had been killed in Paris, and closed the door, telling the group to be gone. A stone came flying through the window with a terrifying crash. Inside, Charles Hugo's widow, Alice, and the two infants, Georges and Jeanne (one of whom was sick), cowered and wept. The crowd outside shouted: "Down with Victor Hugo! Down with Jean Valjean! Down with the communard!" Their shouting continued for some time.

An hour later, toward one in the morning, they returned and renewed their shouting and stone throwing, as Hugo testified. In the darkness of an interior room the old man sat with his weeping family around him, wondering if the crowd outside would grow in numbers and violence. Victor Hugo, like other prophets, was being stoned, and in the city where he was a property-holder and a long-time resident. At last the police came and drove the crowd away.

The midnight assault in Brussels left an ineffaceable impression on his mind, and he returned to it often in later years, in writings which touched on the "terrible year." Vehemently he protested and asked for punishment of the marauders, but the police authorities maintained that the aged poet had lent literary and romantic exaggeration to a small scuffle. In the press of Paris, where "order" was now re-established, it was said that he merely sought publicity and "picked up all the stones that were flung at his window in order to use them as a pedestal for his vanity." Yet public opinion in Belgium was sufficiently aroused to bring about a relaxation of the ban on political refugees—who were freely admitted to England and the United States as such. Once more the tumult over Hugo had brought help to the unfortunate.

A few weeks later, in July, 1871, though he was absent from France, his name was presented in an election for the Seine Department, and amid the terrible hue and cry against him he was badly defeated, with only 58,000 votes against 200,000 for his opponent of the extreme Right. It was an experience previously unknown to Hugo and extremely humiliating.

To his old acquaintance Alphonse Karr, who wrote him advising that he quit politics, Hugo answered in terms that were a little sad, yet full of pride:

The word "politics" has always seemed to me ill-defined. For my part, I have always tried, to the best of my abilities, to introduce into that which is called politics the moral question and the question of humanity. On moral ground, I fought Louis Bonaparte; in the name of humanity I raised my voice in aid of the oppressed of all lands and all parties. I feel that I have done right. My conscience bears me out.

He had not tried to be a practical politician, as some men of letters have tried, but felt that, in his public life, he had championed the only policies that a man wedded to civilization and the humanities could support.

Yet, though he still held himself erect, he was threescore and ten. The latter half of his career sometimes seemed all strife and tragedy—in 1873, François-Victor, his only remaining child, died suddenly, leaving him alone with his little grandchildren. He turned then to the more tranquil literary labors that he had lately neglected.

After the stoning of his house in Brussels, he had been asked by the local authorities to leave the city, but upon his refusal to do so was formally expelled, on May 30, 1871. He passed across the border into the little neighboring Duchy of Luxemburg, stopping at the little town of Vianden. Here, near the Ardennes Forest, by the banks of the charming Ourthe River, he spent the summer peacefully, taking walks, drawing sketches, writing every day, and holding himself in seclusion. For he was unwilling to return to France, where his enemies triumphed, where a fanatical reaction imposed law and order again. All this he desired, for the moment, to forget.

CHAPTER XX

The Art of Being a Grandfather

In his peaceful Luxemburg retreat at Vianden, Victor Hugo returned to his writing. He could not change the habits of fifty years: each morning he rose early and wrote a hundred lines of poetry, or from ten to twenty pages of prose. At intervals, even during the thunderous siege of Paris by the Germans, he had continued with his writing.

So many fearful things had happened to him and to France in the past year. His mind was full of the catastrophic war, the siege, the political turmoil at Bordeaux, the insurrection, the death of his elder son, Charles, his second flight from France, the second siege of Paris by the troops of Versailles, the subsequent incendiarism and blood bath in the great capital, the stoning in Brussels, and his second expulsion from Belgium.

A witness of the defense of Paris against the Germans, he had planned to write a book in commemoration of that tragic season, which he first called "Paris Besieged." But then the expanding social tragedy of civil war superimposed upon national war far exceeded anything he had conceived possible. *L'Année terrible* he called the year beginning in July, 1870, and ending with his arrival in Luxemburg in June, 1871. To this year he dedicated a whole book of poems, conceived in the epic style, narrating its fearsome succession of events month by month: the fragments of poems inspired by news or experience, which he had begun during the siege, were completed; added to these were the poems written in Brussels, the elegies to Charles Hugo, and those he wrote at Vianden, in retrospect, then placed in the chronological order of the events they treated.

In its time, *L'Année terrible* was a work of tremendous popular interest. It had the effect mainly of a journal of the year of war and revolution (rather than of epic poetry), seen, of course, through the eyes of Hugo. It embodies his fluctuating opinions and emotions, from appeals for universal peace and fraternity to savage war poems. The truth was that the Franco-Prussian War of 1870 at first embarrassed Victor Hugo considerably: for years previously he had been preaching opposition to the military dictator, Bonaparte, and yet also had spoken as a pacifist, abhorring war; he had been a decided friend and admirer of Germany. But these moral difficulties were easily suppressed, when, after the demise of Napoleon III, the Republic found itself fighting for its life against the new German Empire.

Once more he celebrated the courage of the people of Paris. But the insurrection and its inhuman suppression became the most urgent theme of his book. The ill-fated but significant social revolution launched in Paris, in March, 1871, was little understood at the time—though later it served as a form of historical laboratory for the leaders of the Russian revolution of 1917. But Victor Hugo, no "scientific" socialist (though far more widely read by proletarians than was Karl Marx), viewed the insurrection and its defeat as a pacifist, as one who longed for conciliation and "universal pardon." Though the humanity and sense of pity of the author of *Les Misérables* led him to the side of the socialists, his deepest instincts (as often happens to writers) disposed him to be neutral, to stay "above the battle," and, while blaming the Thiers Government for its provocation, to lament the violence and hatred shown on both sides.

But even such humane neutrality was dangerous in 1871, as Hugo learned. The first editions of *L'Année terrible,* published in France in May, 1872, had many passages suppressed, blanks marked with asterisks, which were restored only seven years later, in a new edition. This volume of "timely" poems was a great popular success in 1872; once more Hugo, with his "crystal soul" reflected the experiences and sufferings of his era; though half of literate France condemned the book, the other half read him avidly. However, as with newspaper editorials done in a time of crisis, its value was not permanent; it appears now much weaker as poetry than *Les Châtiments,* and marks, almost for the first time, a decline in his artistic powers.

He had returned quietly to Paris, at the end of September, 1871, to make arrangements for the publication of his book, and also to help win the release of his friend Henri Rochefort, who had been treated as a partisan of the communards, a mission in which Hugo was successful. But France was still under a state of siege conducted by Thiers, the first President of the Third Republic; many familiar landmarks—the ancient Town Hall, the Tuileries Palace, the old Porte Saint-Martin Theater, where so many of his plays had been produced—had disappeared in flames. This Republic was not yet free, though Thiers swore that he would loyally re-establish civil rights, and for the moment Hugo felt himself distinctly unwelcome in it. He turned his steps again toward the soil of England:

> *. . . A stranger in my own city . . .*
> *For holding the victory of love to be the only victory,*
> *Therefore let me return to my old, bleak Guernsey.*

He was in a black humor, feeling the "breath of hatred too close." Was it for this he had returned as an old man, after so many years of exile, to find himself hounded by an infamous pack? "Dark heaven, here I am alone!"

The impressions of the terrible civil struggle in Paris remained so strongly fixed in the old poet's mind that during 1872 and most of 1873, at Guernsey, he occupied himself exclusively with a historical novel, placed in the time of the French Revolution. It was called *'Quatre-Vingt-Treize* (" 'Ninety-Three") in allusion to the terroristic phase of the First Republic. Its theme was the bloody civil conflict between the Catholic Royalists of the Vendée and the forces of the Republic, a theme that was used to symbolize the parallel civil struggle of 1871. In his romantic-symbolist style Hugo gives a picture of the night of horror and chaos over France in 1793; he describes both parties to the conflict, Royalists and Revolutionists, as fanatically brave, and celebrates the heroes and martyrs of each in many lyrical pages, like a Chateaubriand writing of the martyrs of the Church and the triumph of the Christian religion. Hugo's novel proclaimed, one might say, the triumph of the French Revolution—as a religion. The Republican Convention is represented, after all, as "the summit" of human history; as in his occult and prophetic poems Hugo ends by professing the mystic faith that man's deliverance, "the new social order," must come inevitably out of horror and suffering itself. Neither the siege nor the tragedy of the Commune altered this conviction.

However, as historical romance or as fiction, " 'Ninety-Three," with its idealized characters (actually symbols), its unreal and de-clamatory dialogue, its long and diffusely mystical digressions, was unfavorably compared with the firmly organized works of realism that were winning public favor in 1874, the year when it was published. The disappointing reception it had discouraged the aging author from further fiction writing, and " 'Ninety-Three" was his last novel.

As he finished writing it in the late summer of 1873, his younger son François-Victor lay sick in Paris, with chronic consumption, and the father returned to watch by his bedside. In December, François-Victor suddenly sank to his death after an attack of pneumonia. All of his family were now removed from him—for Adèle, with clouded mind, remained always secluded in a sana-torium—and of his own kin he had only the two grandchildren, Georges and Jeanne, aged five and four, who since the days of the siege were his inseparable companions.

The atmosphere of Paris was calmer by 1874, and Victor Hugo now established himself there again in permanent fashion in a small, private house at number 21 rue de Clichy. He had his apartment on an upper floor, Alice Hugo and the two children were established on the floor below, and on the ground floor Mme. Drouet resided. There was a garden in back of the house and here every afternoon he played with the grandchildren, whom he was resolved to bring up himself.

In rural Vianden, following his expulsion from Brussels in 1871, the Luxemburgers would see old *Père* Hugo every day on the main street of the town, pushing little Jeanne in her perambulator while he tugged Georges along by the arm. In Paris he conducted them to the public gardens or zoo. His unpublished diaries of this period show, along with reflections upon war and revolution, very numer-ous, detailed, and tender observations of the two children. One of the notes of 1871 reads: "At all my leisure moments I take Georges and Jeanne out for walks. . . . I may now be called *representative of the people* and *children's nurse.*" Another dating from Guernsey somewhat earlier, in 1868, reads: "Georges is doing very well. He now suckles at both his mother's breasts. For a long time he suckled only at the *left* breast. Inherited radical tendencies?"

Growing very old, his life spanning almost three-quarters of a century, he felt more closely drawn to the tiny children; with them he forgot his many sorrows; turning from his social and political preoccupations, he wrote long poems for their entertainment, or about them, or about the joy of being a grandfather. Something "primitive" in Hugo made him, like Dickens, both fascinated by children and fascinating to them. The poems that he wrote for them, which he gathered together under the happy title: "The Art of Being a Grandfather," though often extremely sentimental, embodied the strongest paternal emotion. Many were simply entertaining, or told mischievous anecdotes, or were fantasies woven around the elephants, seals, and lions in the zoo. In one, for example, there is the account of how little Georges, for wrongdoing, has been spanked and put in a closet by his mother. The grandfather, distressed by his cries, steals in with some jam and crackers, but is discovered in the act and scolded by the mother. Confessing his error, Victor Hugo declares that he himself ought now to be punished with confinement:

> And from the dark depths of the closet, Georges
> Exclaims: Then I shall bring you jam!

Other poems, however, were seriously intended for the instruction of the children when they grew bigger: they were counseled to be prepared to defend their country, to champion the Republic, to believe in God—but to beware of priests. For their grandfather's convictions on this subject were unchanging.

When *L'Art d'être grand-père,* as a small book, was published in 1877, it touched the hearts of readers belonging to all parties in France. No controversy such as usually followed the appearance of his books was aroused, and it contributed richly to the growing Hugo cult in France. His readers marveled at the many-sided gifts of Victor Hugo, at the freshness and simplicity of this new and unexpected work, and at the quality of bubbling youth in this grandfather of seventy-five years.

2

To the grandchildren he was a "good ogre," as Georges Hugo recollected. In astonishment they watched him seize the claw of a lobster to crack it with his strong teeth. His inexhaustible energy and zest for life caused legends of all sorts to be attached to him, some of them superstitious and salacious, crediting him with a miraculously prolonged masculine virility.

That he was held to be still a devotee of the god Pan, a snowy-haired, ruddy, and stout Silenus, was owing largely to his own indiscretions. While in exile at Guernsey, and supposedly absorbed in social politics and occult religion, he had published in 1865 a volume of collected poems called *Chanson des rues et des bois* ("Songs of Street and Forest"), consisting mainly of amatory and lusty songs, full of the chase of earthy nymphs in secluded meadows, of nudities beside woodland pools, of "glimpses even above the knee" through flying skirts, and "secret letters warmed in bodices." Some of the poems dated apparently from earlier years, when Victor Hugo was a noble Peer sitting in the Luxembourg Palace every day. Others, alas, introduced themselves even during the heroic period of exile; into the austere life of the aging political martyr they brought salty allusions to a round of fleshly pleasure and the intermittent pursuit of servant maids and tavern waitresses. Boldly they celebrated the libertinage of man, which was likened to the singing lubricity of nature, insects, birds, trees, and flowers! In short, as one disapproving critic said, "The goat's hoof of the satyr was permitted to peep out of the trailing cloak of Olympio." What was worse, these songs were written in Hugo's best vein; they were full of an anacreontic wit and added new, pagan laurels to his lined brow.

So now, in the last years of his life, incredible stories of his green old age clung to him at Guernsey, pursued him in Belgium and in France wherever he went. There was Eva, for instance, a pretty serving maid at Hauteville House, who forever pranced about, her hips at play, breaking dishes, and darting flaming looks at the guests and especially at the handsome old master. Then one day, Mme. Drouet arranged to have the girl sent away to France. They told Victor Hugo that she was a spy of Napoleon's and he was easily reconciled to her disappearance.

After the death of Mme. Hugo, it was thought that he would at last legalize his connection with Juliette Drouet by marriage. For a time she desired this and spoke of it. But he, out of reverence for his dead wife and partly out of indifference to convention, did nothing about it, though he continued always as before to formulate declarations of undying love in verse and prose, and also now made her publicly the head of his family establishment. To this order of things Juliette resigned herself with good grace. She was compelled also to resign herself to the increasing liberties that her aged philanderer now insisted upon. Although seventy, and in weak health, she was consumed by passionate jealousy!

There were many scenes that stirred her jealousy. The more the legends of his magic powers were spread, the more ladies besieged him. At one evening party in Paris, a very pretty young woman, engaged in conversation with the poet, leaned close to him at one moment and whispered earnestly: "Ah, my dear master, how I long just to touch you!" Whereupon Mme. Drouet, overhearing, said: "There, there, madame, he already touches you only too much!"

On another occasion, a lady of a certain age, who feigned that the old poet had been guilty of some impertinence, drew back from him and said haughtily: "Remember that in the old days you used to lie at my feet!" He replied briskly: "And pray do not forget that sometimes I also used to hold you by your foot."

Sometimes poor Juliette would attempt to close her eyes and ears, which was not easy. Sometimes she would try to banter him on his behaving like an old Triton, centaur, satyr, or simply "an old rascal" who tripped about "pinching the ladies." Even reading his verses she saw danger on all sides:

Tell me, sir poet! to what lovely nurses are those gallant lines dedicated that you did not think it proper for me to copy them for you? That little twinge of conscience probably hides some big misdeed for which my poor heart, alas, will no doubt suffer sorely. . . . How wrong it is for me to love you with the same ardent passion and jealousy in 1872 with which I loved you in 1833. It is more than an anachronism; it is an absurdity. I must expiate the sin of it.

At times she had the harrowing fear that she might finally lose him in her last declining years, and she prayed more fervently than she ever had in the days when she was a pupil of the Bernardine-Benedictines Sisters. Her prayers, however, were now cast in the Hugolian terminology. "Oh God, help us to live together forever," she wrote in her journal on January 1, 1873. "Grant this to me, grant this to him. May he never be lacking to me in the days of my life and for no moment of all eternity. May I be his forever, and useful and beloved by him. Save us, transfigure us, unite us."

Alas, the worn Juliette had need of all the power of prayers.

Amid the storm of exile, revolution, siege, and war, his eye wandered away. In his ripe old age incontinence had become a fixed principle with him. Among the various comforting doctrines he now embraced was one holding that a taste for women was good for old graybeards. He recommended to others "that this feeling be kept ever young, in spite of years and the sorrows of life," and, at an age when other men were normally sated, his desire, his hunger, remained noticeably alive, to the amusement of the public and the consternation of his doctors, relatives, and friends.

As he escaped from Belgium, at the end of May, 1871, a number of communard refugees joined his party and were charitably given aid by him—among them a handsome young woman of twenty, widow of an insurrectionist leader whom Victor Hugo had known. He showed great pity for the weeping widow and invited her to join his expedition to Luxemburg. There, he wandered off with her into the Ardennes Forest, stopping at tiny village inns, and was gone for days. The lines preserved in his posthumous volume, *Toute la lyre,* which celebrate love rites by a forest pool with a sorrowing young "nymph," are a testimonial to this excursion of 1871.

Returning to Guernsey, in 1872, Mme. Drouet brought with her from Paris, as her personal maid, a young girl of about twenty, who was known as Blanche. Soon a lecherous attraction drew the irrepressible grandfather and the pretty young Blanche together. The intimates and guests, who were aware of their connection, for a long time tried to keep it from the attention of Mme. Drouet. But in Paris she discovered the whole affair, and there were stormy scenes, as always before.

In the rue de Clichy, Alice Hugo, now married to Edouard Lockroy, the editor of *Le Rappel* and a close friend of her late husband, warned the old man that his Juliette was making preparations to leave him. "What will you do if she goes?" asked his daughter-in-law. "In that case," he replied gloomily, "I shall have to follow her."

Blanche was dismissed after a time, but her venerable lover settled some money upon her and established her in a little modiste's shop. Later she married, but her husband proved to be a knave. Learning of her affair with Victor Hugo and her continued meetings with the old man, he turned to blackmail. After a time Blanche's rascally husband was smoothed off with a little additional money. But Blanche mourned for her old Triton. For

several years, when his presence was advertised at public ceremonies or political meetings in Paris, she appeared like a wraith at
the back of the audience, waiting for a sight of him.

The family doctor now cautioned the author of *Les Misérables*
upon the need for restraint and discretion at his advanced age.
Hugo was then over seventy-six, but he replied obstinately: "It
seems to me that nature ought to give us warnings; I am still waiting for them."

He had lately been taking a most active part in the preparation for a great national ceremony in honor of the centenary of
Voltaire's death, and writing as if he were a youth of thirty. At a
large gathering in the rue de Clichy, following many courses of
food and wine, he clashed in argument with his old friend Louis
Blanc over the relative merits of Voltaire and Rousseau—Blanc,
as opinionated as Hugo, holding Rousseau to be the superior
genius. Such downright contradiction was too much for the aged
poet, and he suddenly collapsed under a slight stroke that was described as cerebral congestion, news of which was kept out of the
newspapers.

Now the Doctors Allix and Sée, joining with the family circle,
strongly pressed him to leave Paris and retreat to Guernsey for rest
and a change of air. This time he obeyed.

3

The Third Republic, "the republic nobody wanted," persisted at
first in a precarious balance between hostile political groups. The
years passed, and the bourgeois Republic slowly relaxed its repressive measures; the rebels of 1871 gradually drifted back or
were released from prison; under the steady pressure of popular
opinion civil liberties were restored, and France recovered from
military disaster, civil strife, and burdensome reparations with
surprising speed.

Victor Hugo was not happy over this highly bourgeois and sometimes venal Republic. Returning permanently to France in 1873
he had begun at once to appeal for amnesty for the imprisoned
communards. Thanks to his enormous sway over the masses, he
played an influential part in turning the government's policy
toward greater tolerance. In 1876, when a Senate was created
under the slowly evolving Constitution, and while more liberal
trends showed themselves in recent elections, Victor Hugo was

named a member of the higher chamber, with general approval. Here his first speech was a plea for indulgence toward the political prisoners, which remained a bitterly contested issue up to 1880.

In 1877, a first sudden thrust was directed against the Republic by its internal enemies on the Right, provoked by the question of public education. A Liberal Ministry was in power, but the President was Marshal MacMahon, one of the "heroes" of Sedan, who had been elected in much the same fashion as was Marshal von Hindenburg, after a German defeat in a later European war. Mac-Mahon, partially descended from Irish *émigrés,* was a devout Catholic, and a Royalist by conviction. On May 16, 1877, he attempted a virtual *coup d'état* by dismissing Jules Simon, the Liberal Premier, dissolving the Chamber of Deputies, and appointing a pro-clerical and reactionary Ministry, headed by the Duc de Broglie, without any parliamentary backing.

By the "MacMahon movement" all France was plunged again into a fierce political controversy between clericals and anti-clericals. Gambetta, the foremost orator of the day, took the stump with his ringing war cries against "our enemy within, clericalism." In this conflict Victor Hugo instantly joined, sensing that the republican form of government was in danger. His speech on the centenary of Voltaire, traditional enemy of the Church, was inspired by the urgency of the moment. From this period also date many of his bitterly anti-clerical writings, chiefly in satirical verse, such as *Le Pape, L'Ane, Religions et religion,* and others which he now began to publish.

He had also in his drawer, in the spring of 1877, the unpublished two-volume account of "The Story of a Crime," which twenty-five years earlier he had happily decided to replace with a briefer account of the *coup d'état* of December, 1851, "Napoleon the Little." Now he finished the preparation of the earlier, unpublished version. The parallel it drew in such vigorous style between the Bonaparte conspiracy against the Second Republic in 1851 and the "movement" of Marshal MacMahon against the Third Republic in 1877 had a startling effect. Hugo issued the old work on October 1, 1877, with the introductory words: *"This book is more than timely; it is urgent. I publish it."* Within a few weeks, over fifty thousand copies were sold. On October 16, 1877, while the great anti-clerical controversy agitated all France, the new elections took place. Despite the strenuous efforts of the party in power to control the vote, a republican majority was elected to the Chamber of

Deputies. The new Liberal Ministry soon prepared reform measures that worked toward the final separation of Church and State
in France in matters of education, and toward the discouragement
of Jesuit schools. The President, after a face-saving delay of a year,
resigned, though it was considered an abdication, and Jules Grévy,
one of Victor Hugo's old comrades in the underground Committee of Resistance of 1851, was elected in his place. In this
victory the publication of Hugo's book had played a substantial
part. Thenceforth a more conciliatory and Liberal ministry ruled
France—one might almost say a pro-Hugo government—and
there were scarcely honors enough it could pay to the old poet, now
the national hero and "one of the glories of France."

4

For five years, up to 1878, Hugo lived in the small house at
number 21 rue de Clichy, "so disproportionate to the glory of its
great inhabitant," as Mme. Alphonse Daudet thought. Almost
every night its small salon was thronged to the doors by political
and literary friends. But on his return from the stay in Guernsey
in November, 1878, the master, now restored in health, established himself in a much larger private residence far uptown, at
number 130 Avenue d'Eylau, in the Champs Elysées quarter. His
daughter-in-law, with her husband and Hugo's grandchildren, came
to live next door.

At this period Victor Hugo admitted to Meurice: "My fortune
has got out of hand, and I can no longer give my time to it." It
was reported by an English writer that Hugo's investments in
England alone amounted to 92,000 pounds sterling; by others,
such as Meurice, his total fortune was estimated at about three
times that figure, or $1,400,000. He increased his regularly dis-
tributed charities several times over, and also augmented his allowance to Mme. Drouet, giving her 3,000 francs a month for her
table and 1,200 francs a month for wine. Almost every night during the season, up to thirty guests joined them in an informal dinner.

The house in the Avenue d'Eylau (later named the Avenue
Victor-Hugo) was decorated by its master most lavishly in the
baroque-romantic style he always preferred: the main salon was
carpeted with Aubusson rugs; its décor centered about a vast fireplace designed like a Renaissance altar; the small salon adjacent

was rebuilt in an oval shape to conform with panels of antique Cordovan leather, embossed with figures, which Hugo had collected. The great dining room was done in the Venetian manner; the poet's study on the second story overlooked both the street and a spacious private flower garden, with a fountain and fine shade trees. Here, in his old age, Victor Hugo lived not only with good cheer but in relative splendor. Here the world beat a path to his door; as his secretary related, here came "princes, dukes, Presidents of Republics, like Manin, makers of revolutions, like Louis Blanc, great popular leaders like Garibaldi and Kossuth, soldiers, diplomats, artists and peasants."

It was the time of *Hugolatry*. The handsome old man, with the huge forehead and snow-white beard, was idolized by the literati and the lion-hunters who came to see him almost in fear and trembling. As he stood by his fireplace, or sat on his green divan, they would vie with each other in plying him with compliments. Turgenieff, a long-time resident of Paris, has told the somewhat apocryphal yet illuminating tale of how, at one of these séances, an admirer began to wonder out loud what fitting honors might be awarded France's great poet. It was proposed first that a street be named after him, but that seemed too small. A public square, someone suggested. "A whole city," cried another. And Hugo is reported to have nodded his head and said reflectively: "That will come, that will come some day, my dear friends."

Yet other witnesses found him extremely simple in manner, ever courteous in an old-time way, and essentially democratic. One very sensitive observer who was a frequent guest, Mme. Alphonse Daudet, described him after his return from exile as "dazzling in conversation and full of reminiscences that were brought forth and told with inexhaustible animation. . . . In his manner was something noble and dignified; there was the kindly smile of a grandfather under those thick locks which I have seen whiten through all the shades from dark gray to the pure snow of the octogenarian."

The Third Republic has sometimes been called "the republic without great men." Gambetta, its bellwether, died prematurely in 1882. But there was still Hugo as the old knight of the young Republic, and there he had always been, nigh on to a hundred years, people realized, while all his famous contemporaries had one by one gone to their graves. For almost a decade he lived out his days as the idol and figurehead of France. In England men spoke of him as the "first citizen of France."

On February 26, 1881, he celebrated his seventy-ninth birthday, receiving a great number of visits and complimentary cards. On the following morning, as he entered upon his eightieth year, the municipality of Paris held a vast popular and democratic festival both in honor of Hugo and of the democratic system he symbolized. The plans for the procession, oddly enough, were in charge of the same men who had managed those pompous Imperial parades with which Napoleon III had formerly tried to entertain the populace. The whole length of the Avenue d'Eylau was decked with flowers and banners. Before the door of the poet's house, upon a pedestal banked with red and blue flowers, they set up a great gilded laurel wreath reaching to the second story. From early morning a huge crowd lined the street, and toward noon the deputations began to arrive. Children marched with banners, one of them reciting a poem written in honor of Victor Hugo by Catulle Mendès. Then local and national government officials came to pay their respects, while from his window, before the great crowd filling the street, the poet gave an address.

"I salute Paris," he said, "I salute the immense city." What Athens and Rome were to antiquity Paris represented for the civilization of Europe and America, "the place consecrated to a divine labor."

The French people have always loved ceremony, despite their adoption of democratic forms. Although the sun of Austerlitz was lacking on that day of triumph, for it rained intermittently, a monstrous parade marched by the poet's house; it consisted of the Society of Men of Letters (of which he was president), trade associations, student clubs, the Society for the Benefit of Poor Orphans, many masonic lodges in full uniform, gymnastic clubs and tradeunions of tailors, shoemakers, carpenters, vintners, bakers. All that afternoon they defiled past him, while he came out from time to time to greet them. It was estimated that marchers and onlookers numbered 700,000 persons. The press reported that it was a demonstration that an "Emperor might well have envied." To the nation the venerable old man assumed a legendary character of grandeur and genius, while his errors and shortcomings were forgotten. He was, as the British Laureate Tennyson had said in a sonnet recently written in his honor: "Victor in poetry, Victor in romance, Victor in life."

5

Up to the very end, almost, he continued his lifetime habits of regular work, rising a little after dawn, putting on, over his red woolen undergarment, a long gray dressing gown, tied by a cord, and writing until midday. His study floor would be littered with papers that had fallen off the tables, but he gave orders that they were to be left undisturbed. Then he would take lunch and, putting on a soft felt hat, without coat or raincoat, go off on his daily rambles about Paris, or along the Champs Elysées toward the Bois de Boulogne. This was his routine during the 1870's, when, in a brilliant sunset glow, he prepared and published at intervals of one or two years a series of ten volumes of prose or poetry.[1]

Victor Hugo, it used to be said disparagingly, wrote "a million lines of poetry." Though this is somewhat exaggerated, it is true that in the sprawling mass of his later work there is much repetition and evidence of declining power. This is particularly true of the later and more mystical pieces added to the enlarged three-volume edition of *La Légende des siècles*. Yet even here one finds many of the poems (perhaps originating from earlier periods) that have become features of nearly all anthologies of French poetry. It is evident that much of his later poetic work, chiefly those of a religious tone, he intended as a kind of preparation of his readers for the great prophetic books, "God" and "The End of Satan," which he reserved for publication after his death, as his last testament of faith. In *Le Pape* he tells of a Pope who leaves the Vatican, wanders about the world like Jesus, spreading the word of God among the poor, among children, mothers, and suffering workers; a Pope who witnesses and experiences poverty for the first time, and who chases the money changers out of the Temple for a sec-

---

[1] These included *L'Année terrible* (1872); the novel *'Quatre-Vingt-Treize* (1874); *Actes et Paroles,* his speeches and public letters in two volumes (1875–1876); the Second Series of the *Légende des siècles* (1875); *L'Histoire d'un crime* and *L'Art d'être grand-père* (1877); *Le Pape* (1878); *La Pitié suprême* (1879); *L'Ane* (1880); and *Religions et religion* (1880). Finally, in 1881, he issued a large collection of his later verse in two large volumes: *Les Quatre Vents de l'esprit* ("The Four Winds of the Mind"), containing some ten thousand lines of poetry falling into four categories: the Satirical Book; the Dramatic; the Lyrical; and the Epic. Not all of this was done during the last years; most of it came from the trunk he had had in Guernsey which he called "Ocean," and into which he had thrown unfinished pieces, or work to be put aside for later use, during his last great phase of poetic production, 1852–1859.

ond time. *Religions et religion* is another poetic dissertation assailing the rigmarole of established churches, yet ending with an eloquent affirmation of faith in God—thus a prelude to *Dieu*. (Hugo tended to reproach his friends, the socialists, for failing to see the "abyss of eternity" that surrounded man's life.) His religious thought generally seems concerned with finding a metaphysics and ethics, and a conception of divinity more explicative of the duties of real life than is orthodox religion. Hence the unwearying crusade against the clerics. He said at this period: "The priests hate me because I poach on their preserves. Like them I speak of the soul and God, but I would strip their fictions down to truth."

His memory these days was prone to wander a little in conversation, or even in public speech. Looking back over the long span of his life he would decorate its more stirring events with the suggestions of his imagination. Thus when for the first time, at a banquet of exiles in Brussels, he spoke of his escape from Paris in December, 1851, he placed his hand on the shoulder of his colleague Victor Schoelcher, one of the most heroic members of the Committee of Resistance, and said:

"Ah, my brave Schoelcher! How much better we feel here than in the omnibus that carried us out of Paris beyond the reach of the usurper. Do you remember how you lowered the window, seeing soldiers passing, and cried: 'Down with Bonaparte!' and I pulled you by the coat tails, saying, 'Hush! You will put us all in the jug!'?"

The next time he recalled this incident, at a similar reunion of exiles a few years later, he said: "Ah, Schoelcher, do you remember when we were on the omnibus and the regiment passed by, and how we both yelled through the window, clenching our fists at the soldiers: 'Down with Bonaparte! Violator of the Constitution! Criminal!'"

A third banquet of the former comrades in exile took place some years after the fall of the Empire, and the white-haired, dim-sighted Victor Hugo reminisced of the same adventures: "Ah, my poor Schoelcher! How reckless we were when we were young! Do you remember how, lowering the window of the omnibus, I shook my fist at the soldiers and shouted: 'Down with Bonaparte!' And you, you pulled me by the coat tails, saying: 'Be quiet! You will put us all in the jug!' Ah, my good Schoelcher, I shan't forgive you for that! You were too easily frightened!" Schoelcher would merely sit nodding and smiling at everything his great friend said. For had not *Père* Hugo been noble enough in 1851?

After his slight heart attack of 1878, he moved about more slowly and warily. His literary labor involved mainly revision of earlier unpublished work rather than new writings. Nowadays he no longer walked all over Paris, but preferred to ride on the horse-drawn omnibus line that circled the city. Either alone or with Mme. Drouet, he would mount to the imperial, or uncovered upper deck, at the same hour each day, ride to the end of the line and back. Some of his fellow passengers, recognizing him, would lift their hats, and he would respond with a stiff little bow. Others would pretend not to notice him, knowing that he was composing lines in his head as he rode about the town, rocked by the plunging omnibus.

Juliette Drouet too had become almost a figure of legend after nearly fifty years' connection with the poet. They were Philemon and Baucis. Once when Victor Hugo insisted upon trying an ascent in a captive balloon, poor Juliette, though petrified with fear, insisted on accompanying him. Hugo was full of a child's gaiety as they floated up together, stared out at this unimaginable Jules Verne view over Paris, and came down.

To the Hugo intimates, Juliette's virtue was thoroughly known. Evidence exists that at one time the old poet transferred to her securities valued at 200,000 francs in order to leave her with independent means. In this instrument he states again that he owes her his life. However, a document of later date shows that Juliette returned the funds, indicating that she had no need for them and wished them bequeathed to his grandchildren or to suitable charities.

Late in November, 1882—she was now seventy-five—Mme. Drouet, after attending a revival of one of her lover's plays, returned home and took to her bed. She wrote to Victor Hugo: "I dare not look forward or backward, for thee or for myself; I am afraid." She learned now that her illness was cancer of the stomach and that she had but a brief time to live, but told him nothing of her condition. "For him his friend is not seriously ill, but indisposed," wrote one of Victor Hugo's intimates in 1883.

On February 17, 1883, the old gallant wrote in her *livre de l'anniversaire:* "This book contains your life and mine. . . . Let us begin our fiftieth year together, saying: 'I love you.' "

The wife of Alphonse Daudet tells of the decline of the aged lovers in her memoirs:

In health and in mental vigor the grand old man had now gone one step lower down the final stair. He still loved to receive his friends, and one of the charms of the open house was its boundless hospitality. The guests still gathered around his groaning table. . . . Mme. Drouet, her face drawn into that dolorous effigy which the painter Bastien Lepage has preserved for us, still presided there. And in these later times the master would look sorrowfully at her noble and ravaged countenance as she sent away dish after dish untasted.

"Madame Drouet! You are eating nothing! You must eat. A little courage!"

Eat? She was dying!

Up to the end, like a nurse, she had continued to care for his daily needs, for he too was growing weaker. But now she languished, all spent. On May 11, 1883, she died.

He could not follow her to her grave; he could only stand by his window, as his doctor had ordered, watching the funeral cortège depart. Now, for the first time, he felt all his strength leave him. He had once written, in honor of the wife of a friend of his, words that applied well to his lost mistress:

He was her glory; she was his delight. She fulfilled the great, obscure function of woman, which is love. . . . Man strives, endeavors, invents, creates, sows and reaps, destroys and builds, thinks, fights, meditates; woman loves. And what does she do with her love? She makes the strength of man.

Only the year before, at the age of eighty, he had gone out to a midnight supper with the actors and actresses who had played in the stage production of his novel, "'Ninety-Three," and had enjoyed himself so much that he had not returned till three in the morning. But now, after Juliette's death, he lost his appetite for pleasure; he suffered from insomnia, and hardly ever left his house. Mme. Lockroy, the former Alice Hugo, with her husband and children, came to live with him; together with other old friends, Meurice and Vacquerie, they formed a sort of guard of honor around Victor Hugo and watched over him. Reclining in his armchair after dinner, he would say sometimes: "I am ready, Dei voluntate. I have lived already a hundred years."

On February 26, 1885, another imposing festival, a banquet in honor of his eighty-third birthday, was held at the Hotel Continental. The plan for a National Edition of his collected works, in forty quarto volumes, to be enriched with illustrations by leading French painters, was announced in commemoration of his birthday. He could not speak that night, and retired at nine o'clock, saying: "These parties are not for a man of my age." But the next day he rallied and came to his door to receive the compliments of delegations of workingmen in blue blouses, shaking hands with as many of them as possible, and showing himself to a large crowd of thousands of persons outside.

It was his last public appearance. Only a few old friends came to see him once or twice a week thereafter. In the hands of Auguste Vacquerie, one of the executors of his will, he had placed his final instructions: "I leave fifty thousand francs to the poor. I wish to be borne to the cemetery in a pauper's coffin. I refuse the prayers of all churches; I ask a prayer from all." To Paul Meurice he confided careful instructions for the publication of his posthumous work.

One night, after dinner, on May 15, 1885, he felt ill and took to bed with what seemed but a heavy cold. Then pneumonia showed itself. For a week, three noted doctors attended him. His resistance was powerful and after severe sinking spells he had phases of recovery when his breathing seemed quite easy. Bulletins were published morning and evening in the press of Europe, giving news of his fluctuating condition.

The Cardinal Archbishop of Paris, though he was ill himself, offered to come in person to administer the last rites. But Edouard Lockroy wrote him at once that this would violate the express orders Victor Hugo had given him in the last days.

Departing, he struggled lustily as always for breath, for life. In calm moments his mood was one of resignation; he said to Paul Meurice: "How hard it is to die. Yes, this time it is death, and it will be most welcome to me." To the doctors he exclaimed: "Ah me! How long death is in coming." Sometimes, in fever, he sprang out of bed, struggled with his attendants, and could only be quieted with a drug. Waking at one interval, he sat up and cried out a line of verse: *"This is the struggle between the day and the night!"*

On May 22, 1885, toward one-thirty in the afternoon, while he lay in coma, night finally overtook him.

All France seemed to wear marks of mourning. As his life was tumultuous and his death was strenuous, so was his gigantic funeral, which by government decree was turned into a huge national and democratic ceremony. By a further government measure it was ordered that his remains be placed in the Panthéon. Floral testimonials came from many foreign lands, two of them from the English poets Tennyson and Browning. Thousands of tourists also arrived in Paris to see the colossal spectacle.

On the evening before the funeral, the simple pauper's coffin of Hugo lay under the Arch of Triumph, veiled in crepe, on a lofty dais, while the green flames of great bronze lamps threw weird lights and shadows against the imperial monument and glittered upon the helmets and breastplates of the dragoons guarding it all night.

All the great institutions of France—Army, Chamber, Senate, and Academy—were fully represented at the funeral, and marched in the procession. Detachments of soldiers and huge floral floats followed them. From the Place de la Concorde to the Arch a million people were assembled in an endless cortège, proceeding confusedly toward the Panthéon, while ten thousand soldiers struggled for five hours to control them. With such a mob flooding all the central avenues of Paris, the heads of the government that day were actually gripped by the fear of some explosion that would lead to insurrection. Once more the learned societies and trade associations, the labor unions, the freemasons, and even the members of the Gymnastic Society of Belleville, in tights, marched in Hugo's honor. It was scarcely a funeral ceremony; the people seemed to rejoice because Hugo, though dead, was one of the immortals, and belonged to them.

"A whole people follows him to his grave," said Prime Minister Brisson in his panegyric. "For what man of our time is not indebted to him? Democracy everywhere laments his passing."

And one of the plain people in this turbulent mass festival exclaimed: "Oh, how pleased he would have been to see this, *le Père Hugo!*"

APPENDIX NOTES

I. *Hugo's Mother*

More than a century was to pass before the real portrait of Sophie Hugo emerged for us and an unvarnished account of the causes of her separation from her husband became available. This was furnished chiefly in Louis Guimbaud's *La Mère de Victor Hugo,* with its candid study of legal records of the separation suit of 1814–18, as well as of old reports still circulating among the descendants of the Trébuchets and Hugos.

II. *Mme. Hugo and Sainte-Beuve*

For almost a century French scholarship, with a fairly obscene curiosity not often encountered in Anglo-American literary research, has investigated the celebrated "affair" between Sainte-Beuve and Mme. Hugo. During the late 1840's it was erroneously assumed that Mme. Hugo's connection with Sainte-Beuve became "adulterous" following her husband's liaison with Juliette Drouet in 1833. This was the explanation furnished, in somewhat veiled language, by the gossiping journalist, Alphonse Karr, a former lover of Juliette Drouet.

However, it soon became evident through the publication of a portion of Hugo's letters to Sainte-Beuve that the two men had severed their friendship in 1831, in a crisis *preceding* the appearance of Juliette by two years. The letters of Sainte-Beuve when they were published also corroborated this view.

In general, since the 1880's, French commentators have held two opposing theories of the "affair." One school, headed by the late Louis Barthou, who collected Hugo letters indefatigably and at great cost, speaks for the *chute intégrale,* the complete fall of Adèle Hugo. The opposing school of thought, fostered by Gustave Simon, denies the occurrence of an actual illicit union. Simon was an intimate friend of the Hugos in their later years, and probably had most opportunity to study the papers both husband and wife committed partly to his care. In his sympathetic biographical study of Adèle Hugo, *La Vie d'une femme*, Gustave Simon exonerates her from all charges of wrongdoing, but reproaches her for indiscretion in encouraging the intimate friendship of a man of Sainte-Beuve's shifty character. Barthou's arguments to the contrary (in *Les Amours d'un poète*) are mainly based on papers and letters left by the unscrupulous Sainte-Beuve, sometimes on mere copies of letters which were perhaps never mailed to Mme. Hugo.

The whole story has been sifted very completely in recent years, almost in the manner of a judicial inquiry, by a noted French lawyer, Bénoit-Lévy, in his *Sainte-Beuve et Mme. Hugo*. Bénoit-Lévy in his long study of all the facts and evidence bearing on the case systematically disproves the thesis of *une chute intégrale*, and holds Mme. Hugo to be the artless victim of a great literary artificer. I have leaned to agreement with Simon and Bénoit-Lévy in a disinterested spirit and with no moralistic ax of my own to grind here.

III. *Hugo and the Utopian Socialists*

The ablest study of Victor Hugo's evolution as a political personality and of the gradual application of his romantic doctrines to democratic and socialist objectives is to be found in H. J. Hunt's *Le Socialisme et le romantisme en France*. While some of the early socialists criticized Hugo for accepting a peerage from the King, other utopians in 1842 "saluted the elevation to the peerage of a man of such real merits. . . . They saw him as a future Minister and expected that he would help their 'universal unity,'" as H. J. Hunt relates after studying the contemporary Saint-Simonian periodicals. Hugo told his socialist friends that "but little distance" separated him from them; however, he was not a man for systems and, before 1851, feared that the socialists were in some ways "the founders of new convents." It was only later that he became decidedly a socialist-humanitarian.

NOTES ON SOURCES, WITH SOME ACKNOWLEDGMENTS

The Hugolian literature is vast: among the leading personalities of French history only Napoleon had more books written about him than Victor Hugo. The Hugolian literature is also full of the swirling crosscurrents of partisanship and controversy. To French democracy, after the crisis of the middle nineteenth century, Hugo, besides being a subject of perennial popularity, was a sort of literary-political "father Abraham Lincoln" who fortunately escaped assassination; for this very reason he was anathema to those substantial elements in France who opposed democracy (and who are now in the saddle). Therefore it is necessary to study the Hugolian literature with an eye to the successive historic shiftings of opinion and controversy.

Before 1851 the critical and biographical literature concerning Hugo was divided along classical and romantic lines. After the *coup d'état* of 1851, commentators execrated or idolized him for twenty years according to their political and religious doctrines. One of the world's leading Jesuit writers, Louis Veuillot, for example, exhausted his most vitriolic and often diverting invective upon the exiled poet and orator whom the democrats and anti-clericals in France all profoundly venerated. But upon his triumphal return in 1870, and after the reactionary phase of the Third Republic had passed by, Hugo was immitigably idolized. Shortly after his death in 1885, however, a reaction set in; this was partly owing to the rise of the important Zolaist, or naturalist, literary school which, in somewhat doctrinary fashion, claimed to be antithetical to Hugolian romanticism (though it was in reality much the same thing). The reaction was also partly due to the renewed political crisis of the Dreyfus case, during which Right and Left parties strove for control of the Republic. It was in the atmosphere of the 1890's that Edmond Biré published the last volume of his biography of Hugo—the longest work on the subject—which was promptly crowned by the old boys of the French Academy.

Biré was a pious Royalist and Catholic, and was a younger contemporary of his subject. He had begun by issuing the first of his four volumes, *Victor Hugo avant 1830,* in the year 1880, while his "hero" was still alive. Thereafter the succeeding volumes of his lifelong study followed, making up the testimony of one who was a Boswell-in-reverse, and piling up 1,500 pages of denigration and hatred. For a long time this curious performance dominated the Hugolian literature by its weight and accumulated arguments. Biré does not deny the importance of Hugo as a writer and artist, but endeavors to paint him as a fraud and as an irresponsible destroyer of political and religious authority. Biré used to point out that Hugo was long-winded and enumerated 300 pages of digression in *Les Misérables.* But I would estimate that there are more than 300 pages of the most tiresome carping and wailing in his own four-volume biography of Hugo. Yet even today Biré's fifty-year-old work is used more than any other writer's by American and English literary scholars, and the most complete existing biography in the English language—that of A. F. Davidson, published thirty years ago (London, 1912)—is a faithful copy of Biré's debunking job and incorporates all of Biré's mistakes as well as his animus.

The literary executors of Hugo, such as Paul Meurice and Gustave Simon, gave reply in their own somewhat partisan fashion. Around 1889 the project was conceived of issuing a monumental "national edition" of all the poet's work in quarto volumes illustrated with pictures and manuscript facsimiles and embellished with voluminous selections from his private papers and correspondence, of which only a small portion had been available to Biré and his English imitator, Davidson. This "national" (Ollendorf) edition did not begin to appear until about the turn of the century; Paul Meurice died and Gustave Simon continued to edit the successive volumes. By 1939, forty volumes had appeared—the series was, of course, interrupted by the debacle of 1940. They contain, as a large appendix, along with the Hugo text (about three quarters of his complete works) some 2,000 pages of his previously unpublished letters, notes, and journals (*Océan* and *Moi*), most of which was made available only during the 1930's. They offer us their candid revelation of a Hugo who was no plaster saint, and not without human contradictions, but a far greater man than the mere fraud Biré and others had concocted. The last installments of the private papers and notes available in the "national" edition, touching on Hugo's later and more public life, give strong evidence refuting the work of later denigrators of Hugo's political career, such as Pierre de Lacretelle (in *La Vie politique de Hugo*, 1928).

In great measure my own work is one of rehabilitation of Hugo's character before the English-reading world—much of this had already been accomplished in France in recent years, between 1918 and 1940, by later and juster scholars such as Professor Paul Berret. In another sense my work has attempted to draw together all the new material (some of it enormously important) that even in French has been available only in separate monographs treating special phases of Hugo's life and has never been summed up altogether in any one biography. The complete story of Sainte-Beuve and the Hugos, for example, unknown fifty years ago to Biré, has only been reconstituted since the 1920's, thanks to the late Louis Barthou's collecting activities. The 50,000 letters of Juliette Drouet, furnishing a far more intimate picture of the great man, only became available after 1912, and like many other documentary materials were still being sifted in 1940. The true story of Hugo's mother was not available until 1930.

In many respects this study deviates sharply from all previous accounts of Hugo's life. I beg the learned or specialized reader to assume that these divergencies are the result of my own judgment, mature or otherwise, and not of ignorance of the work of the more important of my predecessors. In the main my book has been based on direct study and examination of Hugo's own writings in prose and poetry, and his speeches, all of which contain so many rich suggestions to the biographer—these of course verified as far as possible against other and more objective contemporary evidence.

One of the younger American scholars of French literature, Professor Elliott M. Grant of Williams College, by his able monographs has helped in an important degree to repair some of the injustice done to Victor Hugo by earlier writers, especially with respect to the phase of political action. But I am further indebted to Professor Grant because, though he has a study of his own on Hugo's life and works under preparation, he has, like a generous citizen of the republic of letters, furnished me with advice and suggestions and undertaken the drudgery of reading proofs for this book. I trust that my book but emphasizes the need for a somewhat more comprehensive critical and biographical volume on Hugo, one destined for a scholarly audience, such as is to be expected from Professor Grant's pen.

I am also under obligation to the Library of Columbia University, and especially to Mrs. D. M. Peake, Chief of its Loan Division, for permitting me an extended loan of its choice Hugo collection at a time when French books were difficult to obtain. Finally I must express my gratitude to Thomas B. Costain, advisory editor to Doubleday, Doran and Company, for his Hugolian enthusiasm and his unflagging encouragement of this work.

SELECTIVE LIST OF BOOKS, MONOGRAPHS, AND ARTICLES CONSULTED

AMICIS, EDMONDO DE. *Studies of Paris.* New York, 1879

ANCELOT, M. L. *Les Salons de Paris.* Paris, 1867

ARAGON, LOUIS. *Pour un réalisme socialiste.* Paris, 1935

ASSELINE, ALFRED. *Victor Hugo intime.* Paris, 1885

BALZAC, HONORÉ DE. *Correspondance, 1819–1850.* Paris, 1876

BARBOU, ALFRED. *Victor Hugo.* Paris, 1885

BARROT, ODILON. *Mémoires posthumes.* 3 vols. Paris, 1879

BARTHOU, LOUIS. *Les Amours d'un poète.* Paris, 1922. Chateaubriand et Victor Hugo. *La Revue Bleue,* September 2, 1911. *Le Général Hugo, après des documents inédits.* Paris, 1928. *Victor Hugo, élève de Biscarrat.* Paris, 1924

BELLESORT, ANDRÉ. *Victor Hugo: essai sur son oeuvre.* Paris, 1930

BELTON, LOUIS. *Victor Hugo et son père.* Paris, 1902

BÉNOIT-LÉVY, E. *La Jeunesse de Victor Hugo.* Paris, 1928. *Sainte-Beuve et Mme. Hugo.* Paris, 1926

BERRET, PAUL. *Victor Hugo*. Paris, 1927. *La Légende des siècles*. (Edited after the original MSS. and Hugo's unpublished notes and letters.) 6 vols. Paris, 1920–1927

BIRÉ, EDMOND. *Victor Hugo avant 1830*. (2nd ed.) Paris, 1883. *Victor Hugo après 1830*. 2 vols. Paris, 1891. *Victor Hugo après 1852*. Paris, 1894

CASSAGNAC, GRANIER DE. *Souvenirs du Second Empire*. 2 vols. Paris, 1879–1881

CHENAY, PAUL. *Victor Hugo à Guernesey: souvenirs inédits de son beau-frère*. Paris, 1887

CLARETIE, JULES. *Victor Hugo*. Paris, 1882. Les Causeries de Hugo. *Revue de Paris*, July 1, 1894

CLEMENT-JANIN, NOËL. *Victor Hugo en exil*. Paris, 1922

Conservateur Littéraire: 1819–1821. 3 vols. Containing the early prose and poetry of Victor Hugo. Yale University Library: Collection Hugolienne

DAUDET, MME. ALPHONSE. *Souvenirs autour d'un groupe littéraire*. Paris, 1910

DAVIDSON, A. F. *Victor Hugo*. London, 1912

DUBOIS, PAUL-FRANÇOIS. *Mémoires inédites: le Correspondant*. Paris, 1900

DUBOIS, PIERRE. *Bio-Bibliographie de Victor Hugo de 1802 à 1825*. Paris, 1913

DUCLAUX, MARY R. *Victor Hugo*. London, 1920; New York, 1921

DUFAY, P. *Victor Hugo à vingt ans*. Paris, 1908

DUMAS, ALEXANDRE. *Mes Mémoires*. 10 vols. Paris, 1863

DUPUY, ERNEST. *La Jeunesse des romantiques*. Paris, 1905

ESCHOLIER, RAYMOND. *La Place Royale et Victor Hugo*. Paris, 1933. *La Vie glorieuse de Victor Hugo*. Paris, 1928

FAGUET, EMILE. *Amours des hommes de lettres*. Paris, 1914

FOUCHER, PIERRE. *Souvenirs de Pierre Foucher, 1772–1845; introduction de Louis Guimbaud*. Paris, 1929

GAUTIER, THÉOPHILE. *Souvenirs romantiques*. (New ed.) Paris, 1929

GIESE, WILLIAM F. *Victor Hugo; the Man and the Poet*. New York, 1926

GLACHANT, PAUL ET VICTOR. *Papiers d'autrefois: les manuscripts de Victor Hugo*. Paris, 1899

GRANT, ELLIOTT M. *Victor Hugo During the Second Republic*. Northampton, Mass., Smith College, 1935. The Exile's Return: 1871. *Romanic Review* (Columbia University), 1939

GUIMBAUD, LOUIS. *Juliette Drouet et Victor Hugo*. Paris, 1914 and 1927. *La Mère de Victor Hugo*. Paris, 1930

HOOKER, KENNETH. *Victor Hugo in England*. New York, 1938

HUGO, CHARLES. *Les Hommes de l'exil.* Brussels, 1868

HUGO, MME. VICTOR. *Victor Hugo Raconté par un témoin de sa vie.* 2 vols. Paris, 1863. Unpublished letters of Adèle Hugo. *Annales Politiques et Littéraires,* Feb. 4–Mar. 10, 1912

HUNT, H. J. *Le Socialisme et le romantisme en France.* Oxford, 1935. L'Impulsion socialiste dans la pensée politique de Victor Hugo. *Revue d'Histoire Littéraire de la France,* 1933

JANIN, JULES. *Histoire de la littérature dramatique en France.* 4 vols. Paris, 1853–1857

JULLIEN, ADOLPHE. *Le Romantisme et l'éditeur Renduel.* Paris, 1897

KARR, ALPHONSE. *Le Livre du bord.* 4 vols. Paris, 1879–1880

LACRETELLE, PIERRE DE. *La Vie politique de Victor Hugo.* Paris, 1928

LATOUCHE, HENRI DE. L'Amitié littéraire. *Revue de Paris,* October, 1829

LE CANU, A. *Chez Victor Hugo par un passant.* Paris, 1864

LESCLIDE, RICHARD. *Propos de table de Victor Hugo.* Paris, 1885

MARECHAL, CONSTANTIN. *La Clef de "Volupté."* Paris, 1912

MARSAN, EUGÈNE. *La Bataille romantique.* Paris, 1909

MARTIN-DUPONT, N. *Victor Hugo anecdotique.* Paris, 1904

MARZIALS, SIR FRANK T. *Victor Hugo.* London, 1876 and 1888

MAUPAS, CHARLEMAGNE EMILE DE. *Mémoires sur le Second Empire.* 2 vols. Paris, 1884–1885

MEURICE, PAUL. *Correspondance entre Victor Hugo et Paul Meurice.* Paris, 1909

MICHAUT, G. M. A. *Sainte-Beuve, amoureux et poète.* Paris, 1911

PELLETAN, CAMILLE. *Victor Hugo, homme politique.* Paris, 1907

PONS, ALEXANDRE. *Sainte-Beuve et ses inconnues.* Paris, 1879

RENOUVIER, CHARLES. *Victor Hugo, philosophe.* Paris, 1900

RIVET, GUSTAVE. *Victor Hugo chez lui.* Paris, 1877

ROCHEFORT, HENRI. *Les Aventures de ma vie.* Paris, 1896

RUDWIN, M. J. *Le Satanisme dans l'oeuvre de Victor Hugo.* Paris, 1926

SAINTE-BEUVE, CHARLES-AUGUSTIN. *Portraits littéraires.* Paris, 1829. *Portraits contemporains.* Paris, 1846. *Les Premiers Lundis.* 3 vols. Paris, 1875. *Chateaubriand et son groupe littéraire.* Paris, 1860. *Joseph Delorme.* Paris, 1829. *Le Livre d'amour.* Paris, 1843 and 1912. *Volupté.* Paris, 1834. *Correspondance générale.* 3 vols. Paris, 1935–1938. *Nouvelle Correspondance.* Paris, 1880. *Mes Poisons.* Paris, 1926

SALOMON, MICHEL. *Charles Nodier.* Paris, 1924

SAURAT, DENIS. *La Religion de Victor Hugo.* Paris, 1929

SCHENCK, E. M. *Charles Nodier et les idées romantiques de Victor Hugo.* Paris, 1914

SCHINZ, ALBERT. L'Unité dans la carrière politique de Victor Hugo. *Revue de l'histoire littéraire de la France*. Vol. 39 (1932)

SECHÉ, LÉON. *Sainte-Beuve*. 2 vols. Paris, 1904. *La Cénacle de Joseph Delorme*. Paris, 1921

SIMON, GUSTAVE. *Les Tables tournantes de Jersey*. Paris, 1923. *L'Enfance de Victor Hugo*. Paris, 1904. *La Vie d'une femme: Adèle Hugo*. Paris, 1914. *Le Roman de Sainte-Beuve*. Paris, 1926. Lamartine et Hugo. *Revue de Paris*, April 15, 1904

SOUCHON, PAUL. *Autour de Ruy Blas, avec lettres inédites de Juliette Drouet*. Paris, 1939

SOURIAU, MAURICE. *La Préface de Cromwell*. Paris, 1897

STAPFER, PAUL. *Victor Hugo à Guernesey*. Paris, 1905

SWINBURNE, ALGERNON C. *A Study of Victor Hugo*. London, 1886.

TROUBAT, JULES. *Sainte-Beuve intime*. Paris, 1903

VACQUERIE, AUGUSTE. *Mes Premières années à Paris*. Paris, 1872

VIANEY, JOSEPH. (Ed.) *Les Contemplations de Hugo*. Paris, 1922

WEILL, ALEXANDRE. *Introduction à mes mémoires*. Paris, 1890

EDITIONS OF HUGO'S WORKS

The most relatively complete and "authorized" edition of the *Oeuvres complètes* is that of Hetzel-Quantin in 48 vols., 1880–1889. The *Oeuvres posthumes* were issued after 1886. The *Correspondance,* in 2 vols., 1896–1898, and *Lettres à la fiancée* (edited by Gustave Simon) appeared in 1901.

The complete works of Hugo would run to between sixty and eighty volumes according to the format used, and have never been embraced in one edition. An attempt at this, begun in 1889, resulted in the issuance of forty quarto volumes individually, year after year, of a "national illustrated edition," edited by Paul Meurice, Gustave Simon, and other scholars. This series, issued by Ollendorf of Paris, which was halted in 1939, embraces now about three fourths of Victor Hugo's complete works, and is of utmost value to scholars for its voluminous collection of unpublished letters and private papers of the author.

INDEX